ENCYCLOPEDIA OF
WORLD CITIES

Volume One   A–L

ENCYCLOPEDIA OF
WORLD CITIES

Volume One A–L

IMMANUEL NESS

SHARPE REFERENCE
an imprint of M.E. Sharpe, Inc.

SHARPE REFERENCE

Sharpe Reference is an imprint of ℳ.E. Sharpe INC.

ℳ.E. Sharpe INC.
80 Business Park Drive
Armonk, NY 10504

Library of Congress Cataloging-in-Publication Data

Ness, Immanuel.
Encyclopedia of world cities / Immanuel Ness.
p. cm.
ISBN 0-7656-8017-3 (set: alk. paper)
1. Cities and towns--Encyclopedias. I. Title.
HT108.5.W47   1999
307.76'03--dc21
98-29844
CIP

Printed and bound in the United States of America

The paper used in this publication meets the minimum requirements of
American National Standard for Information Sciences--Permanence of
Paper for Printed Library Materials,
ANSI Z 39.48.1984.

MV (c) 10 9 8 7 6 5 4 3 2 1

Vice President and Publisher: Evelyn M. Fazio
Vice President and Production Director: Carmen P. Chetti
Production Editor: Wendy E. Muto
Editorial Coordinator: Aud Thiessen
Editorial Assistants: Esther Clark and Patricia Loo
Fact Checker: Monique Widyono
In-house Typesetter: Wilford Bryan Lammers
Cover Design: Lee Goldstein
Cartographer: Chris Agee

CONTENTS

Volume 2

Editor

Immanuel Ness
Brooklyn College, City University of New York, Brooklyn, New York

Contributors

James Ciment
New School University
New York, New York

Chris Agee

Clare Newman

ACKNOWLEDGMENTS

This work could not have been initiated without the foresight and enthusiastic support of Evelyn Fazio, who recognized the true need for an encyclopedia of world cities that would be accessible to both students and scholars. The actual compilation and writing of the book is another matter, for which I am entirely responsible. In researching and writing the encyclopedia, I received invaluable help from James Ciment, who wrote the entries for all of the African cities and most of the European cities, as well as cities in the Middle East and South Asia. Chris Agee created the detailed maps that place the cities in their respective regions and countries, and wrote the entries for the Latin American cities. Clare Newman was mainly responsible for assembling the tables, a tireless and tedious task that benefited from her precision, organization, and strong quantitative skills. I also received helpful research assistance from Jeffrey Eastby and Ron Friedman. A project of this magnitude cannot be completed without a skilled and tenacious production staff. In particular, I would like to thank Wendy Muto for her diligent management of this challenging project by coordinating the copyeditors, proofreaders, graphic artists, typesetters, and me. Thanks are also due to Aud Thiessen for her help in managing the project at M.E. Sharpe, and to Sue Warga, the copyeditor, who worked on this entire project.

Immanuel Ness

ABOUT THIS ENCYCLOPEDIA

This encyclopedia examines 132 of the world's leading cities and answers several basic questions about them. Where are they located? How big are they? What is their history? How are they governed? How do their residents make a living, and how do they get around? What kind of health, housing, and educational and cultural institutions do their citizens enjoy? It is a critical moment for such an examination, as the century coming to a close has witnessed the greatest and most rapid urban growth in human history.

Paleontologists, who study early humans, believe that our species emerged in its modern form—*Homo sapiens*—about 100,000 years ago. For roughly 90 percent of that time, humanity lived in small hunting-and-gathering bands scattered across the Eastern Hemisphere, spreading to the Americas and Australia between 15,000 and 40,000 years ago. The dawn of historical time—and the first cities—arrived about 10,000 years ago in the Middle East.

Still, until about 200 years ago, the vast majority of humanity lived in rural areas. With the advent of the industrial revolution in eighteenth-century England, a trend toward more rapid city growth began. A century later, urban development had spread to North America, Western Europe, and Japan. By the late twentieth century, the movement of people to urban areas had become a global phenomenon, and today about 50 percent of human beings live in urban areas. It is expected that in 2025 about two thirds of humanity will live in cities.

To put these time spans in perspective, imagine humanity's existence as a single year. From January 1 to roughly the end of October, we lived as hunters and gatherers. Through November and most of December, increasing numbers of us farmed, and a tiny minority lived in urban areas. Then, around Christmas, the rate of urban growth began to climb, reaching 50 percent around midnight on December 31. In short, urban living is largely a very recent phenomenon.

Urbanization has been a mixed bag for humanity. On the one hand, city living often offers better-paying employment, higher standards of living, and increased access to educational, health, and cultural institutions. On the other hand, urban crowding foments social discord and can increase economic inequality. With the enormous growth in cities, urban, regional, and national government officials and planners face major challenges. Specifically, how do they meet the economic, social, environmental, and cultural needs of this vast wave of new arrivals? This is particularly critical in the developing countries of Asia, Africa, and Latin America, where the growth of cities is especially acute and financial resources are in short supply.

In selected urban areas—the so-called megacities—the challenges are even greater. A megacity, according to demographers—that is, those who study population growth—is an urban area that contains 10 million or more persons. Megacities amplify existing urban problems and create new ones of their own. For example, planning becomes particularly acute in megacities because the metropolitan areas encompass various municipal and regional governments. By early in the next century, there are expected to be some 23 megacities, with most of them in the developing world, including Cairo, Dhaka, Jakarta, Karachi, Lagos, Manila, Mexico City, Mumbai, Rio de Janeiro, and São Paulo.

GLOBALIZATION AND URBANIZATION

What causes cities to grow? As with immigration, there are both push and pull factors behind urbanization. The push comes from the land. With the growth of commercial agriculture—particularly in its large plantation or corporate form—subsistence farmers and those who produce small amounts of crops for sale are driven off the land, either through changing laws or because they cannot compete effectively. Not surprisingly, this trend began in England during the industrial revolution and has since spread to virtually all parts of the globe. The pull factor concerns manufacturing and trade. Since both are primarily located in urban areas, they represent a draw for displaced rural persons looking for jobs and a better standard of living.

While these factors have not necessarily changed since the beginning of the industrial revolution, the pace at which they spread has accelerated greatly, particularly in the late twentieth century as commercial farming and industrialization have spread to ever-greater portions of the planet. These economic factors do not exist in a political vacuum, however. That is to say, they are encouraged by government and corporate decision makers. This effort to push economic modernization and integrate the world's economies into a single market has come to be called "globalization," and its effects on urban growth cannot be overestimated.

Globalization involves breaking down restrictions on trade, allowing for the free flow of capital and goods (and, more rarely, labor) across national borders, without government-imposed restrictions such as tariffs, regulations, or laws that restrict land or business ownership to citizens only. Since cities tend to be the primary points of trade, finance, and manufacturing, globalization encourages their economic growth. This growth, then, encourages migration from the countryside, where the push factors of globalization—that is, more land being devoted to corporate-controlled export crops rather than food for local consumption—come into play as well. In addition, globalization leads to new waves of immigrants, most of whom tend to settle in the urban areas of the developed world, which includes Western Europe, North America, Japan, Australia, and a few other countries.

Like urbanization itself, globalization offers a mixed bag for humanity. On the one hand, it has unleashed tremendous economic growth. This has been especially evident in the (until recently) booming export economies of East and Southeast Asia. On the other hand, it greatly increases the potential for financial instability, as the recent economic calamity in Asia also proves. Massive and sudden shifts in capital can undermine entire national economies, and there is little that governments and national economic planners can do about it.

Moreover, as financial crises deepen, international lending institutions come to have more influence over economic policies than national governments, since much of the growth in developing economies is financed by foreign capital. Not surprisingly, these lending institutions frequently place their own inter-est in being repaid over the needs of developing economies. As they impose restrictions on government spending—including subsidies on food, fuel, and other items necessary to urban life—they increase human suffering and heighten the potential for social discord. The recent violence in Indonesia, centered largely in urban areas, offers the best example of this pattern.

Globalization's mixed bag is also evident in that it has created great wealth but failed to distribute it equitably. This inequity emerges along two major divides. First, globalization has deepened the divide between wealthy developed nations, where most capital is controlled, and the more impoverished developing world. Second, it increases the divide between social classes within both developed-world and developing-world societies. That is to say, globalization tends to benefit the elites of the world—the monied, the educated, or members of dominant ethnic groups. This tends to be most pronounced in urban areas, where the chances for taking advantage of globalization—or suffering its consequences—are greatest. To illustrate this point, take a look at virtually any city on the planet: more limousines and more homeless in the developed world, gleaming high-rises beside squalid slums in the developing world.

BASIS FOR CITY SELECTION

Several criteria were used in the selection of cities in this encyclopedia. First and foremost was size. With a few exceptions, only major urban areas were chosen. Second was location. An effort was made to be geographically inclusive, covering all the major cities of each continent. The third basis for selection was a city's historical and cultural importance. For those reasons, smaller cities such as Jerusalem and Kyoto were selected.

Finally, an emphasis was placed on cities in North America and Europe for two reasons. In the case of the former, the large number of U.S. and Canadian cities selected reflects their importance in twentieth-century urban history and life. With their characteristic sprawl, low-density housing, and heavy dependence on the automobile, these cities have become models for much of the world. In the case of Europe, the emphasis took into account the various cities' long-standing political, economic, and cultural influence in their respective nations' histories and contemporary life.

DATA PROBLEMS AND INCONSISTENCIES

Gathering data on urban areas presents several problems. First, most data are gathered for nation-states, not cities. Second, there is a general lack of statistics for many of the world's poorer cities. Third, data are often noncomparable. That is to say, different national and international data-collecting institutions focus on different aspects of urban life. Moreover, some data-collecting institutions focus on metropolitan areas rather than municipalities. (The tables and summaries indicate which geographic area is being discussed.) In short, the reader should take note of, but not be too distracted by, discrepancies in the city summaries and tables.

Two rules of thumb apply here. First, the data presented reflect the data available. Second, the data presented reflect the city being examined. For example, religious differences are emphasized in the discussions of African cities because these are key factors in urban life there. On the other hand, race is a key focus in the discussions of North American cities because of its importance there.

Overall, it is important to keep in mind that city comparisons can be tricky. While comparing cities between the developed and developing worlds can be useful, they are of such different types that this must be done carefully. It is best, then, to compare cities in the developing world as a whole against cities in the developed world. For more precise comparisons, it is best to choose cities from the same region and level of economic development. For these reasons, this encyclopedia follows a pattern. That is to say, while all city summaries contain the same ten categories (see "How This Encyclopedia Is Organized"), each category may have a different focus and contain different data.

HOW THIS ENCYCLOPEDIA IS ORGANIZED

This encyclopedia examines ten key areas of life in the urban areas of the contemporary world. These include location; population and demography; history; government and politics; economy; transportation; health care; education; housing; and culture, the arts, and entertainment.

Location

The location, topography, and environment of a city play important roles in the development of cities, their economies, their relations to surrounding regions, and the quality of life of their inhabitants. Though modern communications are rapidly breaking down geographic distances, location remains critical in shaping urban centers in several ways. Important questions about city locations include: Where do they lie in relation to other cities? What kind of impact have natural features such as rivers had in their development? How do the topography and climate affect the quality of life?

Population and Demography

When it comes to modern cities, size does matter, as do other factors, including growth rates, density, gender ratios, and such vital statistics as birth and death rates (including infant mortality) and marriage and divorce rates. In general, these population statistics vary greatly between cities of the developing and developed worlds, and many of these factors are interrelated. For example, the lower growth rates of cities in the developed world are usually the result of lower birth rates and aging populations. The rapid growth of developing-world cities is largely caused by declining death rates, sustained high birth rates, and a generally young population. At the same time, marriage and divorce rates are influenced by the proportions of the various age groups. A younger population is more likely to have a higher marriage rate than an older one.

Of course, other factors are critical in assessing these statistics. For instance, in-migration is often a more important ingredient in growth rates than natural increase, while bureaucratic efficiency plays a role in marriage rates, since cities without effective bureaucracies often fail to record all marriages and divorces, many of which are conducted informally.

In all of these statistics, relative poverty plays an important role, especially in such key statistics as infant mortality and death rates. Of course, the pattern of urban poverty varies greatly from city to city. For example, most U.S. cities have seen a rise in poverty because of the out-migration of the middle class to the suburbs. Not surprisingly, then, some urban areas of the United States have infant mortality rates similar to those of the developing world, much higher than the U.S. average. In most European cities, the opposite is true, as governments built public housing projects for the poor in surrounding suburbs.

In developing-world cities, the influx of vast numbers of poverty-stricken people from the countryside has had contradictory statistical effects. On one hand, people tend to have smaller families in cities, because of housing shortages and because there is no need for family labor to work the land. At the same time, increased numbers of poor people raise death and infant mortality rates, even though overall national statistics in these areas may decline because health care is usually more available in urban areas.

History

The cities listed in this encyclopedia have had very different histories, and much can be understood about their current situation by studying their past. Cities such as Damascus (Syria), Rome (Italy), and Kyoto (Japan) have ancient roots and are often divided into older, more densely populated sections and newer, more open areas. Other urban areas, such as Birmingham (United Kingdom) and Chicago (United States), are products of the industrial revolution. Older cities were typically established along strategic transportation and trade crossroads. Thus many older cities throughout the world are port cities and highway centers located on important waterways and roadways. Most of these cities retain their stature as important transportation centers. Innovations in urban transportation encourage growth. Intercity transportation or transportation between rural and urban areas has historically played a key role in the development of cities. The three largest cities in the United States offer the best example. New York became America's leading city during the age of water transport because with the completion of the Erie Canal in 1825, it lay at the intersection of the Atlantic Ocean and the Great Lakes region. Chicago grew to predominance during the railroad age as it became the transportation hub for the growing Midwest. Los Angeles grew to maturity in the age of the automobile and airplane. Its vast distance from other urban areas became less critical with the growth of interstate highways and jet travel.

Some older industrialized cities have experienced significant declines in population and quality of life with the shift of manufacturing to developing countries. Cities in many parts of the developing world are the by-products of imperialism. Such urban areas as Hong Kong (China) and Calcutta (India) largely grew up as administrative centers for colonial regimes. Finally, some of the world's most important cities, though founded centuries ago, have grown into full-sized urban areas only in this century. Recently expanded cities such as Calgary (Canada) and São Paulo (Brazil) tend to be more spread out, reflecting the impact of the automobile.

Government and Politics

Throughout history, cities have played a disproportionate role in the politics and governing of nations. Because urban populations are concentrated and, in the case of capital cities, concentrated around the centers of political power, national leaders have had to be careful not to inflame the sentiments of their urban constituents. From the French Revolution of 1789, which overthrew King Louis XVI, to the recent Indonesian unrest that toppled the dictator Suharto, urban peoples have played a key role in influencing governments and governmental policies.

Not surprisingly, in many developing-world countries where the government plays a major role in regulating economic affairs, the interests of rural peoples have often been sacrificed in the face of urban demands. Thus in many African countries the urban masses were placated with cheap food prices that kept their rural counterparts living in poverty or else forced them to move to cities and join their urban compatriots.

At the same time, the rapid growth in urban areas has forced changes in urban governments, especially in the developed world. There has been a tendency in recent years, for example, to set up governing and planning bodies that deal with entire metropolitan areas. In this instance, European cities are generally ahead of their North American counterparts, where urban sprawl has left city governments to cope with the poorest, the least educated, and the underskilled, who are left behind. Moreover, suburban municipalities have generally resisted incorporation into metropolitan councils, for fear of having to share their relatively substantial tax bases with their poorer urban neighbor.

Economy

Cities are generally the centers of regional, national, or international economic development for essentially two reasons. First, they are where money tends to be made. Large cities in particular benefit greatly from national and international trade, labor migration, and investment. Second, they tend to be where money is spent. Though often slum-ridden and impoverished, urban areas have more of the things—such as schools, health facilities, and cultural institutions—that money can buy. And these factors tend to build upon one another. Because there is more money to be made, cities attract the young, the healthy, the skilled, and the educated. And because these are the kinds of people cities attract, money gravitates there as well.

Still, cities face enormous economic problems, the most important of which is jobs.

Globalization plays a key role here. Because developing-world countries offer cheaper labor costs, many industries have abandoned the cities of the developed world, leading to job loss, poverty, and crime. At the same time, the impact of globalization has forced rural inhabitants of developing countries to move to urban areas in numbers too great for new industries to absorb. Many workers, then, are channeled into the underground or informal economy, making goods and providing services that go unregulated and untaxed. This lack of tax revenues and absence of regulation, of course, make it more difficult for urban governments to provide basic social services or watch over the welfare of their citizens.

Transportation

Intracity transport has also been key in the growth of cities. The development of the streetcar, elevated railway, subway, and freeway has allowed metropolitan areas to expand outward, as workers can enjoy less crowded living conditions while commuting to work.

Despite these universal qualities of transportation innovations, there are great differences among the cities of the world when it comes to moving people and goods around. While most developed-world cities have been able to build elaborate public transportation systems (or, in the case of North America, a complex system of highways), the developing world lags behind. Indeed, a key measurement of economic development is transportation, as the rise of highways and subways in Asian cities attests. Still, in the least developed regions of the world, such as Africa and Latin America, people are forced to make due with overcrowded buses or travel by foot.

Health Care

A critical element in the quality of life in any city, health care differs greatly around the world, though, in general, health care facilities and public health tend to be better in urban areas than in rural ones. In most of the developed world—with the major exception of the United States—governments offer universal health care to their citizens, frequently paid for by tax revenues.

In the developing world, there are usually two health care systems—a generally up-to-date one for the nation's elite and an overcrowded, poorly staffed and poorly supplied one for the vast majority of the less well-off. This is because health care in the developing world has inherited two negative legacies. Under colonial regimes, little was done to promote health care. Then, after independence, many developing-world governments in Africa, Asia, and Latin America put most of their meager financial resources into prestige hospitals in the capital, leaving many poorer urban areas—as well as much of the countryside—without even the most primitive of clinics. In much of the former Communist world, a different pattern emerges—a good distribution of health care facilities and well-trained staff, but little in the way of medical supplies.

Education

Since ancient times, cities have been centers of learning. This is where the first great universities and libraries were located and, in the past century or two, this is where the first experiments in universal public education were attempted. By the early part of the twentieth century, primary and even secondary education was widely available in the cities of the developed world. Though not as universally available as in Europe and North America, a growing proportion of developing countries' population was gaining access to secondary education. Since World War II, near-universal primary education and even some secondary education has spread to even the poorest of developing-world countries.

In short, this is because education—particularly at the primary level—is relatively cheap to provide, though in most developing world schools, students are required to pay for their own books, supplies, and even teacher fees. Still, the overall effect has been more literate populations, with the biggest gain in recent years coming in the realm of the education of girls and women.

Housing

Not surprisingly, the growth of urban populations has led to housing shortages in virtually all of the world's major cities, though the specifics vary from place to place. The decline in public housing expenditures in much of the developed world has led to a shortage of low-cost housing that largely affects the poor and working class. With more emphasis on private financing of housing, investment tends to gravitate toward housing for the middle and upper classes, where the profit margin is greater.

In developing-world cities, the situation is even more acute, and this for two reasons. First, the growth in urban population is much more rapid, as people pour in from the countryside. Second, there is a much higher proportion of poor. Consequently, most cities in the developing world have come to be surrounded by vast rings of shantytowns. Consisting of self-built housing and with little access to utilities, they are called by different names in different cities: *favelas* in Rio de Janeiro (Brazil); *geçekondus* in Istanbul (Turkey); and *bidonvilles* in Algiers (Algeria).

Culture, the Arts, and Entertainment

As with education, cities have long been centers of culture, the arts, and entertainment. Indeed, urban culture and cultural institutions are often a draw for rural residents. Still, there are wide disparities in the cultural life of cities, and for several reasons. First, the relative age of a city determines the depth and breadth of its culture. Older cities tend to have a more developed cultural scene, with numerous institutions such as museums, concert halls, theaters, and even zoos and botanical gardens. Relative wealth plays a role as well. More money means more disposable income, which is often spent on the arts and culture. Galleries, concert venues, and dance repertory companies cannot thrive without government and private financial support.

Age and wealth are less critical when it comes to such popular forms of entertainment as film and music. Many impoverished cities in Africa and the Caribbean have vibrant musical scenes, while newer cities in the developed world often boast scores of cinemas. Finally, mass entertainment via radio and TV is a near-universal aspect of urban life, even in the poorest cities of the world, where entire neighborhoods share a single set.

ICON KEY

 Service

 Trade

 Health Care

 High Tech

 Government

 Finance

 Transportation

 Historical

 Population Center

 Manufacturing

 Education

 Agriculture

 Natural Resources

 Cultural

 Maritime

 Sports

 Communications

Abidjan
CÔTE d'IVOIRE/IVORY COAST

LOCATION

The largest city and port in Ivory Coast, Abidjan is situated on a number of islands and parts of the mainland in series of lagoons along the southeast coast of the country. The city has an area of 215 square miles (580 square kilometers). It is roughly 525 miles west of Lagos, Nigeria, and 1,050 miles southeast of Dakar. Located at sea level and several degrees north of the equator, Abidjan has a hot and humid tropical climate. The year-round average is 80.5 degrees Fahrenheit (26.9 degrees Celsius), with little variation between seasons. January temperatures average 80.5 degrees Fahrenheit (26.9 degrees Celsius) and July temperatures average 78 degrees Fahrenheit (25.5 degrees Celsius). The city receives roughly 77.1 inches (1,958 millimeters) of rain annually, mostly in the summer months.

POPULATION AND DEMOGRAPHY

With a population of just 60,000 in 1950, the Abidjan metropolitan area had grown to 2.9 million inhabitants by 1996. From 1950 to 1975, the annual growth rate of 11 percent was among the highest in Africa. Growth slowed to about 5 percent in the 1980s and 1990s and is expected to decline to about 2.5 percent in the twenty-first century. The increase in years past was largely due to an influx from the countryside, as well as to immigration from other French-speaking West African countries. The population—over half of whom are under the age of 19—is expected to reach 5.3 million by about 2015.

The metropolitan area is relatively built-up, with a density of 11,637 persons per square mile (4,310 persons per square kilometer). The city's population is largely African, with a cross section of ethnic groups from Ivory Coast and French-speaking West Africa. There is also a small community of Lebanese traders and French businesspersons. Much of the city's population is Roman Catholic, but there are substantial minorities of Muslims and practitioners of traditional religions.

HISTORY

Abidjan was founded as a French trading post late in the nineteenth century and was declared a separate municipality in 1903. A year later, the city became a terminus for a railway that extended to the interior of the colony. Despite this important eco-

nomic position, the city remained village-sized in population until it was made the administrative capital of the colonial government in 1934. In 1951, Abidjan's central lagoon was connected to the Atlantic by the Vridi Canal, eventually making the city the largest deepwater port in West Africa. With Ivory Coast's independence in 1960, Abidjan was made the capital, a role it played until 1983, when the government was moved to the more centrally located city of Yamoussoukro, though most administrative functions of the central government remain in Abidjan.

GOVERNMENT AND POLITICS

Really a collection of small communities grown into a single city, greater Abidjan was in 1986 administratively divided into ten municipalities, each governed by an elected council and mayor. There is also an overall mayor and council for the greater metropolitan area. Through most of independent Ivory Coast's history, the country was dominated by its first president, Félix Houphouët-Boigny—a conservative, pro-French, strongly Roman Catholic leader—until his death in 1993. Houphouët-Boigny, who emphasized close ties with Paris and an export-oriented economy, made Ivory Coast a model of economic prosperity for West Africa.

ECONOMY

Until the 1980s, Ivory Coast was hailed by international economists as a model of successful development, with an annual growth rate in excess of 10 percent through the 1960s and 1970s. Under the leadership of Houphouët-Boigny, the government emphasized agriculture over major industrial projects. In particular, the country became a major exporter of cocoa, coffee, timber, and other tropical products. With a collapse in world prices for its agricultural exports and a severe drought, the economy went into decline, shrinking by about 2 percent annually through most of the 1980s. Agriculture generates approximately 75 percent of the export earnings and employs 60 percent of the economically active proportion of the population of the country.

Abidjan's own economic fortunes are closely linked to that of the country generally. Most of the city's industries are involved in processing agricultural products or producing consumer items for the country, including automobile assembly, agricultural machinery, textiles, shoes, and clothing. In addition, a large segment of the economy revolves around the port. While Abidjan is no longer the political capital, it remains the financial center of the country and a major business center for much of French-speaking West Africa. Many of the city's modern skyscrapers house national and international banking institutions. The city also has a small tourist sector, mostly catering to beach-bound travelers from France.

TRANSPORTATION

Abidjan is well served by one of the finest highway networks in West Africa. The city has good bus service, which handles 51 percent of all commuter trips. Another 18 percent of the population travels by car or taxi. The remainder commute on bikes or foot. Other than rush hour, there is little in the way of traffic jams in Abidjan. The city also has a single railroad connecting it to Ouagadougou, in Burkina Faso, and its international airport is a major travel hub for the region, with connections to Europe and other African countries. Air Afrique, an airline run by a consortium of West African countries and other international carriers, serves the international market, while Air Ivoire connects the city to provincial capitals and neighboring African capitals.

HEALTH CARE

The growing inadequacy of the sewage system in the city has led to a resurgence in water-borne diseases, including guinea worm and diarrhea, in recent years. Malnutrition, measles, and respiratory ailments are responsible for about one third of all infant deaths. The infant mortality rate is 73 per 1,000 live births. AIDS is also a growing problem. A 1988–89 study found that 41 percent of males and 32 percent of females who died in those years were infected with HIV. It is estimated that AIDS is the leading cause of death among men and the second leading cause among women. Life expectancy is an average 56 years for all citizens.

EDUCATION

Among the better-educated countries of West Africa, Abidjan has an extensive, though basic school system, that provides classes for approximately 69 percent of all primary school-age children. Secondary education is much less available, with only 23 percent of school-age students attending. Of course, rates are much higher in the Abidjan metropolitan area.

HOUSING

With its relatively low density, Abidjan has a large proportion of traditional dwellings, which house over 50 percent of the metropolitan area's population. Another third of the population lives in modern housing, including a number of high-rises and low-rise public housing projects. Approximately 16 percent of the people live in shantytowns and other irregular housing. The government built 72,000 subsidized housing units in the early 1980s, about 25 percent of the total housing stock. Still, continuing demand for about 25,000 units annually is going largely unmet due to cutbacks in government spending.

Abidjan's water supply system is quite good. About 60 percent of the population enjoys access to tap water. The city also has the best utility infrastructure in western Africa, though only about 35 percent of the population is connected to the sewer network, while 45 percent use septic tanks. To protect the central lagoon from contaminants, a $50 million World Bank water treatment project was initiated in 1989. The city has a steady electrical supply.

CULTURE, THE ARTS, AND ENTERTAINMENT

Abidjan has a number of libraries and several museums, and it is home to the national university. The city is also well served by extensive green areas and parks, and many of the main streets and boulevards are thickly lined with shade trees. The city also features several large markets selling local handicrafts.

CATEGORY	DATA	YEAR	AREA
LOCATION & ENVIRONMENT			
Area	215 square miles		City
	580 square kilometers		City
Elevation	Sea level		City
January Temperature	80.5 degrees Fahrenheit		City
	26.9 degrees Celsius		City
July Temperature	78 degrees Fahrenheit		City
	25.5 degrees Celsius		City
Annual Precipitation	77.1 inches/1,958 millimeters		City
POPULATION & DEMOGRAPHY			
Population	2,900,000	1996	City
Projected Population	5,300,000	2015	City
Growth Rate	4.9%	1990–1995	City
Growth Rate	88.3%	1995–2015	City
Density	11,637 per square mile	1991	City
	4,310 per square kilometer		
Gender			
Male	52%	1991	City
Female	48%	1991	City
Age			
Under 20	52.9%	1990	City
20–59	45.9	1990	City
Over 60	1.3%	1990	City
VITAL STATISTICS			
Life Expectancy	56 years	1989	City
Fertility Rate	5.7 births per woman	1989	City
Infant Mortality Rate	73 per 1,000 live births	1989	City
TRANSPORTATION			
Trips by Bus	51%	1988	City
Trips by Foot	30%	1988	City
Trips by Taxi	7%	1988	City
Trips by Car	11%	1988	City
Trips by Bike	1%	1988	City
HOUSING			
Demand for New Housing	25,000	1988	City
New Housing Units	18,000	1981–1984	City
Traditional Housing	54%	1986	City
Modern Housing	30%	1986	City
Shanty Housing	16%	1986	City

(continued)

CATEGORY	DATA	YEAR	AREA
EDUCATION			
Completed Primary School			
Males	35.6%	1994	City
Females	37.4%	1994	City
Completed Secondary School			
Males	33.0%	1994	City
Females	17.9%	1994	City
Completed Higher Education			
Males	6.8%	1994	City
Females	1.3%	1994	City

Sources: Department of Economic and Social Affairs, Population Division. *Urban Agglomerations, 1996.* New York: United Nations, 1997; *Statistics of World Large Cities.* Tokyo, Japan: Tokyo Metropolitan Government, 1992 and 1994; and United Nations Center for Human Settlements. *Compendium of Human Settlements Statistics.* New York: United Nations, 1995.

Addis Ababa

ETHIOPIA

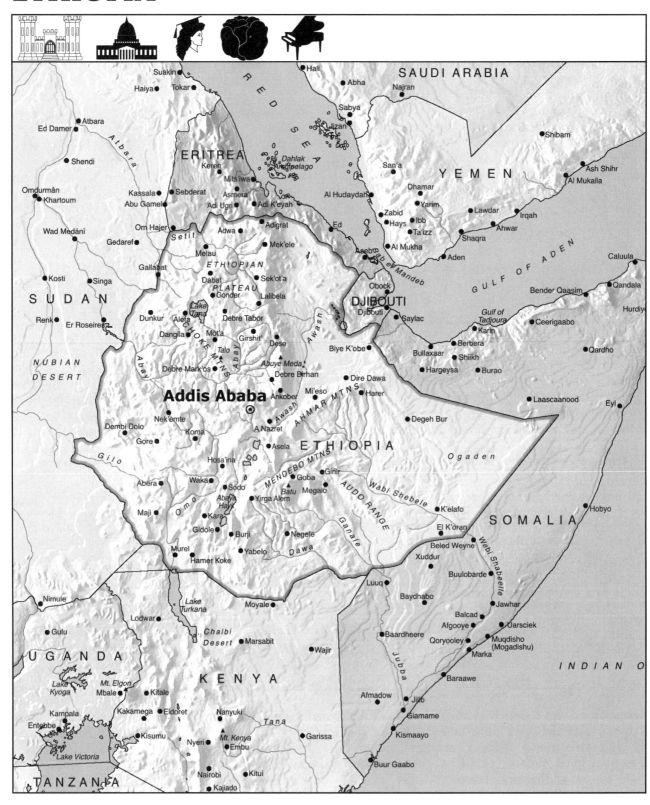

LOCATION

Addis Ababa is the largest city in Ethiopia and the nation's capital. The city is located 750 miles north of Nairobi and 1,500 miles south-southeast of Cairo. Situated at 8,038 feet (2,894 meters) in the Ethiopian highlands, the city enjoys cool temperatures of about 60 degrees Fahrenheit (15 degrees Celsius) year round and moderate rainfall, the latter occurring mostly in the summer months. Temperatures range from 59.8 degrees Fahrenheit (15 degrees Celsius) in January to 59.5 degrees Fahrenheit (15.3 degrees Celsius) in July. Altogether, Addis Ababa receives about 48.7 inches (1,237 millimeters) of precipitation annually.

POPULATION AND DEMOGRAPHY

Addis Ababa's population was estimated at 2.6 million in 1996, having grown from 1.75 million at the beginning of the decade. Its growth rate of 4.8 percent annually is high by Western standards but not unusual for African cities. It is estimated that the population will grow to approximately 6.6 million by the year 2015. The city is also crowded, with a population density of 21,638 persons per square mile (8,014 persons per square kilometer).

The crowding and high growth rate reflect two trends. First, there is a high natural increase, since the city's population is young: 53.3 percent are under 20 years of age. Second, the city has seen a major influx from the countryside over the past several decades, a migration caused by lengthy armed conflicts, natural disasters, and rural impoverishment.

The high rate of migration from the countryside—almost 50 percent of the population was born somewhere else—means that the city includes a melange of the country's major ethnic groups, though the majority of the population comes from the Amharic- and Tigrean-speaking peoples. Most of the city's inhabitants practice a form of Coptic Christianity or Islam.

HISTORY

Addis Ababa was founded by the Emperor Menelik II and his wife, Empress Taitu, in 1887. Located near the geographic center of the country, it served as a seasonal capital. Because of the cold mountain climate, the expanding population cut down most of the native trees for fuel. As a remedy, the government imported fast-growing eucalyptus trees from Australia, leaving the city with a leafy canopy.

Isolated from the outside world during its first three decades, it was connected by railroad to the French colonial port of Djibouti on the Gulf of Aden in 1917. In 1935, Ethiopia was invaded by Italy, and Addis Ababa became the capital of Italian East Africa from that year until 1941, when the Italians were forced to abandon the city by the Allies. During their occupation, the Italians constructed a number of boulevards lined with large stone houses.

From 1941 until 1960, the city saw little growth. From the 1960s on, however, Emperor Haile Selassie engaged in a major construction program of low-rise housing projects, government buildings, and roads until his overthrow by Marxist-inspired military officers in 1974.

GOVERNMENT AND POLITICS

From 1974 until the early 1990s, the Provisional Military Administrative Council, known popularly as the Derg, ruled the city and country with an iron hand, inspiring revolts among ethnic minorities in Tigre and Eritrea in the eastern parts of the country. During the 1970s and 1980s, wide swaths of the Ethiopian countryside were hit by drought- and war-induced famines, leading to major influxes of country people into the capital.

By 1991, the rebels—now including elements of the dominant Amharic population—controlled most of the country outside the capital. Faced with a bankrupt treasury as well, the Derg surrendered that year. Two years later, Eritrea achieved independence, though it promised Ethiopia free access to the Red Sea. Since 1991, the country has enjoyed a partially democratic government, with relatively free and fair elections.

ECONOMY

As Ethiopia's main transportation hub, Addis Ababa serves as the nation's distribution center for agricultural and consumer goods. Most of the nation's imports and exports pass through the city on their way to ports in Djibouti and Eritrea. A significant proportion of Addis Ababa's population—approximately 20 percent—is engaged in wholesale and retail trade. Many of those involved in retail trade are women.

In addition, the city contains the largest concentration of manufacturing establishments in the country. About 13 percent of the city's population is involved in light manufacturing, including textiles, shoes, food and beverages, furniture, and wood products. There are also several plants for the production of chemicals and plastics.

Because it is the nation's capital, about 45 percent of Addis Ababa's inhabitants are employed in the national and international agencies headquartered there. In addition, approximately one third of the population is listed by the government as "own-account workers," indicating a large sector of workers who are not integrated into the formal economy. Addis Ababa is also the center of the country's small but growing tourism trade. The total civilian labor force is approximately 1 million, roughly evenly divided between men and women.

The inflation rate over the past two decades has been modest by African standards. As of the mid-1980s, the cost of living had risen some 450 percent over two decades.

TRANSPORTATION

Because Addis Ababa is the nation's transport hub, 6.5 percent of the city is engaged in that sector. There were approximately 77,000 buses serving the city in the late 1980s, while the number of cars and trucks was 88,822. This relatively large number of vehicles makes for severe traffic problems, since only 683 miles (1,120 kilometers) of the city's roads are paved. Many older parts of the city have decaying cobblestone streets and the center of the city is a web of tiny, twisting streets, which means that there is no regular address system. In addition, vehicular traffic is forced to navigate through thick crowds of humans and animals. One major railroad connects the city to the port of Djibouti, 900 kilometers away.

HEALTH CARE

Health conditions in Addis Ababa have improved significantly in the past several decades. Between 1967 and the late 1980s, life expectancy climbed from 40 to 63 years, while infant mortality fell from 170 to 75 per 1,000 births. As of 1987, the city had thirteen hospitals and eleven clinics; there was 1 physician for every 6,000 inhabitants. Still, the cool highland climate makes it impossible for malaria-carrying mosquitoes to breed, and it eliminates the tse-tse fly, the source of African sleeping sickness and a number of fatal diseases afflicting livestock.

EDUCATION

Education facilities in the city have seen a dramatic improvement over the past several decades as well. Approximately 90 percent of both boys and girls between 7 and 15 attended school in the mid-1980s, and the literacy rate for those age 15 to 19 was well over 94 percent. Of those older than 65, however, only about one fourth can read and write, as a result of a decade of war between rebels and government that siphoned needed school funds into defense and saw many underaged youths forcibly recruited into the various armies.

HOUSING

Decades of war, economic mismanagement, and rapid population growth have left the city's housing stock in a precarious condition. Well over half the dwellings in the city consist of one or two rooms, with an occupancy rate of approximately 5.5 persons per dwelling as of the mid-1980s.

In addition, the housing stock is of poor quality. Only 10 percent of the buildings are constructed of concrete or steel, though over 90 percent have tin roofing. Approximately half of all dwellings have earthen flooring. Approximately 80 percent have separate kitchens.

Access to utilities is low as well. While well over half of all dwellings have running water, less than 1 percent include sewer-connected toilet facilities. Access to electricity is more widespread, with approximately 90 percent of all dwellings wired, though frequent power shortages continue to plague the city.

CULTURE, THE ARTS, AND ENTERTAINMENT

Addis Ababa boasts several major tourist attractions, particularly in the form of nineteenth-century Coptic churches and several elaborate palaces built by Emperor Haile Selassie and his predecessors in the late nineteenth and twentieth centuries. The city has two libraries, three museums, and twenty-four parks. Seven cinemas showing films from Egypt, the United States, India, and Europe were open as of 1988. Haile Selaisse Stadium hosts national and international soccer matches. TV and radio ownership is low; as of 1988, there was only 1 radio and 1 TV for every 10 and 40 inhabitants, respectively.

CATEGORY	DATA	YEAR	AREA
LOCATION & ENVIRONMENT			
Area	80 square miles		City
	217 square kilometers		City
Elevation	8,038 feet/2,894meters		City
January Temperature	59.8 degrees Fahrenheit		City
	15.0 degrees Celsius		City
July Temperature	59.5 degrees Fahrenheit		City
	15.3 degrees Celsius		City
Annual Precipitation	48.7 inches/1,237 millimeters		City
POPULATION & DEMOGRAPHY			
Population	2,600,000	1996	City
Projected Population	6,600,000	2015	City
Growth Rate	4.8%	1990–1995	City
Growth Rate	170.7%	1995–2015	City
Density	21,638 per square mile	1989	City
	8,014 per square kilometer	1989	City
Gender			
Male	52%	1991	City
Female	48%	1991	City
Age			
Under 20	53.3%	1990	City
20–59	26.2%	1990	City
Over 60	20.5%	1990	City
ECONOMY			
Total Workforce	430,486	1984	City
Manufacturing	13%	1984	City
Construction	3%	1984	City
Utilities	1%	1984	City
Agriculture	1%	1984	City
Mining	0.3%	1984	City
Wholesale, Retail, Hotel	19.5%	1984	City
Finance, Insurance, Real Estate	1.5%	1984	City
Community Social Services	54.2%	1984	City
Transport and Communications	6.5%	1984	City
TRANSPORTATION			
Trips by Bus	100%	1988	City
Total Number of Private Vehicles	88,822	1988	City
COMMUNICATIONS			
Telephones per 1,000 Residents	48	1988	City
Televisions per 1,000 Residents	26.8	1988	City

(continued)

CATEGORY	DATA	YEAR	AREA
HOUSING			
Total Occupied Units	259,555	1984	City
Owner-Occupied Units	32%	1984	City
Renter-Occupied Units	9%	1984	City
Persons per Housing Unit	5.5	1984	City
HEALTH CARE			
Hospitals	13	1987	City
Clinics	11	1987	City
Physicians per 1,000 Residents	0.2	1987	City
EDUCATION			
Population 5–24 in School	719,625	1984	City
% 5–24 in School	78.2%	1984	City
% Male	79%	1984	City
% Female	77.5%	1984	City

Sources: Department of Economic and Social Affairs, Population Division. *Urban Agglomerations, 1996.* New York: United Nations, 1997; *Statistics of World Large Cities.* Tokyo, Japan: Tokyo Metropolitan Government, 1992 and 1994; and United Nations Center for Human Settlements. *Compendium of Human Settlements Statistics.* New York: United Nations, 1995.

Algiers
ALGERIA

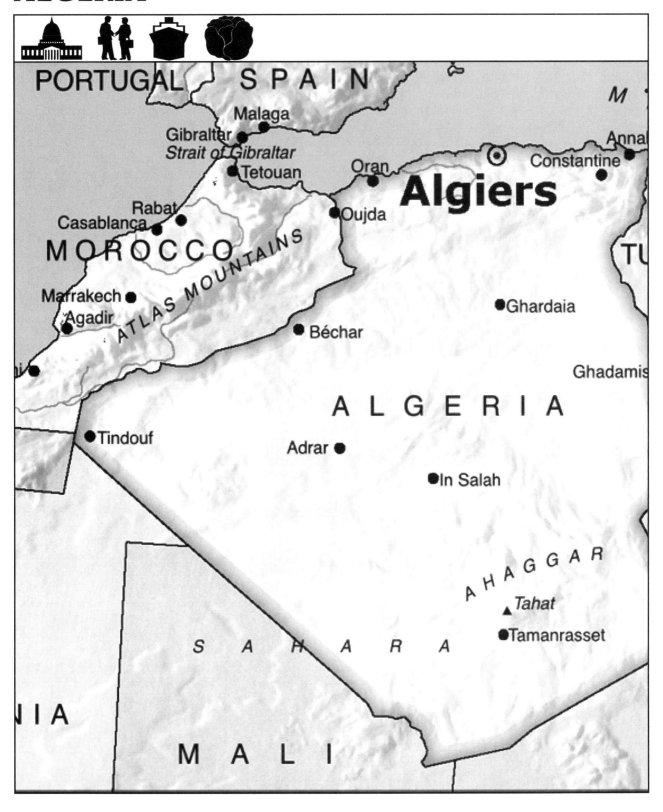

PORTUGAL S P A I N

Malaga

Gibraltar
Strait of Gibraltar

Tetouan

Oran

Annal

⊙ Constantine

Algiers

Rabat
Casablanca

Oujda

M O R O C C O

TU

ATLAS MOUNTAINS

Marrakech

●Ghardaia

Agadir

Béchar

Ghadamis

i

A L G E R I A

Tindouf

Adrar ●

In Salah

A H A G G A R

▲ *Tahat*

●Tamanrasset

S   A   H   A   R   A

NIA

M A L I

LOCATION

Algiers is the largest city, main port, and capital of Algeria, the second most populous country in North Africa, after Egypt. The city is located approximately 1,700 miles west of Cairo, Egypt, and 850 miles south of Paris, France. Situated on the Sahel Hills along the Bay of Algiers, at 194 feet (59 meters) above sea level, the city's layout has been compared to a gigantic amphitheater. The city enjoys a Mediterranean climate with hot, dry summers and cool, wet winters. January and July temperatures average 54 and 76.5 degrees Fahrenheit (12.2 and 24.7 degrees Celsius), respectively. Annual rainfall is about 30 inches (762 millimeters), with the bulk falling in the winter months.

POPULATION AND DEMOGRAPHY

Approximately 3.8 million people currently live in the Algiers metropolitan area, which has grown rapidly in the past several decades. During most of the period since independence in 1962, the city has grown at a rate of 4 percent annually, the result of migration from the countryside and a high natural rate of increase (about 70 percent of the country's population is under the age of 21). While growth rates are expected to decline in the next century to about 1.5 percent annually, it is projected that the metropolitan area's population will rise to about 6.4 million by 2015.

Algiers's population is divided into two main groups. The largest represents Arabs, but about 25 percent of the population is Berber in origin, an ethnic group with its own language and culture. In addition, the city is sharply divided along class lines as well, with a minority of elite, French-speaking businesspersons and government officials and a majority of working-class Berber- and Arab-speaking inhabitants. Virtually the entire population is Sunni Muslim, but they are divided into traditional and fundamentalist sectors. Indeed, Algiers has been the epicenter of a violent conflict between the secular-oriented military government and fundamentalist Islamic guerrillas that has killed an estimated 100,000 Algerians since the conflict began in 1992.

HISTORY

Algiers is an ancient city, originally settled by Phoenicians a millennium before Christ. The city was subsequently occupied by the Carthaginians and Romans but was destroyed by Vandal armies in the fifth century A.D. Arab invaders arrived in the seventh century, and a revived Berber dynasty in the tenth century made the city a center of commerce in the Mediterranean. To combat the piracy of Moors who made Algiers their home after their expulsion from Spain in 1492, the Ottomans took control of the city and ruled it for more than three hundred years.

A revival of piracy led to French counterattacks in the early nineteenth century, but it was imperial ambitions that led Paris to occupy the city in 1830. That invasion became the basis for an increasingly ambitious colonizing plan that aimed to Gallicize Algeria and eventually populate it with a million emigres from France and southern Europe. As early as the 1870s, however, native Algerian forces were rising up to drive the French from the country. But it was not until the post–World War II period that the real struggle for independence began. From 1954 to 1962, the National Liberation Front (FLN) of Algeria fought the French in a brutal and exhausting conflict that left approximately 1 million Algerians dead.

GOVERNMENT AND POLITICS

From independence until 1992, the FLN led Algeria as a socialist state, with a heavy emphasis on economic centralization. At the same time, the FLN expanded the welfare state, promoted secular education, and co-opted political forces. Much of this program was financed by the country's vast gas and oil reserves. But the drop in world energy prices in the 1980s—as well as increasing corruption in Algeria—led to protests and demands for democratization. When national elections appeared to be leading to an Islamist victory in early 1992, the military intervened. Over the next six years, the government tried to crush an underground Islamist army, even as it attempted to return the country to democratic rule. Neither policy has truly succeeded, and the country remains economically crippled and racked by conflict.

Since the 1970s, the central government has attempted to rein in the uncontrolled growth of the city and preserve the rich agricultural land on its periphery. In 1984, the city was divided into eight sectors, each with its own center and planning council.

ECONOMY

Once at the top of the list of developing countries, Algeria has seen serious economic decline in the 1980s and 1990s due to civil conflict, corruption, increasing debt, unequal distribution of wealth, inefficient industry, declining agriculture, and a drop in gas and oil prices. While Algeria was a net exporter of food at independence, it has become increasingly reliant on food imports in the past several decades.

The government remains the major employer in Algiers; 73 percent of the workforce labored for government agencies and industries in 1980, though this number has declined in recent years. Industries include food processing, oil and gas refining, metalworking, cement, toiletries, and shoes. In addition, Algiers is a major port and banking center. But unemployment has risen dramatically in recent years. Officially, it was listed at 16 percent in 1987, but most experts say it was probably double that then and has risen since. As a consequence, a large underground sector has developed that may account for as much as 50 percent of the city's economy.

TRANSPORTATION

Algiers is the center of the nation's transportation infrastructure and, as such, has a fine system of highways and secondary roads, some 257 miles (421 kilometers) in the city itself. However, privatization policies of the 1980s led to an increase in luxury imports, including automobiles. At the same time, the decline in public revenues meant that transportation spending lagged. Public transport deteriorated, and automobile traffic became increasingly congested. The ongoing war between the government and Islamist militants has put many modernization projects on hold. The port in Algiers, one of the largest in North Africa, handles over 6 million tons of goods annually, though the country's main exports—oil and gas—are transported by pipelines to other ports or, under the Mediterranean, to Europe itself.

There are approximately a quarter of a million telephones in the city, one for every 12.7 residents. But the inefficient government telecommunications company has a hard time keeping up with demand. There are an estimated 100,000 people on the waiting list for new telephones.

HEALTH CARE

The French colonialists left little in the way of an educational or health infrastructure when they abandoned the country in 1962. And while the socialist government of the FLN made these social sectors a priority—and achieved substantial gains in social in-

dices—corruption and economic hard times have made it difficult to keep health and education facilities growing to meet population needs. Because of the foreign debt and a lack of hard currency, the city's clinics and hospitals find themselves short of equipment and medicine. In addition, many of the doctors are underpaid and so moonlight as private practitioners, leaving the government health facilities understaffed.

EDUCATION

At the same time, educational levels remain high in the city. Most school-age children attend classes and the literacy rate for adults is high, though women's literacy lags significantly behind that of men. But better educational opportunities, say many experts, has led ironically to more social unrest. High school and university graduates often cannot find jobs commensurate with their skills. In addition, some mosques—both those sponsored by the government and those that are antigovernment—offer limited educational regimens, while others run full-scale primary and secondary schools.

HOUSING

Aside from unemployment, the most significant problem facing Algiers is a lack of adequate housing. It is estimated that the city's housing stock is adequate for perhaps 800,000, though the population tops 4 million. Nor is the government making a serious effort to alleviate the shortage. In 1992, for example, there were only 1,950 new housing starts. The lack of housing is seen as one of the major causes for the rise in opposition politics. Many young Algerians are unable to find housing of their own and are unable to leave their parents' home. This has forced many to postpone marriage, raising frustration levels. Occupancy in the city's housing is so high that many families—and Algerian families tend to be large—are forced to share apartments.

Population growth has also caused major water shortages. Most people are forced to keep water in cisterns or even bathtubs, filling these vessels when the water system is running for the many hours when it is not. Unfortunately, the hills and mountains behind Algiers are not high enough to support a major snowpack, and there are few steady streams or rivers. The city's sewage system is also overwhelmed by the population, and much of the city's sewage is dumped into the Mediterranean untreated.

CULTURE, THE ARTS, AND ENTERTAINMENT

Algiers was once a very cosmopolitan city, with a heavy French emphasis. Wide boulevards and numerous squares boasted cafes, nightclubs, and bars. But the recent conflict and the rise in Islamic fundamentalism has hurt the city's nightlife. Moreover, economic troubles have made it more difficult for many residents to partake of the city's numerous museums and cinemas, though many continue to visit the fine beaches on the outskirts of the capital. The rise in Islamist cultural influence has led to more restricted dress codes and even to sex-segregated beaches.

TV ownership is widespread, and the introduction of satellite dishes has ended the government's monopoly on media. Algiers is also home to a vibrant, semifree press. The major dailies are published in French and Arabic.

CATEGORY	DATA	YEAR	AREA
LOCATION & ENVIRONMENT			
Elevation	194 feet/59 meters	1995	City
January Temperature	54 degrees Fahrenheit		City
	12.2 degrees Celsius		City
July Temperature	76.5 degrees Fahrenheit		City
	24.7 degrees Celsius		City
Annual Precipitation	30 inches/762 millimeters		City
POPULATION & DEMOGRAPHY			
Population	3,800,000	1995	City
Projected Population	6,400,000	2015	City
Growth Rate	4.0%	1990–1995	City
Growth Rate	71.4%	1995–2015	City
VITAL STATISTICS			
Births per 1,000 Residents	13.9	1990	City
Infant Mortality Rate	25.5 per 1,000 live births	1990	City
Deaths per 1,000 Residents	2.7	1990	City
ECONOMY			
Public Administration	73%	1980	City
Unemployment Rate	16%	1987	City
COMMUNICATIONS			
Telephones	260,000	1980	City
Persons per Telephone	12.7	1992	City
HOUSING			
Housing Units	402,688	1987	City
Persons per Housing Unit	8.5	1987	City
HEALTH CARE			
Hospitals	2	1991	City
Clinics	25	1991	City
Physicians per 1,000 Residents	0.3	1991	City

(continued)

CATEGORY	DATA	YEAR	AREA
EDUCATION			
Total Students	347,060	1993	City
Primary	67.3%	1993	City
Secondary	32.7%	1993	City

Sources: Algerian Census. Algiers, Algeria: 1990; Department of Economic and Social Affairs, Population Division. *Urban Agglomerations, 1996.* New York: United Nations, 1997; and United Nations Center for Human Settlements. *Compendium of Human Settlements Statistics.* New York: United Nations, 1995.

Almaty (Alma-Ata)
KAZAKHSTAN

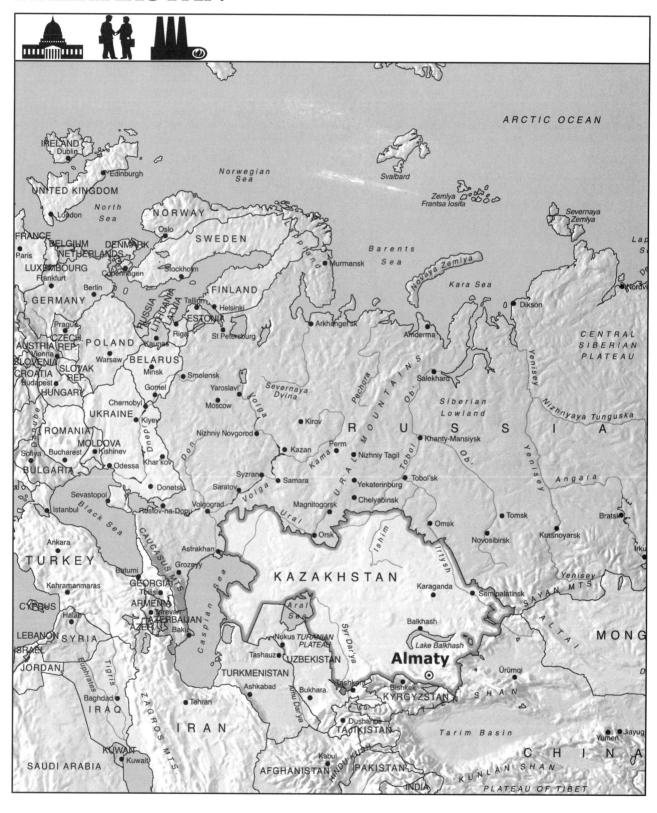

LOCATION

Almaty, formerly known by its Russian name, Alma-Ata, is the capital and largest city of Kazakhstan, one of the newly independent republics created out of the former Soviet Union in 1991, and now a member of the Commonwealth of Independent States (CIS). Covering 68 square miles (183 square kilometers), it is situated in the northern foothills of the Trans-Alay mountains at an elevation of 2,543 feet (915 meters), where the Boshaya and Malaya Almaatinka Rivers emerge onto the plains. Almaty is located roughly 1,800 miles southeast of Moscow, Russia, and about 750 miles north-northeast of the Afghan capital of Kabul. Almaty has a temperate climate, with freezing temperatures in winter and mild summers. The 28.1 inches (715 millimeters) of precipitation fall throughout the year.

POPULATION AND DEMOGRAPHY

With 1,300,000 inhabitants, Almaty is the largest city in the Central Asian states of the CIS. It has a growth rate of nearly 1.4 percent annually, though this is expected to decline a bit in the second decade of the twenty-first century, when the population will reach a million and a half in the metropolitan area. The city has a population density of 19,117 persons per square mile (7,104 per square kilometer). Approximately one third of its population is under 20 years of age and 9 percent is over 60, leading to a demographic profile slightly older than is typical for the region. Females outnumber males by about 108 to 100, the equivalent of 54 percent to 46 percent.

Under tsarist and Soviet rule, the government made it official policy to populate Almaty and Kazakhstan with Slavic-speaking peoples. Today, the city is roughly 60 percent Slavic-speaking and 40 percent Turkic-speaking. Most of the former are Russian—with small contingents of Ukrainians—and most of the latter are Kazakh, though there are also minorities of Uzbeks, Uighurs, and Tajiks. In addition, the city is home to small communities of Tatars, Germans, and Koreans. Most of the Slavic groups are nominally Christian, though a significant proportion do not practice their faith. The Kazakhs are Muslim, though seventy-five years of Soviet rule has undermined practice of the faith. This may change as the new independent government begins to encourage mosque restoration and other religious programs.

HISTORY

Almaty's origins, though shrouded by time, are believed to stretch back to Scythian settlements in the first millennium B.C. The city, however, was destroyed by the Mongols in the thirteenth century. Soon revived by Cossacks, peasant settlers from Russia and Tatar merchants, the city grew slowly over the next five centuries. The city was under various Central Asian and Chinese regimes during this period, but it came under Russian hegemony in the late eighteenth century. In 1854, the tsarist government established a fort on the site and became the city of Vernyi. It became the administrative center for the Semirechye province of the governate-general of Turkistan, and by 1906, the city had a population of 27,000, about two thirds of whom were Russians and Ukrainians.

Following the Russian Revolution of 1917, to which most Kazakhs remained bystanders, the city came under Soviet rule and the name was changed in 1971 to the Kazakh Almaty, though it was usually called by the Russian name Alma-Ata. Its designation as the capital of the Kazakh Soviet Socialist Republic and the completion of the trans-Siberian railroad, which runs through the city, caused Almaty's population to grow rapidly. With the German invasion of European Russia during World War II, the Soviet government moved a portion of its industrial capacity to the city, resulting in further growth. At the same time, Moscow's efforts to settle the largely nomadic people of the region resulted in terrible population loss among the Kazakhs, due to the destruction of their life-sustaining habitat. About a million and a half died, while several hundred thousand fled to neighboring countries. In addition, the city is located in an active geological zone and has been hit by several major earthquakes and mudslides in the past century. In 1966, the Soviet government created a dam in the nearby Medeo Gorge, which has prevented floods.

GOVERNMENT AND POLITICS

With independence from the Soviet Union in 1991, Almaty became the capital of the Kazakh Republic, though in 1994, the government announced plans to move its administrative facilities to Aqmola over the next decade or so. Under the constitution of 1995, Kazakhstan is ruled by a president—who is eligible to serve for two five-year terms—and a bicameral legislature. The president also appoints a prime minister (to handle domestic affairs) as well as much of the rest of the cabinet. The political situation since independence has been a rocky one. The first parliamentary elections were declared illegal by the constitutional court, the country's highest judicial body. This forced the drafting of the 1995 constitution, which granted extraordinary powers to the president.

ECONOMY

Almaty is a major industrial center, with about half of all production in the heavy industrial sector of steel milling, cement production, and chemicals, particularly the production of fertilizers for the country's large agricultural industry. The other half of the industrial infrastructure is devoted to food products—especially beet sugar and meat—and consumer goods production. While some 20 percent of the workforce labors in the manufacturing sector, most of these are ethnic Slavs. Fewer than one tenth of all Kazakhs work in industry. The city has a relatively small commercial sector, employing just over 7 percent of the workforce. While all industry was developed under state control during the Soviet period, a privatization program has been launched since independence, though due to the uncompetitiveness of much of the industrial capacity, as well as a lack of financial resources, this has been slow going. In 1994, Kazakhstan and two other Central Asian republics— Uzbekistan and Kyrgyzstan—established an economic union that allows for the free movement of labor and capital, as part of an overall economic coordination policy. The recent discoveries of vast new oil reserves in the Caspian Sea basin are expected to boost the economy even though most of these are not in the part of the basin that belongs to Kazakhstan.

TRANSPORTATION

Almaty is well served by the railroad system built under tsarist and Soviet rule. Several main lines— including the trans-Siberian—connect the city to Russia and other Central Asian republics. The city has a major international airport with connections to Russia, Europe, and Asia. In addition, there is an extensive oil pipeline network in Kazakhstan. Metropolitan transportation consists largely of buses. While the city had few private cars during Soviet rule— some 50,000 or so—this fleet has grown substantially since independence. Still, the city experiences little in the way of traffic problems. Under Soviet rule, many

wide boulevards were constructed that far outserved the existing traffic needs. While the city's communications system is quite backward and there is just one telephone for every four persons, the government has begun investing in this sector.

HEALTH CARE

Though better than in other Central Asian cities, the health profile in Almaty is significantly worse than in Western cities and even Russian municipalities. The moderately high death rate of 8.4 per 1,000 residents and infant mortality rate of 18 deaths per 1,000 live births reflect the inadequacy of the health care system, as well as unbalanced diets and environmental factors. While the city boasts relatively low official ratios of hospital beds and physicians to residents, a shortage of equipment, supplies, and training makes these numbers a bit suspect. In addition, there is growing tension over the distribution of scarce health care resources to the various ethnic communities in the city.

EDUCATION

Since just before independence, the educational system in Almaty and Kazakhstan as a whole has been undergoing significant changes. In 1989, the government radically revised the curriculum to more heavily emphasize Kazakh history, literature, and the arts, as well as to reject Marxist teaching. At the same time, it made Kazakh the official language of the republic, though under the 1995 constitution Russian was also included as an official language. However, since few ethnic Russians speak Kazakh, the officializing of the language has seen many Russian teachers replaced with Kazakh ones. The major universities and research centers of Almaty—including the Kazakh al-Farabi State University and the Kazakhstan Academy of Sciences—have begun to emphasize studies that have more pertinence to the country, such as geology and agricultural science.

HOUSING

One of the best-planned cities in the former Soviet Union, Almaty's housing stock consists mostly of low- and high-rise concrete apartment buildings that have largely replaced the old stock of wooden housing. The metropolitan area contains approximately 350,000 dwellings, with an average of about three persons per unit. In 1992, a typical year, an additional 4,500 units were constructed, mostly by the government. The city is well served by its electrical and water supply systems. The average daily use of electricity is approximately 2.5 kilowatt-hours per person, and water use is about 67 gallons (250 liters) per person daily.

CULTURE, THE ARTS, AND ENTERTAINMENT

More than most other Central Asian peoples, the Kazakhs and their culture have been heavily influenced by Russian rule and proximity. Much of their modern literature and arts—as well as daily dress and habits—has been heavily Russified. More recently, there have been efforts to resurrect indigenous Kazakh culture, including poetry, novels, and other literature written in the native language. Almaty is home to a number of modern theaters that offer plays in Russian, Kazakh, and other Central Asian languages. The radio and television studios, while still mostly broadcasting Russian-language programming, are attempting to introduce more Kazakh content. The most significant architectural site in the city is the Ascension Cathedral (now a museum), the second tallest wooden building in the world.

CATEGORY	DATA	YEAR	AREA
LOCATION & ENVIRONMENT			
Area	68 square miles		City
	183 square kilometers	1992	City
Elevation	2,543 feet/915 meters		Metro
January Temperature	27.9 degrees Fahrenheit		Metro
	−2.3 degrees Celsius		Metro
July Temperature	74.1 degrees Fahrenheit		Metro
	23.4 degrees Celsius		Metro
Annual Precipitation	28.1 inches/715 millimeters		Metro
POPULATION & DEMOGRAPHY			
Population	1,300,000	1996	Metro
Projected Population	1,500,000	2015	Metro
Growth Rate	1.4%	1990–1995	Metro
Growth Rate	22.9%	1995–2015	Metro
Density	19,117 per square mile	1992	Metro
	7,104 per square kilometer		Metro
Gender			
Male	46%	1988	Metro
Female	54%	1988	Metro
Age			
Under 20	35.1%	1988	Metro
20 to 59	55.9%	1988	Metro
Over 60	9.0%	1988	Metro
VITAL STATISTICS			
Births per 1,000 Residents	12.4	1992	Metro
Deaths per 1,000 Residents	8.4	1992	Metro
Infant Mortality Rate	18.1 per 1,000 live births	1989	Metro

(continued)

CATEGORY	DATA	YEAR	AREA
ECONOMY			
Workforce	403,600	1992	Metro
Agriculture	0.1%	1992	Metro
Manufacturing	20.7%	1992	Metro
Construction	10.4%	1992	Metro
Finance, Insurance, Real Estate	1.5%	1992	Metro
Trade	5.9%	1992	Metro
Government	3.6%	1992	Metro
Service	0.1%	1992	Metro
Transport	11.3%	1992	Metro
Utilities	3.3%	1992	Metro
TRANSPORTATION			
Total Journeys	619,558	1988	Metro
Bus	93%	1988	Metro
Trolley	8%	1988	Metro
COMMUNICATIONS			
Telephones per 1,000 Residents	292	1992	Metro
HOUSING			
Total Housing Units	354,212	1992	Metro
New Units	4,561	1992	Metro
Persons per Unit	3.1	1992	Metro
HEALTH CARE			
Hospitals	56	1989	Metro
Clinics	109	1989	Metro
Physicians per 1,000 Residents	9.3	1989	Metro
EDUCATION			
Total Students	212,719	1989	Metro
Primary	68.6%	1989	Metro
Higher	31.4%	1989	Metro

Sources: Department of Economic and Social Affairs, Population Division. *Urban Agglomerations, 1996.* New York: United Nations, 1997; Tokyo Metropolitan Government, *Statistics of World Large Cities.* Tokyo, Japan: 1992 and 1994; and United Nations Center for Human Settlements. *Compendium of Human Settlements Statistics.* New York: United Nations, 1995.

Amsterdam
HOLLAND, THE NETHERLANDS

LOCATION

Amsterdam, the largest city and an important administrative center of the Netherlands, is situated on some ninety islands at the head of Lake Ijssel, a former inlet of the North Sea. Located within a complex system of dikes, levees, and canals, the city lies about 20 feet (6 meters) below sea level. Amsterdam is located 35 miles northeast of The Hague, the capital of the Netherlands, and 100 miles north of Brussels, Belgium. The city covers 236 square miles (636 square kilometers) of territory, divided by numerous canals and connected by over a thousand bridges.

The city's climate is temperate, moderated by its proximity to the Atlantic Ocean. Its summers are breezy and cool, with July temperatures averaging about 64 degrees Fahrenheit (17.8 degrees Celsius), and its winters are mild, with typical January temperatures of 37 degrees Fahrenheit (2.8 degrees Celsius). The city receives a great deal of precipitation throughout the year, largely in the form of rain but with occasional snowfalls in winter.

POPULATION AND DEMOGRAPHY

The Amsterdam metropolitan area has a population of approximately 1.1 million people and has been growing at an annual rate of 1 percent during the 1990s. This growth is expected to disappear early in the next century, when the population will stabilize at about 1.2 million. With its numerous waterways, lakes, and parks, the city has a very low density of 4,409 persons per square mile (1,633 per square kilometer). Its age profile is typical for a West European city, with 19.3 percent of the population under age 20 and 18.8 percent age 60 or above.

The vast majority of the citizens of Amsterdam are Dutch by ethnicity and Protestant by religion, though the number of practicing Christians is quite low. The imperial legacy of the Netherlands and the need for low-skilled laborers in the post–World War II economic boom has led to an influx of immigrants from the former Dutch colonies of Indonesia and Suriname, as well as the presence of guest workers from Turkey and southern Europe. The city is also home to small communities of other West Europeans. Its once thriving Jewish community was largely destroyed during the Nazi occupation of World War II.

HISTORY

While stories of settlements in the marshes around Amsterdam date back to the Roman era, the first hard evidence of permanent human settlement in the area situates the city's origins in a fishing village from the thirteenth century A.D. From these first years, the inhabitants were forced to build dikes to keep out the invading sea. In addition, from very early in its history, Amsterdam became a center of trade, with merchant ships sailing to ports throughout northern Europe. The first mention of the name Amsterdam dates back to 1275, though not until 1306 was the city granted an official charter by the Burgundian-Austrian monarchs who ruled the region.

From the fourteenth to the sixteenth century, Amsterdam gradually grew in population and economic importance. Religious conflict, fed by the Reformation and Counter-Reformation, spread through the Low Countries in the 1500s, eventually leading to a nationalist struggle for independence under William I and the House of Orange and culminating in the bloodless revolution against the Hapsburg Empire in 1578.

The years that followed the revolution were the golden age of Amsterdam and Holland. The city quickly grew into one of the great trading, manufacturing, and banking centers of Europe, sending out trading and colonizing fleets to all parts of the world. The city's bourgeoisie became fabulously wealthy, supporting a thriving cultural scene and a remarkably tolerant political and religious society, which included many Jews.

By the late eighteenth century, however, Amsterdam had lost out to the House of Orange, situated in The Hague, in the struggle for political control of the Netherlands. At the same time, Holland was overtaken as the dominant trading and colonial country of northern Europe by England and France. The city was occupied by Prussia in 1787 and was liberated by France in 1795, which incorporated the country into the French Empire in 1810. With the fall of Napoleon several years later, Holland once again became an independent kingdom. In the 1830s, the southern half of the Netherlands, now called Belgium, won its independence in a bloodless political struggle.

While Amsterdam continued to grow during the nineteenth century, its harbor grew increasingly useless as it silted up, a problem that was not effectively solved until the twentieth century. During World War I, the Netherlands was able to maintain its neutrality, but it was invaded by Nazi forces early on in the Second World War. The city was liberated by Canadian troops in May 1945. In the years since, Holland gave up its empire, but only after a bloody struggle in Indonesia. At the same time, the city grew quite wealthy, riding the wave of postwar European prosperity. In the past several decades, Amsterdam has gained a reputation as a freewheeling city, with a liberal attitude toward drugs and prostitution.

GOVERNMENT AND POLITICS

Like all large towns and cities in the Netherlands, Amsterdam is ruled by a city council, with forty-five members elected for a four-year period. The Executive Committee, which handles day-to-day administration, consists of nine aldermen elected by the council and a *burgemeester* appointed by the Crown—usually from the ranks of the dominant party in the council—for six years. The Socialists have dominated the council since World War II, but many other parties are represented, including the Communists. By tradition, all council meetings are open to the public, and members serve without pay. Aside from ordinary city services, the city government of Amsterdam maintains several banks and businesses.

ECONOMY

Amsterdam's economy is dominated by finance and ranks with London and Frankfurt as one of the great financial cities of Europe. More foreign securities are bought and sold in Amsterdam than in any other exchange in Europe, and some 77.9 percent of the workforce is involved in the service sector. After finance comes trade. The city has been a major center of wholesale trade in tropical commodities since the seventeenth century and continues to be a major importing and distribution center. Approximately 19.8 percent of the workforce is employed in the manufacturing industry and 2.3 percent in agriculture.

The city is the largest industrial city in the Netherlands, though much of its manufacturing is in high-end products, including printing and publishing, fine textiles, machine tools, and diamonds. Indeed, most of the world's industrial diamonds are processed here. The final key sector of the economy is tourism. The city is a popular destination for travelers from other countries in Europe and overseas, and a significant percentage of the population works in the city's many fine hotels, restaurants, clubs, and cafes.

TRANSPORTATION

Amsterdam is home to one of the larger and busier harbors in Europe, and the city serves as a major port of entry for overseas goods coming into the continent. An extensive system of canals offers barge connections to much of northwestern Europe. In addition, the city is home to a major international airport, with connections worldwide, and it is an important hub of the West European railroad system.

Metropolitan traffic is served by a mixture of public transport—mostly in the form of buses, commuter railroads, and trolleys—and private automobiles. (Subways are not possible in the city because it is below sea level.) With over 356,000 cars in the metropolitan area and numerous narrow streets, bridges, and canals, traffic is often a problem. But many Amsterdam citizens use bikes to get around, a transportation option made viable by the city's many bike paths and lanes.

HEALTH CARE

As in the rest of the Netherlands, health care in Amsterdam is provided free to all citizens and is financed out of general government revenues. The city is home to thirty-nine hospitals and has a good ratio of 4.9 physicians per 1,000 residents. As the largest city in the Netherlands, the city boasts many of the country's more prestigious and best-equipped specialized medical care facilities. Amsterdam is also renowned for its research institutes on tropical disease, a legacy of the Netherlands' colonial empire in the East and West Indies.

EDUCATION

Amsterdam has an extensive and well-financed primary and secondary school system, and the city's population is among the most literate, well-read, and best-traveled in the world. In addition, the city is home to some fifteen institutions of higher learning. Among these, the oldest and largest is the University of Amsterdam, founded in 1632. Another major institution is the Free University, founded in 1880. The city also boasts several significant art and music academies.

HOUSING

The city's housing stock is largely of excellent quality and there is no real shortage, though rents can be quite high in the more popular and upscale neighborhoods. Since 1935, the city's housing growth has been guided by a metropolitan plan that situates new residential neighborhoods in parkland and establishes public transport connections for them. And while Amsterdam's built-up area has tripled since World War II, the population has not grown much, so the occupancy rate is a low 1.8 persons per dwelling. Most buildings are privately owned and rented out to tenants, though about 5 percent are owned by the state.

CULTURE, THE ARTS, AND ENTERTAINMENT

The city's cultural scene is both lively and diverse. A major center of art since the seventeenth century, Amsterdam's museums—including the Rijksmuseum and the Stedelijk Museum—feature collections of the many artists who have called Amsterdam home over the centuries, including Rembrandt, Steen, Vermeer, and van Gogh. Both Rembrandt and van Gogh have museums dedicated to them as well. In addition, the city is home to many contemporary artists and the galleries that feature their work. Amsterdam is also a major center of music. The city's Concertgebouw Orchestra is renowned throughout the world. Amsterdam's architectural legacy is spectacular and includes such highlights as the thirteenth-century Old Church, the former Jewish quarter, the many fine houses of merchants from the seventeenth century, and the modern Olympic Stadium, built for the 1928 games.

The city's cafe culture is also internationally famous, as is its nightlife. Amsterdam is a popular destination for tourists, young and old. Its beautiful architecture and many fine hotels and restaurants draw many visitors to the city.

CATEGORY	DATA	YEAR	AREA
LOCATION & ENVIRONMENT			
Area	236 square miles	1995	Metro
	636 square kilometers		Metro
Elevation	−20 feet/−6 meters		Metro
January Temperature	37 degrees Fahrenheit		Metro
	2.8 degrees Celsius		Metro
July Temperature	64 degrees Fahrenheit		Metro
	17.8 degrees Celsius		Metro
Annual Precipitation	25.6 inches/650.2 millimeters		Metro
POPULATION & DEMOGRAPHY			
Population	1,100,000	1996	Metro
Projected Population	1,200,000	2015	Metro
Growth Rate	1.0%	1990–1995	Metro
Growth Rate	5.7%	1995–2015	Metro
Density	4,409 per square mile	1989	City
	1,633 per square kilometer		
Gender			
Male	49%	1991	City
Female	51%	1991	City
Age			
Under 20	19.3%	1991	City
20–59	61.9%	1991	City
Over 60	18.8%	1991	City

(continued)

CATEGORY	DATA	YEAR	AREA
VITAL STATISTICS			
Births per 1,000 Residents	13	1992	Metro
Deaths per 1,000 Residents	9	1992	Metro
Infant Mortality Rate	7 per 1,000 live births	1992	Metro
Net Migration per 1,000 Residents	3.6	1992	Metro
ECONOMY			
Workforce			
Agriculture	2.3%	1993	Metro
Industry	19.8%	1993	Metro
Services	77.9%	1993	Metro
TRANSPORTATION			
Passenger Vehicles	356,000	1992	Metro
HOUSING			
Housing Units	374,106	1989	City
New Housing Starts	4,220	1990	City
Persons per Unit	1.8	1989	City
Owner-Occupied	10%	1989	City
Renter-Occupied	90%	1989	City
HEALTH CARE			
Hospitals	39	1990	City
Physicians per 1,000 Residents	4.9	1990	City
Hospital Beds per 1,000 Residents	1.6	1992	Metro
EDUCATION			
Total Students	547,000	1992–93	Metro
Primary	40.0%	1992–93	Metro
Secondary	43.3%	1992–93	Metro
Higher	16.7%	1992–93	Metro

Sources: Department of Economic and Social Affairs, Population Division. *Urban Agglomerations, 1996.* New York: United Nations, 1997; *Statistics of World Large Cities.* Tokyo, Japan: Tokyo Metropolitan Government, 1992 and 1994; United Nations Center for Human Settlements. *Compendium of Human Settlements Statistics.* New York: United Nations, 1995; and Eurostat *Regions Statistical Yearbook.* Brussels, Belgium: Statistical Office of European Communities, 1996.

Anchorage, Alaska
USA

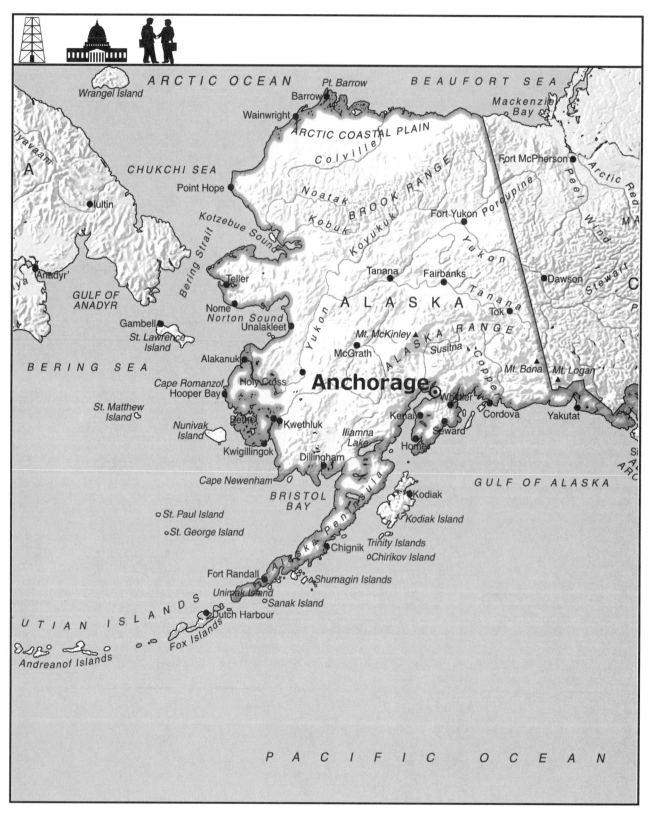

LOCATION

Anchorage, the northernmost American city with a population of over 200,000, is located in southern Alaska on Knin Arm at the head of Cook Inlet, which flows southwest past Kenai Peninsula into the Gulf of Alaska and the Pacific Ocean. The city lies on a lowland coastal plain at an elevation of 85 feet between the Mat-Su Valley and the Kenai Peninsula. To the east are the Chugach Mountains, to the north are the Talkeetna Mountains and the Alaska Range, and to the west are the Kuskokwim Mountains. Anchorage is about 200 miles due south of Denali National Park and Mount McKinley, which, at 20,320 feet above sea level, is the highest point in North America. To Anchorage's south is Kenai Peninsula, across Turnagain Arm of Cook Inlet. At 1,697.6 square miles (4,396 square kilometers), the sprawling municipality of Anchorage has the largest land area of any city in the United States, extending 55 miles north to south. The surrounding metropolitan region includes the municipalities of Eagle River, Kenai, Palmer, Seward, and Soldotna. Anchorage is located 360 miles southwest of Fairbanks, Alaska's second largest city, and about 650 air miles northwest from Juneau, Alaska's capital. The city is 725 road miles west of Whitehorse, in Canada's Yukon Territory. Barrow, the center of Alaska's petroleum range, is located along the coast of the Arctic Ocean, about 800 air miles northwest of Anchorage. From 1961 to 1990, Anchorage's temperature ranged from an average low of 14.9 degrees Fahrenheit (−9.5 degrees Celsius) in January to an average high of 58.4 degrees (14.6 degrees Celsius) in July. The city has an annual average precipitation of 15.91 inches (404 millimeters).

POPULATION AND DEMOGRAPHY

Between 1980 and 1992, Anchorage's population increased by 41 percent (71,435) to 245,866, the eleventh fastest growth rate among major American cities. As a result of the expansion of the city's area to include the entire Anchorage Borough (the borough is the Alaskan equivalent of the typical U.S. county), the city's population increased by over 80 percent, from 48,029 to nearly 250,000, in the twenty-two years between 1970 and 1992. Although Anchorage is the largest city in land area, it is the least dense major city, with 145 persons per square mile (55.9 persons per square kilometer). The city is considerably less demographically diverse than most mainland cities, which have higher concentrations of African-Americans, Asians, and Hispanics. Whites account for about 75 percent of Anchorage's residents. The city's 14,569-member Native American community forms the next largest demographic group, representing 6.4 percent of the city's residents, followed by black residents, who also make up 6.4 percent of the city's population. Asians and Pacific Islanders are the fourth largest minority, with 4.8 percent of the city's population, followed by Hispanics, who constitute 4.1 percent of the city's population. Only 5.9 percent of the city's population is foreign-born, and 9.7 percent speak a language other than English at home. Chiefly as a result of the relatively harsh climate, Anchorage has the smallest percentage of senior citizens—only 3.7 percent of the city's population is 65 years of age or older. Anchorage has a very youthful population, with 29.5 percent of the city's population 18 years of age and under, and 62.5 percent between 18 and 64 years of age. The city has one of the highest concentrations of males relative to females, with 105.8 males for every 100 females.

HISTORY

In the early eighteenth century, Russian sailors explored Alaska and later established outposts there. The United States purchased Alaska from Russia in 1867. The discovery of gold in Alaska in the late 1880s fueled a gold rush that continued in spurts through the 1920s. In 1914, Anchorage was established as a supply station for the Alaska Railroad on its route to Fairbanks. The city was formally incorporated in 1920. In the wake of World War II, the city became a crucial military center as headquarters of the U.S. Alaska Defense Command. Anchorage was virtually completely destroyed by the 1964 Alaska earthquake, the most powerful on record. The rebuilt Anchorage came to economic prominence after the completion of the Trans-Alaska Pipeline, which transported oil from Prudhoe Bay, on the north coast of Alaska, to the Gulf of Alaska. During the last two decades of the twentieth century, Anchorage has developed into a major American city as thousands of young migrants from the forty-eight contiguous U.S. states have settled in the city.

GOVERNMENT AND POLITICS

A mayor and a city council are responsible for the executive and legislative functions of Anchorage's government. The State of Alaska 1975 Anchorage Home Rule Charter provides for the election of an eleven-member legislative assembly responsible for the enactment of budgets and laws of the Municipality of Anchorage. The Anchorage Assembly enacts laws, sets municipal and school board budgets, and confirms appointments to municipal boards and commissions. Members of the Anchorage Assembly are elected to three-year terms on a district basis. Executive and administrative power is vested in a mayor. Anchorage citizens participate directly in issues affecting their neighborhoods through an association of 37 local community councils.

ECONOMY

Anchorage is the primary service center for the oil and gas, finance, real estate, transportation, communications, fishing, and tourism industries. Anchorage is also a leading commercial center in Alaska, and it has many government agencies. The Anchorage metropolitan area is home to Fort Richardson and Elmendorf Air Force Base—two large U.S. government military installations employing a total of 9,000 military personnel.

The Anchorage civilian labor market expanded by 36.2 percent between 1980 and 1990, to a total of 116,738 workers. The labor market is dominated by wholesale and retail trade workers, who comprise 36.2 percent of the workforce, followed by public administration workers, at 11.8 percent; health services workers, at 6.4 percent; and finance, insurance, and real estate workers, at 6.4 percent of the labor force. The city has the smallest percentage of manufacturing workers of any U.S. city with a population over 200,000: Only 3.6 percent of all workers in Anchorage are employed in the manufacturing sector. In the early 1990s, Anchorage's unemployment rate was comparatively lower than that of other major cities, and the percentage of the population living below the poverty line was both significantly lower than for other major U.S. cities and under the national rate. Anchorage's poverty rate was lower than that of any other major U.S. city with the exception of Virginia Beach, and less than half the national rate. After San Jose, California, Anchorage has the second highest median household income in the nation. With 69.5 percent of its female residents in the civilian labor force, Anchorage has the third highest female labor force participation rate in the country.

TRANSPORTATION

The primary means of transportation in Anchorage is the private automobile. The city has a very high average number of vehicles per household—in 1990, there were 1.8 motor vehicles per household in the city. The city operates a public municipal bus system known as People Mover that provides year-round service to neighborhoods throughout the city. The system also helps facilitate carpool transportation and service for people with disabilities. Air passenger and freight transportation is vital to Anchorage's economic vitality, due to the relative remoteness of the city from the 48 contiguous U.S. states. The state-owned Anchorage International Airport and two smaller airfields provide commercial air transport to the city. In recent years the international airport has grown in prominence as a refueling and layover point for trans-Pacific flights. The Port of Anchorage, completed in the 1960s, facilitates the export of marine and natural resource exports and the import of pipe, drilling, construction materials, and automobiles. The Alaska Railroad provides links to major destinations in Alaska, including Seward, Whittier, and Fairbanks. The city is linked to Canada and the lower forty-eight states through the Glenn Highway, which intersects the Alaska Highway to the east.

HEALTH CARE

Anchorage has two hospitals and 579 hospital beds, a rate of 256 hospital beds per 100,000 city residents. The city has an infant mortality rate of 11.4 deaths per 1,000 live births, lower than most other major U.S. cities, but higher than the national rate. With a very youthful population, Anchorage has a high natural growth rate due to the large excess of births over deaths. The city has a rate of 18 live births and a rate of 3 deaths per 1,000 city residents.

EDUCATION

The Anchorage School District operates eighty-four public primary and secondary schools. Anchorage has a school enrollment of 63,357, representing 25.8 percent of the city's population, of which 39,993, or 63 percent, of all students are in grades 1 through 12. Over 29 percent of all students are enrolled in higher educational institutions. A large majority, 95 percent, of the city's students attend public primary and secondary schools, the fourth highest rate of public school enrollment among major U.S. cities. The district's education policy is set by the seven-member Anchorage School Board. The city has a fairly well educated population, with 26.9 percent of all residents who are 25 years and over possessing a bachelor's degree or higher. The major postsecondary institutions in the city are the University of Alaska–Anchorage and Alaska Pacific University.

HOUSING

To accommodate the city's rapidly expanding population, the city's housing stock increased by 33.8 percent, to 94,153 units, between 1980 and 1990. New construction has continued to expand the city's housing stock into the 1990s. Only 0.6 percent of all units were constructed prior to 1940. The city has a very small share of one-person and single-parent households. The smaller share of the population residing in single-person households tends to minimize the demand for housing. Thus, despite the rapid population growth, the city has a relatively high housing vacancy rate of 12 percent. The city's owner occupancy rate is 52.8 percent. The city has comparatively higher median housing values and median rental costs than major cities in the contiguous United States. The city has placed a priority on the development of low-income housing and homeless assistance. However, there is limited federal funding to support the development of affordable housing in the municipality.

CULTURE, THE ARTS, AND ENTERTAINMENT

Anchorage's major cultural facilities are the Museum of Art and History and the Alaska Center for Performing Arts, a regional venue for touring national and international artists, musicians, and entertainers. The city has numerous parks and recreational facilities, including hockey rinks and golf courses. Collegiate and visiting professional basketball and hockey teams play at the George Sullivan Sports Arena.

CATEGORY	DATA	YEAR	AREA
LOCATION & ENVIRONMENT			
Area	1,697 square miles	1995	City
	4,396 square kilometers		City
Elevation	85 feet/27.9 meters		City
January Temperature	14.9 degrees Fahrenheit	1961–1990	City
	−9.5 degrees Celsius	1961–1990	City
July Temperature	58.4 degrees Fahrenheit	1961–1990	City
	14.6 degrees Celsius	1961–1990	City
Annual Precipitation	15.9 inches/404 millimeters	1961–1990	City
POPULATION & DEMOGRAPHY			
Population	245,866	1994	City
Population Growth	41%	1980–1992	City
Density	145 per square mile	1992	City
	55.9 per square kilometer		
Gender			
Males	51.4%	1990	City
Females	48.6%	1990	City
Age			
Under 18	29.5%	1990	City
18–64	62.5%	1990	City
Over 65	3.7%	1990	City
VITAL STATISTICS			
Births per 1,000 Residents	18	1988	City
Death per 1,000 Residents	3	1988	City
Infant Mortality Rate	11.4 per 1,000 live births	1988	City

(continued)

CATEGORY	DATA	YEAR	AREA
ECONOMY			
Total Workforce	116,738	1990	City
Trade	20.7%	1990	City
Manufacturing	3.6%	1990	City
Health Services	7.3%	1990	City
Finance, Insurance, Real Estate	6.4%	1990	City
Public Administration	11.8%	1990	City
TRANSPORTATION			
Passenger Vehicles	145,901	1990	City
HOUSING			
Total Housing Units	94,153	1990	City
Persons per Unit	2.6	1990	City
Owner-Occupied Units	52.8%	1990	City
HEALTH CARE			
Hospitals	2	1991	City
EDUCATION			
Total Students	63,357	1991	City
Primary and Secondary	70.6%	1991	City
Higher	29.4%	1991	City

Sources: U.S. Bureau of the Census. *County and City Data Book 1994.* Washington, DC: U.S. Government Printing Office, 1994.

Ankara
TURKEY

Istanbul

Sakarya

Ankara

Tuz Gölü

Kizil Irmak

B L A C

Izmir

T U R K E Y

Konya

Adana

S Y R I

Nicosia

CYPRUS

Limassol

Tripoli

Hims

LEBANON

Beirut

Damascus

MEDITERRANEAN SEA

Haifa

Ba diy

Tel Aviv

Amman

Alexandria

Port Said

Jerusalem

ISRAEL

JORDAN

Qattâra
Depression

Cairo

Suez

S i n a i

Elat

Al Jawf

A n

LOCATION

Ankara is the capital of Turkey. The city is located at 2,825 feet (861 meters) above sea level, on the northern edge of the central Anatolian Plateau, approximately 180 miles east-southeast of Istanbul. The built-up area of Ankara covers approximately 293 square miles (790 square kilometers). The city has a temperate climate, with cold, wet winters and hot, dry summers. The average temperature ranges from 31.5 degrees Fahrenheit (−0.3 degrees Celsius) in January to 72.5 degrees Fahrenheit (22.5 degrees Celsius) in July. Ankara receives approximately 13.6 inches of snow and rain annually (345.4 millimeters), much of it falling in the winter and spring.

POPULATION AND DEMOGRAPHY

With 2.9 million people in the metropolitan area, Ankara is the second largest urban center in Turkey, after Istanbul. Much of the population is young. About half of the city's residents are under the age of 20. There are 9,698 persons per square mile (3,592 per square kilometer). The city has a moderate growth rate of about 2.3 percent annually, though this rate is expected to drop in the next twenty years to about 1 percent. This will give Ankara a population of approximately 4 million in 2015.

Like Turkey itself, Ankara is dominated by ethnic Turks, but also includes substantial minorities of Arabs, Armenians, and Kurds. Virtually all of its residents are Muslims, though the small Armenian community practices Christianity. There is also a small Jewish population. Well over two thirds of the city's Muslims practice the Sunni form of the religion, while most of the remainder are Alevis, a distinct branch of Islam related distantly to Shiism.

HISTORY

Ankara is one of the oldest cities in the world, with settlements dating back to prehistoric times. It has been ruled by the Hittite, Hellenic, Roman, Byzantine, and Ottoman Empires, each of which has left buildings and streets in its wake. Fought over extensively from the tenth to fifteenth centuries, it came under long-term Ottoman rule in 1403.

Following the collapse of the Ottoman Empire after World War I, Kemal Atatürk, father of the modern Turkish Republic, shifted the capital from the more vulnerable and then recently foreign-occupied Istanbul to more centralized and protected Ankara. From the 1920s on, Atatürk and his successors rebuilt much of the city with large boulevards and extensive government buildings.

GOVERNMENT AND POLITICS

With the fall of the Ottoman Empire after World War I, Turkey was transformed from a monarchy, or more precisely a sultanate, to a republic, ruled by a president, prime minister, and parliament. But the country's experience with democracy has not always been successful. While political parties thrive and there is a relatively free political climate, the army has overthrown the democratically elected government on three occasions since World War II.

In 1995 Turkish voters elected their first Islamist government. Though moderate by Mideast standards, the Islamic Welfare Party, or Refah, offended the pro-secular military. In 1997, the latter pressured Turkey's president to dismiss the Refah prime minister and install a coalition government of center-right parties.

ECONOMY

The Ankara metropolitan area is dominated by government institutions and industry. Of the city's labor force of 1,089,561, 14.1 percent works for the government. Manufacturing enterprises employ another 12.6 percent of the workforce, making a diverse array of products, including food items, wine, construction materials, and agricultural machinery. Centrally located on the Anatolian peninsula, Ankara has been a major transportation hub since ancient times; 4.9 percent of the workforce labors in this sector.

At the same time, Ankara is one of the centers of a rapidly modernizing Turkish economy. Of the workforce, 22.7 percent is involved in trade, finance, insurance, and real estate, and another 11.2 percent labors in the service sector. Like Turkey as a whole, Ankara has been heavily hit by growth-induced inflation and saw prices on all items rise by more than 500 percent in the 1980s.

TRANSPORTATION

Because of urban planning dating back to the 1920s, Ankara has many broad boulevards and does not experience the severe traffic jams common in Istanbul. It also has a number of major highways serving the city's periphery and connecting the metropolitan area to other cities in Turkey, Europe, and the Middle East. As of 1987, the city had 342,000 vehicles, or about one per eleven residents.

Ankara is also located on a major east-west rail line and has a number of shorter commuter rail lines, though much of the public transport consists of buses. A modern telecommunications system connects the city to the outside world, though telephone ownership is low, a result of poverty and slow installation services. As of 1987, there were 256 telephones for every 1,000 persons.

HEALTH CARE

The Ankara metropolitan area is well served by a network of 84 hospitals and clinics. There is a relatively low ratio of physicians to patients, about one for every 375 persons. The city's health care system is heavily subsidized by the government, though the city lacks enough trained medical staff. The major diseases afflicting residents of Istanbul include cardiovascular and respiratory ailments. In general, however, the city has a better health profile in virtually all indices than the country of Turkey as a whole.

EDUCATION

The vast majority of the city's children are in school. Ankara has over 1,600 primary and secondary schools, with a pupil population of over 600,000. As Ankara is the nation's capital, a number of major universities are located in the city, including the University of Ankara, founded in 1946, and the Middle East Technical University, established in 1956. Altogether, the city's seventy large and small institutions of higher education have over 100,000 students in attendance. The nation's literacy rate is roughly 70 per-

cent, with significantly higher figures for Istanbul, although women lag behind men somewhat.

HOUSING

Divided into two sectors, Ankara presents two distinct faces. The old city, situated on the slopes of a great citadel, is marked by narrow, winding streets with mostly two-story houses constructed of mud brick and wood. The newer city is largely dominated by concrete and brick low- or high-rise housing. In 1990, 25,110 new dwellings were built, though there remains a serious housing shortage.

Until the 1980s, Ankara, like most Turkish cities, experienced stress on its electrical and water supplies. The central government embarked upon a major hydroelectric project in the country's southeast, officially known as the Greater Anatolian Project (GAP), and the completion of the largest of several dams has solved much of the electrical problem, though the city still has a problem with water supplies.

CULTURE, THE ARTS, AND ENTERTAINMENT

Ankara is home to many national cultural institutions, including the Turkish State Theater and the Presidential Philharmonic Orchestra. It is the site of the National Library, the Archeological and Ethnographic Museum, and the much-visited Mausoleum of Atatürk. The city is home to nine theaters. There are also nearly 350 parks. In addition, the city is a major media center. Over sixty newspapers and two hundred magazines and journals are published in Ankara. TV and radio ownership is relatively widespread, with approximately one TV and one radio set for every 5.5 and 3 persons respectively, as of 1990.

CATEGORY	DATA	YEAR	AREA
LOCATION & ENVIRONMENT			
Area	293 square miles	1995	City
	790 square kilometers		City
Elevation	2,825 feet/861 meters		City
January Temperature	31.5 degrees Fahrenheit		City
	−0.3 degrees Celsius		City
July Temperature	72.5 degrees Fahrenheit		City
	22.5 degrees Celsius		City
Annual Precipitation	13.6 inches/345.4 millimeters		City
POPULATION & DEMOGRAPHY			
Population	2,900,000	1996	Metro
Projected Population	4,000,000	2015	Metro
Growth Rate	2.3%	1990–1995	Metro
Growth Rate	41.5%	1995–2015	Metro
Density	9,698 per square mile		City
	3,592 per square kilometer		City
Age			
Under 20	44.8%	1988	Metro
20–59	49.8%	1988	Metro
Over 60	5.4%	1988	Metro
VITAL STATISTICS			
Births per 1,000 Residents	6.5	1988	Metro
Deaths per 1,000 Residents	6.1	1988	Metro
ECONOMY			
Total Workforce	1,089,561	1990	Metro
Agriculture	26.5%	1990	Metro
Manufacturing	12.6%	1990	Metro
Construction	5.5%	1990	Metro
Finance, Insurance, Real Estate	15.6%	1990	Metro
Trade	7.1%	1990	Metro
Government	14.1%	1990	Metro
Service	11.2%	1990	Metro
Transport	4.9%	1990	Metro
Utilities	0.2%	1990	Metro
TRANSPORTATION			
Passenger Journeys	325,244,000	1990	Metro
Rail	7.1%	1990	Metro
Bus	92.9%	1990	Metro
COMMUNICATIONS			
Telephones per 1,000 Residents	256	1990	Metro
Televisions per 1,000 Residents	181.8	1990	Metro

(continued)

CATEGORY	DATA	YEAR	AREA
HOUSING			
New Housing Units	25,110	1990	Metro
HEALTH CARE			
Hospitals	26	1992	Metro
Clinics	58	1992	Metro
Physicians per 1,000 Residents	3	1992	Metro
EDUCATION			
Total Students	724,838	1990	Metro
Primary	50.5%	1990	Metro
Secondary	35.2%	1990	Metro
Higher	14.3%	1990	Metro

Sources: Department of Economic and Social Affairs, Population Division. *Urban Agglomerations, 1996.* New York: United Nations, 1997; *Statistics of World Large Cities.* Tokyo, Japan: Tokyo Metropolitan Government, 1992 and 1994; and United Nations Center for Human Settlements. *Compendium of Human Settlements Statistics.* New York: United Nations, 1995.

Athens
GREECE

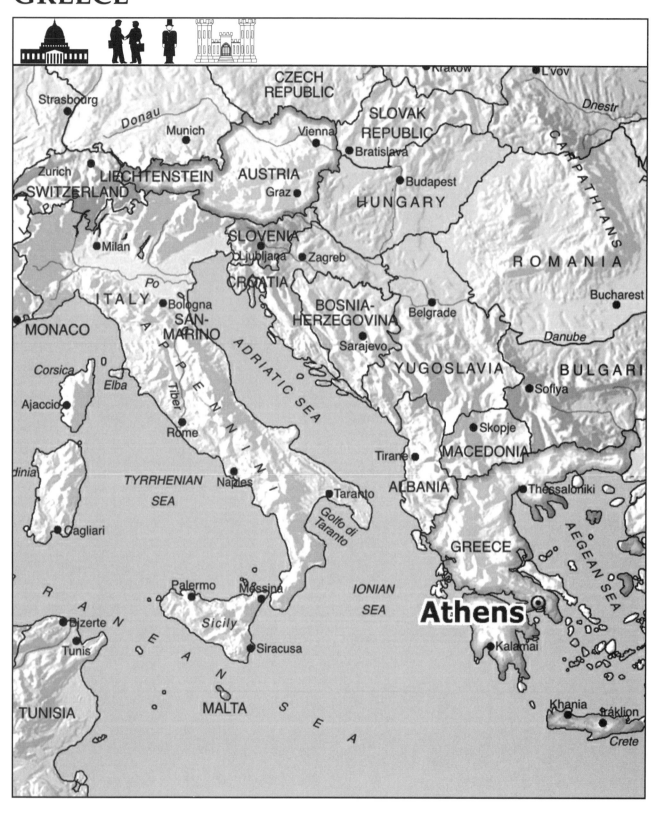

LOCATION

The capital of Greece and the country's largest city, Athens is located approximately 5 miles inland from the Bay of Phaleron, off the Aegean Sea, where its port, Piraeus, is situated. The city is separated from Petalion Bay to the east by the Hymettos Mountains. During the winter and spring, two small rivers run through the city. Approximately 330 feet (108 meters) above sea level, Athens is located 350 miles southwest of Istanbul, Turkey, and 500 miles south-southeast of Belgrade, Yugoslavia. The city covers approximately 170 square miles (450 square kilometers) of hilly territory.

The city has a climate typical for the Mediterranean basin, with hot and dry summers and cool, rainy winters. The January temperature averages 54 degrees Fahrenheit (12.2 degrees Celsius), and the July temperature averages 90 degrees Fahrenheit (32.2 degrees Celsius). The city receives 15.8 inches (401.3 millimeters) of rain annually, virtually all of it falling in the winter and spring months.

POPULATION AND DEMOGRAPHY

The Athens metropolitan area has a population of 3.1 million, making it one of the largest cities on the Mediterranean. Its growth rate is virtually zero, and the city is not expected to grow in population over the next twenty years. Quite crowded, the city has a density of 18,315 persons per square mile (6,783 per square kilometer). Though it has a low growth rate, the city's age profile is younger than that of most other European cities; 33.4 percent of the population is under the age of 20, while 13.2 percent is age 60 or above. The vast majority of the city's inhabitants are ethnically and linguistically Greek, and virtually all are members of the Greek Orthodox Church. There are also small minorities of Turks, Arabs, and Jews.

HISTORY

Athens has one of the most illustrious histories of any city in the world, and it is often considered the birthplace of Western civilization and democracy. The Athens area has been inhabited by humans since prehistoric times. In the second millennium B.C., the city became an administrative and trading center, reaching its pinnacle in the fifth century B.C. under the rule of Pericles, who built many of the spectacular monuments on the Acropolis, a mesa situated in the city center. Having fended off Persian invaders through a coalition of Greek city-states, the city was gradually sapped by a series of wars with its great rival Sparta. In the fourth century B.C., the city became one of the launching points for the conquests of the Hellenistic emperor Alexander the Great.

Several centuries later, the city was incorporated into the expanding Roman Empire and became a major center of culture and an inspiration for Roman culture. Following the collapse of the western Roman Empire in the fifth century A.D., Athens began to go into decline as an increasingly marginal provincial city of the Byzantine Empire. With the fall of that empire and the incorporation of Greece into the expanding Ottoman Empire in the fifteenth century, Athens declined further for the next four hundred years.

In 1827, during the Greek fight for independence against the Turks, Athens was evacuated and six years later there were only 4,000 people living in huts along the north slope of the Acropolis. The city became the capital of the new Hellene Kingdom in the 1830s and grew gradually to about 50,000 inhabitants by midcentury. With the arrival of a railroad to the port of Piraeus in the mid-nineteenth century, the pace of the city's growth quickened. By the turn of the century, Athens had a population of about 150,000.

An explosion in the city's size and population occurred shortly after World War I, when a vast exchange of populations occurred between Greece and the newly founded Republic of Turkey, with huge numbers of Greek-speaking people from Turkey crowding into the city. Occupied during World War II by the Nazi army, the city's population suffered from famine and disease.

GOVERNMENT AND POLITICS

Although Athens is often considered the birthplace of Western-style democracy, its recent history has not reflected this great heritage. Following World War II, the city was a battleground for Communist and royalist partisans during the Greek civil war. With U.S. military aid, the latter triumphed and Greece became a member of NATO. A tumultuous political period, culminating in the rise of a military junta in the 1960s and 1970s, ended with the permanent establishment of democracy and membership in the European Union.

ECONOMY

Athens is far and away the industrial center of Greece, a position it has held since before World War II. Indeed, over half the manufacturing jobs in the country are held by people in the Athens metropolitan area. The city's factories include both heavy and light industry, with major sectors devoted to chemicals, steel, automobile assembly, and ship repair. Light industrial establishments produce pottery, textiles, carpets, consumer items, and food products, including much of the country's cooking oil. The city is also a major publishing center. In recent years, the Greek government has offered financial incentives to get businesses to establish new or move existing factories outside the city. This effort is being made to alleviate congestion and the serious air pollution problem that the city faces.

In addition, Athens is the center of Greek business and includes headquarters for virtually all of the nation's banking, insurance, and commercial firms. It is also a major headquarters city for the shipping business. Over 50 percent of the city's workforce is involved in one form of trade or another.

TRANSPORTATION

The most serious source of air pollution is automobile and truck traffic. More than half of the cars, trucks, and buses of Greece operate in the Athens metropolitan area. In recent years the government has begun to fund a subway and expanded trolley service to supplement the city's thousands of buses and cars.

International transport for Athens includes major highways and rail lines to Istanbul and the Middle East, as well as to Europe via the former Yugoslavia, though the latter were disrupted by the war and sanctions that hit that country in the 1990s. However, Athens is best known as a center of shipping. Piraeus, Athens's port, is home to dozens of major and minor shipping lines, many of which operate ships flying Liberian and Panamanian flags. The port handles approximately 35 million tons of freight and over 12 million passengers annually.

HEALTH CARE

Since World War II, the Greek government has done an excellent job eradicating the many diseases—including malaria and dysentery—that once plagued the citizens of Athens. The infant mortality rate has been brought down to a First World level of 10 per 1,000 live births. The city's ratios of physicians and hospital beds to citizens are also near European averages at 304. In 1992, there were 5.8 physicians and 1.7 hospital beds per 1,000 residents. At the same time, the growth of industry and car ownership has created a major air pollution problem, which contributes to high rates of respiratory illnesses, including emphysema and bronchitis.

EDUCATION

Athens has achieved great strides in education since the end of World War II. While literacy rates were below 50 percent in the prewar period, they have since climbed to over 95 percent for the metropolitan area. Much of this has occurred because of the development of an extensive primary and secondary school system that teaches over 520,000 students, virtually the entire school-age population of the city. In addition, the city is home to several institutions of higher education. Among these, the oldest and largest is the University of Athens, founded shortly after independence in 1837.

HOUSING

Much of Athens has been rebuilt since the 1950s, with new apartment houses erasing the lines that once divided neighborhoods by class and ethnicity. And the city has grown dramatically in size, incorporating numerous small villages over the past fifty years. Much of this construction was done haphazardly and, with the many highways built to connect different parts of the city, gives Athens the jumbled and car-oriented look of an American city. In 1964, the city tried to impose a plan, but this was overwhelmed by rapid growth. The city's housing stock consists of nearly 1.6 million dwellings, most in low- and high-rise concrete apartment buildings, with an occupancy rate of about two persons per unit.

CULTURE, THE ARTS, AND ENTERTAINMENT

Athens is most famous for its many spectacular examples of ancient Greek architecture. Atop the Acropolis, near the center of the city, are the Parthenon, one of the most recognized monuments in the world, the Erechtheum, and the Propylaea. At the foot of the Acropolis are the theaters of Herodes and Dionysus, as well as the Agora, or ancient marketplace. Some of the finest examples of Greek sculpture are displayed in the National Archeological Museum. The city is also home to the Byzantine Museum, featuring arts from that period in the city's history, and the National Library.

While old Athens has largely disappeared, there are still well-preserved sections on Monastriraki Square, near the Agora. Numerous shops and taverns are frequented by locals and tourists alike and remain open late into the night, especially in the warmer months. Another popular neighborhood is the Plaka, on the Acropolis's north slope, with its tiny squares and Turkish-era baths.

CATEGORY	DATA	YEAR	AREA
LOCATION & ENVIRONMENT			
Area	168 square miles	1995	Metro
	454 square kilometers		Metro
Elevation	300 feet/108 meters		Metro
January Temperature	54 degrees Fahrenheit		Metro
	12.2 degrees Celsius		Metro
July Temperature	90 degrees Fahrenheit		Metro
	32.2 degrees Celsius		Metro
Annual Precipitation	15.8 inches/401.3 millimeters		Metro
POPULATION & DEMOGRAPHY			
Population	3,100,000	1996	Metro
Projected Population	3,100,000	2015	Metro
Growth Rate	0.2%	1990–1995	City
Growth Rate	0.8%	1995–2015	City
Density	18,315 per square mile	1983	City
	6,783 per square kilometer		
Gender			
Male	48%	1992	City
Female	52%	1992	City
Age			
Under 20	33.4%	1992	City
20–59	53.4%	1992	City
Over 60	13.2%	1992	City
VITAL STATISTICS			
Births per 1,000 Residents	10.6	1992	Metro
Deaths per 1,000 Residents	8.9	1992	Metro
Infant Mortality Rate	10 per 1,000 live births	1992	Metro
Net Migration per 1,000 Residents	−5.7	1992	Metro
ECONOMY			
Workforce	1,316,000	1992	City
Agriculture	1.2%	1992	City
Manufacturing	21.8%	1992	City
Construction	6.3%	1992	City
Trade	51.5%	1992	City
Service	17.6%	1992	City
Utilities	1.4%	1992	City

(continued)

CATEGORY	DATA	YEAR	AREA
TRANSPORTATION			
Passenger Journeys	998,000,000	1992	City
Passenger Vehicles	284,000	1992	City
HOUSING			
Housing Units	1,597,000	1992	City
Persons per Unit	2	1992	City
HEALTH CARE			
Physicians per 1,000 Residents	5.8	1992	City
Hospital Beds per 1,000 Residents	1.7	1992	City
EDUCATION			
Total Students	520,000	1992–93	Metro
Primary	52.5%	1992–93	Metro
Secondary	30.8%	1992–93	Metro
Higher	16.7%	1992–93	Metro

Sources: Department of Economic and Social Affairs, Population Division. *Urban Agglomerations, 1996.* New York: United Nations, 1997; Eurostat *Regions Statistical Yearbook.* Brussels, Belgium: Statistical Office of European Communities, 1996; and United Nations Center for Human Settlements. *Compendium of Human Settlements Statistics.* New York: United Nations, 1995.

Atlanta, Georgia
USA

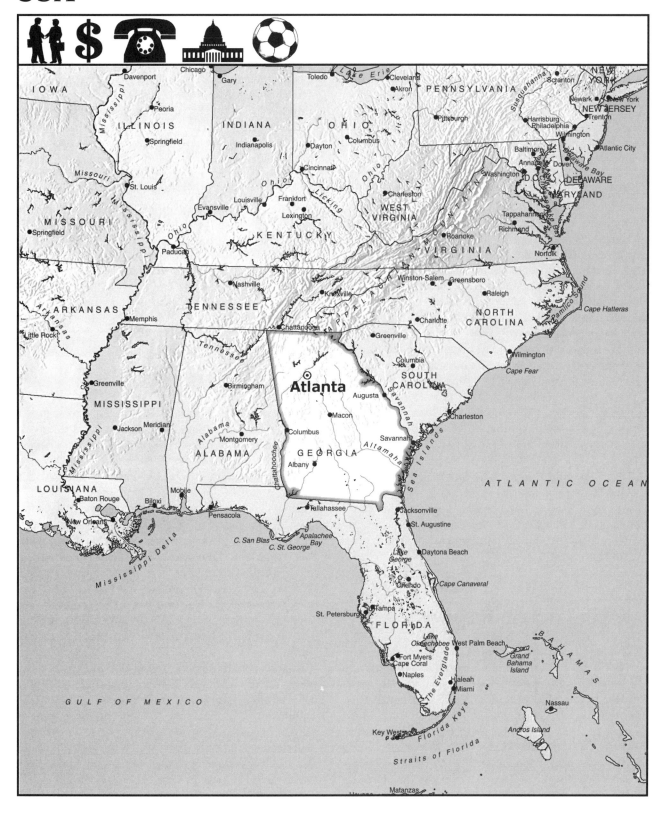

LOCATION

Atlanta, the capital of Georgia, the state's most populous city, and the urban center of one of the most rapidly growing metropolitan regions in the United States, is located in northwest Georgia, on the Piedmont Plateau, at the foot of the Blue Ridge Mountains at an elevation of 1,010 feet above sea level. The Chattahoochee River flows to the southwest from Lake Sidney Lanier, northeast of Atlanta, through the city's northwest side to West Point Reservoir, on Georgia's boundary with Alabama. Atlanta occupies a land area of 131.8 square miles (341.4 square kilometers) in both Fulton County, on the southwest, and DeKalb County, on the northeast. The Atlanta metropolitan statistical area encompasses Fulton County, DeKalb County to the city's east, and Cobb County, to the northwest. The City of Atlanta is the administrative center of Fulton County. Besides Atlanta, the metropolitan area includes the municipalities of East Point, Sandy Springs, and Roswell, in Fulton County; Dunwoody, North Atlanta, Tucker, and Candler-McAfee, in DeKalb County; and Mableton, Smyrna, and Marietta, in Cobb County. Atlanta occupies a central geographic location in the U.S. South. The city is 65 miles west of Athens, Georgia, 150 miles northwest of Augusta, Georgia, 110 miles southeast of Chattanooga, Tennessee, 110 miles northeast of Columbus, Georgia, 150 miles east of Birmingham, Alabama, 240 miles southwest of Charlotte, North Carolina, and 350 miles northwest of Jacksonville, Florida. In the three decades between 1960 and 1991, Atlanta's average temperature ranged from a January low of 41 degrees Fahrenheit (4.5 degrees Celsius) to a July high temperature of 79.6 degrees Fahrenheit (26 degrees Celsius). Over the same period, the city had an average annual precipitation of 49.7 inches (1,938 millimeters).

POPULATION AND DEMOGRAPHY

The Atlanta metropolitan area had a population of 2,500,000 in 1996. Atlanta's central city population declined by 7.1 percent between 1980 and 1992, from 425,022 to 394,848, continuing a two-decade-long urban decline. Atlanta has a density of 2,996 persons per square mile (8,089 persons per square kilometer). The city's population fell by over 20 percent in the twenty-two-year period from 1970 to 1992. While the urban population has dropped over the past two decades, the region as a whole has grown to be one of the largest and most important metropolitan areas in the United States. The central city of Atlanta makes up approximately 13 percent of the metropolitan area's 2.5 million residents. As the central city has lost population due to out-migration, the region has expanded due to the migration from the central city to the outlying suburbs and the in-migration to the Atlanta metropolitan area from other regions of the United States. About 24.1 percent of the population is under 19; 64.6 percent is between 19 and 64; and 11.3 percent is over 65 years of age. Atlanta's 264,262 black residents form a 67.1 percent majority; after Detroit, Atlanta has the highest percentage of blacks in the population of any city with a population exceeding 200,000. Hispanics comprise less than 2 percent of the city's population, and Asian and Pacific Islanders less than 1 percent. Only 3.4 percent of all city residents were born outside of the United States, and 5.8 percent speak a language other than English at home, lower than in most other major U.S. cities. The median age of Atlanta residents is 31.5 years. The gender ratio is 91.5 males for every 100 females.

HISTORY

In the early nineteenth century, the U.S. government formally settled Atlanta as a railroad head following the expropriation of the region from Native Americans. The site, known as Terminus in the 1830s, was situated at the southern extension of a railroad that extended from Chattanooga, Tennessee, to the city's northwest. The rail hub was first incorporated as the town of Marthasville in 1843 and then as a city in 1847; it became the state capital at the end of the Civil War. Atlanta became a major production and supply center for the Confederate war effort during the Civil War. As such, a major goal of the Union Army was to capture and destroy the city. The objective was achieved on September 2, 1864, when General William Tecumseh Sherman captured the city for the Union Army.

Atlanta was rebuilt following the end of the Civil War, and the city's population expanded rapidly in the late nineteenth century. The home of civil rights leader Martin Luther King Jr. from the 1950s through the 1970s, Atlanta was a focal point of African-American civil rights activity. By the 1970s, Atlanta was the largest center of commerce and trade in the American Southeast. In 1996, Atlanta hosted the summer Olympic Games.

GOVERNMENT AND POLITICS

Local government is administered by a mayor, elected every four years, who is responsible for executive functions and coordination of legislative functions with the City Council. The mayor appoints city department and bureau leaders. The eighteen-member Atlanta City Council is the city's principal legislative body, responsible for shaping city policy, appropriating funds, adopting the annual budget, setting tax rates, confirming mayoral appointments, and granting special licenses, contracts, and franchises.

ECONOMY

The Atlanta regional labor market was vibrant in the mid- to late 1990s as a result of the strong local economy. Although regional unemployment remained relatively low by historical standards, industrial restructuring and the shift to contingent part-time and temporary employment has reduced wages in the local labor market. The city's civilian labor market reached 175,126 workers in 1990, an increase of 1.4 percent over the preceding decade. The major employment sectors are wholesale and retail trade, with 20.4 percent of the labor force; manufacturing, with 9.4 percent; finance, insurance, and real estate, with 8.8 percent; health services, with 7.7 percent; and public administration, with 5.7 percent. Atlanta's workforce is economically competitive with those of other major U.S. cities due to the lower labor costs in the city. Although 27.3 percent of Atlanta's residents have incomes below the poverty line—fifth highest among major U.S. cities—the city still has a relatively low unemployment rate since many of those living in poverty have stopped looking for work due to the paucity of jobs that pay a living wage. The regional military installations are a major source of direct and indirect employment in the metropolitan area.

As the center of the largest consumer market in the U.S. Southeast, the city has a large and growing trade and distribution industry. The city's leading manufacturing industries are aircraft, motor vehicles, transportation equipment, food processing, printing and publishing, clothing, lumber, paper products, and chemicals. The city has a large and growing convention industry.

TRANSPORTATION

Private motor vehicles are the primary means of transportation in the Atlanta region and will continue to be into the twenty-first century. A regional transportation plan with $1.3 billion in federal and state funds will increase highway capacity by widening and adding roads. Some transportation analysts suggest that continued road expansion may lead to increased usage of private vehicles, more traffic congestion, and declining air quality. To reduce traffic congestion, the Metropolitan Atlanta Rapid Transit Authority (MARTA) operates a 45.4-mile rail transport system with four lines that converge in central Atlanta. Since MARTA began operations in 1979, ridership on the system has increased dramatically. By the beginning of the 1990s, 20 percent of Atlanta's population commuted to work with public transportation. Hartsfield-Atlanta International Airport—one of the largest airports in the United States—serves the metropolitan region.

HEALTH CARE

Atlanta is the headquarters of the Centers for Disease Control of the U.S. Public Health Service. Atlanta has sixteen community hospitals that provide beds to 5,529 patients, a fairly high rate of 1,403 beds per 100,000 city residents. The city has a natural population increase of 9.1 per 1,000 population, with 20.9 births and 11.8 deaths per 1,000 population. Atlanta's infant mortality rate is 16.4 infant deaths per 1,000 live births, more than double the national average, and tenth highest among America's seventy-seven major cities with populations exceeding 200,000.

EDUCATION

Atlanta's school enrollment is 76,398 students, or approximately 19 percent of the city's population. Students enrolled in grades 1 through 12 make up 59 percent of all students in the city. About 90 percent of Atlanta's primary and secondary students are enrolled in the city's public schools. The city ranks twentieth among major American cities in education, with 26.6 percent of the city's population over 25 years of age possessing a bachelor's degree or higher. The city's postsecondary educational institutions include Emory University, the Georgia Institute of Technology, Georgia State University, and Atlanta

University Center. The city and region are also served by numerous community colleges.

HOUSING

The city's housing stock increased 2.2 percent between 1980 and 1990, to 182,754 units. Due to the population loss over the past two decades, Atlanta has a favorable housing vacancy rate of about 15 percent, significantly higher than most other large urban centers. The high vacancy rate has reduced housing costs for the relatively large number of households who are renters. Owner-occupied housing units comprise 43.1 percent of Atlanta's housing stock. The median value of owner-occupied housing in the city is fairly competitive with values in other major U.S. cities. Atlanta ranks third among major American cities in the percentage of the population living in one-parent families and fourteenth in the percentage of one-person households. The reduction of federal funding to support affordable housing has placed greater stress on the local housing supply for Atlanta's poor and working-class families.

CULTURE, THE ARTS, AND ENTERTAINMENT

The major artistic institutions in Atlanta are the High Museum of Art, the Atlanta Historical Society, the Fernbank Science Center, and the Atlanta Museum. The city is home to major historical sites associated with the civil rights movement, including Ebenezer Baptist Church and the home of Martin Luther King, Jr. The city is served by the Atlanta Symphony Orchestra. After Atlanta was selected to host the 1996 Olympic Games, the region expanded and upgraded its stadiums, arenas, and sports facilities to accommodate the event. Most of the sports venues are located at Olympic Park. Following completion of the games, Olympic Stadium was converted into a baseball stadium for the Atlanta Braves baseball team. Atlanta has two other major league professional sports teams: the Falcons football team, who play in the Georgia Dome indoor sports facility, and the Hawks basketball team. In 1997, the National Hockey League selected Atlanta as a site for an expansion team, to begin play in 1999 in a new arena. The Atlanta metropolitan area is a center of collegiate and high school sports.

CATEGORY	DATA	YEAR	AREA
LOCATION & ENVIRONMENT			
Area	131.8 square miles	1995	City
	341.4 square kilometers		City
Elevation	1,010 feet/308 meters		City
January Temperature	41 degrees Fahrenheit	1961–1990	City
	4.5 degrees Celsius	1961–1990	City
July Temperature	79.6 degrees Fahrenheit	1961–1990	City
	26 degrees Celsius	1961–1990	City
Annual Precipitation	49.7 inches/1,938 millimeters	1961–1990	City
POPULATION & DEMOGRAPHY			
Population	2,500,000	1996	Metro
Projected Population	3,000,000	2015	Metro
Growth Rate	2.5%	1990–1995	Metro
Growth Rate	0.7%	1995–2015	Metro
Density	2,996 per square mile	1992	City
	8,089 per square kilometer		
Gender			
Males	47.3%	1990	City
Females	52.7%	1990	City
Age			
Under 19	24.1%	1990	City
19–64	64.6%	1990	City
Over 65	11.3%	1990	City
VITAL STATISTICS			
Births per 1,000 Residents	20.9	1988	City
Death per 1,000 Residents	11.8	1988	City
Infant Mortality Rate	16.4 per 1,000 live births	1990	City
ECONOMY			
Total Workforce	175,126	1990	City
Trade	20.4%	1990	City
Manufacturing	9.4%	1990	City
Health Services	7.7%	1990	City
Finance, Insurance, Real Estate	8.8%	1990	City
Public Administration	5.7%	1990	City
TRANSPORTATION			
Passenger Vehicles	186,219	1990	City
HOUSING			
Total Housing Units	182,754	1990	City
Persons per Unit	2.2	1990	City
Owner-Occupied Units	43.1%	1990	City
HEALTH CARE			
Hospitals	16	1991	City

(continued)

CATEGORY	DATA	YEAR	AREA
EDUCATION			
Total Students	103,195	1991	City
Primary and Secondary	59.4%	1991	City
Higher	40.6%	1991	City

Sources: Department of Economic and Social Affairs, Population Division. *Urban Agglomerations, 1996.* New York: United Nations, 1997; U.S. Bureau of the Census. *County and City Data Book 1994.* Washington, DC: U.S. Government Printing Office, 1994; and United Nations Center for Human Settlements. *Compendium of Human Settlements Statistics.* New York: United Nations, 1995.

Baghdad
IRAQ

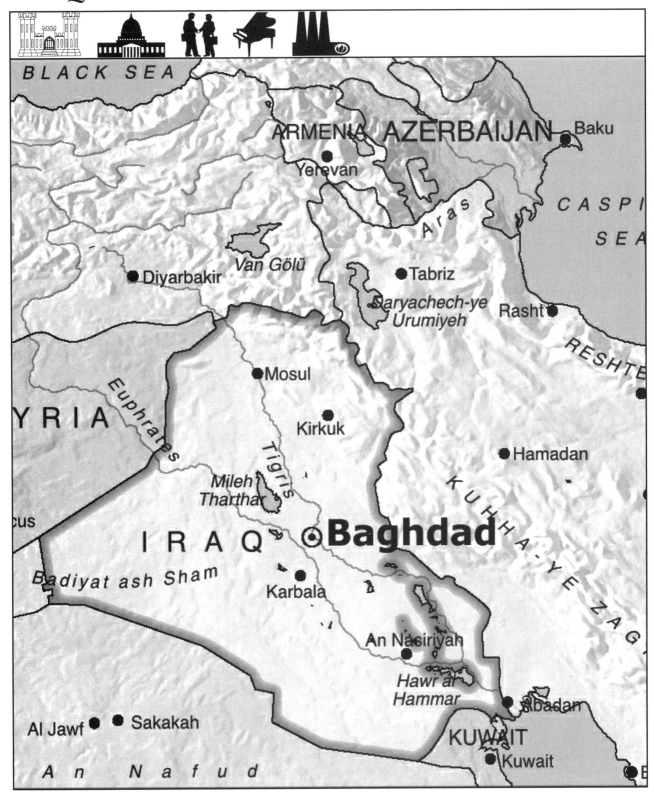

BLACK SEA

ARMENIA AZERBAIJAN • Baku

• Yerevan

CASPI

SEA

Aras

• Diyarbakir

Van Gölü

• Tabriz

Daryachech-ye
Urumiyeh Rasht •

RESHTE

• Mosul

Euphrates

YRIA

Tigris

• Kirkuk

• Hamadan

Mileh
Tharthar

K U H H A - Y E   Z A G

I R A Q   ⊙ **Baghdad**

cus

Badiyat ash Sham

• Karbala

• An Nasiriyah

Hawr al
Hammar

• Abadan

Al Jawf • • Sakakah

KUWAIT

A n   N a f u d

• Kuwait

LOCATION

Baghdad, the capital and largest city of Iraq, is located on the Mesopotamian alluvial plain. The city fronts on the Tigris River, about 330 miles northwest of the mouth of the Persian Gulf, in the center of Iraq. It is situated at an elevation of 111 feet (40 meters) above sea level. Teheran, Iran, is 425 miles to the east-northeast and Damascus, Syria, is roughly 400 miles to the west. The Baghdad metropolitan area covers 320 square miles (863 square kilometers). The city's summer climate is dry and extremely hot, with an average July temperature of 93 degrees Fahrenheit (33.9 degrees Celsius). Prevailing winds from the Gulf, known as *shamals*, can cool things somewhat, but they often bring dust storms in their wake. Winters are mild, with about 6 inches (152 millimeters) of rain and an average January temperature of 49.5 degrees Fahrenheit (9.7 degrees Celsius).

POPULATION AND DEMOGRAPHY

The city has seen major growth since World War II. In 1950, the population stood at about 600,000; in 1996, the metropolitan area's population was estimated at 4.4 million, and it is projected to reach 6.9 million by the year 2015. Since 1990, the annual growth rate has been 1.4 percent annually but it is expected to climb to 2.1 percent after the year 2000 because of the youthfulness of the population. The population density is about 14,580 persons per square mile (5,629 per square kilometer).

The population of Baghdad is largely Arab, though there are significant Kurdish and Turcoman minorities. All three groups are Sunni Muslim, though a number of Arab migrants from the south of Iraq practice Shiism. The city's population is quite young, with 51.4 percent under the age of 20, and only 4.6 percent over 60 years of age.

HISTORY

Human settlements have existed in what is now Baghdad since prehistoric times, and the city is located on the Mesopotamian plain, one of the cradles of Western civilization. With the invasion of Arab armies and the development of the caliphate in 762, Baghdad became the capital of a vast Arab empire stretching from Persia to North Africa.

This unity did not last. Divisions within the Arab world and invasion by Mongols, including the destruction of the city in the thirteenth century, saw the decline of Baghdad. Still, many great monuments from the city's golden era of the early Middle Ages remain, including the Abbasid Palace and the Mustansiriyan School of Islamic Law.

The conquering Ottomans in the sixteenth century divided Iraq into three provinces, or *wilayets*, with Baghdad governing the central one. With the fall of the Ottoman Empire after World War I, Great Britain, which had established extensive economic interests in the country since the early nineteenth century, took over. The League of Nations awarded London a mandate over the country after World War I. Around the same time, vast quantities of oil were discovered in the country.

GOVERNMENT AND POLITICS

Britain granted Iraq nominal independence under a hand-picked Saudi prince in 1932 but kept control of the nation's military and oil industry. A revolution in 1958 ousted the king and established a republic. A decade of turmoil and coups led to the victory of Saddam Hussein and his Ba'ath Party, which has ruled ever since.

The hike in oil prices in the 1970s flooded the government with wealth, much of which was spent building a vast modern infrastructure for the city, including new highways, bridges across the Tigris, government buildings, and health and education facilities. War with Iran during the 1980s diverted wealth, leaving much of the city in shabby condition.

This situation was further exacerbated by the 1991 multinational Gulf War to drive Iraq out of Kuwait, which it had invaded in 1990. Extensive allied bombing ruined much of the city's infrastructure. UN-imposed economic sanctions in the years since have left the nation and city's treasury in dire straits, as well as impoverishing Baghdad's citizens. The result has been deteriorating living conditions and a disintegrating infrastructure.

ECONOMY

Most of Iraq's industrial infrastructure is located in the Baghdad metropolitan area; 10.6 percent of the workforce of 1.04 million is engaged in manufacturing. Key industries include processed food, textiles, wood products, chemicals, plastics, electronics, and metalworking. Construction employs another 8.8 percent, while the trade sector employs 7.9 percent. As Baghdad is the capital of the country, much (in 1987 the estimate was over half) of the city's workforce is employed in the public sector in both national agencies and social services. Until the Gulf War, the city's budget was heavily dependent on oil income, but much of that has disappeared with the international sanctions against Iraqi oil exports imposed since the end of the war in 1991.

Baghdad's economy, once thriving and vibrant, has been hit hard by these sanctions. Not only were transportation, communications, and industrial facilities destroyed by bombing, but repairs have been slowed due to a shortage of necessary imported materials and parts. Inflation and unemployment caused by the sanctions have reduced many families' incomes significantly.

TRANSPORTATION

Transport facilities in Baghdad were generally extensive and well maintained before the Gulf War and the imposition of UN sanctions in 1991. Even during the midst of the long war with Iran, the number of passenger cars in the Baghdad metropolitan area grew from nearly 120,000 in 1980 to 342,561 in 1987, while the number of public buses increased from about 5,600 to over 10,000. A number of plans, the first of which was proposed in 1954, have called for a series of peripheral roads to alleviate traffic congestion in the city center.

Today Baghdad is relatively traffic-free because of the sanctions: Spare parts and new cars are in short supply. Ironically, air pollution has worsened; the lack of new equipment and spare parts for the country's oil refineries means that poorer-quality gas and diesel are being burned by vehicles and industry.

HEALTH CARE

The deteriorating condition of the city's infrastructure, due to a lack of spare parts, in the 1990s has led to serious epidemics. It is estimated that several hundred thousand Baghdad citizens, many of them children, have died because of the sanctions. And while the UN has allowed some medicines and medical equipment to be imported under an oil-barter program, the supplies remain inadequate and the city's extensive health care system, built in the flush days of the 1970s, has deteriorated. Before the war, Baghdad had 58 hospitals and a ratio of 1 physician for every 1,000 persons.

EDUCATION

Education has not been as hard hit, but is also suffering from the lack of revenues caused by the sanc-

tions. Before the war, the city boasted over 1,400 primary and secondary schools, with 817,000 students. Of persons age 5 to 24, 46.7 percent were in school. But many of the schools have gone on part-time schedules because of a lack of books and because many teachers have been forced to moonlight to supplement their lowered wages. The city is also home to several medieval-era and modern universities.

HOUSING

Utilizing the revenues generated by rapidly increasing oil prices in the 1970s, the Baghdad government embarked upon a massive project of low-income housing construction. This caused the Baghdad metropolis area to grow horizontally across the Mesopotamian plain, especially to avoid the effects of the occasional severe flooding of the Tigris River, which runs through the city. A dam-building program on the river in the late 1970s helped alleviate the problem, and the city government reemphasized high-rise construction to avoid metropolitan sprawl. By 1987, the metropolitan area included 419,876 dwellings. Constructions starts averaged nearly 8,000 units annually before sanctions put equipment and materials in short supply. In the early 1990s, only about 2,000 new dwellings went up each year. This shortfall and the fact that Arab households tend to be large means that each dwelling in Baghdad houses an average of about nine residents.

Until the Gulf War, Baghdad was a city well served by electricity and water, with over 90 percent of all homes connected to both grids. Damages resulting from heavy bombing—exacerbated by a lack of imported spare parts—has left sewage, electrical, and water systems in deteriorating condition.

CULTURE, THE ARTS, AND ENTERTAINMENT

Prior to the Gulf War, Baghdad had a lively culture and popular entertainment scene. The city's many coffeehouses were sites of conversation and debate. At the same time, the city was home to a theater and arts community, much of it subsidized by the government, though these artists were also heavily censored by the state. Since the war, the lack of income and the isolation of the country have hurt the arts scene, especially as many artists and performers have been forced into other pursuits to make ends meet.

CATEGORY	DATA	YEAR	AREA
LOCATION & ENVIRONMENT			
Elevation	111 feet/40 meters	1995	City
January Temperature	49.5 degrees Fahrenheit		City
	9.7 degrees Celsius		City
July Temperature	93 degrees Fahrenheit		City
	33.9 degrees Celsius		City
Annual Precipitation	19.3 inches/490.2 millimeters		City
POPULATION & DEMOGRAPHY			
Population	4,400,000	1996	Metro
Projected Population	6,900,000	2015	Metro
Growth Rate	1.4%	1990–1995	Metro
Growth Rate	58.3%	1995–2015	Metro
Density	14,580 per square mile	1987	City
	5,629 per square kilometer	1987	City
Gender			
Male	52%	1987	City
Female	48%	1987	City
Age			
Under 20	51.4%	1987	City
20–59	44.0%	1987	City
Over 60	4.6%	1987	City
ECONOMY			
Total Workforce	1,036,600	1987	City
Manufacturing	10.6%	1987	City
Construction	8.8%	1987	City
Agriculture and Mining	2.3%	1987	City
Trade and Hotels	7.9%	1987	City
Finance, Insurance, Real Estate	1.5%	1987	City
Social and Personal Services	55.6%	1987	City
Transport and Communications	6.4%	1987	City
Utilities	1.1%	1987	City
TRANSPORTATION			
Passenger Vehicles	342,561	1987	City
COMMUNICATIONS			
Telephones per 1,000 Residents	73	1987	City
HOUSING			
Housing Units	419,876	1987	City
New Housing Units	7,970	1989	City
Persons per Unit	9.2	1987	City
HEALTH CARE			
Hospitals	58	1987	City
Physicians per 1,000 Residents	1	1987	City

(continued)

CATEGORY	DATA	YEAR	AREA
EDUCATION			
Total Students 5–24 Years	817,000	1987	City
Males 5–24 Years in School	46.7%	1987	City
Females 5–24 Years in School	42.6%	1987	City

Sources: Department of Economic and Social Affairs, Population Division. *Urban Agglomerations, 1996.* New York: United Nations, 1997; *Statistics of World Large Cities.* Tokyo, Japan: Tokyo Metropolitan Government, 1992 and 1994; and United Nations Center for Human Settlements. *Compendium of Human Settlements Statistics.* New York: United Nations, 1995.

Baltimore, Maryland
USA

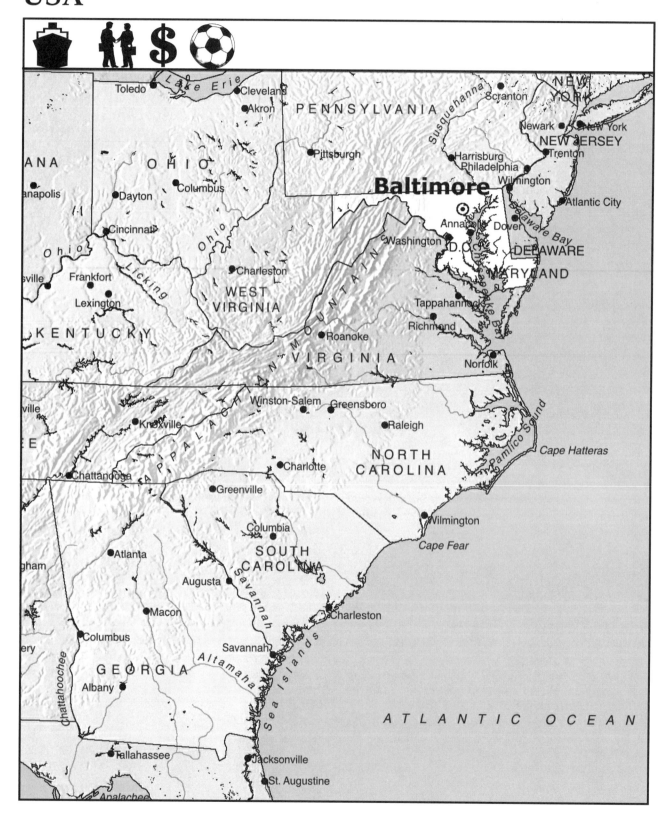

LOCATION

Baltimore is located on a lowland coastal plain in northeast Maryland at the northwest end of the Patapsco River, an inlet of Chesapeake Bay. Baltimore County—which is independent of the City of Baltimore—bounds the city to the east, north, and west. Covering a surface area of 80.8 square miles (209.3 square kilometers), Baltimore is the largest city in Maryland and one of five major population centers in the densely populated corridor extending from Washington, D.C.—40 miles to the southwest—to Boston, 400 miles to the northeast. Between 1961 and 1990, the average temperature in Baltimore ranged from a low of 31.8 degrees Fahrenheit (–0.1 degrees Celsius) in January to a high of 77 degrees Fahrenheit (25 degrees Celsius) in July. Over the same thirty-year period, Baltimore had an average annual precipitation of 40.8 inches (1,035.3 millimeters).

POPULATION AND DEMOGRAPHY

In 1996 the Baltimore metropolitan area had a population of 2 million. However, from 1980 to 1992, Baltimore's central city population declined by 60,645 to 726,096, a total of 7.7 percent. Approximately 59 percent of the city's population is black, 39 percent is white, 1 percent is Asian, and 1 percent is Hispanic. From 1995 to 2015, the Baltimore metropolitan region's population is projected to expand by over 15 percent, to 2,300,000. A large share of the city's population is under 18 years of age or over age 65. Sixty-two percent of all residents are in the 18-to-64 age range. The central city has a population density of 8,986 per square mile (3,470 per square kilometer). Over 53 percent of the central city population are female.

HISTORY

The Baltimore region was inhabited by Native Americans when it was explored by the British in the early seventeenth century. Baltimore was settled in 1729. Over the last two centuries Baltimore became a major port city and manufacturing and trading center. Baltimore's natural harbor contributed to the city's early development as a distribution hub for domestic and foreign goods. Baltimore emerged as a major American manufacturing center in the wake of the early-nineteenth-century expansion of the city's rail, road, and port capacity, which made the city attractive to industries seeking to take advantage of its access to consumer and producer markets. Manufacturers were also attracted to Baltimore by the abundant pool of low-wage labor, a result of migration to the city from the South after the Civil War. In the early 1890s, Baltimore's reputation as a manufacturing center was enhanced with the construction of Sparrows Point on a peninsula on the northern edge of Baltimore. Sparrows Point was the largest steel production complex in the world until the early 1980s, when it was unable to compete with modern steel mills and closed permanently. Baltimore's manufacturing economy has not recovered since the closing of Sparrows Point and suffers from growing competition from modern containerized ports.

GOVERNMENT AND POLITICS

The Office of the Mayor is responsible for the delivery of health services, the criminal justice system, economic development, monitoring of equal opportunity rights for women, and protection for the aged. City government operates the Baltimore public school system, the Enoch Pratt Free Library, fire services, housing and community development, planning, police, public works, recreation and parks, and social services. The Baltimore city government oversees quasi-public and public-private management and development partnerships.

ECONOMY

In the 1980s, Baltimore had high unemployment and rising rates of poverty, particularly in minority neighborhoods. However, the city has retained its industrial base, as some manufacturers have modernized their operations to compete with regional, national, and global producers. The City of Baltimore, in partnership with private business groups, has sought to diversify the local economy and promote the expansion and development of new technology-based industries (pharmaceuticals, medical supplies, biotechnology), trade, health care, personal services, finance, and banking. The modernization and development of the Inner Harbor area has promoted the growth of the business and tourist industries.

The city had a labor force of 347,593 in 1990. By 1990, manufacturing—employing 12.3 percent of the local labor market—had been eclipsed by wholesale and retail trade (17.6 percent) and health services (12.7 percent) as the largest sector of the central city labor market. Public administration and finance, insurance, and real estate accounted for significant shares of the local labor market. However, the transformation of the local economy away from manufacturing has reduced employment opportunities for unskilled and semiskilled workers, who earn significantly lower wages in entry-level retail and service sector jobs than they would in manufacturing. The scarcity of jobs that pay good wages, the persistence of high unemployment, and high poverty rates remain serious problems for the city. Unemployment in the urban areas hovered above the 10 percent rate, and in 1990, nearly 22 percent of all residents in the City of Baltimore had incomes below the poverty line, more than twice as high as the regional 10.1 percent poverty rate.

TRANSPORTATION

The Baltimore region is served by national, state, and local public transportation networks. Amtrak provides regular commuter rail service through Baltimore to major cities in the Washington-to-Boston corridor. The Maryland Mass Transit System operates over sixty bus routes in the Baltimore area. The Central Light Rail Line operates a 22.5-mile electric train route from Baltimore County to the City of Baltimore. Three commuter train lines, operated by the Maryland Rail Commuter Service, provide service to over 20,000 riders a day. The Baltimore Metro, a subway line opened in 1995 by the state transit system, runs a 15.5-mile subway route that carries approximately 44,000 commuters to fourteen stations from Owings Mills to Charles Center in Baltimore. Major interstate and state highway systems link the metropolitan area to national and regional destinations. The Port of Baltimore is modernizing its operations to remain a competitive shipping and distribution center.

HEALTH CARE

Health insurance is provided to most citizens through private insurance companies. To control rising health care costs, employers and health insurance plans in Maryland are shifting coverage to managed-care organizations that seek to regulate costs through limiting the scope of service. The state has already shifted Medicare and Medicaid recipients to managed-care organizations as a means to reduce the growth of spending. The City of Baltimore is served by eighteen hospitals and numerous health care clin-

ics, including several notable hospitals in the region affiliated with major university teaching hospitals.

EDUCATION

The City of Baltimore administers 145 public elementary and middle schools and 13 public high schools. Nearly 21,000 students were enrolled in the city's 123 private schools. The school district also administers vocational-technical, arts, alternative, and adult education programs. A total of 181,558 students were enrolled in Baltimore's schools, of which 119,468 (65.8 percent) were in primary and secondary education programs. Almost 61 percent of city residents are high-school graduates, and 15.5 percent hold postsecondary degrees. The city's leading colleges and universities are Johns Hopkins University, Loyola College, the College of Notre Dame, Coppin State College, Morgan State University, Towson State University, the University of Baltimore, and the University of Maryland at Baltimore. The city is a center of specialized training institutions in the arts, most notably the Peabody Conservatory of Music at Johns Hopkins University and the Maryland Institute College of Art.

HOUSING

In 1990, the City of Baltimore had 303,706 housing units, of which 276,484 were occupied. Owner-occupied housing units comprised 48.6 percent of all occupied housing units. Baltimore's revitalization, which began in the early 1980s, is concentrated in the downtown and Inner Harbor areas, and has largely benefited business and property owners. The many Baltimore urban redevelopment projects have concentrated on the urban core and all but ignored residents in surrounding neighborhoods, where a chronic shortage of safe and affordable housing persists. Critical issues identified by the city's department of housing and community development are the declining supply of adequate affordable housing, the decline in federal support for the development of affordable housing, the deterioration of public housing, the increase in homelessness, and the reduction in the number of middle-income residents. In this adverse environment, city housing officials are seeking to expand ownership opportunities for low- and moderate-income residents and affordable rental housing for low-income residents.

CULTURE, THE ARTS, AND ENTERTAINMENT

Among Baltimore's major museums are the Baltimore Museum of Art, the B&O Railroad Museum, the Baltimore Museum of Industry, and the Edgar Allan Poe House and Museum. The city's other attractions include the Enoch Pratt Free Library, the George Peabody Library, the Fort McHenry Monument, the Laurel and Pimlico race courses, the Maryland Historical Society, the National Aquarium, the Star-Spangled Banner Flag House, and Oriole Park at Camden Yards. The city is home to two professional sports teams—the Orioles baseball club, and the Ravens football team.

CATEGORY	DATA	YEAR	AREA
LOCATION & ENVIRONMENT			
Area	80.8 square miles	1995	City
	209.3 square kilometers		City
January Temperature	31.8 degrees Fahrenheit	1961–1990	City
	−0.1 degrees Celsius	1961–1990	City
July Temperature	77 degrees Fahrenheit	1961–1990	City
	25 degrees Celsius	1961–1990	City
Annual Precipitation	40.8 inches/1,035.3 millimeters	1961–1990	City
POPULATION & DEMOGRAPHY			
Population	2,000,000	1996	Metro
Projected Population	2,300,000	2015	Metro
Growth Rate	0.8%	1990–1995	Metro
Growth Rate	15.1%	1995–2015	Metro
Density	8,986 per square mile	1992	City
	3,470 per square kilometer		
Gender			
Males	46.7%	1990	City
Females	53.3%	1990	City
Age			
Under 18	24.4%	1990	City
18–64	61.9%	1990	City
Over 65	13.7%	1990	City
VITAL STATISTICS			
Births per 1,000 Residents	18	1988	City
Deaths per 1,000 Residents	13	1988	City
Infant Mortality Rate	18 per 1,000 live births	1988	City
ECONOMY			
Total Workforce	347,593	1990	City
Trade	17.6%	1990	City
Manufacturing	12.3%	1990	City
Health Services	12.7%	1990	City
Finance, Insurance, Real Estate	7.3%	1990	City
Public Administration	10.0%	1990	City
TRANSPORTATION			
Passenger Vehicles	257,316	1990	City

(continued)

CATEGORY	DATA	YEAR	AREA
HOUSING			
Total Housing Units	303,706	1990	City
Persons per Unit	2.4	1990	City
Owner-Occupied Units	48.6%	1990	City
HEALTH CARE			
Hospitals	18	1991	City
EDUCATION			
Total Students	181,558	1991	City
Primary and Secondary	72.3%	1991	City
Higher	27.7%	1991	City

Sources: Department of Economic and Social Affairs, Population Division. *Urban Agglomerations, 1996.* New York: United Nations, 1997; U.S. Bureau of the Census. *County and City Data Book 1994.* Washington, DC: U.S. Government Printing Office, 1994; and United Nations Center for Human Settlements. *Compendium of Human Settlements Statistics.* New York: United Nations, 1995.

Bangalore, Karnataka State
INDIA

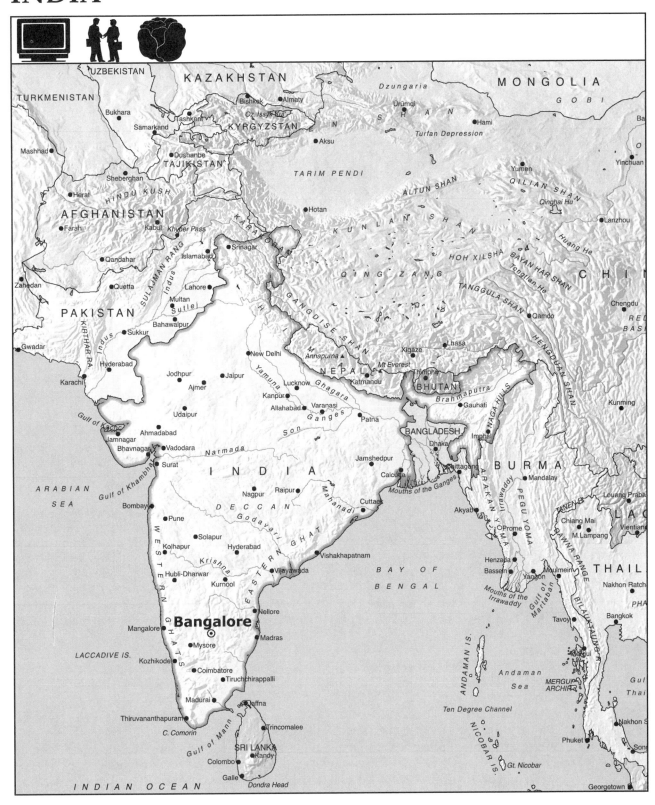

LOCATION

Bangalore is the capital of and largest city in the Indian state of Karnataka (formerly Mysore). Situated at 2,937 feet (895.2 meters) above sea level on the Karnataka plateau of south India, Bangalore is located approximately 200 miles due west of Madras and roughly 1,000 miles south of Delhi. The city limits encompass 56 square miles (151 square kilometers) of rolling hills and plains. Bangalore's elevation somewhat moderates the tropical heat typical of low-lying areas on the coast. The average temperature, which varies little between seasons, is 83 degrees Fahrenheit (28.5 degrees Celsius). Temperatures range from 87.3 degrees Fahrenheit (30.7 degrees Celsius) in January to 79.9 degrees Fahrenheit (26.6 degrees Celsius) in July. The city has a moderate amount of precipitation, receiving approximately 34.2 inches (868 millimeters) of rain annually, virtually all of it in the monsoon rains that wash over the city in the late summer and fall.

POPULATION AND DEMOGRAPHY

The population of the Bangalore metropolitan area was estimated at roughly 5 million in 1996. It has grown rapidly in the past few decades, with an annual increase of 3.5 percent during the 1990s. Much of this growth is due to natural increase—births exceed deaths by roughly 60,000 annually—and migration from the countryside and other Indian cities, the latter a result of Bangalore's thriving economy. While the growth rate is expected to slow to just over 2 percent early in the twenty-first century, population estimates for the year 2015 stand at roughly 8 million. The central portions of the city have a very high density, with 22,735 persons per square mile (8,420 per square kilometer). The city is a meeting point for the Kannada-, Telugu-, and Tamil-speaking populations of south India, though English is widely spoken. The vast majority of the city's population practices Hinduism.

HISTORY

While people have been inhabiting the area since prehistoric times, the modern city of Bangalore was founded in the sixteenth century around a mud fort built by a local ruler named Kempe Gowda. From 1831 to 1881, the city served as Britain's administrative capital for the region. From 1881 until India's independence in 1947, Bangalore was the seat of the raja's government of Mysore, though Britain maintained a significant military and administrative presence. Since independence, when the city was made a state capital, it has grown rapidly.

GOVERNMENT AND POLITICS

Bangalore is one of the nineteen districts of Karnataka state. At the head of the state government is a governor appointed by the president of India. The bicameral legislature consists of a legislative assembly—called the Vidhan Sabha—of directly elected members, and a legislative council, or Vidhan Parishad. The chief minister is assisted by a Council of Ministers. The state High Court is subordinate to the Supreme Court in New Delhi; it consists of a chief justice and several additional judges, who are appointed by the president of India in consultation with the chief justice of India and the governor of the state. There are also district and subordinate courts. A public service commission, whose members are appointed by the governor, functions in an advisory capacity.

ECONOMY

Bangalore has one of the most vibrant economies of any city in India. It is both the industrial and commercial center of Karnataka state, one of the largest in India. Older industries include textiles, pharmaceuticals, glassware, leather goods, footwear, agricultural implements, paper, and watches. But it is Bangalore's new role as a major producer of computer software that has put the city on the maps of the international business community. Known as the "Silicon Valley of India," Bangalore has become home to many software firms utilizing a highly skilled, English-speaking workforce. Over a third of the workers in the city are employed in the manufacturing sector, while approximately half labor in the commercial and service sectors.

TRANSPORTATION

Like most Indian cities, Bangalore is well served by intercity rail lines. In fact, as the southern terminus of the nation's vast rail network, Bangalore is home to one of the Indian railway's major repair yards. The city is served by several paved highways connecting it to Mumbai, Madras, and Kerala state. It also has a major regional airport, located about five miles east of the city, with regularly scheduled flights to Mumbai, Madras, and Colombo, Sri Lanka. The city boasts nearly 800 miles (1,300 kilometers) of paved road, much of it congested by over 500,000 vehicles. There are 37.9 telephones and 40.8 televisions per 1,000 residents.

HEALTH CARE

Several large hospitals and 250 small hospitals and clinics serve the Bangalore metropolitan area. The ratio of persons per physician is relatively low for India, at 2,035 to 1. The many clinics, the low ratio of patients to physicians, and the relatively healthful climate and elevation lend the city a healthy profile. Infant mortality rates are low for India, at 27 per 1,000 live births. The Employees State Insurance Scheme offers free medical treatment—covering work injuries and maternity care—for all workers and their families at state-run factories. A number of family welfare centers for the public are maintained by the government also, specializing in maternity and birth control.

EDUCATION

Bangalore has over 1,700 primary schools, serving nearly 500,000 students, and over 1,000 secondary schools, with a student population of over 400,000. But it is the city's many major universities and technical institutes that have contributed to Bangalore's growth as a center of high-tech industry. There are fifty institutions of higher learning, including the Bangalore University, the University of Agricultural Sciences, the Indian Institute of Science, the Raman Research Institute, the National Aeronautical Research Laboratory, and a division of the National Power Research Institute. Altogether, these institutions instruct over 65,000 students.

HOUSING

Bangalore has a severe housing shortage, largely due to the influx of people from the countryside and the high rate of natural increase among the city's population. There are 233,583 dwellings in the city, with an average of fifteen persons per unit. In 1990, some 6,100 new housing units were constructed. The city has a relatively reliable electricity system, though daily usage is a low 0.3 kilowatt-hour per person. The city's major utility problem, however, concerns water. With no steady rivers on the plateau and relatively light rainfall for south India, the city experiences serious water shortages, particularly in the dry months preceding the monsoon season.

CULTURE, THE ARTS, AND ENTERTAINMENT

Though largely an industrial and commercial center, Bangalore's location in Karnataka puts it within a short distance of major architectural and cultural sites, including Jain temples dating to the seventh century A.D. Bangalore city itself is home to several maharaja's palaces, the Mysore Government Museum, and the Lal Bagh botanical gardens, first landscaped in the eighteenth century. There are an additional two hundred or so parks in the metropolitan area. In addition, Bangalore boasts over fifty libraries and nearly a hundred theaters, largely featuring the rich heritage of Karnatakan drama, dance, and music.

CATEGORY	DATA	YEAR	AREA
LOCATION & ENVIRONMENT			
Area	56 square miles	1995	City
	151 square kilometers		City
Elevation	2,937 feet/895.2 meters		City
January Temperature	87.3 degrees Fahrenheit		City
	30.7 degrees Celsius		City
July Temperature	79.9 degrees Fahrenheit		City
	26.6 degrees Celsius		City
Annual Precipitation	34.2 inches/868.7 millimeters		City
POPULATION & DEMOGRAPHY			
Population	5,000,000	1996	Metro
Projected Population	8,000,000	2015	Metro
Growth Rate	3.5%	1990–1995	Metro
Growth Rate	66.8%	1995–2015	Metro
Density	22,735 per square mile		City
	8,420 per square kilometer	1992	City
Gender			
Male	53%	1990	City
Female	48%	1990	City
VITAL STATISTICS			
Births per 1,000 Residents	25	1990	City
Deaths per 1,000 Residents	7.2	1990	City
Infant Mortality Rate	27 per 1,000 live births	1990	City
ECONOMY			
Workforce	452,490	1984	City
Agriculture	35.1%	1984	City
Manufacturing	4.5%	1984	City
Construction	1.7%	1984	City
Finance, Insurance, Real Estate	19.3%	1984	City
Trade	3.5%	1984	City
Transport	12.7%	1984	City
Service	26.6%	1984	City
Utilities	3.3%	1984	City
TRANSPORTATION			
Total Journeys	517,203	1990	City
COMMUNICATIONS			
Telephones per 1,000 Residents	37.9	1990	City
Televisions per 1,000 Residents	40.8	1990	City
HOUSING			
Total Housing Units	233,583	1990	City
New Housing Units	6,100	1990	City
Persons per Unit	14.7	1990	City

(continued)

CATEGORY	DATA	YEAR	AREA
HEALTH CARE			
Hospitals	250	1990	City
Physicians per 1,000 Residents	0.5	1990	City
EDUCATION			
Total Students	985,292	1990	City
Primary	52.3%	1990	City
Secondary	6.7%	1990	City

Sources: Department of Economic and Social Affairs, Population Division. *Urban Agglomerations, 1996.* New York: United Nations, 1997; *Statistics of World Large Cities.* Tokyo, Japan: Tokyo Metropolitan Government, 1992 and 1994; and United Nations Center for Human Settlements. *Compendium of Human Settlements Statistics.* New York: United Nations, 1995.

Bangkok
THAILAND

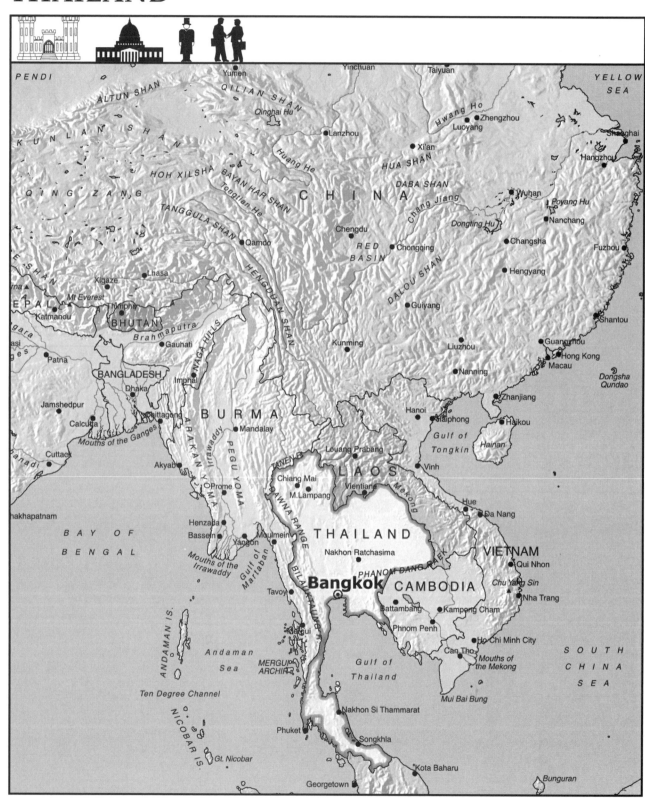

PENDI

YELLOW SEA

ALTUN SHAN
QILIAN SHAN
Yumen
Yinchuan
Taiyuan

Qinghai Hu
Qinghai Hu
Hwang Ho
Zhengzhou
Lanzhou
Luoyang
Shanghai

KUNLAN SHAN
Xi'an
Hangzhou

HOH XILSHA
BAYAN HAR SHAN
HUA SHAN

QING ZANG
Tongtian He
DABA SHAN
Wuhan
Poyang Hu

TANGGULA SHAN
C H I N A
Chang Jiang
Nanchang

HENGDUAN SHAN
Qamdo
RED BASIN
Chengdu
Dongting Hu
Changsha
Fuzhou

Chongqing
Hengyang

Xigaze
Lhasa
DALOU SHAN
Shantou

Mt Everest
Thimphu
Guiyang
Guangzhou

EPAL
BHUTAN
Kunming
Hong Kong
Macau

Katmandu
Brahmaputra
Liuzhou
Dongsha Qundao

Gauhati
Nanning

asi
ges
Patna
BANGLADESH
Imphal
Zhanjiang

Dhaka
NAGA HILLS
Hanoi
Haiphong
Haikou

Jamshedpur
B U R M A
Mandalay
Gulf of Tongkin
Hainan

Chittagong
Irrawaddy
Louang Prabang

Calcutta
ARAKAN YOMA
L A O S
Vinh

Mouths of the Ganges
TANEN R
Chiang Mai

anadi
Cuttack
PEGU YOMA
Vientiane
Mekong

Akyab
M.Lampang
Hue

hakhapatnam
BAWNA RANGE
Da Nang

BAY OF BENGAL
Henzada
Prome
T H A I L A N D
VIETNAM
Qui Nhon

Bassein
Moulmein
Nakhon Ratchasima
Chu Yang Sin

Yangon
PHANOM DANG RAEK
Nha Trang

Mouths of the Irrawaddy
Gulf of Martaban
Tavoy
Bangkok
CAMBODIA

Andaman Sea
Battambang
Kampong Cham

ANDAMAN IS.
Mergui
Phnom Penh
Ho Chi Minh City

MERGUI ARCHIP.
Gulf of Thailand
Can Tho
Mouths of the Mekong
SOUTH CHINA SEA

Ten Degree Channel
Mui Bai Bung

NICOBAR IS.
Nakhon Si Thammarat

Gt. Nicobar
Phuket
Songkhla

Kota Baharu

Georgetown
Bunguran

LOCATION

Bangkok, Thailand's capital, is located in south-central Thailand on the Chao Phraya River. The city is located 25 miles north of the Bight of Bangkok, an inlet of the Gulf of Thailand; the gulf extends about 500 miles southeast into the South China Sea. The city lies on a lowland plain at an elevation of 63 feet above sea level. In 1971, the Metropolis of Bangkok was created through the incorporation of the municipalities of Krung Thep, on the east bank of the Chao Phraya River, and Thon Buri, on the west bank of the river. The consolidated Metropolis of Bangkok has a surface land area of 604 square miles (1,565 square kilometers). The city is located about 100 miles due east of Thailand's western border with Myanmar (formerly Burma), 325 miles northwest of Phnom Penh, capital of Cambodia, 350 miles south-southwest of Vientiane, capital of Laos, and 475 miles northwest of Ho Chi Minh City, Vietnam, Southeast Asia's most populous city. Bangkok's temperature ranges from a January average of 77.4 degrees Fahrenheit (25.2 degrees Celsius) to a July average of 84.0 degrees Fahrenheit (28.9 degrees Celsius). The city averages 56.5 inches (1,435 millimeters) of precipitation per year.

POPULATION AND DEMOGRAPHY

With more than 10 percent of Thailand's population, the Bangkok metropolitan area is the most populous urban center in the nation. In 1996, Bangkok's regional population reached 6,700,000. The regional population is expected to continue to grow over the next twenty years, increasing by 11.5 percent, to 7,320,000, by the year 2000 and by 50.4 percent by the year 2015, when it will reach 9,800,000. The city has a density of 9,209 persons per square mile (3,554 persons per square kilometer). A high and rising birth rate and a low death rate are the primary components of the city's continued population growth. In 1992, Bangkok had 25.8 births and 5.7 deaths per 1,000 residents. The city's population growth is also attributable to migration from the rural countryside. The rapid population growth has contributed to severe overcrowding, placing pressure on the city's already overburdened services and infrastructure. Bangkok's age structure is young and productive: In 1992, 34.2 percent of the city's population was under 20 years of age, 59.2 percent were between 20 and 60 years of age, and 6.6 percent were over 60 years of age. Males account for 50.3 percent of the city's population. Marriages outnumber divorces in Bangkok by a four-to-one ratio. Thais comprise a large majority of Bangkok's population. However, Bangkok is considerably more diverse than Thailand as a whole. Many Chinese emigrated to the city beginning in the late nineteenth century, and persons of Chinese origin are Bangkok's largest ethnic minority. The other ethnic minorities in the city are considerably smaller in number than the Chinese minority. They include Arabs, Malays, Indians, and other South Asians. The city also has a small number of residents from Europe and North America.

HISTORY

The region now encompassing the Bangkok metropolitan area was for many centuries occupied by two port and fishing villages—Bangkok and Thon Buri. In 1782, Bangkok, known by Thais as Krung Thep, emerged as the capital of Siam. The name Bangkok derives from the Thai words for "wild plums district." Subsequently, the city rapidly developed as a major Southeast Asian urban center. From the late eighteenth to the mid-nineteenth century, Bangkok evolved as a major Buddhist religious center, and many Buddhist temples, known as *wats,* and palaces were constructed in the city. The city leaders also constructed an extensive canal transportation system. Beginning in the mid-nineteenth century, Bangkok's transportation infrastructure expanded to include roads and railways. Occupied by Japanese troops during the Second World War, much of Bangkok was destroyed by bombardments by Allied forces. In the period following the end of that war, rapid migration from rural areas contributed to extensive population growth, straining the city's housing, transportation, water supply, and other public services.

GOVERNMENT AND POLITICS

Bangkok is the center of the Thai national government, which takes the form of a constitutional monarchy. The bicameral legislature consists of a senate, which is an appointed body, and a house of representatives, whose members are elected once every four years. A governor and deputies are the chief administrators of the Metropolis of Bangkok, one of seventy-six administrative divisions in Thailand. The national government is responsible for the administration of regional planning and development. Bangkok is a major center of regional and international organizations, including branches of the United Nations, International Monetary Fund, and the Association of South East Asian Nations (ASEAN).

ECONOMY

Bangkok is Thailand's largest center of industry, commerce, finance, and government services. The Bangkok region has a diverse and vibrant economy, led by the service, trade, and finance sectors, which employ 28.4 percent of the regional workforce, and manufacturing, which accounts for 26.6 percent of the local labor force. The leading manufacturing industries in the region are textiles, wood products, food processing, building materials, and petroleum production. In the 1980s and 1990s, the region attracted high-technology production industries, including manufacturers of computer hardware and electronic equipment. Most manufacturing industries are located in Bangkok's outlying areas and suburbs. The majority of the locally manufactured goods are produced for export to North America, Western Europe, and other markets in developed countries. Bangkok's financial sector is dominated by banking, insurance, accounting, and financial services. Until the economic collapse of 1997, Bangkok had developed a thriving stock market and securities industry. Economic growth in the last two decades has increased the size of the government sector. International tourism is a major source of local revenue and employment. However, the informal sector, which is not regulated by the Thai government, accounts for a substantial share of the local economy; in addition, many rural migrants to the city and working poor are forced to resort to the underground economy to survive. The growth in corporate bankruptcies in 1996 contributed to a growing debt crisis and the collapse in the value of the Thai currency, the baht, in the summer of 1997. This placed further pressure on the government's ability to provide jobs that pay a living wage and adequate public services. To repay the debt owed to the international banking community, the International Monetary Fund, along with West European, North American, and Japanese banks imposed strict terms on the local economy, which contributed to a downward spiral in local wages and working conditions.

TRANSPORTATION

For most of the city's modern history, the primary form of transportation in Bangkok was the city's canal system. In recent years, the canals have been almost entirely replaced by roads. The growth in motor vehicle transportation has increased traffic congestion and air pollution in the urban region. Bangkok, unlike many large cities in Southeast Asia, has been slow to develop an integrated urban transportation system, significantly extending the time of local and regional commutes. The major form of mass transportation in Bangkok is the bus system. Highways link Bangkok with outlying towns and villages and with other major cities in Thailand and Southeast Asia. The city is also served by a much less extensive railroad system. The Bangkok port facility is the largest in Thailand. Don Muang International Airport, on the city's fringes, is Thailand's leading airport, serving both domestic and international travelers.

HEALTH CARE

Bangkok is Thailand's leading health care center, with an extensive network of medical institutions. The city is served by 107 local hospitals that provide a range of health care services. The city's medical centers provide specialized procedures and medical care, while basic services and preventive care are provided through smaller hospitals and local clinics. Bangkok has a ratio of 1.03 physicians per 1,000 urban residents. The official infant mortality rate in Bangkok of 9 infant deaths per 1,000 live births in 1992 is significantly lower than the 1996 Thai national average of 33.4 deaths per 1,000 live births. Life expectancy in Thailand is 68.6 years.

EDUCATION

Due to the large percentage of young residents in Bangkok, public schools are under pressure to provide education for the burgeoning population of children. The city's private schools, primarily parochial institutions, take some of the pressure off the public education system. In 1989, of the 1,112,142 students attending school in Bangkok, 88.2 percent were in primary and secondary schools, and 11.8 percent were enrolled in postsecondary institutions. The city's leading colleges and universities are Chulalongkorn University and Thammasat University. The city also has postsecondary institutions specializing in fine arts, agricultural science, medicine, and technology.

HOUSING

Due to the rapid rise in the city's population, Bangkok is facing a severe housing crisis. Many of the city's residents live in overcrowded and substandard housing. Although more-affluent residents have purchased flats in new apartment developments, there continues to be a dire need for public housing for the large number of residents who are unable to afford private housing. The city's inability to provide adequate and affordable housing has contributed to the growth of illegal settlements, known as shantytowns, that do not have basic services such as running water, electricity, and toilet facilities. In 1980, only 77.9 percent of the city's housing had piped water.

CULTURE, THE ARTS, AND ENTERTAINMENT

Bangkok is a leading tourist destination for local and international visitors. Among the city's most-visited sites are Buddhist temples, constructed in the city since the late eighteenth century, including Wat Pho, the oldest Buddhist temple in the city, and Wat Phra Kaeo (Temple of the Emerald Buddha). The city has six major museums, including the National Museum, which houses cultural and artistic relics dating back to the sixth century A.D., and Jim Thompson's Thai House, a center for Thai culture and art. The Silapakorn National Theater, a leading center for traditional and Western dance, theater, and music, is located in Bangkok. The city is also home to eleven libraries.

CATEGORY	DATA	YEAR	AREA
LOCATION & ENVIRONMENT			
Area	604 square miles	1995	City
	1,565 square kilometers		City
Elevation	63 feet/162 meters		City
January Temperature	77.4 degrees Fahrenheit		City
	25.2 degrees Celsius		City
July Temperature	84.0 degrees Fahrenheit		City
	28.9 degrees Celsius		City
Annual Precipitation	56.5 inches/1,435 millimeters		
POPULATION & DEMOGRAPHY			
Population	6,700,000	1996	Metro
Projected Population	9,800,000	2015	Metro
Growth Rate	2.1%	1990–1995	Metro
Growth Rate	50.4%	1995–2015	Metro
Density	9,209 per square mile	1992	City
	3,554 per square kilometer		City
Gender			
Male	50.3%	1992	City
Female	49.7%	1992	City
Age			
Under 20	34.2%	1992	City
20 to 60	59.2%	1992	City
Over 60	6.6%	1992	City
VITAL STATISTICS			
Births per 1,000 Residents	25.8	1992	City
Deaths per 1,000 Residents	5.7	1992	City
Infant Mortality Rate	9 per 1,000 live births	1992	City

(continued)

CATEGORY	DATA	YEAR	AREA
ECONOMY			
Total Workforce	2,978,900	1989	City
Trade and Finance	28.4%	1989	City
Manufacturing	26.6%	1989	City
Services	28.4%	1989	City
Transport and Communications	7.8%	1989	City
Construction	5.0%	1989	City
Utilities	1.1%	1989	City
Agriculture	2.0%	1989	City
Mining	0.4%	1989	City
Nonclassifiable	0.5%	1989	City
TRANSPORTATION			
Passenger Journeys	37,472,000	1990	City
Rail	100.0%	1990	City
Passenger Vehicles	899,161	1990	City
COMMUNICATIONS			
Telephones per 1,000 Residents	243.5	1992	City
Televisions per 1,000 Residents	249.2	1992	City
HOUSING			
Total Housing Units	902,871	1980	City
Persons per Unit	4.3	1980	City
Owner-Occupied Units	30.9%	1980	City
HEALTH CARE			
Hospitals	107	1995	City
Physicians per 1,000 Residents	1	1995	City
EDUCATION			
Total Students	1,112,142	1990	City
Primary	54.3%	1990	City
Secondary	33.9%	1990	City
Higher	11.8%	1990	City
Age 5–24 in School	54.4%	1990	City
Females 5–24 in School	51.7%	1990	City

Sources: Department of Economic and Social Affairs, Population Division. *Urban Agglomerations, 1996.* New York: United Nations, 1997; *Statistics of World Large Cities.* Tokyo, Japan: Tokyo Metropolitan Government, 1992 and 1994; and United Nations Center for Human Settlements. *Compendium of Human Settlements Statistics.* New York: United Nations, 1995.

Barcelona, Catalonia
SPAIN

LOCATION

Barcelona, the second largest city in Spain and the administrative and cultural capital of the Catalan region, is located on the coastal plain of northeast Spain, set between the Mediterranean and a semicircle of mountains an elevation of 312 feet (95.1 meters). Relatively small in area, the city covers just 37 square miles (100 square kilometers) of territory. It is located approximately 320 miles east-northeast of Spain's capital, Madrid, and some 500 miles south of Paris, France.

Typical for a Mediterranean city, Barcelona enjoys a mild climate, with warm and breezy summers and cool and rainy winters. January and July temperatures average 47.1 and 74.1 degrees Fahrenheit (8.4 and 23.4 degrees Celsius), respectively. The city receives approximately 23.5 inches (596 millimeters) of rain annually, most of it falling in the winter and spring months.

POPULATION AND DEMOGRAPHY

The population of the Barcelona metropolitan area is 2.8 million. Due to extreme congestion in the city center, the city has seen a decline in population of about 1 percent annually over the past few years. Natural increase is expected to compensate for this in the next few years, and the city's population is predicted to be stable through the second decade of the twenty-first century. Barcelona's age profile is more typical of northern European cities, with just over 22.2 percent of the population falling under the age of 20 and another 23.8 percent exceeding 60 years of age.

Barcelona's population is divided between Spanish-speaking and Catalan-speaking citizens. Recent laws have emphasized the teaching of Catalan in schools, and so this segment of the population is expected to grow. Virtually the entire population is Roman Catholic, though many do not practice the faith. More religious are the city's minority of North African Muslim immigrants, most of whom have been drawn to jobs in the city in recent years.

HISTORY

Barcelona is among the oldest cities on the Iberian peninsula. According to tradition, it was founded by either Phoenician or Carthaginian traders in the first millennium B.C. The city was incorporated into the Roman Empire in the fourth century B.C. and became a major trading port in the next century. Under the Visigoths, who invaded and captured the city in the fourth century A.D., Barcelona became a major reli-gious center, a role it played until its capture by invading Muslim Moors in 717. Between the early ninth century and the early tenth century, the city changed hands several times between Christian and Moorish forces. After the union of Christian Catalonia and Aragon in 1137, the city gained in importance as a trading center once again.

Hit hard by the plague in the fourteenth century, the city went into further decline when the capital of the Catalan-Aragon kingdom was moved to Naples and the city's trade was undermined by Turkish control of the Mediterranean. During the War of the Spanish Succession in the early eighteenth century, the city became a battleground between the forces of Charles III of Austria and King Philip V of Spain. Though it saw the imposition of rule from Madrid, the reign of Philip V coincided with the growth of Barcelona as a major center of textile production. This helped make Catalonia the richest region of Spain.

Following the Napoleonic occupation from 1808 to 1813, the city grew into Spain's major manufacturing center and a focal point of working-class organization. Anarchist movements flourished, and the city was a major center of republican strength during the war against the Fascists under Francisco Franco in the 1930s. Under Franco's rule, Barcelona's indigenous Catalan culture was suppressed. But with the death of Franco and the restoration of Spanish democracy in the 1970s and 1980s, the city has experienced a renewal of Catalan culture and economic prosperity, and it has become a popular tourist destination.

GOVERNMENT AND POLITICS

Barcelona is the capital of both the province of Barcelona and the autonomous region of Catalonia. The Generalitat, the autonomous government for Catalonia, was restored in 1977. Under an agreement signed with the Spanish government two years later, the city government was given wider control over its own affairs and administration. Barcelona is now ruled as a separate municipality. Its councilors, elected every four years, select a mayor who, in turn, appoints three deputies to assist in the day-to-day operations of the city.

ECONOMY

Barcelona is the second largest manufacturing center in Spain, after Madrid. Despite its smaller size, however, the city's factories tend to be more modern than those of the capital, and they have established themselves as major exporters of textiles, metals, and machinery, the latter two sectors overtaking the former in recent years. Some 29.8 percent of the labor force works in the manufacturing sector. The city is also home to a major artisanal sector that produces fine woven goods and leathers.

The Catalans have always been famous in Spain for their commercial skills, and the city is home to a thriving small business sector. The vast majority of commercial enterprises have fewer than two hundred employees. In addition, there is a free economic zone near the port, which accounts for much of the international investment in the city. Overall, trade employs nearly half the city's workforce. Barcelona is also a major tourist center and is a popular locale for international trade fairs, exhibitions, and conferences.

TRANSPORTATION

Catalonia has the best transportation infrastructure on the Iberian peninsula. Major expressways and high-speed trains connect the city to Madrid and, via France, to the rest of Europe. Among the largest ports in Spain, Barcelona handles over 18 million tons of freight and some 650,000 passengers annually, many of them on ships bound for the Balearic Islands.

Metropolitan traffic is largely handled by the city's subway, opened in 1924. In addition, there are several commuter rail lines and an extensive bus system. Car ownership is widespread, contributing to major traffic problems in the intensely crowded coastal corridor.

HEALTH CARE

The Barcelona municipal government, the Catalan regional government, and the national government in Madrid have made great strides in alleviating the health care problems that once plagued the city. Virtually gone are diseases like malaria and tuberculosis, which were once common. The city's infant mortality rate is among the lowest in the world, at just 3.8 deaths per 1,000 live births. The Barcelona metropolitan area is home to more than sixty-five hospitals and clinics, and the patient-to-physician ratio is a good 120 to 1.

EDUCATION

Barcelona has long had one of the most extensive primary and secondary school systems in Spain. In recent years, there has been a major effort to emphasize primary instruction in the Catalan language, with Spanish relegated to a secondary role. In addition, the city has nearly 100,000 university students, attending some fifteen institutions of higher education. These include the Universidad de Barcelona, founded in 1450, the Universidad Autonoma de Barcelona, established in 1968, and the Universidad Politecnica de Cataluna, first opened in 1971. All three offer courses in both Spanish and Catalan.

HOUSING

While the Barcelona metropolitan area has an adequate stock of housing, the central city is extremely crowded. Apartments are hard to find and expensive to rent. The occupancy rate is relatively high for a West European city, with about 2.5 persons per unit. The government's policy of locating new housing developments outside the city has eased congestion somewhat over the past twenty years.

Much of the city's electrical supply comes from hydroelectric projects in the nearby Pyrenees mountains, as well as from a nuclear power plant. With the rapid growth in population after World War II, the city has experienced a problem in securing an adequate water supply.

CULTURE, THE ARTS, AND ENTERTAINMENT

As the regional capital of Catalonia, Barcelona enjoys a lively cultural scene, especially in recent years with the revival of Catalan literature and arts. The city abounds in private and public libraries. In addition, the city is home to several major dramatic and musical forums, including the Gran Teatro del Liceo, the Teatro Romea, and the Palacio de la Musica, home of the city's symphony orchestra.

A longtime center of fine art, the city boasts several major art museums. These include the Museo de Arte de Cataluna, the Frederico Mares Museum, and the Museo de Arte Moderno, as well as museums dedicated to Catalan artists like Joan Miró and Pablo Picasso. Perhaps best-known for its architecture, Barcelona is marked by elegant apartment buildings set along wide boulevards known as the Ramblas. Highlighting the city's architectural scene are the works of the eccentric modernist Antonio Gaudi, including the Templo Expiatorio de la Sagrada Familia and the Casa Batello and Casa Mila apartment houses. The city's cafe scene is renowned throughout Europe, and its many bookstalls draw bibliophiles from around the Spanish-speaking world.

CATEGORY	DATA	YEAR	AREA
LOCATION & ENVIRONMENT			
Area	36.7 square miles	1995	City
	99 square kilometers		City
Elevation	312 feet/95.1 meters	1995	City
January Temperature	47.1 degrees Fahrenheit		City
	8.4 degrees Celsius		City
July Temperature	74.1 degrees Fahrenheit		City
	23.4 degrees Celsius		City
Annual Precipitation	23.5 inches/596 millimeters		City
POPULATION & DEMOGRAPHY			
Population	2,800,000	1996	Metro
Projected Population	2,800,000	2015	Metro
Growth Rate	−0.7%	1990–1995	City
Growth Rate	0.0%	1995–2015	City
Density	44,439 per square mile	1983	City
	16,459 per square kilometer		
Gender			
Male	47.2%	1992	City
Female	52.8%	1992	City
Age			
Under 20	22.2%	1992	City
20–59	54.0%	1992	City
Over 60	23.8%	1992	City
VITAL STATISTICS			
Births per 1,000 Residents	8.1	1992	Metro
Deaths per 1,000 Residents	9.3	1992	Metro
Infant Mortality Rate	3.8 per 1,000 live births	1992	Metro
Net Migration per 1,000 Residents	−0.1	1992	Metro
ECONOMY			
Workforce	2,198,000	1992	Metro
Agriculture	3.5%	1992	Metro
Utilities	0.8%	1992	Metro
Manufacturing	29.8%	1992	Metro
Construction	8.9%	1992	Metro
Market Services	42.9%	1992	Metro
Nonmarket Services	14.2%	1992	Metro
TRANSPORTATION			
Passenger Journeys	320,238,000	1992	City
Passenger Vehicles	381,000	1992	City
HOUSING			
Housing Units	711,440	1992	City
New Housing Units	4,103	1992	City
Persons per Unit	2.5	1992	City

(continued)

CATEGORY	DATA	YEAR	AREA
HEALTH CARE			
Physicians per 1,000 Residents	4.2	1992	Metro
Hospital Beds per 1,000 Residents	0.9	1992	Metro
EDUCATION			
Total Students	346,521	1990	City
Primary	49.3%	1990	City
Secondary	22.3%	1990	City
Higher	28.4%	1990	City

Sources: Department of Economic and Social Affairs, Population Division. *Urban Agglomerations, 1996.* New York: United Nations, 1997; *Statistics of World Large Cities.* Tokyo, Japan: Tokyo Metropolitan Government, 1992 and 1994; United Nations Center for Human Settlements. *Compendium of Human Settlements Statistics.* New York: United Nations, 1995; and Eurostat *Regions Statistical Yearbook.* Brussels, Belgium: Statistical Office of European Communities, 1996.

Beijing
PEOPLE'S REPUBLIC OF CHINA

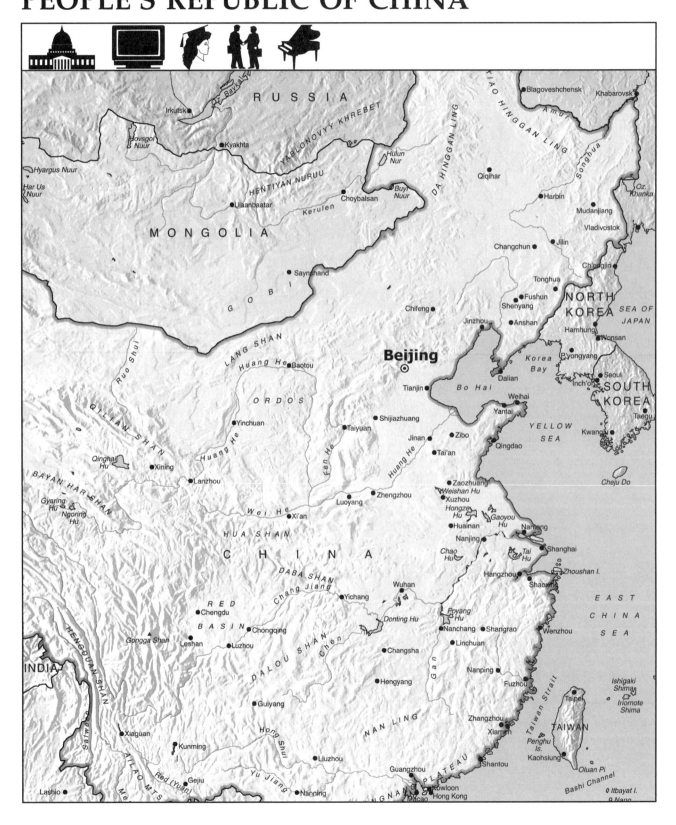

LOCATION

Beijing, capital of the People's Republic of China, is located in northeastern China, about 110 miles northwest of the Bohai Sea, an inlet of the Yellow Sea. The city is situated on the North China Plain, south of the Great Khingan Mountains, at an elevation of 164 feet above sea level. Beijing is intersected by five waterways: the Yongding, Chaobai, Juma, and Juhe Rivers, and the North Canal. The city covers a surface area of 1,043 square miles (2,701 square kilometers). Beijing Municipality, which encompasses a 6,490-square-mile (16,810-square-kilometer) regional area, consists of ten urban districts and eight rural counties. The ten core urban districts are made up of four densely populated neighborhoods and six rapidly expanding suburban zones. Beijing Municipality, a provincial-level municipality, is encircled by Hebei Province, a large industrial and agricultural region with over 61 million residents. The southeastern extremity of Beijing Municipality borders on Tianjin Municipality, a provincial-level unit that includes the industrial port city of Tianjin, 80 miles to Beijing's southeast. Beijing is located about 675 miles north-northwest of Shanghai, China's most populous city, and 1,200 miles north of Hong Kong, China's leading financial and commercial center. Beijing's temperature ranges from an average of 30.7 degrees Fahrenheit (–0.7 degrees Celsius) in January to an average of 78.6 degrees Fahrenheit (25.9 degrees Celsius) in July. The city averages 22.5 inches (572.5 millimeters) of precipitation per year.

POPULATION AND DEMOGRAPHY

After Shanghai, Beijing is China's most populous city. In 1995, the metropolitan area was estimated to have a population of 11.4 million. That population is projected to continue to expand rapidly over the next twenty-year period, ending in the year 2015. Demographers project that the regional population will increase by 37.8 percent, to 15.6 million residents, by the year 2015. In 1991, Beijing's central city population was 10,395,000. Beijing has a relatively low density due to the municipality's large geographic area. In 1991, the regional density was 1,602 persons per square mile (618 persons per square kilometer). Beijing's population structure is skewed toward the young and productive. Young residents under 15 years of age comprise 19.6 percent of the population; persons between 15 and 64 years of age comprise 72.5 percent of the population; and seniors over 65 account for 7.8 percent of the city's population. Bei-

jing's regional dependency ratio is 37.8 persons per 100 residents between 15 and 64 years of age. Family planning programs have significantly reduced the high fertility rates of previous decades. In 1995, the region had 7.9 births and 5.1 deaths per 1,000 residents, producing a natural growth rate of 2.8 percent. The remaining population growth is attributable to migration. However, in Beijing state and regional authorities have curbed the rapid population growth experienced by many other major cities in developing countries in the late twentieth century by placing restrictions on migration from rural areas. Those migrants who arrive from rural areas are typically low-wage unskilled workers who reside in substandard accommodations. Males comprise a 50.8 percent majority of the central city's population. The city is primarily composed of persons of Han Chinese ancestry. The two largest ethnic minorities in Beijing are of Manchu and Mongol origin.

HISTORY

Historians and archeologists believe that the area that now encompasses Beijing on the North China Plain was settled more than five thousand years ago. From the eleventh century B.C. to the third century B.C., the city was the government center of the Chou Dynasty. The city remained an important provincial center between the third century B.C. and the tenth century A.D. From the tenth century to the twelfth century A.D., Beijing became the southern capital of the Khitan Mongols. In the twelfth and thirteenth centuries, Beijing was capital of the Chin and Yuan Dynasties, and in 1272, Kublai Khan came to power. In 1368 the Ming Dynasty moved the capital from Beijing to Nanjing. The capital reverted back to Beijing in 1420 under the Yongle emperor. From the mid-seventeenth century until 1911, Beijing remained China's capital under the Qing Dynasty. With the overthrow of the Qing Dynasty and the founding of the Republic of China in 1911, the capital was again moved back to Nanjing by Chiang Kai-shek, the nationalist leader. The city was occupied by Japanese forces during World War II until the defeat of the Japanese in 1945. After the Chinese nationalists were forced from power in the 1949 revolution, Beijing was reestablished as the capital of the People's Republic of China. Under Communist leadership Beijing expanded in economic and political importance as a major center of industry, transportation, commerce, and government administration. Government planning and restrictions on geographic mobility have controlled urban population growth. However, at the end of the twentieth century, in-migration from the rural areas has placed severe pressure on the city's ability to provide housing and adequate public services. Many residents of the city are "guest workers" from the countryside who have fewer legal rights and more limited access to decent-paying jobs and provisions.

GOVERNMENT AND POLITICS

Beijing is the People's Republic of China's administrative center. The city is home to the executive, legislative, and judicial branches of China's government and is headquarters of the Chinese Communist Party. Local government is administered through the Beijing Municipal District, an independent provincial-level administrative division.

ECONOMY

Beijing is one of China's leading economic centers. Since the 1949 revolution, the region's economic base has been transformed from agriculture to manufacturing, primarily through government industrial planning and direct investment. The regional economy also includes industries managed collectively by their workers; since the early 1980s, private firms have been permitted as well. As part of a national economic restructuring program, the central government is promoting foreign private investment and ownership. At the end of the century, the region's leading local industries are manufacturing, commerce, and finance.

The leading official sectors of Beijing's economy are manufacturing, accounting for 28.2 percent of the local labor force, followed by trade, with 12.1 percent; agriculture and construction, with 10.6 percent; and social services, accounting for 7.7 percent of all workers in the region. The leading manufacturing industries in the local economy are iron and steel production, motor vehicles, machinery, electronics, petrochemicals, petroleum refining, building products, food processing, textiles, printing, and paper products. The city has a growing service sector, led by government services, and an expanding retail and wholesale trade sector.

Although the central government's privatization program is contributing to higher levels of productivity and efficiency, it is also causing permanent factory closures, layoffs, and rapidly growing levels of official unemployment. Rising levels of regional un-

employment are increasing migration to the city, considered illegal by the central government. To survive, many urban workers are forced out of the official economy and into the growing informal sector, which consists of economic activity not regulated or overseen by the government.

TRANSPORTATION

Despite the improvement of public transportation and the growth of motor vehicle use, the bicycle remains Beijing's leading mode of urban transportation. To reduce traffic congestion and facilitate commerce, Beijing authorities have improved and expanded the city's public transportation network. The city is served by an integrated public transit system that includes a thirty-year-old subway system, buses, and trolleys, but nearly all of Beijing's public transit is provided through buses and trolleys: The city has 15.1 buses per 10,000 residents, a higher rate than any other major city in China. Despite continued improvements in Beijing's public transportation system, the city continues to face a serious and growing traffic congestion problem.

Since the 1970s, Beijing's regional transportation network has been substantially upgraded, facilitating the expansion of regional, national, and global trade. The transportation improvements include the construction of a modern road and highway system connecting the region to Tianjin, other nearby coastal cities, and leading urban centers throughout mainland China. Over the last twenty years, the city's rail links to coastal and regional cities have also been refurbished and modernized. Beijing is a major air transportation hub for both international and domestic carriers.

HEALTH CARE

The upgrading and expansion of public access to health care since the revolution in 1949 has substantially reduced the occurrence of infectious diseases and increased life expectancy. Health care is more widely accessible in Beijing than in any other major city in China. Beijing has more hospitals per capita than any other region or municipality in the country. In 1995, Beijing Municipality was served by 629 hospitals, with 4.96 hospital beds and 9 medical personnel per 1,000 residents. The city is China's leading specialized care center, with the nation's most modern health care facilities. Since the early 1970s, local family planning centers have been given responsibility for closely monitoring female fertility. Under Chinese law, females are limited to one child each.

EDUCATION

Beijing has a large municipal school system. Nearly 59 percent of all students attend primary schools, and about 41 percent attend secondary schools. Beijing is China's leading center for postsecondary education, science, and research. The city's colleges and universities attract scholars, researchers, and students throughout China and the world. With 65 postsecondary institutions, Beijing has far more colleges and universities than any other urban center in the nation. The leading institutions are Beijing University, Qinghua University (one of China's leading scientific and technological training institutions), and People's University.

HOUSING

Although family planning programs are slowing Beijing's growth rate, the city is still faced with a major housing crisis due to the continued unauthorized migration of rural residents to the city in search of work. Since the far-reaching introduction of the market-oriented economy in the 1980s, a large and growing number of rural residents, unable to maintain their standard of living in the countryside, have been forced to migrate to Beijing, placing extensive pressure on the urban housing stock. Many inhabitants in the municipality live in severely cramped quarters or in shanties that have been constructed without government permission. In 1995, the official per capita living space in the city was 8.9 square meters per person. While 100 percent of all registered housing units in Beijing have residential tap water and 91.7 percent are hooked up to gas lines, the reality is that many more residents live in unauthorized housing with substandard services or are permanently homeless.

CULTURE, THE ARTS, AND ENTERTAINMENT

Beijing is one of the leading centers of Chinese culture and arts. Many of the city's landmarks, such as palaces, temples, and monuments, date back to the imperial period. Beijing has more museums than any other major urban center in China. In 1991, the city had fifty-three museums, including the five-hundred-year-old Palace Museum, a popular cultural attraction located in the Forbidden City that encompasses the old imperial city. The city is also home to the Museum of China's History and Revolution, which houses documents and artifacts from the 1949 revolution. Beijing is a center of Chinese and Western performance and has many theaters and concert halls. In 1991, the city had eighty-nine cinemas.

CATEGORY	DATA	YEAR	AREA
LOCATION & ENVIRONMENT			
Area	6,489 square miles/	1995	Metro
	16,807 square kilometers		
Elevation	164 feet/50 meters		Metro
January Temperature	30.7 degrees Fahrenheit		Metro
	−0.7 degrees Celsius		Metro
July Temperature	78.6 degrees Fahrenheit		Metro
	25.9 degrees Celsius		Metro
Annual Precipitation	22.5 inches/572.5 millimeters		Metro
POPULATION & DEMOGRAPHY			
Population	11,400,000	1996	Metro
Projected Population	15,600,000	2015	Metro
Growth Rate	0.9%	1990–1995	Metro
Growth Rate	37.8%	1995–2015	Metro
Density	1,602 per square mile	1992	Metro
	618 per square kilometer		Metro
Gender			
Male	50.8%	1992	Metro
Female	49.2%	1992	Metro
Age			
Under 15	19.6%	1995	Metro
15 to 64	72.5%	1995	Metro
Over 65	7.8%	1995	Metro
VITAL STATISTICS			
Births per 1,000 Residents	7.9	1995	Metro
Deaths per 1,000 Residents	5.1	1995	Metro
ECONOMY			
Total Workforce	6,695,000	1995	Metro
Trade	12.1%	1995	Metro
Manufacturing	28.2%	1995	Metro
Services	7.7%	1995	Metro
Finance, Insurance, Real Estate	2.0%	1995	Metro
Transport and Communications	4.3%	1995	Metro
Construction	10.6%	1995	Metro
Government	4.7%	1995	Metro
Utilities	0.6%	1995	Metro
Agriculture	10.6%	1995	Metro
Mining	0.7%	1995	Metro
TRANSPORTATION			
Passenger Journeys	3,384,440,000	1990	Metro
Buses and Trolleys	98.9%	1990	Metro
Rail	1.1%	1990	Metro
Passenger Vehicles	3,685,000	1995	Metro

(continued)

CATEGORY	DATA	YEAR	AREA
COMMUNICATIONS			
Telephones per 1,000 Residents	47.9	1992	Metro
HOUSING			
Total Housing Units	3,431,000	1991	Metro
Persons per Unit	3	1991	Metro
HEALTH CARE			
Hospitals	629	1995	Metro
Physicians per 1,000 Residents	9	1995	Metro
EDUCATION			
Primary	58.7%	1995	Metro
Secondary	41.3%	1995	Metro

Sources: Department of Economic and Social Affairs, Population Division. *Urban Agglomerations, 1996.* New York: United Nations, 1997; William T. Liu. *China Urban Statistics 1988.* New York: Praeger, 1988; United Nations Center for Human Settlements. *Compendium of Human Settlements Statistics.* New York: United Nations, 1995; and *Statistics of World Large Cities.* Tokyo, Japan: Tokyo Metropolitan Government, 1992 and 1994.

Beirut
LEBANON

LOCATION

Once known as the "Paris of the Middle East" for its elegance and cosmopolitan way of life, Beirut was laid low by over a decade of civil war. Still, it remains the capital and largest city in Lebanon. Located on a shelf extending into the Mediterranean on the country's central coast, Beirut extends away from the shore to the slopes of Mount Lebanon to the east and has an elevation of 111 feet (33.8 meters). It is located about 140 miles north of Tel Aviv and 50 miles to the northwest of Damascus. The city limits encompass 25 square miles (67 square kilometers) of territory.

Its climate is typical for the region, with hot, dry summers and cool, wet winters. January and July temperatures average 62.8 and 87.8 degrees Fahrenheit (17 and 31 degrees Celsius), respectively. The city receives 36 inches (914 millimeters) of rain annually, most of it in the winter and early spring.

POPULATION AND DEMOGRAPHY

The Beirut metropolitan area has an estimated population of 2.1 million, with about 400,000 in the city itself. With an annual growth rate of approximately 2.6 percent, the metropolitan area is expected to grow to 3.5 million by 2015. The density is 15,330 persons per square mile (5,678 per square kilometer).

Beirut's population is young, with 47.6 percent under the age of 20. Its inhabitants reflect the religious and cultural diversity of Lebanon. The majority of citizens are Muslims, divided equally between Shiites and Sunnis. There is also a large Christian population, a majority of whom practice a distinct variant called Maronism, while a minority are Roman Catholic. There is also a small population of Druze, who practice a syncretic religion somewhat akin to Islam. Because of the long years of civil war, the territory of the metropolitan area is highly segregated, with various religious groups tending to live in homogeneous neighborhoods.

HISTORY

Like many other cities in the region, Beirut has ancient origins. It was a Canaanite settlement in the second millennium B.C.—Beirut means "wells" in that ancient language—but it did not become an important city until it was colonized by the Romans around the time of Christ. A series of natural disasters devastated the city during its Byzantine period in the sixth century A.D., and it was conquered by Arab

Muslim armies in 635. However, it remained a small garrison town for several centuries until the revival of Mediterranean sea trade in the tenth century.

Briefly conquered by Christian crusaders in the early twelfth century, Beirut reverted to Muslim rule around 1200. It then came under Ottoman rule in 1516 and remained part of that empire, where it flourished as a center for Asian, Middle Eastern, and European trade. With the collapse of the Ottoman Empire in World War I, Beirut was turned over to France as part of its mandate of Greater Syria.

For political and religious reasons, France carved the then-Christian-dominated Lebanon out of Syria and made Beirut its capital. The city's Muslim population resented being dominated by Christians, especially after the French solidified the latter's rule. Lebanon declared independence in 1941 and the French troops finally left in 1946. Disparities between the wealthier Christians and poorer Muslims—combined with the faster growth rates among the latter population—sowed the seeds of conflict, which first exploded in the crisis of 1958.

GOVERNMENT AND POLITICS

The temporary settlement of Christian-Muslim power sharing in 1958 was upset when the Palestine Liberation Organization was forced to abandon Jordan and make Beirut its center of operations in 1970. The rising tensions in the city broke out into open civil war among the various factions in 1975 and drew in Syrian troops. Syria has always considered Lebanon within its sphere of influence. The presence of Syrian troops and the PLO led to an Israeli invasion in 1982 and a siege of the city. Peace has gradually returned to the city since 1990, and Beirut has been rapidly rebuilding itself into the capital of culture and finance that it once was. Like Lebanon itself, Beirut's city government is divided up among the various factions, with each holding a proportion of offices commensurate with its share of the population.

ECONOMY

Despite over a decade of civil war, Beirut never completely lost its position as a major banking center in the Middle East. Its highly educated and highly motivated population continued to maintain the city as a safe haven for Arab capital. In addition, its large population of skilled artisans continued to produce high-quality textiles, shoes, and handicrafts even in the midst of war.

With the return of peace, Beirut is rebuilding itself at a frantic pace. Foreign and domestic capital is being used to rebuild office and residential towers. The fashionable boutiques, nightclubs, restaurants, and hotels that made the city the most popular destination for Arab and European businesspersons and tourists in the Middle East are returning. Moreover, Lebanon has never given up the secrecy-in-banking and free-trade laws, gold-backed currency, and favorable interest rates that made Beirut a safe place for foreign capital and investment, much of it from expatriate Lebanese communities around Africa and the Middle East. Industry is also returning to the city, with factories being refurbished or built from scratch. Some of the industries that are returning include quality metalworking, textiles and clothing, leather goods, food products, and beverages.

TRANSPORTATION

Much of the excellent transportation and communications infrastructure that existed before the war is being rebuilt. A highway system that connects Beirut to other Lebanese cities as well as the Syrian capital of Damascus was always maintained during the war for the purposes of troop movements. The telecommunications system is being refurbished to 1990s specifications, with an emphasis on mobile, wireless phones.

HEALTH CARE

Ironically, the civil war resulted in an expansion of medical services even as the medical infrastructure was being destroyed. Small clinics and mobile services were established to deal with the many accidents and injuries caused by the fighting and the deterioration of the city's infrastructure. Presently, the major hospitals and clinics of Beirut are being rapidly restored to their prewar excellence, when the city offered some of the finest medical care in the Middle East.

EDUCATION

Though Beirut's children suffered during the war from disruptions in education, schooling continued even amidst the worst of the fighting. In 1984, at the height of the war, nearly 90 percent of all residents had some schooling, with fully 16 percent of the population university-educated. It is this high level of education and skills that has made Beirut's rapid postwar revival possible. Beirut has long been home to major universities offering instruction in Arabic and French. In addition, the English- and Arabic-language American University—run by Protestant missions—is considered to be one of the finest institutions of higher learning in the Middle East.

HOUSING

Nothing suffered more during the civil war than the city's housing stock. In 1985, it was estimated that fully 144,000 units were in need of major repairs or complete reconstruction. But rebuilding is proceeding apace. In 1993, permits for construction had risen 95 percent over the previous year. Much of the debris being cleared from damaged and destroyed buildings is being used as landfill for a proposed maritime park on the shores of the Mediterranean.

Electricity and water systems were heavily damaged, and provision of these services was sporadic at best during the conflict. With peace has come revival of services. By 1991, electricity was available six hours a day. It is now provided twenty-four hours a day in much of the city. Most of the city's population has been connected to a series of sixty-two major water tanks, and sewage lines are being repaired rapidly.

CULTURE, THE ARTS, AND ENTERTAINMENT

With its relatively relaxed moral standards and the penchant for fine living among its citizens, Beirut was always a popular destination for Middle Eastern and European tourists before the war, a role the city is determined to reclaim in the postwar era. Its elegant French-style boulevards, once home to world-class restaurants, boutiques, and nightclubs, are coming back to life. The city is also embarked on a major reconstruction of its waterfront, with a new park, new hotels, and new marinas. Its beaches are among the finest on the Mediterranean.

CATEGORY	DATA	YEAR	AREA
LOCATION & ENVIRONMENT			
Area	25 square miles	1996	City
	67 square kilometers		City
Elevation	111 feet/33.8 meters		City
January Temperature	62.8 degrees Fahrenheit		City
	17 degrees Celsius		City
July Temperature	87.8 degrees Fahrenheit		City
	31.0 degrees Celsius		City
Annual Precipitation	36.0 inches/914 millimeters		City
POPULATION & DEMOGRAPHY			
Population	2,100,000	1996	Metro
Projected Population	3,500,000	2015	Metro
Growth Rate	2.6%	1990–1995	Metro
Growth Rate	35.9%	1995–2015	Metro
Density	15,330 per square mile	1996	City
	5,678 per square kilometer		City
Gender			
Male	48%	1995	City
Female	52%	1995	City
Age			
Under 20	47.6%	1984	City
20–59	43.3%	1984	City
Over 60	9.1%	1984	City
VITAL STATISTICS			
Infant Mortality Rate	32 per 1,000 live births	1966–1984	City
ECONOMY			
Skilled Labor	24.9%	1984	City
Business	19.9%	1984	City
Administration	32.2%	1984	City
Professional	16.2%	1984	City
Unskilled	3.6%	1984	City
Police and Army	3.2%	1984	City
HOUSING			
Damaged Houses	144,000	1985	City
Units with Adequate Water	74.6%	1984	City
HEALTH CARE			
Total Hospital Visits	29,442	1984	City
Hospital Visits per Capita	6.2%	1984	City
EDUCATION			
Completed Primary School	18.6%	1984	City
Completed Secondary School	28.4%	1984	City
Completed Higher Education	16.0%	1984	City

Sources: Department of Economic and Social Affairs, Population Division. *Urban Agglomerations, 1996.* New York: United Nations, 1997; United Nations Center for Human Settlements. *Compendium of Human Settlements Statistics.* New York: United Nations, 1995; and Zurayk, Huda et al. *Beirut 1984: A Population and Health Profile.* Beirut, Lebanon: American University of Beirut, 1984.

Belfast, Northern Ireland
UNITED KINGDOM

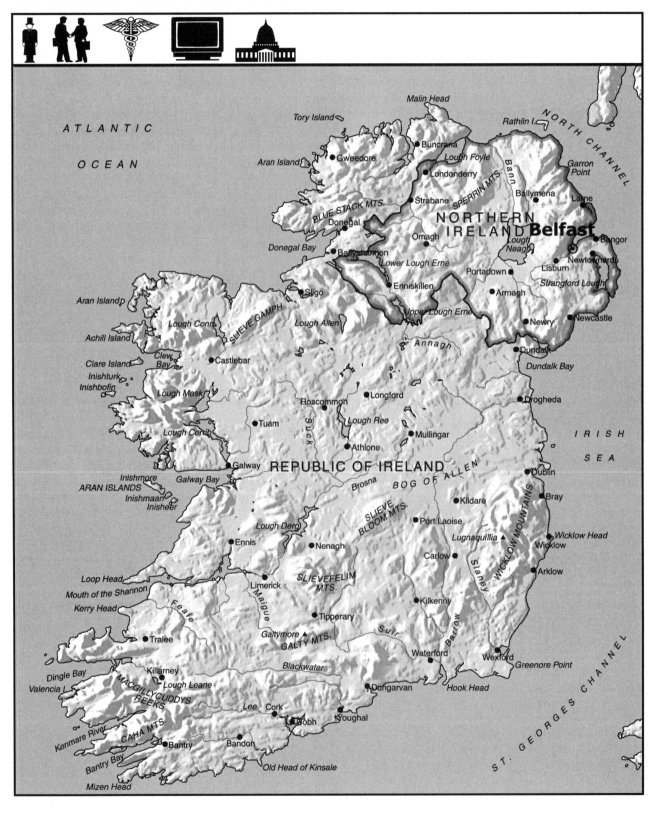

ATLANTIC

OCEAN

Malin Head

Tory Island

NORTH CHANNEL

Rathlin I.

Aran Island

Buncrana

Gweedore

Lough Foyle

Garron Point

Londonderry

SPERRIN MTS.

Ballymena

Larne

BLUE STACK MTS.

Strabane

NORTHERN

Bann

Donegal

IRELAND Belfast

Omagh

Lough Neagh

Bangor

Donegal Bay

Ballyshannon

Lower Lough Erne

Newtownards

Portadown

Lisburn

Aran Island

Sligo

Enniskillen

Strangford Lough

Armagh

Lough Conn

SLIEVE GAMPH

Lough Allen

Upper Lough Erne

Newry

Newcastle

Achill Island

Annagh

Dundalk

Clare Island

Clew Bay

Castlebar

Dundalk Bay

Inishturk

Inishbofin

Lough Mask

Roscommon

Longford

Drogheda

Lough Corrib

Tuam

Suck

Lough Ree

Mullingar

IRISH

SEA

Athlone

Galway

REPUBLIC OF IRELAND

Dublin

Inishmore

Galway Bay

Brosna

BOG OF ALLEN

Bray

ARAN ISLANDS

Inishmaan

Inisheer

Kildare

WICKLOW MOUNTAINS

Lough Derg

SLIEVE BLOOM MTS.

Port Laoise

Lugnaquillia

Wicklow Head

Ennis

Nenagh

Carlow

Wicklow

SLIEVEFELIM MTS.

Slaney

Arklow

Loop Head

Limerick

Kilkenny

Mouth of the Shannon

Maigue

Kerry Head

Feale

Tipperary

Suir

Barrow

Galtymore

GALTY MTS.

Tralee

Waterford

Wexford

Greenore Point

Dingle Bay

Killarney

Blackwater

Hook Head

Valencia I.

Lough Leane

Dungarvan

MACGILLYCUDDYS REEKS

Lee

Cork

Youghal

ST. GEORGES CHANNEL

Kenmare River

CAHA MTS.

Cobh

Bantry

Bandon

Bantry Bay

Old Head of Kinsale

Mizen Head

LOCATION

Belfast is the capital and largest city of Northern Ireland, a region that is part of the United Kingdom but claimed by Irish nationalists as part of the Republic of Ireland. The city lies in a lowland region at an elevation of 57 feet above sea level. It is located in the southwest corner of the Belfast Lough at the head of the Lagan River, a strait facing the North Channel and Scotland to the east. Belfast is located in Castlereagh, one of twenty-six districts in Northern Ireland. It is bounded on the southeast by Down District, on the northeast by the Belfast Lough, on the north by Carrickfergus District, on the northwest by Antrimt District, and on the southwest by Lisburn District. Belfast is 60 miles southeast of Londonderry, Northern Ireland's second largest city, and 110 miles north-northeast of Dublin, the capital of the Republic of Ireland. The city is located 10 miles east of Lough Neagh, the largest inland lake in Ireland. Belfast lies just 40 miles from the Galloway Region in southeast Scotland, across the Belfast Lough and the North Channel. Commonly known internationally as Northern Ireland, the disputed territory is designated as Ulster by the Protestant majority and as Northern Ireland by the Catholic minority. As an administrative unit of the United Kingdom, Northern Ireland is divided into four boards. Belfast is located in the Eastern Board, a region that includes the municipalities of Ards, Castlereagh, Down, Lisburn, and North Down. The city has a surface land area of 44 square miles (115 square kilometers). The average January low temperature is 38 degrees Fahrenheit (3.3 degrees Celsius), and the average July high is 58.5 degrees Fahrenheit (14.7 degrees Celsius). The annual average precipitation is 38.2 inches (970 millimeters).

POPULATION AND DEMOGRAPHY

The Belfast metropolitan region had a population of 1,602,400 in 1992. The central city of Belfast is the second most populous city in Ireland. From 1981 to 1991, Belfast's population expanded by 5.9 percent, to 297,000. The central city of Belfast accounts for about 45 percent of the Eastern-Board population of 668,000 and 18 percent of the population of Northern Ireland. The Belfast regional density is 307.8 persons per square mile (119 persons per square kilometer). According to British statistics, Northern Ireland has a young population, with proportionately more children and fewer pensioners than any other region in the United Kingdom. The Belfast metropolitan area's age distribution is balanced among population groups: 24.3 percent of the population is under 16 years of age, 63 percent of the population is between 16 and 65, and 12.7 percent is over 65 years of age. The major form of identity differentiation is on the basis of religion. The two leading religious groups are Protestants, who are primarily loyal to the United Kingdom, and Catholics, who are primarily loyal to the Republic of Ireland. Although Protestants are the majority, the Catholic minority population is expanding at a faster pace due to higher rates of fertility. The Eastern Board birth rate declined from 15.9 percent in 1991 to 13.4 percent in 1995, reflecting an overall decline in the Northern Ireland birth rate. Males comprise 48.8 percent of the regional population.

HISTORY

The first known settlement in Belfast dates to 1177, when the Normans established a castle in the city. In 1315, the Irish conquered the city and retained control for the next three hundred years. In the early sixteenth century, the English regained control over Belfast and established the settlement as a corporate borough in 1613. Over the next two centuries the town was controlled by the descendants of Sir Arthur Chichester, who was made a baron by King James I and granted the municipality a charter. From the end of the seventeenth century to the early nineteenth century, Belfast expanded in economic importance as a commercial and transportation center. In 1832, the Reform Act created a council of ten aldermen and thirty councilors. Rapid industrialization transformed the small market town into a bustling textile manufacturing center and increased Belfast's population to 350,000 by the end of the century. In 1888, Belfast was officially chartered as a city. By the turn of the twentieth century, large segments of the city's population resided in impoverished, overcrowded neighborhoods. In response to the urban blight, city officials endeavored to build new parks, public buildings, museums, and libraries. In the first two decades of the century, divisions between the region's Catholic minority and Protestant majority intensified rivalries and conflict. About 56 percent of Northern Ireland's population is Protestant and 41 percent is Roman Catholic. The partition of Ireland between north and south intensified Catholic nationalist efforts to unify the country, desires that were strongly resisted by the Protestant population, which favors union with the United Kingdom. The rise of the Irish Republican Army, a militant wing of the Irish Catholic nationalist movement, in the late 1960s intensified civil conflict in the region. By the end of the century, despite intermittent mediation efforts and cease-fires, relations between the two groups remain hostile and tense.

GOVERNMENT AND POLITICS

Belfast has a city council form of municipal government. The fifty-one-member Belfast City Council is responsible for municipal safety, health, environmental policy, economic development, tourism, and arts. The Lord Mayor, Deputy Lord Mayor, and High Sheriff are elected members of the city council. The city council has four-year corporate development plans aimed at improving service delivery and the urban environment.

ECONOMY

Led by strong growth in the manufacturing sector, the Northern Ireland regional economy rebounded in the 1990s. This economic growth contributed to a slight drop in unemployment, historically a persistent problem in the region. Still, in 1995, the unemployment rate hovered between 11 percent and 12 percent, and unemployment is even higher among poor and working-class residents, many of whom are Catholic. Unemployment in Northern Ireland was relatively higher than in most other regions in Ireland, the United Kingdom, and the European Union. Public authorities have launched various strategies to reduce unemployment, thus far to little avail. Additionally, Northern Ireland fares worse than the United Kingdom in average income per capita and in gross weekly wages. The disparities in wealth and income are even greater when comparing Northern Ireland's minority population with other regions.

The major industries in Belfast and the Northern Ireland region are manufacturing, services, health care, and tourism. The primary manufacturing industries are engineering, guided missiles, aircraft, tobacco, food processing, and garment and textile production. The engineering sector includes shipbuilding, aerospace, telecommunications, and automobile parts production. The city is an important petroleum refining center. The Belfast region is the leading global producer of linen products. Secondary regional industries are carpet production, chemicals, printing and packaging, plastics, cement, furniture, pottery, rope-making, industrial ceramics, tire manufacturing, crystal glassware and china. About half of the manufacturing sector is employed in British, European Community, East Asian,

and other foreign-controlled industries. The government of Northern Ireland provides local industries with support services aimed at improving the region's economic competitiveness, promotes industrial technological development, and administers programs to improve worker skills.

The region's scenic environment has long attracted tourists to the region. However, the ongoing civil war between the region's Protestant and Catholic population has sharply curtailed the growth of the tourist industry. Peace efforts between the Irish Republican movement and the British government that began in the early 1990s have contributed to stronger growth in tourism. In 1994, Northern Ireland attracted nearly 1.3 million visitors. Still, the continuation of hostilities in the region reduces Northern Ireland's popularity as a tourist destination.

A major dilemma for public authorities has been to promote economic development among the Catholic minority population, which historically has had significantly higher rates of unemployment than the Protestant majority. In 1989, the government passed a Fair Employment Act that monitors employers and assists minorities facing employment discrimination. According to government authorities, from its inception in 1989 through 1994, the fair employment program achieved modest success in increasing employment among Irish Catholics. Since the mid-1980s, Belfast and Northern Ireland authorities have initiated efforts to rehabilitate the areas that have fallen into disrepair as a result of high poverty rates. However, much of this urban regeneration effort is focused on redeveloping the riverfront area near the city center to promote business and investment. The Making Belfast Work program, which began in 1988, has generated 3,000 small businesses and 4,000 industrial jobs. Other efforts have sought to target business development in the strife-torn areas of Belfast.

TRANSPORTATION

Belfast is the leading transportation center in Northern Ireland, with a deepwater port and major road and rail links. The city's port is the largest in Ireland and a leading northern European shipping and repair center. Belfast City Airport is one of the fastest-growing regional airports in the British Isles, with connections to the United Kingdom. Belfast International Airport provides flights to mainland Europe and North America. The city also has a ferry service that reaches Scotland in an hour, and a rail line that has been upgraded to transport passengers between Belfast and Dublin in less than two hours.

In 1995–1996, 68 percent of all households in Northern Ireland had at least one car.

HEALTH CARE

As a jurisdiction of the United Kingdom, health care is universally guaranteed in Northern Ireland, regardless of one's ability to pay. The Health Service is Northern Ireland's largest employer. The region has a rate of 1 physician per 1,000 residents. Through a system of hospitals and local community clinics, the Health Service provides comprehensive medical care throughout Northern Ireland. The health care industry includes pharmaceutical, diagnostic, and medical packaging manufacturers. The region has two medical teaching facilities, Queens University Belfast and the University of Ulster. The average infant mortality rate between 1993 and 1995 for the metropolitan area was 7.4 infant deaths per 1,000 live births, higher than the Northern Ireland average of 6.8 infant deaths per 1,000 live births and the United Kingdom average of 6.2 infant deaths per 1,000 live births. The British government recognizes Northern Ireland as having the lowest percentage of heavy drinkers than any other region under British control.

EDUCATION

Primary and secondary education in Belfast is administered centrally through the Department of Education for Northern Ireland and locally through education and library boards. In 1993, 454,000 students were enrolled in the region's educational institutions, of which nearly 42 percent were enrolled in primary schools, 50 percent in secondary schools, and 7.7 percent in higher educational institutions. The Department of Education administers four categories of schools: controlled schools, run by local governing boards; maintained schools, operated by nondenominational management; voluntary grammar schools, under Roman Catholic management; and integrated schools, which seek to jointly educate Protestant and Roman Catholic students. Northern Ireland has twenty-eight integrated schools that educate approximately five thousand students. According to the British National Statistics Office, Northern Ireland's students have a high rate of educational attainment compared to students in other regions of the United Kingdom. The region has four institutions of higher learning: Queens University of Belfast, the University of Ulster, Belfast College of Technology, and Union Theological College. Belfast's publicly fi-

nanced schools have a low pupil/teacher ratio. In 1995 and 1996 there were 19.5 pupils per teacher in Belfast primary school and 14.6 pupils per teacher in Belfast secondary schools, a lower ratio than the Northern Ireland or British national average.

HOUSING

An ongoing problem in the region has been housing. While conditions have improved somewhat, the regional and local governments' attempts to reduce the disparity in housing conditions between the Protestant and Catholic districts have not been fully successful. The Northern Ireland Housing Executive operates 151,500 housing units throughout the region. The executive was formed in 1971 to improve the large numbers of dilapidated public housing units in the region. The authority claims to have reduced unfit housing stock from 20 percent in 1974 to less than 9 percent in 1991. Regional private housing construction in the mid-1990s has increased by fairly high rates. Recent efforts have sought to increase the number of owner-occupied housing units. From 1978 to 1996, the owner-occupied housing stock increased from 51 percent to 65 percent, in part due to the sale of public-sector housing to tenants. Although housing prices are lower than in any other region under British control, housing prices increased by 25 percent between 1993 and 1996, 2.5 times the increase in any other region.

CULTURE, THE ARTS, AND ENTERTAINMENT

The holdings of the Ulster Museum, located in the Botanic Gardens, include contemporary international art, Irish art, furniture, glass, silver, ceramics, and costume. The city has a number of art galleries exhibiting the work of major Irish artists. Other leading cultural sites include the Linen Hall Library, the Botanic Gardens, the Home Front Heritage Centre, the Belfast Zoo, Cave Hill, Dixon Park, and the Crown Liquor Saloon Museum. The leading theaters and concert halls are the Grand Opera House, the Belfast Civic Arts Theatre, the Lyric Theatre, the Group Theatre, the Old Museum Arts Centre, the Garden Thread Theatre, Ulster Hall, Whitla Hall–Queens University, and King's Hall. The city also has over a dozen musical pubs offering live traditional, folk, jazz, blues, and rock music. The city hosts a number of annual outdoor festivals, including Rose Week and the Spring and Autumn Flower Showers.

CATEGORY	DATA	YEAR	AREA
LOCATION & ENVIRONMENT			
Area	44 square miles	1996	City
	115 square kilometers		City
Elevation	57 feet/17.4 meters		City
January Temperature	38 degrees Fahrenheit		City
	3.3 degrees Celsius		City
July Temperature	58.5 degrees Fahrenheit		City
	14.7 degrees Celsius		City
Annual Precipitation	38.2 inches/970.3 millimeters		City
POPULATION & DEMOGRAPHY			
Population	1,602,400	1992	Metro
Density	307.8 per square mile	1995	Metro
	119 per square kilometer		
Gender			
Males	48.8%	1992	Metro
Females	51.2%	1992	Metro
Age			
Under 16	24.3%	1992	Metro
16–64	63.0%	1992	Metro
Over 65	12.7%	1992	Metro
VITAL STATISTICS			
Births per 1,000 Residents	13.4	1992	Metro
Deaths per 1,000 Residents	9.3	1992	Metro
Infant Mortality Rate	6 per 1,000 live births	1992	Metro
ECONOMY			
Manufacturing	17.9%	1992	Metro
Construction	6.0%	1992	Metro
Utilities	1.4%	1992	Metro
Agriculture	7.7%	1992	Metro
TRANSPORTATION			
Passenger Vehicles	523,000	1995	City
HOUSING			
Total Housing Units	572,000	1991	Metro
Persons per Unit	2.8	1991	Metro
Owner-Occupied Units	65.0%	1991	Metro
EDUCATION			
Total Students	454,000	1993	Metro
Primary	41.9%	1993	Metro
Secondary	50.20%	1993	Metro
Higher	7.70%	1993	Metro

Sources: Eurostat *Regions Statistical Yearbook.* Brussels, Belgium: Statistical Office of European Communities, 1996. Office for National Statistics. *Regional Trends 32.* London, England: The Stationery Office, 1997.

Belgrade, Serbia
YUGOSLAV FEDERATION

LOCATION

Belgrade, the largest city in Serbia and the capital of the Yugoslav Federation, is situated at the confluence of the Danube and Sava Rivers, at the southern end of the Pannonian Basin. The city covers 133 square miles (360 square kilometers) of territory and is located at an elevation of 453 feet (165 meters) above sea level. Two hundred miles inland from the Adriatic Sea, the city is located approximately 110 miles northeast of the Bosnian capital of Sarajevo and 280 miles west of the Romanian capital of Bucharest.

The city has a temperate climate, with January temperatures averaging about 34 degrees Fahrenheit (1 degree Celsius) and summer temperatures in the low 70s Fahrenheit (low 20s Celsius). The city receives 24.6 inches of precipitation annually, much of it falling in the spring and summer months.

POPULATION AND DEMOGRAPHY

The Belgrade metropolitan area has a population of 1.2 million and has been growing at a rate of 0.5 to 1 percent annually. United Nations projections put the population at about 1.3 million early in the twenty-first century. The city has a density of around 8,800 persons per square mile (3,250 per square kilometer). Typical for a European city, one fourth of the population is under 20 years of age and just over 10 percent is 60 and older. The gender ratio in Belgrade is roughly even.

Most of the city's population is of south Slavic origin. Indeed, the name Yugoslavia means "land of the southern Slavs." Since ancient times, ethnic origins have been a point of contention for the people of the region, a situation exacerbated by the civil war that gripped the former Yugoslavia in the 1990s. Approximately 80 percent of Belgrade's population identifies itself as Serbian. The second largest group consists of ethnic Hungarians, followed by Germans and Albanians. Belgrade once had significant communities of Croatians and Bosnians, but most of these have fled since the fighting began. The city also once had a significant Jewish community, but much of this was destroyed when Nazi armies occupied the city during the Second World War. A small Jewish population still lives there, as does an even smaller community of Roma people, better known as Gypsies.

The predominant language is Serbo-Croatian, though Albanian and Hungarian are also spoken. Most of the population are members of the Eastern Orthodox Church, though years of Communism have diminished the numbers of those who practice the faith. Ethnic Albanians and Bosnians are usually Muslim, while Croatians are largely Roman Catholic.

HISTORY

The city's origins date back to a fortress first built by Celtic peoples in the region during the fourth century B.C. It came under Roman rule in the first century A.D. and was called Singidunum. Huns conquered and destroyed the city in 442, though it was eventually recaptured by the Roman emperor Justinian and remained part of the Byzantine Empire—with short periods under Frankish and Bulgar rule—until the thirteenth century. In 1284, it was captured by Serbs, and the city was made their capital in 1402. The Turks laid siege to the city off and on from 1440 until they finally captured it in 1521. It remained under their rule—except for short periods of Austrian governance in scattered years from 1688 through 1791—until the Serbian uprising of 1804, when it once again became the Serb capital. This lasted only nine years until the Turks captured it again, controlling it until it was ceded to the Serbs for the last time in 1867.

At the Versailles Peace Conference following World War I, the Allied victors decided to create a state out of the southern Slavic lands, and Belgrade became the capital of the newly created Yugoslavia. The city was captured by the Nazis in World War II and was heavily damaged in the fighting between Germans and Yugoslav partisans, as well as by Allied bombing. From 1945 until the collapse of Yugoslavia in 1991, the city grew rapidly in population and industrial capacity. It became the capital of both Serbia and the truncated Yugoslav Federation—consisting of Serbia and Montenegro—in 1992. Since then, the city has been hard hit by economic sanctions aimed at ending Serbian support for Serb separatists in Bosnia.

GOVERNMENT AND POLITICS

Once capital of Communist Yugoslavia, Belgrade was home to the Communist Party headquarters and the federal-style government created by Josip Broz Tito after World War II. With the 1991 multiple declarations of independence by the constituent republics of Yugoslavia—including Slovenia, Croatia, and Bosnia—the government of the newly truncated Yugoslav Federation adopted a set of rules called the "Essentials of the Organization and Functioning of Yugoslavia as a Common State."

Under this quasi constitution, many powers were given to the governments of the two constituent republics of Serbia and Montenegro. The federal government maintains responsibility for fiscal management, civil rights, foreign policy, defense, environmental protection, and social welfare. The head of state is elected by the parliaments of the two republics, in alternating turns. The president then appoints a prime minister, who is subject to approval or dismissal by the bicameral parliament of the federation. The president and prime minister are not permitted to come from the same republic. While the basic rules of the country call for the honoring of human rights, there has been severe repression under the regime of Serbian president Slobodan Milosevic, a by-product of the long and bloody wars Serbia has fought by proxy in Croatia and Bosnia. Like other localities in Serbia, Belgrade is governed as a commune, with responsibility for basic services and tax collection.

ECONOMY

The Belgrade metropolitan area is not only the capital of the Yugoslav Federation but also its largest industrial center. Factories in the city—most of them dating from Communist times and now somewhat obsolete, a problem compounded by the economic sanctions imposed on the country—produce electrical equipment, machine tools, motors, tractors, chemicals, and building materials. In addition, the city has a major light industrial sector producing food products and textiles. The city is also a major smelting center for the many ferrous and nonferrous minerals found in the country. Slightly less than one fourth of the labor force works in the manufacturing sector. The commercial sector, though more developed than in most former Communist countries due to Yugoslavia's history of nontraditional socialism, still lags behind cities in the West. Still, about 13 percent of the workforce is employed in trade, with some 7 percent involved in finance, real estate, and insurance.

TRANSPORTATION

Belgrade has been an important transportation hub since ancient times, serving the trading routes connecting Western Europe to the Middle East. In the modern era, the city saw its first railroads in the mid-nineteenth century, and soon had lines connecting it to Greece, Austria, and countries in Eastern Europe,

including the famous Orient Express from Paris to Istanbul. Since then, the network has been expanded to connect Belgrade to all the major cities in what used to be Yugoslavia, though rail connections to Bosnia and Croatia have been disrupted by warfare.

Metropolitan transport is handled mainly by bus, though there is also a system of commuter trains and trolleys. Car ownership is relatively high for a former Communist city. There were an estimated 350,000 automobiles in Belgrade in 1990. Telephone and television ownership is also rather widespread. There is approximately one telephone for every two citizens and one television for every three inhabitants.

HEALTH CARE

The health care system has also been a victim of sanctions and the war. Once a major breeding ground for malaria, typhus, typhoid, and dysentery, Serbia saw these diseases virtually eradicated during the administration of Tito from the 1950s to the 1970s. But some of these diseases have been making a reappearance in recent years. Under the plan developed by the Communist government, all citizens are part of a national health insurance scheme, though about 10 percent of the population remains outside of it today. The city has some seventy-five hospitals and clinics—many of them now suffering from a shortage of equipment and supplies—and a ratio of 1 physician for every 225 citizens.

EDUCATION

Education up through the age of 13 is compulsory, and secondary education is provided free. While illiteracy was high before World War II, the Communist regime made education a priority, lowering the rate to European levels in a generation. Currently less than 5 percent of the city's population cannot read and write. The city is also home to several major universities, and about one in ten citizens has a college degree. The largest institution of higher education is the University of Belgrade, founded in 1863. There are approximately 65,000 university students in the Belgrade area.

HOUSING

Most of Belgrade's population lives to the south and southeast of the city in developments built since the end of World War II. Many of these consist of low- and high-rise apartment buildings. There were approximately 500,000 dwellings in the city in 1990, with an average occupancy of 2.2 persons. New construction has slowed to a crawl due to the economic sanctions and the war in Bosnia. Most of the energy in the city comes from hydroelectric facilities or coal-burning power plants. Citizens consume an average 3.9 kilowatt-hours of electricity and use approximately 40 gallons (150 liters) of water daily. Much of the once excellent utility infrastructure has decayed due to a lack of spare parts, again a problem created by the economic sanctions placed on the government for its participation in the Bosnian war.

CULTURE, THE ARTS, AND ENTERTAINMENT

Belgrade is home to most of the national cultural institutions, including the Serbian National Theater, which reflects the great theatrical tradition of the country. The city is also home to Yugoslavia's film industry, once quite prolific and renowned, but now suffering from the financial constraints of war. Much of the music, art, theater, film, and dance in Serbia reflects a melding of fine art and folk art traditions. Architecturally, the city is not particularly distinguished, though the old fortress of Kalemegdan is a popular tourist spot and there are many fine examples of nineteenth-century residential and commercial construction.

CATEGORY	DATA	YEAR	AREA
LOCATION & ENVIRONMENT			
Area	133 square miles	1995	City
	360 square kilometers		City
Elevation	453 feet/165 meters		City
January Temperature	34.3 degrees Fahrenheit		City
	1.3 degrees Celsius		City
July Temperature	71.2 degrees Fahrenheit		City
	21.8 degrees Celsius		City
Annual Precipitation	24.6 inches/624.8 millimeters		City
POPULATION & DEMOGRAPHY			
Population	1,200,000	1996	Metro
Projected Population	1,300,000	2015	Metro
Growth Rate	0.7%	1990–1995	Metro
Growth Rate	7.9%	1995–2015	Metro
Density	8,767 per square mile		City
	3,247 per square kilometer		City
Gender			
Male	49%	1990	City
Female	52%	1990	City
Age			
Under 20	25.4%	1981	City
20–59	62.9%	1981	City
Over 60	11.7%	1981	City
VITAL STATISTICS			
Births per 1,000 Residents	9.9	1990	City
Infant Mortality Rate	15.4 per 1,000 live births	1990	City
Deaths per 1,000 Residents	8.5	1990	City

(continued)

CATEGORY	DATA	YEAR	AREA
ECONOMY			
Total Workforce	518,036	1990	City
Agriculture	0.4%	1990	City
Manufacturing	22.9%	1990	City
Construction	13.8%	1990	City
Finance, Insurance, Real Estate	7.1%	1990	City
Trade	13.7%	1990	City
Government	2.8%	1990	City
Service	2.5%	1990	City
Transport	8.8%	1990	City
Utilities	1.9%	1990	City
TRANSPORTATION			
Passenger Journeys	855,084,000	1990	City
Rail	4.2%	1990	City
Trolley	12.9%	1990	City
Bus	82.9%	1990	City
COMMUNICATIONS			
Telephones per 1,000 Residents	526	1990	City
Televisions per 1,000 Residents	357	1990	City
HOUSING			
Housing Units	526,571	1990	City
New Housing Units	8,583	1990	City
Persons per Unit	2.2	1990	City
HEALTH CARE			
Hospitals	44	1990	City
Clinics	32	1990	City
Physicians per 1,000 Residents	4.4	1990	City
EDUCATION			
Total Students	211,581	1990	City
Primary	53.8%	1990	City
Secondary	15.9%	1990	City
Higher	30.3%	1990	City

Sources: Department of Economic and Social Affairs, Population Division. *Urban Agglomerations, 1996.* New York: United Nations, 1997; *Statistics of World Large Cities.* Tokyo, Japan: Tokyo Metropolitan Government, 1992 and 1994; and United Nations Center for Human Settlements. *Compendium of Human Settlements Statistics.* New York: United Nations, 1995.

Berlin
GERMANY

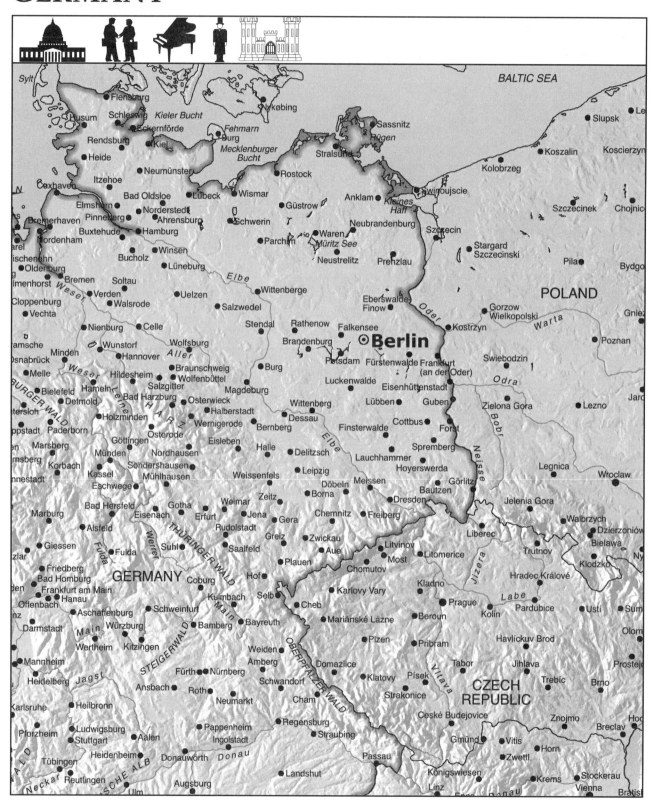

LOCATION

Berlin, Germany's capital and most populous city, is located on the North German Plain of east-central Germany at an elevation of 50 feet (15 meters) above sea level. Berlin was divided from the end of World War II until October 1990, when it was formally reunited following the collapse of East Germany and its reunification with West Germany. Prior to November 1989, the eastern part of Berlin, under East German control, had been separated from the western part, under West Germany's control, by the Berlin Wall. Following reunification of East and West Germany, Berlin was named the new capital and administrative center of Germany. The city is located at the junction of the Havel River, which flows southwest of the city, and the Spree River, which flows southeast from the Havel to the border of the Czech Republic. The city is located approximately 40 miles west of the Oder River, on the border with Poland, and about 80 miles south of Stettin Bay, an inlet of Pomeranian Bay and the Baltic Sea. The reunited city occupies a surface land area of 548.6 square miles (883 square kilometers). Berlin's temperature ranges from a January average of 35 degrees Fahrenheit (1.6 degrees Celsius) to a July average of 68 degrees Fahrenheit (19.8 degrees Celsius). The city averages 23.5 inches (595.9 millimeters) of precipitation per year.

POPULATION AND DEMOGRAPHY

Berlin is Germany's largest city. Before German unification in 1990, the populations of the eastern and western districts of the city were measured individually by the East German and the West German governments, respectively. The population of West Berlin has always been larger, encompassing from 60 to 65 percent of the combined city's population from 1970 until unification. Between 1980 and 1995, Berlin's population has increased by a cumulative 2.2 percent, from 3,247,000 to just over 3.3 million inhabitants. The city's 1992 age structure was older than that of most cities in the world, but comparable to that of Central European cities. Berlin's population is projected to remain at 3.3 million over the twenty-year period ending in the year 2015. About 20.4 percent of the population was 20 years or under, 61.4 percent was 20 to 59 years of age, and 18.2 percent was 60 years of age or older. Owing to the older age structure and the tendency for females to live longer than males, females comprise more than 52 percent of all inhabitants. Due to the excess of deaths over births, the city had a natural population decrease of

3.6 per 1,000 residents in 1992. However, this decrease was more than compensated for by a net inmigration of 9.3 per 1,000 residents—a trend that is expected to continue as the city gains in stature as the capital of the unified Germany. Some German demographers predict that, due to growth in migration, Berlin's population will increase by over 30 percent by the year 2020. In 1992, the city had 17,895 marriages and 6,644 divorces. Turks are the largest minority in Berlin. Other ethnic minorities residing in the city include Poles and Yugoslavs.

HISTORY

The region that now encompasses Berlin is believed to have been occupied for more than ten thousand years. Records indicate that in the first century A.D. the region was inhabited by the precursors to the Germanic peoples who are now the primary residents in the area. In the eighth century, the region was conquered by Charlemagne, the Frankish leader who had seized control of large swaths of land in Germany to Berlin's south and west. German tribes regained control of the region by the tenth century. It was not until the twelfth century that Berlin and Cöln were founded as two merchant settlements on either side of the River Spree. The earliest documentary evidence of the city dates to the year 1244. In 1359 the city joined the Hanseatic League of Cities. In 1415, Berlin became part of the Hohenzollern Dynasty. The city was made capital of Brandenburg and forced to withdraw from the Hanseatic League. The city's economic and political development was greatly set back by the hostilities during the Thirty Years' War (1618-1648). In 1709, King Frederick I of Prussia incorporated the cities of Berlin and Cöln into the consolidated city of Berlin, and named the city capital of Prussia. In 1709, the city's population stood at some 57,000 residents. Berlin came under French occupation in 1806 during the Napoleonic Wars. Shortly thereafter, Prussians gained sovereignty over Berlin and declared the city their capital. During the bourgeois revolution of March 1848, German authorities instituted political reforms that established a national assembly. In 1871 the German Empire was established and Berlin was named its capital, after which Berlin's population exploded to new heights. During the nineteenth century, Berlin industrialized and the city's population expanded dramatically to over 3 million by the turn of the twentieth century. The city's prosperity was set back again by Germany's defeat in the First World War. After the establishment of a German Republic in 1918 by the

Social Democrats, the city continued to expand, albeit more slowly than in previous decades. Germany and the city suffered from an economic depression that included high rates of poverty, and this was a factor in the rise of German nationalism and right-wing fascism.

In the Second World War (1939-1945), Berlin's buildings and infrastructure suffered extensive damage as a consequence of Allied bombing. During World War II, Berlin's population declined by over 1.6 million, in part as a consequence of the mandatory deportation of Jews and ethnic minorities from the city to ghettos in Eastern Europe and to concentration camps. Other residents left the city to escape the war. From the war's end in 1945 to the end of the century, Berlin's population did not increase appreciably from its wartime low of 2.8 million. In 1948, the Soviets attempted to force the victorious Western powers (United States, Britain, and France) from Berlin through a blockade that compelled the Western countries to airlift supplies into the city. In November 1948, a separate city administration was established in East Berlin. In 1949, following the establishment of two German states, the eastern part of Berlin came under Soviet Russian occupation, and the western part was divided between the United States, Britain, and France.

East Berlin, under the control of the Soviet-led East German government, instituted a planned economy controlled by the state. West Berlin, under the control of West Germany, instituted a mixed market economy that included significant government involvement and regulation. In 1961, after repeated efforts to restrict migration to the west, the East German government constructed the Berlin Wall. The Berlin Wall remained up until 1990, when Germany was unified. Unification has come under economic and political terms dictated largely by the Federal Republic of Germany, with a democratic form of government and a market-oriented economy. However, the incorporation of East Berlin and eastern Germany into the Federal Republic has come at great cost to West Germans, who had to pay for the modernization of East Berlin and the integration of the two countries.

Due to Berlin's growing national and international prominence as the capital of Germany, government and private sector leaders have initiated a vast rebuilding program. The construction of government buildings and dwellings to accommodate public offices and a large residential population became a pressing need. By the mid-1990s, Berlin was considered a city "under construction," with new developments throughout the city center and beyond.

GOVERNMENT AND POLITICS

In June 1991, the German Bundestag (legislature) voted to make Berlin the capital of a united Federal Republic of Germany. While Bonn will continue to maintain several ministries, the parliament and government began to relocate to Berlin beginning in 1996. The German national legislature will relocate to Berlin sometime between 1998 and the end of the century.

Growing speculation increased real estate values—particularly in the eastern part of the city, which had fairly low-priced living accommodations prior to reunification. Although government officials are attempting to bridge the gap between east and west, there is growing resentment among westerners, who feel forced to pay for the development of the east, and easterners, who feel nostalgic for the days when housing was ample and living expenses low. In 1994, the Party of Democratic Socialism, the reformed Communists, came to prominence as the leading political force in the region.

Berlin is one of sixteen administrative units in Germany that are known as *Länder*. The Berlin House of Representatives has a minimum of 150 members, who are elected to four-year terms. The house elects a mayor as chief administrator and a senate to run city government services and departments. However, Berlin's mayor does not have power equivalent to that of the prime ministers of other *Länder* in Germany.

ECONOMY

When Germany was partitioned in 1949, Berlin's economy was divided between eastern and western control, with strikingly different market systems. West Berlin assumed the German Federal Republic's mixed economic system that combined government regulation with a private market. Under the American-sponsored Marshall Plan, West Berlin's war-torn economic infrastructure was rebuilt. East Berlin took on an economic system directed by the German Democratic Republic, which gave the state control over industry, wages, prices, and public services. East Berlin matured into East Germany's leading manufacturing, commercial, and transportation center. After the Soviet blockade, Western support maintained West Berlin as a flourishing center of international finance, research, and development. The city maintained its stature as one of Europe's leading cultural, musical, and artistic centers, with an eminent film and television production industry.

In the reunified Germany, East Berlin's industrial base has undergone modernization and economic restructuring. Industries that were essential to the local economy but were not subject to standards of profitability under East German rule have been privatized, and many have been closed.

Moreover, the reunified Germany inaugurated major rebuilding and economic redevelopment, modernizing East Germany's economy to match the standards of the advanced economies of Western Europe and North America. The introduction of the market economy contributed to considerable job loss among residents of the eastern part of Berlin. Many in the eastern part of Berlin have not benefited from the expansion of the private market and also have lost the basic protections guaranteed by the former socialist government. Moreover, privatization has fomented worker unrest due to higher rates of unemployment.

The city's leading manufacturing industries are iron and steel, rubber, electrical and electronic equipment, machinery, motor vehicles, textiles, clothing, transportation equipment, chemicals, printing and publishing, and processed foods. Berlin's growing importance has expanded the presence of international firms, which have established branch offices in the city. The city has experienced a construction boom as a result of the growing need for office space, multiunit residential apartments, hotels, and government buildings. Moreover, following the collapse of the state-dominated economies in other East European countries that had followed a Soviet economic planning model, the city became increasingly important to the growing East European markets. Prior to unification, the leading sectors of the local economy were services, government, manufacturing, and transport and communications. However, since unification market services and construction have expanded dramatically and manufacturing has declined, due to the closure of unprofitable facilities in East Berlin. Today, the service sector accounts for about 66 percent of the local economy. The relocation of the federal capital to Berlin is expected to contribute to an increase in the number of government employees in the local labor market.

TRANSPORTATION

From 1949 to 1989, the eastern and western portions of the city established separate transportation infrastructures linked to their respective republics. Since unification, the government has sought to create an integrated road and public transport system to accommodate the needs of residents of the city. Prior to unification, West Berlin had an extensive subway and bus system. East Berlin's key transit system consisted of rail and subway services. Since unification, the rail network from East Berlin to West Berlin has been upgraded, expanded, and modernized.

Berlin is one of Europe's busiest inland ports. Waterways link the city's port on the Spree River to the Baltic Sea. Extensive road and rail systems that intersect the city facilitate regional and continental trade. The two airports of East Berlin and West Berlin, respectively Schoenfeld and Telgel, accommodate domestic and international air carriers. In 1994, construction started on a third, much larger airport.

HEALTH CARE

The German Federal Republic's social insurance system guarantees residents of Berlin universal health and medical care services. The combined city has a total of ninety-eight hospitals and a ratio of 4.6 physicians and 1.6 hospital beds per 1,000 urban residents. The city's hospitals include specialized treatment and care facilities. In 1992, Berlin had a death rate of 12.2 per 1,000 urban residents. Diseases of the circulatory system and cancer were the leading causes of death. In 1992, the city had an infant mortality rate of 6.3 infant deaths per 1,000 live births.

EDUCATION

Education is provided to residents of Berlin from preschool to adulthood. By 1991–1992, the East and West Berlin school systems had been integrated into a single system. The united system has instituted efforts to integrate the buildings, equipment, and teaching standards of east and west Berlin. Of the 618,000 students enrolled in the city's school system in the 1992–1993 academic year, 24.3 percent are in primary institutions, 49.8 percent are in secondary institutions, and 25.9 percent are in higher education. For higher education, the vocational colleges have been reorganized to provide technical and specialized education for a single city in leading industries. They had previously been affiliated with the factories in East Berlin. The city's leading postsecondary institutions are the Free University of Berlin, the Technical University of Berlin, and Humboldt University. The city is home to specialized postsecondary institutions, including the European Business College, the German Institute for Economic Research, the Max Delbrück Center for Molecular Medicine, the Fraunhofer Society for the Advancement of Applied Research, the Konrad Zuse Center for Information Technology, the Max Planck Society, and the Central Academy for Social Research. The city is also home to leading artistic and musical institutions, including the German Film and Television Academy and the College of the Arts.

HOUSING

Berlin's housing stock has increased steadily since unification, from about 1.75 million units at unification to about 1.8 million units in 1998. However, the city is still suffering from an acute housing shortage, particularly of affordable units. Government experts have estimated the city currently has a shortfall of 100,000 units, and this is projected to grow to 143,000 units by the year 2000. The primary causes of the housing shortage are the growing importance of the city, which attracts more migrants to the city, and the conversion of low-cost units, primarily in East Berlin, to market-rate housing. To alleviate the shortage, government authorities planned to initiate construction of 72,000 new units by 1998. New housing units are planned for residential neighborhoods and underutilized commercial areas that have been largely abandoned. Additionally, efforts are under way to restore older residential buildings that have fallen into disrepair. The vast majority of the city's

dwelling units are rental units. About 11 percent of the former West Berlin's housing stock is owner-occupied, compared to about 8 percent of the former East Berlin's.

CULTURE, THE ARTS, AND ENTERTAINMENT

Even after four decades of separation, Berlin has retained its distinction as the center of German culture and arts. The city has about 270 libraries and 125 museums, which attract millions of visitors. Among the city's museums and artistic attractions are the Bauhaus Archives and Museum, the Museum of Applied Arts, the New National Gallery, the Pergamon Museum, the Bode Museum, the National Gallery of Decorative Arts, the Humboldt Museum, the Ethnological Museum, the Sculpture Gallery, the German Folklore Museum, the Bridge Museum, and museums of Greek, Roman, and Egyptian antiquities. Berlin also has museums of Indian, Islamic, and East Asian art. The city is home to leading musical organizations, including the Berlin Philharmonic Orchestra. The city has 62 performing arts theaters and 133 cinemas.

Noted theater companies include the Comic Opera and the Berliner Ensemble, the latter founded by Bertolt Brecht.

CATEGORY	DATA	YEAR	AREA
LOCATION & ENVIRONMENT			
Area	548.6 square miles	1996	City
	883 square kilometers		City
Elevation	50 feet/15 meters		City
January Temperature	35 degrees Fahrenheit		City
	1.6 degrees Celsius		City
July Temperature	68 degrees Fahrenheit		City
	19.8 degrees Celsius		City
Annual Precipitation	23.5 inches/595.9 millimeters		City
POPULATION & DEMOGRAPHY			
Population	3,300,000	1996	City
Projected Population	3,300,000	2015	City
Growth Rate	0.2%	1990–1995	City
Growth Rate	0.0%	1995–2015	City
Density	10,524 per square mile	1992	City
	3,898 per square kilometer		
Gender			
Males	47.8%	1992	City
Females	52.2%	1992	City
Age			
Under 20	20.4%	1992	City
20–59	61.4%	1992	City
Over 60	18.2%	1992	City
VITAL STATISTICS			
Births per 1,000 Residents	8.6	1993	City
Deaths per 1,000 Residents	12.2	1993	City
Infant Mortality Rate	6.3 per 1,000 live births	1992	City
ECONOMY			
Total Workforce	1,066,000	1992	City
Manufacturing	20.1%	1992	City
Construction	7.8%	1992	City
Utilities	1.0%	1992	City
Agriculture	0.6%	1992	City
Market Services	44.7%	1992	City
Nonmarket Services	25.7%	1992	City
TRANSPORTATION			
Passenger Journeys	1,376,000,000	1987–1989	City
Subway	32.6%	1987–1989	City
Rail	12.5%	1987–1989	City
Buses and Trolleys	40.2%	1987–1989	City
Passenger Vehicles	229,000	1992	City

(continued)

CATEGORY	DATA	YEAR	AREA
HOUSING			
Total Housing Units	1,800,000	1998	City
New Housing Units	8,360	1992	City
Persons per Unit	2	1991	City
HEALTH CARE			
Hospitals	98	1992	City
Physicians per 1,000 Residents	4.6	1992	City
Hospital Beds per 1,000 Residents	1.6	1992	City
EDUCATION			
Total Students	618,000	1993	City
Primary	24.3%	1993	City
Secondary	49.8%	1993	City
Higher	25.9%	1993	City

Sources: Department of Economic and Social Affairs, Population Division. *Urban Agglomerations, 1996.* New York: United Nations, 1997; Eurostat *Regions Statistical Yearbook.* Brussels, Belgium: Statistical Office of European Communities, 1996; *Statistiches Jahrbuch 1996 für die Bundesrepublik Deutschland.* Wiesbaden, Germany: Federal Statistical Office, 1996; and United Nations Center for Human Settlements. *Compendium of Human Settlements Statistics.* New York: United Nations, 1995.

Birmingham, West Midlands
ENGLAND, UNITED KINGDOM

LOCATION

Birmingham, the second largest city in the United Kingdom, lies in a densely populated industrial region on central England's midland plains, at an elevation of 535 feet above sea level. The City of Birmingham occupies a land area of 98 square miles (265 square kilometers). Birmingham is located in West Midlands Metropolitan County, in the heart of the West Midlands region. Unlike major coastal or inland port cities, Birmingham is not intersected by a major waterway. However, the city is surrounded by four major waterways—the Penk, Trent, Tame, and Severn Rivers. The Severn River, to Birmingham's west, serves as the primary regional waterway. The development and expansion of road and rail transport in the eighteenth and nineteenth centuries greatly expanded transportation access to and from the Birmingham region. The West Midlands region also includes Hereford and Worcester, Shropshire, Staffordshire, and Warwickshire Counties. Birmingham is the industrial, commercial, and administrative center of West Midlands Metropolitan County. The other major municipalities in the county are Coventry, Dudley, Sandwell, Soilhull, Walsall, and Wolverhampton. Birmingham is located approximately 130 miles northwest of London, the capital city, 80 miles southeast of Liverpool, and 75 miles due south of Manchester. The city has an average January low temperature of 38.5 degrees Fahrenheit (3.6 degrees Celsius) and an average July high of 61.5 degrees Fahrenheit (16.4 degrees Celsius). Birmingham's average annual precipitation is 29.7 inches (754.4 millimeters).

POPULATION AND DEMOGRAPHY

Birmingham's metropolitan area population of 2.3 million grew by 0.3 percent between 1990 and 1995. The regional population is projected to remain constant between 1995 and 2015. Between 1981 and 1995, as the United Kingdom's population expanded by 4 percent, to 58.6 million, the West Midlands Metropolitan County population declined by 1.3 percent, to 2.6 million. Over the same period, the population of the central city of Birmingham declined by 0.3 percent, to 1,017,000. The population decline reflects a migratory trend from the industrial West Midlands region to the growth cities in northern and southeastern England. However, in the mid-1990s, the number of migrants into the region began to eclipse the number of migrants leaving the region. The region's population decline is tempered by an increase

in the birth rate and a decrease in the death rate, contributing to a natural increase rate of 2.7 per 1,000 residents. Birmingham has a relatively high population density of 6,628 persons per square mile (2,558 persons per square kilometer), considerably higher than that of Manchester or Leeds. Birmingham's population age distribution is comparable to other English regions: 19.7 percent of all urban residents are under 16 years of age, 61.6 percent of the city's residents are in their productive years, and 15.3 percent are 65 years and over. After London, West Midlands has a higher proportion of ethnic minorities than any other region in the United Kingdom. The ethnic minority population comprises 8 percent of the total population. The leading population minorities are Indian, Pakistani/Bangladeshi, and black residents. Males comprise 49.3 percent of the central city's population.

HISTORY

In 1166, Birmingham was chartered as a market town. Due to the absence of major rivers or water transportation routes in the region, through the Middle Ages Birmingham did not expand in population or economic importance. Its proximity to the coalmining region contributed to Birmingham's growth as a burgeoning manufacturing center in the sixteenth century. Over the next two hundred years, the city grew into a major British manufacturing city. The manufacturing sector was led by the growth in the iron and steel industry. The development of modern transportation in the eighteenth century made it easier to export the metal products fabricated in Birmingham. By 1838, railroad lines connected Birmingham to the major port cities of London, to the southeast, and Liverpool, to the northwest. Unregulated industrial development contributed to poor working conditions and growing levels of labor unrest by the end of the century. In addition, living conditions were cramped and overcrowded. At the turn of the century, city authorities began to improve public services and housing conditions. The city suffered from German air raids during the Second World War, contributing to significant damage. In the postwar years, the expansion of British social services improved labor and living conditions for the city's poor and working-class population. However, over the last quarter of the twentieth century, the decline in the manufacturing industry significantly increased unemployment, particularly among ethnic minorities and older urban residents.

GOVERNMENT AND POLITICS

The Birmingham City Council, an elected body, is responsible for enacting local policy and ordinances in the city. In addition, the city council is responsible for administering municipal services. The city council oversees economic development, education, environment, finance, housing, recreation, government employees, social services, and transportation.

ECONOMY

Situated in the heart of the English coal-mining region, Birmingham emerged as a major industrial city by the early nineteenth century. However, low-wage foreign competition in the twentieth century has accelerated the decline in the manufacturing sector. Nonetheless, the sector continues to be a mainstay of the regional and local economy. In 1995, 38 percent of the total West Midlands male labor force was employed in manufacturing, a higher proportion of manufacturing workers than any other region in the United Kingdom. In 1996, 29.8 percent of the total West Midlands Metropolitan County labor force, both male and female, was employed in manufacturing. Manufacturing accounts for an even smaller share of the central city labor force. In 1991, just 25.2 percent of all Birmingham's workers were employed in the sector. According to British National Statistics, production industries account for a higher proportion of gross domestic product in the West Midlands than any other industry. The major industries in the region produce iron and steel, automobiles, aircraft, machinery, textiles, rubber, electrical equipment, glass, chemicals, brassware, household utensils, sporting goods, and jewelry. Foreign competition has greatly increased unemployment in the manufacturing sector, which traditionally had been concentrated in basic industries. In 1995 and 1996, West Midlands Metropolitan County's unemployment rate of 11.3 percent was significantly higher than the national 8.5 percent unemployment rate. After Merseyside and North East, the West Midlands regional unemployment rate was the highest in the United Kingdom. The long-term unemployed—those who are jobless for longer than twelve months—comprise a large 45.5 percent of all unemployed people in Birmingham, one of the highest ratios in the United Kingdom. Manufacturing workers who are unlikely to find employment make up a large share of Birmingham's long-term unemployed. Disposable household income is considerably lower in West Midlands Metropolitan County than elsewhere in the country.

The Birmingham City Council's economic development strategy is aimed at resuscitating local industries to reduce unemployment caused by recurrent national recessions that have hurt the local manufacturing industries. The sustained decline in the manufacturing sector has contributed to greater reliance on the service sector. However, economists continue to consider the revival of manufacturing to be crucial to the city's economic recovery. Local officials consider the growth of engineering and high-technology manufacturing to be essential for a sustained long-term recovery. In addition, economists believe that the city will need to continue to diversify into transportation, communications, and business and financial services in order to regain its competitiveness. However, even if this economic development strategy is realized, local officials believe that the city will continue to suffer from high unemployment.

A significant problem is the growing disparity between social classes in the city. The city is seeking to close the gap that is developing between the unemployed and low-income residents and the more affluent residents. The disadvantaged population in Birmingham includes large numbers of ethnic minorities, women, older residents, and the disabled. The city's strategy seeks to close the gap through improving education, skills, and employment opportunities for these populations. In addition, the plan calls for the regeneration of impoverished local communities, encouraging development and investment in neighborhoods of Birmingham, including Birmingham Heartlands, City Centre, Handsworth/Soho, Castle Vale, and West Northfield.

TRANSPORTATION

Unlike other major world cities, Birmingham is relatively landlocked, as it is not intersected by a major waterway. Thus, much of the city's growth in economic importance occurred in the nineteenth and twentieth centuries with the development of railroads and motor vehicles. Today, Birmingham is served by major railways and national and regional highways. As in other regions, passenger vehicles are the leading form of transportation in the West Midlands. The trend toward greater motor vehicle use is projected to increase further into the next century. In 1996, 71 percent of households in the West Midlands had at least one car. Birmingham residents utilize regional airports for domestic and international air transport.

HEALTH CARE

The West Midlands Metropolitan County death rate increased from 10.6 deaths per 1,000 residents in 1981 to 11 deaths per 1,000 residents in 1995. Heart and other circulatory system problems were the leading causes of death in 1992 in the West Midlands, followed by cancer. The regional infant mortality rate between 1993 and 1995 was 7.9 infant deaths per 1,000 live births, considerably higher than the national infant mortality rate of 6.2, but considerably lower than the rates in the Leeds and Manchester metropolitan areas.

EDUCATION

The West Midlands Metropolitan County student/teacher ratio is close to the national average: 23 students per teacher in primary school and 16.1 students per teacher in secondary schools. Students are required to attend school between the ages of 5 and 15; in 1994-1995, 75 percent of all 16-year-olds went on to continue their education. Of the metropolitan student population, 39.4 percent are in primary schools, 51.8 percent are in secondary schools, and 8.9 percent attend higher-education institutions. The leading postsecondary educational institutions serving the city are the University of Aston in Birmingham, the University of Birmingham, and the University of Central England in Birmingham.

HOUSING

Housing conditions have improved appreciably since the turn of the twentieth century, when large families lived in small, cramped quarters with little light. Frequently, more than one family would live in overcrowded dwellings, and there was little privacy. Following the end of the Second World War, a large number of public housing units were built to accommodate the growing population. But, under the conservative national leadership that governed the United Kingdom from the late 1970s to the mid-1990s, the private sector assumed a larger role in housing development and ownership. But, in Birmingham, public housing authorities continue to maintain control over much of the housing stock. In 1995, public housing authorities were responsible for 44.1 percent of all new housing stock in the City of Birmingham. The average household size in Birmingham is 2.5 persons, and single-person households comprise 31.4 percent of all households. Rental units account for 32 percent of the regional housing stock. According to the Office of National Statistics, average rental costs in West Midland were about 25 percent lower than the English average rental cost; however, Birmingham's rental costs are slightly higher than the metropolitan average.

CULTURE, THE ARTS, AND ENTERTAINMENT

The leading museums are the Birmingham Museum and Art Gallery and the Museum of Science and Industry. The city has a number of historic churches, including St. Philip's Cathedral, Saint Margin's Parish Church in the Bull Ring (a historic 800-year-old market site), and Saint Chad's Roman Catholic Cathedral. Other historic sites include Town Hall and the Council House. Birmingham is home to a leading international orchestra, the City of Birmingham Symphony Orchestra, and the Birmingham Repertory Theatre.

CATEGORY	DATA	YEAR	AREA
LOCATION & ENVIRONMENT			
Area	98 square miles	1996	City
	265 square kilometers		City
Elevation	535 feet/163 meters		City
January Temperature	38.5 degrees Fahrenheit		City
	3.6 degrees Celsius		City
July Temperature	61.5 degrees Fahrenheit		City
	16.4 degrees Celsius		City
Annual Precipitation	29.7 inches/754.4 millimeters		City
POPULATION & DEMOGRAPHY			
Population	2,300,000	1996	Metro
Projected Population	2,300,000	2015	Metro
Growth Rate	−0.3%	1990–1995	Metro
Growth Rate	0.0%	1995–2015	Metro
Density	6,628 per square mile	1995	Metro
	2,558 per square kilometer		
Gender			
Males	49.3%	1992	Metro
Females	50.7%	1992	Metro
Age			
Under 16	19.7%	1992	Metro
16–64	61.6%	1992	Metro
Over 65	15.3%	1992	Metro
VITAL STATISTICS			
Births per 1,000 Residents	13.6	1992	Metro
Deaths per 1,000 Residents	10.6	1992	Metro
Infant Mortality Rate	7.9 per 1,000 live births	1993–1995	Metro
ECONOMY			
Trade	17.1%	1991	City
Manufacturing	25.2%	1991	City
Services	31.3%	1991	City
Finance, Insurance, Real Estate	13.5%	1991	City
Transport/Communications	5.8%	1991	City
Construction	3.8%	1991	City
Utilities	1.0%	1991	City
Agriculture	2.1%	1991	City
Mining	2.3%	1991	City
TRANSPORTATION			
Passenger Journeys	4,830,000,000	1990	City
Rail	11.2%	1990	City
Buses & Trolleys	88.8%	1990	City
Passenger Vehicles	2,426,000	1995	City

(continued)

CATEGORY	DATA	YEAR	AREA
HOUSING			
Total Housing Units	2,089,000	1991	Metro
Persons per Unit	2.5	1991	Metro
Owner-Occupied Units	68.0%	1991	Metro
HEALTH CARE			
Hospitals	30	1992	City
EDUCATION			
Total Students	983,000	1993	Metro
Primary	39.4%	1993	Metro
Secondary	51.8%	1993	Metro
Higher	8.9%	1993	Metro

Sources: Department of Economic and Social Affairs, Population Division. *Urban Agglomerations, 1996.* New York: United Nations, 1997; United Nations Center for Human Settlements. *Compendium of Human Settlements Statistics.* New York: United Nations, 1995; Eurostat *Regions Statistical Yearbook.* Brussels, Belgium: Statistical Office of European Communities, 1996; and Office for National Statistics. *Regional Trends 32.* London, England: The Stationery Office, 1997.

Bogotá
COLOMBIA

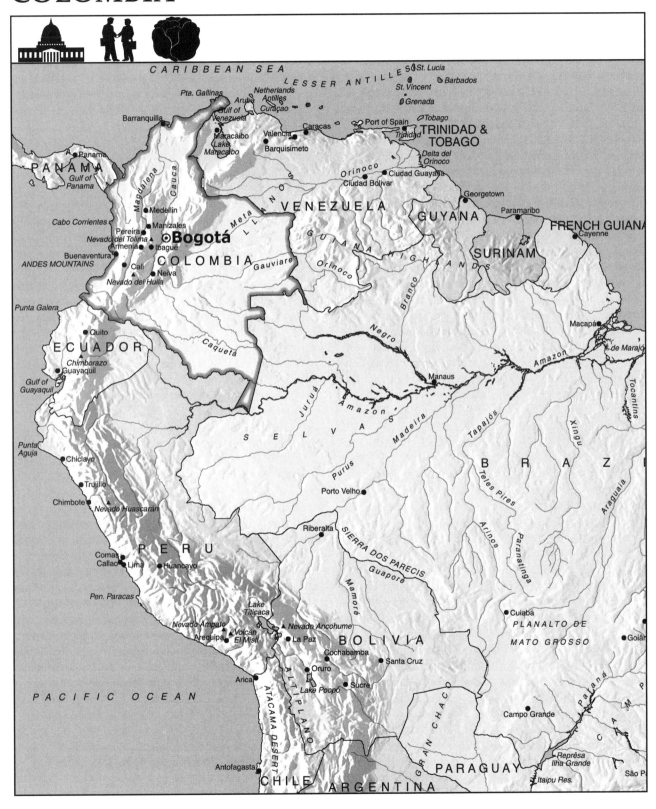

LOCATION

Bogotá, officially referred to as Santa Fe de Bogotá, is located high in a fertile basin on a mountain-rimmed plateau of the Cordillera Oriental in the Andes Mountains. As Colombia's largest city, located in the central portion of the country, Bogotá serves as both the capital and the manufacturing center.

Bogotá is located at an altitude of 8,355 feet (2,547 meters). January and July temperatures remain fairly static at 57.2 degrees Fahrenheit (14.0 degrees Celsius), with an average annual precipitation of 37.5 inches (952 millimeters) per year. Due to its high altitude, the city gets cold in the evenings and shuts down early at night. Flanked by steep mountains on its eastern rim, the city has expanded in other directions and now spans an area of 613 square miles (1,587 square kilometers). As is typical with most Latin American cities, Bogotá is characterized by downtown high-rise buildings, crowded boulevards, sprawling affluent suburbs, and expanding squatter settlements. Bogotá is one of South America's fastest-growing metropolitan areas.

Bogotá competes economically with other cities including Medellín, Cali, and Barranquilla. Furthermore, Bogotá, which grew rapidly during the 1980s, suffered less from the economic recession of that decade than most of its regional counterparts.

POPULATION AND DEMOGRAPHY

Bogotá's population has expanded rapidly during the twentieth century, growing 3 to 6 percent annually for much of that time. From a base of 100,000 in 1900, the population had tripled, to 300,000, by the late 1930s, and then more than doubled, to 676,000, by 1950. Bogotá went from 1,697,000 inhabitants in 1964 to 2,855,000 in 1973, 4,268,000 in 1985, and 5,898,000 in 1993. In the 1960s, the growth rate began to decrease; it now stands at 2.4 percent, and it is estimated that the population will reach 8.4 million in the year 2015.

But while the population in Bogotá is growing at a slower rate, smaller towns in the surrounding areas are now growing at faster rates, and migration—from all parts of Colombia, but especially from neighboring towns—has played a major role in the growth of Bogotá. Due to the high numbers of women migrating to Bogotá in search of work, there is a high ratio of women to men. The city has seen a dramatic drop in the infant mortality rate, from 50 deaths per 1,000 live births in the 1970s to 31.7 deaths per 1,000 births in 1987, and an increase in life ex-

pectancy, from 66 years in the 1970s to 71 in the 1990s. The infant mortality rate is expected to continue to decline.

Bogotá's population is also very young, which is another major cause of its rapid growth. Forty percent of the population is under 20, 54 percent is between the ages of 20 and 59, and only 5.7 percent is over the age of 60. Family size has been decreasing, however, due to increased literacy rates, more widespread use of family planning methods, and an increased rate of female participation in the workforce.

HISTORY

Bogotá was founded near the populous Chubcha Indian center near Bacata in 1538. The location of Bogotá was ideal because of the rich agricultural area around it and the fact that there was plenty of water and space to grow. In 1717, the city became the capital of Greater Colombia, which encompassed present-day Colombia, Ecuador, Panama, and Venezuela. Simón Bolívar liberated the territory in 1819 from the Spanish, and in 1830, it became the capital of present-day Colombia.

Bogotá's remote location has mitigated its ability to dominate Colombia's political and economic life. Turbulent struggles for political power in the capital city, as well as geographic isolation, stunted Bogotá's growth and prosperity in the nineteenth century.

In the 1930s, after a series of political struggles, the Liberal Party was able to introduce modern social legislation that supported the labor movement. Conservatives resorted to violence to regain power. High inflation, static wages, and growing unemployment in the post–World War II period led to anger and frustration among workers and peasants.

Many peasants moved to Bogotá to flee the violence in the countryside. Riots subsequently broke out in Bogotá, culminating in a series of clashes that resulted in many deaths and caused widespread damage to the city. Unrest continued in Bogotá until 1958, when a Liberal-Conservative coalition formed a pact in which both parties agreed to alternate the presidency and share public office for sixteen years. This arrangement ended sectarian violence, though it failed to end rural guerrilla activity, which continues to this day.

GOVERNMENT AND POLITICS

Colombia is divided into twenty-three departments, four intendencies, five commissariats, and one special district, which includes Bogotá. Like other administrative units, the Bogotá special district is headed by a governor who is appointed by the president of the republic. In addition, Bogotá has a municipal government, headed by a mayor who is appointed by the governor.

ECONOMY

As recently as 1945, Medellín still had one third more industrial jobs than Bogotá. While import-substitution strategies implemented in the 1950s diversified the nation's economic structure, trade restrictions fostered a national manufacturing base, providing an opportunity for the capital to grow in economic importance. Bogotá has become the economic heart of the country, increasing its share of the country's gross domestic product from 15 percent in 1960 to 25 percent in 1985. Due to its isolated location in the mountainous highlands of the Andes and its decades-old protectionist policies, Bogotá was left relatively untouched by the economic downturns experienced throughout the region in the 1980s.

The manufacturing industry, which is domestically oriented, is focused on printing and publishing, motor vehicle and transport assembly, food processing, and the manufacturing of textiles, metals, electrical equipment, cement, chemicals, and plastics. Bogotá currently generates little in terms of exports. These include flowers (41 percent of total exports), emeralds (29 percent), agricultural products (12 percent), leather goods (7 percent), and clothing (5 percent).

Bogotá's strength lies in services, manufacturing for the domestic market, higher education, research, and commerce. With a growth rate of 25 percent annually, the economy is strong and diversified. Services (27.4 percent), trade (23.7 percent), and manufacturing (23.5 percent) comprise the bulk of the economic activity. Government is a vital component of the economy, accounting for 15 percent of the gross domestic product and employing 34,000 people, a third of the country's total public employees.

Financial services, insurance, and real estate constitute the fourth most important sector, accounting for 9.1 percent of the economy. Transport and communications comprise 6.8 percent. National and international banks and corporations maintain their headquarters in Bogotá. With all major railroads and highways, including the Pan American Highway, passing through Bogotá, and an international airport, Bogotá is well positioned as a major hub in the country.

Notwithstanding, there are not enough jobs for Bogotá's workers; the working-age population in the region doubled from 2.4 million in 1976 to 4.8 million in the mid-1990s, and labor-force participation rose across all age groups, but particularly among women (during the mid-1990s, women were 50 percent of the labor force, up from 36 percent in the mid-1970s). During the 1980s, unemployment reached an average of 11 percent, rising to 14 percent in 1986. Recent unemployment figures are half of the 1980s averages, but this is due to the fact that increasing numbers of workers are employed in the informal sector of the economy at lower wages. Typically, these jobs are found in commerce, construction, services, and manufacturing. As a result, the proportion of workers earning less than the minimum wage rose from 50 percent in 1976 to 58 percent in 1990.

While overall poverty rates have fallen dramatically since the early 1970s, from 57 percent to 17 percent in the early 1990s, some 800,000 people lack basic services, and 200,000 live in poverty. In 1985, the poorest fifth of the population earned only 4 percent of the city's income, while the top tenth received 37 percent. These gross disparities are visibly notable in the segregated neighborhoods.

TRANSPORTATION

Bogotá's public transport system has been entirely privatized. Buses and trolleys are the primary form of mass transit. By 1990, public transport provided for about 4.5 million trips. While 90 percent of residents travel by public transport, traffic congestion still is a serious problem in Bogotá. There were 336,056 passenger vehicles in 1989. Each day, 200,000 workers commute to the city center. A medium-range trip of 3 to 6 miles can take as long as one or two hours. Many companies are using small minibuses, following similar routes to the city center, but regular bus fares are rising.

HEALTH CARE

Health care is provided by the public sector, social security funds, and the private sector. The public sector's hospitals and clinics have suffered from poor administration and inefficiency. Notwithstanding the continued rise in population, the number of hospital beds is decreasing. In 1990, there were 8,425 hospital beds, down from 9,378 in 1970. There is also a serious shortage of emergency-room beds. The city has a rate of 2.8 physicians per 1,000 urban residents. The long lines, impolite treatment, and corresponding low morale in the public health care institutions are further exacerbating their notoriety for poor care.

EDUCATION

Bogotá is Colombia's main educational center, hosting the National University of Colombia, founded in 1867, as well as many other universities and educational facilities. In 1980, 17 percent of all students attended institutions of higher education, up from 2 percent in 1960. Primary school attendance was up to nearly 100 percent in 1980, from 77 percent in 1960. Secondary school attendance, however, is still low; it was 39 percent in 1980, although up from 12 percent in 1960. The city's illiteracy rate was at 10 percent in 1984.

While most primary school students (62 percent) attended public schools in the late 1980s, 60 percent of secondary school students and 79 percent of those enrolled in postsecondary institutions attended private schools. Public school education suffers from large numbers of dropouts, and many students are forced to repeat years. This is in part due to high student-teacher ratios. In 1988, there were thirty-four students per teacher in public primary schools on average, while there were twenty-four per teacher in public secondary schools.

HOUSING

Bogotá has decent housing stock, particularly in the middle-class and well-to-do neighborhoods of the north and northwest. By the standards of most Third World cities, much of the working class lives in relatively well-constructed housing. Of the city's 1 million housing units, 72 percent are single-family units and 27 percent are apartments.

Nevertheless, the rapid population growth has led to a persistent housing shortage. In 1980, there was a reported deficit of 210,000 housing units; 13 percent of homes in Bogotá were overcrowded, and 4 percent were in serious disrepair. Furthermore, Bogotá is segregated along class lines. The poor live mostly in the south and southwest parts of the city, where land invasions and self-built housing are the norm, as compared to the northern suburbs, which have majestic houses surrounded by concrete walls.

Since the mid-1930s, 31 percent of the housing in Bogotá has been developed without government regulation. Between 1987 and 1991, 42 percent of the city's total new housing land involved self-built homes. It is difficult to provide infrastructure after the fact to housing that is self-built. In 1993, 11.7 percent of homes in Bogotá lacked running water, 10 percent lacked electricity, and 13.7 percent lacked drainage; most of these were in the south and southwest sections. One percent of housing had no services at all.

Policy regarding illegally developed housing has vacillated between attempts to ignore the problem and outright efforts to eradicate the units. Neither policy has worked, and recently the city has begun to look at the situation as an efficient solution to the shortage of low-income housing. The government is instead now trying to legalize the settlements and provide basic infrastructure and amenities.

CULTURE, THE ARTS, AND ENTERTAINMENT

Bogotá has a wealth of museums and historic buildings. Indeed, the stately colonial architecture of historic Bogotá, the National University, the National Museum, the National Library, and the National Conservatory of Music are testaments to Bogotá's position as Colombia's cultural center. But most renowned is the city's Gold Museum, home to the largest collection of pre-Columbian gold artifacts in the world. Other interesting cultural sites include San Francisco Church (built in 1567), the National Astronomical Observatory, the Columbus Theater, the planetarium, and the Museum of Natural History. The restored Casa de Poesia Silva, built in 1720, is solely devoted to promoting poetry. For a breathtaking view of the city from a steep mountainside, residents and visitors travel by cable car to the shrine of Monserrate.

CATEGORY	DATA	YEAR	AREA
LOCATION & ENVIRONMENT			
Area	613 square miles	1989	City
	1,587 square kilometers		City
Elevation	8,355 feet/2,547 meters		City
January Temperature	57.2 degrees Fahrenheit		City
	14.0 degrees Celsius		City
July Temperature	57.2 degrees Fahrenheit		City
	14.0 degrees Celsius		City
Annual Precipitation	37.5 inches/952 millmeters		City
POPULATION & DEMOGRAPHY			
Population	6,200,000	1996	City
Projected Population	8,400,000	2015	City
Growth Rate	3.0%	1990–1995	City
Growth Rate	38.1%	1995–2015	City
Density	7,622 per square mile	1989	City
	2,944 per square kilometer		
Gender			
Males	47.6%	1989	City
Females	52.4%	1989	City
Age			
Under 20	40.2%	1991	City
20–59	54.1%	1991	City
Over 60	5.7%	1991	City
VITAL STATISTICS			
Births per 1,000 Residents	15.6	1987	City
Deaths per 1,000 Residents	4.4	1987	City
Infant Mortality Rate	31.7 deaths per 1,000 live births	1987	City
ECONOMY			
Total Workforce	1,769,146	1989	City
Trade	23.7%	1989	City
Manufacturing	23.5%	1989	City
Services	27.4%	1989	City
Finance, Insurance, Real Estate	9.1%	1989	City
Transport and Communications	6.8%	1989	City
Construction	6.8%	1989	City
Utilities	0.4%	1989	City
Agriculture	1.5%	1989	City
Mining	0.6%	1989	City
Nonclassifiable	0.6%	1989	City
TRANSPORTATION			
Passenger Journeys	4,498,000	1990	City
Buses and Trolley	100%	1990	City
Passenger Vehicles	336,056	1989	City

(continued)

CATEGORY	DATA	YEAR	AREA
COMMUNICATIONS			
Telephones per 1,000 Residents	214	1990	City
HEALTH CARE			
Hospitals	20	1988	City
Physicians per 1,000 Residents	2.8	1988	City
EDUCATION			
Primary	46.1%	1990	City
Secondary	36.6%	1990	City
Higher	17.3%	1990	City

Sources: Department of Economic and Social Affairs, Population Division. *Urban Agglomerations, 1996.* New York: United Nations, 1997. United Nations Center for Human Settlements. *Compendium of Human Settlements Statistics.* New York: United Nations, 1995.

Boston, Massachusetts
USA

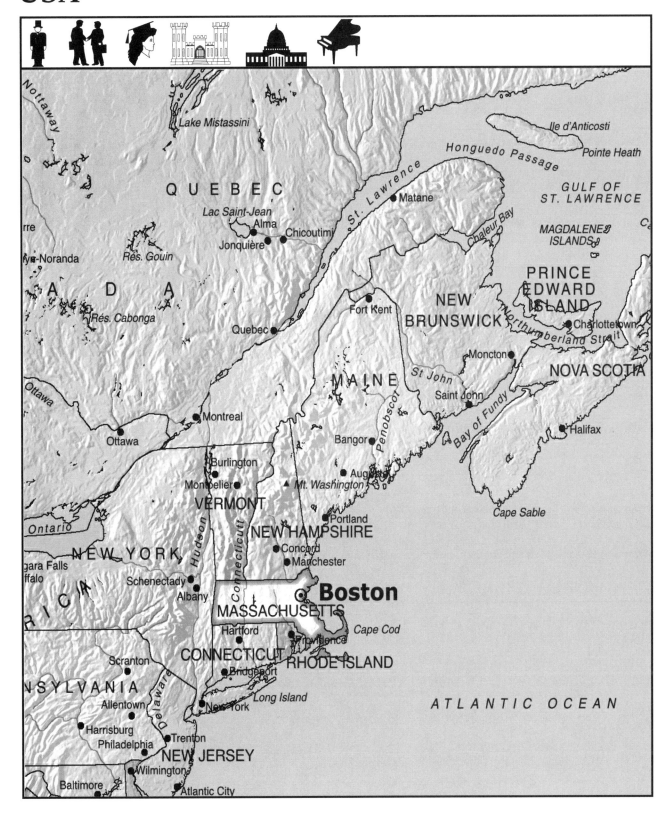

LOCATION

Boston, the capital of Massachusetts and New England's most populous city, is located in Suffolk County in east-central Massachusetts. Boston lies at the northeastern end of the largest population concentration in the United States, a corridor extending 450 miles southwest to Washington, D.C. The city is located on a natural harbor at the western shore of Boston Bay, which extends east into Massachusetts Bay and the Atlantic Ocean. The Charles River flows into Boston Harbor from the northeast, and the Neponset River runs along the city's southwestern boundary. Boston's relatively small land area expanded in the early nineteenth century through dredging and the filling of tidal flats and the annexation of nearby areas, and now totals 46 square miles (124 square kilometers). The Boston metropolitan statistical area is one of America's largest centers of population, a sprawling area, with a 30-mile radius, extending into southeastern New Hampshire. The Boston consolidated metropolitan statistical area (the area extending beyond the central city region) extends south to Rhode Island and Connecticut. The city's temperature ranges from an average low of 28.6 degrees Fahrenheit (-1.8 degrees Celsius) in January to an average high of 73.3 degrees Fahrenheit (23.1 degrees Celsius) in July. Boston's average annual precipitation is 41.5 inches (1,054 millimeters).

The city of Boston prides itself as a livable urban environment with preserved older buildings in established neighborhoods, well-maintained parks, clean air and water, and a modern and efficient waste-removal system. In the late 1990s, Boston instituted an environmental blueprint through a coalition of governmental, nongovernmental, and community agencies, and neighborhood groups that seeks to expand the quality and sustainability of the urban environment. The key elements of the blueprint involve improving the environment in poor and minority neighborhoods; expanding open spaces; renovating historic buildings, places, and parklands; and expanding recycling programs.

POPULATION AND DEMOGRAPHY

Over the last several decades, Boston's metropolitan area population has expanded even as the central city's population has declined and stabilized. From 1950 to 1982, Boston's central city population declined by over 250,000, a 30 percent drop from its high of over 800,000. In 1995, the central city population of 551,675 was just 19 percent of the total regional population of 2,842,000. Between 1980 and 1992, the City of Boston's population declined by 11,319, representing a cumulative 2 percent decline. Conversely, Boston's metropolitan area population is projected to expand by 12.6 percent to 3,200,000 over the next twenty years, due to continued growth of the suburbs and outlying areas. In 1990, the consolidated metropolitan statistical area, a region that surrounds Boston and encompasses all or part of the New England states of Massachusetts, New Hampshire, Maine, and Connecticut, had a population of 5,455,403. The central city has a density of 11,398 persons per square mile (4,300 per square kilometer).

In the three centuries since the Boston metropolitan area was originally colonized by British settlers, the region was settled by Irish, Canadian, Russian, and Italian immigrants, African-Americans, and more recently Hispanic and Asian immigrants. Boston's black, Hispanic, Irish, and Italian populations reside in mostly segregated neighborhoods. Unlike many other northeastern and midwestern American cities, a majority of Boston's population is white (65.4 percent). Blacks comprise 26.6 percent of the central city's population. Hispanics make up 11.2 percent, and Asians and Pacific Islanders are 5.5 percent. A relatively large proportion of Boston residents is in the productive 18-to-64 age group. Seniors 65 years and older comprise 11.4 percent of the city's population, while youth under age 18 make up 19.2 percent of all city residents.

HISTORY

Before European colonization and settlement, the Boston region was inhabited by Algonquian Indians, whose numbers dwindled following the arrival of Europeans. The area that is now Boston was settled in 1630 and named capital of the Massachusetts Bay Colony. The city had become an important settlement by 1750 and was a major battle site in the 1770s, during the American War of Independence against Britain. By the eighteenth century, Boston became a leading port city for foreign trade. The city's stature grew in the nineteenth century as a result of the influx and settlement of European immigrants and the growth of manufacturing. Boston was incorporated as a city in 1822.

GOVERNMENT AND POLITICS

The city of Boston is governed through a city council (the legislative branch) and the mayor (the chief executive and administrator of local government). Laws are enacted with the approval of a majority of city council members and the mayor. The Boston City Council consists of four councilors elected on an at-large basis and nine councilors who are elected in specific districts. Each member of the council is assigned certain legislative responsibilities. As the chief executive, the mayor is responsible for the delivery of municipal services, economic development, collecting taxes, and enhancing the city's social and physical environment. The chief function of the mayor's office is to formulate and plan policy, municipal government operations, housing, education, and drug policy. The mayor's office encourages local participation by residents of the diverse neighborhoods through local coordinators and liaisons. The mayor is also responsible for coordinating affairs with federal, state, and other local governments.

ECONOMY

The character of the Boston regional economy has changed significantly over the last half of the twentieth century through a transformation from manufacturing to high-technology industries. Traditional textile and footwear manufacturing industries have been replaced by high-technology and information-based computer software and biomedical industries. Even the once-promising computer hardware industry has lost its competitive edge in the 1990s to lower-cost producers elsewhere in the United States and abroad. Boston's high-technology sector benefits from its proximity to the major research institutions in the region, which encourage venture capital investments and spur the development of new products and services. The Port of Boston, one of the busiest ports in the United States during the nineteenth century, remains an important element of the city's economy. The terminals have been modernized to accommodate containerized cargo.

Although the region has gained many new high-wage jobs associated with new technologies, finance, insurance, and real estate, the loss of older industries has reduced the number of jobs that once provided decent wages for unskilled and semiskilled workers. Manufacturing jobs have been replaced by much lower-paying service-sector jobs in fast-food restaurants, retail stores, maintenance, and health care. In 1990, less than 10 percent of Boston's workforce was employed in manufacturing, while nearly 17 percent was employed in wholesale and retail trade, 13.3 percent in health services, and 10.8 percent in finance, insurance, and real estate. In 1989, the U.S. Census

Bureau reported that nearly 19 percent of the city's population, the vast majority of them children, was living below the poverty line.

In 1997, the city inaugurated Boston 400 as its first comprehensive planning process since 1965. The key elements involve determining what physical foundations are needed to serve Boston's economy, and which cultural institutions can help to build Boston's reputation as a livable city. The plan calls for stimulating the local economy through economic development programs and improving the city's planning and design of streets, sidewalks, parks and open spaces, plazas and public buildings, museums, and convention centers. A major component of the city's plan for the twenty-first century is to embrace the global economy and to expand Boston as a center of international business and trade.

TRANSPORTATION

Like many other major American cities, Boston suffers from serious traffic congestion. However, the region has developed an advanced public transit system and is planning new programs to improve movement in the region. The Massachusetts Bay Transportation Authority provides Boston-area residents with one of the most modern bus, subway, and commuter rail transportation systems in the United States. The city's subway system has four major routes. A new $1 billion central artery tunnel project is under construction, and the city has inaugurated the Downtown Plan and other programs aimed at reducing traffic congestion through improving pedestrian and bicycle access to the downtown, waterfront, and neighborhood areas through the redesign of selected streets. The city is served by nearby Logan Airport, which accommodates airlines flying to domestic and international destinations.

HEALTH CARE

In Boston, as in most other cities in the United States, there is no universal guarantee of health care services to all citizens. In recent years, federal and state government budget cuts have reduced access to health care through Medicaid, the federally mandated health insurance program providing access to the poor and indigent. Budget cuts and the declining commitment to the poor have placed added pressure on Boston government authorities to deliver services more efficiently. Oversight of public health and the health care system is provided by the Boston Public

Health Commission (BPHC), whose mission is to protect, preserve, and promote the health and well-being of Boston residents, particularly the most vulnerable ones. The BPHC provides public-health education, addiction, domestic violence prevention, school-based health, AIDS prevention, and communicable disease services. To improve access to health services in underserved local communities, the Boston Department of Public Health is collaborating with existing community-based organizations. The Boston metro area is a center for medical research and specialized health care services.

EDUCATION

Boston's public school system serves nearly 66,000 primary and secondary school students. The racial and ethnic composition of Boston's public schools is considerably more diverse than in the 1970s, when school desegregation was instituted and many white middle-class families moved to the suburbs or enrolled their children in private and parochial schools to avoid desegregation. Almost half of all school enrollees are black; more than 25 percent are Hispanic, 18 percent are white, and 9 percent are of Asian origin. A growing number of children in the public schools are the sons and daughters of recent immigrants from Latin America, Haiti, China, and Cape Verde. Many of America's leading postsecondary institutions are in the Boston metropolitan area, including Boston College, Boston University, Brandeis University, Emerson College, Harvard University, the Massachusetts Institute of Technology, Northeastern University, Suffolk University, Tufts University, the University of Massachusetts, and Wellesley College. The region is also served by local community colleges.

HOUSING

The acceleration of gentrification trends in the 1980s has contributed greatly to a crisis in affordable hous-

ing. New construction and rehabilitation in Boston's older neighborhoods have created more housing for upper-middle-class residents but have pushed poor and working-class residents out of these neighborhoods. Most new housing construction is concentrated in the outlying suburbs. The decline in new public housing development has further reduced housing availability. The elimination of a housing price stabilization program has further increased rental costs. These factors are contributing to an increasingly inadequate housing supply, the doubling up of families in housing units meant for one family, and homelessness among vulnerable populations, particularly among the elderly. The city of Boston alone has lost over 30,000 units of affordable housing in the thirty-year period ending in 1996.

CULTURE, THE ARTS, AND ENTERTAINMENT

Boston is New England's center of arts, culture, and entertainment. The leading museums in the Boston area are the Museum of Science, the Museum of Fine Arts, the Institute of Contemporary Art, the Harvard University Art Museums, the Computer Center, the New England Science Center, and many private art galleries. The city is also home to the John F. Kennedy Library. The region has four orchestras, including the internationally recognized Boston Symphony Orchestra, a ballet company, and several theater and repertory companies. The Boston metropolitan area has five major league sports teams, including the Boston Red Sox baseball team, the Boston Celtics basketball team, the Boston Bruins hockey team, the New England Patriots football team, and the New England Revolution soccer team. The Boston Marathon, the preeminent long-distance foot race in the United States, is run every spring.

CATEGORY	DATA	YEAR	AREA
LOCATION & ENVIRONMENT			
Area	48.4 square miles	1995	City
	125.4 square kilometers		City
Elevation	21 feet/6.9 meters		City
January Temperature	28.6 degrees Fahrenheit	1961–1990	City
	−1.8 degrees Celsius	1961–1990	City
July Temperature	73.3 degrees Fahrenheit	1961–1990	City
	23.1 degrees Celsius	1961–1990	City
Annual Precipitation	41.5 inches/1,054 millimeters	1961–1990	City
POPULATION & DEMOGRAPHY			
Population	2,900,000	1996	Metro
Projected Population	3,200,000	2015	Metro
Growth Rate	0.5%	1990–1995	Metro
Growth Rate	12.6%	1995–2015	Metro
Density	11,398 per square mile	1992	City
	4,399 per square kilometer		
Gender			
Males	48.1%	1990	City
Females	51.9%	1990	City
Age			
Under 18	19.2%	1990	City
18–64	69.4%	1990	City
Over 65	11.4%	1990	City
VITAL STATISTICS			
Births per 1,000 Residents	17	1988	City
Death per 1,000 Residents	10	1988	City
Infant Mortality Rate	13.9 per 1,000 live births	1988	City
ECONOMY			
Total Workforce	316,162	1990	City
Trade	16.6%	1990	City
Manufacturing	9.9%	1990	City
Health Services	13.3%	1990	City
Finance, Insurance, Real Estate	10.8%	1990	City
Public Administration	5.6%	1990	City
TRANSPORTATION			
Passenger Vehicles	198,930	1990	City
HOUSING			
Total Housing Units	250,863	1990	City
Persons per Unit	2.2	1990	City
Owner-Occupied Units	31.0%	1990	City
HEALTH CARE			
Hospitals	19	1991	City

(continued)

CATEGORY	DATA	YEAR	AREA
EDUCATION			
Total Students	166,508	1991	City
Primary and Secondary	49.1%	1991	City
Higher	50.9%	1991	City

Sources: Department of Economic and Social Affairs, Population Division. *Urban Agglomerations, 1996.* New York: United Nations, 1997; U.S. Bureau of the Census. *County and City Data Book 1994.* Washington, DC: U.S. Government Printing Office, 1994; and United Nations Center for Human Settlements. *Compendium of Human Settlements Statistics.* New York: United Nations, 1995.

Brussels

BELGIUM

LOCATION

Brussels is the capital and largest city in Belgium, as well as the administrative center for the European Union. It is located on the central plateau of the country, approximately 190 feet (58 meters) above sea level and about 60 miles inland from the North Sea coast. Brussels, covering a land area of 60 square miles (161 square kilometers), is situated approximately 100 miles south of Amsterdam and some 160 miles northeast of Paris.

Brussels has a temperate climate, modified by its proximity to the sea. Summers tend to be cool, at 63.5 degrees Fahrenheit (17.5 degrees Celsius) on average, while winters average 36 degrees Fahrenheit (2.2 degrees Celsius). The city receives an abundance of precipitation, on the order of about 32.7 inches (830.6 millimeters) annually.

POPULATION AND DEMOGRAPHY

The Brussels metropolitan area has a population of approximately 1.1 million. This has been shrinking at about 0.5 percent annually over the past decade, though this trend is expected to reverse itself early in the next century. Still, the population is not predicted to grow above its current level for at least the next twenty years. Densely congested, with 16,376 persons per square mile (6,065 per square kilometer) in the city center, the city has a typical age profile for a European city: 30.3 percent of the population is under the age of 20, and almost 17.5 percent is 60 or above.

Like Belgium itself, Brussels is divided between Flemish and French speakers, though the city's population is dominated by the latter. This has represented a change over the pre–World War II era, when most spoke Flemish. The change has occurred for several reasons, including the influx of immigrants from the French-speaking part of the country, of which Brussels is a part, and the prestige of speaking an international language. Still, the issue of language remains sensitive in the city and country. For political reasons, no poll of language preference has been conducted since 1947. Beyond language, most Flemish are more Dutch in their cultural and religious orientation, tending toward Protestantism, while the French-speaking Belgians generally are Catholics. Overall, however, most people in Brussels are not overtly religious in practice.

On top of this basic split, Brussels has seen its population become increasingly diverse over the past few decades, a result of two different causes. First, the headquarters of the European Union has brought bureaucrats and others from all over the union to live in Brussels. In addition, and like other West European cities, Brussels has seen a massive influx of immigrants and guest workers from southern Europe and North Africa since World War II. Virtually all of these immigrants speak or adopt French as their second language, and many of the North Africans are Muslim.

HISTORY

The city of Brussels dates back to a fortified castle established on the site in the sixth century A.D. Over the next six hundred years, the city grew slowly as a trading place and ford across the small tributary of the Ypres that runs through it. From the twelfth to fourteenth centuries, the city became a major town in the Duchy of Brabant, specializing in the production of textiles. In 1430, the city was incorporated into the Duchy of Burgundy and became an important administrative, cultural, and economic center of the Low Countries. The wealth that came from textiles was partially spent on the construction of large municipal buildings during the fifteenth and sixteenth centuries, especially after the city became the capital of the Low Countries provinces of the Hapsburg emperor Charles V. In 1561, a canal was built connecting the city to the Rhine River and the ocean.

During the wars of the reformation and the Dutch war of independence, the city changed hands several times, ultimately being returned to the Spanish Hapsburgs at the end of the sixteenth century. During the late seventeenth century, the city came under several sieges and attacks by the armies of Louis XIV of France, reducing much of the central city to ruins. Out of the rubble grew the great guild halls that still mark the city. As the capital of the Austrian Netherlands, Brussels grew as a financial and industrial center in the eighteenth century. The Brabant revolt against the Austrian government was followed by the Napoleonic occupation. Following Napoleon's defeat at nearby Waterloo, Brussels and Belgium were briefly unified with the Netherlands, a union that ended with the division of 1830, when Belgium gained its independence for the first time and Brussels became its capital.

Through the course of the nineteenth century, Brussels and Belgium generally were at the cutting edge of the industrial revolution, the latter becoming second only to England in its output per capita and the percentage of its laboring force employed in manufacturing. Brussels's growth was temporarily stopped by the German invasion of Belgium in 1914, one of the precipitating acts that brought on World War I. The city once again came under German occupation during World War II but did not suffer extraordinary damage by Allied bombers, since much of the heavy industry had been moved out of the city during the course of the late nineteenth and early twentieth centuries. The city was liberated by British forces in late 1944.

Since World War II, the city has been a flashpoint for tensions between the French- and Flemish-speaking Belgians. Massive Flemish demonstrations in the early 1960s pushed for efforts to establish official bilingualism for the country and an end to overt French influence. This inevitably produced a reaction among the French-speakers, who organized the Francophone Democratic Front in 1964. Today, both forces have risen and fallen in popularity, partially for cultural reasons, but also because of the rising and falling fortunes of the Belgian economy. The situation continues to remain in flux, though there is little violence involved in the dispute.

GOVERNMENT AND POLITICS

Under a constitution dating back to 1836, the government of Belgium offers wide latitude and powers to the individual communes of the country; in the Brussels metropolitan area there are nineteen such communes. In 1970–1971, the Belgian parliament amended the local-government provisions of the national constitution. Three regions—Flemish-speaking Flanders, French-speaking Wallonia, and bilingual Brussels—were recognized. However, the nineteen communes of Brussels continued to maintain their own councils, municipal establishments, burgomasters, and aldermen. The council members are elected by universal suffrage, while the aldermen are chosen by the councilors from their own ranks. The burgomaster, appointed by the king, usually comes from the council and represents the executive power in each commune. The burgomaster of Brussels is often a figure of national political importance.

The constitutional amendments of the early 1970s also established a new Council for the Brussels Agglomeration, with its own directly elected assembly. This body has authority over planning issues, the environment, and specific metropolitan-area services like firefighting and ambulances. A 1980 law also established separate councils to handle the cultural affairs of the Flemish- and French-speaking communities in the Brussels metropolitan area.

ECONOMY

Once one of Europe's major industrial centers, Brussels has seen a massive shift toward the service and commercial sectors in the twentieth century. Still, a number of high-tech industries remain, most of which are located around the river port of the city. These industries manufacture specialized machine tools and electrical goods as well as fine textiles. Approximately 8.5 percent of the workforce is employed in the manufacturing sector.

Trade and finance, on the other hand, accounts for nearly three fifths of the employment in the metropolitan area. Most of the country's major banks, insurance companies, and headquarters of manufacturing companies are located in Brussels. In addition, the establishment of the European Union headquarters in Brussels has led many multinational firms to set up offices in the city.

TRANSPORTATION

Brussels is at the hub of the Belgian transportation network, itself heavily integrated into a complex system of railways, highways, and artificial waterways that weave northwestern Europe into one economic unit. The city's central station handles up to a hundred trains an hour during peak periods. In addition, the city's central location in northwestern Europe makes it a popular destination for travelers heading off to all parts of the continent.

Because of the small size of the country and its extensive network of limited-access highways, Belgians from all over the country commute to the city to work. Indeed, many parts of the city that bustle during the day become quiet after work hours. To alleviate the growing traffic problem, the government opened the city's first subway in 1976. Today, five lines extend to all parts of the metropolitan area.

HEALTH CARE

Brussels has an extensive health care system, most of which is provided through national health insurance schemes, largely funded from general government revenues. Under the constitutional changes of the 1970s, many of the basic health services were turned over to agencies established in each commune. The city has health-promoting ratios of 6.5 physicians and 1.2 hospital beds per 1,000 residents. In addition, the city government has made great strides in recent years to lower the levels of water pollution and air pollution, which have plagued the region since the industrial revolution began.

EDUCATION

Like much else in Brussels, the city's educational system is fractured along linguistic and communal lines. About half of the primary students in the city attend so-called free schools, which are actually administered by the Catholic Church but subsidized by the government. State schools are run by local communes. Parents have a choice of sending their children to Flemish- or French-speaking schools. Brussels is also home to several major institutions of higher learning, which are also divided by language. However, the largest university in the city, the Free University of Brussels, has both Flemish- and French-speaking components. Altogether, there are some 68,000 university students in the Brussels metropolitan area.

HOUSING

Brussels has experienced population pressures since the early nineteenth century, when the city first became a major industrial center. During these years, the city exploded out of its medieval core; the walls surrounding the city center were replaced with boulevards, from which radiated wide avenues lined with four- to six-story apartment buildings. By the late nineteenth and early twentieth centuries, many rural villages had become suburbs. Despite this growth, the city includes much open space.

Conditions, however, remain crowded in the city center. With just 394,000 dwellings, Brussels has a relatively high occupancy rate for a West European city, with some 2.4 persons per unit. In addition, many of the older buildings lack some of the basic amenities of modern life. For instance, less than 70 percent are served by central heating; the remainder provided with room heaters.

CULTURE, THE ARTS, AND ENTERTAINMENT

Belgium has an outstanding artistic and architectural heritage and is home to a number of internationally recognized museums displaying many of the great painters in Belgian history, including Rubens, Delvaux, and Magritte. The Palace of Fine Arts, designed by Art Nouveau artist and designer Victor Horta, was opened in 1928 and features film, music, literature, and theater. The Palace is also where most of the city's major cultural exhibitions occur, and it is home to the Philharmonic Society and the National Federation of Youth and Music.

Other cultural institutions, many of them housed in fine Beaux Arts buildings, include the National Archives, the Albert I Royal Library, the French-language National Theater, and the National Opera House. In general, French-language writers and artists tend to dominate the city's cultural scene. Brussels's main sports stadium is located in Heysel, a northern district of the commune.

CATEGORY	DATA	YEAR	AREA
LOCATION & ENVIRONMENT			
Area	60 square miles	1995	City
	161 square kilometers		City
Elevation	190 feet/58 meters		City
January Temperature	36 degrees Fahrenheit		City
	2.2 degrees Celsius		City
July Temperature	63.5 degrees Fahrenheit		City
	17.5 degrees Celsius		City
Annual Precipitation	32.7 inches/830.6 millimeters		City
POPULATION & DEMOGRAPHY			
Population	1,100,000	1996	Metro
Projected Population	1,100,000	2015	Metro
Growth Rate	−0.5%	1990–1995	Metro
Growth Rate	0.1%	1995–2015	Metro
Density	16,376 per square mile	1986	City
	6,065 per square kilometer		
Gender			
Male	47.2%	1992	Metro
Female	52.8%	1992	Metro
Age			
Under 20	30.3%	1992	Metro
20–59	52.2%	1992	Metro
Over 60	17.5%	1992	Metro
VITAL STATISTICS			
Births per 1,000 Residents	13.6	1992	Metro
Deaths per 1,000 Residents	11.6	1992	Metro
Infant Mortality Rate	7 per 1,000 live births	1992	Metro
Net Migration per 1,000 Residents	−2.9	1992	Metro
ECONOMY			
Workforce	647,000	1992	Metro
Manufacturing	8.5%	1992	Metro
Construction	4.3%	1992	Metro
Trade	59.0%	1992	Metro
Service	27.4%	1992	Metro
Utilities	0.8%	1992	Metro
TRANSPORTATION			
Passenger Vehicles	400,000	1992	Metro
HOUSING			
Housing Units	394,000	1992	Metro
Persons per Unit	2.4	1992	Metro

(continued)

CATEGORY	DATA	YEAR	AREA
HEALTH CARE			
Physicians per 1,000 Residents	6.5	1992	Metro
Hospital Beds per 1,000 Residents	1.2	1992	Metro
EDUCATION			
Total Students	183,000	1992–93	Metro
Primary	39.3%	1992–93	Metro
Secondary	23.0%	1992–93	Metro
Higher	37.2%	1992–93	Metro

Sources: Department of Economic and Social Affairs, Population Division. *Urban Agglomerations, 1996.* New York: United Nations, 1997; Eurostat *Regions Statistical Yearbook.* Brussels, Belgium: Statistical Office of European Communities, 1996; *Statistics of World Large Cities.* Tokyo, Japan: Tokyo Metropolitan Government, 1992 and 1994; and United Nations Center for Human Settlements. *Compendium of Human Settlements Statistics.* New York: United Nations, 1995.

Bucharest
ROMANIA

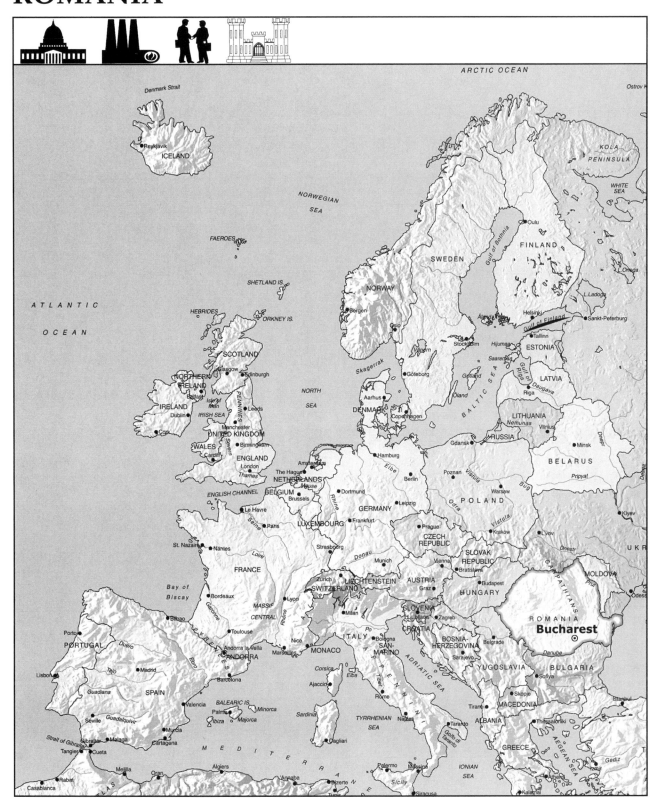

LOCATION

Bucharest, the capital and largest city in Romania, is in the middle of the Romanian Plain on the banks of the Dambovita River, a minor tributary of the Danube that passes approximately 30 miles south of the city. Bucharest covers 84 square miles (228 square kilometers) of territory and lies at an elevation of 269 feet (97 meters). Situated 125 miles west of the Black Sea coast, the city is about 300 miles north-northwest of Istanbul, Turkey. Bucharest has a temperate climate, with January and July temperatures averaging 29.7 and 72.7 degrees Fahrenheit (-1.3 and 22.6 degrees Celsius), respectively. The city receives approximately 22.8 inches of precipitation annually.

POPULATION AND DEMOGRAPHY

The Bucharest metropolitan area has a population of 2.1 million and has been growing at a rate of less than 1 percent for the past ten years, a rate that is expected to drop to zero by 2015, when the population should reach about 2.2 million. The age breakdown of the population is typical of East European cities, with some 27.6 percent under the age of 20 and 11.6 percent above the age of 60. The city has a density of about 24,462 persons per square mile (9,060 per square kilometer).

The vast majority of Bucharest's citizens are Romanians. Minorities—including Hungarians, Roma (Gypsies), Germans, and Ukrainians (in that order)—make up about 15 percent of the population. The city, once home to a major Jewish community, saw this population largely eliminated during the Nazi occupation of World War II. Despite years of secular Communist rule, most of Bucharest's population are adherents of the Romanian Orthodox Church. The Hungarian, German, and Ukrainian minorities are largely Roman Catholic.

HISTORY

Human habitation in what is now the Bucharest metropolitan area dates back to prehistoric times. The first appearance of the name Bucharest in a written historical record goes back to 1459, when Vlad III (Vlad the Impaler), ruler of Wallachia, built a fortress on the site in order to hold back invading Turkish armies.

The tactic failed and the city was soon occupied by the Ottoman Empire. Under Turkish rule, the city developed as a major center of trade and craft production, becoming the capital of the province of Wallachia in 1659. While the Ottomans ruled through local Wallachian princes, by the early 1800s the city was largely governed by Phanariotes (Greeks from Phanar, a district near Constantinople). One uprising in 1821 ended Phanariote rule and another in 1859 led to the union of Wallachia and Moldavia. Three years later, local patriots declared Romania an independent state, with Bucharest as its capital. This move was officially ratified in 1877.

During the first half of the twentieth century, the city continued to grow in size and importance, despite being occupied by Nazis during World War II. Shortly after the takeover of the government by Communists in the mid-1940s, a mass nationalization of industry and land occurred. Under the rule of Nicolai Ceaucescu in the 1970s and 1980s, much of the older sections of the city were bulldozed to make way for wide boulevards and huge government buildings and palaces. Ceaucescu was overthrown and assassinated by reformers around Christmas 1989, the only violent revolution in Eastern Europe during the collapse of Communism at the end of the 1980s.

GOVERNMENT AND POLITICS

With the fall of the Communist regime in 1989, a constituent assembly drafted a constitution that was passed in a general referendum in December 1991. Under this document, a bicameral legislature was established. In addition, it called for a president, elected every four years, who nominates a prime minister and cabinet. While the president is officially the head of government and the armed forces, most of the day-to-day running of domestic and international affairs is handled by the prime minister. Communist Party officials dominated all offices of government before 1989 and remain a major political force in the post-Communist, pluralistic era through their influential positions in the National Salvation Front and the Democratic National Salvation Front parties.

ECONOMY

The Bucharest metropolitan area is the center of Romanian industry. There is a great deal of heavy and light industry. Among the former are factories manufacturing machine tools, vehicles and vehicle parts, and electrical equipment. The city is also home to a large number of food plants processing the produce and livestock grown in Romania's rich agricultural lands. In addition, the city has a number of refineries and metallurgical plants that utilize the country's substantial oil and ore reserves. Virtually all of the industrial sector, however, is quite backward technologically. And while unemployment was officially kept near zero by the Communist government, many of the jobs were redundant, further undermining the competitiveness of Bucharest's industry. Though over 40 percent of the workforce labors in the manufacturing sector, unemployment has grown dramatically since 1989.

Among the rest of the workforce, many work in the public sector, serving in jobs connected to the national government, which is housed in Bucharest. The relatively tiny commercial sector is also a legacy of Communist rule. Less than 10 percent of the workforce is employed in trade and business.

TRANSPORTATION

Bucharest serves as the main transportation hub for Romania's extensive railroad network. Major lines, including many electrified ones, connect the city to the Black Sea port of Constanta, as well as other cities in the Balkans, Eastern Europe, and, via Vienna, to Western Europe. Bucharest is also home to the country's largest airport, with flights to most points in Europe, the Middle East, and North Africa.

Metropolitan transport is handled by buses, trolleys, and subways, each carrying about one third of the transportation load. Two legacies of the Communist era—huge boulevards and a low rate of private car ownership—mean that the city has few traffic congestion problems.

HEALTH CARE

While Bucharest has an extensive health care system on paper—including fifty-two hospitals and nearly five hundred clinics—the health care profile of the population has been declining dramatically over the past decade. Many of the hospitals and clinics lack even the most basic supplies and equipment, and a number of doctors have abandoned the government-run health sector because of low wages and nonpayment of salaries. The death rate in the city has climbed to 10.9 deaths per 1,000 residents and the infant mortality rate is 15.9 deaths per 1,000 live births, among the highest in Europe. In addition, the city has a major problem with orphaned and abandoned children (caused by an official government policy discouraging abortions during the waning days

of the Ceaucescu regime, to boost population) and children with HIV (the result of routinely giving babies transfusions of unscreened blood).

EDUCATION

Under the Communist government, Romania made great strides in the field of education, virtually eliminating the high rates of illiteracy that marked the country's past. All education through the university level is provided free by the government, and schooling is obligatory through the secondary level. The major institution of higher education in Bucharest is the Romanian Academy, founded in 1866 and home to the largest library in the country. Other schools include the University of Bucharest, founded in 1864, and the Technical Institute of Bucharest, established in 1819. Since the revolution of 1989, a number of small private academies at the secondary and tertiary levels have opened, charging tuitions that are affordable only to the nation's elite.

HOUSING

Most of Bucharest's population lives in housing developments on the periphery of the metropolitan area. Many are marked by poorly constructed low- and high-rise concrete apartment buildings. Bucharest's core—which once housed many people in nineteenth-century apartment buildings—was devastated by the vast building projects of Ceaucescu in the 1980s, which cleared some 25,000 acres (10,000 hectares) of the central city. Construction has slowed to a virtual halt in recent years due to the economic collapse of the country. Only some 2,200 new dwellings were built in 1992, adding to the stock of over 750,000 dwellings. There is an occupancy rate of 2.7 persons per unit. Much of the city's electrical supply is provided by coal- and oil-burning plants, and consumption is about two kilowatt-hours per person daily.

CULTURE, THE ARTS, AND ENTERTAINMENT

Much of Bucharest's culture reflects the rich ethnic and folk traditions of the countryside. Theaters and concert halls, often connected to institutions of higher learning or sponsored by the government, perform a wide variety of plays and concerts based on these traditions. Bucharest is also home to a wide variety of architectural styles. These include a number of historical churches in the Byzantine style, dating from the eighteenth century. The focal point of the historic city is Republic Square, surrounded by Palace Hall and the Cretulescu Church. Many visitors also come to marvel at the monumental construction projects built by Ceaucescu, including the mammoth Boulevard of the Victory of Socialism and the huge marble palace known as the House of the People.

CATEGORY	DATA	YEAR	AREA
LOCATION & ENVIRONMENT			
Area	84 square miles	1995	City
	228 square kilometers		City
Elevation	269 feet/97 meters		City
January Temperature	29.7 degrees Fahrenheit		City
	−1.3 degrees Celsius		City
July Temperature	72.7 degrees Fahrenheit		City
	22.6 degrees Celsius		City
Annual Precipitation	22.8 inches/579.1 millimeters		City
POPULATION & DEMOGRAPHY			
Population	2,100,000	1996	Metro
Projected Population	2,200,000	2015	Metro
Growth Rate	0.4%	1990–1995	Metro
Growth Rate	4.4%	1995–2015	Metro
Density	24,462 per square mile		City
	9,060 per square kilometer		City
Gender			
Male	47%	1992	City
Female	53%	1992	City
Age			
Under 20	27.6%	1992	City
20–59	55.8%	1992	City
Over 60	11.6%	1992	City
VITAL STATISTICS			
Births per 1,000 Residents	7.5	1992	City
Infant Mortality Rate	15.9 per 1,000 live births	1992	City
Deaths per 1,000 Residents	10.9	1992	City
ECONOMY			
Total Workforce	1,104,128	1991	City
Agriculture	1.2%	1991	City
Manufacturing	42.7%	1991	City
Construction	10.7%	1991	City
Finance, Insurance, Real Estate	0.6%	1991	City
Trade	8.0%	1991	City
Government	1.4%	1991	City
Transport	7.2%	1991	City

(continued)

CATEGORY	DATA	YEAR	AREA
TRANSPORTATION			
Passenger Journeys	683,544,000	1990	City
Trolley	34.6%	1990	City
Subway	36.1%	1990	City
Bus	29.3%	1990	City
COMMUNICATIONS			
Telephones per 1,000 Residents	294	1992	City
Televisions per 1,000 Residents	250	1992	City
HOUSING			
Housing Units	761,156	1992	City
New Housing Units	2,273	1992	City
Persons per Unit	2.7	1992	City
HEALTH CARE			
Hospitals	52	1993	City
Clinics	478	1993	City
Physicians per 1,000 Residents	3	1993	City
EDUCATION			
Total Students	455,265	1991	City
Primary	58.6%	1991	City
Secondary	24.8%	1991	City
Higher	16.6%	1991	City

Sources: Department of Economic and Social Affairs, Population Division. *Urban Agglomerations, 1996.* New York: United Nations, 1997; *Statistics of World Large Cities.* Tokyo, Japan: Tokyo Metropolitan Government, 1992 and 1994; and United Nations Center for Human Settlements. *Compendium of Human Settlements Statistics.* New York: United Nations, 1995.

Budapest
HUNGARY

LOCATION

Budapest is the capital and largest city of Hungary. Its name, derived from the twin cities of Buda and Pest, reflects its location astride the Danube River. Buda, on the left bank of the river, is built on the slopes of the Buda Hills, which sweep down to the Danube, while Pest lies on a flat and featureless plain. A good portion of the city's 194 square miles (525 square kilometers) of territory is made up of forest and other open land. The city lies 394 feet (121 meters) above sea level and is located approximately 125 miles east-southeast of Vienna, Austria, and 200 miles north of Belgrade, Serbia.

The city's climate has features of both the temperate and continental types. Its winters are mildly cold, with January temperatures averaging about 35 degrees Fahrenheit (2 degrees Celsius) and summer temperatures in the 70s Fahrenheit (20s Celsius). The city receives nearly 24.2 inches (614.7 millimeters) of precipitation annually, most of which falls in the form of rain in the spring and summer months.

POPULATION AND DEMOGRAPHY

The population of the Budapest metropolitan area has been generally stable for the past decade at 2 million and is not expected to grow over the next twenty years. Due to its large areas of undeveloped land, the city has a relatively low density of 10,365 persons per square mile (3,839 per square kilometer). Like most European cities, the population is generally balanced by age. About 24.4 percent of the people are under the age of 20, and 21.6 percent are 60 and above.

While the city was once famous for its linguistic diversity, virtually the entire population speaks Hungarian now, though many citizens trace their roots to Germany. In addition, the city once had a vast Jewish minority, comprising nearly one fourth of the population, but this community was largely destroyed during the Nazi occupation of World War II.

HISTORY

While Budapest's historical roots stretch back to Roman times, the city is really an outgrowth of the urban expansion of the Austro-Hungarian Empire of the eighteenth century. At that time, Hungary was three times larger than it is today, and the city gradually became the administrative, manufacturing, and transportation hub for the region. In addition, many of the central city's architectural monuments date back to this era.

The cities of Buda and Pest were officially joined into a single municipality in 1872. From that year until the advent of Communist rule shortly after World War II, the city was independently governed by its own council and grew at a faster rate than nearly any other city in the empire. The rapid population and industrial growth produced a large and volatile working class who rose up in revolution after the Austro-Hungarian Empire collapsed at the end of World War I. A short-lived democracy was followed by an even shorter-lived Communist regime, which in turn gave way to a dictatorship.

The city stagnated in the interwar years, when it was the capital of an independent Hungary. It avoided capture by Nazi troops until 1945 because the country was governed by a pro-Nazi regime. But occupying German troops put up fierce resistance to the advancing Soviet army at the end of the war, destroying much of the central city in the process. Following the war and the imposition of a pro-Soviet Communist regime, the city grew rapidly. In 1950, the boundaries were extended to include seven satellite towns and sixteen villages. Six years later, the city was the center of a failed uprising against the Communist regime and Soviet domination. Thousands of citizens subsequently fled to Vienna before the border with Austria was closed. During the recapture of the city by the Red Army, much damage was sustained. The city then underwent a period of bloody reprisals. From 1956 until the collapse of the Communist regime in 1989, the country was governed by a strongly pro-Soviet regime that, at the same time, allowed for a greater openness to free-market economics than virtually any other in Eastern Europe. Since 1989, the city has become a center of culture, attracting tourists from around the world.

GOVERNMENT AND POLITICS

Budapest serves as the seat of the Hungarian government. In addition, both Buda and Pest function as the administrative centers of their respective districts. The city itself is divided into twenty-two administrative districts: six on the Buda side, fifteen in Pest, and one consisting of Csepel Island in the Danube River. Each district elects by popular vote a councilor who serves on the Budapest Metropolitan Council. The day-to-day operation of city services is handled by the nonelected Management Committee, which is held responsible to the council.

ECONOMY

Beginning in the nineteenth century, Budapest has been a major industrial center. Since the end of World War II, this has included a vast array of factories manufacturing both capital and consumer goods. The outputs of Budapest's industrial sector include engineered products, electronics, munitions, and agricultural implements for the country's large farming sector. In addition, there are many food-processing and textile factories in the city. Approximately half of the city's workforce labors in the industrial sector.

Unlike most other former Communist countries of Eastern Europe, Hungary has a thriving commercial sector, largely an outgrowth of the "goulash" market-reform laws of 1968. Most of the major banks, insurance companies, and other financial businesses are located in the Pest side of the city. The commercial and financial sectors have been greatly expanded since 1989, when foreign investment funds began pouring into the country. The city also has a large tourist economy, and many workers labor in the numerous national government agencies in the city.

TRANSPORTATION

For ages, Budapest has been a major transportation hub and a popular crossing point on the Danube. As such, it gradually became the center of the country's highway and railroad systems. In addition, the city is a major port on the Danube River, with barges traveling upriver to Vienna and downstream to the Black Sea. The city serves as the headquarters for the international commission that regulates transport on the river. Budapest is home to Hungary's only international airport.

The city's metropolitan traffic is handled by a subway system built in the 1970s, as well as a large fleet of buses and trolleys. There are also several commuter railroads connecting the city center to the industrial and residential satellite towns on the periphery of the metropolitan area. Unlike other East European cities, Budapest has a large fleet of privately owned automobiles, a result of the country's long history of a socialist-market hybrid economy.

HEALTH CARE

The health care system in Budapest is quite good, with some forty hospitals serving the citizenry. The ratio of residents to physicians is relatively high,

about 150 to 1, equivalent to a rate of 7 per 1,000 residents. The city has a low infant mortality rate for Eastern Europe, 12.4 infant deaths per 1,000 live births. While the overall death rate is 12.4 for every 1,000 persons, this reflects the unusually high number of old people in the city. Budapest is home to most of the major specialized medical centers in Hungary as well.

EDUCATION

Budapest has both an extensive primary and secondary school system and a highly literate population. The citizenry purchases more magazines and newspapers than in virtually any other city in Eastern Europe. In addition, the city is home to over 30,000 university students who study at several major state universities, including the Hungarian Academy of Sciences as well as academies for music and the arts. In recent years, Budapest has become a popular place for higher studies among students from other European countries.

HOUSING

Budapest continues to suffer from a major housing shortage dating back to the Communist era. While massive construction of satellite towns helped to alleviate the crowding in the rapidly growing central city, many citizens continued to live in the crowded but picturesque neighborhoods there. Since the fall of the Communist regime in 1989, many residential buildings have been turned into offices for domestic and international businesses. The loss of residential space coincides with a trend that exacerbates a trend in which many younger people are returning to live in the city, closer to the growing number of clubs, cafés, and restaurants. The city has a steady water supply, an effective electrical system, and a well-maintained sewage network.

CULTURE, THE ARTS, AND ENTERTAINMENT

As with population, industry, and commerce, Budapest dominates the cultural life of Hungary. Virtually all of the nation's major museums, cultural institutions, and artists make their home in the capital. These include such facilities as the world-famous Budapest Opera House, the National Theater, the National Historical Museum, and the Hungarian National Gallery of the Arts. The city is also renowned for its many bookstores and literary cafés.

Since ancient times, people have been coming to Budapest to take advantage of the natural hot springs located on both sides of the river. In the nineteenth century, several elegant bathing establishments were built and now cater to many ordinary citizens as well as visitors.

Architecturally, Budapest is spectacular, with many fine examples of medieval and modern building styles. In 1984, the Opera House was returned to its nineteenth-century grandeur. In addition, there is the thirteenth-century fortress on Castle Hill, the medieval Gothic Church of Our Blessed Lady, the baroque eighteenth-century palace built by Maria Theresa, Queen of Hungary, and the modernist National Theater.

CATEGORY	DATA	YEAR	AREA
LOCATION & ENVIRONMENT			
Area	194 square miles	1995	City
	525 square kilometers		City
Elevation	394 feet/121 meters		City
January Temperature	35.6 degrees Fahrenheit		City
	2.0 degrees Celsius		City
July Temperature	73.2 degrees Fahrenheit		City
	22.9 degrees Celsius		City
Annual Precipitation	24.2 inches/614.7 millimeters		City
POPULATION & DEMOGRAPHY			
Population	2,000,000	1996	Metro
Projected Population	2,000,000	2015	Metro
Growth Rate	0.0%	1990–1995	Metro
Growth Rate	0.0%	1995–2015	Metro
Density	10,365 per square mile	1992	City
	3,839 per square kilometer		City
Gender			
Male	46%	1992	City
Female	54%	1992	City
Age			
Under 20	24.4%	1992	City
20–59	54.0%	1992	City
Over 60	21.6%	1992	City
VITAL STATISTICS			
Births per 1,000 Residents	9.6	1992	City
Infant Mortality Rate	12.4 per 1,000 live births	1992	City
Deaths per 1,000 Residents	12.4	1992	City
ECONOMY			
Total Workforce	917,716	1990	City
Production	35.7%	1990	City
Professional	20.9%	1990	City
Management	13.7%	1990	City
Clerical	14.7%	1990	City
Service	8.7%	1990	City
Trade	6.3 %	1990	City

(continued)

CATEGORY	DATA	YEAR	AREA
TRANSPORTATION			
Passenger Journeys	1,833,307,000	1989	City
Rail	5.2%	1989	City
Trolley	30.9%	1989	City
Subway	18.1%	1989	City
Bus	45.8%	1989	City
COMMUNICATIONS			
Telephones per 1,000 Residents	385	1992	City
Televisions per 1,000 Residents	256.4	1992	City
HOUSING			
Housing Units	807,014	1992	City
New Housing Units	3,829	1992	City
Persons per Unit	2.5	1992	City
HEALTH CARE			
Hospitals	39	1992	City
Physicians per 1,000 Residents	7	1992	City
EDUCATION			
Total Students	300,043	1991	City
Primary	65.3%	1991	City
Secondary	23.8%	1991	City
Higher	11.0%	1991	City

Sources: Department of Economic and Social Affairs, Population Division. *Urban Agglomerations, 1996.* New York: United Nations, 1997; *Statistics of World Large Cities.* Tokyo, Japan: Tokyo Metropolitan Government, 1992 and 1994; and United Nations Center for Human Settlements. *Compendium of Human Settlements Statistics.* New York: United Nations, 1995.

Buenos Aires
ARGENTINA

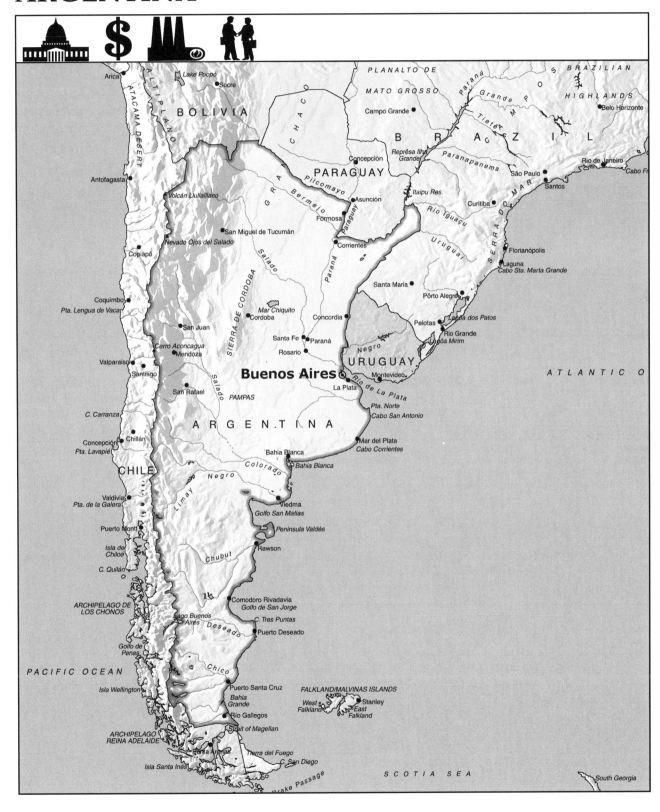

LOCATION

Buenos Aires is the capital city and largest urban agglomeration in Argentina. Located on the western bank of the Rio de la Plata, Buenos Aires (which means "fair winds" in Spanish), is at the mouth of the country's major river and on the edge of the pampas, a grass-covered plain that is one of the most fertile regions in the world.

The metropolitan area spans over 1,500 square miles (3,885 square kilometers) and consists of the Federal capital, a 77-square-mile (200-square-kilometer) area and nineteen surrounding districts. The city is on the coast, with an elevation of 89 feet (27 meters). Temperatures average between 66.2 degrees Fahrenheit (19 degrees Celsius) in January and 45 degrees Fahrenheit (17.2 degrees Celsius) in July. The annual precipitation is 43.2 inches (1,096 millimeters).

The Plaza de Mayo, the downtown area, is next to the waterfront and served as the starting point for the original settlement. The rest of the city expanded in semicircles from the plaza. Since the 1950s, sprawling neighborhoods in the outer rings have developed shopping centers that have become new urban foci. Hotels, restaurants, and theaters as well as financial, commercial, and government offices and luxurious residences are concentrated just west of the plaza. Grand boulevards, elegant open plazas, and lush green parks and diverse neighborhoods embellish the city.

POPULATION AND DEMOGRAPHY

In 1855, the population of the Federal District had reached 93,000, and it began to grow rapidly thereafter at annual rates of between 3.9 percent and 5.7 percent. The population reached 1.5 million in 1914, a result of both natural growth and migration, and by the 1920s, Buenos Aires was one of the largest cities in the world. The population was 5 million in 1950 and 8.4 million in 1970. In 1991, one third of Argentina's population, or some 10.7 million people, lived in the greater Buenos Aires area, which includes the Federal Capital and its twenty-two suburbs; this increased to 11.9 million by 1996. The annual growth rate between 1985 and 1995 has slowed to 1.2 percent, and the projected increase between 1995 and 2015 totals 17.4 percent, with an estimated population in 2015 of 13.9 million.

The city's age structure currently resembles that of a developed country; 27.3 percent of the population is under 20 years of age, while 53.5 percent is between the ages of 20 and 59, and 19 percent is over 60. In the late 1980s, the birth rate was 14.7, while the death rate remained slightly lower at 12.4 per 1,000 residents. The infant mortality rate was 16 deaths per 1,000 live births. There are more females (54.7 percent) than males (45.3 percent).

The population density is 38,512 persons per square mile (14,827 per square kilometer). The population has inhabited the city in concentric circles spreading out from the historic center. The population density decreases sharply from the center out to the periphery.

HISTORY

Buenos Aires was founded by the Spanish in 1536 as a bulwark against Portuguese expansion. Originally an economic backwater, it soon became a center for contraband. During the early colonial period, the economy of the settlement was also tied to the rich silver mines in upper Peru. Throughout the seventeenth and eighteenth centuries, the port became a major Spanish entrepôt on the Atlantic coast of the Americas, and in 1776, the city was declared the capital of the Spanish territory of the Plata. Located on land ideal for farming and grazing, Argentina's prosperity became increasingly tied to agriculture and animal products.

In 1810, Argentina declared independence from Spain, by which time Buenos Aires had already become a prosperous city and begun trading with other countries, including Britain. By the 1860s, a great period of expansion had occurred in trade, including the export of hides, wool, grain, and meat. Ongoing struggles with other parts of the country were resolved, and the city was officially designated the capital of the country in 1880. The city was separated from the province of Buenos Aires, and the Federal Capital district was established at that time.

Foreign capital—mainly British—financed the railroads, port facilities, streetcars, and gas works. European immigrants began arriving in droves in the late nineteenth century, mostly from Italy and Spain. Due to the large number of immigrants, the city developed an international flair. By 1910, Buenos Aires emerged as one of Latin America's leading political, economic, and cultural centers.

GOVERNMENT AND POLITICS

The municipal government of Buenos Aires is headed by a mayor, who is appointed by the president of the republic, as well as an elected city council. Because of the highly centralized nature of the Argentinian federal government, the powers of both the mayor and the council are tightly circumscribed, and the council meets irregularly. In fact, the country's president is technically in control of the municipality and the national congress has veto power over legislation affecting the city. The city is divided into administrative districts, each run by a local council.

ECONOMY

Buenos Aires is Argentina's principal seaport and commercial center. Ship basins and docks extend along the Rio de la Plata, and three major rail lines radiate out of the city to the rest of the country. The stock exchange and the cereal exchange (where grain is bought and sold) are centrally located in the financial district. Most of the industrial plants were originally built within the Federal Capital district but have since been relocated to the outer suburbs of the city.

Principal industries located in Buenos Aires include meat packing and other food processing, petroleum refineries, chemical factories, motor vehicle assembly plants, and various light industries, including printing and textiles. Retail and commercial trade is located near the city center. Altogether, Buenos Aires contributes 24 percent of the Argentine gross domestic product. The city accounts for 14.7 percent of the trade sector and dominates in the service sector, employing 33.3 percent of the labor force. Most of the federal government's offices and the headquarters of many businesses, including trading concerns and financial firms, are located in the Federal Capital.

In 1985, there were 436,000 industrial jobs in the surrounding districts and 231,000 in the Federal Capital. There has been an increase in the productivity of industrial employment and a growth in the participation of women in the labor force in recent years. Yet there has also been an increase in unemployment, which has hit double digits and has led to growth in the informal sector of the economy. Recent growth in the Federal Capital has occurred mostly in the tertiary sector.

During the 1980s, Argentina suffered a combination of debt, recession, hyperinflation, and growing poverty. As a result, the economic health of the city was poor. The 1990s have seen the national economic growth record improve but some say its prospects are integrally linked to the country's ability to both generate new export products and increase sales of traditional exports.

The figures reflect the impact of industrial deconcentration in the metropolitan area; industrial activities declined 9 percent between 1980 and 1989, with a loss of 200,000 industrial jobs in the metropolitan area between 1974 and 1985. Since the 1980s, economic growth has rested on the service sector, which represents 70 percent of all job growth in the metropolitan area. Finance, insurance, and real estate constitute some of city's the most dynamic economic activities.

Poverty and inequality have increased markedly in recent years, and housing conditions have deteriorated. Incomes have fallen, unemployment has risen, and more people are employed in the informal sector. Indeed, labor conditions in the formal sector have been badly affected by deregulation, and the distribution of income has become less equal. There has also been a failure to improve the quality of the water and sewerage systems.

Trade liberalization has played a role in the worsening of labor conditions in Argentina as a whole and Buenos Aires in particular. More manufactured imports have brought about a decline in domestic production. Furthermore, working conditions have deteriorated, and official rules and regulations are increasingly ignored. In the Federal Capital, 33 percent are working without social security coverage, and 55.9 percent have no union affiliation.

The economic problems have led to political unrest, which was met with military rule between 1975 and 1983. The authoritarian government introduced economic models that accentuated income inequality, but the return to democratic elections has not changed the economic situation. The poorest tenth of the population had 2.6 percent of the wealth in 1984 and only 1.8 percent in 1989. Meanwhile, the richest tenth had 27 percent of the wealth in 1984 and had almost doubled it, to 41.6 percent, by 1989. Those below the poverty line in 1990 made up 35 percent of the Buenos Aires population; many of this group previously had been part of the middle class.

TRANSPORTATION

In Buenos Aires, there were nearly 1.8 trillion commuter trips per year in 1988. Primary forms of transport were buses and trolleys, railway, and subway. Overall, one fifth of all journeys in Argentina begin or end in the Federal Capital.

The use of private cars has skyrocketed in recent years, increasing by 58 percent, and now account for one quarter of all journeys. Government policy supports the use of cars, and only recently have new restrictions been imposed. The city suffers from chronic road congestion, and new restrictions allow any given car to be used only six days per week, as designated by the last number of the license plate. Nevertheless, the road system is not well adapted to the growing numbers of cars. Outside the Federal Capital, only the main roads are paved.

The coordination of the public transport system is poor. There are 299 public bus routes, totaling 15,000 miles, and 5 subway lines, totaling 25 miles. The subway has existed since 1913. There are also six metropolitan rail lines, extending over 600 miles, that run out of three stations. As there are few tunnels and bridges, trains often disrupt automobile traffic in the region.

As of the 1990s, the bus services had already been privatized, and both the metropolitan railway system and the subway system are in the process of being privatized. Bus privatization has been widely questioned, since poor areas have limited service and fares remain high, notwithstanding the high profits earned by the companies.

HEALTH CARE

Buenos Aires has a fine system of health care delivery, with a number of municipal and private hospitals. These institutions are augmented by numerous dispensaries, pharmacies, and social hygiene centers located throughout the metropolitan area. In addition, the city has a disproportionate number of hospital beds, which serve the many people from around the country who come to the capital for health care. The city has a high rate of 7 physicians per 1,000 city residents.

EDUCATION

Buenos Aires is home to numerous educational institutions, though some have expanded or moved to outlying areas. The University of Buenos Aires has recently added a new campus outside of the core of the city, near the river. The National Library has been relocated to a northern suburb near the location of

the private University of Belgrano. Other educational institutions include the National Technological University, the Catholic University, the National Conservatory of Music, and the National School of Fine Arts. About 45.9 percent of the city's students attend primary school, 23.4 percent attend secondary school, and 30.7 percent attend higher education institutions.

HOUSING

In 1991, 5 percent of the population of the Federal Capital lived in substandard housing. In the greater Buenos Aires area, the figure is much higher, 28 percent. There are thus acute problems with land use. In the north and west of the Federal Capital, housing is of high quality, with good access to shopping and miscellaneous services. In the rest of the city, however, housing and infrastructure have degenerated, and large slum areas have sprung up, particularly in the south and west. The central city has an average occupancy rate of 2.9 persons per housing unit.

CULTURE, THE ARTS, AND ENTERTAINMENT

Buenos Aires is the cultural capital of the country. The city boasts a number of galleries featuring works of Argentinian artists. In addition, the city is noted for its modern architecture, embracing virtually every movement of the twentieth century. It also boasts one of the finest opera houses in the world in the Colon Theater, which attracts opera companies from Europe and elsewhere. The theater scene is active, with traditional and modern plays performed in the Presidente Alvear Theater, the Cervantes National Theater, and La Boca, among others. Popular entertainment is featured at numerous clubs and cafes, the former hosting many performances of the tango, Argentina's national dance. The city also boasts a number of fine museums, including the National Museum of Fine Arts, the National Museum of Decorative Arts, and the Isaac Fernandez Blanco Municipal Museum of Hispanic-American Art.

CATEGORY	DATA	YEAR	AREA
LOCATION & ENVIRONMENT			
Area	77 square miles	1995	City
	200 square kilometers		City
Elevation	89 feet/27 meters		City
January Temperature	66.2 degrees Fahrenheit		City
	19.0 degrees Celsius		City
July Temperature	45.0 degrees Fahrenheit		City
	17.2 degrees Celsius		City
Annual Precipitation	43.2 inches/1,096 millimeters		City
POPULATION & DEMOGRAPHY			
Population	11,900,000	1996	City
Projected Population	13,900,000	2015	City
Growth Rate	1.2%	1990–1995	City
Growth Rate	17.4%	1995–2015	City
Density	38,512 per square mile	1991	City
	14,827 per square kilometer		City
Gender			
Male	45.3%	1991	City
Female	54.7%	1991	City
Age			
Under 20	27.3%	1991	City
20–59	53.5%	1991	City
Over 60	19.0%	1991	City
VITAL STATISTICS			
Birth Rate per 1,000 Residents	14.7	1988	City
Death Rate per 1,000 Residents	12.4%	1988	City
Infant Mortality Rate	16 per 1,000 live births	1988	City
ECONOMY			
Total Workforce	1,397,133	1989	City
Trade	18.2%	1989	City
Manufacturing	17.0%	1989	City
Services	36.7%	1989	City
Finance, Insurance, Real Estate	12.2%	1989	City
Transport, Communications	5.9%	1989	City
Construction	2.6%	1989	City
Utilities	0.5%	1989	City
Agriculture	0.2%	1989	City
Nonclassifiable	6.7%	1989	City
TRANSPORTATION			
Passenger Journeys	1,778,967,000	1988	City
Buses and Trolley	73.3%	1988	City
Rail	16.6%	1988	City
Subway	10.0%	1988	City
Passenger Vehicles	963,011	1987	City

(continued)

CATEGORY	DATA	YEAR	AREA
COMMUNICATIONS			
Telephones per 1,000 Residents	51.5	1992	City
HOUSING			
Total Housing Units	1,023,464	1991	City
Persons per Unit	2.9	1991	City
HEALTH CARE			
Hospitals	181	1980	City
Physicians per 1,000 Residents	7	1980	City
EDUCATION			
Primary	45.9%	1982	City
Secondary	23.4%	1982	City
Higher	30.7%	1982	City

Sources: Department of Economic and Social Affairs, Population Division. *Urban Agglomerations, 1996.* New York: United Nations, 1997. United Nations Center for Human Settlements. *Compendium of Human Settlements Statistics.* New York: United Nations, 1995.

Cairo

EGYPT

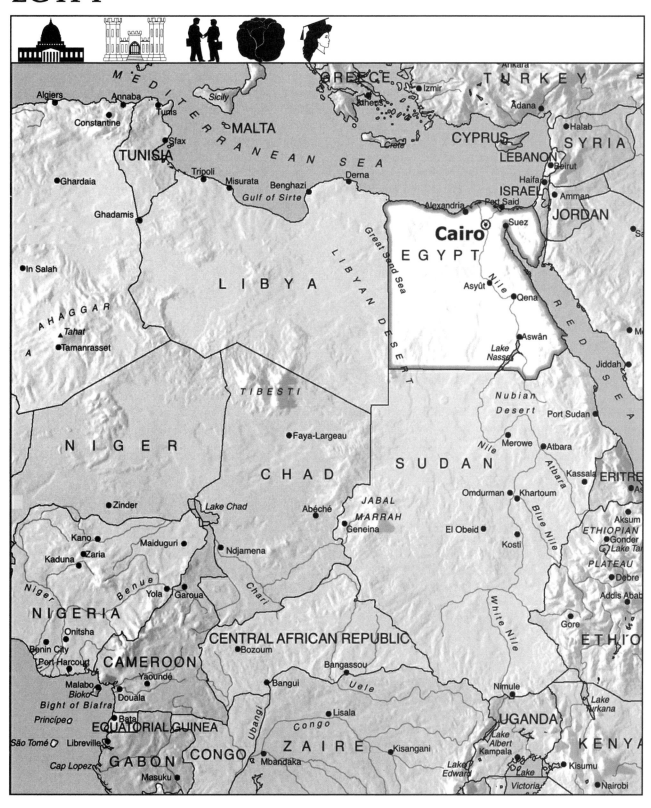

LOCATION

Cairo, located at the top of the Nile delta, is the capital of Egypt. It is a major industrial and trading city, the most populous city in Africa, and the unofficial cultural and political capital of the Arab world. Situated at 381 feet (137 meters) above sea level, and on the borderline between the Mediterranean and Saharan climatic zones, Cairo experiences extremely hot and dry summers and moderately cool and wet winters. January and July temperatures average 66.2 and 95 degrees Fahrenheit (19 and 35 degrees Celsius), respectively. The city is located 275 miles southwest of Jerusalem and 2,100 miles north-northwest of Nairobi, Kenya. Cairo's area is 257 square miles (693 square kilometers).

POPULATION AND DEMOGRAPHY

The city's 9.9 million people live in a metropolitan area that stretches along both banks of the Nile and spreads eastward to the low Mokattam Hills. It is extremely crowded, with approximately 85,109 people packed into each square mile (31,522 in each kilometer).

While the city grew rapidly during the 1950s and 1960s, its rate of expansion has slowed since the 1970s to about 2 percent annually. Still, it is projected that Cairo will have a population of over 14.4 million by the year 2015. Much of this growth reflects an influx from the countryside, and a government economic policy that situated much of Egypt's new industry in the capital region.

The city is ethnically homogeneous. The vast majority of its citizens are Arabic-speaking Sunni Muslims, though a small minority practice the Coptic form of Christianity. Racially, however, the city is a blend of lighter-skinned Mediterranean Arabs and darker-skinned Africans or Arab-African mixed peoples.

HISTORY

By any standard but Egypt's, Cairo is an old city. It came into existence with the invading Arab armies of the seventh century A.D. The city itself, however, was officially founded several centuries later when the Muslim caliph Umar I realized that the annual Nile floods cut off the then-current capital of the region, Alexandria, from the Arab hinterland. He established his capital on the east bank of the Nile. In 968, the new Fatimid dynasty renamed the city El

Qahira, "the victorious." In 1187, the great Kurdish general Saladin joined Cairo with several other settlements to form the rough outline of the current city.

In the Middle Ages, Cairo became a major center for trade between Europe and the Middle East under the rule of the Mameluke dynasty. By 1340, the population exceeded 500,000, making the city the largest in the world outside of China. In 1517, Cairo was conquered by the Turks, who ruled the city, with one interruption in the early nineteenth century, until it came under British rule with the collapse of the Ottoman Empire in the early twentieth century.

Both the Turks and the British began modernizing the city and developing new suburbs outside the city walls built by Saladin in the twelfth century. These developments divided the city into two parts—a modern, commercial sector centered on Heliopolis, and the increasingly isolated and decrepit central city.

Since World War II, and especially following the rise to power of Gamel Abdel Nasser in 1952, the city has undergone a vast expansion, both planned and unplanned. Since 1956, several metropolitan schemes have been implemented to build new business, residential, and industrial districts in the open areas around the central city. Since the Cairo master scheme of 1983, the government of President Hosni Mubarek has sought to limit Cairo's growth and protect valuable agricultural land on the city's periphery.

GOVERNMENT AND POLITICS

Cairo was declared an independently governed municipality in 1949. Ten years later, a national Ministry for Local Administration was established and passed uniform municipal codes for the nation's large cities. Though the ministry was dissolved in 1971, much of the code remains. The governing body of Cairo—which covers the metropolitan area and surrounding territory—is headed by a governor who is appointed by the president. An executive committee made up of the heads of various city agencies assists the governor. A popularly elected assembly also administers the city, though financial control over the budget is largely controlled by the national government.

ECONOMY

Since the tenth century, Cairo has been a major center of trade and production. Its craftsmen specialized in metal, leather, and glass products. Since Egyptian independence in 1922, the government has promoted the development of manufacturing plants throughout the new areas of the city, relying on agricultural products grown in the Nile valley and delta. Major industries include textile manufacturing, sugar refining, paper milling, and tobacco products.

Under the Nasser regime (1956–1970), most of the industrial development was done under government aegis, and many foreign banks and other firms were nationalized. With the accession to power of Anwar Sadat (1970–1981), a new policy of liberalization and privatization—popularly known as *al-intifah*—was undertaken.

With the vast rise in oil prices in the 1970s, the Cairene economy was given a boost by the wages sent home by Egyptians working in the oil-producing states of the Persian Gulf, as well as by banks processing petrodollars. The collapse of oil prices in the 1980s hit Cairo hard, but high economic growth rates of 6 percent annually have nevertheless been sustained by heavy borrowing and government expenditures.

As of the mid-1980s, nearly half of the population was involved in manufacturing, construction, and other producer-oriented sectors. Both wholesale and retail trade involved another third of the people. As the Egyptian capital, Cairo has a large cohort of government workers as well.

TRANSPORTATION

As one of the most densely populated cities in the world, Cairo experiences major traffic problems, and its drivers are renowned for their audacity and their use of the horn. Though a number of expressways have been built since the 1960s, the city still has an extremely high car-to-road ratio. This is partly attributable to the low, subsidized price of gasoline and diesel fuel. Still, car ownership is low, at about twenty-six private vehicles for every thousand Caireans.

Adding to the traffic problem is the ineffective surface public transport system. Rush hour sees passengers clinging to the outside of the city's buses and trams, the latter largely of early-twentieth-century vintage. The public bus system of approximately three thousand vehicles is supplemented by tens of thousands of large and minibuses. To alleviate the crowding problem caused by all of these vehicles, the city has built a 26-mile (42.5-kilometer) underground metro system. Currently serving 60,000 passengers an hour, it is expected to reduce surface transport requirements by 75 percent when completed.

The city also has an effective telephone system, with good connections to the international network. There is approximately one telephone for every 2.5 households.

HEALTH CARE

Cairo's population is a largely healthy one. Twenty-four major hospitals serve the city, and the physician-to-populace ratio is approximately 1.1 to 1,000. Average life expectancy is 65 for males and 68 for females.

Among the major health problems are those caused by the city's serious air and water pollution. The Nile is severely affected by industrial and residential runoff, and the city is often blanketed by a thick layer of smog. Sporadic attempts to limit air pollution by mandatory inspections of vehicles and industry have been largely ineffective. Thus, many of the health problems involve illnesses of the digestive and respiratory tracts.

EDUCATION

Cairo is a center of education for the Arab world. Students from every Arab country, as well as many non-Arab Muslim countries, attend academies in the Egyptian capital. Major universities in the city, including the American University and El Azhar University, the latter among the oldest in the world, have a total attendance in the tens of thousands. Over 1.6 million children attend the city's public and mosque-based schools. Still, poverty and child labor prevent a significant minority from attending school on a regular basis.

HOUSING

Despite its expansion into the Egyptian countryside and the development of major housing schemes by the government, Cairo is facing a severe housing shortage, at least officially. It is estimated that over 80 percent of the city's population lives in informal housing; however, much of this sector is of high quality, surpassing that of older buildings in the city. In addition, the city's famed cemeteries are home to over 10 percent of Cairo's living population, who make their homes in tombs and mausoleums. Still, for all of these problems, the city has, in fact, an adequate housing stock if these unofficial dwellings are taken into account; a moderate 3.5 people live in each dwelling.

The city's water supply is largely obtained from surface water of the Nile. Though this source is more than adequate, many of the city's water mains are of nineteenth- and early-twentieth-century vintage. Because of this, there are numerous breaks and water outages throughout the city. The government has recently embarked on a water infrastructure initiative and is promoting conservation. A massive sewage project in the 1980s has nearly eliminated backups and flooding.

Cairo's electricity supply—based on oil-burning plants as well as the Aswan hydraulic station—is sufficient and steady. Electricity usage in 1990 was 1.2 kilowatt-hours per person daily.

CULTURE, THE ARTS, AND ENTERTAINMENT

As the cultural center of the Arabic-speaking world, Cairo is home to one of the largest television and movie-production industries in the world. Only India and the United States produce more films each year. There are nearly a hundred cinemas in the city.

Cairo's population also has widespread access to TV, with over one set per household. The city also has nearly a hundred libraries and twenty museums, including the world-famous Egyptian Museum, filled with antiquities from Egypt's pharaonic past. The city also boasts over five hundred parks, including extensive tree-lined areas along both banks of the Nile.

CATEGORY	DATA	YEAR	AREA
LOCATION & ENVIRONMENT			
Area	257 square miles	1992	City
	693 square kilometers	1992	City
Elevation	381 feet/137 meters	1996	City
January Temperature	66.2 degrees Fahrenheit		City
	19 degrees Celsius		City
July Temperature	95 degrees Fahrenheit		City
	35 degrees Celsius		City
POPULATION & DEMOGRAPHY			
Population	9,900,000	1995	City
Projected Population	14,400,000	2015	City
Growth Rate	2.3%	1990–1995	City
Growth Rate	48.8%	1995–2015	City
Density	85,109 per square mile	1992	City
	31,522 per square kilometer	1992	City
Gender			
Male	51.3%	1992	City
Female	48.7%	1992	City
VITAL STATISTICS			
Births per 1,000 Residents	20.2	1989	City
Infant Mortality Rate	36.6 per 1,000 live births	1989	
ECONOMY			
Workforce	1,231,053	1986	City
Manufacturing	36.9%	1986	City
Construction	7.1%	1986	City
Mining	3.6%	1986	City
Agriculture	1.0%	1986	City
Utilities	1.0%	1986	City
Trade	30.0%	1986	City
Finance, Insurance, Real Estate	5.3%	1986	City
Transport and Communications	3.5%	1986	City
Public Service	9.5%	1986	City

(continued)

CATEGORY	DATA	YEAR	AREA
COMMUNICATIONS			
Telephones per 1,000 Residents	94.3	1990	City
Televisions per 1,000 Residents	312.8	1990	City
HOUSING			
Total Occupied Units	1,943,300	1990	City
Persons per Unit	3.5	1990	City
HEALTH CARE			
Hospitals	24	1990	City
Physicians per 1,000 Residents	1.1	1990	City
EDUCATION			
Total Students	1,616,719	1991	City
Primary	77.7%	1991	City
Secondary	7.9%	1991	City
Higher Education	14.4%	1991	City

Sources: Department of Economic and Social Affairs, Population Division. *Urban Agglomerations, 1996.* New York: United Nations, 1997; *Statistics of World Large Cities.* Tokyo, Japan: Tokyo Metropolitan Government, 1992 and 1994; and United Nations Center for Human Settlements. *Compendium of Human Settlements Statistics.* New York: United Nations, 1995.

Calcutta, West Bengal
INDIA

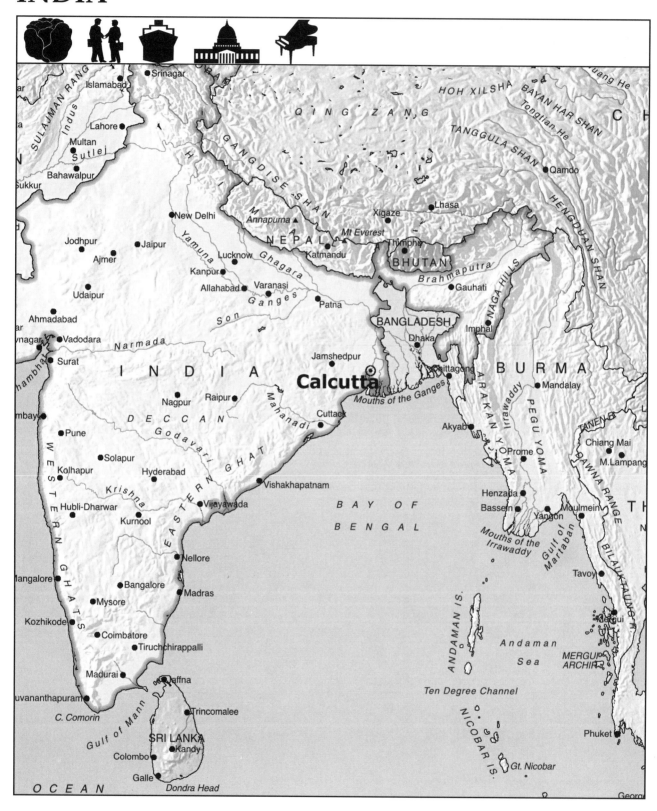

LOCATION

Calcutta is the capital and largest city of India's West Bengal state and the second largest metropolitan area in the country, after Mumbai. It is situated at 20 feet above sea level (6 meters) in the low, swampy delta of the Hooghly River, approximately 100 miles from the Bay of Bengal. India's capital of New Delhi is roughly 800 miles to the northwest. The city covers 197 square miles (533 square kilometers), largely in two strips 5 to 8 miles wide along either bank of the river.

The climate is tropical. Average winter and summer temperatures are 67.5 and 84.5 degrees Fahrenheit (19.7 and 29.2 degrees Celsius), respectively. The city receives an abundance of rainfall, about 63 inches (1,600.2 millimeters) annually, most of which falls during the monsoon months from August to November. The heavy precipitation, combined with an elevation of just 20 feet above sea level, results in frequent flooding during the monsoon months. The city is also vulnerable to cyclones emanating from the Bay of Bengal.

POPULATION AND DEMOGRAPHY

Calcutta is an extremely crowded city, with densities up to 12,200 persons per square mile (33,000 per square kilometer). The population in the metropolitan area is estimated at 12.1 million. While its growth rate has slowed to about 2 percent annually in the last two decades, the metropolitan area's population is still expected to grow to 17.3 million by 2015.

Most of the city's population is Bengali, though there are large minorities of migrants from the nearby states of Bihar, Orissa, and eastern Uttar Pradesh. The city is largely Hindu, though it also has small minorities of Buddhists, Jains, Christians, and Muslims, the last having flooded into the city during the Bangladesh independence war of 1971. Most of the city speaks Bengali, though English is commonly known as well.

HISTORY

As a city, Calcutta dates from the early eighteenth century, when the Mughal emperors that ruled India granted Britain's East India Company the right to establish a trading post on the site. The city was the object of a power struggle between successor Mughal emperors and the British until 1757, when Calcutta was captured by British forces under the leadership of Robert Clive. Fifteen years later, it was turned into the administrative capital of the growing British presence in India, a role it held through the early twentieth century.

The British established lotteries in the early nineteenth century to raise funds to improve the city's infrastructure, though many of the gains were undone by a series of devastating cyclones in the 1860s and 1870s. Still, the city's population and density continued to grow rapidly, spurring the British to move their Indian capital to New Delhi in 1912.

With independence in 1947, the British partitioned Bengal into a Hindu western section, governed by India, and an eastern Muslim section, ruled by Pakistan, 1,500 miles to the west. Tens of thousands of Hindus and Muslims were killed during this strife-laden period and hundreds of thousands were displaced from their homes, flooding the city with refugees. Roughly twenty-five years later, Bangladesh won its independence with the help of India, leading to a further flood of Muslim refugees from the east.

GOVERNMENT AND POLITICS

The city of Calcutta itself is governed by the Calcutta Municipal Corporation. The corporation's council consists of one hundred representatives, one from each of the city's wards. The council members elect a mayor, a deputy mayor, and a number of administrative committees annually. A commissioner responsible for overall administration is responsible to the council. Though governed by this elected municipal government, much of Calcutta's major public services have been administered by the Calcutta Metropolitan Planning Organization since the late 1960s. The organization tried to reorient Calcutta to the east and west to relieve congestion, but this strategy was changed to a "polynodal" strategy in 1976 with the Development Perspective and Investment Plan. Since 1978, the state of West Bengal has been ruled by a Communist-dominated coalition of parties.

ECONOMY

Calcutta is a major industrial center, though it is dominated by traditional manufacturing, much of which suffers from a lack of competitiveness. The government of India has declared over a hundred industries in Calcutta to be "sick," or newly bankrupt, which is approximately half of the total for the whole country. In addition, there is a list of over 7,000 "sick" small-scale units. Among the most important of these "sick" industries are textiles and jute, though Calcutta still remains the world's largest producer of this item, used in the production of rope and burlap. Other manufacturing items produced in Calcutta are food products, beverages, and tobacco products. Approximately one fourth of the workforce labors in the industrial sector.

The city also has a major commercial sector. Its stock exchange is the second largest in India, after Bombay's, and many banks, insurance companies, and other financial firms have headquarters here. Of the over 40 percent of the workforce employed in the commercial sector, most labor in small shops and bazaars.

TRANSPORTATION

Calcutta is the major transportation hub for eastern India. Its port handles over three million tons of freight annually—approximately one tenth of the country's total—and some 40,000 passengers. Like other Indian cities, Calcutta is well served by the national railroad network. The city has two terminals: Howrah, for trains to the west, south, and north, and Sealdah, to points east and Bangladesh. In addition, Calcutta is the eastern terminus for the Grand Trunk Road Number Two, the main highway of the Ganges valley. The city is also served by Dum Dum International Airport, just north of the city.

Metropolitan transport is largely dependent on a fleet of over ten thousand buses, as well as a small number of commuter trains. A short subway was opened in the early 1990s. Surface traffic is extremely dense. Streets and the four-lane Howrah Bridge are often congested by throngs of pedestrians, rickshaws, animal traffic, and two- and four-wheeled motor vehicles.

HEALTH CARE

For all its overcrowding, inadequate sanitation services, and unhealthy locale, Calcutta has a better-than-expected health profile. Smallpox has been eliminated and malaria and enteric fever brought under control. Much of the credit for this is due to the city and state governments' aggressive health care initiatives, including the establishment of hundreds of hospitals and free dispensaries. There are also a small number of important private and charitable hospitals,

including the late Mother Teresa's world-famous Order of the Missionaries of Charity, which aids the blind, the aged, and leprosy sufferers. Still, the city continues to have serious health problems, such as cholera outbreaks during the dry months, when the city's water supply is often polluted, and a relatively high infant mortality rate of 41.1 per 1,000 live births. Respiratory illnesses are perhaps the number one health problem in the city, with some 60 percent of the population suffering from one form of these illnesses or another.

EDUCATION

Calcutta's educational system is administered by a variety of authorities. The city government runs the system of free primary schools, while the state government of West Bengal operates the secondary school system. However, many students attend private academies, many of which are modeled after British schools. Still, poverty keeps many young people from attending school long enough to gain a proper education.

The city is also home to some of India's more prestigious institutions of higher learning, including the University of Calcutta (with nearly 150 affiliated colleges), Jadavpur University, and Rabindra Bharati University. A number of major technical institutes are also located in Calcutta.

HOUSING

The Calcutta metropolitan area has a serious housing problem, with approximately one third of its inhabitants living in slumlike conditions. It is also estimated that as many as 15 percent of the people live on the streets. The city's water supply largely comes from the Farakka Barrage dam, 240 miles upriver on the Ganges, though in the dry summer months the city's several thousand wells supplement this source. The shallow water table, however, means that the wells are vulnerable to contamination by salt water. While Calcutta has several hundred miles of sewer pipes, these do not reach much of the city. This lack of sewers and the unsanitary methods of removing human waste produce many health problems, most notably dysentery and cholera. The city has several sources of electricity, but still suffers from frequent power outages.

CULTURE, THE ARTS, AND ENTERTAINMENT

Any visitor cannot help but note that despite the city's overwhelming poverty, Calcutta is a vibrant cultural and artistic center. Indeed, most Indians acknowledge that the city is the country's center for high arts and culture. The modern Indian literary movement was born there, and the city was home to Rabindranath Tagore, the Nobel Prize winner for literature in 1913. The city has a number of literary academies.

In addition, Calcutta is a center of dance, drama, music, and fine art, with dozens of academies devoted to each. The city is home to hundreds of theaters, concert halls, and art galleries, as well as over thirty museums. And while Mumbai remains the center of India's mammoth popular movie industry, most of the country's more artistic films come from Calcutta. There are scores of cinemas in the city. The city is also well served by an extensive park system, centered on the Maidan, a large open green space in the very heart of the city.

CATEGORY	DATA	YEAR	AREA
LOCATION & ENVIRONMENT			
Area	197 square miles	1995	City
	533 square kilometers		City
Elevation	20 feet/6 meters		City
January Temperature	67.5 degrees Fahrenheit		City
	19.7 degrees Celsius		City
July Temperature	84.5 degrees Fahrenheit		City
	29.2 degrees Celsius		City
Annual Precipitation	63 inches/1600.2 millimeters		City
POPULATION & DEMOGRAPHY			
Population	12,100,000	1996	Metro
Projected Population	17,300,000	2015	Metro
Growth Rate	1.8%	1990–1995	Metro
Growth Rate	45.1%	1995–2015	Metro
Density	12,200 per square mile	1981	Metro
	33,000 per square kilometer	1981	Metro
Gender			
Male	54.7%	1991	Metro
Female	45.3%	1991	Metro
VITAL STATISTICS			
Births per 1000 Residents	15.6	1992	Metro
Deaths per 1,000 Residents	6.6	1992	Metro
Infant Mortality Rate	41.1 per 1,000 live births	1992	Metro
TRANSPORTATION			
All Vehicles	500,000	1989	Metro

Sources: Department of Economic and Social Affairs, Population Division. *Urban Agglomerations, 1996*. New York: United Nations, 1997; *Statistics of World Large Cities*. Tokyo, Japan: Tokyo Metropolitan Government, 1992 and 1994; and United Nations Center for Human Settlements. *Compendium of Human Settlements Statistics*. New York: United Nations, 1995.

Calgary, Alberta
CANADA

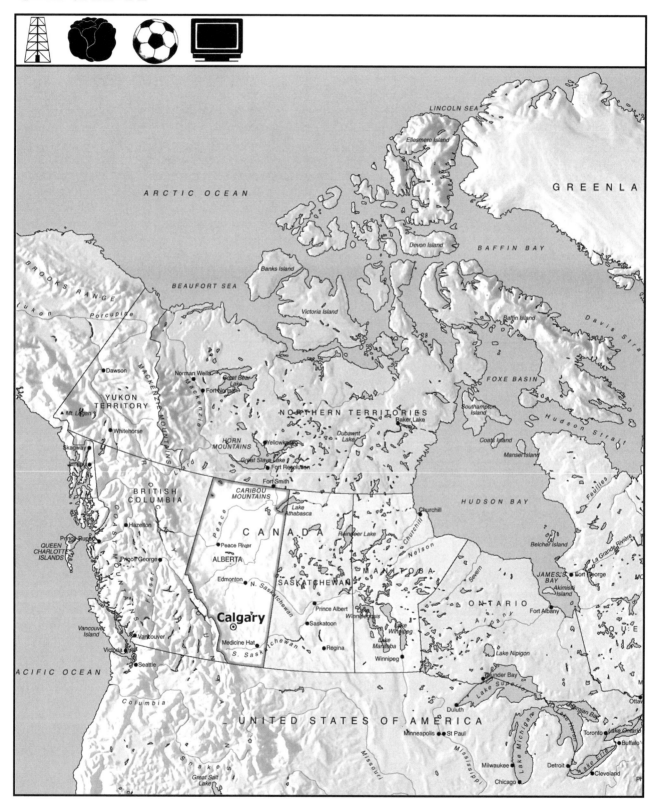

LOCATION

Calgary is Canada's second largest city in land area. The city has expanded in area and population through annexation and incorporation of adjoining communities. The city lies at an elevation of 3,540 feet above sea level. With a surface area of nearly 271.1 square miles (702.2 square kilometers), Calgary is the second largest city in Canada. The city lies about 160 miles south of Edmonton, Alberta's capital, and is the major oil, gas drilling, and production center in western Canada. Calgary is bounded on the south and southeast by a vast prairie and steppe that extends from Alberta into southern Saskatchewan, Manitoba, and the U.S. states of Montana, North Dakota, and South Dakota. The city is approximately 150 miles north of the boundary with Montana. Calgary experiences long, cold winters and short, warm summers. The region frequently experiences chinook winds—a warm, dry air mass that originates in the Pacific Ocean and covers eastern Rocky Mountain slopes. Chinook winds can raise winter temperatures by more than 80 degrees Fahrenheit in a 24-hour period. The city's average temperature ranges from a low of 15.8 degrees Fahrenheit (−9.0 degrees Celsius) in January to a high of 62.4 degrees Fahrenheit (16.9 degrees Celsius) in July. While the rapid temperature swings are a novelty, they sometimes contribute to unpredictable and aberrant weather patterns. For example, a snowstorm occurred in August 1945, and a hailstorm in September 1991 produced severe damage to the city. Frequent rainstorms and torrential downpours periodically swell the area's rivers and creeks and produce flooding. Calgary's average annual precipitation is 16.7 inches (424 millimeters).

POPULATION AND DEMOGRAPHY

The exponential population growth that Calgary has experienced through the first nine decades of the century began to moderate in the 1990s in response to a slowing of growth in the Canadian and regional economy. From 1915 to 1945, Calgary's population nearly doubled from 52,000 to 100,000. The population more than doubled once more between 1945 and 1959, to 218,000, and again to 530,816 in 1979. From 1985 to 1996 the population expanded by 23 percent, to 827,600. However, forecasters expect that Calgary's population will grow more slowly over the next decade, reaching 885,700 by the year 2001, an increase of 6.5 percent. Economic upswings have tended to produce periods of greater population growth. Calgary has a younger age distribution than other regional and Canadian cities, with a larger share of the population 65 years of age and under. The city also has a relatively even number of males and females in the population.

HISTORY

Calgary was founded in 1875 by the North West Mounted Police as a fort and trading post and evolved into a major cattle ranching and rail transportation center. Much of the regional population growth has taken place in tandem with the discovery of new oil and gas reserves in the region and the expansion of the Canadian oil and energy-related industries. Today, Calgary, on the foothills of the Canadian Rocky Mountains, near the confluence of the Bow and Elbow Rivers in southwestern Alberta, is the most populous city in Alberta and the sixth largest Canadian city.

GOVERNMENT AND POLITICS

Unlike most other major Canadian cities, the central city of Calgary alone encompasses most of the regional population, primarily as a result of the annexation of outlying towns and municipalities, whereas in other Canadian cities, a regional authority governs a metropolitan region consisting of a number of towns and municipalities. Therefore, the City of Calgary is also the regional authority that oversees service delivery and economic expansion. The City of Calgary Electric System, the city's public utility, is a wholly owned subsidiary of the City of Calgary.

ECONOMY

Calgary's economy is dominated by the energy and agriculture production and service industries. Calgary is the base of the vast majority of Canada's oil and gas producers, nearly two thirds of the country's coal companies, and a large share of the nation's engineering, geological, and data processing service companies. Many firms provide administrative and financial support services to the oil and gas industries. The leading energy firms include TransCanada Pipelines, Shell Canada, and Petro Canada. The city is also the principal producer services center for the Alberta cattle and grain industries. The key agricultural support services operating in Calgary are food processing, farm equipment and supply marketing, livestock and grain marketing, and agricultural publications, shows, sales, and conventions.

The rapid growth of the local economy came to a standstill in the early 1990s as local corporations sought to increase productivity and profitability by restructuring operations through staff cutbacks. As many as 15,000 workers lost jobs in the oil and gas industry. Cutbacks in the private sector were emulated by public sector efforts to reduce expenditures through layoffs. Nonetheless, the skilled and educated labor force usually limits the magnitude of regional unemployment. Although unemployment moderated in the mid-1990s to the 6.5 percent range, it is still almost double the rate of a decade earlier. Still, Calgary's unemployment rate is significantly lower than that of other major Canadian cities and the national average, which in the mid-1990s hovered around 10 percent.

The manufacturing sector, still dominated by production for the agriculture and energy-related industries, has diversified into lumber and wood processing, food processing, electronics, and publishing. Some locally manufactured goods, such as wood products and electronics, are sold to provincial, Canadian, and foreign markets, while others, such as food products, serve the needs of the growing western Canadian regional market.

The future of the growth of the Calgary economy hinges on the continued expansion of the research and high-tech sectors to support the energy and agricultural industries. Research and advanced technology employ 29,000 workers and generate $5 billion in annual revenues. The leading high-tech growth sectors are energy, seismic image processing and interpretation, telecommunications, supervisory control, data processing, industrial instrumentation, software, and biotechnology. The City of Calgary operates two public industrial parks to promote the growth and expansion of research and high-technology industries. Calgary has a relatively skilled and educated population, with an average income that is 16 percent above the Canadian national average.

TRANSPORTATION

The City of Calgary is divided into four sections, and streets are laid out on a numbered grid system. Calgary has an advanced system of public transportation for a city of its size. In 1981 the city's publicly owned light rail transit system began operation, expanding to include three separate lines that provide service to most parts of the city. A bus system provides public transportation to neighborhoods not served by the rail system. Two major highways intersect Calgary—the Trans-Canada Highway, which provides east-

west service, and the Alberta Highway, which provides service from the American border to Edmonton.

HEALTH CARE

Health care is universally available to all residents of Alberta, which ensures that the health needs of provincial residents are met. Calgary is one of seventeen regional health authorities of the Alberta Department of Public Health. The authority develops services to meet the specific needs of the population, including substance abuse outreach and prenatal nutrition programs.

EDUCATION

Calgary is home to four major universities: the University of Calgary, Mount Royal College, Southern Alberta Institute of Technology, and Athabasca University. Also in Calgary is the Alberta College of Art. The public school system for primary and secondary students is operated by two school boards. A third school board provides education to the city's Catholic students.

HOUSING

Housing construction in Calgary has expanded relatively more rapidly than in other major Canadian cities. The city also has a considerably larger share of owner-occupied dwellings—60.6 percent of all housing units fall into this category. Although the housing stock has expanded, the growth has not been fast enough to meet the needs of a rapidly growing population, and the city requires a larger number of affordable housing units.

CULTURE, THE ARTS, AND ENTERTAINMENT

Calgary was host of the winter Olympic Games in February 1988. In preparation for the Olympic Games, the city constructed world-class skiing, skating, and other winter sports facilities that continue to be available to residents and visitors. Calgary's proximity to the Rocky Mountains and nearby Banff National Park makes it a major destination city for winter and summer sports enthusiasts. Summer outdoor sports include fishing, cycling, hiking, horseback riding, and swimming. The city is home to four professional sports teams, including two major league teams, the Calgary Flames of the National Hockey League and the Calgary Stampeders of the Canadian Football League. The city is the home to the Calgary Stampede Rodeo, a winter sports festival, and is bidding for the World's Fair in the coming years. Calgary has a vibrant arts scene that includes regular concert, theater, and ballet performances.

CATEGORY	DATA	YEAR	AREA
LOCATION & ENVIRONMENT			
Area	271.1 miles	1996	City
	702.2 kilometers		City
Elevation	3,540 feet/1,079 meters		City
January Temperature	15.8 degrees Fahrenheit		City
	−9.0 degrees Celsius		City
July Temperature	62.4 degrees Fahrenheit		City
	16.9 degrees Celsius		City
Annual Precipitation	16.7 inches/424 millimeters		City
POPULATION & DEMOGRAPHY			
Population	827,600	1996	Metro
Growth Rate	23%	1985–1996	Metro
Growth Rate	6.5%	1996–2001	Metro
Density	2,781 per square mile	1991	Metro
	1,074 per square kilometer	1991	Metro
Gender			
Male	49.9%	1995	Metro
Female	50.1%	1995	Metro
Age			
Under 20	28.4%	1991	Metro
20–59	50.7%	1991	Metro
Over 60	11.2%	1991	Metro
VITAL STATISTICS			
Births per 1,000 Residents	15.2	1991	Metro
Deaths per 1,000 Residents	5.3	1991	Metro
ECONOMY			
Total Workforce	441,195	1991	Metro
Manufacturing	9.1%	1991	Metro
Services	13.2%	1991	Metro
Construction	5.8%	1991	Metro
Agriculture	1.5%	1991	Metro
Mining	0.4%	1991	Metro
HOUSING			
Total Housing Units	275,980	1991	Metro
Persons per Unit	2.7	1991	Metro
Owner-Occupied Units	60.6%	1991	Metro

(continued)

CATEGORY	DATA	YEAR	AREA
HEALTH CARE			
Hospitals	5	1991	Metro
Physicians per 1,000 Residents	1.9	1991	Metro

Sources: *Canada Year Book 1994.* Ottawa, Ontario: Statistics Canada, 1995. *Canadian Markets.* Toronto, Ontario: The Financial Post, 1996.

Cape Town, Cape Province
SOUTH AFRICA

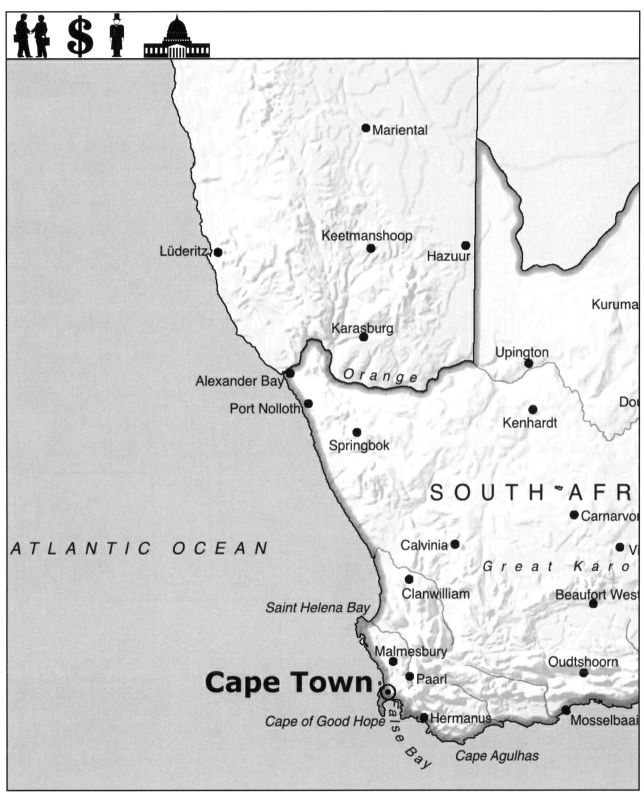

Mariental

Keetmanshoop

Hazuur

Lüderitz

Kuruma

Karasburg

Upington

Orange

Alexander Bay

Port Nolloth

Do

Kenhardt

Springbok

S O U T H ⸙ A F R

Carnarvo

A T L A N T I C   O C E A N

Calvinia

V

G r e a t   K a r o

Clanwilliam

Beaufort West

Saint Helena Bay

Malmesbury

Oudtshoorn

Cape Town

Paarl

Cape of Good Hope

False Bay

Hermanus

Mosselbaai

Cape Agulhas

LOCATION

Situated at the southern tip of the African continent, Cape Town is world-famous for its spectacular natural setting. The oldest part of the city lies on the shore and plains around Table Bay, but many of the suburbs climb the slopes of Signal Hill, Devil's Peak, and the plateau known as Table Mountain. The average elevation is 56 feet (17 meters). The entire metropolitan area extends southward as far as False Bay. The city is located 820 miles southwest of Johannesburg and 2,000 miles south of Kinshasa, Democratic Republic of the Congo. The city covers roughly 111 square miles (300 square kilometers). Cape Town has a Mediterranean-like climate with warm, dry summers and cool, wet winters. January temperatures average 69.8 degrees Fahrenheit (21 degrees Celsius); July temperatures average 55.4 degrees Fahrenheit (13 degrees Celsius). Cape Town receives roughly 25 inches (660 millimeters) of rain annually, most of which falls in the winter.

POPULATION AND DEMOGRAPHY

The Cape Town metropolitan area has a population of approximately 2.8 million and has averaged growth rates of about 3.4 percent annually through the 1990s, much of this in the form of migration from the countryside in the wake of restrictions lifted in the post apartheid era. The population is expected to grow to about 4.4 million by 2015, though the growth rate is expected to drop to about 2 percent annually by then. Of the city's population, 37.1 percent is under 20 years of age, 58 percent is in the 20-to-64 age group, and 4.9 percent is 65 or over. The Cape Town area has a relatively low density of 7,201 persons per square mile (2,667 persons per square kilometer).

Approximately one half the city's population is classified as "colored," an apartheid-era term for mixed-race people; one quarter are white; 20 percent are African; and the rest are Asian, primarily of East Indian origin. Roughly half of the colored and white population speak Afrikaans and the rest speak English. Many of the Africans and virtually all the Asians speak English. Many of the Africans also speak Xhosa and other indigenous South African languages. Most of the population of all races are Protestants, though there are significant Catholic populations among all races and a number of Muslims, largely of East Indian and African origin.

HISTORY

Cape Town was founded initially by survivors of the wreck of a Dutch ship in 1647. Survivors returning to Holland offered glowing agricultural reports, leading to the establishment of a permanent settlement by the Dutch East India Company in 1652. The colony quickly established a representative government and began importing slaves to work the farms that supplied passing ships. To counter French moves, the English occupied the city in 1795, though it reverted to Dutch rule in 1803. Permanent British control began in 1806. In 1840, Cape Town was turned into an official municipality, with a population of 40,000.

During the Boer War of 1899–1902, when Britain fought and defeated the descendants of Dutch settlers for control of South Africa, the British used the city as a base of military supply operations. Since then, the city has grown steadily as an industrial port and popular residential area. During the first half of the twentieth century, Cape Town was largely free of the color bars, prevalent in the rest of South Africa, that separated black from white populations.

GOVERNMENT AND POLITICS

In 1948, the Boer-dominated National Party took control of the South African government and began to institute apartheid policies throughout the country, including Cape Town. With its liberal tradition and heavy population of colored people, however, the city was less vigorous in its application of racial segregation, though the city was divided along racial lines and many colored and black neighborhoods were destroyed. During the 1980s, Cape Town was a center of antiapartheid protest in South Africa.

Cape Town is administered by an elected mayor and city council. There is also a regional council to handle affairs encompassing the entire metropolitan area.

ECONOMY

Until precious minerals were discovered in the Transvaal in northern South Africa, Cape Town was the largest city and economic capital of the colony, a role now assumed by Johannesburg and Pretoria, respectively, though Cape Town is still home to the country's Supreme Court. The city continues to be a major port for freight, ship repairing, and fishing. One of the region's major exports, fruits for the European winter market, passes through Cape Town. It is also an important industrial center, producing petroleum products, chemicals, food products, textiles and clothing, and automobiles. Of the workforce, 23.4 percent is involved in manufacturing. Cape Town is also a popular tourist location for South Africans and, since the fall of apartheid, international visitors as well, who come to the city for its spectacular landscape and beaches. Approximately 20 percent of the city's workforce is involved in trade, finance, and tourism. Another 25 percent work in the public sector.

TRANSPORTATION

Cape Town has a modern and extensive transportation system. Two radial freeways lead southward to the suburbs of False Bay, supplemented by a beltway around the city and several major highways leading to the city center. Most whites and a substantial proportion of coloreds own automobiles. Public transport is extensive and reliable and includes suburban trains and buses. There is also a major private bus company serving the city.

The city is well connected to other points in South Africa via a network of intercity railroads. The port of Cape Town handles 5 million tons of cargo annually, though the shallow harbor cannot handle ships with a draft of more than 40 feet during low tide. The harbor has extensive container-handling facilities. The city is also served by a major international airport, with flights to other parts of South Africa, Africa, Europe, and Asia.

The city has a high rate of telephone ownership, with approximately one line for every household. The city has several television and radio stations, and more are being added in the wake of apartheid's fall. Cape Town is also a major publishing center, with several daily newspapers in English and Afrikaans.

HEALTH CARE

Cape Town has a mixed record on health. Infant mortality rates for whites are at First World levels of 8.8 per 1,000 live births, while the black rate is 44 and the colored rate is 19.3. Birth rates are three times higher for blacks than whites, with coloreds falling somewhere in the middle. While death rates are higher for whites than blacks or coloreds, this is a reflection of the older age of white residents; Cape Town being a popular retirement center for white South Africans.

EDUCATION

The city has a relatively extensive educational system, and the literacy rate for all races is 80.4 percent. In general, however, literacy rates and educational level tend to be highest among whites and significantly lower for the colored and African population. The postapartheid government of Nelson Mandela and the African National Congress has made school integration and a more equitable distribution of educational revenues to schools with predominantly colored, Asian, and African student bodies a priority. This has produced a backlash in the white community, with many parents pulling their children out of the public school system and into private academies. The city's main institution of higher education is the University of Cape Town, founded in 1829.

HOUSING

Many colored, black, and Asian neighborhoods were bulldozed in the wake of the 1966 Group Areas Act and their residents forced to move to townships on the outskirts of the city, including such neighborhoods as the Cape Peninsula, Cape Flats, and Mitchells Plain. White families took their place in the old city neighborhoods. This policy of forced removal was ended in 1990 and all neighborhoods were opened to citizens of all races, though lower incomes among coloreds and blacks mean that most remain in the poorer townships.

With the end of apartheid-era influx controls in the late 1980s, the city witnessed a major migration of blacks and coloreds from the countryside who settled in shantytowns ringing the city. While the African National Congress government of Nelson Mandela—in power since 1994—has made housing a major priority, little progress has been made. Still, most of the city and suburbs are well serviced with utilities. Over 90 percent of the metropolitan area's housing is served by piped water.

CULTURE, THE ARTS, AND ENTERTAINMENT

Several history and art museums are located in Cape Town, including the South African Cultural History Museum and the South African Maritime Museum. The city also has an orchestra, ballet, and opera company. Much of the city's cultural events and institutions are run by the Cape Performing Arts Board. TV ownership is widespread, with about one set for every six people.

Cape Town is best known for its many sports and outdoor facilities. It has several track facilities and stadiums. Popular spectator sports include rugby, soccer, and cricket. Numerous beaches and harbors are popular with bathers, surfers, and sailors. The city also has an extensive park system, and its mild climate makes it ideal for its several public botanical gardens.

CATEGORY	DATA	YEAR	AREA
LOCATION & ENVIRONMENT			
Area	111 square miles	1996	City
	300 square kilometers	1996	City
Elevation	56 feet/17 meters	1996	City
January Temperature	69.8 degrees Fahrenheit		City
	21 degrees Celsius		City
July Temperature	55.4 degrees Fahrenheit		City
	13 degrees Celsius		City
Precipitation	25 inches (660 millimeters)		City
POPULATION & DEMOGRAPHY			
Population	2,800,000	1995	City
Projected Population	4,400,000	2015	City
Growth Rate	3.4%	1990–1995	City
Growth Rate	60.3%	1995–2015	City
Density	7,201 per square mile	1994	City
	2,667 per square kilometer	1994	City
Gender			
Male	52.2%	1990	City
Female	47.8%	1990	City
Under 20	37.2%	1990	City
20–64	58.0%	1990	City
65 and over	4.9%	1990	City
Race			
Colored (Mixed Race)	50.0%	1996	City
White	25.0%	1996	City
African	20%	1996	City
Asian Indian	5%	1996	City
VITAL STATISTICS			
Birth Rate per 1,000 Residents			
Black	33.1	1989–1990	City
White	12.2	1989–1990	City
Colored	21.3	1989–1990	City
Infant Mortality Rate			
Black	44 per 1,000 live births	1989–1990	City
White	8.8 per 1,000 live births	1989–1990	City
Colored	19.3 per 1,000 live births	1989–1990	City
Death Rate per 1,000 Residents			
Black	7	1989–1990	City
White	10.3	1989–1990	City
Colored	7.7	1989–1990	City

(continued)

CATEGORY	DATA	YEAR	AREA
ECONOMY			
Workforce	825,598	1985	City
Manufacturing	23.4%	1985	City
Construction	8.7%	1985	City
Agriculture	4.7%	1985	City
Utilities	0.9%	1985	City
Mining	0.3%	1985	City
Trade	14.0%	1985	City
Finance, Insurance, Real Estate	6.2%	1985	City
Public Service	25.0%	1985	City
Transport and Communications	5.9%	1985	City
TRANSPORTATION			
Vehicles	458,800	1991	City
COMMUNICATIONS			
Telephones per 1,000 Residents	227	1985	City
Televisions per 1,000 Residents	152	1991	City
HOUSING			
Total Occupied Units	484,121	1985	City
Persons per Unit	5.4	1985	City
EDUCATION			
Primary	1,063	1991	City
Secondary	297	1991	City
Higher Education	17	1991	City
Literacy Rate 15 years and over	80.4%	1991	City

Sources: Department of Economic and Social Affairs, Population Division. *Urban Agglomerations, 1996.* New York: United Nations, 1997. United Nations Center for Human Settlements. *Compendium of Human Settlements Statistics.* New York: United Nations, 1995.

Caracas
VENEZUELA

LOCATION

Located in a series of narrow valleys, Caracas is a city of tree-lined streets, parks, and lush gardens, surrounded by the striking natural beauty of coastal mountains and punctuated with hundreds of skyscrapers and numerous highways.

As the largest city and capital of Venezuela, Caracas serves as the national center for industry, manufacturing, commerce, education, and culture. Caracas is linked by air, railroad, and highways to western Venezuela, Ciudad Bolívar, and the nearby Caribbean port of La Guaira.

This sprawling metropolis occupies every available foot of land in the Río Guaire region, contributing to a shortage of land and a high population density. Self-built housing, referred to as *ranchos*, is scattered on the outer slopes of the valley in close proximity to the city's modern skyscrapers.

Earthquakes have destroyed most of what remained of the city's colonial past. Yet the old historic hub, centered around Plaza Bolívar, is a testimony to the fact that Caracas is the official hometown of Simon Bolívar, leader of the Latin American independence struggles against Spain in the early nineteenth century.

The city is located at an altitude of 3,418 feet (1,042 meters). While there is not much variation in temperature throughout the year, it is always cool at night. Temperatures range from 66 degrees Fahrenheit (18.9 degrees Celsius) in January to 69 degrees Fahrenheit (20.6 degrees Celsius) in July. The city averages 32.9 inches (835.7 millimeters) of precipitation per year.

POPULATION AND DEMOGRAPHY

The city's explosive population growth in the twentieth century has accompanied the industrial development that grew out of the country's oil boom. In 1941, the population of Caracas was 300,000. Beginning in the early 1940s, the population began to expand rapidly due to internal and international migration and a high rate of natural increase. In 1950, the population had more than doubled to 676,000, and it doubled again, to 1.3 million, by 1961. By 1996, there were 3 million citizens. The average rate of population growth has declined since its peak at 6.4 percent in the 1950s, falling to 4.7 percent in the 1960s to 1 percent in the early 1990s. In 2015, the population is projected to reach 3.8 million, a growth rate of 25.6 percent. About 39.9 percent of the population is under 20 years of age, 55.4 percent between 20 and

59 years of age, and 4.6 percent over 60 years of age. Females comprise 51.7 percent of Caracas's population.

HISTORY

Caracas was founded in 1567 by Spanish gold explorers, led by Diego de Losada. The original name of the city was Santiago de Leon de Caracas. The town was built up from the historic center, which is now called Plaza Bolívar. The city has endured numerous setbacks, including pirate attacks, earthquakes, and plagues, in its history. In 1595, it was sacked by English buccaneers under the command of Sir Francis Drake. Various earthquakes have demolished the city: In 1812, a tremor killed more than 10,000 residents and left the city in rubble. The most recent earthquake, in 1967, killed 277 people and damaged many buildings.

Notwithstanding these catastrophes, Caracas has always bounced back, and early on it became one of the most prosperous Spanish colonial communities in South America. During the seventeenth century, people inhabiting the valley grew cacao and maize and traded with nearby towns, including the port, La Guaira. Eventually one company, called the Spanish Caracas Company, was granted a monopoly on trade with Spain and became very prosperous.

Outraged residents staged protests and demonstrations against the corrupt policies of the company. The rebellions eventually led to the city's revolt against Spain, which sparked the nineteenth-century South American wars of independence. Caracas became the center of the first revolts against Spain, which began in 1810 and lasted through 1821, when Venezuela secured its independence from Spanish rule. Most of the rest of Latin America then followed suit.

The city was recognized as the capital of Venezuela in 1829 and grew slowly until the early twentieth century. The city's development changed dramatically when oil was discovered nearby in 1917. The city and nation went through an economic boom, with the dollars generated from oil exports leading to the modernization of the colonial town.

GOVERNMENT AND POLITICS

Caracas is governed through the Libertador Department of the Federal District. At the same time, the rapid growth of the city has meant that many parts of the metropolitan area fall under the jurisdiction of the surrounding state of Miranda. As with state governors, the head of the federal district is appointed by the president of Venezuela. The district runs its own police department. While basic municipal services are run by the Municipal Council, larger planning issues are handled by the Metropolitan Commission of Urbanization.

ECONOMY

Caracas serves as the country's center of industry, manufacturing, and commerce. The city's main industries include auto assembly, sugar refining, meat packing, leather tanning, oil refining, wood processing, paper manufacturing, tobacco, food processing, glassware, textiles and clothing, rubber goods, and pharmaceuticals. Important sources of employment in Caracas include government agencies, construction, and the oil industry. Thirty percent of the country's industrial labor force is located in the metropolitan region of Caracas.

The most important sectors remain commerce and services, however. These include wholesale and retail trade, transport, public utilities, education, health care, and public administration. Tourism is also growing. The construction industry has led to the expansion of auxiliary industries, including cement production and construction materials. As the principal center of petroleum-related activities, Caracas also serves as the center for domestic and foreign commerce and banking activities.

TRANSPORTATION

The major means of transport in Caracas is the private automobile. The oil boom initiated massive investments in highways and the automobile industry. As a result, most citizens feel dependent on private cars, and this has made Caracas one of the most congested cities in Latin America. The old historic city center has become increasingly insignificant as highways and modern planning bypass the old quarters. Buses and taxis also serve the metropolis, as well as a subway system, built in 1983, that is clean, cheap, comfortable, and punctual.

HEALTH CARE

While the public health care facilities in the low-income districts of Caracas are insufficient to handle the large numbers of residents there, they are deficient in rich neighborhoods as well. Since the 1940s, the city has had water shortages. This has led to continuing searches for other sources of water, as well as the construction of two dams and an aqueduct. The discharge of raw sewage into the river and the air pollution caused by industry and automobiles have aggravated environmental problems. Other city problems include waste collection and disposal.

EDUCATION

As the capital and largest city of Venezuela, Caracas has one of the finest and most comprehensive school systems in the country. Its educational statistics are somewhat above those for the country at large. Overall, Venezuela has an extensive school system at the primary level, much of it paid for by the revenues generated from the country's large oil reserves. Nationwide, more than 90 percent of all school-age children attend primary school, though only about one-third attend secondary institutions. The biggest gains have come at the university level, where the percentage of university-age students has climbed from roughly 5 percent in 1965 to more than 25 percent in 1995. Both figures include many students who are older than most university students (18–25), thereby inflating the numbers. The literacy rate is roughly 90 percent throughout Venezuela, slightly higher in Caracas.

HOUSING

The rapid population growth during the latter half of the twentieth century has led to a severe housing shortage, as well as to problems with the delivery of basic services. As a result, many residents have taken to the hillsides and built *ranchos* using corrugated metal, cardboard, and other scrap materials. The government has responded by forcibly relocating such communities and by building large-scale apartment complexes to house the poor. Nevertheless, the housing situation remains problematic. In one case, a housing project that was initially intended to go for low-income families became so costly that the city had to abandon the low-income aspect and subsidize the units even when they went for sale to upper-income families. The city has 416,125 housing units and an occupancy rate of 7.2 persons per housing unit.

CULTURE, THE ARTS, AND ENTERTAINMENT

Caracas is rich in art, music, and theater. The Teresa Cerreo Cultural Complex hosts ballets, concerts, and plays. The nearby Museum of Contemporary Art collects and displays art by Venezuelan and international artists. Caracas is endowed with a number of historical buildings and plazas, including the Plaza Bolívar and the nearby National Pantheon, where Bolívar is buried; the seventeenth-century Roman Catholic cathedral; the Central University of Venezuela; and the gold-domed capitol building and city hall.

CATEGORY	DATA	YEAR	AREA
LOCATION & ENVIRONMENT			
Elevation	3,418 feet/1,042 meters	1995	City
January Temperature	66 degrees Fahrenheit		City
	18.9 degrees Celsius		City
July Temperature	69 degrees Fahrenheit		City
	20.6 degrees Celsius		City
Annual Precipitation	32.9 inches/835.7 millimeters		City
POPULATION & DEMOGRAPHY			
Population	3,000,000	1996	City
Projected Population	3,800,000	2015	City
Growth Rate	1.0%	1990–1995	City
Growth Rate	25.6%	1995–2015	City
Gender			
Male	48.3%	1995	City
Female	51.7%	1995	City
Age			
Under 20	39.9%	1995	City
20–59	55.4%	1995	City
Over 60	4.6%	1995	City
HOUSING			
Total Housing Units	416,125	1995	City
Persons per Unit	7.2	1995	City

Sources: Department of Economic and Social Affairs, Population Division. *Urban Agglomerations, 1996.* New York: United Nations, 1997. United Nations Center for Human Settlements. *Compendium of Human Settlements Statistics.* New York: United Nations, 1995.

Casablanca
MOROCCO

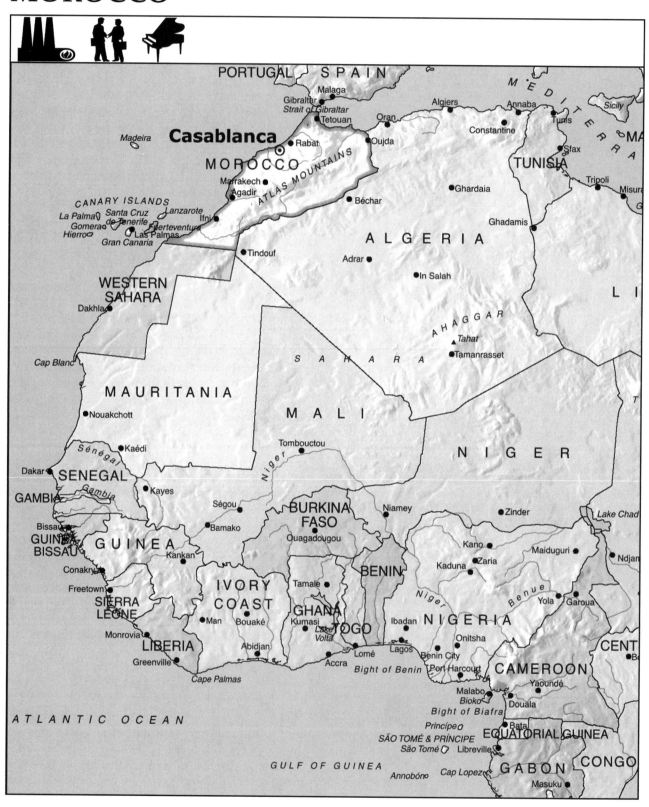

LOCATION

Casablanca is the largest city and principal port of Morocco, situated at an elevation of 164 feet (50 meters) on the Atlantic coastal plain in the north of the country. The city is located 180 miles south-southwest of Tangier and 640 miles west-southwest of Algiers, Algeria. Greater Casablanca covers a vast area of approximately 675 square miles (1,750 square kilometers). It has a desert-type climate of dry, hot summers and cool, wet winters. The average temperature in January is 63 degrees Fahrenheit (17.2 degrees Celsius) and in July, 79 degrees Fahrenheit (26 degrees Celsius), and annual rainfall averages roughly 15.9 inches (403.9 millimeters).

POPULATION AND DEMOGRAPHY

The population of the Casablanca metropolitan area is 3.2 million and has been growing at the rate of approximately 2.5 percent for the past several decades. While growth is expected to slow to about half that in the next century, the population of the metropolitan area will reach 4.8 million by 2015. The population is relatively balanced by age, with about 40 percent of the people under the age of 20. This contrasts with other African cities which often have more than 50 percent of the population under 20.

The city's population is almost entirely Sunni Muslim, though there is a small Jewish community as well. Ethnically, the city is divided between Arabic- and Berber-speaking peoples, while French is used in government offices and many schools.

HISTORY

Known in Arabic as Dar el-Bayda, Casablanca received its Occidental name in 1515, when Portuguese forces destroyed the old city—founded as a Berber village in the thirteenth century—and rebuilt a new one. The city was abandoned after a massive earthquake in 1755, but was again rebuilt by the Ottoman-appointed Sultan Sidi Muhammad ibn Abd Allah. By the late eighteenth century, the city became home to numerous Spanish and French merchants.

Part of the independent kingdom of Morocco, the city was occupied by French forces in 1907, who made the city the main port of their protectorate from 1912 to 1956. In the early years of World War II, the city was divided between Vichy and Free French forces, but was occupied by the Allies in 1942. The city was the site for one of the most important Allied conferences of the war in 1943. Since World War II, and especially following independence in 1956, the city has grown rapidly.

GOVERNMENT AND POLITICS

Since its independence in 1956, Morocco has been ruled as a constitutional monarchy, headed by the conservative King Hassan II. While the prime minister and parliament have some independence, the king has the power to veto legislation. The king also dominates foreign policy and defense issues. Under the rule of King Hassan, Morocco has pursued a pro-Western foreign policy and market-oriented economic development, with a heavy emphasis on tourism and commercial crop export. Casablanca has an independent city council and mayor, the latter appointed by the king and prime minister of Morocco.

ECONOMY

Casablanca is the commercial center of Morocco, producing about half the industrial output of the country. Major manufacturing products include textiles, electronics, leather goods, food and beverage products, and bus bodies and railroad cars. Approximately one third of the workforce is employed in the manufacturing sector, while another quarter works in trade and finance. Casablanca is also a major port for fishing, freight, and cruise ships. Over 20 million metric tons of freight are handled annually, and the port continues to dominate the city's revenues despite efforts to diversify, though only about 6 percent of the workforce is involved in transport.

Casablanca is also an important financial center, accounting for about half of all Moroccan bank transactions. The city is home to the country's main stock market, which has grown dramatically in the past decade. It is also a major tourist destination or point of embarkation for travel to the interior cities and countryside of Morocco.

TRANSPORTATION

Buses are the principal means of transportation in the city, accounting for about half of all commuter and intercity trips. There are 5,359 large buses operating in the city. Highways connect the city to the other major cities of Morocco and the rest of the Maghreb (another name for North Africa). Most of these are two-lane roads, but a major project to replace them with four-lane, limited-access highways is expected to be completed by 2010. The city's 374,089 cars represent almost half the total for the country and contribute heavily to the air pollution problem plaguing the city. There are also 85,652 trucks on the roads of Casablanca. A single railway line connects Casablanca to cities in the interior of the country, as well as Algeria and Tunisia to the east. A subway and surface tram system are in the planning stages.

HEALTH CARE

The population of Casablanca suffers from a host of respiratory and gastrointestinal illnesses. The former are largely caused by the city's serious air pollution problem, exacerbated by the heavy quantity of particulates produced by the large stone quarries just outside the built-up areas. Lack of adequate sewage and water treatment contributes to the occurrence of gastrointestinal illness. Eighty hospitals and clinics serve the greater Casablanca metropolitan area, and the ratio of persons to physicians is approximately 1,500 to 1, or 0.7 per 1,000 residents.

EDUCATION

The city's population is relatively well educated. In 1996, the city's literacy rate was 69.1 percent. Nearly 90 percent of children between the ages of 8 and 13 attend school, and the general literacy rate for men is approximately 80 percent. Women lag behind, with a literacy rate of roughly 60 percent. However, because of poverty and child labor, many of the city's school-age children are able to attend school only on a part-time basis. The city is also home to two major universities, with a student population of over 45,000.

HOUSING

Rapid population growth has led to a serious housing problem in the city. While over 3,500 new hous-

ing units are constructed annually, there is still a significant shortage of low-income housing. Each dwelling houses over five people, and approximately 10 percent of the city's population lives in shanties. Of the rest, almost 60 percent live in houses, and 20 percent are housed in apartments. The metropolitan area has a homeless population of approximately 50,000. The region's nearly century-old, 600-mile-long (1,000-kilometer) sewage system has not kept up with population growth, and raw sewage is often dumped directly into the Atlantic, polluting many of the city's once-fine beaches. While over 90 percent of the homes have toilets, much of the 2,000 tons of solid waste produced daily is dumped in landfills outside the city, polluting ground and surface water sources. Nearly 80 percent of the city's homes have running water and electricity. The city government is engaged in a major planning program to improve the city's sewage and water systems.

CULTURE, THE ARTS, AND ENTERTAINMENT

Casablanca is a popular tourist destination, with many visitors attracted by the city's old marketplaces and its whitewashed Arabic architecture. The medina, the old Arab town, is still enclosed by its medieval-era walls. Newer areas of the city—those built during the French and independent eras—are noted for their broad boulevards and French-style urban architecture. Toward the south of the city are the extensive gardens of the Park of the Arab League. Casablanca is also noted for its many beaches and is home to a major library, fine arts institute, and archeological museum. A 1985 urban rehabilitation plan—only partly implemented—calls for a refurbishing of the old city, creation of facilities for water sports, construction of a major convention center, and a number of new parks and sports centers. The city is also home to nearly fifty cinemas, largely featuring films from Egypt, France, and the United States.

CATEGORY	DATA	YEAR	AREA
LOCATION & ENVIRONMENT			
Elevation	164 feet/50 meters	1996	City
January Temperature	63 degrees Fahrenheit		City
	17.2 degrees Celsius		City
July Temperature	79 degrees Fahrenheit		City
	26 degrees Celsius		City
Annual Precipitation	15.9 inches/403.9 millimeters		City
POPULATION & DEMOGRAPHY			
Population	3,200,000	1995	City
Projected Population	4,800,000	2015	City
Growth Rate	2.6%	1990–1995	City
Growth Rate	48.8%	1995–2015	City
Density	4,946 per square mile	1996	Metro
	1,832 per square kilometer	1996	Metro
Age			
Under 19	40.4%	1996	City
20–59	52.9%	1996	City
Over 60	6.7%	1996	City
VITAL STATISTICS			
Single over 15	44.1%	1996	Metro
Married	48.0%	1996	Metro
Widowed	5.3%	1996	Metro
Divorced	2.6%	1996	Metro
ECONOMY			
Manufacturing	34.2%	1996	Metro
Agriculture	1.0%	1986	Metro
Mining	0.4%	1996	Metro
Trade	21.8%	1996	Metro
Finance, Insurance, Real Estate	5.4%	1996	Metro
Transport and Communications	6.0%	1996	Metro
Services	14.0%	1996	Metro
TRANSPORTATION			
Cars	374,089	1996	Metro
Trucks	85,652	1996	Metro
Buses	5,359	1996	Metro
HOUSING			
Total Housing Units	592,592	1996	Metro
Persons per Unit	5.4	1996	Metro
New Housing Units	3,752	1990	City
Residents Living in Shanties	12%	1996	Metro

(continued)

CATEGORY	DATA	YEAR	AREA
HEALTH CARE			
Hospitals and Clinics	80	1990	Metro
Physicians per 1,000 Residents	0.7	1990	Metro
EDUCATION			
Ages 8–13 in School	1	1996	Metro
Literacy Rate 15 Years and Over	69.1%	1996	Metro
University Students	45,197	1996	Metro

Sources: Annuare Statistique du Maroc. Rabat, Morocco: Bureau des Statistiques, 1996; Department of Economic and Social Affairs, Population Division. *Urban Agglomerations, 1996.* New York: United Nations, 1997; and United Nations Center for Human Settlements. *Compendium of Human Settlements Statistics.* New York: United Nations, 1995.

Chicago, Illinois

USA

LOCATION

Chicago, the third largest urban region in the United States, lies on a coastal plain in northeastern Illinois's Cook County on Lake Michigan, at an elevation of 607 feet above sea level. The 227.2-square-mile (588.5-square-kilometer) city extends 29 miles along the southwest shore of Lake Michigan, from the border of Indiana, on the southeast, to Evanston, on the city's north. Chicago is located 70 miles due south of Milwaukee, Wisconsin. Chicago is strategically located on an extensive water transportation system. The Chicago River crosscuts the downtown area and divides into the North and South Branches. To Chicago's west, a canal links the city to the Des Plaines River, meeting the Illinois and Mississippi Rivers to the southwest. On the city's south, the Calumet River flows into Lake Calumet. Lake Michigan links Chicago to the St. Lawrence Seaway and the Atlantic Ocean. The Chicago metropolitan area extends from Gary, in northwest Indiana, through northeast Illinois to Kenosha, in southwest Wisconsin. The primary Chicago metropolitan area includes Cook County, Lake County, and DuPage County, all in Illinois. The city is located approximately 185 miles northwest of Indianapolis, Indiana, 275 miles west of Detroit, Michigan, 290 miles northeast of St. Louis, Missouri, 310 miles northwest of Columbus, Ohio, 350 miles west of Cleveland, Ohio, and 400 miles southeast of Minneapolis, Minnesota. Between 1961 and 1990, Chicago's average temperature ranged from a low of 22.4 degrees Fahrenheit (−5.3 degrees Celsius) in January to a high of 75.1 degrees Fahrenheit (23.9 degrees Celsius) in July. Over the same thirty-year period, Chicago had an average annual precipitation of 37.38 inches (949 millimeters).

POPULATION AND DEMOGRAPHY

During the 1970s, Los Angeles eclipsed Chicago as the second largest city in the United States. However, Chicago remains the third largest city and metropolitan region in the country. From 1980 to 1992, the city's population declined by 236,589 persons, a total of 7.9 percent. Overall, the city's population declined by 17.8 percent between 1970 and 1992. The city has a density of 12,185 persons per square mile. The Chicago central city population of 2,768,483 is 40.4 percent of the urban region's 6,900,000 residents. The regional population declined by about 2 percent from 1970 to 1995. However, from 1995 to the year 2015, the region is projected to grow by 9 percent, to 7,500,000. Chicago's urban population is more di-

verse than that of other cities in the U.S. Midwest. Whites remain the largest racial population group in Chicago, making up 45.6 percent of the population. Black residents are the leading minority population, with 39.3 percent of all city residents, followed by Hispanics, with 19.7 percent of the city's population, and Asians and Pacific Islanders, who make up 3.7 percent of all residents. Foreign-born residents comprise 16.9 percent of Chicago's population. The city's age distribution is balanced between dependent and productive generations. The population between 18 and 64 is 62.1 percent all urban residents, followed by those under age 18, with 26 percent of the population, and senior citizens over age 65, with 11.9 percent of all residents. The city has a ratio of 92.1 males per 100 females.

HISTORY

Native Americans originally inhabited the region of what is now Chicago prior to their displacement by Europeans in the seventeenth and eighteenth centuries. The city was first explored by the French and became the site of a U.S. army fort in the early nineteenth century, beginning a period of wars with the Native American population. Incorporated as a town in 1833 and as a city in 1837, Chicago was first settled by Scandinavian and Irish immigrants. The major periods of the city's expansion followed the growth of the city as a transportation hub—first as a seaport in the 1830s, then as a railroad link in the 1850s and 1860s, and next as a road freight center at the beginning of the twentieth century. The city was virtually destroyed in the great fire of October 1871. Major waves of immigrants from the eastern and southern parts of Europe migrated to the city in the forty-year period from the 1880s to the 1920s. Many of these immigrants worked in the city's burgeoning manufacturing industries, and the city became a site of large-scale worker revolts—most notably the Haymarket Square Riot of May 4, 1886, which is now commemorated throughout the world as the May Day workers' holiday. Chicago's population continued to expand until the second half of the twentieth century, when an out-migration trend to the suburbs and the Southwest began.

GOVERNMENT AND POLITICS

The mayor holds primary executive and administrative responsibilities. The city council, consisting of fifty aldermen who are elected from local wards, holds primary legislative responsibility. The mayor has veto power over the council, and the council must approve mayoral appointees. Both mayor and aldermen are elected to four-year terms. A 1990 referendum transferred governance over Cook County from an at-large board of commissioners to a seventeen-member Cook County Board, elected to four-year terms from local districts.

ECONOMY

Chicago's labor market has remained relatively stable during the 1980s, with the number of jobs declining by 0.6 percent between 1980 and 1990. The two leading industries in the city are trade and manufacturing. With nearly 20 percent of the workforce, wholesale and retail trade is the city's leading sector, followed by manufacturing, with 18.7 percent of the workforce. The city's other leading sectors are finance, insurance, and real estate; health services; and public administration. The city has a poverty rate of 21.6 percent, comparable to other major industrial cities of the American Midwest and Northeast. Unemployment continues to be a persistent problem, due to the decline in manufacturing and other sectors of the economy that employ less-skilled workers. Even as the economy recovered following the recession of the early 1990s, the city continued to experience an official unemployment rate of about 10 percent. Unemployment is particularly severe among minority and younger residents in the central city. The official unemployment rate among residents between 16 and 19 years of age was nearly 30 percent.

Chicago has the largest metropolitan economy in the U.S. Midwest and, despite the restructuring of industrial production, remains one of the leading manufacturing centers in the country. The major economic activities in the region are distribution (including road, rail, air, and sea transport), which facilitates national and international trade of the manufactured goods produced in the area, and retail trade. The key manufacturing industries are electrical products, industrial machinery, transportation equipment, chemical products, agricultural products, instruments, fabricated metals, primary metals, rubber and plastics, food processing, printing and publishing, and furniture and fixtures. McCormick Place is the largest convention and trade center in the United States, with over 2.4 million square feet of exposition space. Chicago is the leading commodity trading center in the world, with 80 percent of the world's commodities traded through three of the city's exchanges. The city is headquarters of the Chicago Board of Trade

and Chicago Mercantile Exchange, the Chicago Options Exchange, the Mid-America Commodity Exchange, and the Midwest Stock Exchange. The city is a major national and international banking center.

TRANSPORTATION

The Regional Transportation Authority has jurisdiction over the three public transportation agencies: the Chicago Transit Authority, which operates bus, elevated trains, and subways in the city, Metra (Metropolitan Rail), which operates a commuter railroad between Chicago and the suburbs, and the Pace Suburban Bus Service. Chicago has one of the highest rates of public transportation use in the nation, with nearly 30 percent of the city's population using the public transportation system. The Chicago metropolitan area is the nation's leading air, rail, sea, and highway freight distribution center. Chicago's O'Hare International Airport serves the largest number of passengers in the nation.

HEALTH CARE

Chicago is the headquarters of the leading U.S. professional health care associations, including the American Medical Association, the American Hospital Association, the American Dental Association, and the American College of Surgeons. Five medical institutions offer specialized degrees in medicine, including the University of Illinois at Chicago College of Medicine, the largest medical school in the United States. In 1991, the central city area of Chicago had a total of forty-two community hospitals with a total of 12,896 beds, a rate of 463 hospital beds per 100,000 persons. The Chicago metropolitan area had ninety-five hospitals, with over 27,000 beds. Despite the relative plethora of medical facilities, the city had a rate of 15.2 infant deaths per 1,000 live births in 1988, the thirteenth highest infant death rate among the seventy-seven largest American cities.

EDUCATION

In 1990, a total of 744,193 central city students attended Chicago public and private schools, of which 492,184 are enrolled in primary and secondary schools. Approximately 79.5 percent of all schoolchildren in the city attend public schools. The Chicago public school system operates 450 schools, educating over 400,000 students, and 180 parochial schools, with an enrollment of over 75,000 students. The leading city and regional postsecondary institutions are the University of Chicago, Northwestern University, the Illinois Institute of Technology, Roosevelt University, Loyola University of Chicago, De Paul University, Chicago State University, Northeastern Illinois State University, the University of Illinois at Chicago, Malcolm X College, Wilbur Wright College, and Harold Washington College. The city is also home to artistic, theological, engineering, and scientific postsecondary institutions. The central city of Chicago has a considerably lower level of educational attainment than the surrounding metropolitan area. In 1990, only 19.5 percent of the city's population 25 years of age or over had a bachelor's degree or higher, lower than in New York City and Los Angeles.

HOUSING

Chicago has a mean of 2.4 persons per household. Of the city's over 1 million households, 60 percent are headed by a married couple, 32 percent are headed by single females, and 8 percent are headed by single males. From 1980 to 1990, Chicago's housing stock declined by 3.5 percent to 1,133,039 dwelling units. Owner-occupied units comprise 41.5 percent of the city's occupied housing stock, a relatively lower percentage of owner occupancy than the national rate. Housing costs are considerably lower than in the U.S. coastal cities. In 1990, the median cost of owner-occupied housing units was about one third of the median cost in Los Angeles, and less than half the cost in New York City. Rental costs were also comparatively lower than New York City and U.S. West

Coast cities. However, housing values in the city vary considerably between poor and working-class neighborhoods and more affluent neighborhoods. For example, in 1995, the average home value ranged from more than $1.3 million in the Gold Coast neighborhood to $52,000 in the Pullman and North Pullman districts.

CULTURE, THE ARTS, AND ENTERTAINMENT

The city is home to numerous artistic, cultural, and scientific institutions, including the Art Institute of Chicago, the Museum of Science and Industry, the Museum of Contemporary Art, the Field Museum of Natural History, the Du Sable Museum of African-American History, and the John G. Shedd Aquarium. The city's most important performing arts institutions include the renowned Chicago Symphony Orchestra (considered by many to be one of the three best orchestras in the United States), the Lyric Opera of Chicago, and leading dance and theater companies. The Chicago Public Library is the second largest municipal library in the United States. The city has over five hundred parks, with nearly 7,000 acres of parkland. Chicago has five professional sports teams, including the internationally renowned Chicago Bulls basketball team, the Cubs and White Sox baseball clubs, the Bears football team, and the Black Hawks hockey team. Nearby Milwaukee, Wisconsin is home to professional baseball and basketball teams. The city is also a major collegiate sports center—six regional universities have nationally competitive major basketball programs.

CATEGORY	DATA	YEAR	AREA
LOCATION & ENVIRONMENT			
Area	227.2 square miles	1995	City
	588.5 square kilometers		City
Elevation	607 feet/185 meters		City
January Temperature	22.4 degrees Fahrenheit	1961–1990	City
	−5.3 degrees Celsius	1969–1990	City
July Temperature	75.1 degrees Fahrenheit	1961–1990	City
	23.9 degrees Celsius	1961–1990	City
Annual Precipitation	37.4 inches/949 millimeters	1961–1990	City
POPULATION & DEMOGRAPHY			
Population	6,900,000	1996	Metro
Projected Population	7,500,000	2015	Metro
Growth Rate	0.20%	1990–1995	Metro
Growth Rate	9.0%	1995–2015	Metro
Density	12,185 per square mile	1992	City
	4,704 per square kilometer		
Gender			
Males	47.9%	1990	City
Females	52.1%	1990	City
Age			
Under 18	26.0%	1990	City
18–64	62.1%	1990	City
Over 65	11.9%	1990	City
VITAL STATISTICS			
Births per 1,000 Residents	20	1988	City
Deaths per 1,000 Residents	11	1988	City
Infant Mortality Rate	15.2 per 1,000 live births	1988	City
ECONOMY			
Total Workforce	1,419,487	1990	City
Trade	19.5%	1990	City
Manufacturing	18.7%	1990	City
Health Services	8.4%	1990	City
Finance, Insurance, Real Estate	9.2%	1990	City
Public Administration	5.0%	1990	City
TRANSPORTATION			
Passenger Journeys	668,637,000	1990	City
Subway	22.0%	1990	City
Rail	14.8%	1990	City
Buses & Trolley	63.1%	1990	City
Passenger Vehicles	999,797	1990	City
HOUSING			
Total Housing Units	1,133,039	1990	City
Persons per Unit	2.4	1990	City
Owner-Occupied Units	41.5%	1990	City

(continued)

CATEGORY	DATA	YEAR	AREA
HEALTH CARE			
Hospitals	42	1991	City
EDUCATION			
Total Students	744,193	1991	City
Primary and Secondary	72.1%	1991	City
Higher	27.9%	1991	City

Sources: Department of Economic and Social Affairs, Population Division. *Urban Agglomerations, 1996.* New York: United Nations, 1997; U.S. Bureau of the Census. *County and City Data Book 1994.* Washington, DC: U.S. Government Printing Office, 1994; and United Nations Center for Human Settlements. *Compendium of Human Settlements Statistics.* New York: United Nations, 1995.

Cleveland, Ohio

USA

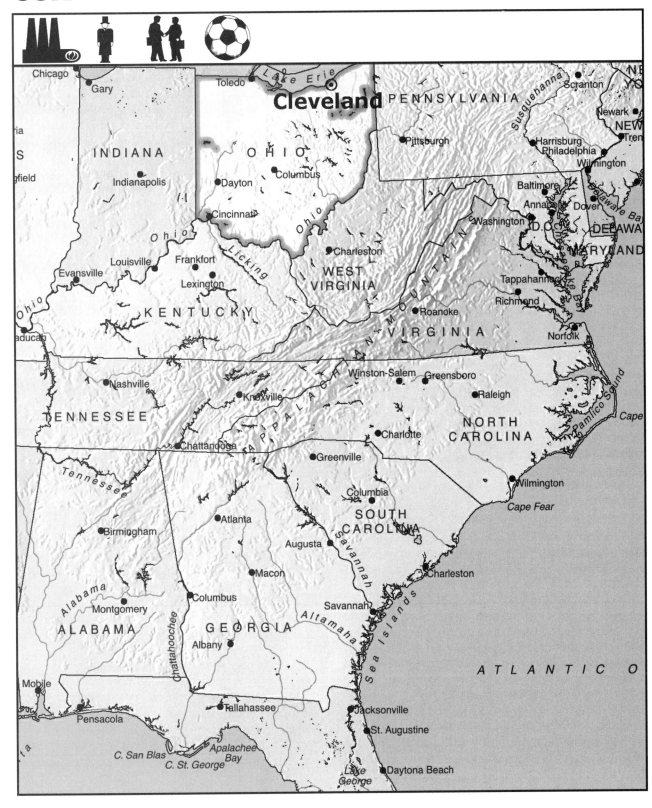

LOCATION

Cleveland, the central city in the largest metropolitan area in Ohio, lies on a flat plain in northeast Ohio on the south shore of Lake Erie, at the mouth of the Cuyahoga River, which divides the city between east and west. Cleveland, the seat of Cuyahoga County, lies on a surface land area of 77 square miles (199.4 square kilometers), 471 miles west of New York City, 129 miles northwest of Pittsburgh, and 348 miles due east of Chicago. Cleveland's metropolitan statistical area has spread to the northeast, south, and west. The metropolitan area is the fourteenth largest in the United States when combined with Ashtabula County and the nearby cities of Akron and Lorain. From 1961 to 1990, Cleveland's temperature ranged from an average low of 24.8 degrees Fahrenheit (−4.0 degrees Celsius) in January to an average high of 71.9 degrees Fahrenheit (22.2 degrees Celsius) in July. Over the same period, the city had an average annual precipitation of 36.6 inches (930 millimeters).

POPULATION AND DEMOGRAPHY

In 1996, the Cleveland metropolitan area had a population of 1.7 million. From 1960 to 1992, Cleveland's central city population declined by 43 percent, from 876,050 to 502,539. The city's population declined by about 12 percent (71,283 residents) between 1980 and 1992 and is expected to decline at a more moderate pace over the coming fifteen to twenty years. Due to projections for a continuation of the population decline in the central city, the metropolitan area is expected to grow by a cumulative 12.9 percent in the twenty-year period from 1995 to 2015, more slowly than comparable U.S. regions. The central city's population density was 6,526 persons per square mile (2,520 persons per square kilometer) in 1992. The central city's population is only slightly younger than the region's, and its age structure is comparable to that of the United States as a whole. Nearly 27 percent of the population is under the age of 18, and 14 percent is over 65 years of age. Although the vast majority of regional residents are white, about half of the residents of the central city are (49.7 percent). Blacks comprise the vast majority of minority residents (46.8 percent), followed by Hispanics (4.6 percent) and Asians (about 1 percent). The city is home to eighty ethnic/racial groups, the largest of which are of German, Italian, Slovenian, Slovakian, Hungarian, and Lithuanian origin. More recently, the city has attracted a large number of immigrants from the Philippines, China, Taiwan, Indochina, and India.

HISTORY

The city, initially inhabited by Native Americans, became a French trading post in the eighteenth century and was incorporated as a village in 1814 and as a city in 1836. The city grew rapidly in the second half of the nineteenth century to become one of America's largest urban and commercial centers. In the hundred years from 1850 to 1950, immigrants from Eastern Europe and African-American migrants from the U.S. South settled the region. However, Cleveland has declined relative to other major U.S. cities since the end of the Second World War, due mainly to the decline of older steel and heavy manufacturing industries. The city's population shrank further in the wake of the 1966 urban uprisings and the flight of many white residents to the suburbs.

GOVERNMENT AND POLITICS

The city is governed by a mayor elected at large and a city council. The city council president presides over the city council elected by each of Cleveland's twenty-one political wards. The mayor's office is responsible for local service delivery and encouraging economic development. When Carl Stokes was elected mayor in 1967, Cleveland became the first major city in American to be governed by a black mayor. Although most Cleveland voters still tend to vote on the basis of the candidate's race, in recent years there is evidence that racial identity has become less important in selecting a mayor. A recent political debate has centered on the extent and nature of commercial development that is desirable in Cleveland's downtown area. Some city council members have favored affordable housing, while others have promoted the construction of hotels, entertainment facilities, and luxury apartments.

ECONOMY

Cleveland emerged as an industrial center in the 1850s, a major shipment point for iron ore and coal from Minnesota and Wisconsin. The steel, oil refining, and garment industries became mainstays of Cleveland's economy during the latter half of the nineteenth century. Although heavy manufacturing industries have declined significantly since the early 1970s, they continue to remain surprisingly resilient and important to the economy at the end of the century. The continued importance of the manufacturing sector can be explained in part by the diversified nature of industry in the northern Ohio region. The manufacturing sector consists of steel, machine tools, automobile and airplane parts, hardware, trucks, electronic equipment, appliances, oil refining, garments, light bulbs, batteries, paints, chemicals, publishing, printing, medical supplies, and biomedical technology. The city is a center for tourism and entertainment, legal services, and industrial research. The Cleveland area is home to ten Fortune 500 companies, chiefly in the manufacturing, banking, and insurance industries.

From 1950 to 1990, the Cleveland and northeast Ohio economies have declined relative to other major American cities, due to the effects of industrial relocation to lower-cost labor markets in the Sunbelt and foreign countries. As the industrial base has declined, many regional residents have migrated to the South and Southwest in search of employment and opportunity. Regional manufacturing firms have restructured their operations to remain competitive with lower-cost producers. Although manufacturing remains important to the regional economy, far fewer workers are employed in the sector than in past decades, due to increased productivity and the utilization of new labor-saving technology. Economists believe that through diversifying the industrial base, the region will better insulate itself from future economic recessions. Much of the regional economic activity is concentrated in the suburbs and in the nearby cities of Akron, Lorain, and the city of Ashtabula, which are beyond the formal metropolitan area while the core city of Cleveland continues to lag behind.

The central labor market contracted by nearly 12 percent in the 1980s. Manufacturing remains the dominant industry in Cleveland and northeast Ohio, but a growing number of workers have entered the service sector. In 1990, 23.1 percent of the labor force was employed in manufacturing, 20.3 percent in wholesale and retail trade, 10.6 percent in health services, 5.6 percent in finance, insurance, and real estate, and 4.6 percent in public administration. Cleveland has a diverse, skilled, and educated workforce. The city has a lower cost of living than most other major American cities; however, Cleveland's workers across a large number of industrial sectors are paid considerably lower wages relative to other major U.S. markets. Thus while the cost of living is low for workers, so are wages. Poverty remains a critical problem in both the central city and region. In 1990, the region had the twelfth highest poverty rate among thirty-five major metropolitan areas. However, the vast majority of the poverty is concentrated in the central city. In 1989, 28.7 percent of Cleveland's population lived below the poverty line.

TRANSPORTATION

The Cleveland bus and rail transit system provides commuter service throughout Cuyahoga County and parts of neighboring counties. The Regional Transit Authority serves an average of 210,000 passengers per day through ninety-eight regional bus routes and three rapid-transit rail lines. The 33-mile rail system serves suburban commuters to the downtown area. Cleveland is an important national and regional transportation center. The city is served by three major interstate highways, major railway links, and a port with a foreign trade zone that serves over fifty countries. Cleveland has over a hundred major freight carrier companies, three major railroad companies, and an international airport.

HEALTH CARE

Health care costs in Cleveland are lower than the national average, an important advantage to local residents, since health care in the United States is not considered a right for most citizens. Cleveland and northeast Ohio more generally are a leading biomedical research and health care center. Cleveland has four leading hospitals with a national reputation: the Cleveland Clinic, Mount Sinai Medical Center, Rainbow Babies and Children's Hospital of University Hospitals of Cleveland, and University Hospitals. The Cleveland Clinic, which specializes in cardiology, is ranked as one of nation's top ten hospitals. Over 125,000 health care workers are employed in fifty regional hospitals and health care institutions, contributing $9 billion to the economy. The central city has fifteen community hospitals

EDUCATION

The Cleveland Public School system has initiated efforts to improve education by including parents, educators, students, and business and civic leaders in a comprehensive education plan intended to improve educational outcomes and administration and to build partnerships among schools, families, and communities. One ongoing program is a partnership that provides work experience to students interested in manufacturing and automotive-related careers. The northern Ohio region has twenty-two universities and colleges, with a total enrollment of 143,000. The area's leading institutions are Case Western Reserve University, John Carroll University, Notre Dame College, Ursuline College, the Cleveland Institute of Art, Baldwin-Wallace College, Cleveland State University, Cleveland Institute of Music, Kent State University, the University of Akron, and Oberlin College. The Cleveland metropolitan region is also served by local community colleges.

HOUSING

In 1990, Cleveland had a total of 224,311 housing units, a decline of 6.4 percent from the previous decade. Owner-occupied units comprised less than 50 percent of all occupied housing units. Despite the decline in the number of units, the Cleveland area has significant housing cost advantages due to a relatively ample housing market. A number of surveys conducted in the mid-1990s found Cleveland metropolitan area housing costs to be considerably lower than those in comparable U.S. metropolitan areas. The city estimates that average housing costs are 40 percent lower in the Cleveland region. Recent studies found the average price of a single-family home to be 35 percent lower than in other major metropolitan areas. The city was also found to have the second lowest median housing cost among major metropolitan areas—the average price for single-family houses was half that of homes in Los Angeles. While much of the recent housing development is in the suburbs, growing demand for downtown housing has spurred new luxury apartment construction. Growing demand among young urban professionals for spacious dwellings in the downtown districts in the 1990s has stimulated the renovation of Cleveland's historic warehouse district and older downtown area buildings. The city has set a goal to build 10,000 new housing units by the year 2000.

CULTURE, THE ARTS, AND ENTERTAINMENT

Cleveland's leading artistic and cultural institutions are the Cleveland Museum of Art, Severance Hall (home to the Cleveland Orchestra), the Cleveland Museum of Natural History, the Garden Center of Greater Cleveland, Karamu House, and the Rock and Roll Hall of Fame. The city is home to three professional sports teams, including the Indians, who play baseball at Jacobs Field, a new 42,000-seat downtown stadium; the Cavaliers, who play basketball at the new Gund Arena, and the Lumberjacks, a minor-league hockey team. In 1996, Cleveland lost its football team to Baltimore. However, in the wake of the move, Cleveland's mayor, Michael White, secured an agreement to acquire a new team from the National Football League to begin play in a new stadium in 1999.

CATEGORY	DATA	YEAR	AREA
LOCATION & ENVIRONMENT			
Area	77 square miles	1995	City
	199.4 square kilometers		City
Elevation	660 feet/216.5 meters		City
January Temperature	24.8 degrees Fahrenheit	1961–1990	City
	−4.0 degrees Celsius	1961–1990	City
July Temperature	71.9 degrees Fahrenheit	1961–1990	City
	22.2 degrees Celsius	1961–1990	City
Annual Precipitation	36.6 inches/930 millimeters	1961–1990	City
POPULATION & DEMOGRAPHY			
Population	1,700,000	1996	Metro
Projected Population	1,900,000	2015	Metro
Growth Rate	0.2%	1990–1995	Metro
Growth Rate	12.5%	1995–2015	Metro
Density	6,526 per square mile	1992	City
	2,520 per square kilometer		
Gender			
Males	46.9%	1990	City
Females	53.1%	1990	City
Age			
Under 18	26.9%	1990	City
18–64	59.6%	1990	City
Over 65	14.0%	1990	City
VITAL STATISTICS			
Births per 1,000 Residents	21	1988	City
Deaths per 1,000 Residents	12	1988	City
Infant Mortality Rate	17 per 1,000 live births	1988	City
ECONOMY			
Total Workforce	212,443	1990	City
Trade	20.3%	1990	City
Manufacturing	23.1%	1990	City
Health Services	10.6%	1990	City
Finance, Insurance, Real Estate	5.6%	1990	City
Public Administration	4.6%	1990	City
TRANSPORTATION			
Passenger Vehicles	217,284	1990	City
HOUSING			
Total Housing Units	224,311	1990	City
Persons per Unit	2.2	1990	City
Owner-Occupied Units	47.9%	1990	City

(continued)

CATEGORY	DATA	YEAR	AREA
HEALTH CARE			
Hospitals	15	1991	City
EDUCATION			
Total Students	124,443	1991	City
Primary and Secondary	77.7%	1991	City
Higher	22.3%	1991	City

Sources: Department of Economic and Social Affairs, Population Division. *Urban Agglomerations, 1996.* New York: United Nations, 1997; U.S. Bureau of the Census. *County and City Data Book 1994.* Washington, DC: U.S. Government Printing Office, 1994; and United Nations Center for Human Settlements. *Compendium of Human Settlements Statistics.* New York: United Nations, 1995.

Copenhagen
DENMARK

LOCATION

The capital and largest city in Denmark, Copenhagen is situated on the islands of Zealand and Amager, at the southern end of the sound that connects the Skagerrak, an arm of the North Sea, and the North Sea to the Baltic. Lying at 43 feet (13 meters) above sea level, Copenhagen covers some 1,960 square miles (5,260 square kilometers) of territory. The city is located approximately 160 miles northeast of Hamburg, Germany, and some 300 miles southwest of Stockholm, Sweden.

Though located relatively far north, the city has a surprisingly mild climate, tempered by its proximity to the sea. Average temperatures in summer are 72 degrees Fahrenheit (22.2 degrees Celsius), while winter temperatures usually remain above freezing on average. The city receives about 23.3 inches (591.8 millimeters) of precipitation annually, most of it in the form of rain, with the occasional winter snowfall.

POPULATION AND DEMOGRAPHY

The Copenhagen metropolitan area has a population of approximately 1.3 million. With a growth rate hovering around zero, the city's population is not expected to increase over the next twenty years. The county of Copenhagen, with its many open spaces and even farmland, has a density of just 1,800 persons per square mile (670 per square kilometer), though conditions in the city center are far more crowded. The city's age profile is typical for northern European cities. About one fourth of the city is under 20, and another 23.2 percent is over 60. In addition, Copenhagen has one of the highest rates of single-parent families in the world, with some 40 percent of all births occurring out of wedlock.

Danes make up the vast majority of the city's population, though there are also significant minorities of other Scandinavian peoples, as well as large immigrant and guest worker communities from southern Europe and Turkey. Virtually all Danes are Protestant, while many of the immigrant workers are Catholic or Muslim. Except among the latter, religious practice is low in the city. Copenhagen's small Jewish community is one of the best-preserved in Western Europe, having been saved from the Nazis by the heroic efforts of the non-Jewish population of the city.

HISTORY

While humans have been inhabiting the islands that now make up Copenhagen since prehistoric times, the first historical references to the site come from the tenth century, when the presence of a small fishing village is mentioned. In the late twelfth century, the Bishop Absalon of Roskilde built a castle on an islet in the harbor and fortified the town with ramparts and a moat. In 1445, Copenhagen was made the capital of the early Danish state. During the wars of the Protestant Reformation of the seventeenth century, the city was sacked several times by both Protestant and Catholic armies.

Even so, the city continued to thrive as a major trading center in the Baltic Sea area, a position it established for itself by the late sixteenth century. Numerous municipal buildings, religious institutions, private dwellings, and commercial establishments were built during this period. During the wars with Sweden in the mid-seventeenth century, the city was besieged for two years. Being constructed largely from wood, the city suffered two serious fires in the eighteenth century.

The medieval-era ramparts were torn down in 1856, when the city began to expand rapidly in population. Copenhagen was occupied for much of World War II but was a center of passive resistance to the Nazi regime. In the years since, Copenhagen has shifted from a fishing and sea-going economy to a largely commercially oriented one. In 1973, Denmark joined the European Union, though its people have resisted full integration.

GOVERNMENT AND POLITICS

As the capital of Denmark, Copenhagen has a reputation for participatory democracy and lenient laws on drug use and prostitution. Copenhagen is situated inside one of the *amtscommuner*, or counties, that make up the country. The *amtscommuner* are governed by a council, elected by universal suffrage. In addition, the city itself is run by a council, also elected by universal suffrage, which chooses an executive from its own members. Most of the long-term planning and environmental issues are handled by the *amtscommune*, while day-to-day municipal functions are handled by the city council.

ECONOMY

Like Denmark itself, Copenhagen's economy supports one of the highest living standards and most egalitarian distributions of wealth in the world. Both of these things are aided by the fact that the national government provides a wide array of public services. In addition, the workforce has one of the highest union membership rates of any country in the world.

Copenhagen's economy has been dominated by trade and finance since the end of World War II. Virtually all of the nation's major companies, banks, and insurance companies are headquartered in the city. All banks are under government supervision, with representatives of the public serving on their boards of directors. Copenhagen's position as a trading city goes back to medieval times, as does its reputation as a major fishing port.

Its industrial sector is small, but with a high value-added component. Most of the manufacturers are small and specialize in light consumer goods, like textiles, electronics, and fish and food processing, the latter utilizing output from the nation's highly productive farmland. The city is also a major port and tourist center. Most of the city's import and export trade is conducted with the United Kingdom and Germany.

TRANSPORTATION

Copenhagen is well connected to the rest of Scandinavia and Europe by a complex system of highways, railways, and ferries. The country's rail system is government-owned and -operated, as are many of the intercity bus lines. Numerous bridges connect the islands on which the city is located with the Danish mainland, as well as with Sweden, across the sound. The city's harbor handles over 6,000,000 metric tons of freight annually. Much of Copenhagen's international air connections are handled by Scandinavian Airlines (SAS), owned by a Danish-Norwegian-Swedish consortium. There are also long-distance ferry lines connecting the city to the Danish-administered Faroe Islands.

Metropolitan traffic is handled largely by buses, trolleys, and commuter railways. City inhabitants own 503,540 cars, roughly one for every two persons. Bicycles remain a popular form of transportation, and an extensive system of bike lanes and paths runs through the metropolitan area.

HEALTH CARE

As in all of Denmark, health care is provided free to all inhabitants. The medical system is quite modern and the city has an extremely good health profile. The death rate is an exceptionally low 4.8 per 1,000 and the infant mortality rate is just 7.9 per 1,000 live births. The city has one hospital bed for every 125 citizens. And while the patient-to-physician ratio is a relatively high 357 to 1 (equivalent to 2.8 physicians per 1,000 residents), this fact is compensated for by the healthy lifestyle of the city's inhabitants and the thousands of alternative health care practitioners who work in the metropolitan area.

EDUCATION

Copenhagen has an extensive primary and secondary school system, as well as one of the finest network of day care centers in Europe. This latter system is made necessary by the high proportion of single-parent households. In addition, the city is home to some 65,000 university students. The largest number attend the University of Copenhagen. Other institutions of higher education include the Technical University of Denmark, founded in 1829, the Royal Veterinary and Agricultural College, established in 1856, the Engineering Academy of Denmark, founded in 1957, and the Copenhagen School of Economics and Business, established in 1917 and considered to be one of the finest such schools in the world.

HOUSING

Copenhagen has one of the finest and best-maintained housing stocks of any city in Europe. Much of the population lives in small apartment buildings scattered throughout the metropolitan area, most of them built since World War II. Because of the high rate of single-family households, the occupancy rate is a low two persons per unit. The city's layout has been planned with plenty of green spaces interspersed among built-up areas.

CULTURE, THE ARTS, AND ENTERTAINMENT

Copenhagen is famous throughout the world for its liberal attitude and tolerance of alternative lifestyles. Cohabitation is as common as marriage, and births out of wedlock are quite high even by northern European standards. Thus, the city has a rather relaxed style of living.

The city is also home to most of the major cultural institutions of Denmark, including the Royal Theater, the Royal Danish Ballet, the Danish Radio Symphony Orchestra, the Royal Danish Conservatory, and the Royal Danish Academy of Fine Arts. Its arts and crafts scene is highly developed, with its specialty being modern furniture and decorative objects for the home.

The city's population is also highly involved in recreational activities. Shooting clubs, gymnasiums, and rowing associations are quite popular, as are spectator and participatory soccer games. The many waterways make sailing and windsurfing popular as well.

CATEGORY	DATA	YEAR	AREA
LOCATION & ENVIRONMENT			
Area	1,960 square miles	1997	City
	5,260 square kilometers		City
Elevation	43 feet/13 meters		City
January Temperature	36 degrees Fahrenheit		City
	2.2 degrees Celsius		City
July Temperature	72 degrees Fahrenheit		City
	22.2 degrees Celsius		City
Annual Precipitation	23.3 inches/591.8 millimeters		City
POPULATION & DEMOGRAPHY			
Population	1,300,000	1996	Metro
Projected Population	1,300,000	2015	Metro
Growth Rate	−0.3%	1990–1995	Metro
Growth Rate	0.0%	1995–2015	Metro
Density	1,800 per square mile	1983	City
	670 per square kilometer		
Gender			
Male	48.5%	1997	City
Female	51.5%	1997	City
Age			
Under 20	23.1%	1997	City
20–59	55.8%	1997	City
Over 60	23.2%	1997	City
VITAL STATISTICS			
Births per 1,000 Residents	6.2	1997	City
Deaths per 1,000 Residents	4.8	1997	City
Infant Mortality Rate	7.9 per 1,000 live births	1997	City
ECONOMY			
Workforce	308,782	1997	City
Agriculture	0.5%	1997	City
Manufacturing	12.7%	1997	City
Construction	5.0%	1997	City
Finance, Insurance, Real Estate	16.7%	1997	City
Trade	18.7%	1997	City
Services	37.1%	1997	City
Transport	8.9%	1997	City
Utilities	0.7%	1997	City

(continued)

CATEGORY	DATA	YEAR	AREA
TRANSPORTATION			
Cars	503,540	1996	City
Passenger Vehicles	310,000	1992	Region
HOUSING			
Housing Units	274,785	1995	City
New Housing Units	992	1995	City
Persons per Unit	2	1995	City
HEALTH CARE			
Physicians per 1,000 Residents	2.8	1992	Region
Hospital beds per 1,000 Residents	0.5	1992	Region
EDUCATION			
Total Students	170,000	1997	City
Primary	38.8%	1997	City
Secondary	22.9%	1997	City
Higher	38.2%	1997	City

Sources: *Annual Statistics Denmark.* Copenhagen, Denmark: Denmark Statistical Bureau, 1997; Department of Economic and Social Affairs, Population Division. *Urban Agglomerations, 1996.* New York: United Nations, 1997; United Nations Center for Human Settlements. *Compendium of Human Settlements Statistics.* New York: United Nations, 1995; and Eurostat *Regions Statistical Yearbook.* Brussels, Belgium: Statistical Office of European Communities, 1996.

Dakar
SENEGAL

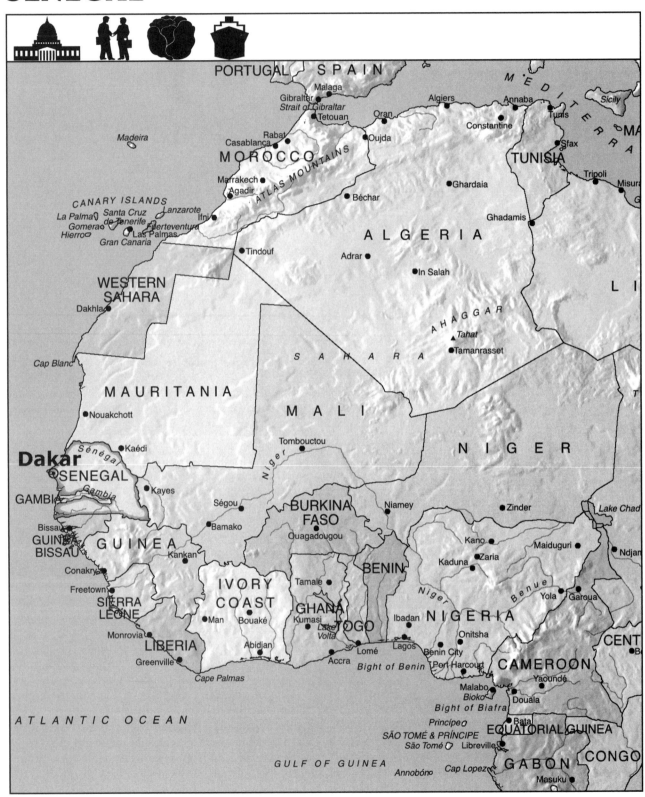

LOCATION

Located near the westernmost tip of Africa, Dakar is the capital, main port, and largest city of Senegal. The city, at an elevation of 131 feet (40 meters), is located 1,700 miles south-southwest of Casablanca, Morocco, and 1,420 miles west-northwest of Lagos, Nigeria. It has a warm, tropical climate and is semiarid. Summer is hot, with daytime temperatures of 88 degrees Fahrenheit (31.1 degrees Celsius), while the winter climate is mild, with temperatures averaging 79 degrees Fahrenheit (26.1 degrees Celsius). Precipitation is light, at about 21.3 inches (541 millimeters) annually, most falling in the summer months.

POPULATION AND DEMOGRAPHY

With its population of 1.8 million, the Dakar metropolitan area dominates Senegal demographically; over 50 percent of the nation's population lives in and around the city. Its high growth rate—about 5 percent annually from 1950 to 1990—has begun to slow in recent years. During the 1990s, the city has grown by only 4.0 percent annually, a rate that is expected to drop below 2 percent early in the next century. The natural population increase has been augmented by large flows of people from the countryside, at a rate of between 15,000 and 60,000 annually. Much of this influx is a result of the severe and lasting drought that has affected the region over the past two decades. And, like many African cities, Dakar has a predominantly young population, with well over half the city's residents under the age of 20. Dakar is relatively spacious and uncrowded, with a density of just over 2,700 persons per square mile (1,000 per square kilometer).

As a magnet for people from all over the country, Dakar's population is a mix of Wolof, Fulani, Serer, and Tukulor peoples, with the first two groups predominating. French, however, is the language of government and is spoken by much of the city's population, though in varying degrees of fluency. About 90 percent of the population is Islamic, with small Catholic and traditional religious groups.

HISTORY

Dakar was founded by the French in 1858 as a way to safeguard the interests of its merchants who had been settling there for decades. Through the early nineteenth century, much of the trade conducted in the region was in slaves. Gorée Island, an infamous slave trading fort and now a UNESCO World Heritage site, is located just off the coast. From 1904 until Senegal's independence from France in 1960, Dakar served as the administrative center of French West Africa. Wide boulevards and elegant, Parisian-inspired buildings are a legacy of that era.

The city has experienced major expansion since the end of World War II, when it served as a temporary headquarters for the Free French forces. The city has several contrasting districts, including a modern southern district of public institutions, a northern business district, and industrial areas to the north and east of the city.

GOVERNMENT AND POLITICS

From 1960 until 1980, Senegal was ruled by the leader of the independence movement, Leopold Senghor, a world-renowned poet and statesman. A brief confederation with Gambia has led to joint defense, foreign, and monetary policies.

Like the other nine regions in the country, greater Dakar is divided into departments and arrondissements. Each region is ruled by a governor, whose rule is coordinative and who is served by two deputy governors, one dealing with planning and the other with administration. An elected regional assembly deals with taxation. Dakar city has its own elected municipal council.

ECONOMY

Approximately 90 percent of Senegal's manufacturing capacity and wage-paying jobs are located in the Dakar metropolitan area. Nearly half of the city's production is in peanut-processing—the major commercial crop in the Senegalese countryside—and textiles, much of which are manufactured from locally-grown cotton. Other industries include food processing, electronics, metal-working, paper, timber, and fish canning and drying.

With its magnificent harbor—perhaps the finest in West Africa—Dakar is also an important shipping and transportation hub for products going into and out of Francophone, West Africa. In 1885, the French completed the first major railway in western Africa, which eventually connected Dakar to the Niger River valley. Major exports include agricultural oils—most especially peanut—phosphates and aluminum. Imports include foodstuffs and energy products. The city's Leopold Senghor Airport is a major hub for flights between West Africa and Europe.

As the center of the national government, Dakar supports a large government sector. It also boasts a significant tourist industry, attracting French travelers in search of sun and sea and black American tourists interested in African history.

HEALTH CARE

After experiencing a major upsurge in infant and child mortality rates in the 1980s, the government embarked upon a large and successful vaccination program. Some 62 percent of the city's children have now been immunized against tuberculosis, diphtheria, measles, and yellow fever. While Dakar boasts six major hospitals and seven major clinics, these are not evenly distributed throughout the city, over half being located in the well-to-do areas. The ratio of physicians to patients was 0.2 per 1,000 residents as of 1988.

EDUCATION

The city has seen some improvement in its educational numbers. Over half the population above the age of 6 has had some schooling; school enrollment for boys age 7 to 12 is about 80 percent, and for girls in this age group it is about 65 percent. Still, only about 30 percent of the population over the age of 15 can read and write, with the rates for older citizens and women lagging significantly behind. The University of Dakar, founded in 1957, is the country's major institution of higher learning.

HOUSING

Like many African cities, Dakar has a central core of permanent housing and a vast periphery of shantytowns, known by the French term *bidonvilles*. To deal with the vastly expanding population, the government has embarked on several major housing projects.

This process began under the French in the 1950s and has continued after independence. These projects usually involved giving plots of land to people willing to build their own houses. As of 1989, approximately 11,000 plots had been distributed, though a waiting list for another 39,000 remained. In 1979, the government established a housing bank to help provide low-interest loans to those interested in building a home of their own. Other housing projects have been initiated by the World Bank and the European Community Fund for Development. Because of high construction costs, however, a severe housing crisis continues to plague the city.

Dakar's sewage system serves only the oldest and wealthiest parts of the central city, and the most densely packed peripheral areas suffer from serious sewage problems. Only about half the city enjoys regular trash pickup.

Water represents another serious problem for the city. Located in a semiarid climate suffering from drought, the city has experienced a major water shortfall of about 6.2 million gallons daily since the end of the 1980s. Only middle- and high-income areas have indoor plumbing, with the rest of the city forced to resort to public water taps. About 80 percent of the dwellings in the city are connected to the electrical grid.

CULTURE, THE ARTS, AND ENTERTAINMENT

Among Dakar's most popular tourist destinations is nearby Gorée Island. Not only the site of Africa's largest trading fort from the slaving era, the island also boasts several archeology and ethnography museums, as well as a village of working craftspeople. There is one major park in the city and a zoo. In addition, the city is well known for its elegant tree-lined boulevards and its many fine beaches. Dakar is also the center of Senegal's small but productive filmmaking industry, the largest in French-speaking Africa.

CATEGORY	DATA	YEAR	AREA
LOCATION & ENVIRONMENT			
Elevation	131 feet/40 meters	1995	City
January Temperature	79 degrees Fahrenheit		City
	26.1 degrees Celsius		City
July Temperature	88 degrees Fahrenheit		City
	31.1 degrees Celsius		City
Annual Precipitation	21.3 inches/541.0 millimeters		City
POPULATION & DEMOGRAPHY			
Population	1,800,000	1995	City
Projected Population	3,500,000	2015	City
Growth Rate	4.0%	1990–1995	City
Growth Rate	104.3%	1995–2015	City
Density	2,700 per square mile	1995	City
	1,000 per square kilometer		
Age			
Under 20	56.8%	1988	City
20–59	38.2%	1988	City
Over 60	18.7%	1988	City
VITAL STATISTICS			
Deaths per 1,000 Residents	7.6	1988	City
ECONOMY			
Commercial Foods	26.0%	1985	Metro
Mechanics and Electronics	15.0%	1985	Metro
Construction	13.0%	1985	Metro
Chemicals	11.0%	1985	Metro
Wood and Paper Products	7.0%	1985	Metro
Mining	6.0%	1985	Metro
HOUSING			
Residents in Permanent Housing	89%	1988	Metro
HEALTH CARE			
Hospitals	6	1988	City
Clinics	7	1988	City
Physicians per 1,000 Residents	0.2	1988	City
Youth Vaccinated	62%	1990	City
EDUCATION			
Educational Enrollment (7–13)			
Males	79%	1988	Metro
Females	64%	1988	Metro

Sources: Department of Economic and Social Affairs, Population Division. *Urban Agglomerations, 1996.* New York: United Nations, 1997; Pison et al. *Population Dynamics of Senegal.* Washington, DC: National Academy Press, 1995; and United Nations Center for Human Settlements. *Compendium of Human Settlements Statistics.* New York: United Nations, 1995.

Dallas, Texas

USA

LOCATION

Dallas, the second most populous city in Texas and the seventh most populous city in the United States, lies on the edge of the Edwards Plateau in northeastern Texas. The city covers a land area of 342.4 square miles (886.8 square kilometers) at the center of Dallas County. The Trinity River flows south through the center of Dallas to Lake Livingston and Galveston Bay and empties into the Gulf of Mexico. The city is the largest population center of Dallas–Fort Worth, a metropolitan area that encompasses Dallas County and extends west to Tarrant County. The metropolitan area's major municipalities include Fort Worth, Arlington, Irving, Grand Prairie, Mesquite, and Richardson. Dallas is 160 miles west of Louisiana and Arkansas, 70 miles south of Oklahoma, 250 miles northwest of Houston, Texas's largest city, and about 200 miles northeast of Austin, Texas's state capital. From 1961 to 1990, Dallas had an average low temperature of 44.6 degrees Fahrenheit (7.0 degrees Celsius) in January and an average high temperature of 85.9 degrees Fahrenheit in July (30.0 degrees Celsius). Over the same thirty-year period, the city had an annual average rainfall of 36.1 inches (916 millimeters).

POPULATION AND DEMOGRAPHY

In the twelve years from 1980 to 1992, Dallas's population grew by 13 percent to 1,022,497, making the city the eighth largest in the United States. The city's population encompasses about one third of the regional population, and Dallas itself has a density of 2,986 persons per square mile (1,153 persons per square kilometer). Dallas's population growth reflects that of the region as a whole, which expanded by 57 percent in the twenty-five-year period from 1970 to 1995, to over 3,612,000 residents. In 1996, the regional population totalled 3.7 million. The prodigious regional population growth over the past two decades is projected to continue at a more modest rate into the next century, reaching 4,400,000 by the year 2015. Whites are the largest population segment in the city, with 54.5 percent, followed by blacks, with about 29 percent, and Asians and Pacific Islanders, who are about 2 percent of all city residents. Approximately one of every five Dallas residents (210,240) is of Hispanic origin, and one of every eight city residents is foreign-born. Dallas is home to about 5,000 Native Americans. The city's age distribution is skewed toward the young. About 25 percent are under 18 years of age, 65 percent are between ages 18 and 64, and less than 10 percent are over 65 years of age. There are 96.8 males for every 100 females in Dallas, a higher ratio of males to females than is found in most major American cities.

HISTORY

Dallas was settled by Europeans in the early 1840s and incorporated as a town in 1856 and as a city in 1871. The city expanded rapidly in the second half of the nineteenth century as a major distribution center for the area's agricultural exports. The city's importance grew with the coming of the railway in the 1870s. The discovery of oil reserves in the region during the 1930s enhanced the city's economic importance, continuing well into the twentieth century. Although the city's population continued to grow at the end of the century, most of the regional growth in the 1980s and 1990s has taken place in the city's suburbs and rapidly expanding outlying cities.

GOVERNMENT AND POLITICS

City government consists of a mayor, serving as chief elected official and presiding officer of the city government, and a fifteen-member city council, the primary legislative body for municipal affairs. The mayor's primary responsibilities are to preside over council meetings, represent the city at official and ceremonial occasions, and create committees and appoint their members. The city council sets policy, approves annual budgets, plans capital improvements, and determines tax policy. The city manager, a non-elected official, is the chief administrative and executive officer over Dallas's government. The city manager implements policy decisions made by the mayor and council, prepares a recommended budget, and coordinates city operations and programs.

ECONOMY

Dallas is the center of one of the largest and most diverse economic regions in the United States. The primary industries in the region are agribusiness and oil and gas production, distribution, and marketing. The city and its surrounding region are a major finance, banking, and insurance center. The regional economy is diversifying into production industries, including electronic and electrical equipment, aircraft, food processing, machinery, electrical and metal products, automobile assembly, chemicals, clothing, meat packing, transportation equipment, and publishing.

From 1980 to 1990, Dallas's civilian labor force expanded by 14.8 percent, to 641,739 workers. The city has developed a diversified economy that has reduced its traditional dependence on the oil and gas industries. Much of the new workers entered the wholesale and retail trade sector, which accounted for 22.9 percent of all workers. The manufacturing sector, which remains important to the city, employed 14.1 percent of all workers, followed by finance, insurance, and real estate, with 10.9 percent; health services, with 6.8 percent; and public administration, with 2.7 percent of the labor force. In the early 1990s, the city's unemployment rate was lower than those in competing large urban centers of the Midwest and Northeast. The city's poverty rate of 18 percent is considerably lower than in most other regional and national cities.

TRANSPORTATION

The private motor vehicle is the predominant mode of transportation in the Dallas–Fort Worth metropolitan area. Only 6.7 percent of Dallas's population uses public transportation, about the same percentage as in Houston, but a considerably smaller share than other major U.S. and international cities with much smaller populations. There is little support for the expansion of public transit to moderate the growth of private automotive traffic on the region's roads. In 1983, the Dallas Area Rapid Transit (DART) system began a 20-mile light rail service in the city. DART is expected to be extended over the next ten years; however, there is growing public opposition to expanding the system through a rail corridor between Dallas and Fort Worth. The city is a major railway and highway center for regional and intercontinental freight traffic. Dallas–Fort Worth International Airport is a major national airline hub.

HEALTH CARE

Dallas has twenty-two community hospitals and 5,555 hospital beds, a rate of 552 hospital beds for every 100,000 residents in the city. The city has a relatively youthful population compared to other major U.S. cities; this tends to moderate the growth in health care costs. Dallas has the third lowest infant mortality rate among the ten largest U.S. cities. In 1988, the city reported an infant mortality rate of 9.3

infant deaths per 1,000 live births. The Dallas Department of Environmental and Health Services is responsible for disease prevention and health education. The department coordinates city resources for the promotion of health, maintains the Bureau of Vital Statistics, is responsible for environmental services (including air pollution and smoking ordinances), overseas food and commercial sanitation, and operates two multipurpose health centers and an adolescent health center. Other department responsibilities also cover child health services, including immunization, low-birth-weight-baby services, maternal health, planning and evaluation, and the Women, Infants, and Children (WIC) program.

EDUCATION

A nine-member board of education presides over the Dallas public school system. The elected board sets policy, identifies needs, establishes goals and priorities, and oversees the 208 schools and over 9,000 teachers in the school system. The city has a total of 245,901 students enrolled in its schools, of which 164,072 (67 percent) were primary and secondary students. Students enrolled in the city's higher education institutions account for 27 percent of the enrolled population. About 90 percent of all primary and secondary school students are in public schools. The student body is primarily composed of minorities—Hispanic students, who are about 45.5 percent of the student body, and African-Americans, who comprise 41.5 percent of students. Whites comprise 10.9 percent of school students. A relatively sizable 27.1 percent of the city's population over 25 years of age has a bachelor's degree or higher. The major postsecondary educational institutions in the region are Southern Methodist University, the University of Dallas, University of Texas–Dallas, and the Baylor University Nursing School. The city is also home to three major theological training schools, including Dallas Baptist University, Dallas Christian College, and Dallas Theological Seminary.

HOUSING

The Dallas Department of Housing is responsible for the revitalization, stabilization, and maintenance of neighborhoods to stimulate the production of affordable housing. The department provides home-ownership assistance, administers programs for housing revitalization, and supports the development of affordable rental units. Various programs provide temporary shelter for the recently homeless and target low-income neighborhoods that have abandoned and substandard housing. The Dallas Housing Authority assists residents in identifying low-income public housing and rentals. Since the early 1990s, federal funding directed at expanding the supply of public and subsidized housing has diminished, seriously straining the supply of affordable housing for the city's low-income population.

To accommodate Dallas's rapidly growing population, the number of housing units increased by 19.2 percent between 1980 and 1990, to 465,600 units. Dallas has a housing vacancy rate of over 13.6 percent. Owner-occupied units comprise over 44 percent of the city's occupied housing units.

CULTURE, THE ARTS, AND ENTERTAINMENT

The city's major museums are the Dallas Museum of Art and the Dallas Museum of Natural History. Dallas has a major symphony orchestra, an opera company, and a major theater venue. The city has 396 public parks, with nearly 22,000 acres of parkland. The Dallas metropolitan area has four major league professional sports teams, including the well-known Dallas Cowboys football team, which plays in the nearby suburb of Irvine; the Texas Rangers baseball team, which plays in the rapidly growing city of Arlington; and the Dallas Mavericks basketball team and Dallas Stars hockey team, which both play in Reunion Arena. The region is a major center for high school and collegiate football and baseball.

CATEGORY	DATA	YEAR	AREA
LOCATION & ENVIRONMENT			
Area	342.4 square miles	1995	City
	886.8 square kilometers		City
Elevation	435 feet/142.7 meters		City
January Temperature	44.6 degrees Fahrenheit	1961–1990	City
	7.0 degrees Celsius	1961–1990	City
July Temperature	85.9 degrees Fahrenheit	1961–1990	City
	30 degrees Celsius	1961–1990	City
Annual Precipitation	36.1 inches/916.0 millimeters	1961–1990	City
POPULATION & DEMOGRAPHY			
Population	3,700,000	1996	Metro
Projected Population	4,400,000	2015	Metro
Growth Rate	2.3%	1990–1995	Metro
Growth Rate	21.3%	1995–2015	Metro
Density	2,986 per square mile	1992	City
	1,153 per square kilometer		
Gender			
Males	49.2%	1990	City
Females	50.8%	1990	City
Age			
Under 18	25.0%	1990	City
18–64	65.3%	1990	City
Over 65	9.7%	1990	City
VITAL STATISTICS			
Births per 1,000 Residents	20	1988	City
Deaths per 1,000 Residents	8	1988	City
Infant Mortality Rate	9.3 per 1,000 live births	1988	City

(continued)

CATEGORY	DATA	YEAR	AREA
ECONOMY			
Total Workforce	641,739	1990	City
Trade	22.9%	1990	City
Manufacturing	14.1%	1990	City
Health Services	6.8%	1990	City
Finance, Insurance, Real Estate	10.9%	1990	City
Public Administration	2.7%	1990	City
TRANSPORTATION			
Passenger Vehicles	598,733	1990	City
HOUSING			
Total Housing Units	465,600	1990	City
Persons per Unit	2.2	1990	City
Owner-Occupied Units	44.1%	1990	City
HEALTH CARE			
Hospitals	22	1991	City
EDUCATION			
Total Students	245,901	1991	City
Primary and Secondary	73%	1991	City
Higher	27.0%	1991	City

Sources: Department of Economic and Social Affairs, Population Division. *Urban Agglomerations, 1996.* New York: United Nations, 1997; U.S. Bureau of the Census. *County and City Data Book 1994.* Washington, DC: U.S. Government Printing Office, 1994; and United Nations Center for Human Settlements. *Compendium of Human Settlements Statistics.* New York: United Nations, 1995.

Damascus
SYRIA

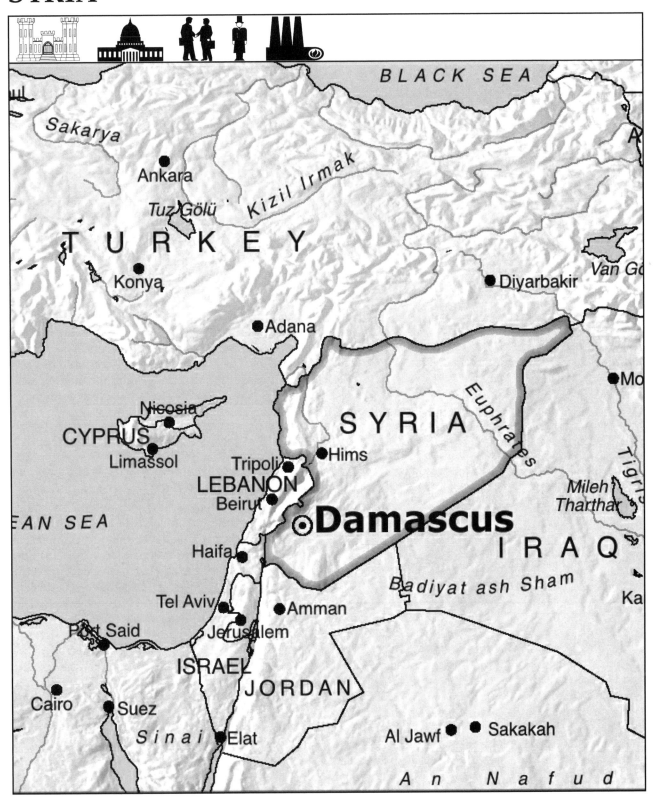

LOCATION

Damascus, Syria's capital and largest city, is located in the southwestern section of the country. Situated on a broad plain 2,362 feet (850 meters) above sea level with the Qasiyun Mountains to the west, the city has been called the "Pearl of the East" for the beauty of its medieval Islamic architecture. It is located approximately 140 miles northeast of Jerusalem and about 100 miles north of Amman, Jordan. The city's climate is a desert one, with dry and extremely hot summers and moderate winters. Average January and July temperatures are 44.5 and 80 degrees Fahrenheit (6.9 and 26.7 degrees Celsius), respectively. Damascus receives only 8.6 inches (152 millimeters) of rain annually, usually in the winter months.

POPULATION AND DEMOGRAPHY

The city of Damascus has a population of about 1.4 million, with another 700,000 in the surrounding suburbs. Like many other Middle Eastern cities, Damascus has seen rapid growth since 1960, when its population numbered about 550,000. The metropolitan area has a growth rate of approximately 2.6 percent annually and is expected to grow to about 3.5 million by 2015. The population of Damascus is almost entirely Arab, with small populations of Kurds and Druze and tens of thousands of Palestinians exiled from Israel and the Occupied Territories. Most Damascenes are Muslim, though there is a small population of Eastern Orthodox and Catholic Christians and a tiny community of Jewish residents. Most of the city's Muslims are Sunni, but a minority practice the Shiite and Alawite variants. The latter group includes many important government officials, including Syrian president Hafez al-Assad.

HISTORY

Along with Jericho in Palestine, Damascus is believed to be one of the oldest continuously inhabited cities in the world, dating back to at least the second millennium before Christ. Ruled by the Assyrian, Hellenistic, Roman, and Byzantine Empires, the city came under the rule of invading Arab armies in the seventh century A.D. From 661 to 750, it served as the capital of the Islamic caliphate and ruled much of the Middle East and North Africa. The city was conquered by the Ottomans in 1516, who ruled until World War I, when Damascus and Greater Syria (including Lebanon) were handed over to the French by a League of Nations Mandate. The French ran the city until 1946, when Damascus was made the capital of independent Syria.

GOVERNMENT AND POLITICS

From independence until the 1960s, Syrian politics were tempestuous, with numerous rebellions in the provinces and a succession of weak governments. Gradually, the Baath Party—eventually led by Hafez al-Assad—took control and stabilized the country's politics, though at the cost of some political freedoms. It has ruled continuously since. Up through the 1990s, the state-administered economy has taken major responsibility in providing for the population's basic economic needs. During the 1967 and 1973 wars with Israel, Damascus was attacked from the air and bombed by Israeli warplanes, though damage was light.

Damascus is ruled by a governing board known as the *muhafazah*, one of fourteen in the country. The nation's president appoints a governor who administers the city with the assistance of a council made up of elected and appointed members. The powers of both the governor and council are limited, however, since Syria is a strongly centralized state, with most decisions made by the national government.

ECONOMY

Since World War II, the city has become a major industrial center, largely through government initiative. All large enterprises in virtually all sectors of the economy are state-owned and-run. The Syrian government plays a dominant role in the Damascus economy, administering major services, building new infrastructure, and subsidizing basic food, medical, and housing needs. Thus far, Syria has resisted Western pressure to privatize the economy even as the privatization trend sweeps through neighboring countries in the Middle East. Thus, although the private sector is relatively small, the government involvement in the economy has allowed the country to escape the high poverty rate that often prevails in other developing countries in the Middle East.

Primary manufactured goods produced in the Damascus metropolitan area include textiles and garments, leather products, food and beverage products, tobacco, aluminum products, and petrochemicals. Most of the products manufactured in the metropolitan area are consumed domestically or exported to Western Europe and nearby Arab countries.

Damascus has retained its reputation for fine artisanry, which dates back to the Middle Ages. Many skilled craftspersons produce finely worked metal products and elegant textiles. It is also the main distribution point for Syrian imports and exports, with much of the latter going to the countries of the Arabian peninsula and the Persian Gulf. The city hosts a major international trade exposition each autumn.

TRANSPORTATION

Only in the past two decades have motor vehicles replaced the once-dominant horse, donkey, and camel as a primary form of transportation. The city is currently served by a network of 1,800 miles (3,000 kilometers) of paved roads, though the enormous growth in private and public vehicles has put them under great pressure. Public transportation remains the primary means of getting around the city. Most commuters get to and from work by bus. Thousands of private minibuses supplement the public transport system, most following fixed routes. Damascus is connected to the Syrian port of al-Ladiqah by a railroad. The international airport, located 20 miles east of the city, accommodates both domestic and international air passengers.

HEALTH CARE

Damascus has a relatively modern and extensive health care system. Forty-six hospitals serve the metropolitan area, and the city has a ratio of 2 physicians per 1,000 residents. About half the country's doctors live in the capital and divide their services between government hospitals and private clinics. The ratio of hospital beds to population is rising, but still below that of most developed countries. Some of the main diseases that afflict Damascenes include respiratory diseases and gastrointestinal illnesses.

EDUCATION

The vast majority of Damascus's school-age children attend public, private, or religious-run institutions. There are approximately 2,400 primary and second-ary schools in the metropolitan area. In addition, there are a number of schools run by the United Nations for the children of Palestinian refugees. The city is host to the University of Damascus, founded in 1923. There are also a number of technical academics and teacher colleges that provide specialized postsecondary education.

HOUSING

Rapid population growth has led to a vast expansion of the city's area. Both planned and unplanned suburbs continue to encroach on agricultural lands and forests. Damascus is divided into several districts that surround an old walled city of medieval origins. Some inner areas of the city were laid out by the French and feature wide boulevards; many of the city's elite inhabitants reside in large houses in these districts. As far as utilities are concerned, many experts believe that Damascus's limited water supplies cannot support any more people. The city receives most of its supply from the nearby Barada River through a system of aqueducts and pipes originally constructed centuries ago but updated over the years. It gets most of its electricity from a hydroelectric plant on the Euphrates River in the northwest part of the country.

CULTURE, THE ARTS, AND ENTERTAINMENT

Damascus is a center of culture as well as politics and industry. Much of the cultural life of the city is supported by the government, including several museums featuring antiquities, crafts, and modern art. The government also manages much of the publishing industry; three of the country's dailies and most of its magazines are published in the city, which is also a center of book production. TV and radio ownership is widespread. Radio broadcasts are generally in Arabic, though there are programs in English, French, and Turkish. TV content is generally in Arabic, with local productions being supplemented by Egyptian programming. The city boasts three major sports stadiums, and soccer is the number one spectator and participant sport, though basketball has been increasing in popularity in recent years.

CATEGORY	DATA	YEAR	AREA
LOCATION & ENVIRONMENT			
Elevation	2,362 feet/850 meters	1995	City
January Temperature	44.5 degrees Fahrenheit		City
	6.9 degrees Celsius		City
July Temperature	80 degrees Fahrenheit		City
	26.7 degrees Celsius		City
Annual Precipitation	8.6 inches/218.4 millimeters		City
POPULATION & DEMOGRAPHY			
Population	2,100,000	1996	Metro
Projected Population	3,500,000	2015	Metro
Growth Rate	2.6%	1990–1995	Metro
Growth Rate	71.9%	1995–2015	Metro
Gender			
Male	52%	1994	City
Female	48%	1994	City
VITAL STATISTICS			
Births per 1,000 Residents	38.5	1987	City
Deaths per 1,000 Residents	5	1987	City
ECONOMY			
Total Workforce	341,000	1984	City
Official Unemployment	3.0%	1984	City
HOUSING			
New Housing Units	869	1987	City
HEALTH CARE			
Hospitals	46	1987	City
Physicians per 1,000 Residents	2	1987	City
EDUCATION			
Total Students	482,077	1987	City
Primary	44.9%	1991	City
Secondary	39.7%	1991	City
Higher	15.4%	1991	City

Sources: Department of Economic and Social Affairs, Population Division. *Urban Agglomerations, 1996.* New York: United Nations, 1997; *Statistics of World Large Cities.* Tokyo, Japan: Tokyo Metropolitan Government, 1992 and 1994; United Nations Center for Human Settlements. *Compendium of Human Settlements Statistics.* New York: United Nations, 1995; and *United Nations WLC.* New York: United Nations, 1984.

Delhi, Union Territory of Delhi
INDIA

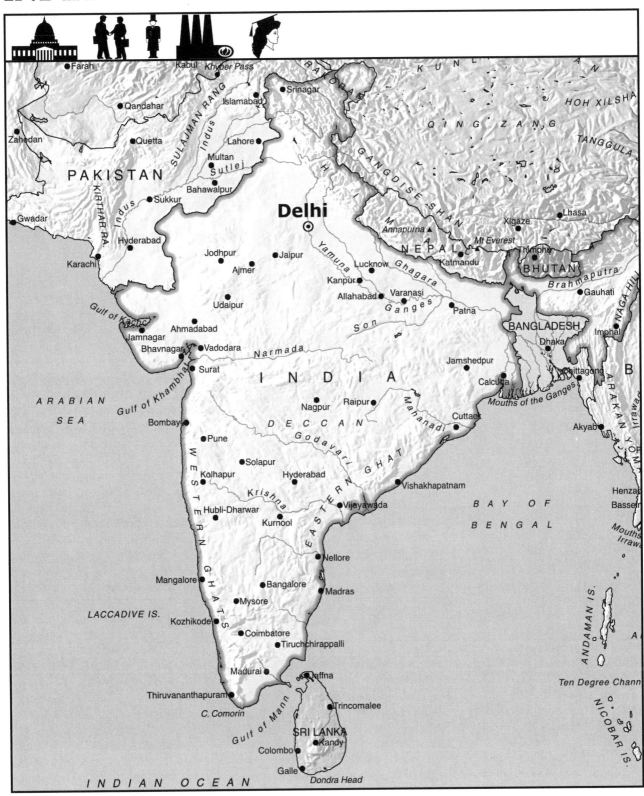

Farah, Kabul, Khyber Pass, Srinagar, Qandahar, Islamabad, Zahedan, Quetta, Lahore, Multan, PAKISTAN, Indus, Sutlej, Bahawalpur, KIRTHAR RA., Sukkur, Delhi, Gwadar, Hyderabad, Karachi, Jodhpur, Jaipur, Yamuna, Lucknow, Ghagara, NEPAL, Annapurna, Mt Everest, Thimphu, Xigaze, Lhasa, QING ZANG, GANGDISE SHAN, TANGGULA, HOH XILSHA, KUNL, Ajmer, Kanpur, Katmandu, BHUTAN, Udaipur, Allahabad, Varanasi, Ganges, Patna, Brahmaputra, Gauhati, Gulf of Kachch, Ahmadabad, Son, BANGLADESH, Imphal, Jamnagar, Dhaka, NAGA HIL, Bhavnagar, Vadodara, Narmada, INDIA, Jamshedpur, Chittagong, Surat, Calcutta, Mouths of the Ganges, ARABIAN SEA, Gulf of Khambhat, DECCAN, Nagpur, Raipur, Mahanadi, Cuttack, Akyab, ARAKAN YOM, Bombay, Godavari, EASTERN GHAT, Vishakhapatnam, Henza, Basse, Pune, BAY OF BENGAL, Solapur, Krishna, Hyderabad, Kolhapur, Vijayawada, Mouths Irrawa, Hubli-Dharwar, Kurnool, EASTERN GHATS, ANDAMAN IS., WESTERN GHATS, Nellore, Mangalore, Bangalore, Madras, Ten Degree Chann, Mysore, LACCADIVE IS., Kozhikode, Coimbatore, NICOBAR IS., Tiruchchirappalli, Madurai, Jaffna, Thiruvananthapuram, Trincomalee, C. Comorin, Gulf of Mann, SRI LANKA, Kandy, Colombo, Galle, INDIAN OCEAN, Dondra Head

LOCATION

Delhi is the largest metropolitan area in north India and the third largest in the country as a whole, after Mumbai and Calcutta. The city is situated on the banks of the Yamuna River, a branch of the Ganges River. Delhi, at 695 feet (212 meters) above sea level, is approximately 700 miles north-northeast of Bombay and about 800 miles northwest of Calcutta. The greater Delhi metropolitan area covers 549 square miles (1,483 square kilometers).

Delhi's climate is subtropical, but with great ranges of temperatures between winter and summer months. The average temperatures in winter and summer are 57 and 87.5 degrees Fahrenheit (13.9 and 30.8 degrees Celsius), respectively, though the thermometer frequently tops 100 degrees in the hot, dry summer months preceding the monsoon rains. Delhi receives approximately 25.2 inches (640 millimeters) of rain annually, mostly during the monsoon season, which lasts from August to November.

POPULATION AND DEMOGRAPHY

The population of the Delhi metropolitan area is estimated at 10.3 million, with a density of approximately 17,763 persons per square mile (6,579 per square kilometer). During the early 1990s, the growth rate was nearly 4 percent annually, though this figure is expected to drop to about half that early in the next century. It is estimated that the population will reach 16.9 million in 2015. The city's population is unevenly balanced by gender, with approximately 110 men for every 100 women. In addition, the city's population is quite youthful, with 46.1 percent under the age of 20. The city includes a variety of ethnic groups from northern India. The population majority is Hindu, with a substantial minority of Muslims.

HISTORY

Unlike the other great cities of India, which were largely founded by the British for purposes of trade, Delhi has a much longer history. A settlement named Indraprastha on the site of the modern city was mentioned in the Hindu epic the Mahabarata, in 1400 B.C. The first reference to the name *Delhi* dates to the first century B.C., when Raja Dhilu gave his name to his new capital city. The city then served as the capital of a series of Hindu kingdoms through the fourteenth century A.D., when Timur destroyed the city and the Hindu kings moved their capital to nearby Agra. Ba-

bur reestablished the city as the capital of the first great Mughal Muslim empire in India in 1526. While the capital of subsequent Mughal rulers was moved to other cities, Emperor Shah Jehan—builder of the Taj Mahal—returned Delhi to prominence when he situated his capital there in 1638. The collapse of the Mughal Empire in the mid-eighteenth century led to fifty years of relative anarchy in the Delhi area, until the region was captured by British forces in 1803.

The British expanded the city but were expelled for several months during the great Indian Mutiny of 1857. In 1912, the British moved their capital from Calcutta to the newly laid-out city of New Delhi, on Delhi's southern perimeter. New Delhi was completed in 1931. Sixteen years later, New Delhi became the capital of independent India. Since independence, both Delhi and New Delhi have grown dramatically in population and built-up territory.

GOVERNMENT AND POLITICS

From independence until 1956, Delhi was administered as a separate state. In 1956, Delhi and New Delhi were proclaimed a special Union Territory, with a unified corporation set up to govern both rural and urban areas of the territory. Under the 1966 Delhi Administration Act, a three-tier administration was established, consisting of a lieutenant governor served by an executive council, an elected metropolitan council, and a municipal corporation. Both the lieutenant governor and executive council, which administer the territory, are appointed by India's president. The metropolitan council is a purely deliberative body, while the popularly elected municipal corporation has authority over most of the territory's autonomous bodies. New Delhi, however, has separate committees, appointed by the president, to administer its municipal services.

ECONOMY

While public and private services are the main basis of the territory's economy, employing 26.3 percent of the 1.8-million-person workforce, Delhi's industrial base has grown dramatically in recent decades. Manufacturing, which employs about 33.9 percent of the workforce, includes industries involved in food and beverage production, electrical equipment, metal products, rubber and plastic goods, transport equipment, machinery, paper products, agricultural implements, and transport equipment. Delhi is also a major commercial center, with a host of major financial institutions headquartered there or maintaining branches in the city. Of the 26.2 percent of the workforce employed in the commercial sector, however, most are involved in retail trade.

TRANSPORTATION

Delhi is the major transportation hub for northern India. Some five railway lines and nine major roads connect the city to other metropolises in India, as well as Nepal and Pakistan. Intracity transportation is dominated by 16,000 public buses, commuter railroads, taxis and motorized rickshaws, and private automobiles. Though the metropolitan area has some 16,000 miles (24,400 kilometers) of paved roads, congestion remains a major problem, with approximately 2.2 million vehicles sharing those roads, the largest figure for any Indian city. The territory's administrative bodies have been trying to move industries and commercial enterprises to the periphery of the city, where many of the workers live. This plan is intended to alleviate some of the congestion and the serious air pollution problem that plagues the city. The city government is also trying to promote the use of bicycles by subsidizing their price.

HEALTH CARE

The government of the Union Territory of Delhi has made health care a high priority. The metropolitan area has 127 hospitals and clinics, with a ratio of patients to physicians of 2,665 to 1. Because of the heavy burden of air and water pollution, a high percentage of the city's inhabitants suffer from gastrointestinal and respiratory illnesses. The infant mortality rate is roughly 33 deaths per 1,000 live births, a relatively low rate for major Indian cities.

EDUCATION

Delhi has an extensive educational system. As of 1989, there were over 1,800 primary schools, with a student population of 700,000, and almost 700 secondary schools, educating nearly 300,000 pupils. Approximately 22 percent of the population of the city

was attending school in the early 1980s. The city also hosts several important institutions of higher learning, including the University of Delhi and its many affiliated colleges and research institutions, the Indian Agricultural Research Institute, the Indian Institute of Technology, and the All India Institute of Medical Sciences.

HOUSING

Though significantly less crowded than Mumbai and Calcutta, Delhi nevertheless suffers from a serious housing shortage. While the city has nearly two million dwellings, the occupancy rate is relatively high, at over five persons per housing unit. Since the 1950s, the government has removed over a million citizens from slums to new housing projects, the largest such shift in the world. Still, the city faces major problems in the provision of utilities. Water is in short supply, especially during the premonsoon months in the late spring and early summer, and the major source, the Yamuna River, is polluted by untreated sewage and industrial waste. Approximately 70 percent of the city's population lives in homes that are not connected to the sewage system. Of the 212 million liters pumped through the city's sewage system, only about half was treated even partially.

CULTURE, THE ARTS, AND ENTERTAINMENT

With its population from various parts of India, Delhi has a cosmopolitan culture. However, much of the traditional dance, music, and poetry forums have given way to more modern forms of entertainment. Western influence is strong in the cultural life of the city's population today. Cinemas and nightclubs often feature Western films and music. At the same time, however, the city still has an exceptional network of libraries and museums, including the national library and archives in New Delhi. Delhi is also a city of gardens, fountains, and notable examples of Mughal architecture, the latter highlighted by the internationally renowned Red Fort. The city also hosted the Asian Games of 1982 and had many facilities built for that event. Delhi is home to the largest zoological gardens in the country.

CATEGORY	DATA	YEAR	AREA
LOCATION & ENVIRONMENT			
Area	549 square miles	1995	Metro
	1,483 square kilometers		Metro
Elevation	695 feet/212 meters		Metro
January Temperature	57 degrees Fahrenheit		Metro
	13.9 degrees Celsius		Metro
July Temperature	87.5 degrees Fahrenheit		Metro
	30.8 degrees Celsius		Metro
Annual Precipitation	25.2 inches/640.1 millimeters		Metro
POPULATION & DEMOGRAPHY			
Population	10,300,000	1996	Metro
Projected Population	16,900,000	2015	Metro
Growth Rate	3.9%	1990–1995	Metro
Growth Rate	69.5%	1995–2015	Metro
Density	17,763 per square mile		Metro
	6,579 per square kilometer		Metro
Gender			
Male	54.8%	1990	Metro
Female	45.2%	1990	Metro
Age			
Under 20	46.1%	1981	Metro
20–59	49.3%	1981	Metro
Over 60	4.6%	1981	Metro
VITAL STATISTICS			
Births per 1,000 Residents	30.7	1992	Metro
Deaths per 1,000 Residents	6.9	1992	Metro
Infant Mortality Rate	33 per 1,000 live births	1992	Metro
ECONOMY			
Total Workforce	1,760,955	1990	Metro
Manufacturing	33.9%	1990	Metro
Agriculture	0.7%	1990	Metro
Construction	0.3%	1990	Metro
Trade	15.8%	1990	Metro
Finance, Insurance, Real Estate	10.4%	1990	Metro
Services	26.3%	1990	Metro
Transport	6.0%	1990	Metro
TRANSPORTATION			
Total Vehicles	2,200,000	1993	Metro
COMMUNICATIONS			
Telephones per 1,000 Residents	64	1992	Metro

(continued)

CATEGORY	DATA	YEAR	AREA
HOUSING			
Housing Units	1,860,748	1992	Metro
New Housing Units	2,865	1992	Metro
Persons per Unit	5.2	1992	Metro
HEALTH CARE			
Hospitals	82	1992	Metro
Clinics	45	1992	Metro
Physicians per 1,000 Residents	0.5	1992	Metro
EDUCATION			
Total Students	981,766	1989	Metro
Primary	71.0%	1989	Metro
Secondary	29.0%	1989	Metro

Sources: Department of Economic and Social Affairs, Population Division. *Urban Agglomerations, 1996.* New York: United Nations, 1997; *Statistics of World Large Cities.* Tokyo, Japan: Tokyo Metropolitan Government, 1992 and 1994; and United Nations Center for Human Settlements. *Compendium of Human Settlements Statistics.* New York: United Nations, 1995.

Denver, Colorado

USA

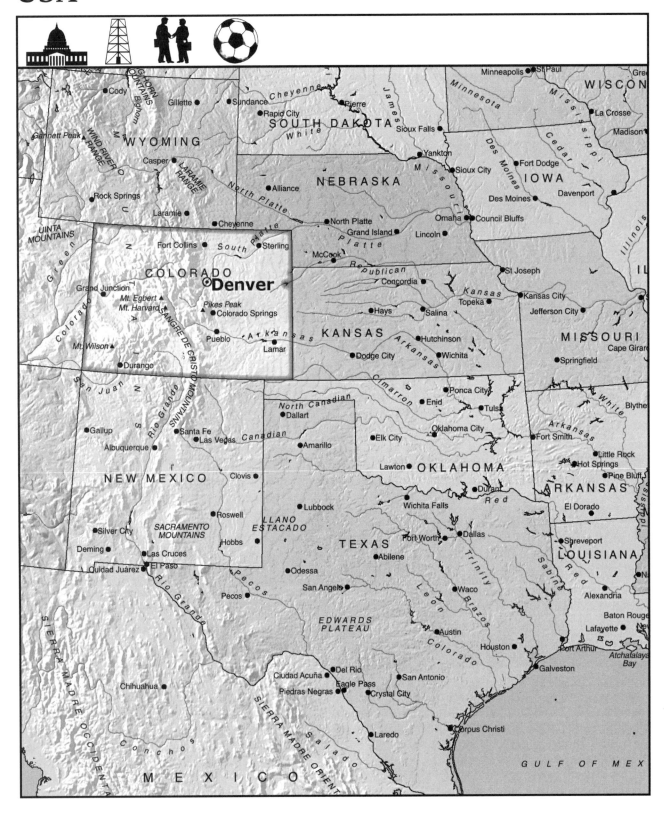

LOCATION

Denver, the capital of Colorado and the state's most populous city, lies on a plain 15 miles east of the Front Range and the eastern side of the Rocky Mountains in northeast Colorado. The city is situated at the intersection of the South Platte and Cherry Rivers, about 350 miles west of the geographic center of the United States. The city, which encompasses Denver County, occupies a land area of 153.3 square miles (397.1 square kilometers) at an elevation of 5,280 feet (1,600 meters) above sea level. To Denver's north, south, and west are the Rocky Mountains, which rise to altitudes of greater than 10,000 feet above sea level. To the city's east is the Great Plains of Colorado, extending into the states of Kansas and Nebraska. The Denver metropolitan area radiates from Denver County to Adams, Arapahoe, Boulder, Douglas, and Jefferson Counties. The region includes the rapidly growing suburban municipalities of Arvada, Boulder, Commerce City, Englewood, Lakewood, Littleton, Longmont, Thornton, Westminster, and Wheat Ridge. The city is located 25 miles southeast of Boulder, 60 miles due south of Fort Collins, 70 miles north of Colorado Springs, and about 100 miles south of Cheyenne, Wyoming. The Rocky Mountain ski resort region is located about 100 to 200 miles to the city's west. From 1960 to 1991, the average temperature ranged from a low of 29.7 degrees Fahrenheit in January (-1.3 degrees Celsius) to a high of 73.5 degrees in July (23.1 degrees Celsius). Over the same thirty-year span, Denver's average annual precipitation was 15.4 inches (391 millimeters).

POPULATION AND DEMOGRAPHY

Between 1980 and 1992, Denver's population declined by 8,834, or 1.8 percent, to 483,858. The central city of Denver has a density of 3,156 persons per square mile (1,218 persons per square kilometer). Although the central city population has declined over the past decade, the metropolitan area is growing at a faster rate than major American metropolitan areas. Between 1970 and 1995, the metropolitan area population grew by nearly 24 percent, to 1.6 million. The regional population is projected to expand to 1.9 million by the year 2015. Many new residents are moving into rural settlements beyond the city's metropolitan area. A major factor in the region's population growth is the migration trend from California to the Rocky Mountain West that began in the 1980s and accelerated in the 1990s. As a major commercial

and transportation center with an expanding economy, Denver is a primary beneficiary of much of the population growth. The central city population, which in 1996 was 23.5 percent of the metropolitan area's population, is predominantly white: 70 percent of the city's population is white, 12 percent is black, and just over 2 percent is Asian and Pacific Islander. One of every five Denver residents is of Hispanic descent. Foreign-born residents make up 7.4 percent of the population, and the city has a ratio of 94.8 males per 100 females. The city's age distribution is spread fairly evenly: 22 percent of city residents are under 18, 64 percent are between ages 18 and 64, and 13.8 percent are over 65 years of age.

HISTORY

In 1858, gold was found in the Denver region, and a gold rush ensued during the 1860s. The city was settled in the 1860s and became the capital of Kansas Territory in 1867. In the two decades between 1870 and 1890, the city's population expanded from under 5,000 to over 100,000. The 1893 economic depression severely undermined the economy by exposing the city's dependence on gold. Subsequently, gold production peaked, and the city's economic base diversified into manufacturing, oil, sugar, and cattle industries. In 1902, Denver was incorporated as a city and county, and in 1906, the U.S. Mint was built in Denver.

GOVERNMENT AND POLITICS

Denver's city government is comprised of a mayor and city council. The mayor is responsible for administration and management, and the city council is responsible for enacting laws and regulations governing the city. The mayor is elected at large. The thirteen-member city council is made up of eleven officials who are elected from local districts and two officials who are elected at large.

ECONOMY

The six-county Denver regional area is the center of commerce and industry in the U.S. Rocky Mountain region. The labor market in the central city contracted by 3.6 percent between 1980 and 1990, to 266,486 workers. However, the labor market showed signs of expansion in the 1990s. Wholesale and retail trade was the leading sector in the central city, employing 20.4 percent of all workers, followed by manufacturing, with 10 percent, health services, with 9.2 percent, finance, insurance, and real estate, with 8.8 percent, and public administration, with 5.6 percent of the labor market. The city has a poverty rate of 17.1 percent, higher than the national average, but considerably lower than the rate in competing American cities in the Northeast, Midwest, and Pacific coast. Over the last decade, Denver's unemployment rate has been consistently lower than the national average and those of competing major cities. Much of the city's economic vitality can be attributed to its relatively diverse economic base. The city's largest employers are telecommunications, hospitals and health care, food services, air transportation, aerospace, defense, computer software, beverages, and electrical utilities. The largest manufacturing industries are food processing, rubber products, railroad equipment, machinery, mining, metal products, missile parts, instruments, chemicals, plastics, furniture, and luggage.

With the support of state and local governments, the information technology industry has emerged as a major industry of the regional economy in the 1990s. The key sectors of the industry are computer equipment manufacturing, cable television, and telecommunications. The region has a lower cost of living and lower state and local taxes than coastal cities.

TRANSPORTATION

The Denver area's public transportation system includes a short light rail transit line and an extensive public bus system. Since the mid-1970s, civic leaders have debated the value of expanding the public transportation network in the region. The regional highways are becoming more congested due to rapid population growth and the lack of a regional rapid transit network that could take some of the pressure off the overcrowded road and beltway system. In 1980, a referendum to build a $1 billion 73-mile regional light rail system was rejected by voters. A smaller 5.3-mile rail line in the central city region was constructed, but regional planners see an urgent need for a more extensive system. Still, there remains strong opposition among business leaders to expanding the rail system into Denver's outlying suburbs. In the mid-1990s, Denver gained prominence as a major air transportation center with the construction of the new Denver International Airport, the first ma-

jor airport built in the United States since the early 1970s. The $5 billion airport replaced Stapleton International Airport, which had experienced serious traffic congestion. However, startup mechanical and software difficulties of the automated baggage handling system delayed the airport's opening and significantly increased startup costs. About 13 percent of Denver's labor force uses public transportation to commute to work, higher than major Texas cities, but a significantly lower rate than European and U.S. coastal cities.

HEALTH CARE

The city has a total of eleven hospitals with 3,487 hospital beds, a rate of 746 hospital beds per 100,000 Denver residents. Health care delivery in the region is primarily through managed-care organizations. Although health care is delivered efficiently, there are growing questions about the quality of and access to health care, as in other U.S. regions. In addition, a large number of younger moderate- and low-income residents continue to lack health insurance coverage. Two serious public health problems identified by civic leaders are the growth in unsafe drug use and HIV infection. City leaders have reversed their long opposition to the distribution of clean needles to help reduce the transmission of HIV that occurs through sharing of needles. The city is also attempting to grapple with environmental hazards, including the long history of hazardous wastes and radioactive materials that are produced and disposed of in the region.

EDUCATION

In 1990, Denver's school enrollment was 108,999, or about 22 percent of the city's population. Students enrolled in primary and secondary schools comprised nearly 60 percent (64,453) of all students. The number of students in Denver's public schools continued to rise during the 1990s. Public school students now make up 85.9 percent of all students. The Denver public school system is expanding cooperative programs with Head Start and local government leaders to improve child care and early childhood education and to provide comprehensive year-round learning by expanding educational programs into the summer. The Denver school system is seeking to educate local primary and secondary school students to eventually form a productive part of an advanced high-technology regional economy. With approximately 29 percent of residents over 25 years of age holding a bachelor's degree or higher, the city has one of the most educated populations among major U.S. cities. The region's largest postsecondary educational institutions are the University of Denver, the University of Colorado at Denver, Regis University, Metropolitan State College of Denver, and the Colorado Institute of Art. The region is also served by local community colleges.

HOUSING

In 1990, the central city of Denver had a total of 239,636 housing units, an increase of 5 percent over ten years earlier. The central city has a housing vacancy rate of 12 percent. Owner-occupied housing units comprise 49.2 percent of all occupied housing units in the city. A large share of the central city's housing growth is due to the growing attractiveness of the older downtown area to younger affluent migrants from the suburbs. As a result, much of the new housing growth consists of expensive luxury units that many long-term residents cannot afford to buy. However, compared to other major U.S. urban regions, the Denver metropolitan area as a whole has relatively moderate housing costs.

CULTURE, THE ARTS, AND ENTERTAINMENT

Over the past decade, government leaders in the metropolitan Denver area have endeavored to expand the area of its parkland and open spaces to protect and enhance the region's physical environment. The region has over a hundred parks; several museums, including the Denver Art Museum, the Museum of Western Art, and the Denver Museum of Natural History; several amusement parks; the U.S. Mint; and the Botanic Gardens. The city is just 15 miles east of the Rocky Mountains. The decline in government support for the arts has seriously reduced access to classical music and the arts in the city. Due to a shortage of funds, the Denver Symphony filed for bankruptcy in 1989 and was replaced by the Colorado Symphony. However, the city has recently supported the revitalization of the central city through building new sports facilities and renovating entertainment venues to encourage the growth of the arts, cultural, and sports communities. The goal of the efforts is to promote the downtown area as an attraction to local residents and tourists. The city has major league professional teams in five sports, including the Denver Broncos football team, the Denver Nuggets basketball team, the Colorado Rockies baseball team, the Colorado Avalanche hockey team, and the Colorado Rapids soccer team.

CATEGORY	DATA	YEAR	AREA
LOCATION & ENVIRONMENT			
Area	153.3 square miles	1995	City
	397.1 square kilometers		City
Elevation	5,280 feet/1,645 meters		City
January Temperature	29.7 degrees Fahrenheit	1961–1990	City
	−1.3 degrees Celsius	1961–1990	City
July Temperature	73.5 degrees Fahrenheit	1961–1990	City
	23.1 degrees Celsius	1961–1990	City
Annual Precipitation	15.4 inches/391 millimeters	1961–1990	City
POPULATION & DEMOGRAPHY			
Population	1,600,000	1996	Metro
Projected Population	1,900,000	2015	Metro
Growth Rate	1.1%	1990–1995	Metro
Growth Rate	17.3%	1995–2015	Metro
Density	3,156 per square mile	1992	City
	1,218 per square kilometer		City
Gender			
Males	48.7%	1990	City
Females	51.3%	1990	City
Age			
Under 18	22%	1990	City
18–64	64%	1990	City
Over 65	13.8%	1990	City
VITAL STATISTICS			
Births per 1,000 Residents	17	1988	City
Death per 1,000 Residents	9	1988	City
Infant Mortality Rate	10.7 per 1,000 live births	1988	City
ECONOMY			
Total Workforce	266,486	1990	City
Trade	20.4%	1990	City
Manufacturing	10.0%	1990	City
Health Services	9.2%	1990	City
Finance, Insurance, Real Estate	8.8%	1990	City
Public Administration	5.6%	1990	City
TRANSPORTATION			
Passenger Vehicles	297,578	1990	City
HOUSING			
Total Housing Units	239,636	1990	City
Persons per Unit	2	1990	City
Owner-Occupied Units	49.2%	1990	City
HEALTH CARE			
Hospitals	11	1991	City

(continued)

CATEGORY	DATA	YEAR	AREA
EDUCATION			
Total Students	108,999	1991	City
Primary and Secondary	66.5%	1991	City
Higher	33.5%	1991	City

Sources: Department of Economic and Social Affairs, Population Division. *Urban Agglomerations, 1996.* New York: United Nations, 1997; U.S. Bureau of the Census. *County and City Data Book 1994.* Washington, DC: U.S. Government Printing Office, 1994; and United Nations Center for Human Settlements. *Compendium of Human Settlements Statistics.* New York: United Nations, 1995.

Detroit, Michigan

USA

LOCATION

Detroit, Michigan's most populous city, is located on the southeastern Michigan glacial lowland plain of the North American Great Lakes region. The city is located in northeastern Wayne County on the western bank of the Detroit River, opposite Windsor, Ontario, on a land area of 138.7 square miles (359.2 square kilometers). Detroit, the seat of Wayne County, is located approximately 20 miles north of the western shore of Lake Erie and 40 miles southwest of the southern shore of Lake Huron. Lake St. Clair is on the northeastern fringes of the city. The Detroit metropolitan area includes the municipalities of Canton, Dearborn, Dearborn Heights, Livonia, Redford, Taylor, and Westland, in Wayne County; Farmington Hills, Pontiac, Rochester Hills, Royal Oak, Southfield, Troy, Waterford, and West Bloomfield Township, in Oakland County; and Clinton, Roseville, St. Clair Shores, Sterling Heights, and Warren, in Macomb County. Detroit is approximately 40 miles northeast of Toledo, Ohio. Between 1961 and 1990, the average temperature ranged from a low of 24.7 degrees Fahrenheit (−4.1 degrees Celsius) in January to a high of 74.2 degrees Fahrenheit in July (23.4 degrees Celsius). Over the same thirty-year period the city had an average annual precipitation of 32.1 inches (815 millimeters).

POPULATION AND DEMOGRAPHY

After Chicago, Detroit is the largest city in the American Midwest, with a population of 1,012,110. The city's density is 7,297 persons per square mile (2,818 persons per square kilometer). From 1980 to 1992, Detroit's population declined by 15.9 percent, as nearly 200,000 residents fled the city for the suburbs and the American Sunbelt region. By the mid-1990s, the central city had 27.2 percent of the metropolitan area's population of 3,700,000. Between 1995 and 2015, the regional population is expected to grow by 10.5 percent, to 4,100,000. Since the late 1970s, white urban residents have migrated in droves to the suburbs, and blacks have emerged as a sizable majority population in Detroit. Based on 1990 census data, African-Americans comprised 77 percent of Detroit's population, followed by whites, with 22 percent, and Hispanics, with nearly 3 percent of the city's population. Foreign-born residents comprise 3.4 percent of the population. Detroit's age distribution is skewed toward the young—residents under 18 years of age are nearly 30 percent of all city residents. Older residents, over 65 years of age, make up 12.2 percent of the population. There are 86.5 males for every 100 Detroit females.

HISTORY

When French explorers reached Detroit in the early eighteenth century, indigenous Native Americans inhabited the region. In 1701, the French established Fort Pontchartrain on the Detroit River, which later reverted to British control. In 1796, the British ceded the fort to the Americans. Detroit became the capital of Michigan in 1805 and was formally incorporated as a city in 1815. Michigan gained statehood in 1837, and Lansing was named the state's capital in 1847. The defeat of the Native Americans and the expropriation of their territories in the early nineteenth century stimulated the region's growth. The city's importance expanded as new forms of transportation facilitated more rapid commercial transport and passenger travel in the nineteenth century. Major improvements in transportation during the nineteenth century began with the expansion of the canal system in the early part of the century, the development of railroads at midcentury, and the mass production of the automobile at the end of the century. Detroit became the industrial center of motor vehicle production in the early twentieth century, and in the 1930s and 1940s it became a major site of industrial strife between workers seeking union representation and manufacturers. In the late 1960s, Detroit's black residents revolted against police brutality and for greater economic opportunity, leading to the expansion of government programs. However, white flight to the suburbs and the general neglect of the central city followed in the 1970s through the 1990s, reducing tax revenue and resulting in a corresponding deterioration in education and housing.

GOVERNMENT AND POLITICS

Detroit has a mayoral and city council form of government. The mayor is responsible for administrative and executive affairs, and an eighteen-member city council is responsible for legislative affairs. In 1997, Detroit residents approved a referendum that allows the establishment and operation of casinos in the city. The mayor and city council members are elected officials.

ECONOMY

Detroit is the center of the U.S. automobile manufacturing industry and the headquarters of the three major U.S. automobile firms: General Motors, Ford, and Chrysler. Between 1980 and 1990, Detroit's civilian labor force contracted by 13.7 percent, to 444,898, reflecting the erosion of manufacturing employment. Manufacturing, with 20.5 percent of all city jobs, continues to dominate the local economy. The other leading sectors of the economy are wholesale and retail trade (18.5 percent), health services (11.4 percent), and public administration (7.7 percent). The creation of low-wage service sector jobs has reduced the city's high unemployment rate, which exceeded 13 percent in the early 1990s, to single digits. However, the city suffers from a very high rate of poverty—32.4 percent of all urban residents live below the poverty line, the highest poverty rate in the nation.

The major manufacturing industries in the region are automobiles and automobile parts and accessories, machinery and machine tools, iron and steel, metal products, pharmaceuticals, chemicals, tires, office machines, food processing, distilled liquor, and printing and publishing. Unemployment is higher in the central city than in the metropolitan area as a whole, where job growth has produced a tight labor market and reduced the jobless rate below the national average. Between January 1992 and June 1997, unemployment declined in the metropolitan area from a peak of nearly 11 percent to 4 percent. However, even as the regional economy has improved, employment in the automobile manufacturing industry, long the cornerstone of economic prosperity in the region, has continued to stagnate and decline.

The diversification out of basic manufacturing that has taken place in the Detroit metropolitan area through the 1990s has improved employment prospects. The key growth sectors are business services, engineering and management consulting firms, construction, health care services, producer services for the automobile industry, retailing, and services industries. The construction industry is benefiting from major public infrastructure projects under development, including a baseball stadium and football stadium in Detroit, three casinos, and a $1.6 billion expansion and upgrade of Detroit Metro Airport. Although technological advancement and economic restructuring have significantly increased efficiency and profitability in automobile production, the number of manufacturing jobs has actually declined. Since automobile production jobs tend to pay far higher wages than most service and retail jobs, average personal income has declined significantly over the past twenty years. Continued employment decline in automobile production and basic manufacturing into the late 1990s is projected to offset the strong job growth that has recently occurred in the construction, retail, and service industries. Regional economic forecasters predict that the services industry will be a major source of job growth in the twenty-first century. However, it remains to be seen if the region can educate and attract a highly skilled labor force and whether the recent employment growth in services will be accompanied by higher wages. To encourage greater economic activity in the Detroit downtown region, the city has approved casino gambling.

TRANSPORTATION

Greater Detroit area residents are more highly dependent on the motor vehicle for transportation than are inhabitants of other large U.S. and European cities. Only 10.7 percent of the city's labor force uses public transportation as a means to commute to work. Significantly smaller percentages use public transport in the suburbs and outlying municipalities. Detroit Metro Airport, a major North American air transport hub, is now undergoing expansion and renovations. Greater Detroit has major highways that link the city with major Midwest, Northeast U.S., and Canadian cities.

HEALTH CARE

Detroit's eighteen community hospitals and 6,245 hospital beds give the city a rate of 608 hospital beds per 100,000 persons. The greater Detroit area is served by sixty-four hospitals and two teaching and research centers: Detroit Medical Center and the University of Michigan Medical Center in Ann Arbor. The city's 1988 infant mortality rate of 21 deaths per 1,000 live births is significantly higher than the suburban infant mortality rate and about three times as high as the national average. After Washington, D.C., Detroit has the highest infant mortality rate among U.S. cities with over 200,000 residents.

EDUCATION

In 1990, approximately 71 percent of Detroit's 290,367 students attended primary and secondary schools, and 87.3 percent of these were in public educational institutions. The city's traditional reliance on manufacturing historically did not require the same degree of formal education required in most other industries. Only 9.6 percent of Detroit adults over age 25 have a bachelor's degree, the third lowest percentage among U.S. cities with populations exceeding 200,000. To improve the educational attainment of Detroit students, the Detroit public schools have embarked on a five-year strategic plan for the district. However, despite the relatively low percentage of educated adults, the region has nationally respected universities and colleges. The major postsecondary educational institutions in the metropolitan area are Wayne State University, the University of Detroit Mercy, the Detroit College of Law, Oakland University, and the University of Michigan at Dearborn. The University of Michigan at Ann Arbor is one of the leading public universities in the United States.

HOUSING

In 1990, Detroit had a total of 410,027 housing units, a 13 percent decline from the previous decade. Owner-occupied units comprised 52.9 percent of all occupied housing units. Although housing costs vary throughout the Detroit metropolitan area, the city had the lowest median housing value among the nation's seventy-seven cities with populations exceeding 200,000. During the 1990s, Detroit's poorly maintained 9,000 public housing units, which have provided housing for low-income, elderly, and disabled residents, have deteriorated significantly, causing many residents to move in search of alternative housing.

CULTURE, THE ARTS, AND ENTERTAINMENT

The major cultural institutions are the Detroit Symphony Orchestra, the Fort Wayne Military Museum, the Great Lakes Indian Museum, the Detroit Historical Museum, and the Detroit Institute of the Arts. The Detroit metropolitan area has major league professional sports teams in four competitive sports. The Detroit Tigers baseball team is moving into a new stadium slated for completion in the year 2000. The Detroit Lions football team is moving back to Detroit from Pontiac to a new stadium scheduled for completion in the year 2001. The Detroit Red Wings hockey team plays in the city, and the Detroit Pistons basketball team plays in the suburbs. The Detroit metropolitan area is also a center for major collegiate basketball and football.

CATEGORY	DATA	YEAR	AREA
LOCATION & ENVIRONMENT			
Area	138.7 square miles	1995	City
	359.2 square kilometers		City
Elevation	585 feet/191.9 meters		City
January Temperature	24.7 degrees Fahrenheit	1961–1990	City
	−4.1 degrees Celsius	1961–1990	City
July Temperature	74.2 degrees Fahrenheit	1961–1990	City
	23.4 degrees Celsius	1961–1990	City
Annual Precipitation	32.1 inches/815 millimeters	1961–1990	City
POPULATION & DEMOGRAPHY			
Population	3,700,000	1996	Metro
Projected Population	4,100,000	2015	Metro
Growth Rate	0.2%	1990–1995	Metro
Growth Rate	10.5%	1995–2015	Metro
Density	7,297 per square mile	1992	City
	2,818 per square kilometer		City
Gender			
Males	46.4%	1990	City
Females	53.6%	1990	City
Age			
Under 19	29.5%	1990	City
19–64	48.5%	1990	City
Over 65	12.2%	1990	City
VITAL STATISTICS			
Births per 1,000 Residents	19	1988	City
Deaths per 1,000 Residents	12	1988	City
Infant Mortality Rate	21 per 1,000 live births	1990	City
ECONOMY			
Total Workforce	444,898	1990	City
Trade	18.5%	1990	City
Manufacturing	20.5%	1990	City
Health Services	11.4%	1990	City
Finance, Insurance, Real Estate	6.2%	1990	City
Public Administration	7.7%	1990	City
TRANSPORTATION			
Passenger Vehicles	395,086	1990	City
HOUSING			
Total Housing Units	410,027	1990	City
Persons per Unit	2.5	1990	City
Owner-Occupied Units	52.9%	1990	City
HEALTH CARE			
Hospitals	18	1991	City

(continued)

CATEGORY	DATA	YEAR	AREA
EDUCATION			
Total Students	290,367	1991	City
Primary and Secondary	77.4%	1991	City
Higher	22.6%	1991	City

Sources: Department of Economic and Social Affairs, Population Division. *Urban Agglomerations, 1996.* New York: United Nations, 1997; U.S. Bureau of the Census. *County and City Data Book 1994.* Washington, DC: U.S. Government Printing Office, 1994; and United Nations Center for Human Settlements. *Compendium of Human Settlements Statistics.* New York: United Nations, 1995.

Dhaka (Dacca)
BANGLADESH

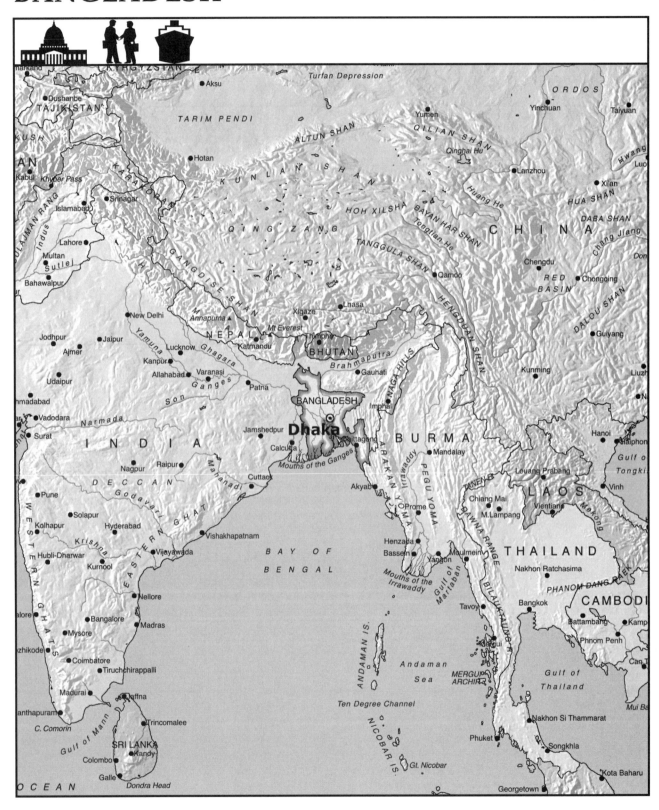

LOCATION

The capital and largest city in Bangladesh, Dhaka is located in the delta of the Ganges and Brahmaputra Rivers, approximately 125 miles from the Bay of Bengal. Situated at just 20 feet (6 meters) above sea level, the city is located roughly 160 miles to the northeast of Calcutta, India, and approximately 600 miles north-northwest of Yangôn, Myanmar. The metropolitan area of Dhaka covers roughly 2,800 square miles (7,500 square kilometers) of territory.

Dhaka has a tropical climate. Temperatures in summer and winter average 88 and 73.9 degrees Fahrenheit (31.1 and 23.3 degrees Celsius), respectively. The city receives an abundance of precipitation, some 98.4 inches (2,500 millimeters) per year, most falling in the monsoon months between August and November. The city is also in the path of cyclones generated in the Indian Ocean—including the great cyclone of 1970 that killed over 200,000 East Pakistanis—and its site in a river delta makes it prone to flooding, particularly in the monsoon season.

POPULATION AND DEMOGRAPHY

Dhaka had a population estimated at 9 million in 1996. This figure represents dramatic growth over previous decades: As late as 1950, the population was just 335,000. During the early 1990s, the city grew at a rate of 6.4 percent annually, though this figure is expected to diminish to half that early in the next century. Still, the population of the metropolitan area will more than double by the year 2015, reaching 19.5 million. Much of this growth has resulted from migrants from the countryside fleeing impoverished conditions and frequent flooding. Despite this influx, the metropolitan area has a relatively low density of roughly 613 persons per square mile (1,657 persons per square kilometer). The city's population has a ratio of 116 men for every 100 women, and 49.8 percent of the population is under the age of 20. The vast majority of the city's residents speak Bengali and practice the Islamic faith. English is widely spoken, particularly among the educated population.

HISTORY

While Dhaka's history can be traced as far back as the first century A.D., the city did not rise to prominence until the seventeenth century, when it served as the Mughal capital of Bengal, displacing Calcutta. It also grew into a major trading port in these years,

with important posts for British, Dutch, and French traders. The return of the capital to Calcutta and the decline of Mughal Muslim power reduced the city to a relative backwater in the eighteenth century. In 1765, Dhaka came under British rule, and it was organized as a municipality in 1864. It was the capital of Eastern Bengal and Assam province from 1905 until independence in 1947.

During the independence period, the city was racked by rioting and massacres as the minority Hindu population was forced to flee to West Bengal. Bangladesh was incorporated into Pakistan as East Pakistan. Under West Pakistani rule from 1947 to 1971, the city received a lower share of resources from the government, and repression of dissidents grew. Rising protests in favor of independence led to massacres by troops from West Pakistan and a war involving Bengali freedom fighters and Indian troops against the West Pakistan army.

GOVERNMENT AND POLITICS

In 1971, Bangladesh was declared an independent state and Dhaka was made its capital. Originally divided into 464 unequal subdistricts, Bangladesh moved to a more centralized form of government in 1991. The new plan lowered the number of districts and made them more equal in size. At the same time, the Dhaka metropolitan area was given its own overall administrative structure. The city itself is governed by a municipal council, which is elected by the citizens, and an executive appointed by the national government.

ECONOMY

While Dhaka was a major manufacturing city under Mughal rule, two hundred years of British rule undermined its industrial capacity by turning Bengal into a region producing commercial crops for export. Another twenty-five years of West Pakistani rule saw continued stagnation of the Dhaka and East Bengal economy, though industrialization did begin, a process that accelerated after Bangladeshi independence in 1971. The major industries include jute mills (for rope and burlap production), textile mills, rubber factories, woodworking shops, publishing, electrical equipment plants, and fertilizer factories. In recent years, the city's garment industry has grown dramatically, employing about a half million people, mostly women, by the mid-1990s. Of the workforce in 1981, 48.2 percent labored in the manufacturing sector. Dhaka is also the major commercial hub of Bangladesh. Most of the country's financial institutions are headquartered there. Just over one third of the workforce is involved in the commercial sector. As Dhaka is the country's capital, a significant portion of the workforce—some 14 percent—labors in the public sector.

TRANSPORTATION

Dhaka serves as the hub of Bangladesh's transportation network and is closely integrated into neighboring India's rail and highway system. Major rail lines connect Dhaka to the country's number two city, Chittagong, as well as Calcutta and Assam Province in India. Dhaka is also a major port, particularly for the heavy boat traffic that utilizes the country's complex and extensive river systems. Some 70,000 vessels carry half a million tons of freight and over ten million passengers annually.

Metropolitan traffic is highly congested. By a 1983 measure, 80,094 vehicles share crowded streets with rickshaws, pedicabs, motorcycles, pedestrians, and draft animals. While the city has an extensive public bus system and thousands of private minibuses, much of the population is too poor to afford them, and commutes by foot instead. Telephones, televisions, and radios are relatively rare, with a ratio of 93, 55, and 37 persons, respectively, for one of these items.

HEALTH CARE

Due to the high level of poverty, Dhaka suffers from severe health care problems. It is estimated that as much as 85 percent of the population suffers from mild to acute malnutrition. While the government has built dozens of neighborhood health care clinics, most are understaffed and lacking in supplies and equipment. The poor care offered in these clinics leads many sufferers to flood the city's fourteen hospitals. The ratio of citizens to physicians is a high 7,900 to 1 (equivalent to 0.1 physicians per 1,000 residents). The infant mortality rate is an extremely high 100 per 1,000 live births, higher than virtually any other city in Asia. The city's swampy locale and poor waste disposal lead to a high frequency of gastrointestinal illnesses.

EDUCATION

Dhaka has an extensive educational system. Approximately 800 primary and secondary schools in 1981 served 369,449 students. Still, poverty and the extensive use of child labor prevent the majority of the city's children from attending. The city is home to several major universities, including the University of Dhaka and its many affiliated colleges, and Jahangirnagar University. The population of university students in 1981 was just under 20,000.

HOUSING

While the national government has heavily emphasized family planning in recent years and while Dhaka receives a disproportionate share of government grants per capita, the city suffers from a severe shortage of housing, caused by the fact that much of the territory in and around the capital is frequently flooded and thus unsuited for construction. Because of the high price of land in the city center, most of the squatters and slums are situated on the periphery of the city, and make up a significant portion of the built-up area of the metropolitan area.

The city's water supply—plagued by leaks—is insufficient to keep up with population growth. Less than 40 percent of the city's dwellings are hooked up to the underground sewage system. This situation is exacerbated by the low-lying nature of the territory and by frequent flooding. Electrical supplies are inadequate, and the city experiences frequent outages.

CULTURE, THE ARTS, AND ENTERTAINMENT

The city has a vibrant cultural life and is home to the majority of the country's national cultural institutions. Like Calcutta, its counterpart in West Bengal, India, Dhaka is a major center of Bengali culture. There are numerous venues for dance, theater, and music, as well as galleries featuring both folk and fine arts. Dhaka is also home to thirty-four library branches and four museums. Cinemas are popular as well; the twenty-eight movie houses feature films from India, Hong Kong, and the United States.

CATEGORY	DATA	YEAR	AREA
LOCATION & ENVIRONMENT			
Area	2,767 square miles	1995	Metro
	7,470 square kilometers		Metro
Elevation	20 feet/6 meters		Metro
January Temperature	73.9 degrees Fahrenheit		Metro
	23.3 degrees Celsius		
July Temperature	88 degrees Fahrenheit		Metro
	31.1 degrees Celsius		
Annual Precipitation	98.4 inches/2,500 millimeters		Metro
POPULATION & DEMOGRAPHY			
Population	9,000,000	1996	Metro
Projected Population	19,500,000	2015	Metro
Growth Rate	6.4%	1990–1995	Metro
Growth Rate	128.1%	1995–2015	Metro
Density	613 per square mile	1993	Metro
	1,657 per square kilometer		
Gender			
Male	58.2%	1988	Metro
Female	41.8%	1988	Metro
Age			
Under 20	49.8%	1981	Metro
20–59	35.3%	1981	Metro
Over 60	14.9%	1981	Metro
VITAL STATISTICS			
Births per 1000 Residents	26.9	1981	Metro
Deaths per 1,000 Residents	7.8	1981	Metro
Infant Mortality Rate	100 per 1,000 live births	1981	Metro
ECONOMY			
Total Workforce	297,906	1981	Metro
Manufacturing	48.2%	1981	Metro
Trade	37.1%	1981	Metro
Services	14.0%	1981	Metro
TRANSPORTATION			
Cars	67,759	1983	Metro
Trucks	12,335	1983	Metro
COMMUNICATIONS			
Telephones per 1,000 Residents	11	1983	Metro
Televisions per 1,000 Residents	18	1983	Metro

(continued)

CATEGORY	DATA	YEAR	AREA
HOUSING			
Housing Units	518,612	1982	Metro
New Housing Units	7,002	1982	Metro
Persons per Unit	10.4	1982	Metro
HEALTH CARE			
Hospitals	14	1982	Metro
Clinics	41	1992	Metro
Physicians per 1,000 Residents	0.1	1982	Metro
EDUCATION			
Total Students	369,449	1981	Metro
Primary	50.7%	1981	Metro
Secondary	43.9%	1981	Metro
Higher	5.4%	1981	Metro

Sources: Department of Economic and Social Affairs, Population Division. *Urban Agglomerations, 1996.* New York: United Nations, 1997; *Statistics of World Large Cities.* Tokyo, Japan: Tokyo Metropolitan Government, 1992 and 1994; and United Nations Center for Human Settlements. *Compendium of Human Settlements Statistics.* New York: United Nations, 1995.

Dublin, Leinster
IRELAND

ATLANTIC
OCEAN

Malin Head

Tory Island

Aran Island · Gweedore

Rathlin I.

NORTH CHANNEL

Buncrana

Lough Foyle

Garron Point

Londonderry

Bann

Ballymena

Laune

Strabane

SPERRIN MTS.

NORTHERN IRELAND

BLUE STACK MTS.

Donegal

Omagh

Lough Neagh

Belfast · Bangor

Donegal Bay

Ballyshannon

Lower Lough Erne

Portadown

Lisburn

Newtownards

Enniskillen

Armagh

Strangford Lough

Sligo

Upper Lough Erne

Newry · Newcastle

Aran Island

SLIEVE GAMPH

Lough Allen

Annagh

Dundalk

Lough Conn

Dundalk Bay

Achill Island

Longford

Drogheda

Clare Island

Clew Bay

Castlebar

Roscommon

Lough Ree

IRISH SEA

Inishturk
Inishbofin

Lough Mask

Tuam

Mullingar

Lough Corrib

Athlone

Galway

REPUBLIC OF IRELAND

Brosna

BOG OF ALLEN

⊙ Dublin

Inishmore

Galway Bay

Bray

ARAN ISLANDS

Kildare

Inishmaan
Inisheer

SLIEVE BLOOM MTS.

Port Laoise

WICKLOW MOUNTAINS

Wicklow Head

Lough Derg

Lugnaquillia ▲

Wicklow

Ennis

Nenagh

Carlow

Slaney

Arklow

Loop Head

SLIEVEFELIM MTS.

Mouth of the Shannon

Limerick

Kilkenny

Barrow

Kerry Head

Maigue

Tipperary

Feale

Galtymore ▲ GALTY MTS.

Suir

Tralee

Waterford

Wexford

Dingle Bay

Killarney

Blackwater

Greenore Point

Valencia I.

MACGILLYCUDDYS REEKS

Lough Leane

Dungarvan

Hook Head

Lee · Cork

Youghal

ST. GEORGES CHANNEL

CAHA MTS.

Cobh

Kenmare River

Bantry

Bandon

Bantry Bay

Old Head of Kinsale

Mizen Head

LOCATION

Dublin, the capital and largest city in the Republic of Ireland, is located in east-central Ireland on Dublin Bay and the coast of the Irish Sea. The city is located on a lowland coastal plain in Dublin County, Leinster Province, at an elevation of 155 feet above sea level. Dublin lies at the mouth of the Liffey River, which flows northeast from Kildare through the north and south sides of the city before emptying into Dublin Bay. Dublin is located 110 miles southwest of Belfast, Northern Ireland, and 140 miles northeast of Cork, the Republic of Ireland's second largest city. Liverpool, England, is 140 miles due east of Dublin, across the Irish Sea. The city lies in the center of Dublin County, which is bounded by Meath, Kildare, and Wicklow Counties. The Dublin metropolitan region includes the municipalities of Balbriggan, Clondalkin, Glasnevin, Kingstown, Lucan, Malahide, Portmarnock, Rathgar, Rathmines, Stepaside, and Swords. The Dublin region has an area of 82 square miles (221 square kilometers). Dublin averages a January maximum temperature of 41 degrees Fahrenheit (5 degrees Celsius) and a July maximum temperature of 59 degrees Fahrenheit (15 degrees Celsius). The city has an annual average of 29.7 inches of rainfall (754.4 millimeters).

POPULATION AND DEMOGRAPHY

Dublin occupies the core of Leinster Province, the population center of the Republic of Ireland. More than 50 percent of the Republic of Ireland's population reside in Leinster, one of 4 provinces of the Irish Republic. From 1991 to 1996, the population of Dublin County Borough increased by a modest 0.7 percent from 478,389 to 481,854. Over the same period, greater Dublin's population, encompassing Dublin County and Dublin County Borough, increased by 3.2 percent, from 1,025,304 in 1991 to 1,058,264 in 1996. The county and region have expanded at a slower pace than the Republic of Ireland, which in the thirty-five years from 1961 to 1996 grew by 28.7 percent, to 3,626,087. Still, in 1996, Eastern Ireland (an area encompassing Dublin and adjoining counties in eastern Ireland) had a significant 29 percent of the nation's population. Dublin is about three times as large as Belfast, the largest city of Northern Ireland. Dublin is more than five times as populous as Cork, Ireland's second largest city, with a population of 180,000, and twelve times as large as Limerick, Ireland's third largest city. During the 1980s and 1990s, Dublin's urban population has declined relative to

the suburbs and outlying regions of Leinster Province, which has expanded extensively over the last two decades of the twentieth century. Females comprise a 50.3 percent majority of greater Dublin's population.

HISTORY

The area surrounding Dublin Castle was an indigenous settlement in the second century. Dublin gets its name from Dubh Linn (meaning "dark pool"), a region that lies at the confluence of the Liffey and Poodle Rivers in Eastern Ireland. Patrick, the patron saint of Ireland, is believed to have converted local residents to Christianity in 450. According to archaeological data, Viking explorers captured the region and established a settlement near Dublin in 841. Dublin developed as a medieval city in 1170, following the Anglo-Norman invasion and the defeat of the Danes. Following the defeat of local leaders by the English in the early sixteenth century, Dublin became embroiled in four hundred years of violent conflict between English imperial power and native peoples, culminating in 1921, when Dublin became capital of the newly established Irish Free State. In the eighteenth century, Dublin's architecture developed a distinctive Georgian character that remains prominent in the city's buildings.

POLITICS AND GOVERNMENT

A county borough council, known as the Dublin Corporation, governs the greater Dublin area. The Dublin region is governed by the Dublin Regional Authority, which consists of twenty-nine elected members nominated by the local authorities, including five from South Dublin; five from Dun/Laoghaire Rathdown; five from Fingal; and five from Dublin Corporation. The Dublin Regional Authority is one of eight regional authorities in Ireland established under the Local Government Act of 1991. The Dublin Regional Authority coordinates economic and social linkages between Ireland and Wales and Europe. The authority has responsibility for improving regional transport links and infrastructure; enhancing the area's tourist potential; developing the area's economic potential; and assisting human resources and cultural development. Through its European Union Operational Committee, the Dublin Regional Authority reviews the implementation of structural funds in the region and participates in European Union activities and events. The Republic of Ireland's social welfare functions are carried out by ten social welfare agencies, called regions, including three regions in the Dublin area.

ECONOMY

Dublin is the capital and the major commercial and transportation center of the Republic of Ireland. The region's principal manufacturing industries are shipbuilding, steel plants, automobile assembly, electrical and electronic equipment, engineering, footwear and leather products, textiles, clothing, glass, pharmaceuticals, food processing, breweries, and distilleries. The Greater Dublin area has historically been the center of Ireland's manufacturing industries. However, recent national efforts to decentralize industrial output have contributed to the growth of manufacturing outside the area. Although gross domestic product continues to lag behind that of other countries in the European Union, between 1988 and 1994 the region has grown significantly. Although manufacturing remains important to the local economy, the vast majority of the regional workforce is employed in the service and government sectors, which employ about 75 percent of workers.

Dublin's status as Ireland's capital city contributes to regional economic stability. Major regional employers include the national, provincial, and regional governments. The region's economy is also stimulated by the presence of offices of foreign enterprises, international banks, corporate offices, and support services. Dublin's economic growth is also sustained by its increasing importance as a point of entry for the European Union.

The tourist industry is a major component of the national and regional economies. In particular, greater Dublin is a major destination for British, European, and North American visitors. The leading sectors of Ireland's labor force in 1977 were commerce, insurance, and finance, with 21 percent of the labor force; manufacturing, with 20.3 percent; agriculture, with 10 percent; and building and construction, with 7.2 percent. Despite a recent national and regional economic recovery, unemployment remains on average higher than in other European Union regions. The unemployment rate in April 1994 was 15.2 percent.

TRANSPORTATION

The Republic of Ireland has 242 passenger vehicles per 1,000 persons. Commuters and regional residents in the greater Dublin area rely more heavily on the public transportation system. The growth of motor vehicle use has contributed to traffic congestion and increased levels of air pollution. To respond to the need for improved access throughout the region, Dublin regional authorities have initiated the construction of an integrated public transportation system that will link Dublin and its suburbs to Heuston Station, the busiest regional rail station. The new light rail transit system and improved transfers between bus lines is expected to greatly improve public access and reduce the duration of commuter transportation trips. Dublin Airport, located 18 miles north of the city, serves the greater Dublin area. Dublin is a major national and international port city that accommodates large ships. Two canals to the Shannon River in Ireland's interior connect to the greater Dublin area.

HEALTH CARE

Prior to the creation of the Department of Health by the Irish government in 1947, health functions were the responsibility of the Department of Local Government and Public Health. While the national government retains responsibility for coordinating public health policy, regional authorities have responsibility for delivering public health services to local areas. Local authorities had administered public health services until the Health Act of 1970 established eight health boards throughout the nation and abolished the Hospitals Commission, increasing the Department's direct involvement in the execution of health policy. Local health boards and agencies are given responsibility for providing direct and indirect health and personal social services. The Eastern Health Board administers health services to 1,295,939 residents in the greater Dublin region. Ireland has a faster national growth rate than most European countries. In 1992, the region had a natural growth rate of 5.8 persons per 1,000 residents, reflecting a birth rate of 14.5 per 1,000 residents and a death rate of 8.7 per 1,000. However, the natural population increase is moderated by a net migration of 1.2 persons per 1,000 residents. In the same year, the infant mortality rate was 7 deaths per 1,000 live births. Greater Dublin is the nation's leading center of hospitals, medical facilities, and medical training institutes. The city is also home to leading pharmaceutical and medical equipment companies.

EDUCATION

The Republic of Ireland requires children between the ages of 4 and 15 to attend school. Some 45.5 percent of the nation's students are in primary schools, 42.3 percent are in secondary schools, and 12.1 percent attend institutions of higher education. The leading postsecondary institutions in the greater Dublin area are the University of Dublin, which includes Trinity College; University College of the National University of Ireland; Dublin City University; and several regional technical training institutions. The Dublin region also has specialized training institutions in the arts, business, and medicine.

HOUSING

The moderation of population growth in the Republic of Ireland and the greater Dublin area has significantly reduced pressure on regional housing stock. In 1991, based on European Union statistics, the region had an occupancy rate of 2.9 persons per housing unit, considerably lower than in previous decades. In the last five years, the government reported that the region's housing stock has grown as a result of an increase in public housing and private housing construction. The number of new regional units went up from 19,539 in 1990 to 33,735 in 1996. Owners occupy the vast majority of Ireland's housing stock. In 1991, renters occupied less than 2 percent of the nation's housing. However, the greater Dublin region has a larger share of housing units occupied by renters.

CULTURE, THE ARTS, AND ENTERTAINMENT

The greater Dublin area is a major center of culture, arts, music, and architecture. Dublin's leading museums are the National Gallery, the National Museum, the National History Museum, the Municipal Gallery of Art, and the Dublin Writers Museum. The city's leading theatres and performance halls are the Abbey Theatre, the Gate Theatre, and the James Joyce Cultural Center. Dublin's churches, libraries, colleges, and other public buildings are reminders of the city's Georgian architectural heritage. The leading parks and public spaces in the city are Phoenix Park and the National Botanic Gardens. Residents in the Dublin region are avid sports fans, and the greater Dublin area is home to soccer, rugby, and cricket teams.

CATEGORY	DATA	YEAR	AREA
LOCATION & ENVIRONMENT			
Area	82 square miles	1996	City
	221 square kilometers		
Elevation	155 feet/47 meters		City
January Temperature	41 degrees Fahrenheit	1992	City
	5 degrees Celsius		
July Temperature	59 degrees Fahrenheit	1992	City
	15 degrees Celsius		
Annual Precipitation	29.7 inches/754.4 millimeters	1992	City
POPULATION & DEMOGRAPHY			
Population	1,058,264	1996	Metro
Density	2,972 per square mile	1995	Metro
	1,148 per square kilometer		
Gender			
Males	49.7%	1992	Metro
Females	50.3%	1992	Metro
Age			
Under 15	26.3%	1992	Metro
15–64	62.2%	1992	Metro
Over 65	11.4%	1992	Metro
VITAL STATISTICS			
Births per 1,000 Residents	14.5	1992	Metro
Deaths per 1,000 Residents	8.7	1992	Metro
Infant Mortality Rate	7 per 1,000 live births	1992	Metro
ECONOMY			
Total Workforce	1,338,000	1992	Metro
Manufacturing	20.3%	1992	Metro
Finance, Insurance, Real Estate	21.0%	1992	Metro
Construction	7.2%	1992	Metro
Agriculture	10%	1992	Metro
TRANSPORTATION			
Passenger Vehicles	242,000	1995	City
HOUSING			
Total Housing Units	1,020,000	1991	Metro
Persons per Unit	2.9%	1991	Metro
Owner-Occupied Units	82.00%	1991	Metro
EDUCATION			
Primary	45.5%	1990	Metro
Secondary	42.3%	1990	Metro
Higher	12.1%	1990	Metro

Sources: Department of Economic and Social Affairs, Population Division. *Urban Agglomerations, 1996.* New York: United Nations, 1997; United Nations Center for Human Settlements. *Compendium of Human Settlements Statistics.* New York: United Nations, 1995; and Eurostat *Regions Statistical Yearbook.* Brussels, Belgium: Statistical Office of European Communities, 1996.

Edmonton, Alberta
CANADA

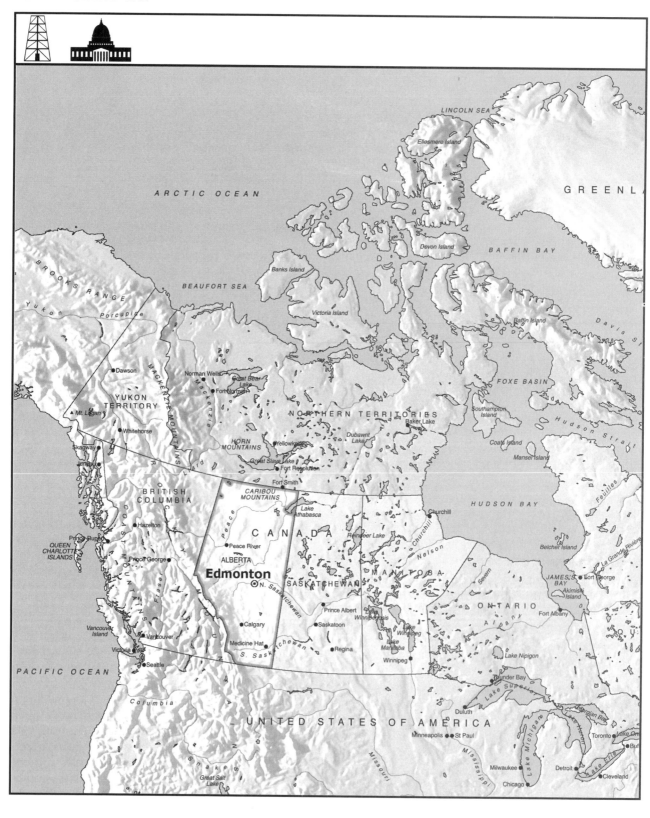

LOCATION

Edmonton, the capital and second most populous city of Alberta, lies on the North Saskatchewan River in central Alberta. The city lies east of the foothills of the Canadian Rocky Mountains at an elevation of 2,219 feet above sea level, 160 miles north of Calgary, Alberta's largest city. To the north of Edmonton are some of the world's richest oil and gas reserves, which are a major source of economic activity in the region. To the city's south and east is a vast stretch of prairie and steppe region where cattle ranching and wheat farming predominate. The central city occupies a land area of 270.5 square miles (700.6 square kilometers). Like Calgary to the south, Edmonton experiences relatively long, cold winters and short, warm summers. As the northernmost largest city in North America, Edmonton is known as the "Gateway to the North." Average temperatures in Edmonton range from a low of 2.3 degrees Fahrenheit (−16.5 degrees Celsius) in January to a high of 60.4 degrees Fahrenheit (15.8 degrees Celsius) in July. The city experiences average annual precipitation of 18.4 inches a year (467 millimeters).

POPULATION AND DEMOGRAPHY

The central city of Edmonton comprises almost 90 percent of the regional population. The adjoining cities of St. Albert and Sherwood Park and Strathcona County account for the remaining regional population. Between 1985 and 1996, the city's population expanded by 12.3 percent. Edmonton's regional population was 991,000 in 1995 and is projected to expand by 27.6 percent, to 1,369,000, by the year 2015, considerably faster than most other Canadian cities. Edmonton has a relatively larger share of younger residents and a smaller proportion of older residents than other major Canadian cities. Nearly 17.7 percent of the city's population is under 20 years of age, 58.3 percent is between the ages of 20 and 59, and 12 percent is over 65 years of age. Females comprise about 50 percent of the population. Edmonton is less ethnically diverse than Montreal, Toronto, or Vancouver. The four largest linguistic minorities are speakers of Chinese, German, French, and Ukrainian.

HISTORY

The growth of the Edmonton metropolitan area is closely linked to the abundant natural resources in the central Alberta region. The city initially origi-

nated around fur trading posts that were built by the North West and Hudson Bay companies. The city was founded in 1891, a year after the Canadian Pacific Railroad established a transportation link to the area. After gold was discovered in the Yukon Territory in the 1890s, Edmonton's economy and population grew significantly. In 1904 Edmonton was formally established as a city. The discovery of abundant oil and gas reserves in the region in the twentieth century further contributed to the region's economic importance and population growth.

GOVERNMENT AND POLITICS

Government services in Edmonton are administered on a city level. However, since the city encompasses nearly 90 percent of the metropolitan area, most services and economic planning can be considered regional. Edmonton participates in the Capital Region Forum, a relatively powerless informal organization that attempts to address shared regional concerns through deliberation and consensus. The major functions of the government are parks and recreation, planning and development, transportation and streets, community and family services, police services, and public works. Edmonton's government is administered through a city manager and a city council, which, along with department managers, examine and coordinate policy and major issues facing the city.

ECONOMY

The dominant economic activity in the Edmonton region is related to the extraction of oil and gas production of energy-related products. The Edmonton region contains immense reserves of oil, gas, and tar sands, and the Province of Alberta contains the vast majority of Canadian oil reserves. While Calgary, to Edmonton's south, is the major financial center for the energy industry, Edmonton is the production center. The Edmonton region is home to major petroleum and petrochemical refineries. Edmonton also serves as an important transshipment center for oil and natural gas products from western and northern Canada. Other major natural resource-related industries in the Edmonton area are coal, uranium, and precious metal mining, processing, and distribution.

Although energy and natural resources are the most important component of the economy, dollarwise the industry is not a major source of jobs. In 1991, less than 3,000 workers were directly employed in mining, quarrying, and extracting oil and gas. Many more were employed in natural resource processing, and transport equipment operating. Most workers in the region are employed in service sector jobs (managerial, administrative, clerical, teaching), health care, wholesale and retail trade, and manufacturing. In the mid-1990s, Edmonton suffered through a deep economic recession that contributed to significantly higher unemployment than in preceding decades. In the 1990s, Edmonton's unemployment rate was more than double the rate of the 1980s.

TRANSPORTATION

Edmonton has a comprehensive bus and rail transportation system. The bus system provides service throughout the city. In 1978, Edmonton became the first North American city with a population below 1 million residents to open a light rail transit system. The adjacent regional municipalities of St. Albert, Sherwood Park, and Strathcona County also provide service to and from Edmonton. Two major highways link Edmonton with Winnipeg, Vancouver, Calgary, and the United States. Edmonton is the southern terminus of the McKenzie Highway, which connects up with the Alaska Highway in British Columbia. Specialized highways serve the oil and tar sands mining operations north of the city. Edmonton International Airport provides vital access to passengers traveling to and from other major destinations in Canada and the United States.

HEALTH CARE

The provincial government provides health care services to all residents of Alberta. The health care system is administered by Capital Health, one of seventeen regional health authorities formed in 1994 by the Alberta provincial government to cut costs by amalgamating hospital, continuing care, and public health. Capital Health's mission is to coordinate health services among agencies in each community and to shift the health care mission from treatment to prevention. The relative youth of Edmonton's population has contributed to a greater emphasis on preventive care. The regional health system serves residents through two tertiary-care hospitals, three community hospitals, and a rehabilitation hospital. Thirty-five percent of all patients admitted to Capital Health's hospitals reside outside the region, chiefly in north and central Alberta. The system also provides home care, community rehabilitation, health promotion, and disease

prevention services. With approximately 15,000 workers, Capital Health is the largest employer in the region.

EDUCATION

Edmonton's leading postsecondary educational institutions are the University of Alberta, Alberta College, the Northern Alberta Institute of Technology, Grant MacEwan College, Alberta Vocational College, a community college, and two specialized petroleum training institutes. In 1995 the Edmonton public school system enrolled 75,000 students in 201 primary, secondary, and continuing-education schools. The school system provides specialized education programs to gifted students in the arts, technology, and languages. A Catholic school board also provides parochial school education.

HOUSING

The City of Edmonton had a total of 306,180 dwelling units in 1991, of which 59 percent were owner-occupied units. Single-family detached houses made up 57 percent of the housing stock, followed by apartment units, which comprised 26 percent of the housing stock. The number of new housing units constructed declined steadily in the mid-1990s due to the effects of the lingering regional economic recession and slower population growth, which depressed local demand for new homes. Between 1993 and 1995, the number of new housing units declined by more than 50 percent, from 6,751 to 3,103. In Edmonton, as in other western Canadian cities, there are fewer affordable housing units available for low- and moderate-income residents. The Office of the Commissioner of Housing operates approximately 4,300 community social housing units and 950 lodge units for seniors, and enforces minimum housing standards for rental units.

CULTURE, THE ARTS, AND ENTERTAINMENT

Edmonton and its environs is a region of many museums. The leading museums in the metropolitan Edmonton region are the Alberta Aviation Museum, the Alberta Railway Museum, the Edmonton Art Gallery, the Edmonton Police Museum and Archives, the Edmonton Space and Science Center, the Musée Heritage Museum, the Provincial Museum of Alberta,

Rutherford House, and the Ukrainian Cultural Heritage Museum. The city is home to three professional sports teams, including the Edmonton Oilers hockey club, the Edmonton Eskimos football club, and the Edmonton Trappers baseball club. The city is home to a large number of public parks and open spaces. The region's location east of the foothills of the northern Rocky Mountains makes it a major attraction for skiers and outdoor sports enthusiasts in western Canada and throughout North America.

CATEGORY	DATA	YEAR	AREA
LOCATION & ENVIRONMENT			
Area	270.5 square miles	1996	City
	700.6 square kilometers		City
Elevation	2,219 feet/676.4 meters		City
January Temperature	2.3 degrees Fahrenheit	1992	City
	−16.5 degrees Celsius	1992	City
July Temperature	60.4 degrees Fahrenheit	1992	City
	15.8 degrees Celsius	1992	City
Annual Precipitation	18.4 inches/467 millimeters	1992	City
POPULATION & DEMOGRAPHY			
Population	991,000	1995	Metro
Growth Rate	12.27%	1986–96	Metro
Growth Rate	2.6%	1996–2001	Metro
Density	3,105 per square mile	1996	Metro
	1,199 per square kilometer		Metro
Gender			
Male	49.8%	1995	Metro
Female	50.2%	1995	Metro
Age			
Under 20	17.7%	1991	Metro
20–59	58.3%	1991	Metro
Over 60	12.0%	1991	Metro
VITAL STATISTICS			
Births per 1,000 Residents	14.8	1995	Metro
Deaths per 1,000 Residents	6.1	1995	Metro
ECONOMY			
Total Workforce	472,915	1991	Metro
Manufacturing	11.5%	1991	Metro
Services	13.6%	1991	Metro
Construction	6.4%	1991	Metro
Agriculture	2.2%	1991	Metro
Mining	0.6%	1991	Metro
HOUSING			
Total Housing Units	306,180	1991	Metro
Persons per Unit	2.7	1991	Metro
Owner-Occupied Units	59.2%	1991	Metro

(continued)

CATEGORY	DATA	YEAR	AREA
HEALTH CARE			
Hospitals	12	1991	Metro
Physicians per 1,000 Residents	2	1991	Metro

Sources: Department of Economic and Social Affairs, Population Division. *Urban Agglomerations, 1996.* New York: United Nations, 1997; *Canadian Markets.* Toronto, Ontario: The Financial Post, 1996; and United Nations Center for Human Settlements. *Compendium of Human Settlements Statistics.* New York: United Nations, 1995. *Canada Year Book 1994.* Ottawa, Ontario: Statistics Canada, 1995.

Frankfurt am Main, Hesse
GERMANY

LOCATION

Frankfurt, Germany's leading financial center, is located in the west-central state of Hesse, at an elevation of 312 feet (95.1 meters) above sea level. The city is located on the Main River, southeast of the Taunus Mountains and west of the Spessart and Rhon Mountains. The city covers a relatively small surface area of 96 square miles (249 square kilometers). Frankfurt is divided into two districts—Anstadt, an old medieval neighborhood that borders the Main River, and Neustadt, a modern community north of Anstadt that is at the center of Frankfurt's financial and commercial operations. Frankfurt's financial and commercial status is enhanced by the city's strategic location on a major German waterway that provides excellent access to West European markets. The city is located approximately 75 miles northeast of the German border with France, and about 80 miles southeast of Bonn, the former capital of West Germany. Frankfurt is about 300 miles southwest of Berlin, the capital and administrative center of the reunited Germany. The city's temperature ranges from an average of 36 degrees Fahrenheit (2.4 degrees Celsius) in January to an average of 68 degrees Fahrenheit (19.7 degrees Celsius) in July. The city has an annual average precipitation of 28 inches (760 millimeters).

POPULATION AND DEMOGRAPHY

Frankfurt is Germany's fourth largest city and the center of the country's second largest urban agglomeration. The primary demographic trend in the metropolitan area is the contraction of the urban core and the gradual expansion of the urban region as a whole. Between 1972 and 1990, the central city's population has declined by 2.9 percent, from 660,410 to 641,300. However, since 1982, Frankfurt's central city population has increased by more than 16,000. The Frankfurt urban agglomeration has expanded in population in recent decades and is projected to continue to grow in the coming years. From 1995 to the year 2015, the Frankfurt metropolitan area is expected to grow from 3.6 million to 3.7 million inhabitants. Like many other German regions, the regional population distribution is older than that in many other large world urban centers. In 1992, 14.5 percent of the regional population was 15 years of age or under, 70.5 percent was between 16 and 64 years of age, and 15 percent was 65 years of age or over. In the same year, females accounted for 51.2 percent of the

region's inhabitants. The region has a natural population decrease of 0.3 per 1,000 residents, owing to the excess of deaths over births. However, migration makes up for this loss. Frankfurt's location in the heart of Central Europe and the city's wealth and prosperity have been a magnet to immigrants and foreigners. Before the start of the Second World War, the city was home to a large Jewish community. In the postwar years the city has become a home to foreigners and guest workers from the Middle East. Turks have become the predominant ethnic minority at the end of the century.

HISTORY

In the first century A.D., the region now encompassing the state of Hesse was a northern Roman outpost. In 794, Frankfurt was founded as a theological meeting place for Franconian aristocrats, and between 800 and 814 Charlemagne held imperial councils in the city. In 1372, Frankfurt was declared a free imperial city, accountable only to the kaiser. By the early sixteenth century, Frankfurt became a center of the Protestant Reformation. The city's central location contributed to Frankfurt's growth as a center of commerce and trade, and in 1585 a stock market was established in the city. With the defeat of the Holy Roman Empire by Napoleon's forces in 1806, the reign of the Holy Roman Empire came to a close. In 1815, following Napoleon's defeat, the city became part of the German Bund between 1816 and 1866. In 1848, the first democratically elected parliament in Germany convened in Frankfurt. In 1866, during the Seven Weeks' War, Frankfurt was seized and annexed by Prussia. During Bismarck's wars of unification, Hesse was divided into four principalities and duchies, one county, and the free city of Frankfurt. The city was extensively damaged in World War II by Allied bombing. In the postwar years, Frankfurt was rebuilt and became West Germany's leading banking center.

GOVERNMENT AND POLITICS

With the division of Germany in the aftermath of World War II, government officials debated naming Frankfurt capital of the German Federal Republic. Although Bonn became the national capital, Frankfurt was selected as headquarters of the leading German monetary institutions—the German Federal Bank and the Federal Court of Audits, organizations that remain in the city even after the relocation of the nation's capital to a unified Berlin. Frankfurt is the capital of Hesse, one of sixteen administrative divisions in Germany known as *Länder,* with powers equivalent to those of states in the United States; Hesse has an elected legislative body and an administrative arm responsible for enacting laws and implementing policy for the entire region. Frankfurt government administrative and legislative authorities are responsible for local government policy.

ECONOMY

As one of the world's leading banking and finance centers, Frankfurt is home to Germany's stock exchange and central bank. The city has a large financial sector that includes about 400 banks and 770 insurance companies. In 1993, Frankfurt was chosen as headquarters of the European Monetary Institute. After the creation of a unified European currency, Frankfurt will become the headquarters of the European Central Bank. The region has one of the strongest economies in the European Union, with the highest per capita gross domestic product. The leading industrial sectors in the region are chemicals, manufacturing, motor vehicles, and mechanical engineering and electronics. Other significant industries in the metropolitan area are machinery, electrical equipment, pharmaceuticals, textiles and garments, leather, and printing and publishing. The city is a leading trade and conference center that by the late 1990s held 50,000 annual conventions and meetings. The city is the home of the world's largest book fair, which brings about 8,000 exhibitors and 250,000 visitors annually. Frankfurt alone has about five hundred publishing and printing companies. The advertising industry plays a key role in the local economy. The state government is an important force in the regional economic development and innovation.

The leading sectors of the regional labor force are service, manufacturing, and government. Since the mid-1990s, unemployment has grown in the manufacturing sector, primarily due to growing regional and international competition from low-cost producers.

TRANSPORTATION

Frankfurt has a modern mass transit system that includes rail and bus service, though urban sprawl and the growth of the city's suburbs have increased the use of private motor vehicles. The modernization and expansion of the regional highway system has facilitated the growing use of automobiles as the primary form of regional transportation. In 1992, there were 533 passenger vehicles per 1,000 regional inhabitants. Transportation from Frankfurt to other German cities is facilitated by the German *autobahn* and an intercity rail network. Frankfurt has the largest airport in Europe.

HEALTH CARE

The German public health system, administered on a regional level by the State of Hesse, guarantees universal medical and health care to all residents. The region has a ratio of 3.4 physicians and 1.1 hospital beds per 1,000 inhabitants. Due to the older age structure in the region, the number of deaths tends to exceed the number of births; in 1992, the region had 10.2 births and 10.5 deaths per 1,000 residents. The region has an infant mortality rate of 5 infant deaths per 1,000 live births. The central city of Frankfurt, with a relatively large population of young immigrants from the Middle East, has a greater need for preventive health care services and clinics. Circulatory system diseases and cancer account for over 70 percent of all causes of death in the Frankfurt region.

EDUCATION

The region has a highly educated and skilled population. Universal public education is provided to all residents between 5 and 18 years of age. In addition, continuing education is provided to adults seeking to learn new skills. In the 1992–1993 school year, 24.6 percent of all regional students attended primary schools, 59.2 percent attended secondary schools, and 18.3 percent were enrolled in institutions of higher education. Educational needs in the central city of Frankfurt tend to be more acute due to the large presence of a large immigrant minority in the municipality. About one third of all children attending Frankfurt's schools are foreigners, with children of Turkish immigrants making up the largest proportion of these. The city is home to leading postsecondary schools, including Johann Wolfgang Goethe University, an institution that enrolls about 35,000 students. The city is home to a number of leading specialized scientific and technical research institutions.

HOUSING

In the aftermath of World War II, Frankfurt's housing stock was rebuilt. A primary trend in the region since the 1960s has been the expansion of the suburbs at the expense of the urban core. However, since the early 1980s, Frankfurt's housing supply has increased to accommodate a growing central city population. Of the region's 1,543,000 housing units, only 24 percent are single-family units. The vast majority of housing units in the central city are located in multiunit complexes. The state government regulates the regional housing supply. A growing housing problem in Frankfurt is the shortage of adequate and affordable housing for the community of foreign guest workers who reside in the city.

CULTURE, THE ARTS, AND ENTERTAINMENT

Frankfurt is a regional center of German culture and arts. Museums and art galleries are the leading cultural and artistic institutions in the city. Frankfurt's museums are concentrated in the Museum Embankment, a center that consists of seven museums, including the German Postal Museum. Other leading museums located in the city are the Museum of Applied Arts, the Museum of Modern Art, Schirn Art Hall, and the Jewish Museum. Frankfurt is also home to numerous art galleries and a zoological garden. The city has a number of old churches and cathedrals that date back to the ninth century. The city attracts leading national and international orchestras, ballets, and theater groups. The city also has many small theater performance groups and a thriving jazz and pop music scene.

CATEGORY	DATA	YEAR	AREA
LOCATION & ENVIRONMENT			
Area	96 square miles	1996	City
	153.6 square kilometers		
Elevation	312 feet/95.1 meters		City
January Temperature	37 degrees Fahrenheit		City
	2.7 degrees Celsius		
July Temperature	75 degrees Fahrenheit		City
	23.8 degrees Celsius		
Annual Precipitation	24.1 inches/612 millimeters		City
POPULATION & DEMOGRAPHY			
Population	3,600,000	1996	Metro
Projected Population	3,700,000	2015	City
Growth Rate	0.9%	1990–1995	City
Growth Rate	2.7%	1995–2015	City
Density	1,312 per square mile	1992	Region
	486 per square kilometer		
Gender			
Males	48.8%	1992	Metro
Females	51.2%	1992	Metro
Age			
Under 15	14.5%	1992	Metro
15–64	70.5%	1992	Metro
Over 65	15.0%	1992	Metro
VITAL STATISTICS			
Births per 1,000 Residents	10.2	1993	Metro
Deaths per 1,000 Residents	10.5	1993	Metro
Infant Mortality Rate	5 per 1,000 births	1993	Metro

(continued)

CATEGORY	DATA	YEAR	AREA
ECONOMY			
Total Workforce	2,733,000	1992	Region
Manufacturing	28.2%	1992	Region
Construction	6.4%	1992	Region
Utilities	1.0%	1992	Region
Agriculture	1.8%	1992	Region
Market Services	44.7%	1992	Region
Nonmarket Services	17.9%	1992	Region
TRANSPORTATION			
Passenger Vehicles	533,000	1992	Metro
HOUSING			
Total Housing Units	1,543,000	1992	Metro
Persons per Unit	2.3	1992	Metro
HEALTH CARE			
Physicians per 1,000 Residents	3.4	1992	Metro
Hospital Beds per 1,000 Residents	1.1	1992	Metro
EDUCATION			
Total Students	953,000	1993	Metro
Primary	24.6%	1993	Metro
Secondary	59.2%	1993	Metro
Higher	18.3%	1993	Metro

Sources: Department of Economic and Social Affairs, Population Division. *Urban Agglomerations, 1996.* New York: United Nations, 1997; Eurostat *Regions Statistical Yearbook.* Brussels, Belgium: Statistical Office of European Communities, 1996; United Nations Center for Human Settlements. *Compendium of Human Settlements Statistics.* New York: United Nations, 1995; and *Statistiches Jahrbuch 1996 für die Bundesrepublik Deutschland,* Wiesbaden, Germany: Federal Statistical Office, 1996.

Glasgow, Scotland
UNITED KINGDOM

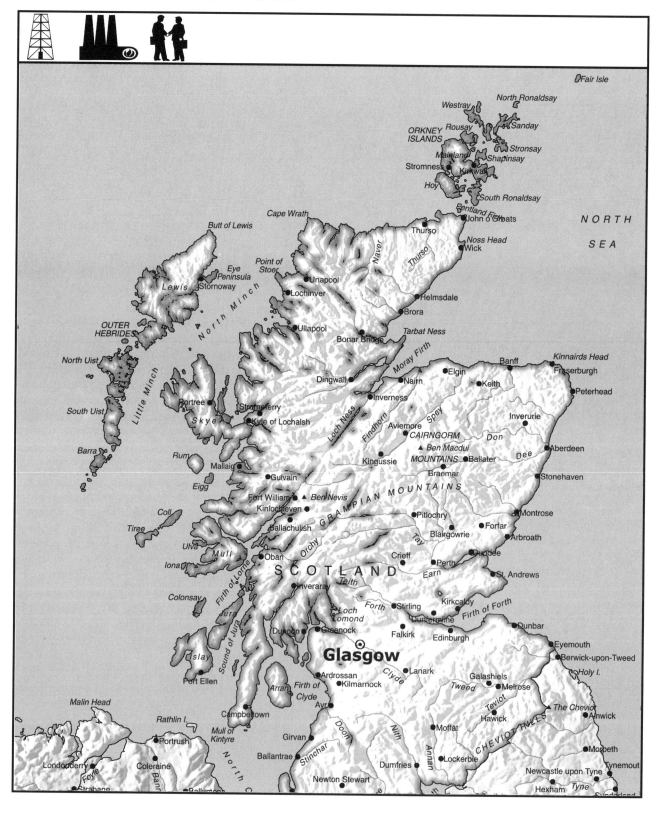

LOCATION

Glasgow, Scotland's major population and industrial center, is located in south-central Scotland, at an elevation of 45 feet on a lowland plain in Strathclyde, one of Scotland's twelve regions. The 65-square-mile (175-square-kilometer) city is situated on the north and south banks of the Clyde River, a major waterway that flows from the Lowther Hills in the Southern Uplands of southern Scotland, 80 miles to the southeast, into the Clyde Estuary, 20 miles to the north of the city. Bordering Glasgow are East Dunbartonshire on the north, West Dunbartonshire on the northwest, Renfrewshire on the west, East Renfrewshire on the southwest, South Lanarkshire on the south, and North Lanarkshire on the east. The Clyde Estuary flows into the Firth of Clyde, a major bay on Scotland's southwestern coast that extends to the North Channel and the Irish Sea. The city is located approximately 40 miles southwest of Edinburgh, Scotland's capital and second largest city. Glasgow is located approximately 350 air miles northwest of London, the United Kingdom's capital and economic center. The average annual temperature measured at Scotland's capital of Edinburgh ranges from a low of 35 degrees Fahrenheit (1.7 degrees Celsius) in January to a high of 65 degrees Fahrenheit (18.3 degrees Celsius) in July. The average annual precipitation is 27.6 inches (701 millimeters).

POPULATION AND DEMOGRAPHY

In 1995, Glasgow had over 12 percent of Scotland's population. Between 1981 and 1995, Glasgow's population declined by 13.2 percent, to 618,000. While most of Glasgow's population loss occurred in the 1980s, the population decline moderated in the 1990s. Glasgow's population shift reflects a downward trend that has occurred throughout the region. However, Glasgow and other urban industrial areas experienced a significantly steeper decline than the region as a whole. In the fifteen-year period between 1981 and 1995, Scotland's population declined by a more modest 0.8 percent. Most of the region's population loss is caused by natural population decrease. In 1995, the City of Glasgow had a natural population decrease of 1.7 percent, reflecting the excess of deaths over births (14.3 deaths and 12.6 births per 1,000 residents). Internal and international migration accounts for only a small proportion of the regional population decline. Despite the substantial population loss, Glas-

gow remains the largest city in the region. According to national statistics, the City of Glasgow, with a population density of 1,309 persons per square mile (3,533 per square kilometer), is the most densely populated local government area in the United Kingdom. The city's population age distribution closely parallels that of the United Kingdom as a whole: 18.9 percent of the population is under 16 years of age, 66.1 percent is between 16 and 65 years of age, and 15 percent is over 65 years of age. Due to longer female life expectancy, males are a 47.6 percent minority of Glasgow's population. Ethnic minorities make up just 1 percent of Scotland's population. Pakistanis, Bangladeshis, and Indians are the region's leading ethnic minorities.

HISTORY

Glasgow was originally settled as a salmon-fishing village at a crossing point on the Clyde River. The Christian missionary St. Mungo founded Glasgow and established the city as a religious center. The cathedral was destroyed in local wars and rebuilt in 1116. In 1451, Glasgow University was established. Following a union with England in 1717, the city expanded as a commercial center. Glasgow merchants became major importers of sugar, rum, and tobacco from the Americas. The proximity to iron ore deposits enabled Glasgow to develop into a major production center for basic manufactures. In the nineteenth and twentieth centuries, the city emerged as a leading shipbuilding and locomotive production center. However, by the nineteenth century, much of Glasgow's population lived in poverty in cramped housing. The subsequent development of public housing in the twentieth century greatly ameliorated substandard housing conditions in the city and region. In the postwar period, Glasgow's heavy manufacturing industries were superseded by foreign competitors. Although Glasgow has attempted to diversify into electronics and high-tech industries, the city has continued to suffer economic decline. The discovery of North Sea oil reserves in the 1970s shifted regional economic growth to northeast Scotland.

GOVERNMENT AND POLITICS

Glasgow's government is administered by a popularly elected city council. Regional autonomy demands in the 1980s and 1990s have led to higher levels of regional authority. In 1997, Prime Minister Tony Blair of Great Britain greatly expanded Scotland's authority over regional affairs.

ECONOMY

Following the discovery of iron ore reserves in the region in the nineteenth century, Glasgow became a major heavy manufacturing center. Today, the major industries in the region are iron and steel, machinery, shipbuilding, printing, textiles, carpets, aircraft engines, electronic equipment, chemicals, food processing, breweries and distilleries. In the early 1990s, foreign tourism has increased while tourism from the United Kingdom has declined. The discovery and development of rich oil reserves in the North Sea revitalized the regional Scottish economy. However, much of the regional economic growth is concentrated on the North Sea coast in the north and northeast. Although the oil and petroleum exploration and production industries have benefited the regional economy, Glasgow residents have not reaped a substantial share of the benefits. From 1990 to 1996, Scottish regional unemployment figures have paralleled the national unemployment rate. Scotland's unemployment rate hovered between 9 and 10 percent in the early 1990s. By the mid-1990s, Scottish regional unemployment declined to about 8 percent. The decline in the manufacturing sector in major urban and industrial centers has contributed to the region's job loss. However, the decline in manufacturing has been offset by a rise in employment in the natural resource industry. In particular, the Aberdeen region in northeast Scotland, abutting the North Sea, has benefited from the discovery and development of oil in the region. Unemployment remains an endemic problem in both Glasgow and the region. In January 1997, the long-term unemployed comprised 36.4 percent of all jobless claimants.

TRANSPORTATION

Scotland has one of the highest percentages in the United Kingdom of households who do not have access to a car. In the year ending 1996, 38 percent of Scottish residents had no car, compared to 30 percent nationally. The rate of automobile ownership is even lower in Glasgow and other highly populated urban areas, where larger proportions of residents rely on public transportation. The region as a whole had a significantly greater reliance on public transport as a mode of transportation than the national average. In 1995–1996, 38 percent of the region's households did not have ready access to an automobile. According to national statistics, Scotland has had higher rates of pedestrian accidents than the national average, due to the relatively low rate of car ownership in the region. In 1995, pedestrian casualties accounted for nearly 21 percent of all road accidents. The city has an integrated bus, train, and subway system. The subway system, known as the Glasgow Underground, opened in 1896 and modernized and upgraded in the 1980s, is the only subway system in the United Kingdom outside of London. The subway system links fifteen stations in twenty-four minutes. The region is an important freight and shipping transportation center. The region ranks third in rail freight tonnage in the United Kingdom. After Heathrow, Glasgow International Airport ranks first in the United Kingdom in domestic passenger arrivals and departures.

HEALTH CARE

The British government provides universal health coverage to all inhabitants. Scotland has a higher proportion of public medical insurance users than any other region in the United Kingdom and the lowest percentage of private medical insurance users. The infant mortality rate in Glasgow exceeded that in both the United Kingdom and Scotland between 1993 and 1995, with 8.1 infant deaths per 1,000 live births.

EDUCATION

Glasgow has one of the lowest student/teacher ratios in the United Kingdom. The student/teacher ratio in Glasgow is 19.0 in primary schools and 12.2 in secondary schools, compared with the United Kingdom figure of 22.7 students per teacher in primary school and 16.1 in secondary schools. Primary students comprise 53.6 percent and secondary students make up 38.5 percent of the regional student population of 823,000. Schooling is compulsory until the age of 16, and the region has one of the highest rates in the United Kingdom of 16-year-olds continuing their education in postsecondary schools or government-supported training. On average, Scotland spends more per pupil than any other region in the United Kingdom. The leading postsecondary educational institutions in the Glasgow region are Caledonian University, the Glasgow School of Art, the College of Nautical Studies, the Royal Scottish Academy of Music and Drama, Stow College, Strathclyde University, and the University of Glasgow. A higher percentage of undergraduate and postgraduate students in Scotland attend regional institutions than in any other British region.

HOUSING

Between 1981 and 1995, the Scottish regional housing stock increased by 13.3 percent, to 434,000 units. Over the same period, owner-occupied housing units increased from 52 percent to 58 percent of the total. Still, owner occupancy in Scotland continues to lag behind the British national average of 67 percent. The region had the highest percentage of publicly controlled rental units in the United Kingdom. The decline in the average household size has placed added pressure on housing in the region. In 1995, Scotland had the lowest average household size (2.38 persons) in the United Kingdom outside of London. Despite national government efforts to reduce public housing, Glasgow and Scotland as a whole have a higher percentage of public housing than any other region

in the United Kingdom. In 1995, nearly as many housing starts were initiated by housing associations and local authorities (1,026) as by private enterprise (1,108). After Edinburgh, local authority tenants in Glasgow City paid a significantly higher average weekly rent than those in other Scottish localities.

CULTURE, THE ARTS, AND ENTERTAINMENT

The Glasgow metropolitan area is a leading center for art, architecture, and design. The city's leading museums are the Burrell Collection, the Art Gallery and Museum, Kelvingrove, the Hunterian Art Gallery, Pollok House, the Gallery of Modern Art, the Museum of Transport, Provand's Lordship, the St. Mungo Museum of Religious Life and Art, the McLellan Galleries, People's Place, and Fossil Grove. The city is a regular host to international arts festivals and design shows. Glasgow has four major British soccer clubs.

CATEGORY	DATA	YEAR	AREA
LOCATION & ENVIRONMENT			
Area	65 square miles	1996	City
	175 square kilometers		
Elevation	45 feet/13.5 meters		City
January Temperature	35 degrees Fahrenheit	1992	City
	1.7 degrees Celsius		
July Temperature	65 degrees Fahrenheit	1992	City
	18.3 degrees Celsius		
Annual Precipitation	27.6 inches/701 millimeters	1992	City
POPULATION & DEMOGRAPHY			
Population	618,000	1995	Metro
Population Change	−13.2%	1981–1995	Metro
Density	1,309 per square mile	1995	Metro
	3,533 per square kilometer		
Gender			
Males	47.6%	1995	City
Females	52.4%	1995	City
Age			
Under 16	18.9%	1992	Metro
16–64	66.1%	1992	Metro
Over 65	15.0%	1992	Metro

(continued)

CATEGORY	DATA	YEAR	AREA
VITAL STATISTICS			
Births per 1,000 Residents	12.6	1995	City
Deaths per 1,000 Residents	14.3	1995	City
Infant Mortality Rate	8.1 per 1,000 live births	1995	City
ECONOMY			
Total Workforce	434,000	1996	Metro
Manufacturing	19.3%	1992	Metro
Construction	7.7%	1992	Metro
Utilities	2.4%	1992	Metro
Agriculture	3.0%	1992	Metro
TRANSPORTATION			
Passenger Vehicles	1,618,000	1995	City
HOUSING			
Total Housing Units	434,000	1991	Metro
Persons per Unit	2.38	1991	Metro
Owner-Occupied Units	58%	1995	Metro
EDUCATION			
Total Students	823,000	1993	Metro
Primary	53.6%	1993	Metro
Secondary	38.5%	1993	Metro
Higher	7.9%	1993	Metro

Sources: Eurostat *Regions Statistical Yearbook.* Brussels, Belgium: Statistical Office of European Communities, 1996. Office for National Statistics. *Regional Trends 32.* London, England: The Stationery Office, 1997.

Guadalajara, Jalisco State
MEXICO

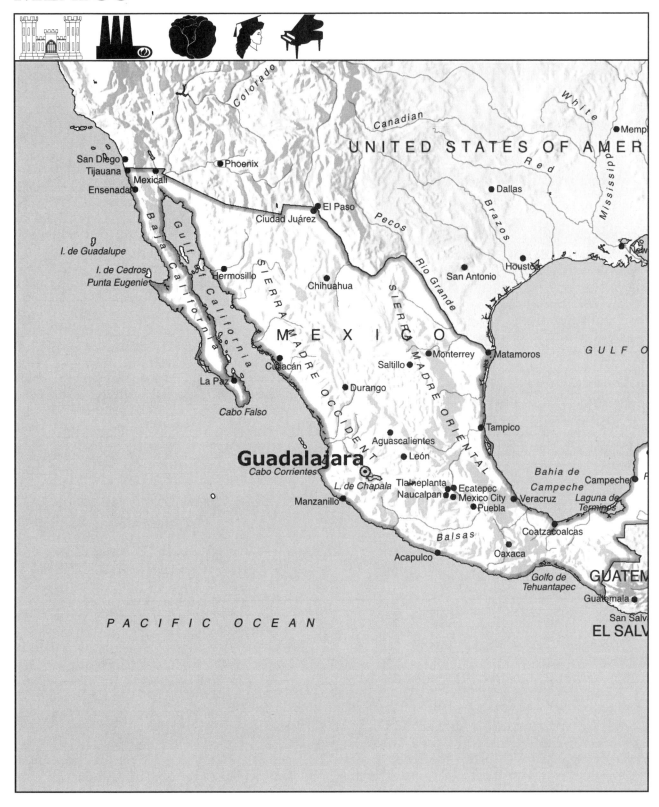

LOCATION

Guadalajara is the capital of the state of Jalisco and the second largest city in Mexico. Founded in 1530 and endearingly referred to as the "City of Roses," Guadalajara's picturesque surroundings have little in common with the squalor and disorder of Mexico City.

Located in a rich farming region at an altitude of 5,194 feet (1,583 meters), Guadalajara has a dry, mild climate throughout the year. Temperatures range from 59 degrees Fahrenheit (15 degrees Celsius) in January to 69 degrees Fahrenheit (20.6 degrees Celsius) in July. The annual precipitation averages 39.7 inches (1,008 millimeters). The metropolitan area spans an area of 72.6 square miles (188 square kilometers) and includes the three small municipalities of Zapopan, Tlaquepaque, and Tonala.

Guadalajara's historic center is organized around four majestic squares that are flanked by governmental buildings and the cathedral. While giant statues and fountains adorn the shady plazas, there is an imaginative mixture of architecture that combines such modern elements as department stores with colonial buildings, including the jewel of the city, the Hospice of Cabañas. The business community regularly invests in infrastructure and services and other public projects. Large numbers of squares, fountains, tree-lined streets, and public monuments adorn both the city center and the suburbs.

Beginning in the 1940s, Guadalajara quickly grew to become an important commercial center. Its image as a traditional city has nevertheless begun to change. Together with U.S. corporations, Guadalajara has turned from an exclusive colonial town into a modern city with much the same layout as a U.S. city. The affluent from the southwest quarters, for example, enjoy new residential facilities and a major new shopping complex. It was chosen as a location by U.S. corporations for its low wage workforce, pleasant climate, and desirable urban image.

As the recession hit Mexico in the 1980s, unemployment rose. Many working-class residents of Guadalajara migrated to the United States, and drug trafficking increased. In the early 1990s, two traumatic events shook the city of Guadalajara. In 1992, a massive explosion caused by negligence at a local Pemex refinery tore up twenty-two city blocks and killed two hundred people. A year later, a dramatic shootout among drug traffickers outside of the airport left a Roman Catholic cardinal and six others dead.

POPULATION AND DEMOGRAPHY

The population of Guadalajara was 3,500,000 in 1996. The annual growth rate is 2.6 percent, and by 2015 the city is projected to grow by a total of 29.9 percent, to 4,500,000. The population density is 22,797 persons per square mile (8,803 per square kilometer). In 1992, 46.3 percent were under the age of 20, 45.6 percent were between 20 and 59, and 7.1 percent were over 60 years old.

Guadalajara has a birth rate of 33.6 per 1,000 residents and a death rate of 6.1 per 1,000 residents; 18.6 infants die per 1,000 live births. There are more females (52 percent) than males (47 percent).

While Guadalajara has experienced steady population growth since its founding, the rate was particularly low during the nineteenth and early twentieth centuries. After 1940, however, the growth rate rose due to natural increase, urban migration, and extension of geographic boundaries.

The first census, in 1784, recorded a population of 22,163. After the war of independence in the 1820s, the population increased to 45,500 in 1838 and 75,000 in 1857. A wave of new migration occurred after the revolutionary war of 1910–1920. Guadalajara expanded in all directions after 1940 and grew by 64.5 percent between 1940 and 1950, reaching a population of 400,000. Between 1950 and 1960, the population nearly doubled, reaching a total of 880,000. During the 1970s, the average population increase was 7.8 percent annually, mostly due to in-migration.

HISTORY

Guadalajara was founded in 1532 after a vicious campaign of conquest by Nuño de Guzmán. The city thrived after being officially recognized by Charles V in 1542 as "one of the most Spanish cities." This was due in part to the fact that the indigenous population had either been killed or fled the area. Set off from the mining centers, Guadalajara developed as a regional center for trade and agriculture. As the colonial monopolies began to crumble toward the end of the eighteenth century, local industry started to develop and the city became known for its export of wheat, hides, cotton, and wool.

After the War of Independence from Spain, it was named capital of Jalisco. In the late nineteenth and early twentieth centuries, Guadalajara developed rapidly, particularly because of the railroad connections to California and the United States. After the 1940s, the population of Guadalajara expanded rapidly, and recent attempts to relocate people from the Mexico City area have brought more migration to Guadalajara.

GOVERNMENT AND POLITICS

Guadalajara is the capital of Jalisco, one of thirty-one states composing the Federal Republic of Mexico. Like other states, Jalisco is run by a governor and a unicameral legislature, the former appointed by the federal government and the latter elected by popular vote. The city of Guadalajara, like other municipalities, is governed by a mayor and a council, both of which are elected by popular vote.

ECONOMY

The contemporary urban economy is dominated by commerce, services, and light industry. Centered in a rich industrial and agricultural area, Guadalajara produces chemicals, footwear, textiles, and pottery. It is also an important mining center. Other manufactured products include textiles, leather goods, furniture, hats, and cordage. Agricultural products include wheat, hides, cotton, and wool. Native Americans make their own high-quality pottery and glassware. Near the Juanacatlán Falls, there is a hydroelectric plant that generates power to operate the factories of the city.

Guadalajara is also an important university center and host to the second largest public university in the country, the University of Guadalajara. Tourism ranks as another important source of revenue.

Of the 870,183 persons who are economically active, most (32.4 percent) work in the service sector, 28.2 percent are employed in manufacturing, and 20.5 percent are employed in trade. Notwithstanding the city's impressive economic growth, unemployment is a serious problem in Guadalajara.

Over the past decade, the secondary and tertiary sectors have expanded considerably. While the municipality of Zapopan is primarily engaged in the production of corn, Tonala focuses on pottery and manufacturing. Tlaquepaque is also an important pottery center and attracts tourists. Guadalajara is the site of an important Catholic sanctuary, attracting million of worshipers annually.

TRANSPORTATION

Nearly 98 percent of public transit passengers travel by bus and trolley, and 84 percent of those buses pass through the city center. In the 1970s, a subway was built to link up, among others, the working-class areas in the northeast with the industrial sector in the southwest. The subterranean system has been augmented by an improved highway system and rapid surface transport. There are 700,594 passenger vehicles in Guadalajara. While Guadalajara is connected by railroad to Mexican cities, its direct lines to the United States have proved to be an essential source of trade for the city.

HEALTH CARE

There are twelve hospitals in Guadalajara and 1.5 physicians per 1,000 residents. Seasonal heavy rains produce chronic flooding, and so an underground tunnel has been constructed to improve drainage and the sewage system. Air pollution has been a problem in Guadalajara, and efforts to combat it have included the permanent or temporary closure of factories, changes in the production process, reforestation campaigns, and the rehabilitation of green areas.

EDUCATION

Guadalajara is a university town. Several universities and colleges, including the University of Guadalajara and the Autonomous University of Guadalajara, are located in the city. There are a total of 489,293 pupils in primary, secondary, and higher education. Most (57.5 percent) students attend primary schools, while 18.7 percent are enrolled in secondary schools, and 23.8 percent attend one of the universities.

HOUSING

Large flows of migrants from other parts of the state of Jalisco have set up legal and illegal settlements, creating complex social and urban problems. Initially, local government policy restricted the building of shantytowns, although it was not as acutely problematic in Guadalajara as elsewhere in Mexico, since the industrial structure of the city hinders their development. While small- and medium-sized plants have fostered the development of artisans and small-business communities, the city government has facilitated the development of miniaturized middle-class communities: small, closely built houses built of brick and concrete.

Nevertheless, shantytowns began to appear after 1940. The city provided the new settlements with better services and infrastructure than other Mexican municipalities. After 1970, the process of low-income housing development deteriorated seriously as plots became smaller and services less generous, and the land that was sold to new settlers was in fact common land that belonged to rural communities.

A housing shortage has developed due to commercial and industrial development as well as rising urban land values. By the mid-1980s, this process had forced 500,000 Guadalajarans into high-density squatter settlements that lack basic utilities. The government has responded by building public housing projects in outlying areas such as Libertad and Proyecto Sur.

CULTURE, THE ARTS, AND ENTERTAINMENT

Many cultural traditions considered characteristically Mexican were created in Guadalajara. These include mariachi music, tequila, the Mexican hat dance, broad-brimmed *sombreros*, and the Mexican rodeo.

Guadalajara has a vibrant culture, fine museums and galleries, exciting nightlife, and good places to stay and eat. Landmarks in Guadalajara include the cathedral's mural and the governor's palace, both of which are excellent examples of Spanish colonial art and architecture. Other sites of interest include the University of Guadalajara and the Autonomous University of Guadalajara; the museum, which houses the works of José Clemente Orozco; and the Degollado Theater, where the symphony orchestra plays.

CATEGORY	DATA	YEAR	AREA
LOCATION & ENVIRONMENT			
Area	72.6 square miles	1995	City
	188 square kilometers		
Elevation	5,194 feet/1,583 meters		City
January Temperature	59 degrees Fahrenheit		City
	15 degrees Celsius		
July Temperature	69 degrees Fahrenheit		City
	20.6 degrees Celsius		
Annual Precipitation	39.7 inches/1,008 millimeters		City
POPULATION & DEMOGRAPHY			
Population	3,500,000	1996	City
Projected Population	4,500,000	2015	City
Growth Rate	2.6%	1990–1995	City
Growth Rate	29.9%	1995–2015	City
Density	22,797 per square mile	1992	City
	8,803 per square kilometer		
Gender			
Male	47.7%	1992	City
Female	52.3%	1992	City
Age			
Under 20	46.3%	1992	City
20–59	45.6%	1992	City
Over 60	7.1%	1992	City
VITAL STATISTICS			
Births per 1,000 Residents	33.6	1992	City
Deaths per 1,000 Residents	6.1	1992	City
Infant Mortality Rate	18.6 per 1,000 live births	1992	City

(continued)

CATEGORY	DATA	YEAR	AREA
ECONOMY			
Total Workforce	870,183	1992	City
Trade	20.5%	1992	City
Manufacturing	28.2%	1992	City
Services	32.4%	1992	City
Transport, Communications	5.7%	1992	City
Construction	5.1%	1992	City
Utilities	0.6%	1992	City
Mining	0.8%	1992	City
Government	3.4%	1992	City
Nonclassifiable	3.2%	1992	City
TRANSPORTATION			
Passenger Journeys	1,024,368,000	1991	City
Buses and Trolley	97.8%	1991	City
Passenger Vehicles	700,594	1991	City
COMMUNICATIONS			
Telephones per 1,000 Residents	413.1	1992	City
Televisions per 1,000 Residents	199.6	1992	City
HOUSING			
Total Housing Units	328,439	1991	City
Persons per Unit	5	1991	City
HEALTH CARE			
Hospitals	12	1992	City
Physicians per 1,000 Residents	1.5	1992	City
EDUCATION			
Total Students	489,293	1992	City
Primary	57.5%	1992	City
Secondary	18.7%	1992	City
Higher	23.8%	1992	City

Sources: Department of Economic and Social Affairs, Population Division. *Urban Agglomerations, 1996.* New York: United Nations, 1997. United Nations Center for Human Settlements. *Compendium of Human Settlements Statistics.* New York: United Nations, 1995.

Guangzhou
PEOPLE'S REPUBLIC OF CHINA

LOCATION

Guangzhou (formerly known as Canton), the capital and most populous city in Guangdong Province, is located on the Zhu Jiang (Pearl River) in south China. The city has a major port on the Zhu Jiang, one of South China's busiest waterways. The city lies on a lowland plain at an altitude of 59 feet above sea level, south of the Nan Ling Mountains, which border Hunan and Jiangxi Provinces. The 2,870-square-mile (7,434-square-kilometer) city is located 100 miles northwest of Hong Kong and the South China Sea. Guangzhou lies 1,150 miles south of Beijing, capital of the People's Republic of China; 750 miles west-southwest of Shanghai, China's largest city; and 500 miles east-northeast of Hanoi, Vietnam's capital.

Guangzhou's temperature ranges from a January average of 56.3 degrees Fahrenheit (13.5 degrees Celsius) to a July average of 83.8 degrees Fahrenheit (28.8 degrees Celsius). The city averages 69 inches (1,753 millimeters) of precipitation per year.

POPULATION AND DEMOGRAPHY

Guangzhou is China's sixth largest city, after Shanghai, Beijing, Tianjin, Hong Kong, and Shenyang. In 1996, Guangzhou's regional population was 4,600,000. The city's population is projected to increase by 15.3 percent, to 4,676,000, by the year 2000 and by 61.0 percent, to 7,200,000, by the year 2015. The municipality has a population density of 2,173 persons per square mile (839 persons per square kilometer). The city has a higher birth rate than most other major Chinese urban centers. In 1995, Guangzhou had a rate of 18.1 births and 5.7 deaths per 1,000 residents, equaling a natural growth rate of 12.4 per 1,000 residents. Males are a 51.5 percent majority of the municipality's residents. Due to the high fertility rate, the region has a significantly higher young and dependent population than Beijing, Shanghai, and Hong Kong. In 1995, the young (those under age 15) comprised 30.9 percent of the regional population, persons between 15 and 64 made up 61.2 percent, and seniors over 65 accounted for 7.1 percent of the regional population. In 1995, the region had a ratio of 61.4 dependents per 100 persons in their productive years.

HISTORY

For many centuries, Guangzhou has come under global influence as a leading Chinese commercial and trading center. In the third century B.C., the city was incorporated into the Chinese Empire. Subsequently, the city became a major commercial center for merchants from South Asia and the Middle East. Between the sixteenth century A.D., when Portuguese explorers reached East Asia, and the nineteenth century, Guangzhou was ruled by a succession of imperial powers, coming under the influence of the British in the seventeenth century and being dominated by the French and the Dutch in the eighteenth century. In most instances, European powers established an entrepôt relationship with the city. By the late nineteenth century, Guangzhou had become a major zone of European foreign trade.

In the early twentieth century, Guangzhou became a center of the Chinese nationalist movement. In 1911, the Chinese nationalist Sun Yat-sen and the Kuomintang established headquarters in the city. Guangzhou was occupied by the Japanese from 1938 until 1945. Following the war, the city reverted to the control of Chinese nationalists. The 1949 revolution ousted the nationalists from power.

GOVERNMENT AND POLITICS

Guangzhou is capital of Guangdong Province, a large southeastern region that is one of twenty-eight administrative divisions in the People's Republic of China. Guangdong's provincial government is responsible for regional industrial and economic planning and service delivery. A major urban redevelopment and industrial revitalization program was carried out under Communist rule. The redevelopment efforts included the modernization and expansion of the city's port facilities and the improvement of the city's appearance. Since the early 1980s, national and regional authorities have promoted foreign investment and privatization of state enterprises.

ECONOMY

The local economy of Guangzhou, like that of other major cities in China, has been transformed by the Communists from a backward economy serving the interests of foreign concessions to a diversified industrialized economy. For nearly four decades after the revolution, the central government took primary responsibility for planning and investing in local production industries. However, beginning in the early 1980s, the central government has encouraged private ownership and investment to supplement the public sector's role in the economy. As in other Chinese cities, the private sector's role in the local economy has accelerated productivity and efficiency, but has also contributed to higher rates of unemployment for workers displaced by the efforts of industrial enterprises to become competitive in the global economy. A large segment of production now is for export to the economically developed countries of North America, Western Europe, and Japan.

The leading industrial products in the local economy are textiles, garments, iron and steel, motor vehicles, machinery, and petrochemicals. The local economy also includes production primarily for the regional market—including food and agricultural products, cement, and fertilizer. The economy of Guangdong Province continues to be dominated by agriculture, accounting for 37.5 percent of all workers, followed by manufacturing, making up 20.4 percent of all workers, and trade, with 9.1 percent of all regional employees. Officially Guangdong Province had a very low unemployment rate, less than 3 percent in 1995, but unofficial estimates of unemployment in the region are considered by experts to be significantly higher, perhaps over 20 percent. Unemployment among youth is considered to be a particularly acute problem for the region.

TRANSPORTATION

Like most major cities in China, bicycles provide the primary form of vehicular transportation in Guangzhou. While private motor vehicle use has increased in Guangzhou during the 1980s and 1990s, the city still has a scarcity of automobiles. Most residents traveling longer distances rely on public transportation. Guangzhou's primary means of public transportation are bus and trolley, accounting for 97.6 percent of all recorded public-transport journeys; rail transport is used 2.4 percent of the time. Guangzhou is a leading center for freight and cargo exports, with an estimated 20 percent of all Chinese trade flowing through the city. The city has an important seaport and rail links to Hong Kong and Beijing.

HEALTH CARE

Although Guangdong Province's residents are entitled to free and universal access to health care, there is a limited number of health care facilities and personnel. In 1995, the metropolitan region had an average of only 1.95 hospital beds and 3.2 medical care practitioners per 1,000 area residents. Health services are available in Western and traditional Chinese medicine.

EDUCATION

Nearly 70 percent of all Guangdong Province's students attend primary schools, and 30 percent are enrolled in secondary schools. The region has forty-two postsecondary institutions that provide specialized higher education in technical, scientific, and agricultural fields. Zhongshan University, located in Guangzhou, is the leading regional postsecondary educational institution.

HOUSING

Housing availability in Guangdong is coming under greater pressure as the city attempts to accommodate the city's rapidly rising population. The Chinese government's reform policies of the 1980s and 1990s have contributed to the decline of rural areas and the concentration of economic growth in Guangzhou, leading to a growing need for affordable housing. Due to the housing shortage, a large and growing share of the city's inhabitants are living in cramped quarters, and many rural migrants to the city are homeless. Guangzhou residents live in quarters with an average of 8.5 square meters per person. About 98 percent of all city housing units have tap water, and 86.6 percent are connected to gas lines.

CULTURE, THE ARTS, AND ENTERTAINMENT

As a major center in the Chinese nationalist movement in the first decade of the twentieth century, Guangzhou is home to a number of historic sites and monuments associated with the independence movement, including Sun Yat-sen Memorial Hall. The city is also home to ancient temples dating back to the fourteenth century. The central city of Guangzhou is home to nineteen museums and eleven libraries. Guangzhou Museum, which includes a fourteenth-century watchtower, is the leading cultural institution in the city. In 1993, Guangzhou had a total of fifty-two cinemas showing both popular and art films, and there were 338.7 televisions per 1,000 city residents.

CATEGORY	DATA	YEAR	AREA
LOCATION & ENVIRONMENT			
Area	2,870 square miles	1995	Metro
	7,434 square kilometers		
Elevation	59 feet/18 meters		Metro
January Temperature	56.3 degrees Fahrenheit		Metro
	13.5 degrees Celsius		
July Temperature	83.8 degrees Fahrenheit		Metro
	28.8 degrees Celsius		
Annual Precipitation	69 inches/1,753 millimeters		Metro
POPULATION & DEMOGRAPHY			
Population	4,600,000	1996	Metro
Projected Population	7,200,000	2015	Metro
Growth Rate	2.7%	1990–1995	Metro
Growth Rate	61.0%	1995–2015	Metro
Density	2,173 per square mile	1992	Metro
	839 per square kilometer		
Gender			
Male	51.5%	1992	Metro
Female	48.5%	1992	Metro
Age			
Under 15	30.9%	1995	Metro
15–64	61.2%	1995	Metro
Over 65	7.1%	1995	Metro
VITAL STATISTICS			
Births per 1,000 Residents	18.1	1995	Metro
Deaths per 1,000 Residents	5.7	1995	Metro
Infant Mortality Rate	18.8 per 1,000 live births	1993	Metro
ECONOMY			
Total Workforce	36,568,000	1995	Metro
Trade	9.1%	1995	Metro
Manufacturing	20.4%	1995	Metro
Services	1.6%	1995	Metro
Finance, Insurance, Real Estate	0.9%	1995	Metro
Transport and Communications	3.6%	1995	Metro
Construction	7.3%	1995	Metro
Government	1.8%	1995	Metro
Utilities	0.5%	1995	Metro
Agriculture	37.5%	1995	Metro
Mining	0.4%	1995	Metro
TRANSPORTATION			
Passenger Journeys	697,190,000	1990	Metro
Buses and Trolleys	97.6%	1990	Metro
Rail	2.4%	1990	Metro
Passenger Vehicles	4,473,000	1995	Metro

(continued)

CATEGORY	DATA	YEAR	AREA
COMMUNICATIONS			
Telephones per 1,000 Residents	147.7	1993	Metro
Televisions per 1,000 Residents	338.7	1993	Metro
HEALTH CARE			
Hospitals	2,267	1992	Metro
Physicians per 1,000 Residents	3.2	1992	Metro
EDUCATION			
Primary	69.7%	1995	Metro
Secondary	30.3%	1995	Metro

Sources: William T. Liu. *China Urban Statistics 1988.* New York: Praeger, 1988; *Statistics of World Large Cities.* Tokyo, Japan: Tokyo Metropolitan Government, 1992 and 1994; and United Nations Center for Human Settlements. *Compendium of Human Settlements Statistics.* New York: United Nations, 1995.

Halifax, Nova Scotia
CANADA

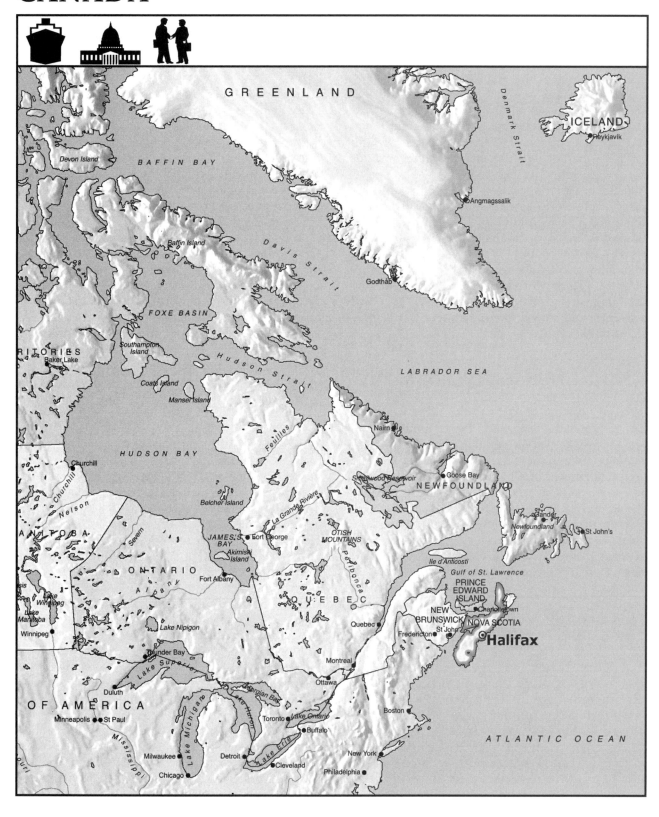

LOCATION

Halifax is the largest city of the Canadian Maritime Provinces of Nova Scotia, Prince Edward Island, and New Brunswick. The port city lies in Halifax County, on the east south-central seaboard of Nova Scotia Province, on the southwestern shores of Halifax Harbor, an inlet of the Atlantic Ocean. The regional land area encompasses 82.9 square miles (325 square kilometers). The central city covers a relatively small land area of 24 square miles (65 square kilometers) and has an elevation of 83 feet above sea level. The city forms part of a metropolitan region that includes the city of Dartmouth, located across Halifax Harbor. Halifax, the easternmost major city in North America, lies 350 miles northeast of Boston, Massachusetts, and about 500 miles east-northeast of Montréal, Québec. Halifax is linked to Dartmouth by two suspension bridges and by ferry. Average temperatures range from a low of 24.4 degrees Fahrenheit (−4.2 degrees Celsius) in January to a high of 65 degrees Fahrenheit (18.3 degrees Celsius) in July. The city has a fairly high average annual precipitation of 53.7 inches (1,364 millimeters).

POPULATION AND DEMOGRAPHY

Between 1985 and 1996, the Halifax Regional Municipality population expanded by a cumulative 13.6 percent, to 336,300. The population is expected to increase by 3.8 percent to 349,000 by the year 2001. Just under 20 percent of all area residents are under 15 years of age, 70.6 percent are in the 15-to-64 age group, and 9.5 percent are over 65 years of age. Females make up 51.3 percent of the area's population. Halifax's population is less heterogeneous than that of most other major Canadian cities. In 1991, 93.1 percent of all the region's residents spoke English as their native language and 2.7 percent spoke French.

HISTORY

Halifax was founded by English settlers and named after George Montagu Dunk, the Earl of Halifax, in 1749, the same year 1,200 British citizens volunteered to emigrate to the settlement. The city was formally incorporated in 1842. On December 6, 1917, a fire set off by an explosion caused by the collision and explosion of two warships carrying munitions destroyed much of the city and killed two thousand people. The explosion and fire were considered the worst nonmilitary disaster in the era prior to the nu-

clear age. On two separate occasions, in 1969 and 1996, Halifax expanded in size through the annexation and incorporation of outlying municipalities into the city.

GOVERNMENT AND POLITICS

Halifax is the capital region of the Province of Nova Scotia. In 1996, the Nova Scotia Provincial Government established the Halifax Regional Municipality through the amalgamation of the cities of Halifax and Dartmouth, the Town of Bedford, and Halifax County Municipality. Government powers are exercised by a council and mayor elected at large. The regional municipality united all major service delivery functions that previously had been administered by four local government authorities. The rationale for creating a regional government was to improve the effectiveness and economic efficiency of service delivery and economic planning by streamlining local programs into a larger authority that is accountable to citizens in the entire metropolitan area. The elected mayor and council also administer transportation, health care, education, sanitation, and environmental protection services.

ECONOMY

The Port of Halifax and the shipping industry dominate the regional economy. Halifax is one of the world's leading ports and the biggest and deepest natural harbor on North America's eastern seaboard. The Port of Halifax contributes 7,000 jobs to the local economy. The Halifax Port Corporation is responsible for building and maintaining port facilities, which are rented to operators. The city is positioning itself to be a major port city in the twenty-first century and is ensuring that Halifax remains a first-class port through modernization and investments in new technology to enhance the efficiency of cargo operations. The port is funding the development of rail and road links to improve land transportation to and from the facilities. The port is also a major port of call for the cruise liners. In 1997, forty-seven cruise ships carrying 45,000 passengers berthed at the Port of Halifax, contributing significantly to the regional tourist industry. Global integration and the growing importance of regional trading alliances such as NAFTA are expected to enhance the importance of Halifax's port facilities to the U.S. market. The city's leading local employers are the Department of National Defense, the MT&T telephone company, and IMP, an aerospace company. The province has the highest level of applied and basic research and the second highest concentration of research scientists in Canada.

The Greater Halifax Partnership, a partnership between public and private sectors, is responsible for economic development and promoting local industry. The partnership, consisting of the local business community, the Halifax Regional Municipality, and the provincial and federal governments, seeks to assist existing businesses, attract new investment, and promote business in the greater Halifax area. The partnership also provides business with market information, nurtures internal economic growth, and provides a single point of contact for clients. Other manufacturing industries important to the Halifax economy are food processing, printing, publishing, petroleum refining, shipbuilding, motor vehicle assembly, electronic equipment, plastic goods, clothing, cordage, and furniture manufacturing. Halifax is also the Maritime Provinces' largest financial, banking, and commercial center.

TRANSPORTATION

To reduce motor vehicle traffic congestion, encourage more sustainable forms of transportation, and moderate the growth of automobile ownership and use, national and regional authorities have encouraged the use of more efficient transportation. The Halifax Regional Municipality is served by a public transit system that provides bus service reaching more than 75 percent of the area's residents. A ferry service provides additional public transportation service to area residents. The Halifax regional airport provides direct flights to two U.S. cities, four European cities, and three major Canadian cities. The city's strategic location as the largest northern city on the North American eastern seaboard contributes to its importance as a leading freight and shipping center. Public officials are promoting efforts to upgrade and expand the port and rail facilities to accommodate the expected increase in European trade.

HOUSING

Owner-occupied housing accounts for 58 percent of the Halifax region's 118,320 housing units. Nearly half the housing units in the region are single-family detached houses, and over 30 percent are units in apartment buildings. Due to significantly higher levels of migration to suburban and rural areas in Nova Scotia during the late 1980s and early 1990s, pressure

for new housing development in Halifax is not as great as in other major Canadian cities.

HEALTH CARE

The Canadian federal government guarantees access to health care to all residents as a right of citizenship. The Canadian national health insurance system is administered on a provincial level by Nova Scotia health authorities. Halifax is served by eight regional hospitals. Due to the scarcity of health care services in the rural areas of Nova Scotia, residents who live outside the Halifax metropolitan region frequently travel to the city to utilize the more plentiful and advanced medical service facilities there.

EDUCATION

Halifax has seven degree-granting postsecondary institutions: Dalhousie University, the University of King's College, Saint Mary's University, the Nova Scotia College of Art and Design, Mount Saint Vincent University, and the Technical University of Nova Scotia. Halifax has a relatively high proportion of residents who have completed postsecondary degree programs. In 1991, 16.3 percent of metropolitan Halifax's population had a university degree. To enhance regional planning, the metropolitan area amalgamation plan of 1996 merged the three district school boards of Halifax, Dartmouth, and Halifax County/Bedford into a single regional school board.

CULTURE, THE ARTS, AND ENTERTAINMENT

Halifax is the leading center of art and culture in the Maritime Provinces. The leading museums are the Bedford Institute of Oceanography, the Halifax Citadel National Historic Site, the Nova Scotia Museum, the Nova Scotia Museum of Natural History, the Nova Scotia Public Archives, and the Thomas McCulloch Museum. The leading art galleries are the Art Gallery of Nova Scotia, the Dalhousie Art Center, the Dartmouth Public Art Gallery, and the Nova Scotia Centre for Craft and Design. The city is home to a symphony orchestra, a jazz performance group, and several theater companies. Halifax is also home to the Halifax Mooseheads ice hockey team. Other organized sporting activities in Halifax include football, synchronized swimming, and bicycling.

CATEGORY	DATA	YEAR	AREA
LOCATION & ENVIRONMENT			
Area	82.9 square miles	1996	City
	325 square kilometers		
Elevation	83 feet/25.3 meters		City
January Temperature	24.4 degrees Fahrenheit	1992	City
	−4.2 degrees Celsius		
July Temperature	65 degrees Fahrenheit	1992	City
	18.3 degrees Celsius		
Annual Precipitation	53.7 inches/1,364 meters	1992	City
POPULATION & DEMOGRAPHY			
Population	336,300	1996	Metro
Growth Rate	13.6%	1985–1996	Metro
	3.8%	1996–2001	Metro
Density	10,016 per square mile	1991	Metro
	3,866 per square kilometer		
Gender			
Male	48.7%	1995	Metro
Female	51.3 %	1995	Metro
Age			
Under 20	19.9%	1991	Metro
20–59	70.6%	1991	Metro
Over 60	9.5%	1991	Metro
VITAL STATISTICS			
Births per 1,000 Residents	14.1	1995	Metro
Deaths per 1,000 Residents	7	1995	Metro
ECONOMY			
Total Workforce	180,165	1991	Metro
Manufacturing	7.2%	1991	Metro
Services	16.2%	1991	Metro
Construction	5.2%	1991	Metro
HOUSING			
Total Housing Units	118,320	1991	Metro
Persons per Unit	2.7	1991	Metro
Owner-Occupied Units	58.0%	1991	Metro
HEALTH CARE			
Hospitals	8	1991	Metro
Physicians per 1,000 Residents	3.5%	1991	Metro

Sources: *Canada Year Book 1994.* Ottawa, Ontario: Statistics Canada, 1995. *Canadian Markets.* Toronto, Ontario: The Financial Post, 1996.

Hamburg
GERMANY

LOCATION

Hamburg, Germany's leading port and second most populous city, is located on the Elbe River in north-central Germany at the junction of the Alston River, 65 miles southeast of the North Sea. The city lies on the North German Plain at an elevation of 43 feet (13.1 meters) above sea level. The city occupies a surface area of 292 square miles (755 square kilometers). Hamburg is one of sixteen states, or *Länder*, in the Federal Republic of Germany. The city-state, formed in 1815 as the Free and Hanseatic City of Hamburg, is composed of seven administrative districts. The greater Hamburg region extends into the states of Schleswig-Holstein, to the city's north, and Lower Saxony, on the city's south. Hamburg has two primary districts, an old section east of the Alston River and a commercial and business center west of the river. The city is located approximately 150 miles northwest of Berlin, the capital and largest city of the reunited Germany, 90 miles south of the German border with Denmark, and about 50 miles southwest of Lübeck, a major German port city near Mecklenburg Bay, an inlet of the Baltic Sea. Hamburg's temperature ranges from an average low of 36 degrees Fahrenheit (2.4 degrees Celsius) in January to an average of 67 degrees Fahrenheit (19.7 degrees Celsius) in July. Hamburg has an annual average of 30 inches (761 millimeters) of precipitation.

POPULATION AND DEMOGRAPHY

Although Hamburg is Germany's second largest city, the city's residential population has declined over the past two decades due to urban sprawl and suburban migration. In 1995, the regional population was 2.6 million. The population is expected to grow to 2.7 million by the year 2015. From 1972 to 1992, the city of Hamburg's population declined by a cumulative 8.1 percent, from 1,817,122 to 1,640,000, although the city's population decline has slowed to 3 percent between 1982 and 1992. The city-state has a density of 6,040 persons per square mile (2,237 persons per square kilometer). The population density of Hamburg's city center is considerably higher. Hamburg's population structure is considerably older than that of most major global cities. About 22 percent of the city's population is under 20 years of age, 60 percent are between 20 and 59 years old, and 17.8 percent are 60 or over. In 1992, the city had a birth rate of 9.8 per 1,000 residents and a death rate of 12.2 per 1,000 residents, constituting a natural population decrease of 2.4 per 1,000 city residents. Females comprise 52.4

percent of the city's population. Marriages exceed divorces in Hamburg by a ratio of about 2 to 1.

HISTORY

Hamburg was founded by Charlemagne in 808 as a fortress and Christian religious center and subsequently emerged as a leading North Sea port and trading center. In 1189 the Holy Roman Empire formally chartered Hamburg as a city, and by the early thirteenth century Hamburg, along with Lübeck and Bremen, formed part of the Hanseatic League of Cities. The city was a focal point of Lutheranism in the German Reformation movement a century later. However, due to hostilities initiated against Protestant adherents by the Holy Roman Empire, Hamburg's economic prosperity declined significantly during the Thirty Years' War, which reduced trade and commerce in Europe and ravaged the northern German population. Hamburg was occupied by Napoleon's forces in 1811, but with his defeat in 1815, Hamburg became part of the German Confederation. The city's reemergence in the mid-nineteenth century was interrupted by a fire in 1842 that destroyed much of the city. Subsequently, Hamburg was rebuilt and regained its prominence as a trade and shipping center. The large port spawned industrial development, initially shipbuilding and repairing, and subsequently the development of heavy industry, including iron and steel production, metal fabrication, and electrical engineering. The growth of industrial production engendered the development of a large market and the growth of food and tobacco production, pharmaceuticals, and printing production. By the turn of the twentieth century, a strong labor movement allied to the Socialist and Communist parties emerged. In 1938, the boundaries of the city were expanded to incorporate the outlying suburbs. The city was used as a German submarine base during World War II. Frequent air raids by Allied forces destroyed large sectors of the city's residential areas and harbor facilities. Hamburg was rebuilt at the end of the war.

GOVERNMENT AND POLITICS

Hamburg is both a city and a federal state of the German Federal Republic, and so state and local government administration are fused. The central city is divided into seven districts. Executive power is held by a senate, which sets administrative policy for the Hamburg region and represents the state in affairs with the Federal Republic. The Hamburg Senate must be made up of at least ten members but must not exceed fifteen members. The Senate is selected by the Metropolitan Council, an elected parliamentary body. A mayor, who serves a one-year term, is selected from among the members of the Senate. Hamburg has an independent judicial system.

ECONOMY

Hamburg is the leading commercial, transportation, and media center in northern Germany and the hub of the German media industry. The city's leading industries are associated with Hamburg's role in commerce, transportation, and foreign trade and include engineering, copper, petroleum and oil refining, shipbuilding, pharmaceuticals, machinery, chemicals, metal goods, electronics, food processing, printing, and publishing. Due to growing international competition, many of Hamburg's basic industries—steel, shipbuilding, and electrical engineering—have declined since the 1960s. The growth of the local aerospace industry has replaced some of the industrial decline, but the city continues to endure a high rate of unemployment that has persisted through the last two decades of the twentieth century. Still, Hamburg has one of the highest per capita incomes in the European Union—while the city has only 2 percent of the German population, it generates 4 percent of the national gross domestic product. Hamburg has about 935,000 workers. The service sector is the largest sector of the local labor force, accounting for 27.2 percent of all workers, followed by trade (18 percent), manufacturing (15.5 percent), government (14.1 percent), and transport and communications (10.3 percent).

Hamburg's importance as Germany's center of trade and commerce is advanced through the presence of over 3,500 branch offices of transnational companies in the city. Many of the firms are concentrated in the City Nord, a business center for the banking, insurance, and information industries that is located outside the city center.

Since the end of World War II, Hamburg has become a leading media center in Germany with the growth of the printing and publishing, film, and radio and television broadcasting industries.

TRANSPORTATION

Hamburg has an integrated public transportation system that consists of buses, a subway, and a regional rail network. In 1992, subways accounted for 57.4 percent and buses and trolleys 42.6 percent of all mass transit passenger journeys in the city. Urban sprawl and the growth of the city's suburbs since the 1960s contributes to greater reliance on motor vehicles and the decline of mass transit. In 1992, the city had 523 passenger vehicles per 1,000 residents.

Hamburg, Germany's leading foreign trade center, handles a large share of the country's foreign trade through the city's transportation facilities. The city's seaport facilities, which include extensive docks, a container port, and warehouses, are linked by rail and waterways to other points in central and northern Europe. Hamburg's international airport is located about 10 miles north of the city.

HEALTH CARE

The Hamburg Government administers health care, guaranteed as a right to all citizens by the Federal Republic of Germany. The universal health care system covers both routine procedures and catastrophic illnesses. The system supports residents who are aged, infirm, or disabled by providing comprehensive care services and economic assistance. In 1993, Hamburg had a relatively high death rate of 9.8 per 1,000 residents, owing to the city's large number of elderly residents. In the same year, the city's infant mortality rate was 6.8 infant deaths per 1,000 live births. In 1992, Hamburg had 0.8 hospital beds and 4.7 physicians per 1,000 residents, a higher ratio of doctors to patients than Berlin, Frankfurt, or Munich.

EDUCATION

The Hamburg state government provides free compulsory education for children between 5 and 18 years of age. Primary school students accounted for 19.2 percent of the city's school enrollees in the 1992–1993 academic year. Secondary school students comprised 54.6 percent and higher education students made up 26.1 percent of all students in the city. The city's schools provide both academic and vocational training. Hamburg is a leading center of postsecondary education and research. Hamburg University, with about 50,000 students, is the leading university. Other schools in the city include an economics institute, technical schools, a college of music and theater, a fine arts school, and theological institutions.

HOUSING

During World War II, Hamburg lost over 50 percent of its residential housing stock as a result of aerial bombardments by Allied forces. Much of the housing stock was rebuilt in the immediate postwar period. By 1960, all of Hamburg's housing stock that was lost in the Second World War had been rebuilt. Much of the new housing construction was of better quality than the housing lost during the war. The limited supply of affordable housing for the city's middle- and working-class population spurred the state government to regulate private housing and develop a large stock of public housing units. However, a sizable housing stock remains for affluent residents. Since the 1960s, the trend in Hamburg has been the growth of residential housing in the city's outlying areas. In 1992, the city had 801,000 housing units, of which 15 percent were single-family homes. Between 1991 and 1992, Hamburg's housing stock grew by 0.9 percent.

CULTURE, THE ARTS, AND ENTERTAINMENT

Hamburg is home to Germany's leading artistic museums. The city's most well-known gallery is the Kunsthalle Museum, which houses an extensive collection of nineteenth- and twentieth-century art. The city is home to numerous private galleries. Other museums include historical, cultural, anthropological, zoological, and arts and crafts institutions. As the birthplace of composers Johannes Brahms and Felix Mendelssohn, Hamburg has a rich musical legacy that continues into the late twentieth century. The city is home to the Hamburg State Opera, the Hamburg Symphony, the Hamburg State Philharmonic Orchestra, and the Norddeutschen Rundfunks Symphony Orchestra. The city has a concert hall, opera house, and over forty theaters for the performing arts. Leading spectator sports in Hamburg are soccer, tennis, and horse racing.

CATEGORY	DATA	YEAR	AREA
LOCATION & ENVIRONMENT			
Area	292 square miles	1996	City
	755 square kilometers		
Elevation	43 feet/13.1 meters		City
January Temperature	36 degrees Fahrenheit		City
	2.4 degrees Celsius		
July Temperature	68 degrees Fahrenheit		City
	19.7 degrees Celsius		
Annual Precipitation	28 inches/760 millimeters		City
POPULATION & DEMOGRAPHY			
Population	2,600,000	1996	City
Projected Population	2,700,000	2015	City
Growth Rate	0.7%	1990–1995	City
Growth Rate	0.0%	1995–2015	City
Density	6,040 per square mile	1992	City
	2,237 per square kilometer		
Gender			
Males	47.6%	1992	City
Females	52.4%	1992	City
Age			
Under 20	22.0%	1994	City
20–59	60.0%	1994	City
Over 60	17.8%	1994	City

(continued)

CATEGORY	DATA	YEAR	AREA
VITAL STATISTICS			
Births per 1,000 Residents	9.8	1993	City
Deaths per 1,000 Residents	12.2	1993	City
Infant Mortality Rate	6.8 per 1,000 births	1993	City
ECONOMY			
Total Workforce	935,000	1992	City
Trade	18.0%	1992	City
Manufacturing	15.5%	1992	City
Services	27.2%	1992	City
Transport and Communications	10.3%	1992	City
Government	14.1%	1990	City
TRANSPORTATION			
Passenger Journeys	558,000,000	1990	City
Subway	57.4%	1990	City
Buses and Trolley	42.6%	1990	City
Passenger Vehicles per 1,000 Residents	523	1992	City
HOUSING			
Total Housing Units	801,000	1992	City
New Housing Units	7,471	1992	City
Persons per Unit	2.1	1992	City
HEALTH CARE			
Hospitals	43	1992	City
Physicians per 1,000 Residents	4.7	1992	City
Hospital Beds per 1,000 Residents	0.8	1992	City
EDUCATION			
Total Students	287,000	1993	City
Primary	19.2%	1993	City
Secondary	54.6%	1993	City
Higher	26.1%	1993	City

Sources: Department of Economic and Social Affairs, Population Division. *Urban Agglomerations, 1996.* New York: United Nations, 1997; Eurostat *Regions Statistical Yearbook.* Brussels, Belgium: Statistical Office of European Communities, 1996; and *Statistiches Jahrbuch 1996 für die Bundesrepublik Deutschland,* Wiesbaden, Germany: Federal Statistical Office, 1996.

Harbin, Heilongjiang Province
PEOPLE'S REPUBLIC OF CHINA

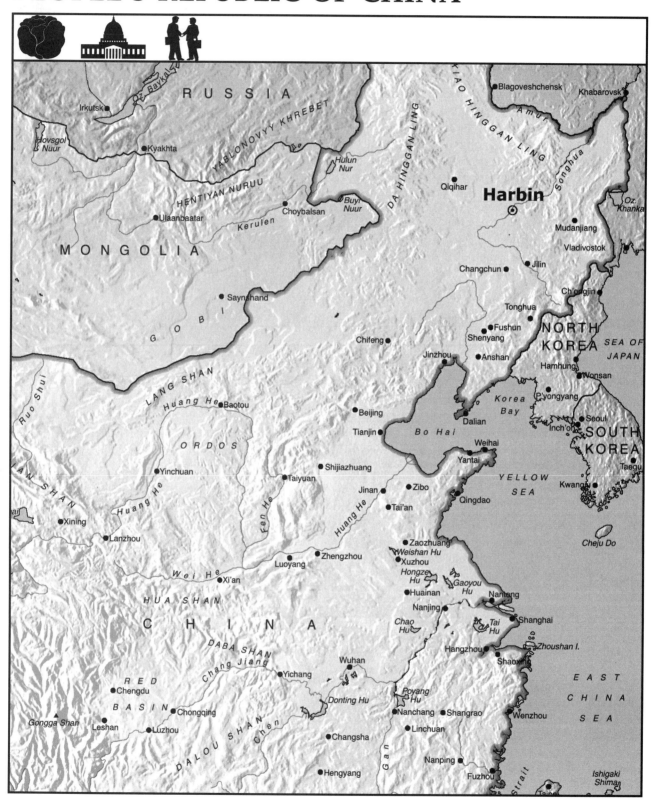

LOCATION

Harbin, the capital of Heilongjiang Province, in northeastern China, is about 250 miles northwest of China's border with North Korea and 300 miles northwest of the Russian port city of Vladivostok, on the Sea of Japan. Harbin has a surface land area of 6,323 square miles (16,375 square kilometers) at an elevation of 476 feet above sea level. The city is located in south-central Heilongjiang Province, on the Sungari (Songhua) River, which flows northwest from the Changbaek-Sanmaek Highlands on the Chinese–North Korean boundary to the Nen River, east of China's Great Khingan Mountains. The older part of the city lies on the south bank of the Sungari River. Newer developments are situated on the north bank of the river. Harbin lies approximately 700 miles northeast of Beijing, the capital of the People's Republic of China. Harbin's temperature ranges from a January average of 4.9 degrees Fahrenheit (−15.1 degrees Celsius) to a July average of 73 degrees Fahrenheit (22.8 degrees Celsius). The city averages 16.7 inches (424 millimeters) of precipitation per year.

POPULATION AND DEMOGRAPHY

Harbin is the most populous city in Heilongjiang Province. Over the past two decades, vigorous national and regional government efforts to reduce high fertility rates have moderated the city's population growth. In 1996, the metropolitan area had a population of 4,700,000. The central city density is 4,872 persons per square mile (1,881 persons per square kilometer). The metropolitan area population is projected to increase by 81.5 percent to 8.1 million by the year 2015. Harbin has a rate of 13.2 live births per 1,000 residents, higher than Beijing and Shanghai but lower than Guangzhou, and a rate of 5.3 deaths per 1,000 residents. The region has a natural growth rate of 7.9 percent. The regional age structure in Heilongjiang Province is significantly younger than China's other major population centers: 23.4 percent of all residents are under 15 years of age, and 72 percent are between 15 and 64 years of age. Only 4.6 percent of the province's residents are over 65 years of age. The region has a ratio of 38.95 young and senior dependents for all residents between 15 and 64 years of age. Males account for a 50.6 percent majority of Harbin's central city residents. The vast majority of the city's residents are of Han Chinese origin. Due to the legacy of Russian influence over Harbin during the last two centuries, the city continues to have a relatively large Russian ethnic minority.

HISTORY

At the end of the nineteenth century, Harbin was a small fishing village. In 1896, Russian investors financed the development of the city as a major rail transportation center. Following the completion of the railway, Harbin became the most prominent stop on the Chinese Eastern Railway, a major branch of the Trans-Siberian Railroad, which extended between Lake Baikal, to the city's east, and the Russian port city of Vladivostok, on the Sea of Japan. After the Russian surrender to the Japanese at the end of the Russo-Japanese War of 1904–1905, the city came under the greater Japanese influence. Between 1932 and the defeat of the Japanese in 1945, Harbin became known as Pinkiang, the name given to the city by the Japanese occupying government. In the aftermath of the Bolshevik Revolution, Harbin attracted a wave of refugees, significantly increasing the size of the Russian ethnic minority population. Following the defeat of the Chinese nationalists by the Red Army in 1949, Communist government policies helped transform the city into a major Chinese industrial center.

GOVERNMENT AND POLITICS

Harbin is the capital and administrative center of Heilongjiang Province, one of twenty-three administrative units in the People's Republic of China. The provincial government is responsible for industrial planning throughout the region, although the private sector is assuming a larger share of local productive activity. The regional authorities also administer basic service delivery throughout the region, including education, transportation, and public health. Like other major regional centers in China, to spur economic development regional authorities have encouraged foreign capital investment and privatization programs to increase productivity.

ECONOMY

Harbin is the leading industrial center in Heilongjiang Province. Much of Harbin's importance stems from the city's access to the major markets in Russia and the Far East. The city continues to be dominated by the rural agricultural industry, which accounts for 36.8 percent of the regional labor force. Manufacturing, employing 18.8 percent of all workers, is the region's second leading economic sector, followed by trade, with 12 percent, and the mine industry, which employs 9.6 percent of all regional workers.

The region's major industries include agricultural and food processing (sugar refining, grain, tobacco), machine tools, mining, metallurgical equipment, agricultural equipment, plastics, electrical equipment, ball bearings, and cement. Other regional industries include leather and soap production. In 1995, unemployed youth accounted for more than two thirds of Harbin's official regional unemployment rate of 3 percent; however, actual unemployment is considered to be significantly higher.

TRANSPORTATION

The major forms of public transportation in Harbin are buses and trolleys, which account for 96.8 percent of all passenger journeys; rail passengers comprise the rest. Harbin has an average of 8.2 buses per 10,000 residents, lower than Beijing, Shanghai, and Guangzhou, but significantly higher than Tianjin. The bicycle is Harbin's major form of vehicular transportation. Motor vehicles are relatively scarce in Harbin and the region. Heilongjiang Province has an average of 3.2 passenger motor vehicles per 100 regional residents. Harbin is an important transportation center for the regional agricultural industry and a key railway center, linking northeast China with the Pacific Ocean, Russia, and the Commonwealth of Independent States (Russian Federation and the former Soviet republics of eastern Europe and central Asia). The city is also served by a regional airport.

HEALTH CARE

While health care is guaranteed to all citizens in China, the region has a shortage of medical institutions and health care personnel. In 1995, Heilongjiang Province had numerous hospitals and health care institutions and an average of 3.9 hospital beds and 4.2 physicians per 1,000 regional residents. Both Western and Chinese traditional medicine are practiced in the region.

EDUCATION

Harbin is a leading center of provincial and regional postsecondary education. In 1995, Heilongjiang Province had a total of thirty-eight postsecondary education institutions providing specialized scientific, agricultural, and technical education. Agricultural education and research institutions are important to the region, due to the prominence of farming in the regional economy. Excluding postsecondary students, approximately 58.2 percent of students in Heilongjiang Province attend primary school, and 41.8 percent of students attend secondary school.

HOUSING

Due to the past and anticipated rapid rise in population, Harbin is facing a severe housing shortage and overcrowding. Although local government authorities have attempted to address the housing shortage through the construction of large apartment complexes on the city's fringes, the new developments have not kept pace with rapid population growth. Harbin's housing shortage stems in part from continued migration to the central city and higher-than-average fertility compared to the national average. The average resident in Harbin occupies 7 square meters of living space. About 94.3 percent of the city's housing stock has access to residential tap water and 91.3 percent has access to residential gas.

CULTURE, THE ARTS, AND ENTERTAINMENT

As a relatively new city, constructed in the last century, Harbin has few architectural and historic sites that attract local, regional, or national visitors. In fact, the relative absence of cultural, artistic, and entertainment institutions is striking. Harbin has no museums of importance, and there are only eight libraries in the city. Although Harbin's population exceeds 3 million inhabitants, the city is served by only fifteen cinemas. In 1992, there were 308.1 television sets per 1,000 city residents. The region's relatively cold climate is conducive to winter sports.

CATEGORY	DATA	YEAR	AREA
LOCATION & ENVIRONMENT			
Area	6323 square miles	1995	Metro
	1,637 square kilometers		Metro
Elevation	476 feet/145.1 meters		Metro
January Temperature	4.9 degrees Fahrenheit		Metro
	−15.1 degrees Celsius		Metro
July Temperature	73.0 degrees Fahrenheit		Metro
	22.8 degrees Celsius		Metro
Annual Precipitation	16.7 inches/424 millimeters		Metro
POPULATION & DEMOGRAPHY			
Population	4,700,000	1996	Metro
Projected Population	8,100,000	2015	Metro
Growth Rate	4.3%	1990–1995	Metro
Growth Rate	81.5%	1995–2015	Metro
Density	4,872 per square mile	1992	Metro
	1,881 per square kilometer		Metro
Gender			
Male	50.6%	1992	Metro
Female	49.4%	1992	Metro
Age			
Under 15	23.4%	1995	Metro
15–64	72.0%	1995	Metro
Over 65	4.6%	1995	Metro
VITAL STATISTICS			
Births per 1,000 Residents	13.2	1995	Metro
Deaths per 1,000 Residents	5.3	1995	Metro
ECONOMY			
Total Workforce	15,524,000	1995	Metro
Trade	12.0%	1995	Metro
Manufacturing	18.8%	1995	Metro
Services	2.4%	1995	Metro
Finance, Insurance, Real Estate	0.9%	1995	Metro
Transport/Communication	4.2%	1995	Metro
Construction	4.9%	1995	Metro
Government	2.6%	1995	Metro
Utilities	0.8%	1995	Metro
Agriculture	36.8%	1995	Metro
Mining	9.6%	1995	Metro
TRANSPORTATION			
Passenger Journeys	507,710,000	1990	Metro
Buses and Trolleys	96.8%	1990	Metro
Rail	3.2%	1990	Metro
Passenger Vehicles	1,243,000	1995	Metro

(continued)

CATEGORY	DATA	YEAR	AREA
COMMUNICATIONS			
Telephones per 1,000 Residents	39.6	1992	Metro
Televisions per 1,000 Residents	308.1	1992	Metro
HOUSING			
Total Housing Units	691,705	1992	Metro
Persons per Unit	4.5	1992	Metro
HEALTH CARE			
Hospitals	1,975	1992	Metro
Physicians per 1,000 Residents	4.2	1992	Metro
EDUCATION			
Primary	58.2%	1995	Metro
Secondary	41.8%	1995	Metro

Sources: Department of Economic and Social Affairs, Population Division. *Urban Agglomerations, 1996.* New York: United Nations, 1997; *Statistics of World Large Cities.* Tokyo, Japan: Tokyo Metropolitan Government, 1992 and 1994; and United Nations Center for Human Settlements. *Compendium of Human Settlements Statistics.* New York: United Nations, 1995.

Havana
CUBA

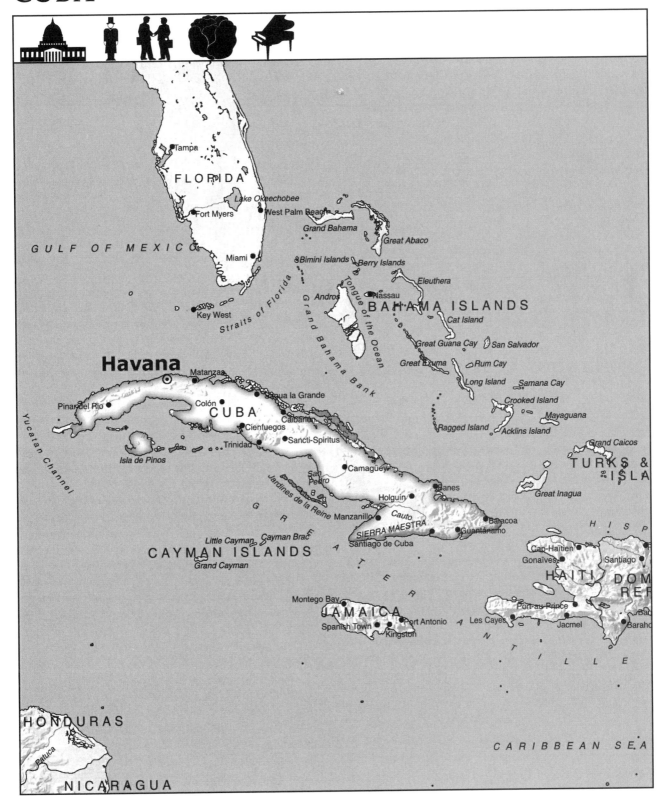

LOCATION

Havana is the capital, chief seaport, commercial hub, and cultural center of Cuba. One of the oldest cities in the Western Hemisphere, Havana features narrow streets and old houses with overhanging balconies. Its historical landmarks include colonial churches, palaces, and fortresses. Newer areas feature broad, tree-lined boulevards.

Situated approximately 80 feet above sea level, the city stretches south from its harbor to cover 281 square miles (727 square kilometers) of territory. The city is located on the western side of Havana Bay and is built on a traditional Spanish grid pattern. The city is approximately 200 miles southwest of Miami, Florida, and some 400 miles northeast of Merida in Mexico.

Havana enjoys a warm and tropical climate. The mean temperature varies from 73.4 degrees Fahrenheit (23 degrees Celsius) in winter to 80.4 degrees Fahrenheit in summer (26.9 degrees Celsius). It has a rainy climate, with some 58.2 inches (1,479 millimeters) annually.

POPULATION AND DEMOGRAPHY

The Havana metropolitan area has a population of approximately 2.2 million people, making it the largest city in the Caribbean basin. Between 1950 and 1970, the city grew rapidly at a rate of approximately 2 percent annually, but that growth has dropped off in recent years to just over 1 percent between 1990 and 1995, reflecting government policies designed to discourage urban-bound migrants from the countryside. Still, the population is projected to grow to 2.4 million by the year 2015.

While virtually all of Havana's citizens speak Spanish, there is a wide ethnic mix in the city, reflecting the vicissitudes of Cuban history. While no group is numerically dominant, the population includes people of European, African, and mixed European and African descent. While Roman Catholicism has been the overwhelming faith of Havana's citizens, there has been a major decline in the number of practitioners since the revolution of 1959.

HISTORY

San Cristobal de Havana was originally founded on the southern coast of Cuba at the mouth of the Mayabeque River, where the modern town of Batabono

is located. A few years later, it was moved to the Almendares River delta. Finally, in 1519, the town was reestablished yet again at the entrance of Havana Bay, its current location. While Havana was one of seven original cities established by Diego Velázquez, the city's strategic maritime location favored its role as a command post. Fleets carrying the riches collected from Spanish conquests in Mexico and Peru stopped at Havana on their way back to Spain. Indeed, the town is strategically located along the path of trade winds that channel boats across the Atlantic.

With such busy ocean-going traffic, Havana became the target of French buccaneers in 1555. To protect the port, the Spanish built three fortresses between 1558 and 1630. In 1556, Havana replaced Santiago de Cuba as the seat of the Spanish Captains General, and by the early 1600s, the city had become the capital of Spanish Cuba. For the next two hundred years, Havana served as the most important port in Latin America.

During the Seven Years' War between France and England in the mid-eighteenth century, the British captured the port, then traded Florida for it. New fortresses were built to protect the city against invaders, making it among the most fortified cities in the world.

Economic liberalization triggered by the British occupation allowed Havana to prosper in the late eighteenth and early nineteenth centuries. At the same time, the city modernized, with the first railway coming in 1832, gas lighting in 1848, the telegraph in 1851, and electric lighting by 1890.

While most Latin American countries had established independence from Spain in the 1820s, Cuba remained under Spanish colonial rule. Widespread protests escalated in the late nineteenth century and culminated in the Spanish-American War. In 1898, the United States forced a rapid Spanish surrender. Political instability and a series of U.S.-supported dictators ruled the country until 1959. After years of insurgency, Fidel Castro and the 26th of July Movement took power on January 1, 1959 and began a series of revolutionary reforms.

Immediately seeking to liberate Cuba from U.S. economic control, he nationalized many assets, alienating Washington, DC, in the process. For the next forty years, the United States imposed a boycott against the island but was largely unable to prevent other countries from trading with it. Meanwhile, President Castro established a socialist government and extended health care and education to the Cuban masses.

GOVERNMENT AND POLITICS

Havana includes fifteen separate municipalities, which in turn are divided into ninety-three official neighborhoods. These neighborhoods are run by people's councils and serve as a link between residents and the municipal governments. To improve the delivery of social services to the neighborhoods and ensure more community participation, the government has made a major effort to decentralize authority in recent years.

ECONOMY

Havana is the center of industry and commerce in Cuba. Light industries include processing plants for the country's sugar and tobacco crops. Heavy industries include refineries, paper mills, textile plants, and metal fabrication factories. In addition, the port area is the site of shipbuilding enterprises as well as fishing fleets.

Following the revolution of 1959, the government set forth long-term plans for the country's economic development. Under the first set of such plans—roughly up to the mid-1970s—Havana was deemphasized, as the government invested heavily in the countryside. By the mid-1960s, salaries and social indices were roughly equal between the capital and the hinterland.

More recently, government planners have emphasized high-technology industries—including biotechnology and medicine—and tourism. In addition, the government is actively encouraging foreign companies to set up factories in the city through the establishment of free trade zones.

Altogether, Havana's workforce includes nearly 771,000 people, of whom about 26 percent labor in manufacturing and 13 percent in trade. Most of the rest are in services. The city is recovering from the withdrawal of Soviet trade in the early 1990s. By the late 1990s Havana has become a vibrant economy due to the encouragement of trade with the Americas and western Europe.

TRANSPORTATION

Havana is the main rail, highway, and air terminus for the country. Within the metropolis, buses and taxis remain the sole forms of public transit. Unlike most Latin American cities, Havana does not suffer from heavy traffic jams, largely because private car ownership remains relatively uncommon, with less than 100,000 such vehicles in the city.

Since the collapse of the Soviet Union in the early 1990s and the subsequent loss of Soviet-subsidized oil, the government in Havana has encouraged the use of bicycles for transport. Because of lack of spare parts, many buses do not run, while those that do suffer from overcrowding. The country is now compensating for the loss of trade with the former Soviet Union by expanding linkages with East Asia, now a major source of automobile and commercial vehicle imports.

HEALTH CARE

Since the 1959 revolution, health care has been provided free by the government to all Cubans. Moreover, the government has developed a system of neighborhood health clinics throughout the island. Thus, local doctors know their patients and their patients' living patterns intimately. Indeed, Cuba has made enormous strides in health care delivery since the revolution, raising itself up to First World standards. There are sixty hospitals and clinics in Havana and more than 7 physicians per 1,000 citizens. Moreover, life expectancy has risen from 60 to 74 since the revolution.

EDUCATION

As a result of a nationwide literacy campaign begun shortly after the revolution, the citizens of Havana are remarkably well educated. In recent years, there has also been a major effort to prepare more young people for college. This new emphasis, however, has not fully displaced the old focus on vocational and agricultural skills. Most secondary students still spend part of the year at boarding schools in the countryside. Altogether, there are over 300,000 students in Havana's schools—45 percent of whom are in primary schools, 30 percent in secondary schools, and another 25 percent at the university level. The city is home to the University of Havana, one of Latin America's leading research institutions.

HOUSING

In the first two decades following the 1959 revolution, housing construction in Havana was deemphasized in favor of the countryside. Since the mid-1970s, however, there has been a growing realization that the city's housing stock was in serious decay. Since that time, there has been new construction on the periphery of the city, as well as major efforts to rehabilitate the old colonial and early independence-era buildings in the center of the city. Special policies to help people build their own homes have also been inaugurated in recent years. Still, housing shortages remain and migration from the countryside is still discouraged, except for educational reasons. The central city has a housing occupancy rate of 3.8 persons per unit.

CULTURE, THE ARTS, AND ENTERTAINMENT

Havana is home to a number of major educational and cultural institutions, including the National University and the Great Theater, the oldest continuously functioning dramatic establishment in the Americas. The city also has a wealth of historical and revolutionary monuments. Significant examples of the latter include the Granma Pavilion, the Museum of the Revolution, and a memorial to José Martí, a nineteenth-century Cuban nationalist. The downtown Plaza of the Revolution is home to the National Library, and the famous relief of Che Guevara. In addition, the city has an exciting nightlife with old nightclubs and cabarets from the prerevolutionary era that feature floor shows with elaborately costumed dancers.

CATEGORY	DATA	YEAR	AREA
LOCATION & ENVIRONMENT			
Area	281 square miles	1995	City
	727 square kilometers		City
Elevation	80 feet/24 meters		City
January Temperature	73.4 degrees Fahrenheit		City
	23 degrees Celsius		City
July Temperature	80.4 degrees Fahrenheit		City
	26.9 degrees Celsius		City
Annual Precipitation	58.2 inches/1,479 millimeters		City
POPULATION & DEMOGRAPHY			
Population	2,200,000	1996	City
Projected Population	2,400,000	2015	City
Growth Rate	1.0%	1990–1995	City
Growth Rate	9.0%	1995–2015	City
Density	7,541 per square mile	1990	City
	2,915 per square kilometer	1990	City
Gender			
Male	47.8%	1987	City
Female	52.2%	1987	City
Age			
Under 20	28.3%	1990	City
20–59	57.1%	1990	City
Over 60	14.6%	1990	City

(continued)

CATEGORY	DATA	YEAR	AREA
ECONOMY			
Total Workforce	770,893	1985	City
Trade	13.0%	1985	City
Manufacturing	26.0%	1985	City
Services	5.0%	1985	City
Finance, Insurance, Real Estate	1.0%	1985	City
Transport, Communications	10.2%	1985	City
Agriculture	1.3%	1985	City
Nonclassifiable	32.0%	1985	City
TRANSPORTATION			
Passenger Journeys	1,207,895,000	1990	City
Buses and Trolley	100%	1988	City
Passenger Vehicles	96,713	1988	City
COMMUNICATIONS			
Telephones per 1,000 Residents	71.4	1990	City
HOUSING			
Total Housing Units	555,036	1990	City
Persons per Unit	3.8	1990	City
HEALTH CARE			
Hospitals	60	1990	City
Physicians per 1,000 Residents	7.2	1990	City
EDUCATION			
Total Students	316,707	1991	City
Primary	45.7%	1991	City
Secondary	29.1%	1991	City
Higher	25.2%	1991	City

Sources: Department of Economic and Social Affairs, Population Division. *Urban Agglomerations, 1996*. New York: United Nations, 1997. United Nations Center for Human Settlements. *Compendium of Human Settlements Statistics*. New York: United Nations, 1995.

Ho Chi Minh City
VIETNAM

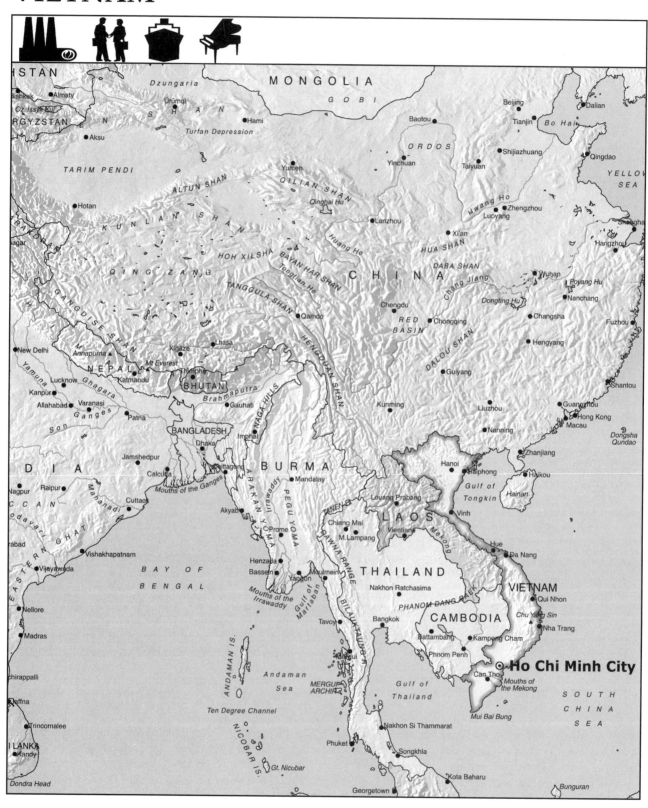

LOCATION

Ho Chi Minh City (known as Saigon until 1976), the most populous city in Vietnam, is located on the Saigon River, north of the Mekong River delta. The 794-square-mile (2,057-square-kilometer) port city lies at an elevation of 33 feet above sea level, about 50 miles northwest of the South China Sea. The former capital of South Vietnam is located approximately 875 miles south-southeast of Hanoi, Vietnam's capital, 160 miles east-southeast of Phnom Penh, capital of Cambodia, and 475 miles east-southeast of Bangkok, Thailand. The climate in Ho Chi Minh City ranges from a January average temperature of 78.1 degrees Fahrenheit (25.6 degrees Celsius) to a July average of 81.9 degrees Fahrenheit (27.7 degrees Celsius). The city has an average of 85.2 inches (2,163 millimeters) of rainfall per year.

POPULATION AND DEMOGRAPHY

The Vietnamese national government policy of rural resettlement since the end of the Vietnam War has moderated the rapid population growth that has occurred in other major cities of Southeast Asia. In the decade between 1985 and 1995, the central city population has increased by a modest 3.7 percent, to an estimated 3,600,000. In part due to the relaxation of the national government's rural resettlement policies, demographers are projecting that Ho Chi Minh City's regional population will increase at a much faster rate over the next two decades. The city has a density of 5,312 persons per square mile (1,947 persons per square kilometer). Between 1995 and the year 2015, Ho Chi Minh City's population is expected to increase by 36.3 percent, to 4,800,000. The city's structural profile is significantly younger than most Southeast Asian cities: 18.8 percent of the city's residents are 15 years or younger; 76.6 percent are between 15 and 64 years of age; and 4.7 percent are under 65 years of age. Unlike large cities of Southeast Asia, females comprise a 53.6 percent majority of Ho Chi Minh City's residents.

HISTORY

Ho Chi Minh City originated as the capital of the kingdom of Cambodia. The city came under Vietnamese control in the seventeenth century as an important commercial and trading center. In the mid-nineteenth century, French traders and missionaries settled in the region. The city was captured by French troops in 1859, and the city was ceded by the Vietnamese to the French colonial authorities in 1862. From 1862 to the end of French colonial rule in Southeast Asia in 1954, Saigon was the capital of the French protectorate of Cochin China.

Under French colonial rule, Saigon expanded from a small trading center to a major Southeast Asian commercial and population center. In particular, Saigon's economic growth stemmed from the expansion of the city's port facilities and the development of regional railways. The growth in transportation facilities greatly enhanced the regional agricultural industry. The city was occupied by Japanese troops during World War II. The French colonial government regained control of the city in 1945, when the Japanese government surrendered to Allied forces. However, the declaration of independence by Vietnamese nationalists led to the First Indochina War, between French colonial forces and the Viet Minh independence movement. The war ended in 1954 with the division of Vietnam between North and South at the Geneva Conference.

Vietnamese efforts to unite the nation were resisted by the United States, which began a military operation in the region in the early 1960s. Saigon became the center of the American military operations. The war between Vietnamese nationalists and the United States expanded during the mid-1960s as the American government vastly increased the size of its operations. The North Vietnamese captured the city of Saigon from fleeing American forces in 1975 and reunited the nation. Large sections of the city were destroyed in the war.

Following the American defeat, the new government nationalized private enterprises. The city's population declined following the end of the war due to the defection of wartime collaborators with the United States and opponents of the new socialist-oriented government. The city's population declined further due to the government's focus on agricultural development and the promotion of resettlement efforts in rural areas. But Vietnamese government efforts to promote foreign investment in the 1980s and 1990s have led to the dramatic expansion of the city.

GOVERNMENT AND POLITICS

In 1976, Saigon was renamed Ho Chi Minh City in honor of the Vietnamese nationalist leader who led the struggle for unification with North Vietnam, and Hanoi, the former capital of North Vietnam, became capital of the united nation. Ho Chi Minh City is one of fifty-three administrative municipalities in Vietnam, including fifty provinces and three municipalities. Along with Hanoi and Haiphong, Ho Chi Minh City's government has a status equivalent to that of a province. Many of the urban planning programs are created by the national government, which has sought to achieve a balanced system of development between the regions and between the urban and rural zones.

ECONOMY

Following the American withdrawal from Vietnam, the economy reverted to centralized control. During the 1970s, Vietnamese government planners emphasized agricultural development in the rural areas to help provide for the country's basic food needs rather than industrial development for export. However, since 1986, the Vietnamese government has sought to attract foreign investment in order to encourage industrial development, primarily for export purposes. The nation and the city are moving away from a government-administered economy to a private economy. As a consequence, many of the new industries in the Ho Chi Minh City region established since the late 1980s are privately controlled and have substantial foreign investment. A major attraction to foreign investors is the relatively low cost of labor—even lower than labor costs in mainland China, Indonesia, and the Philippines. Moreover, the Vietnamese government prohibits workers from improving their working conditions through the formation of independent unions. In particular, low labor costs in the Ho Chi Minh City region have attracted investors to the textile, garment, and rubber industries. Other leading industries in the Ho Chi Minh City region are food processing (rice, coffee, seafood), basic machinery and industrial goods, plastics, chemical products, construction, and building materials. In the 1990s, the region became a leading Southeast Asian tourist destination for North American and West European visitors.

In 1989, Ho Chi Minh City had a labor force of 1,089,650. Manufacturing, mining, and utilities workers accounted for nearly 44 percent of the city's labor force, followed by workers in the trade sector, with 27.4 percent of the labor force, and transport and communications workers, with 9 percent of the city's workers. Construction workers accounted for 4.4 percent of all urban employees. Although the new market economy will attract greater foreign investment, privatization programs could also lead to higher unemployment in the rural areas and encourage migra-

tion to the city, increasing the problem of urban joblessness.

TRANSPORTATION

Bicycles are the primary form of vehicular transport in Ho Chi Minh City. The city is also served by a bus system. Although the regional transportation infrastructure sustained extensive damage during the Vietnam Wars, the government has repaired and modernized the network of roads and railways to accommodate domestic and international freight and cargo transportation. In the late 1990s, Ho Chi Minh City was the leading transportation center in southern Vietnam, with major railway links, highways, and a nearby port facility. An international airport nearby the city serves both domestic and international air carriers.

HEALTH CARE

Ho Chi Minh City has a system of health clinics dispersed throughout the region that serve the basic health care needs of the local population. Ho Chi Minh City residents have relatively greater access to health care facilities and services than do rural residents. The life expectancy and infant mortality rates in Vietnam are comparable to those of cities in the Philippines and Indonesia, but higher than the mortality rates in Japan, Singapore, Korea, and China. In 1989, Ho Chi Minh City had 20.7 births per 1,000 residents and, owing to the city's youthful population structure, only 5.5 deaths per 1,000 residents.

EDUCATION

About 45.6 percent of all urban residents between 5 and 24 years of age in Ho Chi Minh City attended school in 1989. The city has a very high literacy rate, exceeding the national level of 93.7 percent in 1995. Females accounted for almost 44 percent of all Ho Chi Minh City students attending school in 1989. The city is a leading Vietnamese center of higher education and research institutions. The University of Ho Chi Minh City, formerly the University of Saigon, is the city's leading postsecondary educational institution.

HOUSING

The Vietnamese government has played a major role in constructing housing in Ho Chi Minh City, and much of the city's housing stock is owned by the state. Still, more than two thirds of the city's housing stock is privately owned. The Vietnamese government's economic liberalization program, which began in earnest during the early 1990s, has contributed to increased in-migration from the rural hinterland to the central city, placing added pressure on the city's already strained housing stock. Although new building has expanded in Ho Chi Minh City, most new construction is of new roads and infrastructure, along with hotels and commercial establishments financed through foreign capital. Real estate costs are so high that they threaten foreign investment. The urban population influx has created a great need for housing, and many newcomers have been forced to build shanties and other temporary housing in the city's open spaces and outlying areas. These informal dwellings have eased the housing shortage but represent a potentially serious health and sanitation problem, due to the limited availability of clean water and sanitary facilities in such nonstandard housing.

CULTURE, THE ARTS, AND ENTERTAINMENT

Ho Chi Minh City is a leading center of culture and the arts in Vietnam, with temples, pagodas, churches, and historical landmarks dating back to the eighteenth and nineteenth centuries. The city is home to several history and art museums, including the Museum of the Revolution, the Museum of American and Chinese War Crimes, and the Museum of Fine Arts. In 1990, the city had nineteen libraries. Ho Chi Minh City is home to a number of theaters, including the well-known National Theater. Since the late 1980s, government leaders have increasingly opened the city to western cultural influence.

CATEGORY	DATA	YEAR	AREA
LOCATION & ENVIRONMENT			
Area	794 square miles	1995	City
	2,057 square kilometers		City
Elevation	33 feet/10.1 meters		City
January Temperature	78.1 degrees Fahrenheit		City
	25.6 degrees Celsius		City
July Temperature	81.9 degrees Fahrenheit		City
	27.7 degrees Celsius		City
Annual Precipitation	85.2 inches/2,163 millimeters		City
POPULATION & DEMOGRAPHY			
Population	3,600,000	1996	Metro
Projected Population	4,800,000	2015	Metro
Growth Rate	1.7%	1990–1995	Metro
Growth Rate	36.3%	1995–2015	Metro
Density	5,312 per square mile	1992	Metro
	1,947 per square kilometer		Metro
Gender			
Male	46.4%	1989	Metro
Female	53.6%	1989	Metro
Age			
Under 15	18.8%	1989	Metro
15–64	76.6%	1989	Metro
Over 65	4.7%	1989	Metro

(continued)

CATEGORY	DATA	YEAR	AREA
VITAL STATISTICS			
Births per 1,000 Residents	20.7	1990	Metro
Deaths per 1,000 Residents	5.5	1990	Metro
ECONOMY			
Total Workforce	1,089,650	1988	Metro
Trade	27.4%	1988	Metro
Services	2.4%	1988	Metro
Finance, Insurance, Real Estate	1.0%	1988	Metro
Transport and Communications	9.0%	1988	Metro
Construction	4.4%	1988	Metro
Mining, Manufacturing, Utilities	43.9%	1988	Metro
Nonclassifiable	9.5%	1988	Metro
COMMUNICATIONS			
Telephones per 1,000 Residents	128	1985	Metro
HEALTH CARE			
Hospitals	33	1990	Metro
Physicians per 1,000 Residents	0.5	1990	Metro
EDUCATION			
Total Students	693,257	1990	Metro
Primary	62.1%	1990	Metro
Secondary	37.1%	1990	Metro
Age 5–24 in School	45.6%	1990	Metro
Females 5–24 in School	43.9%	1990	Metro

Sources: Department of Economic and Social Affairs, Population Division. *Urban Agglomerations, 1996.* New York: United Nations, 1997; *Statistics of World Large Cities.* Tokyo, Japan: Tokyo Metropolitan Government, 1992 and 1994; and United Nations Center for Human Settlements. *Compendium of Human Settlements Statistics.* New York: United Nations, 1995.

Hong Kong
PEOPLE'S REPUBLIC OF CHINA

LOCATION

Hong Kong, the business and commercial center of China, is located in southeast China on the South China Sea. The city was a colony of Britain from 1842 to July 1, 1997, when Hong Kong was returned to China. Hong Kong consists of Hong Kong Island, Kowloon Peninsula, Stonecutters Island, the New Territories, and 230 islands. Hong Kong Island has just 35 square miles of the city's surface area of 416 square miles (1,078 square kilometers). The New Territories, bordering the Chinese Province of Guangdong, make up about 90 percent of Hong Kong's land area. The city's geography varies sharply between the steep and mountainous terrain of the New Territories and Hong Kong Island to lowland plains near Hong Kong Harbor. Tai Mo Shan, located in central New Territories, is Hong Kong's highest point, with an elevation of 3,140 feet (957 meters) above sea level. To the north of the city is Guangdong Province. Guangzhou (Canton), capital of Guangdong, is located 100 miles to the city's northwest. Beijing, capital of the People's Republic of China, is located 1,200 miles north of the city. Hong Kong has a seasonal climate, with a cool and humid winter season, hot and rainy springs and summers, and warm and sunny autumns. Temperatures range from lows of 58.3 degrees Fahrenheit (14.6 degrees Celsius) in January to highs of 84.9 degrees Fahrenheit (29.4 degrees Celsius) in July. Average annual rainfall is 92.3 inches (2,344 millimeters).

POPULATION AND DEMOGRAPHY

Although Hong Kong's population is expected to continue to increase over the next two decades, the region's population is projected to grow at a significantly lower rate than the 20.9 percent growth experienced between 1980 and 1995. Between 1995 and the year 2000, Hong Kong's 1995 population of 5,574,000 is expected to grow by a cumulative rate of 2.5 percent, to 5,712,000. From 1995 to 2015, the city's population is projected to increase by 4.9 percent, to 5,849,000. About 95 percent of Hong Kong's population lives on Hong Kong Island and Kowloon Peninsula. A small and declining number of residents continue to reside on boats and junks. Persons of Chinese descent account for the vast majority of Hong Kong's population. Recent Chinese immigrants have migrated to the city from nearby Chinese provinces (Fukien, Shanghai, Chekiang, Kiangsu, and Taiwan). The remaining 5 percent of Hong Kong's population is British, Americans, Vietnamese, Japanese, Indians, Pakistanis, Australians, or New Zealanders. Since the end of World War II, the region has experienced significant population growth due to natural increase and migration from nearby Chinese provinces and East Asian countries.

The age structure of Hong Kong's population, although younger than that of Japanese cities, is older than that of cities of nearby Southeast Asia. In 1996, an estimated 19 percent were under 15 years of age, 70 percent were between 15 and 64 years of age, and 11 percent were 65 years of age or older. In 1996, Hong Kong had 10.5 births and 5.2 deaths per 1,000 inhabitants. The net in-migration rate was 12.4 per 1,000 residents. Males comprise 50.9 percent of all residents.

HISTORY

For over two thousand years, Hong Kong was settled intermittently by people of Chinese ancestry. Hong Kong was a relatively small fishing village for many centuries, until the beginning of the nineteenth century, when British colonial authorities sought to gain control over the city as a strategic outpost. In particular, the British coveted Hong Kong's protected harbor as a potential naval station to protect and enhance East Asian commerce and trade. In 1839, hostilities began when the Chinese Special Commissioner imprisoned British merchants and seized opium warehouses, beginning the First Opium War (1839–1842). Upon defeat at the hands of a superior British naval force, China ceded control over Hong Kong Island to Britain in the Treaty of Nanking. Continued conflicts between the British and Chinese authorities brought the two nations to war again in the Second Opium War (1856–1860). Chinese forces were defeated a second time, and they subsequently ceded Kowloon Peninsula to the British in the 1860 Peking Convention.

In 1898, the British colonial authorities signed a ninety-nine-year lease for the entire region, including Hong Kong, the New Territories, and nearby islands. Hong Kong's commercial and economic importance expanded under British control. Following the creation of the Republic of China in 1911, nationalists unsuccessfully sought to abrogate the treaty and regain control over Hong Kong. The city became a focal point of hostilities during World War II. In 1939, Japanese forces attacked Hong Kong, and subsequently occupied the territory from 1941 to 1945, until the Japanese surrender. The Japanese occupation forced residents from the territory and depressed the local economy. British forces regained control over Hong

Kong in 1945 and restored civilian government in 1946. Displaced persons returned to Hong Kong after the Second World War. However, the expansion of hostilities between Nationalists and Communists in the late 1940s led to further social and economic instability. The Hong Kong local economy was also damaged by the Korean War.

By the early 1960s, Hong Kong was a major attraction to foreign investors seeking access to a low-wage labor force and the lack of local labor regulations. The local economy became a major exporter of garments, textiles, toys, and trinkets. In 1967, poor working conditions led to labor unrest, including protests and mass insurrections. In response to the public protests, local living and working conditions gradually improved, but some investors moved to other regions—Korea, Taiwan, and subsequently Indonesia, Thailand, the Philippines, and Vietnam—where labor costs were lower. Over the last two decades of the twentieth century, Hong Kong became a major center of commerce, banking, and finance, servicing the regional East Asian economy.

In December 1984, China agreed to create a Hong Kong Special Administrative Region, which would preserve a local capitalist economy for fifty years after the 1997 transfer. Under the agreement, Hong Kong local authorities were granted control over local affairs, but gave the central government control over foreign policy and defense.

GOVERNMENT AND POLITICS

Under a 1994 agreement between the United Kingdom and China, China agreed to continue the city's economic and social system after the transfer of Hong Kong to China on July 1, 1997. China would gain sovereignty over the region and have control over foreign policy. Previously, Hong Kong was a dependent territory of the United Kingdom under the control of a governor, an executive council, and a legislative council. The executive council was filled by appointment only. The Queen of England appointed the president of the elected council. Local affairs in Hong Kong were directed by district boards and management committees drawn from the region's eighteen administrative units. After Hong Kong formally reverted to Chinese control, Chinese government officials appointed by Beijing had primary responsibility over the region.

ECONOMY

Hong Kong was one of the leading economies in East Asia before control reverted to the People's Republic of China in 1997; by the late 1970s, Hong Kong's economy rivaled those of much larger states in the region. In the post–World War II years, the city's economy was dominated by textile and garment production, electronics, and other basic manufacturing industries. Thereafter, Hong Kong developed thriving toy, jewelry, and appliance industries. Initially, the Hong Kong economy flourished on the basis of its relatively easy access to cheap labor, which could lure foreign capital and investors to the region. However, as local labor costs gradually increased in the 1970s and 1980s, the economy diversified into more capital-intensive industries such as shipbuilding, metal fabrication, and machine tools production. More important, Hong Kong became a major center of finance and banking for foreign investors seeking to invest throughout the region. The city developed a leading international currency exchange and one of the most active stock markets in East Asia. Before the transfer of political power from the British colonial authorities to the Chinese government, some investors left the city, fearing that the Chinese policies would smother the local capitalist economy. However, many fears were put to rest before the transfer and Hong Kong's economy boomed in the mid-1990s, as land speculation fueled a vibrant local real estate industry. Unfortunately, the East Asian financial crisis that began in 1997 has taken a toll on Hong Kong's financial community; fears of a regional economic crisis eroded confidence, causing local stock prices to collapse at the end of 1997.

Historically, the local economy was dependent on foreign trade for petroleum products and raw materials, but with reunification with mainland China, the city's access to these products remains assured into the foreseeable future. Tourism is an important component of the local economy. Before reverting to Chinese control in 1997, Hong Kong's leading trading partners were mainland China, the United States, Germany, Japan, and the United Kingdom.

Based on 1989 statistics, the leading component of Hong Kong's labor force is manufacturing, accounting for 28.5 percent of all workers, followed by trade (27.9 percent), services (17.7 percent), finance, insurance, and real estate (9.2 percent), transport and communications (4.5 percent), and construction (2.5 percent). In 1993, production increased at an annual rate of 2 percent.

TRANSPORTATION

The primary modes of public mass transportation are buses and trolleys, rail, and ferry service. Due to the city's relatively small geographic size, the British government had restricted motor vehicle ownership. However, many of Hong Kong's more affluent citizens own automobiles. Hong Kong is a major trade and commercial center with no tariffs on most imports. The city's modern containerized port can accommodate large ocean-going ships. A major rail line links China with Guangzhou in mainland China. Following the transfer of power from the United Kingdom to China, Hong Kong's foreign trade came under Chinese government supervision. Hong Kong has two major airports that accommodate domestic and international carriers. A new airport is scheduled to open at the end of the century.

HEALTH CARE

Hong Kong has a comprehensive system of hospitals and clinics that provide modern treatment and services to the city's residents. The health care system has greatly reduced the prevalence of many communicable diseases. The regional government operates public health programs that are directed at minimizing infectious diseases and improving preventative health care. In 1996, Hong Kong had an estimated infant mortality rate of 5.1 infant deaths per 1,000 live births, a comparable rate to leading Japanese cities, which have the lowest levels of infant mortality in the world. In the same year, life expectancy at birth for Hong Kong residents was 82.2 years.

EDUCATION

Before reverting to Chinese control, education was compulsory in Hong Kong, and the city had a mixed public and private school system. About 60 percent of Hong Kong's primary and secondary schools are operated privately. Only about 30 percent of Hong Kong's schools are administered publicly. In 1992, among Hong Kong's residents 15 years of age or older, 92 percent have attended school, of which 96 percent are male and 88 percent female. Under Chinese control, Hong Kong's educational system has not appreciably changed. The region's leading universities are the Chinese University of Hong Kong, City Polytechnic of Hong Kong, Hong Kong Polytechnic, Hong Kong Baptist College, and the University of Hong Kong. The city also has postsecondary institutions for specialized training.

HOUSING

Residential housing costs in Hong Kong are among the highest in the world, due to real estate speculation and the limited supply of affordable housing. The highest housing costs are concentrated in the central city, where most of the city's affluent residents reside. To ease the housing crunch, British authorities constructed public housing units, most of which are in outlying areas. The serious shortage of affordable housing is not expected to be ameliorated by Chinese authorities. The vast majority of Hong Kong's new housing under construction during the 1990s has not been subsidized by public authorities and is expected to be sold at high market rates.

CULTURE, THE ARTS, AND ENTERTAINMENT

Hong Kong's leading museums are the Academy of Museums and the Art Center. The city has many leading classical and popular music, dance, and theater groups, including the Hong Kong Philharmonic Orchestra, the Hong Kong Chinese Orchestra, the City Contemporary Dance Company, and the Chung Ying Theatre Company. Hong Kong is an internationally recognized center of the East Asian film production industry, with works produced in the city distributed throughout the region and the world. Since 1977, the Hong Kong International Film Festival has been held annually in the city. Soccer matches and other spectator sports take place at Hong Kong Coliseum and Queen Elizabeth Stadium.

CATEGORY	DATA	YEAR	AREA
LOCATION & ENVIRONMENT			
Area	416 square miles	1996	City
	1,078 square kilometers		City
Elevation	3,140 feet/957 meters		City
January Temperature	58.3 degrees Fahrenheit		City
	14.6 degrees Celsius		City
July Temperature	84.9 degrees Fahrenheit		City
	29.4 degrees Celsius		City
Annual Precipitation	92.3 inches/2,344 millimeters		City
POPULATION & DEMOGRAPHY			
Population	5,070,000	1996	City
Projected Population	5,849,000	2015	City
Growth Rate	12.7%	1990–1995	City
Growth Rate	15.4%	1995–2015	City
Density	13,640 per square mile	1991	City
	5,385 per square kilometer		
Gender			
Males	50.9%	1994	Metro
Females	49.1%	1994	Metro
Age			
Under 15	19%	1996	Metro
15–64	70%	1996	Metro
Over 65	11%	1996	Metro
VITAL STATISTICS			
Births per 1,000 Residents	10.5	1996	Metro
Deaths per 1,000 Residents	5.2	1996	Metro
Infant Mortality Rate	5.1 per 1,000 live births	1996	Metro
ECONOMY			
Total Workforce	2,873,000	1989	City
Trade	27.9%	1989	City
Manufacturing	28.5%	1989	City
Services	17.7%	1989	City
Finance, Insurance, Real Estate	9.2%	1989	City
Transport and Communications	4.5%	1989	City
Construction	2.5%	1989	City
COMMUNICATIONS			
Telephones per 1,000 Residents	530.1	1980	City
HOUSING			
Total Housing Units	1,582,215	1993	City

(continued)

CATEGORY	DATA	YEAR	AREA
HEALTH CARE			
Hospitals	81	1993	City
Hospital Beds per 1,000 Residents	4.5	1993	City
EDUCATION			
Total Students	1,003,136	1993	City
Primary	48.4%	1993	City
Secondary	45.5%	1993	City
Higher	6.2%	1993	City

Sources: Department of Economic and Social Affairs, Population Division. *Urban Agglomerations, 1996.* New York: United Nations, 1997; *Statistics of World Large Cities.* Tokyo, Japan: Tokyo Metropolitan Government, 1992 and 1994; and United Nations Center for Human Settlements. *Compendium of Human Settlements Statistics.* New York: United Nations, 1995.

Honolulu, Hawaii
USA

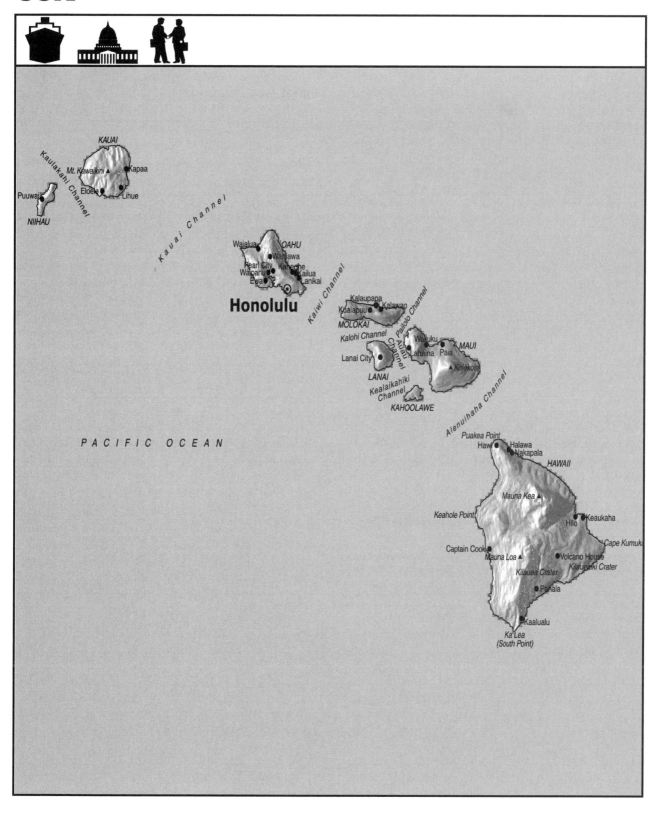

LOCATION

Honolulu, the capital of Hawaii and the most populous urban region in the Hawaiian Islands, is located in Honolulu County, on the coast of Mamala Bay, on the southeastern shore of Oahu Island in the Pacific Ocean. The island of Oahu lies at the approximate geographic center of the Hawaiian Island archipelago. Honolulu occupies a land area of 82.8 square miles (214.5 square kilometers) in southeastern Honolulu County, on a narrow coastal plain. The city is governed by Honolulu County; the county administers public policy on the island of Oahu, which includes the municipalities of Ewa, Haleiwa, Kailua, Kaneohe, Nanakuli, Pacific Palisades, Pearl City, Wahiawa, and Waipahu. To the city's east is Makapuu Point and the Kaiwi Channel. Molokai Island is to the city's southeast. To the city's west is Pearl Harbor, an inlet comprised of three locks north of Mamala Bay. The Koolau Mountain Range runs northeast to northwest near the city, rising to heights exceeding 3,000 feet above sea level. Honolulu is located 217 air miles from Hilo, the state's second largest city, located on the eastern island of Hawaii. Diamond Head and Punchbowl, two extinct volcanic craters, are located in Honolulu. Between 1961 and 1990, the city had a warm average climate with temperatures that ranged from a low of 71.4 degrees Fahrenheit (22 degrees Celsius) in January to a high of 79.9 degrees Fahrenheit (27 degrees Celsius) in July. Over the same thirty-year period, Honolulu had an average annual precipitation of 21.5 inches (547 millimeters).

POPULATION AND DEMOGRAPHY

Between 1980 and 1992, Honolulu's population increased by a modest 6,272, or 1.7 percent, to 371,320. The central city has a density of 4,485 persons per square mile (1,731 persons per square kilometer). In those years, Honolulu's population growth slowed from its rate in the previous decade, when it expanded by a rate of 11 percent. Between 1970 and 1990, the population of the Honolulu metropolitan area, comprising the entire island of Oahu, increased from 630,528 to 863,117, a 26.9 percent rate of growth over the preceding twenty-two-year period. Honolulu is the only major American urban center with a population over 200,000 that has an Asian or Pacific Islander majority. Over 70 percent of the city's population is Asian or Pacific Islander. Over 25 percent of the city's population is white, but only 1.3 percent is black—the lowest concentration of black residents

in a major American city. The 16,700 Hispanic residents comprise 4.6 percent of the city's total population. Over 21 percent of the city's population is foreign-born, and nearly 34 percent speak a language other than English at home. Honolulu's gender ratio is 97.5 males per 100 females. The city has an older population profile than most major cities, with 16 percent 65 years of age or older (ranking sixth highest among major American cities), 19.1 percent 18 years and under, and 65 percent between 18 and 64 years of age.

HISTORY

Although there are no precise historical records on Honolulu's settlement, archaeologists date the city's founding to about 1100 A.D. Other historians contend that Polynesian migrants first settled the area nearly two thousand years ago. In 1804, King Kamehameha I moved his court from Hawaii Island to Waikiki after conquering the island of Oahu in a battle fought in the Nuuanu Valley. Five years later, the king's court was relocated to what is now downtown Honolulu. *Honolulu* is the Polynesian translation of "sheltered harbor." English explorers first discovered Honolulu Harbor in the late eighteenth century, and by the early nineteenth century, the city had become an important Pacific shipping center. Since the early nineteenth century, the regional population has been influenced by North American and East Asian cultural traditions: In the 1820s, New England missionaries arrived in the city, leaving an important cultural and religious imprimatur on the area's population, and later in the century, Asian immigrants influenced the cultural character of the local population. In 1850, Honolulu became the capital of Hawaii.

GOVERNMENT AND POLITICS

The United States annexed the Hawaiian Islands in 1898. In 1905, Oahu became one of the territory's five counties, governed locally by boards of supervisors. In 1907, the County of Oahu was renamed the City and County of Honolulu. Under the new city charter adopted in 1959, executive power was conferred on a mayor, who is assisted by an appointed managing director. Legislative powers were granted to a nine-member city council, elected on a local district level. Both the mayor and city council are elected to four-year terms. Honolulu's government structure is relatively unique among U.S. cities. Because Honolulu County has jurisdiction over regional government services, disparities in education and social services that frequently occur among U.S. cities that are divided among independent municipal governments with great imbalances in wealth and tax revenue are reduced. The city and county government has jurisdiction over public safety and welfare, culture and recreation, community and human development, and general government operations. Honolulu has formed thirty-one neighborhood boards to improve citizens' access to government services on a local basis.

ECONOMY

The Honolulu economy has been mired in a recession through the late 1990s that has contributed to higher than usual levels of unemployment, particularly in the construction industry. Honolulu's civilian labor market expanded 3.3 percent between 1980 and 1990, to 203,498 workers. Wholesale and retail trade workers comprise the largest share of the urban area's workforce, with 24.6 percent of all employees, followed by finance, insurance, and real estate employees, with 9.2 percent; public administration workers, with 7.3 percent; and health services workers, with 7.1 percent. Manufacturing workers make up just 5.7 percent of the labor market, the fourth lowest percentage of manufacturing workers among America's largest cities. The primary manufacturing industries are food processing (pineapples, refined sugar), machinery, printing and publishing, and garment production. Honolulu has the fourth highest median household income and the lowest unemployment rate among major American cities with populations exceeding 200,000. The city's poverty rate of 8.4 percent is among the lowest of major American cities and about half the U.S. national rate.

Honolulu's most important industry is tourism. Honolulu and Oahu remain a major resort destination for U.S. and international tourists, and tourism is the largest source of revenue for the local economy. The U.S. military is a major employer in the region through three primary military installations: Pearl Harbor Naval Base, Hickam Air Force Base, and Tripler Army Medical Center.

TRANSPORTATION

The failure in 1992 to approve a rapid rail transportation system left Honolulu's serious motor vehicle traffic congestion problem unresolved. In the absence of a comprehensive rail transportation system, gov-

ernment authorities are planning to expand and upgrade the city's current fleet of 500 buses to 650. In addition, the transportation authorities are attempting to improve traffic flow by reviewing traffic lanes and intersections and integrating advanced traffic control technology. Honolulu International Airport serves air passengers to and from the mainland United States and other international points. Honolulu is also a major Pacific Ocean cargo center, with a major shipping industry and extensive port facilities.

HEALTH CARE

Honolulu has seven community hospitals and 1,828 hospital beds, a rate of 500 hospital beds per 100,000 urban residents. The city has a very low infant mortality rate of 4.9 deaths per 1,000 live births, the lowest infant mortality rate among major American cities with populations of more than 200,000. Honolulu's infant mortality rate is significantly lower than the U.S. national rate, which has hovered in the 7 percent to 8 percent range during the early 1990s. Hawaii is one of two American states to emphasize universal access to health insurance, regardless of ability to pay.

EDUCATION

Honolulu has a total school enrollment of 88,163, representing 23.7 percent of the urban population. Students in primary and secondary schools represent 54.8 percent of the city's school enrollment. Only 76.1 percent of all urban students are enrolled in public primary and secondary schools, the fourth lowest percentage of public school enrollment among major U.S. cities. A large proportion, about 27.7 percent, of the urban area's residents over 25 years of age have a bachelor's degree or higher. The major postsecondary educational institutions are the University of Hawaii at Manoa, Hawaii Pacific University, and Chaminade University of Honolulu.

HOUSING

Housing is more expensive in Honolulu than it is in virtually any other major urban area in the United States. In 1990, the median value of owner-occupied housing was US$353,900, 15 percent higher than the median value in San Francisco, the second most expensive city. The median price for rental housing ranks sixth among major U.S. cities. The urban area's housing stock increased 2.5 percent from 1980 to 1990, to 145,796 units. Less than 8 percent of Honolulu's housing stock is vacant—a relatively low percentage compared to other major U.S. cities. Owner-occupied housing units comprise 47 percent of the urban area's housing stock. Condominium units account for a large 29.7 percent share of Honolulu's housing stock. Due to the decline in federal and state support for affordable low-income housing and mental health facilities, Honolulu is facing a serious homelessness problem. Although local resources are limited, public officials are supporting the construction of a major facility and service center for homeless people.

CULTURE, THE ARTS, AND ENTERTAINMENT

Honolulu's major artistic and cultural institutions are the Bernice Pauahi Bishop Museum, the Honolulu Academy of Arts, the Alice Cooke Spaulding House, and the Honolulu Symphony. The city also has several theaters. The city is planning to upgrade its recreation centers and play courts and is expanding its parks system. The most popular competitive sports are baseball, soccer, and tennis. Plans are under way to build a sports complex for use as a professional baseball training center and a championship tennis facility, and for the community to use.

CATEGORY	DATA	YEAR	AREA
LOCATION & ENVIRONMENT			
Area	82.8 square miles	1995	City
	214.5 square kilometers		City
Elevation	7 feet/2.3 meters		City
January Temperature	71.4 degrees Fahrenheit	1961–1990	City
	22 degrees Celsius	1961–1990	City
July Temperature	79.9 degrees Fahrenheit	1961–1990	City
	27 degrees Celsius	1961–1990	City
Annual Precipitation	21.5 inches/547 millimeters	1961–1990	City
POPULATION & DEMOGRAPHY			
Population	371,320	1992	City
Average Growth Rule	1.7%	1980–1992	City
Density	4,485 per square mile	1992	City
	1,731 per square kilometer		
Gender			
Males	49.4%	1990	City
Females	50.6%	1990	City
Age			
Under 18	18.1%	1990	City
18–64	65.0%	1990	City
Over 65	16.0%	1990	City
VITAL STATISTICS			
Births per 1,000 Residents	15	1988	City
Deaths per 1,000 Residents	7	1988	City
Infant Mortality Rate	4.9 per 1,000 live births	1990	City
ECONOMY			
Total Workforce	203,498	1990	City
Trade	24.6%	1990	City
Manufacturing	5.7%	1990	City
Health Services	7.1%	1990	City
Finance, Insurance, Real Estate	9.2%	1990	City
Public Administration	7.3%	1990	City

(continued)

CATEGORY	DATA	YEAR	AREA
TRANSPORTATION			
Passenger Vehicles	191,491	1990	City
HOUSING			
Total Housing Units	145,796	1990	City
Persons per Unit	2.5	1990	City
Owner-Occupied Units	47.0%	1990	City
HEALTH CARE			
Hospitals	7	1991	City
EDUCATION			
Total Students	88,163	1991	City
Primary and Secondary	54.8%	1991	City
Higher	38.8%	1991	City

Source: U.S. Bureau of the Census. *County and City Data Book 1994.* Washington, DC: U.S. Government Printing Office, 1994.

Houston, Texas

USA

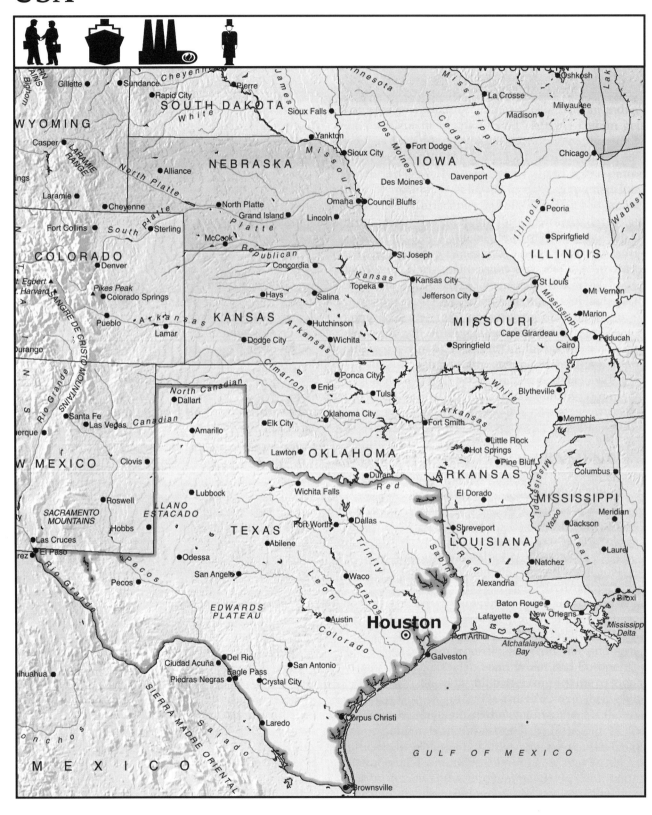

LOCATION

Houston, the most populous city in Texas and the fourth largest American city, is located on the southeast Texas coastal plain, 50 miles north of the Gulf of Mexico. The city covers a land area of 539.9 square miles (1,398.3 square kilometers) within Harris County. Houston, nicknamed the Bayou City, epitomizes the typical American form of urban sprawl, where settlement expands outward from a central city core into the suburbs. However, unlike other major cities, the boundaries of the city of Houston cover a large land region that includes suburban areas. The inland port is located at the western terminus of the Houston Ship Canal, northwest of Galveston Bay and the Gulf of Mexico. Due to the virtual absence of zoning restrictions, land use patterns have often developed haphazardly, with residential, commercial, and industrial areas frequently intermixed. Large skyscrapers dominate the central city; these give way to freeways and residential and light industrial districts on the surrounding south, north, and west sides. The metropolitan area includes Alvin, Galveston, and Texas City to the southeast, Pasadena and Baytown to the east, Katy and Richmond to the west, and North Houston. The city is 200 miles east of San Antonio, 250 miles southeast of Dallas–Fort Worth, 80 miles west of the Louisiana border, and 165 miles southeast of Austin, the state capital. Between 1961 and 1990, the average temperature ranged from a low of 52.2 degrees Fahrenheit in January (11.2 degrees Celsius) to a high of 83.5 degrees Fahrenheit (28.6 degrees Celsius) in July. Over the same thirty-year period, the city averaged 50.8 inches (1,291 millimeters) of precipitation per year.

POPULATION AND DEMOGRAPHY

Between 1980 and 1992, Houston's central city population increased 6 percent, to 1,690,180. Although Houston's population increased moderately in the 1980s, growth during that period was significantly lower than the 30 percent rate of expansion the city experienced during the 1970s. The city has a density of 3,131 persons per square mile (1,209 persons per square kilometer). The central city contains a substantial 53 percent of the metropolitan area population of 3.2 million. The number of people in the Houston metropolitan area is projected to increase by 18.3 percent, to 3.7 million, in the twenty-year period ending in 2015. Houston has a racially and ethnically diverse population. Whites make up a 50 percent majority, blacks comprise 27 percent, and Asians and

Pacific Islanders are 4 percent of all city residents. Almost 27 percent of Houston's population is of Hispanic origin, the majority of whom are of Mexican descent. Foreign-born residents comprise a relatively large 17.8 percent of the central city's residents. Houston has a ratio of 98.5 males for every 100 females. The city's age distribution is skewed toward younger residents: 26.7 percent of the city's population is under 18 years of age, 65 percent is between ages 18 and 64, and only 8.2 percent is over 65 years of age.

HISTORY

Prior to European settlement in the early nineteenth century, indigenous peoples inhabited the southeast Texas region that now encompasses Houston. Augustus C. Allen and John K. Allen, two brothers, founded Houston in 1836 and laid out the plans for the city after the Mexican army overran and destroyed the settlement of Harrisburg. The city was formally incorporated in 1837 and two years later was named the seat of Harris County. Houston gained prominence as a transportation center after the Houston Ship Channel was completed in 1914, connecting the city to the Gulf of Mexico. Rail and highway transportation linkages completed in the nineteenth and twentieth centuries further expanded the city's importance as a transportation and commercial center for the agricultural and petroleum products that were exported from the region.

GOVERNMENT AND POLITICS

The Houston city charter mandates a mayor–city council form of government, consisting of a mayor, city council, and city comptroller. The mayor serves as chief executive officer, is responsible for the general management, appoints city officials, and enforces laws and ordinances. As Houston's legislative body, the fourteen-member city council is responsible for enacting and enforcing ordinances and resolutions. The city comptroller maintains records of city revenues and spending. The mayor, city comptroller, and members of the city council are elected to two-year concurrent terms.

ECONOMY

Houston is the center of the U.S. petroleum, natural gas, and related industries. Many of the largest companies in the region are oil and gas producers or energy servicing and financing companies. These companies are engaged in oil and gas exploration, basic petroleum refining, and petrochemical production. After the depression of global oil prices in the early 1980s contributed to a major recession and large-scale unemployment, the city has sought to diversify its industrial and commercial base. Besides petroleum- and natural-gas-related industries, the major regional manufacturing industries are chemicals, machinery, metal products, synthetic rubber, iron and steel, paper, food processing, and electrical and electronic components. Houston is the home of the Lyndon B. Johnson Space Center, the mission control station for the National Aeronautics and Space Administration (NASA). Other major economic factors are computer, aerospace, environmental, and high-technology industries, medical research and health care, commercial fishing, and international import and export. The city is home to fifteen Fortune 500 corporate headquarters.

In 1990, Houston had a civilian labor force of 1,042,688, approximately equivalent to the number of workers the city had in 1980. The city's unemployment rate has been consistently lower than the national average. However, most new jobs are in the wholesale and retail trade, and they pay considerably lower wages than manufacturing jobs. The wholesale and retail trade sector employs 23.4 percent of all workers; manufacturing has 11.7 percent; health services account for 8.1 percent; and finance, insurance, and real estate employ 7.6 percent. The public sector is responsible for only 2.8 percent of the jobs. The city's poverty rate of 20.7 percent is higher than the national rate but lower than that of most other large American cities.

TRANSPORTATION

The city's development has been based on motor vehicle transportation. Eight major highways and freeways crisscross the city. The city has attempted to reduce congestion and speed traffic flows through the use of high-occupancy-vehicle (HOV) lanes and is installing a vehicle highway monitoring system. Unlike most other major U.S. and world cities with populations exceeding 1 million, Houston has no local or regional rapid rail transit system. Public transportation is provided through the Metropolitan Transportation Authority, which operates 1,000 buses on over 120 routes and serves over 250,000 residents

per day. Still, only 6.5 percent of the city's population commutes to work on the bus system.

Houston is one of the world's major port cities. The Houston Ship Channel, a 52-mile inland waterway that connects Houston to the Bay of Galveston, accommodates large ocean-going vessels. The Port of Houston handles more shipping tonnage than any other U.S. city, and ranks eighth in the world in shipping tonnage. Over six hundred motor freight companies and three major railroad lines serve the city. The city is the major terminus for underground liquid and gas pipelines in North America and is headquarters to four of the ten largest pipeline companies in the United States. Houston has three major airports, including Houston Intercontinental Airport, located 22 miles north of the city.

HEALTH CARE

Houston has thirty-four community hospitals with 10,253 hospital beds, a rate of 629 beds per 100,000 city residents. The Texas Medical Center complex, located south of downtown Houston, is a leading health education, research, and treatment center in the United States. The greater Houston area has over a hundred hospitals. The city's infant mortality rate of 11.3 per 1,000 live births ranks thirty-ninth among the seventy-seven largest U.S. cities, though it is higher than the national rate.

EDUCATION

The greater Houston area has over twenty independent school districts. The Houston Independent School District provides public education through 272 schools in the city. Houston has a total school enrollment of 445,128 students, or 26.3 percent of the city's population. Nearly 73 percent of all students (297,665) are in primary and secondary schools. Over 85 percent of all students in the Houston Independent School District are Latino or African-American, and over 65 percent of the school district's students come from economically disadvantaged backgrounds. Only 12 percent of the student body is white. Houston has a relatively educated population for a large and diverse major urban city. Of the city's population 25 years of age and over, 70 percent have a high school diploma and 25 percent have a bachelor's degree or higher. The major postsecondary institutions in the region are the University of Houston,

Texas Southern University, Rice University, the University of St. Thomas, Houston Baptist University, and the University of Texas and Baylor University Medical Schools.

HOUSING

Median housing and real estate costs in Houston are considerably lower than those in major U.S. cities on the Atlantic and Pacific coasts. The city claims that overall housing costs are 20 percent lower than the U.S. national average. In 1990, Houston had a total of 726,435 housing units, 7.1 percent more than a decade earlier. Nearly 84.9 percent (616,877) of Houston's housing units are occupied. Despite the affordable housing costs, Houston's owner-occupancy rate is a relatively low 44.6 percent.

CULTURE, THE ARTS, AND ENTERTAINMENT

The primary museums and artistic sites in Houston are the Museum of Fine Arts, the Contemporary Arts Museum, and the Museum of Natural Science. Jones Hall and Wortham Center, Houston's two major concert and entertainment halls, accommodate the Houston Symphony Orchestra, the Houston Grand Opera, and the Houston Ballet. The city's two major halls also accommodate local and national theater companies. Houston has two major league professional sports teams. In the coming years, the Astros baseball team will move from the Astrodome, an aging enclosed sports stadium, to a new field. The Rockets basketball team plays at the Summit Arena. The city is also home to professional soccer and hockey teams. The Oilers of the National Football League relocated to Tennessee in 1997.

CATEGORY	DATA	YEAR	AREA
LOCATION & ENVIRONMENT			
Area	539.9 square miles	1995	City
	1,398.3 square kilometers		City
Elevation	40 feet/13.1 meters		City
January Temperature	52.2 degrees Fahrenheit	1961–1990	City
	11.2 degrees Celsius	1961–1990	City
July Temperature	83.5 degrees Fahrenheit	1961–1990	City
	28.6 degrees Celsius	1961–1990	City
Annual Precipitation	50.8 inches/1,291 millimeters	1961–1990	City
POPULATION & DEMOGRAPHY			
Population	3,200,000	1996	Metro
Projected Population	3,700,000	2015	Metro
Growth Rate	1.6%	1990–1995	Metro
Growth Rate	18.3%	1995–2015	Metro
Density	3,131 per square mile	1992	City
	1,209 per square kilometer		
Gender			
Males	49.6%	1990	City
Females	50.4%	1990	City
Age			
Under 18	26.7%	1990	City
18–64	65.0%	1990	City
Over 65	8.2%	1990	City
VITAL STATISTICS			
Births per 1,000 Residents	22	1988	City
Deaths per 1,000 Residents	8	1988	City
Infant Mortality Rate	11.3 per 1,000 live births	1990	City

(continued)

CATEGORY	DATA	YEAR	AREA
ECONOMY			
Total Workforce	1,042,688	1990	City
Trade	23.4%	1990	City
Manufacturing	11.7%	1990	City
Health Services	8.1%	1990	City
Finance, Insurance, Real Estate	7.6%	1990	City
Public Administration	2.8%	1990	City
TRANSPORTATION			
Passenger Journeys	79,514,000	1990	City
Buses	100%	1990	City
Passenger Vehicles	897,035	1990	City
HOUSING			
Total Housing Units	726,435	1990	City
Persons per Unit	2.3	1990	City
Owner-Occupied Units	44.6%	1990	City
HEALTH CARE			
Hospitals	34	1991	City
Physicians per 1,000 Residents	3.4	1991	City
EDUCATION			
Total Students	445,128	1991	City
Primary and Secondary	72.9%	1991	City
Higher	27.1%	1991	City

Sources: Department of Economic and Social Affairs, Population Division. *Urban Agglomerations, 1996.* New York: United Nations, 1997. U.S. Bureau of the Census. *County and City Data Book 1994.* Washington, DC: U.S. Government Printing Office, 1994.

Istanbul
TURKEY

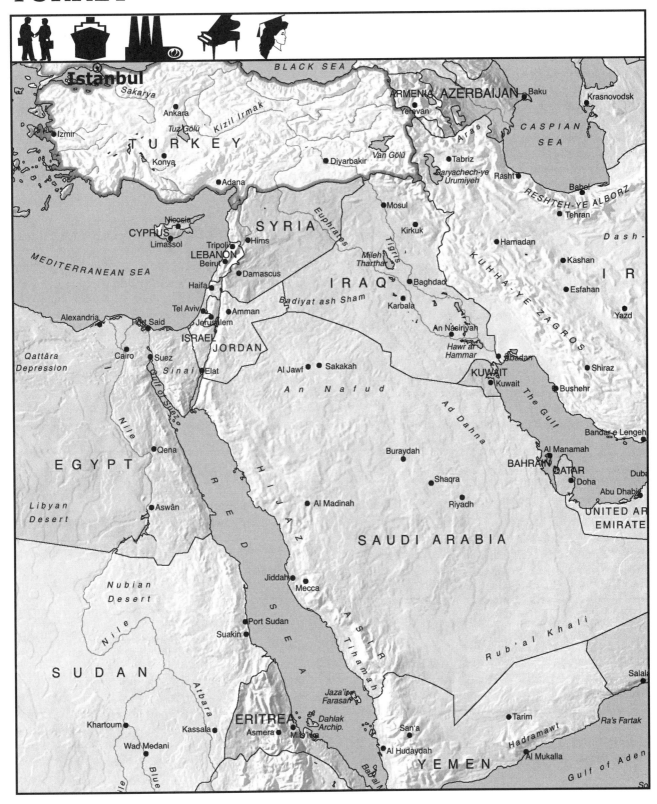

LOCATION

Istanbul, far and away the largest city in Turkey, is situated in one of the world's most spectacular and strategic locations. The Istanbul metropolitan area stretches across a series of low hills along both shores of the Bosporus, a waterway that connects the Black Sea to the Mediterranean. The city itself lies on the western shore, with its ancient center located on the Golden Horn, a peninsula situated at the confluence of the Bosporus and the Sea of Marmara. The city is located 200 miles west-northwest of the capital, Ankara, and approximately 350 miles northeast of Athens, Greece. The metropolitan area is vast, encompassing 604 square miles (1,630 square kilometers). Istanbul has a Mediterranean climate, with cool, wet winters and dry, hot summers. The average temperatures in January and July are 40.5 degrees Fahrenheit (4.7 degrees Celsius) and 73 degrees Fahrenheit (22.8 degrees Celsius), respectively. It receives about 31.5 inches (800.1 millimeters) of rain annually, with most falling in the winter.

POPULATION AND DEMOGRAPHY

The population in 1996 was estimated at 8.2 million, with about 5 million in the city limits alone. During the 1990s, the city grew at a rate of 3.8 percent annually, though this is expected to slow in the next century to about 1 percent. Projection put the Istanbul metropolitan area's population at about 12.3 million in the year 2015. Nearly 42 percent of the city's inhabitants are under the age of 20.

Istanbul is an extremely diverse and cosmopolitan city. Along with its Turkish majority, there are substantial communities of Kurds, Greeks, Armenians, Arabs, Europeans, and Jews. Most of the city's people are Muslims, about two thirds of whom are Sunni and the rest Alevi, a sect akin to Shiism. There are also small cohorts of Christians and Jews.

HISTORY

Because of its strategic location, Istanbul has known human habitation for at least three thousand years. It was a Greek trading city and then fell to the Romans. In A.D. 330, the Emperor Constantine made it the new capital of the Roman Empire. With the fall of the Western Roman Empire in the fifth century A.D., Istanbul, then known as Byzantium, became the capital of the vast Byzantine Empire. Constantine and his successors engaged in vast building projects, in-cluding the construction of the magnificent Hagia Sophia (later converted into a mosque and now a museum). Over the next one thousand years, as it ruled over an ever-shrinking realm, the city's name changed to Constantinople, Greek for "city of Constantine." Beginning in the thirteenth century, local Arabs began to refer to it as *eis ten polin,* meaning "in the city." This gradually was bastardized into the pronunciation Istanbul. In 1453, the millennium of Christian rule came to an end with the capture of the city by Turks. From the sixteenth century until World War I, Istanbul served as the capital of the Ottoman Empire and the last Islamic caliphate. The sultans ruled a huge empire from Istanbul and added to the great architectural legacy of the city.

GOVERNMENT AND POLITICS

In 1908, Istanbul was occupied by the armies of the Young Turks, a group of disgruntled politicians and military officers who all but overthrew the sultanate, maintaining it in name only. During World War I, the city was occupied by Allied armies, including the English, French, and Greeks. To liberate the Turkish homeland, Kemal Ataturk launched a counterattack against Istanbul and the western Anatolian peninsula, successfully driving out the occupying armies. In 1923, he shifted the capital of the new Turkish Republic to Ankara. Since then, however, Istanbul has remained the commercial and cultural capital of Turkey.

Istanbul is governed by a mayor who is appointed by the president of the republic. The mayor also serves as governor of Istanbul province. The city is divided into fourteen districts, or *kazas,* each governed by a subprefect, or *kaymakam.* There is also a newer metropolitan municipality, which handles planning for the entire Istanbul area.

ECONOMY

Istanbul is a major commercial, industrial, and transportation hub, generating approximately 40 percent of the taxable wealth in Turkey. Major industries include textiles, flour milling, tobacco processing, cement, glass, automobiles and trucks, printing, and shipbuilding. The city is also home to major national and international banks, insurance companies, and trading firms. Its port handles the largest share of Turkish imports and exports, as well as a number of Mediterranean and Black Sea cruise ships. Indeed, tourism is a key sector of the city's economy as well.

TRANSPORTATION

Major highways and railroads connect Istanbul to the rest of Turkey, as well as Europe and the Middle East. While its connections to the outside world are excellent, its metropolitan transportation system is overcrowded and in deteriorating condition. While the industrial sections to the south of the city are well served by highways and railroads, much of the new residential expansion to the west and east of the city is poorly served by roads. Public bus fleets cannot adequately handle the traffic. While the modern Bosporus Bridge connects the European and Asian halves of the city, it is often a bottleneck, with traffic moving at a crawl during rush hour. There are also regular ferry services across the Bosporus, though most do not handle vehicles. The city also has a limited subway service.

HEALTH CARE

There are ninety hospitals (half public and half private) serving the Istanbul metropolitan area, half of which are located within the city limits. All primary health care is heavily subsidized by the government, and there is a ratio of 2 physicians per 1,000 persons. At the same time, many of the city's clinics and hospitals lack adequately trained personnel. Along with Ankara, Istanbul is home to Turkey's only two medical schools.

EDUCATION

The vast majority of the city's children attend school, and Istanbul has 3,500 primary and secondary schools. Istanbul's literacy rate is somewhat higher than the overall rate for Turkey of 70 percent, though elderly people and women tend to lag behind. While the public school system is supplemented by private academies, the secular Turkish government frowns upon and discourages religious schools. The city boasts three major universities, including Istanbul University, which was founded in 1453. There are also several technical academies and American-run colleges for men and women.

HOUSING

The city is extremely crowded. The 460,000 existing dwellings mean that occupancy rates are around thir-

teen persons per unit. Vast suburbs have grown up around the city as migrants from the countryside have poured in over the past few decades. Many of these districts are filled with what Turks call *gecekondu*, or night-built houses, after an old Turkish law that says a home put up in a single day cannot be torn down by the authorities.

While Istanbul has a modern chlorinated water treatment system, this has become overwhelmed in recent years by the rapidly expanding population. Water supplies are particularly problematic in the summertime, when the rivers that supply the city tend to run dry. Tap water during these months often slows to a trickle. Electrical shortages have become rare in recent years with the completion of major dams in the southeast of the country, linked to Istanbul by new power lines.

CULTURE, THE ARTS, AND ENTERTAINMENT

Istanbul is one of the great cultural and architectural centers of the world. The old walled city on the Golden Horn is home to the great seraglios (Turkish palaces) built by sultans over the centuries. The city is full of ancient, medieval, and modern mosques, palaces, and monuments, many of which now house museums. The city also boasts many libraries, some with collections dating back over a thousand years. Major museums include the Museum of Istanbul, the Museum of Turkish and Islamic Art, and the Museum of the Janissaries, as well as several significant foreign-run archeological institutes and museums.

The government-run Palais de la Culture is a major center for arts and includes a concert hall, art gallery, and two theaters. It is home to the city orchestra and opera. The ancient Hippodrome is now a major public park. Indeed, Istanbul is home to hundreds of tiny market gardens, located around Byzantine-era cisterns.

The city is also home to most of the Turkish cinema, TV, and radio industries. TV and radio ownership is widespread. Istanbul is also a major publishing center, with a number of presses, several newspapers, and dozens of magazines and journals. The press is largely uncensored.

Sports, both participatory and spectator, are immensely popular in the city. Three major soccer stadiums host national and international matches. Local arenas feature wrestling bouts, a Turkish favorite. There are also extensive facilities in the Istanbul area for golf, sailing, tennis, and other outdoor sports.

CATEGORY	DATA	YEAR	AREA
LOCATION & ENVIRONMENT			
Area	604 square miles	1995	City
	1,630 square kilometers		City
Elevation	59 feet/17.9 meters		City
January Temperature	40.5 degrees Fahrenheit		City
	4.7 degrees Celsius		City
July Temperature	73 degrees Fahrenheit		City
	22.8 degrees Celsius		City
Annual Precipitation	31.5 inches/800.1 millimeters		City
POPULATION & DEMOGRAPHY			
Population	8,200,000	1996	Metro
Projected Population	12,300,000	2015	Metro
Growth Rate	3.8%	1990–1995	Metro
Growth Rate	55.8%	1995–2015	Metro
Density	12,590 per square mile	1990	City
	4,663 per square kilometer		City
Gender			
Male	52.1%	1990	Metro
Female	47.9%	1990	Metro
Age			
Under 20	41.9%	1990	Metro
20–59	51.9%	1990	Metro
Over 60	6.2%	1990	Metro
TRANSPORTATION			
Cars	201,383	1990	Metro
Trucks	20,067	1990	Metro
COMMUNICATIONS			
Telephones per 1,000 Residents	222	1993	Metro
HOUSING			
Housing Units	460,000	1990	Metro
New Housing Units	9,031	1990	Metro
Persons per Unit	13	1990	Metro
HEALTH CARE			
Hospitals	90	1986	Metro
Physicians per 1,000 Residents	2	1986	Metro
EDUCATION			
Total Students	887,056	1980	Metro
Primary	61.7%	1980	Metro
Secondary	29.2%	1980	Metro
Higher	9.1%	1980	Metro

Sources: Department of Economic and Social Affairs, Population Division. *Urban Agglomerations, 1996.* New York: United Nations, 1997; *Statistics of World Large Cities.* Tokyo, Japan: Tokyo Metropolitan Government, 1992 and 1994; and United Nations Center for Human Settlements. *Compendium of Human Settlements Statistics.* New York: United Nations, 1995.

Jakarta
INDONESIA

CHINA

BURMA

Macau Hong Kong

TAIWAN

Hanoi

Haiphong

Bashi Channel

Luang Prabang

Haikou

LAOS

Hainan

Laoag

Vientiane

Luzon

PHILIPPINE
SEA

THAILAND

Da Nang

VIETNAM

Yangoon

Bangkok

ANDAMAN
SEA

CAMBODIA

Nha Trang

Phnom Penh

Ho Chi Minh

Manila

SOUTH
CHINA
SEA

PHILIPPINES

Gulf of
Thailand

Iloilo

Tacloban

Palawan

SULU
SEA

Mindanao

Davao

George Town

Kuala Terengganu

Bandar Seri Begawan

Zamboanga

Sandakan

Isabela

CELEBES
SEA

Ipoh

Kelang

Medan

Kuala Lumpur

BRUNEI

Manado

MOLUCCA SEA

Strait of Malacca

Johor Bharu

SINGAPORE

MALAYSIA

Nantuna Besar

Kapuas

Borneo

MOLUCCAS

Sumatra

Padang

Hari

PEG. BARISAN

Jambi

Pontianak

Balikpapan

Bali

Sulawesi

CERAM

Seram

Ambon

Buru

Bangka

Barito

INDONESIA

Palembang

Belitung

Banjarmasin

Ujung Pandang

Makassar Strait

Baubau

JAVA SEA

Jakarta

FLORES SEA

Wetar

Bandung

Java

Surabaya

Bali

Lombok

Flores

Timor

Malang

Sumbawa

Mataram

Ende

Bathurst

Sumba

Kupang

TIMOR SEA

Wyndham

LOCATION

Jakarta, the capital and most populous city in Indonesia, is located on the northwestern coastal plain of Java, an island southeast of Sumatra, the westernmost major island of the Indonesian Archipelago. The city, once known as Batavia, lies on the shores of the Java Sea, at an elevation of 16 feet above sea level. Fifty miles south of Jakarta is a mountainous upland region dominated by Mount Gede, which rises to an elevation of 9,075 feet above sea level. Jakarta is located about 75 miles east of the Sunda Strait, a major waterway between Java and Sumatra that empties into the Indian Ocean. The city covers a surface land area of 255 square miles (661 square kilometers). The greater Jakarta area includes the municipalities of Bekasi, Bogor, Krawang, Pandeglang, Rangkasbitung, Serang, Tangerang, and Tanjungpriok. The City of Jakarta is located 80 miles west-northwest of Bandung, Indonesia's third most populous city, and about 450 miles west of Surabaya, Indonesia's second most populous city. All three cities are located on Java, Indonesia's most-populated island. Jakarta is located about 800 miles southeast of Kuala Lumpur, Malaysia, and about 1,120 miles south of Ho Chi Minh City, Vietnam. Jakarta's average temperature ranges from 82 degrees Fahrenheit (27.8 degrees Celsius) in January to 74.3 degrees Fahrenheit (23.5 degrees Celsius) in July. The city averages 64.2 inches (1,632 millimeters) of rainfall per year.

POPULATION AND DEMOGRAPHY

Jakarta is projected to become one of the world's most populous cities by the year 2015. In 1996, the metropolitan area's population was estimated at 8.8 million. Jakarta's regional population is projected to increase by 61.5 percent, to 13.9 million, by the year 2015. The city has a comparatively high density of 32,245 persons per square mile (12,435 persons per square kilometer). A dramatic rise in urban migration over the past twenty years is the primary cause of Jakarta's rapidly growing population. The majority of new residents are young people who migrate from outlying regions on Java and Sumatra in search of gainful employment. As a consequence, Jakarta's age structure is skewed dramatically toward the young. About 42.7 percent of the city's population is under 20 years of age, 50.1 percent is between 15 and 64 years of age, and 7.2 percent of all residents are over 65 years of age. The city's young population profile contributes to a high natural population increase, as there are more births than deaths. Jakarta's ethnic majority is Javanese. The leading ethnic minorities are Sundanese, Malays, Arabs, Indians, and other South Asians. The city also has a small number of European and North American residents. Males comprise a 50.5 percent majority of Jakarta's population.

HISTORY

Jakarta originated in the fifth century as a local settlement. In 1527, the Sultan of Bantan defeated Portuguese forces and named the city Jakarta, which in the local Sundanese language translates as "glorious fortress." In 1619, the city came under sustained European domination; Dutch troops captured and razed Jakarta in 1619 and renamed the city Batavia. For more than three centuries, with the exception of a brief interregnum during the Napoleonic Wars, the city remained under the control of the Dutch colonial government. Early in the Dutch occupation, the city became an important trading post for the Dutch East India Company; the authorities built a distinctive wall as a fortress and constructed extensive trading facilities. The Dutch colonial authority had imported slaves from nearby Indonesian islands and migrants from Ceylon (now Sri Lanka), Burma (now Myanmar), and Japan to work as low-wage laborers. The city developed a distinctive Dutch architectural style, with an elaborate system of canals. The construction of a railway from Jakarta to other points on Java and the modernization of the city's infrastructure in the early twentieth century greatly enhanced the city's economic importance, and by 1930, Jakarta's population exceeded 500,000 inhabitants. Jakarta was under Japanese occupation during World War II, between 1942 and 1945. After a brief occupation by Allied troops, the capital was returned to the Dutch.

In August 1945, Batavia was renamed Jakarta by Indonesian nationalists, and on December 27, 1949, when Indonesia formally received its independence from the Dutch authorities, the city became the capital of the new nation. In 1961, Indonesian authorities declared Jakarta a special territory equivalent to a provincial level unit. Since the 1960s, Jakarta has expanded into one of Southeast Asia's leading population and economic centers. However, economic and industrial investment and growth in other regions of Indonesia have reduced the city's economic preeminence. The 1997 collapse of the rupiah, Indonesia's national currency, severely impaired the national and regional economy and sharply reduced living standards. The economic collapse compounded by International Monetary Fund structural adjustment policies imposed in 1998, which included severe austerity programs that further reduced the value of the rupiah and hampered the Indonesian government's already limited ability to respond effectively to the crisis.

GOVERNMENT AND POLITICS

Jakarta is the capital of Indonesia's national government, which consists of an elected executive branch and a legislative branch that is made up of both elected and appointed officials. In 1961, Jakarta was granted the special status of a province. The Jakarta region is administered by a mayor who is granted political power equal to that of a provincial governor. The local government has two branches: the thirty-five-member legislative branch, which includes elected and appointed officials from key government institutions, including the military, and is responsible for local government policy, and the executive branch, which is responsible for local government administration.

ECONOMY

Jakarta is the leading industrial and commercial center in Indonesia. The regional economy is dominated by manufacturing industries that produce for export primarily to North America and Western Europe. Exports pass through the city's port facilities, the largest in Indonesia. The key manufacturing industries in the regional economy are textiles, garments, iron and steel, automobile components, machinery, durable and nondurable consumer goods, and food processing.

The city is the administrative center for west Java's rapidly growing manufacturing economy, and it is Indonesia's preeminent center for internal commerce. Although the regional economy is dominated by manufacturing, the services industry employs the largest number of workers, with a 34.3 percent share. Workers employed in trade comprise the second largest component of the local labor market, with 26.3 percent of all employees, followed by manufacturing workers, who make up 18.4 percent of the local labor market. The city's transport and communications workers account for 7.5 percent of the local labor market. Workers employed in finance, insurance, and real estate make up another 4.2 percent of the labor force.

The economic crisis of 1997, caused by overspeculation and the inability of the government to repay foreign debt, has significantly reduced the regional economy's competitiveness. In the wake of the financial crisis and the austere structural adjustment terms imposed on the Indonesian economy by the international banking community, the national currency has declined in value, forcing down the real value of wages and leading to economic dislocation, rising poverty levels, and mass unrest. In the last years of the century, the region has experienced food riots, militant student protests, and the emergence of an independent labor movement demanding greater economic and political rights. As the Indonesian government has sought improved terms with foreign lenders, it has also repressed local demands for greater democracy and equality. The escalation of the economic crisis contributed to urban protests and insurrections and to the resignation of President Suharto in May 1998 and continued uncertainty over the future stability of the nation.

TRANSPORTATION

As a rapidly growing major urban metropolis, Jakarta is facing serious and growing traffic congestion. The city's public transportation system includes buses and trolleys, which accounts for 95.4 percent of all passenger journeys, and a rail system, which accounts for the remaining 4.6 percent of journeys. A growing number of bus routes serve Jakarta's burgeoning outlying areas and suburbs. While the private automobile is becoming more prevalent in the 1990s, the bicycle remains a leading form of private vehicular transportation.

Jakarta is an important rail freight link for major railroads throughout Java. The railway lines are linked to the city's nearby port at Tanjungpriok, which handles a major share of the nation's exports. The city has a major airport that accommodates carriers providing domestic and international service.

HEALTH CARE

The city is served by modern health care facilities, some operated by the municipal government and others by religious groups and private authorities. Jakarta's neighborhoods have clinics that provide local care to the city's residents. The city had a total of 1,158 health care facilities in 1988, and 2.5 physicians per 1,000 residents. Consequently, compared to major Southeast Asian cities, Jakarta has a much higher infant mortality rate, a higher death rate, and a lower life expectancy. In 1990, despite a relatively young population profile, Jakarta's death rate was 8.4 persons per 1,000 urban residents. In 1985, the city had an infant mortality rate of 33 infant deaths per 1,000 live births.

EDUCATION

Although government officials have authorized funds for new school facilities and additional teachers to meet the growing demand of a young population for primary and secondary education, the city continues to face a serious need for educational services. Among the more than 1.75 million students attending school in the city, 57.9 percent were in primary school, 35.6 percent were in secondary school, and 6.5 percent attended institutions of higher education. The city is home to major universities, including Universitas Indonesia. The national economic crisis of 1998 has spurred the development of a militant student movement, concentrated in the universities in Jakarta, Bandung, Surabaya, and other major cities on Java. Student protests have included demonstrations calling for the provision of food to the city's poor and working-class population, better funding for education, and greater democratization of the national government institutions.

HOUSING

In the 1990s, Jakarta's housing was substandard and overcrowded, with 4.7 persons per housing unit. As Jakarta's population expands uncontrollably over the next two decades, the city will face a serious housing shortage and crisis. Although new apartment developments have been constructed in recent years, they are not expected to grow fast enough to meet the needs of a burgeoning population. The city's population is projected to increase by 61.5 percent in the next twenty years, but the government has made few provisions for public housing to accommodate the city's new inhabitants. Private housing is not expected to fill the gap. More than 95 percent of the city's housing units have access to electricity, and 81.1 percent use coal as the primary form of cooking fuel.

CULTURE, THE ARTS, AND ENTERTAINMENT

As a leading national center of culture and the arts, Jakarta is home to twenty-seven museums, including the National Museum, which has a vast artistic, historical, and cultural exhibition. Jakarta has many mosques and churches, constructed since the end of the seventeenth century, that are testament to the city's diverse Portuguese, Dutch, and South Asian heritage. Western and traditional music, dance, and theater are performed at the Taman Ismail Marzuki Center, the city's leading concert hall. In 1992, the central city of Jakarta had 191 cinemas.

CATEGORY	DATA	YEAR	AREA
LOCATION & ENVIRONMENT			
Area	255 square miles	1996	City
	661 square kilometers		City
Elevation	26 feet/7.9 meters		City
January Temperature	82.0 degrees Fahrenheit		City
	27.8 degrees Celsius		City
July Temperature	74.3 degrees Fahrenheit		City
	23.5 degrees Celsius		City
Annual Precipitation	64.2 inches/1,632 millimeters		City
POPULATION & DEMOGRAPHY			
Population	8,800,000	1996	City
Projected Population	13,900,000	2015	City
Growth Rate	2.4%	1990–1995	City
Growth Rate	61.5%	1995–2015	City
Density	32,245 per square mile	1992	City
	12,435 per square kilometer		
Gender			
Males	50.5%	1990	City
Females	49.5%	1990	City
Age			
Under 15	42.7%	1990	City
15–64	50.1%	1990	City
Over 65	7.2%	1990	City
VITAL STATISTICS			
Births per 1,000 Residents	23.7	1996	City
Deaths per 1,000 Residents	8.4	1996	City
Infant Mortality Rate	33 per 1,000 live births	1985	City
ECONOMY			
Total Workforce	2,868,567	1990	City
Trade	26.3%	1990	City
Manufacturing	18.4%	1990	City
Services	34.3%	1990	City
Finance, Insurance, Real Estate	4.2%	1990	City
Transport and Communications	7.5%	1990	City
Construction	6.4%	1990	City
Utilities	0.6%	1990	City
Agriculture	1.7%	1990	City
Mining	0.6%	1990	City
Nonclassifiable	0.2%	1990	City
TRANSPORTATION			
Passenger Journeys	612,933,000	1988	City
Rail	4.6%	1988	City
Buses and Trolleys	95.4%	1988	City
Passenger Vehicles	398,869	1988	City

(continued)

CATEGORY	DATA	YEAR	AREA
COMMUNICATIONS			
Telephones per 1,000 Residents	60.8	1991	Metro
Televisions per 1,000 Residents	117.9	1991	Metro
HOUSING			
Total Housing Units	1,740,214	1990	Metro
Persons per Unit	4.7	1990	Metro
HEALTH CARE			
Hospitals	1,158	1988	Metro
Physicians per 1,000 Residents	2.5	1992	Metro
EDUCATION			
Total Students	1,776,200	1990	Metro
Primary	57.9%	1990	Metro
Secondary	35.6%	1990	Metro
Higher	6.5%	1990	Metro

Sources: Department of Economic and Social Affairs, Population Division. *Urban Agglomerations, 1996.* New York: United Nations, 1997; *Statistik Indonesia—Statistical Year Book of Indonesia.* Jakarta, Indonesia: Central Bureau of Statistics, 1996; *Statistics of World Large Cities.* Tokyo, Japan: Tokyo Metropolitan Government, 1992 and 1994; and United Nations Center for Human Settlements. *Compendium of Human Settlements Statistics.* New York: United Nations, 1995.

Jerusalem (Al Quds)
ISRAEL/PALESTINE

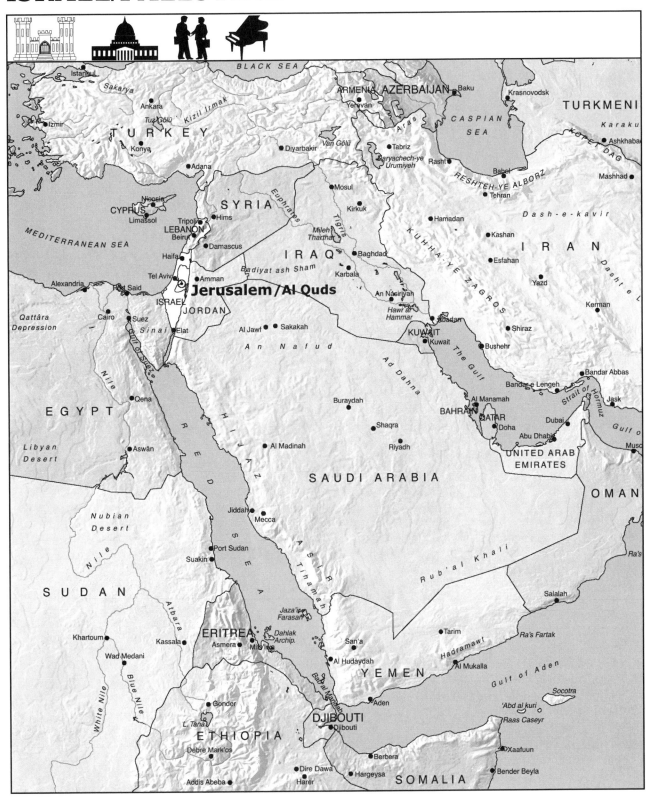

LOCATION

Situated on the heights separating the Jordan River valley and the coastal plain of Israel, Jerusalem is the second largest city in Israel and the largest metropolitan area in the Occupied Territories of the West Bank. The city itself covers approximately 40 square miles (109 square kilometers), but the Jerusalem metropolitan area, including annexed East Jerusalem, covers several times that territory. Jerusalem is approximately 40 miles east of Tel Aviv and 60 miles west of Amman, Jordan.

Located 2,654 feet (955 meters) above sea level, Jerusalem has a Mediterranean climate that plunges into freezing temperatures on many winter evenings. The average temperatures in January and July are 48 and 72 degrees Fahrenheit (8.9 and 22.2 degrees Celsius), respectively. The city receives a moderate amount of precipitation, 19.7 inches (500 millimeters) annually, most of which falls in the winter and spring, largely as rain but occasionally in the form of snow.

POPULATION AND DEMOGRAPHY

The city's population was 544,200 in 1988 and is estimated to be roughly 650,000 in 1998, growing at a rate of 2.2 percent annually. The city is deeply divided between a Jewish western half and an Arab eastern half, though a ring of Jewish housing projects have been constructed in the eastern half of the metropolitan area in the years since Israel annexed the city in 1967, and especially since the victory of the conservative Likud party in the elections of 1977. Approximately three quarters of the city is Jewish and one quarter is Arab, the latter including Muslims, Christian, and Druze. The Jewish population is divided among Orthodox and secular groups.

HISTORY

Jerusalem is one of the oldest continuously inhabited cities in the world. Founded an estimated three thousand years before Christ, the city is believed to be the capital of King David's ancient Hebrew kingdom in the second millennium B.C. According to the New Testament, Jesus Christ preached in Jerusalem and was crucified just outside the walls of the city. The Prophet Muhammed is also said to have visited the city, where he ascended to heaven. Thus, Jerusalem is a holy city to the three major faiths of Western civilization.

Occupied over the centuries by the Babylonians, Persians, Greeks, Romans, Arabs, and Christian Crusaders, the city was conquered by the Ottoman Turks in the early sixteenth century A.D. For the next several centuries, the city became a backwater of the empire until it was captured by British and Arab troops in 1917. Britain promised its Arab allies an independent Palestine with Jerusalem as its capital, but then turned the territory into a mandated colony.

Meanwhile, Jews from Eastern Europe were migrating to Palestine and Jerusalem in a quest to create a Jewish state in the ancient Hebrew lands. This movement was called Zionism. The wave of immigration increased with the victory of the Nazis in Germany in the 1930s. The rising tide of Jews angered many Palestinian Arabs, who saw the newcomers buying up lands and displacing Arabs. A series of conflicts broke out between the Arabs, Jews, and British, culminating in the great Arab uprising of 1937.

Following World War II, Britain could no longer maintain authority in the mandate and turned it over to the UN for administration, which planned to divide Palestine into Jewish and Arab halves and put Jerusalem itself under international administration. But Zionist officials acted first, declaring Israel an independent state in 1948. This action exacerbated the growing conflict between Arabs and Jews and led to a war that Israel won, occupying additional territory in Palestine as well as the western half of Jerusalem. Twenty years later, in 1967, Israel once again fought several neighboring Arab states, seizing East Jerusalem and other territories in the process. Shortly after the war, Israel officially annexed East Jerusalem, a move condemned by the international community.

GOVERNMENT AND POLITICS

In the years since independence, Israel developed West Jerusalem into a modern capital. With the seizure of East Jerusalem, it has tried to surround Arab areas with Jewish settlements and unify the divided city through a master urban plan. These actions have created growing unrest and opposition among Palestinians and have exacerbated tensions with the international community.

Jerusalem serves as the legislative capital of Israel, though this status is not recognized by the United Nations or most of the international community. The vast majority of international embassies are located in Tel Aviv. At the same time, the Palestinian Authority claims the eastern half of Jerusalem as its administrative center, though this is disputed by the

Israeli government, which refuses to allow any offices of the authority to operate in the city.

Jerusalem is ruled by a city council of thirty-one members, who are elected by proportional representation every four years. The council is headed by a mayor, who is elected by a popular vote. The administrative staff of the city government roughly breaks down as 80 percent Jewish and 20 percent Arab. The current mayor of the city is a member of the conservative Likud party.

ECONOMY

The Jerusalem economy is dominated by two sectors: tourism, including religious pilgrimages, and government. Over 40 percent of the workforce is engaged in public and municipal services, both at the municipal and national level. There are also a number of Jewish, Palestinian, and Arab nongovernmental agencies, as well as religious foundations that employ many Jewish and Arab citizens. Transportation, trade, and tourism employ another 21.5 percent of the population. The city had over eight thousand hotel rooms in 1988, and several thousand more have been constructed since.

The city has little in the way of heavy industry; the Israeli government has discouraged it in order to maintain the historical character of the city. Most of the production is done in small shops and includes shoes, clothing, textile, fine metal- and leatherworking, jewelry, religious items, and tourist curios. Several high-tech industrial parks have been established on the outskirts of the city, making software and pharmaceutical products.

TRANSPORTATION

Located atop a series of ridges, Jerusalem has an acute transportation problem. A major four-lane highway and railroad connect the city to Tel Aviv and Ben-Gurion airport, Israel's only major international air terminal. In addition, the Israeli government has built a number of highways connecting Jerusalem to the bedroom suburbs being built— against the protests of Palestinian Arabs and the international community—on the West Bank and annexed territories adjacent to East Jerusalem. Within the city, traffic congestion is acute, owing to the peculiar geography, increasing number of vehicles, and, in the older parts, narrow and winding streets. Bus service, both metropolitan and intercity, is excellent.

HEALTH CARE

Jerusalem boasts one of the finest medical infrastructures in the Middle East. The Hadassah Medical Center, serving patients in both Israel and the Occupied Territories, is considered to be one of the finest hospitals in the world, with state-of-the-art technology and a highly trained medical staff. A host of other government, nonprofit, and religious-run hospitals serve the residents of the city as well. All citizens of Jerusalem, both Arab and Jew, are required to carry medical insurance, and all health services are subsidized by the government.

EDUCATION

While extensive and well run, the educational system of Jerusalem is a complex one, divided by issues of religion, ethnicity, and language. While most children attend government-run schools—where the language of instruction is either Hebrew or Arabic—the city's large Orthodox Jewish and religiously observant Muslim populations has led to the presence of many religious-run schools. Education remains the number one expenditure of the city government. Jerusalem also boasts several world-class institutions of higher learning, including Hebrew University, mainly for Jewish students, and Bir Zeit University, largely catering to Arabs. In addition, many religious orders operate seminaries in the city.

HOUSING

Jerusalem has three basic types of housing. The older parts of the city are dominated by complex multiple-dwelling structures, usually built on several levels and surrounding an inner courtyard. Some of the older neighborhoods have been occupied by Jewish residents who have renovated the homes. Other sections remain Arab, but due to government spending patterns and Arab poverty, these quarters have frequently descended into slumlike conditions. In newer Jewish West Jerusalem, modern apartment blocks line spacious, tree-lined streets. The outskirts of annexed East Jerusalem have become the site of major apartment blocks put up to house Jewish families. Some 180,000 Jewish residents have moved into these sections of Jerusalem since 1967, sparking violent clashes with Arab citizens. The most recent clash occurred in 1997 over a neighborhood known in Hebrew as Har Homa. The average Jewish dwelling is shared by 3.6 persons, while the average Arab house contains 5.4 persons. All parts of the city are served by a modern electrical, water, and sewage system. Few homes remain unconnected to this modern grid of services.

CULTURE, THE ARTS, AND ENTERTAINMENT

Jerusalem is one of the most diverse cities in the world, with fine examples of Roman, Crusader, Islamic, Turkish, and modern architecture. The old walled city contains within it the Western Wall of the Second Temple, Judaism's holiest site; the Church of the Holy Sepulchre, where Jesus's body is said to have been entombed; and the Temple of the Mount,

site of the al-Aqsa Mosque and the Dome of the Rock, where Muhammed is said to have ascended to heaven. Jerusalem is also home to a number of major museums, including institutions devoted to archeology, the arts, and history. Yad Vashem, in West Jerusalem, is devoted to the history of the Holocaust. The city also hosts the Israeli National Archives, which contain the original Dead Sea Scrolls.

In addition, a network of youth, community, and senior citizen centers provide arts, sports, and educational programs for city residents. Immodest dress is generally frowned upon in any part of the city and most especially in Orthodox Jewish and Arab neighborhoods. The Jewish Sabbath is on Saturday, when most stores close and public transport shuts down in many districts of West Jerusalem.

CATEGORY	DATA	YEAR	AREA
LOCATION & ENVIRONMENT			
Area	40 square miles	1995	City
	109 square kilometers		City
Elevation	2,654 feet/955 meters		City
January Temperature	48 degrees Fahrenheit		City
	8.9 degrees Celsius		City
July Temperature	72 degrees Fahrenheit		City
	22.2 degrees Celsius		City
Annual Precipitation	19.7 inches/500 millimeters		City
POPULATION & DEMOGRAPHY			
Population	544,200	1988	City
Jews	399,900	1988	City
Arabs	144,300	1988	City
Growth Rate	2.2%	1988	City
Natural Increase (Jews/Arabs)	12.6%/−1.0%	1988	City
Density	13,481 per square mile	1988	City
	4,993 per square kilometer		City
Age			
Under 20 (Jews/Arabs)	41.0%/48.6%	1988	City
20–59 (Jews/Arabs)	49.9%/47.0%	1988	City
Over 60 (Jews/Arabs)	9.1%/4.4%	1988	City
ECONOMY			
Total Workforce	217,900	1993	City
Public Services	41.4%	1988	City
Trade and Tourism	14.9%	1988	City
Industry	11.2%	1988	City
Finance	10.0%	1988	City
Personal Services	7.2%	1988	City
Construction	6.9%	1988	City
Transport and Communications	6.6%	1988	City

(continued)

CATEGORY	DATA	YEAR	AREA
HOUSING			
Housing Units	62,300	1993	City
New Housing Units	1,806	1988	City
Persons per Unit (Jews/Arabs)	5.4/3.6	1992	Metro
HEALTH CARE			
Hospitals	15	1992	Metro
EDUCATION			
Universities	5	1996	Metro

Source: Population in Localities: Demographic Characteristics by Geographical Divisions. Israel: Central Bureau of Statistics, 1996.

Johannesburg
SOUTH AFRICA

ANGOLA
Neriquinha
ZAMBIA
Lusaka
Kafue
Oncócua
Namacunde
Cuangar
Luiana
Sesheke
Kariba
Lake Kariba
Okavango
Caprivi Strip
Livingstone
Opuwa
Kasane
Victoria Falls
Kad
ZIMBAB
Okaukuejo
Okavango Basin
Maun
Gw
Grootfontein
Bulawayo
Otjiwarongo
Makgadikgadi Pans
Orapa
Francistown
Messina
NAMIBIA
Brandberg
Omaruru
Karibib
Usakos
Ghanzi
BOTSWANA
Serowe
Palapye
Louis Tr
Swakopmund
Windhoek
Gobabis
KALAHARI
Mahalapye
Pietersburg
Walvis Bay
Rehoboth
DESERT
Molepolole
Mochudi
Gaborone
Potgietersrus
Mariental
Kanye
Sun City
Mafikeng
Pretoria
Krugersdorp
Johannesburg
Lüderitz
Keetmanshoop
Hazuur
Vryburg
Vaal
Vereeniging
Vaaldam
SWA
Kuruman
Welkom
Karasburg
Orange
Upington
Harts
Alexander Bay
Kimberley
Ladysmith
Port Nolloth
Kenhardt
Douglas
Bloemfontein
LESOTHO
Maseru
Pieterm
Springbok
Aliwal North
Mafeteng
Dur
SOUTH AFRICA
Carnarvon
Burgersdorp
Port Shep
ATLANTIC OCEAN
Calvinia
Victoria West
Orange
Port St. Johns
Great Karoo
Gt. Fish
Clanwilliam
Beaufort West
Saint Helena Bay
Kirkwood
Grahamstown
East London
Malmesbury
Oudtshoorn
Paarl
Cape Town
Mosselbaai
Port Elizabeth
Cape Recife
Cape of Good Hope
Hermanus
False Bay
Cape Agulhas
Limpopo

LOCATION

Often called the "City of Gold" after its major industry, Johannesburg is the most populous city in South Africa and the world's largest metropolis not located on a navigable body of water. Located on rolling veld, or prairie, in the northeastern portion of the country, and at an elevation of 5,689 feet (2,048 meters), Johannesburg enjoys a mild climate. Its summer temperature averages 66.4 degrees Fahrenheit (19.1 degrees Celsius); its winters average 49.5 degrees Fahrenheit (9.7 degrees Celsius). It has moderate rainfall of about 25 inches (634.6 millimeters) annually. Because Johannesburg is located in the Southern Hemisphere, its seasons are reversed from those of the Northern Hemisphere.

POPULATION AND DEMOGRAPHY

Johannesburg has a population of 900,000, with another 1.3 million located in the surrounding metropolitan area, including many large townships inhabited primarily by black South Africans. This population is divided among Xhosa-, Zulu-, and Venda-speaking peoples, with small minorities of Tswana- and Pedi-speakers. Most South Africans practice the Christian faith, though there are small populations of people practicing traditional religions among blacks, while the East Asian population is Muslim or Hindu.

As of 1986, the city's population was divided into four ethnic groups: whites (Afrikaans- and English-speaking), with 60 percent; blacks, with 25 percent; coloreds, or mixed-race people, with 11 percent; and persons of East Indian ancestry, with 4 percent. Since the dismantling of apartheid laws and residence restrictions in 1990, the city has seen substantial growth in its black population. That factor, and the substantially higher birth rates among black women compared to whites means that the white population will soon represent a minority of the metropolitan area's population.

During the early 1990s, the annual overall growth rate was 2.5 percent, though this is expected to decline to about 2 percent early in the next century. The population of the metropolitan area is expected to reach 3.4 million in 2015, though the city's density will remain near the current relatively low level of about 5,400 persons per square mile (2,000 per square kilometer).

HISTORY

Johannesburg sprang up virtually overnight as the center of the bustling gold-mining business in 1886, after vast deposits of the precious mineral were discovered along the Witwatersrand, or "white water ridge." The city was at the center of the Boer-English disputes that led to the Boer War of 1899–1902 and which resulted in a victory for the English. (Boers are the descendants of early Dutch settlers.) By 1930, the population had grown to 400,000.

The city's history has been marked by the violence and anarchy familiar to any boomtown, a trend exacerbated by serious racial and economic divisions. In 1948, South Africa's all-white electorate put the Afrikaans-speaking and conservative Boer-dominated National Party in power. The National Party then instituted a policy of racial segregation and preference known as apartheid. As part of this initiative, the primarily black Southwestern Townships, more commonly known as Soweto, were legally separated from the city.

GOVERNMENT AND POLITICS

Beginning in the 1960s and accelerating in the following two decades, the blacks and colored persons of Johannesburg and South Africa generally engaged in both peaceful and violent demonstrations against apartheid, leading ultimately to the multiracial elections of 1994 and the accession to power of antiapartheid activist Nelson Mandela and the African National Congress. The Johannesburg metropolitan area is governed by the Greater Johannesburg Metropolitan Board—an elective body created by the 1994 constitution with representatives from the greater Johannesburg metropolitan area. There are also planning councils that institute and run policies connected to the larger Pretoria-Witwatersrand-Vereeniging, or Pretoria-Witwatersrand Union (PWV).

ECONOMY

Johannesburg's economy is dominated by the region's mining industry. Indeed, the nearly 50 miles of ultra-deep gold mines of Witwatersrand, commonly referred to as "the Rand," literally run under the city, and the use of explosives can be felt on the streets of the city above from time to time. While the Rand is perhaps the richest gold-mining area in the world, the importance of this metal to Johannesburg's economy has declined somewhat in recent years as international gold prices have fallen. But the Rand also contains some of the world's richest deposits of other key industrial minerals, including coal, industrial- and jewelry-quality diamonds, uranium, iron, silver, platinum, and chrome.

While mining dominates the economy, much of the city's labor is engaged in other activities. As one of the major manufacturing centers in sub-Saharan Africa, Johannesburg is heavily industrialized, with 34 percent of the labor force engaged in that sector. Much of this industry—nurtured by the isolationist South African government—is not considered particularly competitive. Trade accounts for another 26.7 percent of the workforce. In addition, Johannesburg is a major world financial center. Its stock exchange is the largest in the Southern Hemisphere.

The city's economy began to experience a structural slowdown in the mid-1970s, largely a result of the leap in world energy prices. This slump grew worse with the decline in gold prices in the early 1980s and the growing international sanctions against the apartheid regime imposed in the late 1980s. With the central bank experiencing a severe balance of payments, interests rates climbed, cutting off investment. The city actually saw negative economic growth rates during the mid-1980s. With the lifting of international sanctions in the 1990s, growth rates have returned to about 2 percent in the 1990s, still below historic norms. Other economic problems include a rigid labor market, unequal distribution of wealth, and slow capital growth.

TRANSPORTATION

Johannesburg is a regional transportation hub. Its airport is the largest in southern Africa, and a vast railroad system links Johannesburg to neighboring Zimbabwe and Mozambique, as well as numerous South African cities on the Indian Ocean coastline.

While the city also boasts an extensive commuter railroad system, it was built to serve the needs of apartheid: The black townships are connected to the center of the city, but not to each other. In addition, many black townships are far from the city center, requiring commuting trips as long as three hours a day round-trip.

Most whites own cars, but many blacks do not. Car ownership among the latter is growing, however. In 1975, just 27 blacks per 1,000 owned cars; by the year 2000, that figure is expected to climb to 144. In addition, with the ending of apartheid, many black entrepreneurs have begun to operate group taxi and minibus services, cutting commuting time immensely.

HEALTH CARE

While the Johannesburg metropolitan area boasts thirty-one hospitals and sixty-two clinics, most of the better ones are located in previously whites-only districts. The relatively high ratio of physicians in the population of 2.2 per 1,000 persons disguises the fact that most of the city's doctors are located near—and tend to serve—the city's white population. Infant mortality and death rates among the black population are more like those in the rest of Africa, while white rates are equal to those in Europe. At the same time, much of the African population relies on traditional herbal remedies for common illnesses as well.

EDUCATION

Education is widespread, though much more prevalent and extensive among the white population. The vast majority of the city's population of all races are literate, though far fewer blacks go on to attend secondary schools. Johannesburg is also home to several major universities, including the world-renowned University of Witwatersrand, for English-speaking students, as well as the Rand Afrikaans University, for Afrikaans-speaking pupils. Since the fall of apartheid in the early 1990s, both universities have been integrated racially, though most university-attending blacks prefer to attend English-language institutions.

HOUSING

As with almost everything else in this once legally divided city, Johannesburg's housing stock shows great disparities between rich and poor. Leafy, tree-lined neighborhoods dominate the northern suburbs, while barren tracts of substandard housing lie to the south and west of the city.

Large investments have been made in the past twenty years to improve the city's electricity, water, and sewage systems. Virtually all whites live in houses with indoor plumbing and electricity. Most black homes enjoy electricity, but many lack indoor plumbing. In 1991, the Metropolitan Chamber of Johannesburg was established to deal with problems of black housing, and the government of Nelson Mandela has also made improvements in black housing a priority, though progress has been hampered by slow economic growth.

CULTURE, THE ARTS, AND ENTERTAINMENT

Under the old apartheid regime, the government tried to keep outside media from penetrating South Africa, for fear it would lead to rising demands by blacks for a greater share of the national wealth and a greater say in the country's government. Thus, while the city had a telephone ownership of 1 phone for every 1.3 persons, its TV ownership rates were over 1 to 8. At the same time, the isolation and the struggle against apartheid led to one of the most vigorous theatrical communities in the world.

This isolation has lifted considerably since the repeal of the apartheid laws in the early 1990s. South Africans now enjoy TV and cinema imported from much of the English-speaking world.

Johannesburg boasts an extensive network of libraries and museums. Parkland covers 21 square miles (54.4 square kilometers) of the metropolitan area, though major tracts of wasteland left by gold-mining operations scar the nearby landscape.

CATEGORY	DATA	YEAR	AREA
LOCATION & ENVIRONMENT			
Area	167 square miles	1995	City
	450 square kilometers		City
Elevation	5,689 feet/2,048 meters		City
January Temperature	66.4 degrees Fahrenheit		City
	19.1 degrees Celsius		City
July Temperature	49.5 degrees Fahrenheit		City
	9.7 degrees Celsius		City
Annual Precipitation	25 inches / 634.6 millimeters		City
POPULATION & DEMOGRAPHY			
Population	2,200,000	1996	Metro
Projected Population	3,400,000	2015	Metro
Growth Rate	2.9%	1990–1995	City
Growth Rate	54.7%	1995–2015	City
Density	5,513 per square mile	1990	City
	2,042 per square kilometer		
Age			
Under 20	35.3%	1985	City
20–59	52.4%	1985	City
Over 60	12.3%	1985	City
VITAL STATISTICS			
Births per 1,000 Residents	19.3	1987	City
Deaths per 1,000 Residents	6.5	1989	City
Infant Mortality Rate	25 per 1,000 live births	1984	City
ECONOMY			
Workforce	500,000	1985	City
Manufacturing	34.0%	1985	City
Construction	10.1%	1985	City
Mining	1.2%	1985	City
Agriculture	0.1%	1985	City
Trade	26.7%	1985	City
Real Estate	3.1%	1985	City

(continued)

CATEGORY	DATA	YEAR	AREA
TRANSPORTATION			
Passenger Vehicles	581,920	1990	City
Total Journeys	258,514	1990	City
Rail Journeys	81.5%	1990	City
Bus Journeys	18.5%	1990	City
HOUSING			
Total Housing Units	193,600	1990	City
Persons per Unit	7.02	1990	City
HEALTH CARE			
Hospitals	31	1992	City
Clinics	62	1992	City
Physicians per 1,000 Residents	2.2%	1992	City
EDUCATION			
Total Students	65,297	1992	City
Primary Students	65.4%	1992	City
Secondary Students	34.6%	1992	City

Sources: Department of Economic and Social Affairs, Population Division. *Urban Agglomerations, 1996.* New York: United Nations, 1997; *Statistics of World Large Cities.* Tokyo, Japan: Tokyo Metropolitan Government, 1992 and 1994; and United Nations Center for Human Settlements. *Compendium of Human Settlements Statistics.* New York: United Nations, 1995.

Karachi, Sindh Province
PAKISTAN

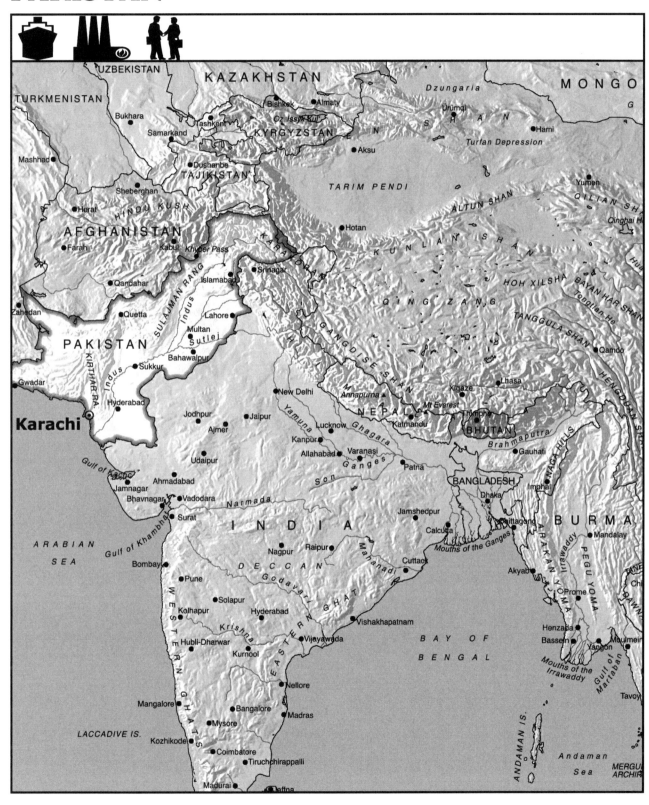

LOCATION

Karachi, the largest city and main port of Pakistan, is located on the Arabian Sea, just to the northwest of the Indus River delta. The city's natural harbor is protected by several islands, and two seasonal rivers run through the metropolitan area. Karachi is located about 550 miles northwest of Mumbai, India, and 650 miles south-southwest of Pakistan's capital, Islamabad. The territory of the metropolitan area is 221 square miles (596 square kilometers) and is located at 13 feet (3.9 meters) above sea level.

The climate of the city is tropical. Average summer and winter temperatures are 86 and 66 degrees Fahrenheit (30 and 18.9 degrees Celsius), respectively, though the highs are often tempered by cooling breezes off the Arabian Sea. The city has a dry climate, with just 7.8 inches (198.1 millimeters) of rain annually, most of which falls during a brief wet season in the early summer.

POPULATION AND DEMOGRAPHY

Karachi has a vast population. The metropolitan area was estimated to have 10.1 million people in 1996. The growth rate of the city has steadily dropped from a high of more than 9 percent annually in the 1940s to 4.1 percent in the 1990s. It is expected to fall to 3 percent early in the twenty-first century, while the population is expected to climb to 19.4 million by 2015. The city bucks the trend of South Asia, with more females than males; there are approximately 112 women for every 100 men (women comprise 56 percent of the city's residents). The population is also young, with 52.5 percent under the age of 20. Population density is 30,434 persons per square mile (11,272 per square kilometer) within the city limits.

The population of Karachi represents a cross-section of Pakistani peoples. Most of the majority Muslim population are of Indo-Pakistani stock, but there are also small minorities of inhabitants of African descent, known as Makranis and Shiddies, as well as Arabs and Persians. Small communities of Hindus, Parsis, and Christians also inhabit Karachi. The official language is Urdu, but many speak other indigenous languages. English is commonly spoken by the educated classes as well.

HISTORY

Karachi was originally founded as a small fishing village over a thousand years ago. But it grew into its modern prominence after a community of traders moved there to take advantage of the site's natural harbor, which protected ships against cyclone-driven waves in the Arabian Sea. The city was occupied by several Muslim emirs in the late eighteenth century, who erected a fort to protect trade and inhabitants against invaders from other parts of Asia and Europe. Karachi was captured by British forces in 1839 and annexed to British-ruled India three years later. It became an administrative and military headquarters and served as the main port for the traffic on the nearby Indus River. The city was connected to the burgeoning Indian railway system in 1878, when a line to Delhi was completed. The port was developed as well during these years, and by 1914, the city had become the largest grain-exporting port in the British Empire. With independence in 1947, Karachi was made the capital of Pakistan, a role it played until 1959, when the capital was temporarily moved to Rawalpindi in anticipation of the completion of a new, planned capital at Islamabad. The city has grown into a major industrial and commercial center since 1947.

GOVERNMENT AND POLITICS

Karachi is governed by five separate institutions, the heads of which are appointed by the government. These include the Karachi Municipal Corporation, which performs a host of civic functions affecting three fourths of the metropolitan area's population; two municipal councils for the various communities in the Karachi area, established in 1966 and 1970; the Karachi Cantonment Board, which administers the extensive military districts in the city; and the Karachi Port Trust, which handles affairs of the harbor.

ECONOMY

The city's manufacturing sector included approximately 1,700 registered industries in 1981. These include textiles, footwear, metal products, food products, paper and printing, wood and furniture, machinery, chemicals and refined petroleum products, leather and rubber goods, and electrical equipment and components. The city is also home to an extensive handicraft industry, producing fine cloth, carpets, metal goods, leather goods, and jewelry. However, the city has been cited as a major violator of international rules against the use of child labor in industry.

Some twenty-five banks make Karachi Pakistan's financial capital. The city is also home to ten insurance companies and the nation's main stock exchange. While most government offices are head-quartered in Islamabad, a number of government agencies maintain offices in Karachi.

TRANSPORTATION

As Pakistan's principal port, and one of the largest in South Asia, Karachi handles over 20,000 tons of freight annually. The city is also connected to the rest of Pakistan, as well as neighboring Iran and India, by three major highways and several rail lines. While the metropolitan area has many fine roads and rela-tively light traffic, congestion is a problem in the cen-tral city. Approximately 75 percent of the population uses public transport, with buses being the principal form of transit. However, the bus fleet remains plagued by repair problems, with only about 1,500 of 2,100 vehicles operating at any one time. In the past two decades, minibuses have helped fill the need unmet by public transport. Private vehicle ownership is low. There are approximately thirty cars and thirty-two motorcycles per thousand persons.

HEALTH CARE

The poor sanitation in the city leads to a high rate of gastrointestinal diseases, including dysentery and cholera, especially during the long dry season, when clean water sources dry up. Tuberculosis, leprosy, and various skin diseases are prevalent. But due to its seaside location, much of the air pollution is swept away by breezes and winds that blow much of the year. This results in a relatively low prevalence of respiratory illnesses. The infant mortality rate is a high 120 per 1,000 live births. The city is served by twenty hospitals, but the ratio of physicians per 1,000 persons is an unhealthful 0.2.

EDUCATION

Karachi has an extensive system of public, private, and religious schools. There are over 2,700 primary schools, with a student population of 640,000, and nearly 1,000 secondary schools, educating over 360,000 pupils. The city is also home to two major universities, including the University of Karachi and its many affiliated colleges, as well as a number of technical institutes. There are approximately 80,000 students in institutions of higher learning in Karachi.

HOUSING

The flood of rural migrants has produced a serious housing shortage in the city. The number of squatter settlements—known as *katchi abadis*—has grown at a rate of 10 percent annually in recent decades, twice the rate for the metropolitan area as a whole. Some 2.6 million people lived in squatter settlements in 1986. Including these squats, some 60 percent of the city's dwellings remain unconnected to the city's wa-ter supply system. The other 40 percent are largely served by standpipes connected to wells. With a ratio of 270 persons for every well and a shallow water table, this water source is occasionally contaminated by salt water. While the city has a workforce of 9,000 municipal sweepers and 150 garbage trucks, fully two thirds of the city's solid waste is not adequately picked up.

CULTURE, THE ARTS, AND ENTERTAINMENT

Much of the drama, music, dance, and fine arts scene in Karachi is supported by the Arts Council of Pak-istan. The Ghanshyam Art Centre and the Bulbul Academy promote traditional dance and other cul-tural activities. The city also hosts several small mu-seums, including one that contains relics from the Indus River Valley, one of the cradles of human civ-ilization. The city has a number of major libraries, including one at the University of Karachi that is the city's largest. Cinema-going is popular, with nearly seventy movie houses showing Indian, Pakistani, and American films. The city has a distinct shortage of open parkland, though there are many fine beaches in the metropolitan area. The city has an extensive network of sports clubs and several major stadiums for spectator sports. Soccer is the city's favorite sport to play and watch. Pakistan is also a major exporter of soccer balls.

CATEGORY	DATA	YEAR	AREA
LOCATION & ENVIRONMENT			
Area	221 square miles	1995	City
	596 square kilometers		City
Elevation	13 feet/3.9 meters		City
January Temperature	66 degrees Fahrenheit		City
	18.9 degrees Celsius		City
July Temperature	86 degrees Fahrenheit		City
	30 degrees Celsius		City
Annual Precipitation	7.8 inches/198.1 millimeters		City
POPULATION & DEMOGRAPHY			
Population	10,100,000	1996	Metro
Projected Population	19,400,000	2015	Metro
Growth Rate	4.1%	1990–1995	Metro
Growth Rate	99.1%	1995–2015	Metro
Density	30,434 per square mile	1989	City
	11,272 per square kilometer		City
Gender			
Male	44%	1989	City
Female	56%	1989	City
Age			
Under 20	52.5%	1989	City
20–59	43.0%	1989	City
Over 60	4.5%	1989	City
VITAL STATISTICS			
Births per 1000 Residents	46	1989	City
Deaths per 1,000 Residents	9	1989	City
Infant Mortality Rate	120 per 1,000 live births	1989	City
TRANSPORTATION			
Cars	339,019	1987	City
Trucks	7,193	1987	City
COMMUNICATIONS			
Televisions per 1,000 Residents	69	1988	Metro
HOUSING			
Housing with Indoor Plumbing	40%	1994	Metro
HEALTH CARE			
Hospitals	10	1987	City
Physicians per 1,000 Residents	0.2	1987	City

(continued)

CATEGORY	DATA	YEAR	AREA
EDUCATION			
Total Students	1,090,179	1987	City
Primary	58.9%	1987	City
Secondary	33.7%	1987	City
Higher	7.4%	1987	City

Sources: Department of Economic and Social Affairs, Population Division. *Urban Agglomerations, 1996.* New York: United Nations, 1997; *Pakistan Statistical Year Book 1994.* Karachi, Pakistan: Federal Bureau of Statistics, 1994; *Statistics of World Large Cities.* Tokyo, Japan: Tokyo Metropolitan Government, 1992 and 1994; and United Nations Center for Human Settlements. *Compendium of Human Settlements Statistics.* New York: United Nations, 1995.

Kiev
UKRAINE

LOCATION

The capital and largest city of the Ukraine, Kiev covers 307 square miles (828 square kilometers) of territory along both banks of the Dnieper River in the middle of the country. The older parts of the city are located on bluffs above the river. Once capital of the Ukrainian Soviet Socialist Republic, Kiev is situated 292 feet (90 meters) above sea level, in the midst of the vast Dnieper River basin. It is about 500 miles upriver from the Black Sea and roughly 600 miles southwest of Moscow, Russia.

The city has a continental climate and its winters can be quite cold. Average January temperatures are 26.4 degrees Fahrenheit (−3.1 degrees Celsius), while summer temperatures average 65.3 degrees Fahrenheit (18.5 degrees Celsius). Much of the city's 21.5 inches (546 millimeters) of annual precipitation falls in the summer months, though there can be heavy snowfall in the winter as well.

POPULATION AND DEMOGRAPHY

The Kiev metropolitan area has a population of approximately 2.8 million. Its annual growth rate was just over 1 percent during the early 1990s, though this should drop to near or below zero in the coming century. Thus, population projections for the next twenty years see the number of inhabitants growing by just 100,000 in total. Kiev has a density of approximately 8,500 persons per square mile (3,100 per square kilometer), and more than one fourth of the population is under 20 years of age, while about 13 percent is over 60.

Like Ukraine itself, Kiev is dominated by Ukrainian-speaking Slavs, though there is a substantial Russian-speaking minority. In addition, the city includes small communities of Bulgarians, Poles, Hungarians, and Romanians. The city had a Jewish population of about 5 percent in 1991, though this has fallen off significantly with mass migration to Israel over the past several years. The predominant religion is Eastern Orthodox Christianity, but there is a substantial minority who practice Catholicism. Under Soviet rule, religion was discouraged, so most of Kiev's inhabitants are not practitioners of their faith, though this has changed somewhat since independence from the Soviet Union in 1991.

HISTORY

Settlements in what is now Kiev date back to prehistoric times. According to traditional accounts, Kiev was founded by three brothers, leaders of an eastern Slavic tribe. Archeologists say that the city was founded in the seventh century A.D. The city was captured by another Slavic tribe, the Varangians, in the mid-ninth century, and they made it their capital. Christianity came to the city in 988, making Kiev a major spiritual center. By the twelfth century, the growing city boasted more than four hundred churches. At this time, Kiev became the capital of the incipient Russian state and was one of the major cities of Europe. A succession of wars weakened the kingdom, leading to the destruction of the city and the massacre of its population by Mongols in 1240.

In the fourteenth century, the city came under control of the expanding Duchy of Lithuania, and in 1569 it was handed over to Poland. Struggles between Polish Catholics and Ukrainian Catholics marked this period. Internal wars as well as attacks by Cossacks weakened Polish rule, and the city was ceded to the growing tsarist empire of Russia in 1686. During the first half of the nineteenth century, Kiev became a center of Ukrainian nationalism and revolution. At the same time, the city became a major industrial center, a role enhanced by the construction of a railroad connecting it to the Black Sea port of Odessa, to the south, and Moscow, to the north. On the eve of World War I, the city had a population of some 350,000.

While a German-controlled independent Ukraine—with Kiev as its capital—was created as a result of the World War I–era Brest-Litovsk Treaty, Kiev came under Red Army control during the Russian civil war. World War II brought much destruction and death to the city with the German conquest in September 1941. Following the war, the city grew rapidly and became heavily industrialized. In 1987, the region around the city was harshly affected by the nuclear disaster at Chernobyl. With the collapse of the Soviet Union in 1991, Kiev became the capital of the independent Republic of Ukraine, part of the Commonwealth of Independent States (CIS).

GOVERNMENT AND POLITICS

The independent republic of Ukraine was declared in Kiev on August 24, 1991. A referendum on the question was passed overwhelmingly in December, when the country also joined the CIS, though the Soviet-era constitution largely remains in force. Under this constitution, the government includes a unicameral legislature known as the Supreme Council of Ukraine. The Presidium of the Supreme Council, once part of the legislature, now functions as an independent executive branch, headed by a popularly elected president who serves for a five-year term. The president appoints a cabinet, whose members are approved by the Supreme Council. There is also an independent judiciary. Major political parties include the former Communist Party, the People's Front of Ukraine for Reconstruction (known as Rukh), and a number of nationalist and neofascist groups.

ECONOMY

Kiev is both a major administrative center, with a good deal of employment in that sector, and a hub for manufacturing. Major industries include iron and steel plants, fed by coal from the massive Donets Basin. In addition, there are important factories making machinery, rubber, linoleum, chemicals, fertilizer, aircraft, elevators, electrical instruments, weapons, river and sea craft, motorcycles, and filmmaking equipment. The city also hosts several major industries manufacturing materials for construction, including lumber, bricks, and reinforced concrete. In addition, there is a substantial light industry sector that produces clothing, shoes, foodstuffs, and precision goods such as watches and cameras. Kiev is also a major publishing center. The commercial sector—largely underfunded in the command economy of the Soviet era—is still truncated. Less than 10 percent of the labor force works in this sector.

TRANSPORTATION

Kiev is a major transportation hub, with all-weather highways and trunk railways connecting it to Moscow, the Donets Basin, and Odessa. In addition, the Dnieper River is a major artery for barge and ship traffic to the Black Sea. The transportation system for the metropolitan area is both modern and extensive. The city has major subway, commuter rail, bus, and trolley systems. Car ownership, discouraged during the Soviet era, is growing from a base of about 150,000 vehicles at the beginning of the independence period. There is approximately one phone for every three people and one radio per person.

HEALTH CARE

The Kiev metropolitan area is host to nearly 100 hospitals and almost 250 clinics. There are approximately 130 persons per physician. The health situation in Kiev and Ukraine has deteriorated significantly since independence in 1991. Facilities built during the Soviet era have not been properly financed, and there has been a resurgence in public health problems, including diphtheria. Life expectancy has decreased and infant mortality has climbed in the past decade.

At the same time, health care is financed by a combination of state and private funding. Low wages for health care providers and underfinanced facilities have led to a further deterioration in the city's health profile. Hospital patients are often required to provide their own food, bed linens, and medicine. In 1991, the social welfare system was restructured and expanded, and benefits were linked to inflation.

EDUCATION

Like other former Soviet republics, the Ukraine has made its native tongue the official language of the independent state, with major implications for the country's educational system. At the same time, most schools have always provided instruction in Ukrainian. The city has an extensive primary and secondary school system, as well as a number of institutions of higher education and research. The latter include the Academy of Sciences and the T. H. Shevchenko State University. The city is also a center for medical, cybernetic, and advanced electrical research.

HOUSING

Most of the population in the Kiev metropolitan area live in housing projects that ring the older sections of the city. Largely built since World War II, these projects—known as microregions—consist of groupings of apartment buildings housing between 2,500 and 5,000 people each, served by shops, schools, cultural facilities, and health care centers, all surrounded by parkland. In the center of the city are a number of newer high-rises of twelve to twenty stories in height. Altogether the city had just over 700,000 housing units in 1988, with 3.7 persons per unit. Most cooking is done with natural gas. The city is also served by hydroelectric, nuclear, and coal-fired power plants. Electricity usage runs about 1 kilowatt-hour per person daily, and maximum water capacity is 53 gallons (200 liters) per person daily.

CULTURE, THE ARTS, AND ENTERTAINMENT

Kiev is a major cultural center, with a number of facilities for drama, music, the fine arts, dance, and literature, many of them sponsored by the vast network of schools connected to the T. H. Shevchenko State University. The city boasts a number of major concert halls and sports arenas, and it is home to a circus and 130 cinemas. The Dnieper River is lined with bathing beaches, though the water itself is quite polluted, and the city is surrounded by extensive parkland.

The architectural heart of the city is the ancient Upper Town, located on a high bluff. This neighborhood includes the eleventh-century Cathedral of St. Sophia, one of the finest examples of Russo-Byzantine architecture in the world. Many of the city's smaller music, drama, dance, and fine arts facilities are also located in the narrow streets of Upper Town.

CATEGORY	DATA	YEAR	AREA
LOCATION & ENVIRONMENT			
Area	307 square miles	1993	City
	828 square kilometers		City
Elevation	292 feet/90 meters		City
January Temperature	26.4 degrees Fahrenheit		City
	−3.1 degrees Celsius		City
July Temperature	65.3 degrees Fahrenheit		City
	18.5 degrees Celsius		City
Annual Precipitation	21.5 inches/546 millimeters		City
POPULATION & DEMOGRAPHY			
Population	2,800,000	1996	Metro
Projected Population	2,900,000	2015	Metro
Growth Rate	1.3%	1990–1995	Metro
Growth Rate	4.5%	1995–2015	Metro
Density	8,535 per square mile	1993	Metro
	3,161 per square kilometer	1993	Metro
Gender			
Male	46.9%	1987	Metro
Female	53.1%	1987	Metro
Age			
Under 20	27.8%	1993	Metro
20–59	59.1%	1993	Metro
Over 60	13.1%	1993	Metro
VITAL STATISTICS			
Births per 1,000 Residents	9.1	1992	Metro
Deaths per 1,000 Residents	8.9	1992	Metro
Infant Mortality Rate	17.4 per 1,000 live births	1992	Metro
ECONOMY			
Total Workforce	1,428,620	1988	Metro
Agriculture	0.1%	1988	Metro
Construction	11.5%	1988	Metro
Finance, Insurance, Real Estate	0.1%	1988	Metro
Trade	7.6%	1988	Metro
Service	35.3%	1988	Metro
Transport	8.4%	1988	Metro

(continued)

CATEGORY	DATA	YEAR	AREA
TRANSPORTATION			
Passenger Journeys	2,163,600,000	1988	Metro
Trolley	21.3%	1988	Metro
Bus	61.8%	1988	Metro
Subway	16.9%	1988	Metro
COMMUNICATIONS			
Telephones per 1,000 Residents	303	1988	Metro
HOUSING			
Housing Units	702,660	1988	Metro
New Housing Units	18,578	1992	Metro
Persons per Unit	3.7	1988	Metro
HEALTH CARE			
Hospitals	96	1992	Metro
Clinics	249	1992	Metro
Physicians per 1,000 Residents	8	1992	Metro
EDUCATION			
Total Students	431,812	1989	Metro
Primary	76.2%	1989	Metro
Higher	23.8%	1989	Metro

Sources: Department of Economic and Social Affairs, Population Division. *Urban Agglomerations, 1996.* New York: United Nations, 1997; *Statistics of World Large Cities.* Tokyo, Japan: Tokyo Metropolitan Government, 1992 and 1994; and United Nations Center for Human Settlements. *Compendium of Human Settlements Statistics.* New York: United Nations, 1995.

Kinshasa
DEMOCRATIC REPUBLIC OF THE CONGO

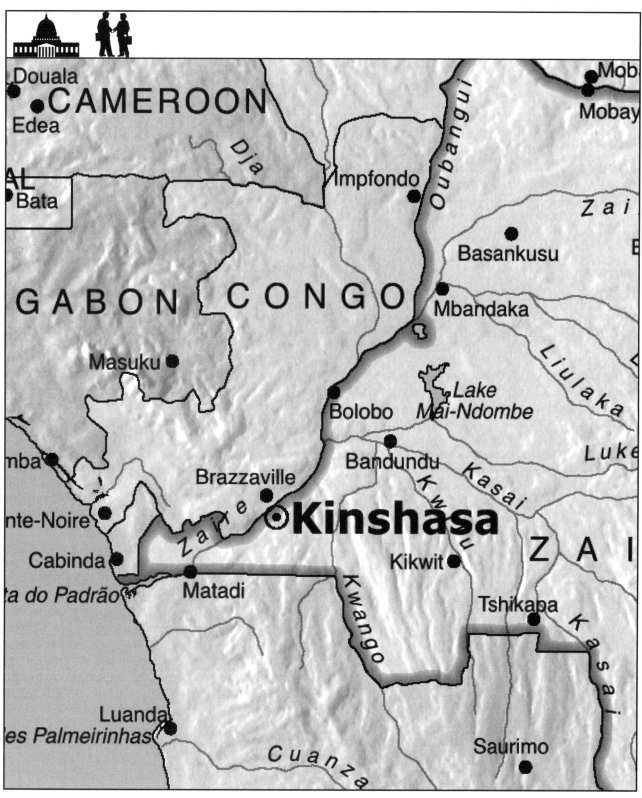

LOCATION

Situated at an elevation of 600 feet (216 meters) on the south bank of the Congo River where it opens up into Malebo Pool, approximately 200 miles upriver from the Atlantic Ocean, Kinshasa is the sprawling capital and the largest city of the Democratic Republic of Congo. The city is located 1,560 miles west of Nairobi, Kenya, and 1,130 miles southeast of Lagos, Nigeria. The metropolitan area covers roughly 3,543 square miles (9,565 square kilometers). Its locale, just below the equator, gives the city a year-round tropical climate. Annual temperatures do not vary much from the mean of 75 degrees Fahrenheit (23.8 degrees Celsius), and the city is humid throughout the year, though it rarely rains during the dry season from May to September. Temperatures range from 78.5 degrees Fahrenheit (25.8 degrees Celsius) in January to 72.5 degrees Fahrenheit (22 degrees Celsius) in July.

POPULATION AND DEMOGRAPHY

The population of Kinshasa is vast and continues to grow rapidly. In 1996, the population of the metropolitan area was estimated at 4.4 million, and it is expected to grow to 9.4 million by 2015. The city has seen growth rates of over 4 percent since 1960 and is expected to continue to grow at that rate well into the next century. This rapid growth is a product both of natural increase—the average woman in Kinshasa has 6.7 children—and massive migration from the Congolese countryside as well as from rural areas in other Central African nations. Indeed, in the early 1980s, just 7 percent of all heads of households had been born in the city.

Kinshasa has a low population density of 721 persons per square mile (267 per square kilometer), though the central city is quite crowded. The population represents a broad cross-section of Central African peoples. Many of its citizens are Roman Catholic, though most practice various traditional religions. The language of government and most educational facilities is French, while Lingala is used more commonly on the streets and in the marketplaces.

HISTORY

People have been inhabiting what is now Kinshasa since prehistoric times. The present city grew out of two fishing villages called Nshasa—which lent Kinshasa its name—and Ntamo. In 1877, the Scottish explorer Sir Henry Stanley Morton formed an alliance with chiefs of these villages and established a trading post. He named it Leopoldville after his patron, King Leopold II of Belgium. At the Berlin Congress of 1885, the territory that is now the Democratic Republic of Congo was granted to Leopold as a personal fiefdom called the Congo Free State. Because of human rights abuses in the Free State, Leopoldville and the Congo were transferred to the Belgian government, which ruled the colony until 1960.

While Leopoldville soon became a base for travel upriver, steamers had to be taken apart and portaged over the rapids downriver. With the completion of a railroad connecting the post to the port of Matadi near the Atlantic in 1898, as well as an oil pipeline in 1914, Leopoldville grew into a city.

With the rising tide of independence sweeping sub-Saharan Africa in the late 1950s, the Congo was granted its independence in 1960 and Leopoldville was made the capital. The lack of preparation for independence, along with cold war politics, led to five years of unrest, until the rise to power of Joseph Mobutu (later Mobutu Sese Seko). As part of his *authenticité*, or return to African origins, campaign of 1971, Mobutu changed the name of the city to Kinshasa and the name of the country to Zaire. Under the corrupt administration of Mobutu, the city grew rapidly and haphazardly. Wealth from the country's vast mineral reserves turned parts of the city into elegant French-style districts, while huge shantytowns known as bidonvilles grew up on the periphery. In 1997, following civil war in neighboring Rwanda, a rebel movement headed by Laurent Kabila fought its way to the capital. Kabila ascended to power—vowing to end the corruption of the Mobutu years—and renamed the country the Democratic Republic of Congo. Since Kabila's ascension to power, civil war and political instability have continued.

GOVERNMENT AND POLITICS

Since 1982, the urban administration of Kinshasa has consisted of a governor and two vice governors, both appointed by the president. They head a city council of twenty-four zone commissioners, also appointed by the president out of a slate elected by the people in each district.

ECONOMY

Kinshasa's economy is largely an underground one. There is a small manufacturing sector, employing about 20 percent of the workforce and producing basic consumer items like food products and textiles. Most people, however, work in the vast informal sector of street marketing, unregistered construction, and unlicensed transport. The rapid population growth has made for a squeeze in food supplies. For the middle and upper classes, this is solved by expensive imports brought in from as far away as South Africa. For the poor majority, however, much of the food and fuel supply is grown or gathered in small plots in the city and nearby countryside. Despite such efforts, inflation as been extreme over the past decade, sometimes exceeding 1,000 percent annually. As the country's capital, Kinshasa employs approximately two thirds of the official workforce in administrative tasks. But again, most of the labor force does not show up in official records.

TRANSPORTATION

Both Kinshasa's and the country's transportation network are in disrepair. Due to a lack of foreign reserves that could pay for spare parts or new vehicles, much of the bus fleet is out of commission at any given time. There are more than 13,000 persons in the city for every bus. About half a million people have no access to transport at all. At the same time, however, wealth flowing to the upper and middle classes has produced an enormous growth in car ownership, leading to congestion on the unimproved roads and highways of the city. There is one railroad, mostly for freight, that connects Kinshasa to the port of Matadi, the country's Atlantic-access port.

At the same time, Kinshasa has a major water transportation system. A number of ferries run between the city and Brazzaville, the capital of the Republic of the Congo, situated on the north shore of the Congo River, opposite Kinshasa. There are also a large number of steamers that travel upriver to Kisangani, Democratic Republic of the Congo's second largest city. Ndkili International Airport is the largest in Central Africa.

HEALTH CARE

Because of its low-lying location and tropical climate, Kinshasa's residents are susceptible to many diseases common in the region, especially malaria. Yellow fever and smallpox have largely been eliminated, but poor sewage management in the city contributes to high rates of cholera and dysentery, especially during the dry season, when clean water sources diminish. Like much else in the city, Kinshasa's health system is largely inadequate to the rapidly growing population. Hospitals and clinics are few and generally located in upper-class areas. Overall, there are approximately 14,000 residents for every physician. Life expectancy is roughly sixty years, and the infant mortality rate is 86 per 1,000 live births.

EDUCATION

The city's public education system is in poor shape, though many children attend church schools. Still, poverty and overcrowding in many schools prevents many school-age children from attending. The language of instruction is usually French, especially at the secondary and university levels, though many primary and secondary schools conduct classes in a number of African tongues. The city is home to several major universities and the world-renowned School of Catholic Theology.

HOUSING

Despite a largely unmet demand for 34,000 new housing units each year, the city's housing situation is generally good, largely because of unregistered building. Most new homes are made of durable materials like concrete and tin roofing. All land belongs to the government and can only be leased. But due to bureaucratic incapacity and corruption, only about 10 percent of the land is registered and therefore subject to official taxes and rent; the rest is controlled unofficially by private individuals. Still, the demand for housing has produced rapidly increasing prices for construction materials and land. Because of the scarcity of land, many residents live in slums on hillsides and riverbanks, which are prone to landslides or flooding in the rainy season. Squatters continue to occupy agricultural land on the outskirts of the city, further undermining food supplies.

CULTURE, THE ARTS, AND ENTERTAINMENT

For all of its confusion and poverty, Kinshasa has one of the most vibrant cultural scenes in all Africa. *Soukous,* the city's signature style of music, is popular worldwide and is played in hundreds of clubs in the city. Oftentimes, names of popular songs are loaned to commercial products. The city also has a thriving art scene, with hundreds of artists offering their work on streetcorners and in local markets. Despite a largely illiterate population, the city has seen a flowering of literature since independence in the form of novels, plays, and poetry, though the few daily newspapers are heavily censored. Kinshasa is also home to several museums of African art and ethnography. TV and radio programs are particularly popular, especially a form of propaganda/entertainment known as *animations*, equivalent to an educational cartoon. The city is also home to dozens of cinemas showing African, Hong Kong, Indian, French, and U.S. films.

CATEGORY	DATA	YEAR	AREA
LOCATION & ENVIRONMENT			
Area	3,543 square miles	1995	City
	9,565 square kilometers		City
Elevation	600 feet/216 meters		City
January Temperature	78.5 degrees Fahrenheit		City
	25.8 degrees Celsius		City
July Temperature	72.5 degrees Fahrenheit		City
	22 degrees Celsius		City
Annual Precipitation	53.3 inches/1,353.8 millimeters		City
POPULATION & DEMOGRAPHY			
Population	4,400,000	1996	Metro
Projected Population	9,400,000	2015	Metro
Growth Rate	4.2%	1990–1995	Metro
Growth Rate	122.3%	1995–2015	Metro
Density	721 per square mile	1984	Metro
	267 per square kilometer		
VITAL STATISTICS			
Life Expectancy	59	1984	Metro
Fertility Rate	6.7 children per woman	1984	Metro
Infant Mortality Rate	86 per 1,000 live births	1984	Metro
ECONOMY			
Official Manufacturing	20%	1994	Metro
Official Trade	67%	1994	Metro
TRANSPORTATION			
Public Buses	58%	1987	Metro
Private Buses	42%	1987	Metro
HOUSING			
Demand for New Housing	34,000	1987	Metro
Units with Piped Water	30%	1987	Metro
HEALTH CARE			
Physicians per 1,000 Residents	0.1	1987	Metro

Sources: Department of Economic and Social Affairs, Population Division. *Urban Agglomerations, 1996.* New York: United Nations, 1997; United Nations Center for Human Settlements. *Compendium of Human Settlements Statistics.* New York: United Nations, 1995; and *United Nations World Large Cities.* New York: United Nations, 1988.

Kuala Lumpur
MALAYSIA

LOCATION

Kuala Lumpur, Malaysia's capital city, is located in an upland plain in the southern region of the Malay Peninsula, 25 miles north of Port Kelang, on the Strait of Malacca. The city covers a surface area of 93.8 square miles (243 square kilometers) at an elevation of 111 feet above sea level. The city is located about 125 miles southwest of the Cameron Highlands, which rise to an elevation of over 7,000 feet above sea level. The greater Kuala Lumpur area includes the municipalities of Kelang, Port Kelang, Seremban, and Shah Alam. The city is located about 200 miles northwest of Singapore, about 750 miles south of Bangkok, Thailand, and about 800 miles northwest of Jakarta, Indonesia. The city's average temperature ranges from 72 degrees Fahrenheit (22.2 degrees Celsius) in January to 90 degrees Fahrenheit (31.1 degrees Celsius) in July. The average precipitation in Kuala Lumpur is 96.1 inches (2,441 millimeters) per year.

POPULATION AND DEMOGRAPHY

Kuala Lumpur is the most populous urban center in Malaysia. In 1995, the city's population reached 1,300,000. In 1992 the city had a population density of 13,670 persons per square mile (5,288 persons per square kilometer). Kuala Lumpur's age distribution is clearly skewed to residents in their young and productive years: 41.7 percent of the city's population is age 19 or under; 53 percent are between 20 and 59 years of age; and 5.3 percent of the city's residents are 60 years and over. Males comprise a 51.5 percent majority of the city's population. A primary cause of the city's relatively youthful profile is migration from the rural hinterland to the central city of Kuala Lumpur. A high birth rate and a low death rate are expected to contribute further to population growth. Suburban residential development on the city's fringes has accommodated much of Kuala Lumpur's growth, but urban infrastructure and services have not kept up with the needs of the city's growing population. The vast majority of the city's residents are of Malay origin. The two largest ethnic minorities in Kuala Lumpur are of Chinese and Indian origin.

HISTORY

Located in the heart of the tin-rich Malay Peninsula, Kuala Lumpur was founded in 1857 by Chinese tin miners and became known as Ampang. In 1885,

Kuala Lumpur became capital of the Federal Malay States, a British protectorate. The city subsequently became an important trading post and warehousing center for the Malay tin industry, growing in population from 2,000 residents in 1880 to 30,000 residents by the turn of the century. The construction of the Klang–Kuala Lumpur Railway by the English colonial government contributed significantly to the city's rapid expansion. In 1895, the British government named the city capital of the Malay States. The central city continued to grow in population, size, and importance over the first half of the twentieth century. The city was occupied by Japanese troops during World War II.

GOVERNMENT AND POLITICS

When the Federation of Malaya declared independence from British colonial authorities, Kuala Lumpur was named capital of the new nation. The city retained its capital upon the founding of the Malaysian Republic in 1963. In 1972, the city was designated the Federal Territory of Kuala Lumpur following the incorporation of suburban settlements that have grown up over the last century, increasing the size and importance of the city. During the last two decades of the twentieth century, settlements have continued to grow on the city's periphery. The Malaysian government, headquartered in Kuala Lumpur, is a constitutional monarchy led by an elected prime minister and a bicameral parliament.

ECONOMY

For almost a century and a half since Kuala Lumpur's founding by tin miners, the city's economic prominence has been overshadowed by Singapore, the economic powerhouse 200 miles to the city's southeast. Singapore's strategic location in the heart of Southeast Asia has made the city the leading commercial center of the region, with a local economy rivaling that of leading global cities. Although the city has not achieved the economic importance of Singapore, Kuala Lumpur's economy has benefited by the rapid expansion of the Malaysian economy over the last three decades of the twentieth century.

Kuala Lumpur's past economic importance was linked to the city's strategic location in the heart of the Malay Peninsula in proximity to the tin mining region. The city's central location contributed to the development of a railway link to the coast in the late nineteenth century and its growing economic importance as a major Southeast Asian transportation and trading center in the twentieth century. Subsequently, the city developed basic manufacturing industries, commercial activities, and a local food products and nondurable-goods manufacturing production capacity to serve the needs of a rapidly growing local population. The city is a major trade and transportation center for agricultural and raw material exports, including rubber and palm oil, tin products, and processed wood. Kuala Lumpur has a growing number of factories that manufacture processed food products and building supplies for the regional and national market. Other local industries produce iron and steel products and fabricated tin and rubber products for the export market. The region's manufacturing facilities are located in outlying neighborhoods zoned specifically for industrial production.

However, the Asian financial crisis that began in 1997 has severely eroded the local economy, as businesses have been unable to generate the capital to pay off foreign debts. The imposition of restrictive monetary policies by the international banking community has severely dampened economic growth, contributing to the erosion of local living standards. In response to the economic crisis, the Malaysian government expelled foreign guest workers from Indonesia and the Philippines who had come to Kuala Lumpur and other localities to work in low-wage jobs, and placed restrictions on currency speculation.

TRANSPORTATION

Kuala Lumpur's rapidly increasing population has produced a greater need for public transportation services to reduce rising levels of traffic congestion on the city's roads. The primary form of mass transit is the local public bus system. A rapid transit system now under construction is expected to ease the city's traffic congestion problem. The historic importance of Kuala Lumpur stems from the construction of a railway to the coast in the late nineteenth century to export the Malay Peninsula's rich tin reserves. Subsequently, the improved access to the region rapidly expanded the city's economic importance and population. In the late twentieth century, the city retains its importance as a major transportation center for the export of raw materials (tin, rubber, cocoa, and timber) and fabricated products to Johor, Kelang, and Malaysia's other coastal port cities. The Malaysian Ministry of Transportation administers the national rail, road, and port facilities. Kuala Lumpur's Subang International Airport accommodates carriers

flying to and from domestic and international destinations; a new $2.5 billion airport opened in July 1998.

HEALTH CARE

The city's health care system is administered by the Federal Territory of Kuala Lumpur. The regional health department oversees disease control, family health, dental health, and health education. With a modern medical and health care system, Kuala Lumpur's population is considerably healthier than Malaysians as a whole. The city's infant mortality rate in 1992 of 9.5 infant deaths per 1,000 live births was less than half the estimated Malaysian national rate in 1996 of 24 infant deaths per 1,000 live births. In 1992, Kuala Lumpur had 25.1 live births per 1,000 residents and 4.0 deaths per 1,000 residents.

EDUCATION

The federal government has primary responsibility for setting education policy and administering the Malaysian education system on the local level. The national education system encompasses preschool through higher education. Although education is not compulsory, virtually all children in Kuala Lumpur attend primary school level. The national school system prepares students for academic or technical careers. National schools in the city teach children in one of three languages: Malay, Chinese, or Tamil. The postsecondary institutions in Kuala Lumpur range from general academic schools to more specialized scientific, technical, and theological institutes. The city's leading universities are the University of Malaya, Universiti Kebangsaan, Federal Technical College, the Language Institute, and Tunku Abdul Rahman College.

HOUSING

The rapid growth of Kuala Lumpur's population has strained the ability of the government and the private sector to meet the expanding need for affordable housing. Although the city's population has not increased as fast as those of Jakarta, Ho Chi Minh City, Bangkok, and other Southeast Asian cities, the city is already facing a severe housing shortage. However, the Malaysian government has taken on a larger role in housing development than in other countries. The national government is developing a nearby city, to be called Putrajaya (Garden City), that will provide housing for 250,000 people for federal government employees and their families. The new city will be a principal government and administrative center.

CULTURE, THE ARTS, AND ENTERTAINMENT

Although Kuala Lumpur is a relatively new city, it is a leading center of culture in Malaysia. The National Museum of Malaysia has the largest collection of art and cultural artifacts from the Malay Peninsula. The collection also includes artifacts from Sarawak, in northern Borneo. The city has a number of mosques and Hindu temples. Kuala Lumpur is home to theater, music, and dance groups performing traditional Malaysian and Western art forms, and it has many cinemas that show films from throughout the world. Numerous leading European, North American, and Asian artists and organizations perform in the city. Kuala Lumpur is a major Southeast Asian sports center; the leading sport is soccer, and the city has a team in the Malaysian Professional Soccer League as well as many amateur soccer teams. Kuala Lumpur was the host of the 1998 Commonwealth Games. Other popular sports include karate, auto racing, golf, tae kwan do, and silat, a national sport of Malaysia.

CATEGORY	DATA	YEAR	AREA
LOCATION & ENVIRONMENT			
Area	93.8 square miles	1995	City
	243 square kilometers		City
Elevation	111 feet/33.8 meters		City
January Temperature	72 degrees Fahrenheit		City
	22.2 degrees Celsius		City
July Temperature	90 degrees Fahrenheit		City
	31.1 degrees Celsius		City
Annual Precipitation	96.1 inches/2,441 millimeters		City
POPULATION & DEMOGRAPHY			
Population	1,300,000	1996	Metro
Projected Population	1,300,000	2015	Metro
Growth Rate	2.0%	1990–1995	Metro
Growth Rate	0.0%	1995–2015	Metro
Density	13,670 per square mile	1992	Metro
	5,288 per square kilometer		Metro
Gender			
Male	51.5%	1992	Metro
Female	48.5%	1992	Metro
Age			
Under 20	41.7%	1992	Metro
20–59	53.0%	1992	Metro
Over 60	5.3%	1992	Metro
VITAL STATISTICS			
Births per 1,000 Residents	25.1	1992	Metro
Deaths per 1,000 Residents	4	1992	Metro
Infant Mortality Rate	9.5 deaths per 1,000 live births	1992	Metro
COMMUNICATIONS			
Telephones per 1,000 Residents	273	1992	Metro

(continued)

CATEGORY	DATA	YEAR	AREA
HEALTH CARE			
Hospitals	48	1992	Metro
Physicians per 1,000 Residents	1.5	1992	Metro

Sources: Department of Economic and Social Affairs, Population Division. *Urban Agglomerations, 1996.* New York: United Nations, 1997; *Statistics of World Large Cities.* Tokyo, Japan: Tokyo Metropolitan Government, 1992 and 1994; and United Nations Center for Human Settlements. *Compendium of Human Settlements Statistics.* New York: United Nations, 1995.

Kyoto
JAPAN

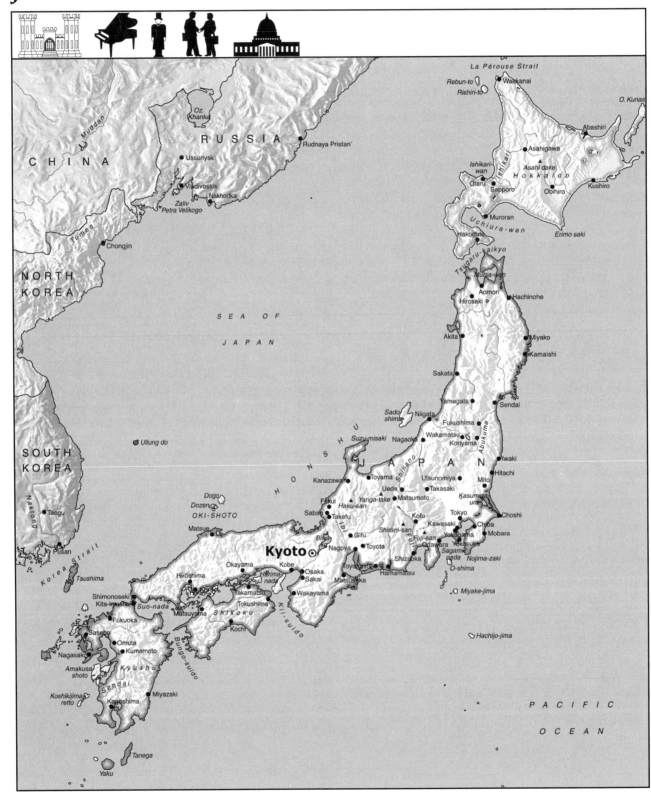

LOCATION

Kyoto, the capital and most populous city of Kyoto Prefecture, lies in south-central Honshu, Japan's largest island, 5 miles southwest of Lake Biwa-ko, Japan's largest lake. The city covers a surface area of 236 square miles (610 square kilometers) at an elevation of 360 feet above sea level. The city lies in the geographic center of one of Japan's largest population corridors: Amagasaki, Kobe, Nagoya, and Osaka all lie within a 60-mile radius of Kyoto. Kyoto is intersected by the Kamo and Katsura Rivers, two tributaries of the Yodo River. The city of Otsu lies less than 5 miles east of the city on the southern shores of Lake Biwa-ko. Kyoto is located on a highland plateau, approximately 310 miles southwest of Tokyo, Japan's capital and largest city, and 30 miles northeast of Osaka, the third most populous city in Japan. Kyoto's temperature ranges from an average of 35.6 degrees Fahrenheit (4 degrees Celsius) in January to an average of 79.7 degrees Fahrenheit (26.5 degrees Celsius) in July. The city averages 77.7 inches (1,973 millimeters) of precipitation per year.

POPULATION AND DEMOGRAPHY

In 1996, the population of the Kyoto metropolitan region was 1,700,000. The central city accounts for the vast majority of all regional residents, though its population declined by 1.2 percent between 1985 and 1990, to 1,461,103. The regional population is expected to remain relatively static through 2015. The central city of Kyoto has a population density of 6,171 persons per square mile (2,387 persons per square kilometer). Kyoto's age structure is fairly balanced among populations in the dependent and productive years: 15.6 percent of the region's population is under 15 years of age, 70 percent of the population is between the ages of 15 and 64, and 14.4 percent are 65 years of age or over. Kyoto Prefecture has a relatively low rate of 9 births per 1,000 regional residents and 7.5 deaths per 1,000 residents. The region's population growth is concentrated in the outlying suburbs of the central city. Females comprise a 51.6 percent majority of Kyoto's residents, primarily due to the older age structure in the central city and the tendency of females to outlive males.

HISTORY

For more than a thousand years, from 794 to 1868, Kyoto served as Japan's imperial capital. In the To-

kugawa period, between 1603 and 1867, government administration was transferred from Kyoto to Edo (now Tokyo). However, the imperial family continued to reside in Kyoto, and the city remained Japan's preeminent religious and cultural center. Nijo Castle, one of the nation's most well-known castles, was constructed in 1803, at the beginning of the Tokugawa period. Unlike other major Japanese cities, Kyoto emerged from World War II unscathed by Allied bombings. In the postwar era, Kyoto became a major destination for domestic and international tourists who visit the city to see the national monuments that were constructed when the city was Japan's national capital.

GOVERNMENT AND POLITICS

In 1868, with the Meiji Restoration, Edo formally replaced Kyoto as Japan's national capital, though Kyoto continued to retain its importance as a cultural center, as many of Japan's national palaces and monuments remain in the city. Kyoto is the capital of Kyoto Prefecture, a 2,014-square-mile (4,612-square-kilometer) region that includes the central city of Kyoto and the outlying cities of Joyo, Kameoka, Nagaokyo, Tanabe, Uji, and Yawata. Kyoto Prefecture is administered by a governor, a vice governor, and a treasurer. Legislative power resides in a sixty-five-member prefectural assembly that is led by a chairman. The City of Kyoto is composed of eleven wards and is administered by a mayor, two deputy mayors, and a treasurer. Kyoto has a seventy-two-member city assembly, which is responsible for legislative affairs that bear on the municipality.

ECONOMY

Kyoto has a modern and diversified economy led by the banking and light manufacturing industries; it also has many corporate headquarters. The city's leading manufacturing industries include medical, precision and electronic machinery, chemicals, textiles, and food and beverage products. Kyoto's manufacturing base also includes porcelain products and traditional Japanese objects that are associated with the city's imperial past. The city is also a major wholesale trading center for the textile and garment industry, and it manufactures many specialty products, including brocades and dyed fabrics. Although

Kyoto is dwarfed by Tokyo and Osaka, the city hosts the headquarters of many of Japan's leading banks and corporations.

Kyoto has a highly skilled and educated labor force. Manufacturing workers make up the largest component of the local labor force, accounting for 25.1 percent of all workers, followed by retail and wholesale trade employees, who comprise 23.9 percent of the labor force, and service sector workers, with 23.2 percent of the labor force. About 7.1 percent of regional workers in Kyoto are employed in the construction sector. In 1990, the region had an unemployment rate of just over 1 percent, one of the lowest jobless rates in the world. Consumer prices in Kyoto in the early 1990s were, on average, about 5 percent higher than the national average, in part due to the higher cost of living in the city than other regions.

TRANSPORTATION

Kyoto is a regional transportation center in central Honshu, although it is overshadowed by nearby Osaka. The city has an integrated rail transportation system that includes railways, subways, buses, and trolley lines. The leading form of urban transportation are railways, encompassing 57.3 percent of all journeys, bus and trolley transportation, comprising 30.5 percent of all journeys, and subways, which carry 12.2 percent of all passengers. High-speed intercity railways link Kyoto to Osaka, Tokyo, and other major Japanese cities throughout Japan.

HEALTH CARE

Kyoto's health care facilities are among the most advanced in the world, and the regional population is very healthy. Additionally, Japan's national health insurance program provides residents universal access to medical care. The prefecture has 212 hospitals and a relatively high rate of 3 physicians per 1,000 residents. In 1993, the prefecture had an infant mortality rate of 5.4 infant deaths per 1,000 live births, one of the lowest among major world cities.

EDUCATION

Due to the relatively low birth rate in Kyoto, the percentage of primary school students is relatively small compared to cities in East Asia that are experiencing rapid population growth. In 1990, 26.4 percent of all students in the city attended primary schools, 35.9 percent attended secondary schools, and 37.7 percent were enrolled in institutions of higher education. Kyoto University is the leading higher educational institution in the city. The city also has specialized technical, scientific, and Buddhist theological institutions.

HOUSING

Kyoto does not have the serious housing shortage that many other cities in East Asia have. All the city's housing units have access to city water and electricity. Owner-occupied units account for 57.9 percent of all regional housing, and the region has an average of 0.6 persons per room, significantly lower than developing cities in East Asia. The major housing problem in Kyoto is the high price of residential real estate, which has become too expensive for working-class and middle-class residents in the region. Although housing prices have declined marginally in the 1990s, the city and region continue to face a shortage of affordable housing.

CULTURE, THE ARTS, AND ENTERTAINMENT

Kyoto, a center of traditional Japanese culture and arts, has a history that dates back 1,200 years. The city has forty-seven museums, including many that specialize in the arts, culture, and history, such as the Kyoto Municipal Museum of Art and the Kyoto National Museum. Kyoto has many imperial castles, temples, and tombs, including Nijo Castle, Katsura Detached Palace, Kyoto Imperial Palace, and numerous Buddhist temples. Kyoto is a center of traditional Japanese music, arts groups, and theater. The city has leading groups that perform Noh and kabuki theater. In 1990, the city had twenty-three theaters showing Japanese and Western films.

CATEGORY	DATA	YEAR	AREA
LOCATION & ENVIRONMENT			
Area	236 square miles	1996	City
	610 square kilometers		City
Elevation	360 feet/109.7 meters		City
January Temperature	35.6 degrees Fahrenheit		City
	4.0 degrees Celsius		City
July Temperature	79.7 degrees Fahrenheit		City
	26.5 degrees Celsius		City
Annual Precipitation	77.7 inches/1,973 millimeters		City
POPULATION & DEMOGRAPHY			
Population	1,700,000	1996	City
Projected Population	1,700,000	2015	City
Growth Rate	−0.1%	1990–1995	City
Growth Rate	0.0%	1995–2015	City
Density	6,171 per square mile	1992	City
	2,387 per square kilometer		
Gender			
Males	48.4%	1990	Metro
Females	51.6%	1990	Metro
Age			
Under 15	15.6%	1994	Metro
15–64	70.0%	1994	Metro
Over 65	14.4%	1994	Metro
VITAL STATISTICS			
Births per 1,000 Residents	9	1993	Metro
Death per 1,000 Residents	7.5	1993	Metro
Infant Mortality Rate	5.4 per 1,000 live births	1993	Metro
ECONOMY			
Total Workforce	1,311,000	1990	Metro
Trade	23.9%	1990	Metro
Manufacturing	25.1%	1990	Metro
Services	23.2%	1990	Metro
Finance, Insurance, Real Estate	4.1%	1990	Metro
Transport and Communications	5.2%	1990	Metro
Construction	7.1%	1990	Metro
Government	3.1%	1990	Metro
Utilities	0.5%	1990	Metro
Agriculture	3.5%	1990	Metro
Mining	0.3%	1990	Metro
TRANSPORTATION			
Passenger Journeys	562,105,000	1990	City
Rail	57.3%	1990	City
Buses and Trolley	30.5%	1990	City
Subways	12.2%		
Passenger Vehicles	792,000	1994	Metro

(continued)

CATEGORY	DATA	YEAR	AREA
COMMUNICATIONS			
Telephones per 1,000 Residents	564	1992	Metro
Televisions per 1,000 Residents	291	1992	Metro
HOUSING			
Total Housing Units	1,030,000	1993	Metro
Persons per Unit	2.8	1993	Metro
Owner-Occupied Units	57.9	1993	Metro
HEALTH CARE			
Hospitals	212	1992	Metro
Physicians per 1,000 Residents	3	1992	Metro
EDUCATION			
Total Students	562,105	1990	City
Primary	26.4%	1990	City
Secondary	35.9%	1990	City
Higher	37.7%	1990	City

Sources: Department of Economic and Social Affairs, Population Division. *Urban Agglomerations, 1996.* New York: United Nations, 1997; Japan Local Government Data Book. Tokyo, Japan: Council of Local Authorities for International Relations, 1995; *Prefecture Japan Yearbook.* Tokyo, Japan: Japan Statistics Bureau, 1996; *Statistics of World Large Cities.* Tokyo, Japan: Tokyo Metropolitan Government, 1992 and 1994; and United Nations Center for Human Settlements. *Compendium of Human Settlements Statistics.* New York: United Nations, 1995.

Lagos, Lagos State
NIGERIA

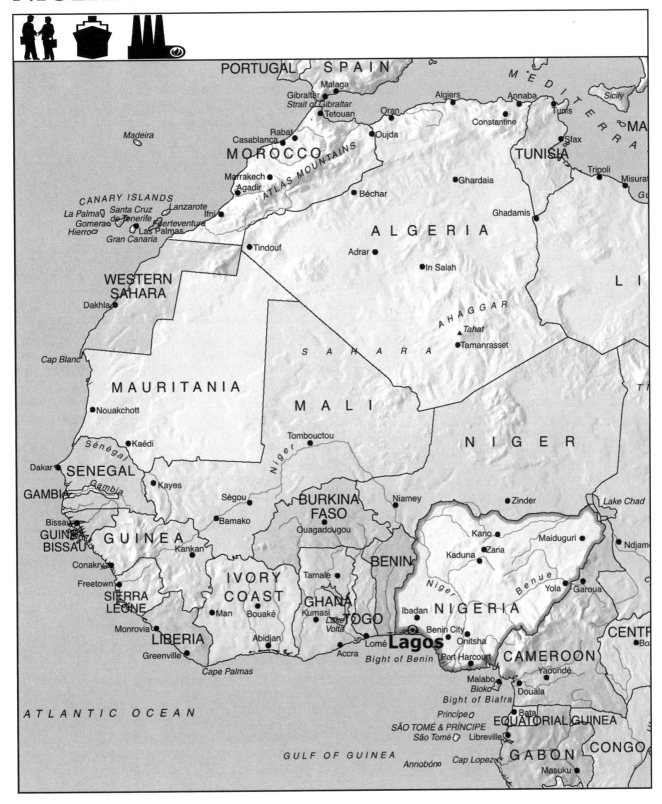

LOCATION

Lagos is the largest city, main port, and primary manufacturing metropolis in Nigeria, the most populous country in Africa. Located on a group of islands around a central lagoon—Lagos means "lagoon" in Portuguese and received its name from explorers—on the Bight of Benin in the Gulf of Guinea. The city covers 98 square miles (264 square kilometers). The city is located 265 miles east-northeast of Accra, Ghana, and 320 miles south of Nigeria's capital, Abuja. Its sea-level elevation and location just north of the equator gives the city an extremely hot and humid climate. There is little variation in temperature between seasons, with a year-round average of about 85 degrees Fahrenheit (29 degrees Celsius). It receives approximately 72.3 inches (1,836.4 millimeters) of rain annually, most of which falls in the summer months.

POPULATION AND DEMOGRAPHY

The population of metropolitan Lagos has grown explosively over the past several decades. Between 1950 and 1985, it grew from 240,000 to nearly 6 million, often at a rate of 10 percent annually. While growth has slowed in recent years, Lagos's population continues to expand rapidly. It was estimated at 10.9 million in 1996 and is expected to climb to 24.6 million by 2015, putting it among the five largest metropolitan areas in the world. Much of the growth has been due to heavy migration from the Nigerian countryside—including a huge influx after the Nigerian civil war of 1967–1969—as well as immigration from neighboring African states. The city is also very crowded; about 54,000 persons inhabit each square mile (20,000 per square kilometer). To help alleviate crowding, institutions of the Nigerian federal government are being moved to the more centrally located city of Abuja.

Like Nigeria itself, the population of the city is extremely diverse, with virtually all of the country's 250 ethnic groups represented. The population includes large Christian, Muslim, and traditional religion cohorts. Most government business and higher education are conducted in formal English; a more pidgin form is spoken on the streets, especially between members of different African linguistic groups.

HISTORY

Lagos's origins are lost in the prehistoric past. The islands that form the city were inhabited by members of the Eko people for centuries. From the late sixteenth century until the mid-nineteenth century, the area was dominated by the Kingdom of Benin, which ceded it to the United Kingdom in 1861. The British made it their administrative capital and trading hub—particularly locally grown palm oil and copra—for Nigeria and surrounding colonies. In 1874, it became part of the Gold Coast (now Ghana), then received a separate status under a British governor in 1886. In 1906, it was rejoined to Nigeria and became the capital of independent Nigeria in 1960, a role it played until 1975. The following year Abuja was made the official capital, though many government offices remained in Lagos. At the same time, the capital of Lagos State—smallest of Nigeria's twenty-one states—was shifted to Ikeja, a suburb of Lagos.

GOVERNMENT AND POLITICS

Nigeria's postindependence political history has been a rocky one. The nation included several major ethnic groups and religions, which led to internal political conflict between the Muslim-dominated north and the Christian and traditional religion south. In 1965, these divisions led to the country's first of many military coups. Assassinations and ethnic massacres furthered poisoned relations with the Ogoni-dominated southeast, a region known as Biafra. A vicious three-year civil war in Biafra, resulting in massive starvation, ended with the victory of the government. Since that time, the country has gone through a series of political upheavals, the most recent being the coup led by General Sani Abacha in the early 1990s. The Abacha regime has been heavily criticized by the international community. General Abacha died suddenly in 1998 and the new military government acceded to new elections and greater civil freedoms.

ECONOMY

Lagos is the commercial, industrial, and transportation hub of Nigeria and several other surrounding states in West and Central Africa. In the 1960s, the city's economy was dominated by government workers and manufacturers of food products, much of which was exported.

With the quadrupling of oil prices in the 1970s, the Lagos economy underwent wrenching change and overheating. Spiraling rents and costs of productions drove many food production firms under, resulting in the need to import billions of dollars' worth of agricultural products. At the same time, the government used some of the petrodollars to finance heavy industry, including steel, automobiles, plastics, and chemicals. Still, despite these developments, light industry continues, and Lagos hosts thousands of small firms manufacturing metal products, electronics, and basic consumer items like soap and paints.

The world recession and decline of oil prices in the 1980s hit the economy of Lagos hard. The city and state governments went deeply into the red, while inflation destroyed the savings of many residents. The massive expansion of the city's infrastructure and social services came to a grinding halt.

TRANSPORTATION

Lagos is infamous for its traffic jams, known colloquially as "go-slows." During much of the day, traffic moves at a crawl, and it comes to a complete halt during morning and evening rush hours. A three-hour journey across the city is not uncommon.

The traffic problem is the result of several causes. First, the oil boom made gasoline prices cheap, leading to a reliance on private automobiles. The decline of oil prices meant that road construction came to a practical halt in the 1980s. In addition, the poor telecommunications system and the slow rate of telephone installation—it takes ten attempts to successfully hook up a new telephone line—mean that people are forced to take trips rather than communicate by phone. The complicated geography of the city adds the final element. Situated on a series of islands, Lagos has many narrow bridges producing serious traffic bottlenecks. While a light rail commuter service was begun in the late 1980s, most of the public transportation system relies on buses, minibuses, and taxis.

HEALTH CARE

Using its oil revenues, the government embarked on a massive expansion of health and education facilities in the 1970s, though many of the gains have become undone by the slowing of growth in these sectors due to declining oil prices and the continuing rapid growth in the city's population. The city's low-lying location and tropical climate result in numerous cases of malaria and encephalitis. In addition, the inadequate sewage system and poor water supply cause a large number of cholera cases, particularly in the dry season, when clean water sources tend to dry up.

The city boasts fifty-five hospitals, but the patient-to-physician ratio remains at nearly 5,000 to 1, equivalent to 0.2 physicians per 1,000 residents. There is one hospital bed for about every 900 persons. While hospital construction was emphasized in the 1970s, the more recent emphasis in public health has been on preventative care. The government's immunization program has reached an estimated 85 percent of the city's children.

EDUCATION

Over 1,000,000 children in Lagos were attending primary and secondary schools in 1993. This impressive number, however, hides the fact that many cannot attend on a regular basis, due to interruptions caused by poverty and labor needs. The adult literacy rate in Nigeria was only 34 percent in the 1980s, but Lagos is believed to have a much higher rate, although figures are not compiled. The city also has several major universities and technical schools, with a student population of nearly 20,000 in 1989.

HOUSING

Lagos has had a severe housing shortage since well before independence, though the problem has been greatly exacerbated by the explosive population growth in the years since. In 1972, some parts of the central city had twenty-two persons per room. Solutions to this problem have been slow in coming. This is due in part to the continually expanding population as well as the complicated federal structure of the Nigerian government. In 1981, the government developed a master plan for metropolitan Lagos, and the Lagos State Urban Renewal Board was created a decade later.

In addition to rehabilitating the city's slums at the rate of about 60,000 units per year, the government has established the Urban Development Bank to help Lagos residents finance their own housing construction.

Though about 90 percent of all residences in the metropolitan area are hooked up to the electrical grid, the city's power system has endemic failures, due largely to a lack of foreign-made spare parts. And despite the region's abundance of subsurface water, Lagos suffers from recurrent shortages. Waste disposal is an even more serious problem. Only the most expensive areas of the city are connected to underground sewers. The remainder of the city's population uses latrines or dumps their waste into the many waterways lacing the region.

CULTURE, THE ARTS, AND ENTERTAINMENT

Lagos is a vibrant cultural hub, particularly for music and dance. The city has thousands of dance and mu-sic clubs, as well as a number of studios that record the popular indigenous–world music hybrids that have become popular around Africa and the globe. At the same time, the city lacks an effective park system and boasts few museums and libraries. The city is also the center of Nigeria's prodigious literary community, which includes Nobel Prize winner Wole Soyinka.

CATEGORY	DATA	YEAR	AREA
LOCATION & ENVIRONMENT			
Area	98 square miles	1988	City
	264 square kilometers		City
Elevation	72.3 feet/1,836.4 millimeters		City
January Temperature	88 degrees Fahrenheit		City
	31.1 degrees Celsius		City
July Temperature	83 degrees Fahrenheit		City
	28.3 degrees Celsius		City
Annual Precipitation	72.3 inches/1,836.4 millimeters		City
POPULATION & DEMOGRAPHY			
Population	10,900,000	1996	Metro
Projected Population	24,600,000	2015	Metro
Growth Rate	5.7%	1990–1995	Metro
Growth Rate	139.5%	1995–2015	Metro
Density	54,000 per square mile	1989	City
	20,000 per square kilometer	1989	City
Gender			
Male	53%	1991	Metro
Female	47%	1991	Metro
VITAL STATISTICS			
Births per 1,000 Residents	14.1	1988	Metro
Deaths per 1,000 Residents	1.3	1988	Metro
TRANSPORTATION			
Large Buses	19,323	1985	Metro
Minibuses	24,843	1985	Metro
Taxis and Cars for Hire	37,169	1985	Metro
HEALTH CARE			
Hospitals	55	1987	Metro
Physicians per 1,000 Residents	0.2	1987	Metro

(continued)

CATEGORY	DATA	YEAR	AREA
EDUCATION			
Total Students	1,382,497	1993	Metro
Primary	63%	1993	Metro
Secondary	35.4%	1993	Metro
University	1.4%	1993	City

Sources: Department of Economic and Social Affairs, Population Division. *Urban Agglomerations, 1996.* New York: United Nations, 1997; *Annual Abstract of Statistics.* Abuja, Nigeria: Federal Bureau of Statistics, 1995; Peil, Margaret. *Lagos: The City is the People.* Boston, Massachusetts: G.K. Hall, 1991; and United Nations Center for Human Settlements. *Compendium of Human Settlements Statistics.* New York: United Nations, 1995.

Lahore, Punjab Province
PAKISTAN

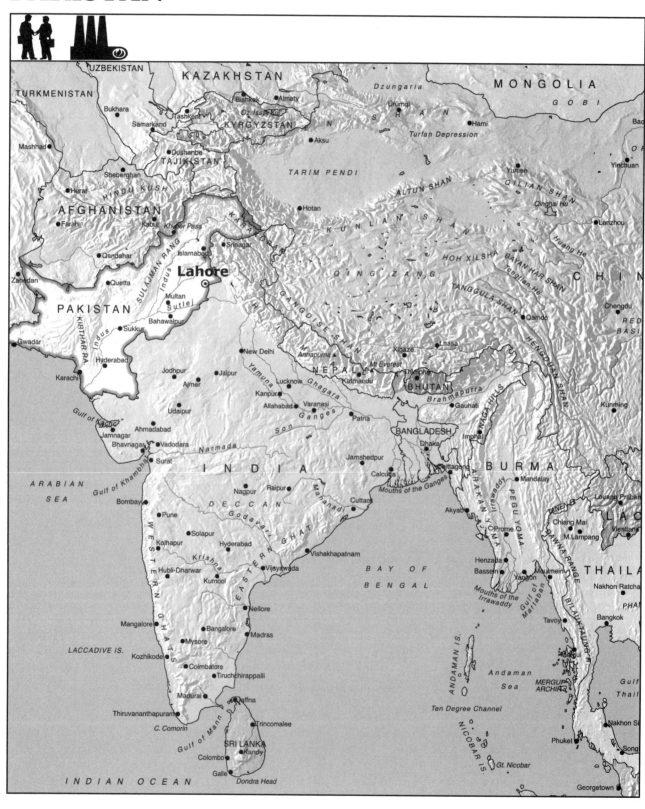

LOCATION

Lahore, the largest city in northern Pakistan and the second largest metropolitan area in the country, is situated on the banks of the Ravi River, a tributary of the Indus River in the upper part of the Indus River Valley at an elevation of 708 feet (216 meters). It is located approximately 650 miles north-northeast of Pakistan's largest city, Karachi, and roughly 150 miles south of the capital, Islamabad. The Lahore metropolitan area encompasses 121 square miles (328 square kilometers). The city has a subtropical climate. The temperature ranges from 60.5 degrees Fahrenheit (26.4 degrees Celsius) in January to 85.8 degrees Fahrenheit (29.9 degrees Celsius) in July. The city receives approximately 18.1 inches (461.1 millimeters) of rain annually, most of which falls in the monsoon season from August through November.

POPULATION AND DEMOGRAPHY

The population of metropolitan Lahore was estimated at 5.2 million in 1996. It grew at a rate of 3.6 percent annually during the 1990s, though this rate is expected to drop to about 3 percent in the next century. The estimate of the metropolitan area's population in 2015 is roughly 10 million. The metropolitan area has a density of 31,352 persons per square mile (11,612 per square kilometer). Much of this growth is due to rural migration from the countryside. The city's population is relatively young, with 43.3 percent under the age of 20.

As Lahore is the capital of Punjab province, which, with its sister state in India, is the home of the Sikh people, the majority of the population practices the syncretic faith of Sikhism (a mixture of religious beliefs) and speaks the Punjabi language, though the national languages of Urdu and English are also widely used. There is also a large population of Muslims, as well as small communities of Hindus, Parsis, and Christians.

HISTORY

While little is known about the origins of the city, Hindu legend says that it was founded by Lava, or Loh, the son of the god Rama (the city's name is a derivative of *Loh*). It became the capital of the Ghaznavid dynasty of Muslim rulers in the twelfth century and was repeatedly attacked by Mongol invaders in the fourteenth century. Lahore was captured by the Mughal emperor Babur in 1524, initiating a golden age in the city's history. On occasion it served as the residence of various emperors, and it was greatly expanded under the Emperor Shah Jehan in the mid-seventeenth century.

For most of the eighteenth century, the city was riven by religious conflict, with the Sikh population in a state of near-constant insurrection against the dominant Muslims. The unrest led to a decline in the city's culture and economy. It became the capital of the Sikh ruler Ranjit Singh in the early nineteenth century and came under British rule in 1849. The British expanded the city, established some industry, and connected Lahore to the expanding railway system of the subcontinent. Upon independence, Lahore was inundated by an influx of Sikhs and Muslims fleeing India. It became the capital of West Punjab province, renamed Punjab in 1970.

GOVERNMENT AND POLITICS

Pakistan is divided into four provinces, including Punjab, of which Lahore is the capital. Each of these provinces is divided into divisions, districts, and sub-districts, or *tahsils*. These various divisions are administered by divisional commissioners, deputy commissioners and subdivisional magistrates, or *tahsildars*. Lahore is a separate district within Punjab. Pakistan itself has undergone a tumultuous political history, shifting back and forth between democratically elected governments and military-run ones. Currently, Pakistan is ruled by a democratically elected head of state, though the military continues to be an influential player.

ECONOMY

Lahore's economy is dominated by manufacturing. Over 40 percent of the workforce is employed in factories and shops producing consumer items, iron, steel, and rubber. The largest industry is textiles, and the city is home to a handicraft industry that makes fine gold and silver items. Overall, the Lahore metropolitan area produces approximately 20 percent of Pakistan's industrial output. The city is also the major commercial and financial center for northern Pakistan. Roughly one fourth of the population is employed in the commercial sector. The city also has a managerial and professional class representing 10 percent of the workforce.

TRANSPORTATION

As the transportation hub for northern Pakistan, Lahore is connected by rail lines and paved highways to other cities in Pakistan, as well as metropolitan areas in northern India. The city has a network of 300 miles (500 kilometers) of paved roads. There were 64,369 cars and 2,176 trucks in 1981. The city has a ratio of 58 televisions per 1,000 residents.

HEALTH CARE

Lahore is served by 32 hospitals, yet much of the population is too poor to take advantage of them. Less than 15 percent of all births are assisted by doctors or nurses. The infant mortality rate is thus quite high, while nearly half of all deaths in the city are of children under the age of 5. Poor sanitation and contaminated water supplies are the causes of much of this problem, with diarrhea being a major cause of childhood deaths. Respiratory illnesses are also a major problem among the elderly.

EDUCATION

Lahore has an extensive school system. The city boasted nearly 2,000 primary and secondary schools in 1987, with a student population in excess of 663,173. Yet poverty prevents many from going to school. While literacy rates are expected to climb as more children attend school, it remains quite low, at just 34.7 percent for males over the age of 10 and 21.9 percent for females. The city is home to the University of the Punjab, the Faisal Shaheed University of Engineering and Technology, and numerous other colleges and institutes.

HOUSING

Lahore has a better housing profile than Karachi. Of the approximately 2 million dwellings in the metropolitan area in 1980, 70.6 percent were owner-occupied, while another 20 percent were rented. About 10 percent of the population lives in squatter settlements, distributed throughout the metropolitan area. While the government has built tens of thousands of modern, subsidized dwellings, much of the housing stock of the city is deteriorating.

CULTURE, THE ARTS, AND ENTERTAINMENT

The cultural heart of Lahore is the old walled city, with its thirteen gates. Within the walls are the mosque of Wazīr Khān, built in 1634, and the Lahore Fort, with its famous *kashi*, or encausted tile work. Other architectural highlights in the city include the Imperial Mosque, the palace of Ranjit Singh, the Shahdara Gardens (containing the tomb of the Mughal emperor Jahangir), and the world-famous Shālīmār Gardens, with their numerous fountains. The city is also the center of Sikh culture in Pakistan. There are four museums and forty-five cinemas in the city.

CATEGORY	DATA	YEAR	AREA
LOCATION & ENVIRONMENT			
Area	121 square miles	1995	City
	328 square kilometers		City
January Temperature	60.5 degrees Fahrenheit		City
	16.4 degrees Celsius		City
July Temperature	85.8 degrees Fahrenheit		City
	29.9 degrees Celsius		City
Annual Precipitation	18.1 inches/461.1 millimeters		City
POPULATION & DEMOGRAPHY			
Population	5,200,000	1996	Metro
Projected Population	10,000,000	2015	Metro
Growth Rate	3.6%	1990–1995	Metro
Growth Rate	100.4%	1995–2015	Metro
Density	31,352 per square mile	1989	City
	11,612 per square kilometer		City
Gender			
Male	54%	1989	City
Female	46%	1989	City
Age			
Under 20	43.3%	1981	City
20–59	51.3%	1981	City
Over 60	5.4	1981	City
VITAL STATISTICS			
Deaths under 5	47.8%	1988	Region
Deaths 5–9	4.4%	1988	Region
Deaths 20–59	18.6%	1988	Region
Deaths over 60	29.2%	1988	Region
ECONOMY			
Manufacturing	44.5%	1988	Region
Trade	24.1%	1988	Region
Clerical	7.8%	1988	Region
Professional and Technical	7.8%	1988	Region
Services	7.6%	1988	Region
Agriculture	5.8%	1988	Region
Management	2.2%	1988	Region
TRANSPORTATION			
Cars	64,369	1987	City
Trucks	2,176	1987	City
COMMUNICATIONS			
Televisions per 1,000 Residents	58	1987	City

(continued)

CATEGORY	DATA	YEAR	AREA
HOUSING			
Housing Units	1,968,371	1981	Region
Owner-Occupied Housing	70.6%	1981	Region
Persons per Unit	6.9	1981	Region
HEALTH CARE			
Hospitals	32	1987	City
EDUCATION			
Total Students	663,173	1987	City
Primary	27.6%	1987	City
Secondary	72.4%	1987	City
Literacy Rate 10 Years and Older			
Male	34.7%	1988	Region
Female	21.9%	1988	Region

Sources: Department of Economic and Social Affairs, Population Division. *Urban Agglomerations, 1996.* New York: United Nations, 1997; *Labor Force Survey.* Islamabad, Pakistan: Statistical Office of Pakistan, 1987–1988; *Pakistan Statistical Year Book 1994.* Karachi, Pakistan: Federal Bureau of Statistics, 1994; *Statistics of World Large Cities.* Tokyo, Japan: Tokyo Metropolitan Government, 1992 and 1994; and United Nations Center for Human Settlements. *Compendium of Human Settlements Statistics.* New York: United Nations, 1995.

Las Vegas, Nevada

USA

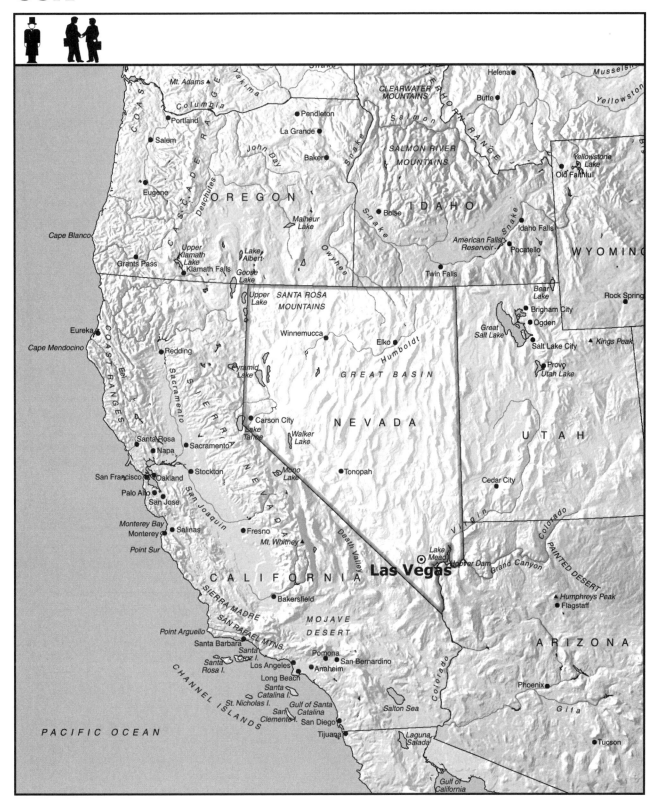

LOCATION

Las Vegas, the most populous city in Nevada and center of one of the nation's most rapidly growing metropolitan areas, is located in Clark County in the southeastern Nevada desert at an elevation of 2,162 feet above sea level. The city, covering a land area of 83.3 square miles (215.7 square kilometers), is located in the arid Great Basin, approximately 20 miles west of the Lake Mead National Recreation Area and about 30 miles northwest of the Colorado River and the Nevada-Arizona border. The Spring Mountains rise to the city's west at elevations exceeding 10,000 feet. The Las Vegas metropolitan area includes the municipalities of North Las Vegas, Sunrise Manor, Paradise, and Winchester. The city is located approximately 440 miles southeast of Carson City, the capital of Nevada, 470 miles southeast of Reno, Nevada, and 275 miles northeast of Los Angeles, California. Death Valley National Monument is 75 miles due west of the city. Phoenix, Arizona, is located about 275 miles to the city's southeast. The city has an extremely hot and dry climate, with temperatures fluctuating from a January low of 45.5 degrees Fahrenheit (7.5 degrees Celsius) to a July high of 91.1 degrees Fahrenheit (32.8 degrees Celsius). In the thirty-year period from 1961 to 1990, with an annual average precipitation of 4.1 inches (105 millimeters), Las Vegas has been the driest American city with a population over 200,000.

POPULATION AND DEMOGRAPHY

Las Vegas, incorporated in 1911, expanded rapidly in the 1930s, after the Hoover Dam was constructed 30 miles to the city's east on the Colorado River. During the 1980s and 1990s, the city's population grew quickly, primarily due to migration from California. From 1980 to 1992, Las Vegas's population expanded by 79.5 percent, from 164,674 to 295,516, representing the highest growth rate of any major U.S. city over the last decade. The city's density is 3,548 persons per square mile (1,370 per square kilometer). From 1980 to 1992, the Las Vegas region, encompassing Clark County, grew from 463,087 to 845,633 residents, an 82.6 percent rate of growth. Nearly 67 percent of Nevada's population lives in Clark County. The city's population is projected to continue to grow rapidly in the 1990s and the first two decades of the twenty-first century. One possible impediment to the continued growth is the limited water supply. Like many other U.S. interior Western cities, Las Vegas has a

significantly larger share of white residents and a smaller share of minorities than large cities on the Atlantic and Pacific coasts. Nearly 70 percent of all city residents are white, while black residents comprise less than 10 percent of Las Vegas's inhabitants. Hispanics account for approximately 11 percent of all city residents, and Asians and Pacific Islanders comprise just over 3 percent. Foreign-born residents comprise 10.3 percent of the city's population. The city has a gender ratio of 102.9 males per 100 females. The larger percentage of male residents is characteristic of rapidly growing cities. Among large American cities described in this book, only Anchorage, Alaska, has a higher ratio of males to females than Las Vegas. The city has a relatively youthful population—residents under 18 make up 25 percent of the population, and only 10.3 percent of the population is over 65 years of age.

HISTORY

The southeast Nevada region was settled initially by Mormons in the 1850s. In 1864, the Fort Baker U.S. army base was established. Las Vegas became a railroad hub in 1905 and in 1911 was incorporated as a city. The construction of the Hoover Dam in the 1930s contributed to the city's growing economic importance. The gaming industry was introduced in 1946 and continued to expand rapidly. By the end of the century, Las Vegas had become a major U.S. metropolis, with a population approaching 1.5 million.

GOVERNMENT AND POLITICS

The City of Las Vegas has a city council–city manager form of government. Four of the five members of the city council are elected from four wards. The mayor, who is elected at large, is the fifth member of the council. The city council is responsible for enacting local laws and ordinances. The city manager, an appointed official, is responsible for the administering city services.

ECONOMY

Las Vegas's economic vitality is linked to the gaming industry. In the last two decades of the century, gaming and tourism have expanded rapidly, spurring economic and employment growth. Between 1980 and 1996, the annual number of visitors to Las Vegas increased from 12 million to nearly 30 million. In 1996, visitors spent over $22.5 billion in the city. The growth in gaming has stimulated economic growth in other major economic sectors of the economy. The construction industry is a major beneficiary of the growth in tourism and gaming in Las Vegas, as casino and hotel companies have expanded their operations to accommodate the expanding demand. In turn, the new gaming venues have attracted even more visitors to the city. The convention industry is a second major beneficiary of the growing popularity of the gaming industry. However, because the Las Vegas economy and labor force remain highly dependent on the growth of gaming, they are subject to severe contraction during periods of economic recession. The city's civilian labor force increased by 61.4 percent between 1980 and 1990, to 145,711 workers. Much of the new job growth has taken place in the tourism, gambling, and construction industries. Many of the new jobs that were created in the last decade have been service jobs in hotels, restaurants, and casinos.

After tourism and gaming, wholesale and retail trade employs 18.7 percent of all workers, followed by finance, insurance, and real estate, which provides jobs for 6.5 percent, and health services, employing 5.2 percent. The manufacturing sector accounts for only 4.3 percent of the labor market and the public administration sector makes up 4.1 percent of all workers. A major regional employer is the military—Nellis Air Force Base, a major military installation, is located in the region. Only 11.5 percent of the city's residents have incomes below the poverty line, a rate lower than the national average and over 50 percent lower than the rate in most cities in the Northeast, Midwest, and South. However, poverty conditions in Las Vegas tend to be concentrated in minority and immigrant neighborhoods. The city's unemployment rate is considerably lower than the national and urban averages and has fallen further since the recession of the early 1990s ended.

TRANSPORTATION

Public transportation in Las Vegas is provided through the Citizen's Area Transit (CAT) bus system. The CAT bus system provides transportation to students, senior citizens, tourists visiting Las Vegas's casino and entertainment attractions, and immigrants and the working poor who cannot afford motor vehicles. Only 2.9 percent of Las Vegas's population use public transportation as a means to commute to work. The city has established a strategic plan to re-

duce the traffic congestion and air pollution that have resulted from the rapid growth in motor vehicle use.

HEALTH CARE

Las Vegas's five community hospitals have a total of 1,776 beds, a rate of 688 beds per 100,000 residents. The city's infant mortality rate of 5.5 deaths per 1,000 live births is lower than the U.S. national rate. In 1988, the city had the second lowest infant mortality rate among cities with populations over 200,000. The rapid growth in Las Vegas's population is likely to put greater stress on the area's already overburdened hospitals and health care institutions.

EDUCATION

The public school system in Las Vegas is under the jurisdiction of the Clark County School District, serving an urban, suburban, and rural population of over 1.1 million residents. In 1996, the school district operated a total of 194 elementary, middle, senior high, and special-education schools, with an enrollment of nearly 192,000. In 1996, the Clark County School District opened nine new elementary schools and a high school to accommodate the region's rapidly growing population. In the coming years, $1.25 billion has been authorized for the construction of forty-one new schools. Public school students comprise 93 percent of all Las Vegas's school enrollees, one of the highest rates in the country. A relatively small portion of the city's population 25 years and over, 13.4 percent, holds a bachelor's degree. Las Vegas's major postsecondary educational institution is the University of Nevada–Las Vegas. The city is also served by a local community college.

HOUSING

Las Vegas can be considered a city under construction. However, new housing construction has not increased as rapidly as construction of hotels and casinos. In the 1980s, the city's housing stock expanded by a prodigious 63.4 percent to accommodate the rapidly growing population, one of the highest new housing growth rates in the country. In 1996, over thirty thousand permits were issued for residential construction, almost four times as many housing permits as in 1980. As Las Vegas's population has continued to increase at meteoric rates into the 1990s, new housing construction has continued apace. The need for even more new housing is reflected in the relatively low vacancy rate, about 9 percent. As a result, median housing purchase and rental costs are relatively higher than other U.S. cities with populations exceeding 200,000, and Las Vegas housing costs continued to rise into the late 1990s. Owner-occupied units comprise 46 percent of the city's occupied housing units.

CULTURE, THE ARTS, AND ENTERTAINMENT

The city's major museums and artistic institutions are the Las Vegas Art Museum and the Las Vegas Museum of Natural History. The city is home to minor league professional sports teams in three leagues.

CATEGORY	DATA	YEAR	AREA
LOCATION & ENVIRONMENT			
Area	83.3 square miles	1995	City
	215.7 square kilometers		City
Elevation	2,162 feet/659 meters		City
January Temperature	45.5 degrees Fahrenheit	1961–1990	City
	7.5 degrees Celsius	1961–1990	City
July Temperature	91.1 degrees Fahrenheit	1961–1990	City
	32.8 degrees Celsius	1961–1990	City
Annual Precipitation	4.1 inches/105 millimeters	1961–1990	City
POPULATION & DEMOGRAPHY			
Population	295,516	1992	City
Density	3,548 per square mile	1992	City
	1,370 per square kilometer		
Gender			
Males	50.7%	1990	City
Females	49.3%	1990	City
Age			
Under 18	25.0%	1990	City
18–64	64.7%	1990	City
Over 65	10.3%	1990	City
VITAL STATISTICS			
Births per 1,000 Residents	23	1988	City
Deaths per 1,000 Residents	7	1988	City
Infant Mortality Rate	5.5 per 1,000 live births	1990	City
ECONOMY			
Total Workforce	145,711	1990	City
Trade	18.7%	1990	City
Manufacturing	4.3%	1990	City
Health Services	5.2%	1990	City
Finance, Insurance, Real Estate	6.5%	1990	City
Public Administration	4.1%	1990	City

(continued)

CATEGORY	DATA	YEAR	AREA
TRANSPORTATION			
Passenger Vehicles	160,284	1990	City
HOUSING			
Total Housing Units	109,670	1990	City
Persons per Unit	2.7	1990	City
Owner-Occupied Units	46.0%	1990	City
HEALTH CARE			
Hospitals	5	1991	City
EDUCATION			
Total Students	192,000	1991	City
Primary and Secondary	67.0%	1991	City
Higher	24.2%	1991	City

Sources: Department of Economic and Social Affairs, Population Division. *Urban Agglomerations, 1996.* New York: United Nations, 1997. U.S. Bureau of the Census. *County and City Data Book 1994.* Washington, DC: U.S. Government Printing Office, 1994.

Leeds, West Yorkshire, England
UNITED KINGDOM

LOCATION

The industrial and commercial city of Leeds is located on the Aire River in North Central England in West Yorkshire, the largest subregion of the Yorkshire and Humber region. The Aire River flows southeast from the northern highlands of North Yorkshire through Leeds before emptying 40 miles downstream into Humber Estuary, an inlet of the North Sea. The city occupies a surface land area of 217 square miles (562 square kilometers) in the Pennine Chain, a mountainous region that extends north from the Scottish Southern Uplands through the Yorkshires and south to the Midlands region. Leeds is the largest city in the West Yorkshire region, which includes the municipalities of Bradford, Calderdale, Kirklees, and Wakefield, the subregional administrative center. Leeds is located about 30 miles due north of Sheffield, South Yorkshire's largest city. The city is located approximately 200 miles north-northwest of London, England's capital, and 40 miles northeast of Manchester. The average annual temperature as measured in Birmingham ranges from a January low of 35 degrees Fahrenheit (1.7 degrees Celsius) to a July high of 69 degrees Fahrenheit (20.6 degrees Celsius). The average annual precipitation is 29.7 inches (754.4 millimeters).

POPULATION AND DEMOGRAPHY

Leeds is the largest city in West Yorkshire and the third largest in the United Kingdom. Between 1981 and 1995, Leeds's population increased by 1 percent, to 725,000 residents. The Leed metropolitan area had a population of 1.4 million in 1996. The population is projected to remain stable over the twenty-year period ending 2025. The central city of Leeds accounts for 34.4 percent of West Yorkshire's 2.1 million residents, a region extending beyond the Leeds metropolitan area. Males comprise 49 percent of the metropolitan area's population. Leeds has a larger share of residents in the economically active age range than most major British cities: 19.3 percent of all residents are under 16 years of age, 64.9 percent are between 16 and 65 years of age, and 15.8 percent are in the retired age range. The major cause of the population increase of 2.3 percent between 1981 and 1995 in the Yorkshire and Humber region was the natural increase of births over deaths. Over the same period, increased levels of internal migration from the area to other British regions have been somewhat compensated for by international migration to the

Yorkshire and Humber region. About 5 percent of the Yorkshire and Humber population is ethnic minorities. Pakistani/Bangladeshi residents comprise 53 percent of the region's ethnic minority population, Indians comprise 18 percent, and blacks comprise 13 percent.

HISTORY

Historical records of Leeds can be traced to 1086, when it was referred to as a small town near the parish church of St. Peter. In 1207, Lord Maurice Paynel founded the town. The city remained an important agricultural establishment through much of the period between the thirteenth and seventeenth centuries. In the late seventeenth century, the city became an important transportation center for the rapidly growing regional cloth market. According to the official city records, the population increased from 10,000 at the end of the seventeenth century to 30,000 by the end of the eighteenth century.

The growth of the clothing manufacturing industry spurred the expansion and development of the city's churches, chapels, meetinghouses, and other urban infrastructure. Leeds became the leading manufacturing, marketing, and communications center in northern England in the early nineteenth century, and by 1840, the city's population had reached over 150,000. A major component of the city's growth was its proximity to major water transportation routes for export of clothing products, textile machinery, chemicals, leather, and pottery. The development of the modern commercial railroad greatly facilitated the growth in the coal mining industry in the middle to late nineteenth century. By the turn of the century, major cultural and educational institutions had been established, including a public library and the Yorkshire College of Science and Medical School, which oversaw colleges of technology, art, commerce, and education. In the post–Second World War II period, the city began to clear slum dwellings and replace them with modern housing. In the late twentieth century, the local economy declined as coal was replaced by oil and petroleum and other sources of energy, and the regional textile industry lost its competitive advantage to lower-cost producers in Asia and Latin America.

GOVERNMENT AND POLITICS

In 1974, the new Leeds City Council, a new form of municipal government, was created through the merger of the Leeds City Council with the Urban District Councils and West Riding of Yorkshire County Council. The city council is responsible for enacting local ordinances and delegating responsibility to committees. The Leeds City Council is the largest employer in the city.

ECONOMY

Leeds is a major British manufacturing and trade center. Leeds's skilled and diverse labor force is a major attraction for domestic and foreign investment. The manufacturing sector is led by the engineering sector. Although the engineering industry declined during the 1980s, the sector continues to provide high-wage employment for the skilled workers. The primary components of the engineering industry are metals, mechanical engineering, electronics, and computers. Other leading industries include printing and publishing, food and drink, chemicals, and furniture. Leeds's industries produce a diverse range of products, including electronic components, battle tanks, heart valves, toiletries, newspapers, magazines, buses, beer, clothing, games, labels, packaging, motor components, and jet turbine blades. Key sectors of the regional economy include a large and growing telecommunications industry, financial and business services, media, and retail sales.

Like other major British cities in the post–World War II period, foreign competition reduced Leeds's relative productivity and increased unemployment in the region. By 1996, 23 percent of West Yorkshire's labor force was employed in the manufacturing sector. However, due to recent employment growth, the West Yorkshire unemployment rate averaged only 7.6 percent between June 1995 and May 1996—lower than the United Kingdom's national rate and significantly lower than Liverpool's and Birmingham's. The long-term unemployed comprised 37.4 percent of the jobless population, a lower rate than in other large British urban centers. A relatively large 63.3 percent of Leeds's population is economically active. Although unemployment is not as high in Leeds as in most other major British urban centers, average household income in the city is comparatively lower than the national average. The integration of the European economies has prompted government and business leaders to develop an initiative to create partnerships and collaborative working relationships with the European Union to enhance the region's economic competitiveness.

TRANSPORTATION

According to the National Statistics Office, on average, people living in the Yorkshire and the Humber region travel a shorter distance to work than those in any other region of Great Britain. Road transportation remains the dominant form of travel in the region. In 1995–1996, 64 percent of all households had access to at least one car. The region is the major British center for road haulage and rail freight. Highways—including the M1 motorway, which connects Leeds to London—link Leeds to other major urban centers in the United Kingdom. The Yorkshire and Humberside region accommodates a larger share of road haulage than any region in the United Kingdom. During the first half of the 1990s, road haulage has grown in importance in the United Kingdom as rail freight transportation has declined. However, rail freight remains a strong component of the Yorkshire and Humberside regional transportation nexus. In 1994–1995, more than 38 percent of all rail freight in the United Kingdom traveled through the region. Although the Leeds Bradford Airport accommodates domestic and international flights, many regional passengers use Manchester Airport for both domestic and international destinations. The region is served by the Humber seaport complex, one of the busiest British port systems. A major intercity passenger rail system connects Leeds to London, Manchester, Liverpool, Newcastle, and Edinburgh. The West Yorkshire Passenger Transport Executive provides regional and local commuter rail service through sixty-five train stations.

HEALTH CARE

The National Health Service guarantees residents of Leeds access to medical care. Health services are administered through local and regional providers. Between 1981 and 1995, West Yorkshire's birth rate and death rate have declined. The birth rate fell from 13.6 to 13.2 per 1,000, and the death rate dropped from 12.4 to 10.6 per 1,000. With an infant mortality rate of 7 infant deaths per 1,000 live births, West Yorkshire has one of the United Kingdom's lowest infant mortality rates. The leading causes of death in the region are circulatory disease (heart and vascular disease), followed by cancer and respiratory diseases. The health care industry is a large and growing generator of jobs in Leeds. About 22,000 employees work in the health sector, representing 7 percent of the labor force. Two medical training institutions provide training for nurses and doctors, St. James's Hospital and United Leeds Hospital.

EDUCATION

The West Yorkshire region had a total of 1,169,000 students enrolled in primary, secondary, and postsecondary schools. West Yorkshire has a student/ teacher ratio of 23.5 primary school students per teacher and 17 secondary school students per teacher. The British educational system requires children between ages 5 and 15 to attend school, and in 1995, 75 percent of all 16-year-olds in West Yorkshire were enrolled in postsecondary educational institutions, lower than the United Kingdom national average of 80 percent. The city of Leeds has 301 primary, secondary, and special schools enrolling over 110,000 students between the ages of 2 and 18. In 1992–1993, West Yorkshire's postsecondary student population constituted about 11.3 percent of all students. The leading postsecondary institutions in Leeds are the University of Leeds, a leading British research institution; Leeds Metropolitan University; and Leeds College of Music.

HOUSING

The Yorkshire and Humber housing stock increased by 9.8 percent between 1981 and 1995, lower than the national United Kingdom housing growth rate of 13.2 percent. The owner-occupancy rate for the region is 66 percent, slightly lower than the national rate of 67 percent. Although a large proportion of housing units in Leeds remain in the hands of housing associations and public authorities, the stock of private dwellings has increased in the 1980s and 1990s. In 1995, nearly 32 percent of new housing starts in Leeds were constructed by housing associations and local authorities, slightly higher than the average rate for the United Kingdom as a whole, but lower than the public housing rates for Glasgow and Birmingham. In 1995, the city had an average of 2.35 persons per household, and 31.1 percent of all households consisted of one person. The regional housing occupancy rate was 2.5 persons in 1991. The declining average household size is increasing pressure to build new accommodations. Average housing rental costs in Leeds are significantly lower than in other major British cities. According to the National Statistics Office, the average local authority rent in the Yorkshire and Humber region in April 1996 was the lowest in the United Kingdom.

CULTURE, THE ARTS, AND ENTERTAINMENT

Leeds is a city of art galleries and cultural and historical museums. The leading museums are Armley Mills, the Henry Moore Institute, the Leeds City Museum, the Temple Newsam House, the Abbey House Museum, Kirkstall Abbey, Middleton Railway, Thwaite Mill, the Royal Armouries Museum, the Thackay Medical Museum, Harewood House, the Horsforth Museum, and Tetley's Brewery Wharf.

CATEGORY	DATA	YEAR	AREA
LOCATION & ENVIRONMENT			
Area	217 square miles	1996	City
	562 square kilometers		City
Elevation	245 feet/80.4 meters		City
January Temperature	35 degrees Fahrenheit	1992	City
	1.7 degrees Celsius	1992	City
July Temperature	69 degrees Fahrenheit	1992	City
	20.6 degrees Celsius	1992	City
Annual Precipitation	29.7 inches/754.4 millimeters	1992	City
POPULATION & DEMOGRAPHY			
Population	1,400,000	1996	Metro
Projected Population	1,400,000	2015	Metro
Growth Rate	−0.2%	1990–1995	Metro
Growth Rate	0.0%	1995–2015	Metro
Density	6,452 per square mile	1995	Metro
	1,291 per square kilometer		
Gender			
Males	49.0%	1992	Metro
Females	51.0%	1992	Metro
Age			
Under 16	19.3%	1992	Metro
16–64	64.9%	1992	Metro
Over 65	15.8%	1992	Metro
VITAL STATISTICS			
Births per 1,000 Residents	13.2	1995	Metro
Death per 1,000 Residents	10.6	1995	Metro
Infant Mortality Rate	7 per 1,000 live births	1992	Metro
ECONOMY			
Total Workforce	1,096,000	1995	Region
Manufacturing	23.0%	1992	Metro
Construction	6.2%	1992	Metro
Utilities	3.8%	1992	Metro
Agriculture	2.4%	1992	Metro
TRANSPORTATION			
Passenger Vehicles	2,426,000	1995	City
HOUSING			
Total Housing Units	2,031,000	1991	Metro
Persons per Unit	2.5	1991	Metro
Owner-Occupied Units	66.0%	1991	Metro

(continued)

CATEGORY	DATA	YEAR	AREA
EDUCATION			
Total Students	1,169,000	1993	Metro
Primary	36.0%	1993	Metro
Secondary	53.0%	1993	Metro
Higher	11.0%	1993	Metro

Sources: Department of Economic and Social Affairs, Population Division. *Urban Agglomerations, 1996.* New York: United Nations, 1997; United Nations Center for Human Settlements. *Compendium of Human Settlements Statistics.* New York: United Nations, 1995; Eurostat *Regions Statistical Yearbook.* Brussels, Belgium: Statistical Office of European Communities, 1996; and Office for National Statistics. *Regional Trends 32.* London, England: The Stationery Office, 1997.

Lima
PERU

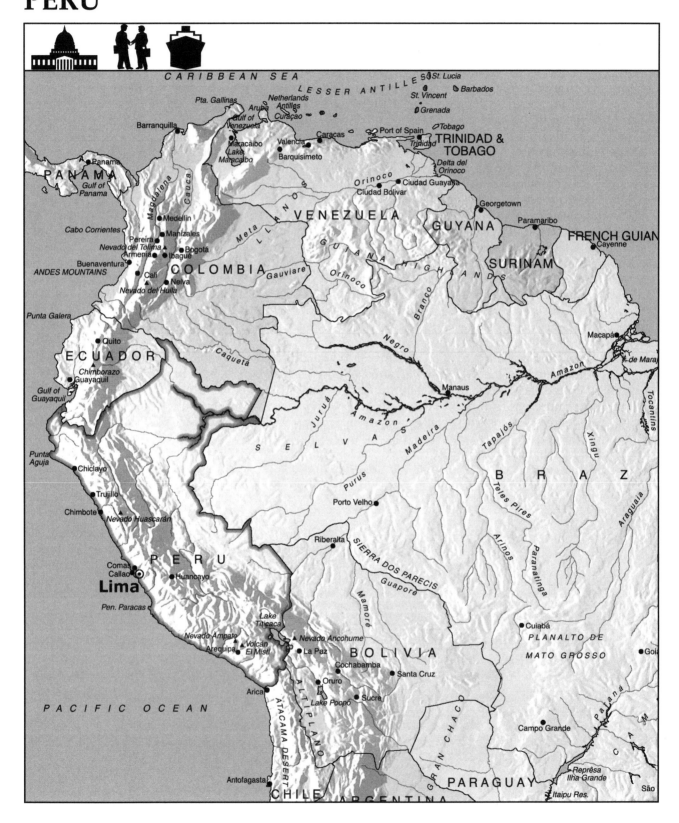

CARIBBEAN SEA

LESSER ANTILLES
St. Lucia
St. Vincent • Barbados
Grenada

Pta. Gallinas
Netherlands Antilles
Aruba Curaçao
Gulf of Venezuela
Barranquilla
Maracaibo
Lake Maracaibo
Valencia
Caracas
Barquisimeto
Port of Spain • Tobago
Trinidad
TRINIDAD & TOBAGO

Panama
PANAMA
Gulf of Panama

Delta del Orinoco
Ciudad Guayana
Ciudad Bolívar
Orinoco

Georgetown

Paramaribo

FRENCH GUIAN
Cayenne

Medellín
Cabo Corrientes
Pereira Manizales
Nevado del Tolima ▲ ● Bogotá
Armenia ▲ Ibagué
Buenaventura
ANDES MOUNTAINS
Cali
● Neiva
Nevado del Hulla ▲

Meta
LLANOS

VENEZUELA

COLOMBIA
Gauviare
Orinoco

GUIANA HIGHLANDS
Branco

GUYANA

SURINAM

Punta Galera

Macapá
de Mara

Quito
ECUADOR
Chimborazo
Guayaquil
Gulf of Guayaquil

Caquetá

Negro

Amazon

Tocantins

Punta Aguja
Chiclayo

SELVAS
Juruá
Amazon

Manaus

Madeira
Tapajós
Teles Pires

BRAZ

Trujillo
Chimbote ●
Nevado Huascarán ▲

Purus

Xingu

Araguaia

PERU
Comas
Callao ◎
Lima ● Huancayo

Porto Velho ●

Riberalta ●
SIERRA DOS PARECIS
Guaporé

Arinos
Paranatinga

Pen. Paracas

Lake Titicaca
Nevado Ampato ▲
Arequipa ▲ Volcán El Misti
Nevado Ancohume
La Paz

Mamoré

Cuiabá ●
PLANALTO DE MATO GROSSO

Goi

BOLIVIA
Cochabamba
Santa Cruz ●

Arica
Oruro
Lake Poopó
Sucre

ATACAMA DESERT
ALTIPLANO

PACIFIC OCEAN

GRAN CHACO

Campo Grande ●

Paraná

Antofagasta ●

CHILE **ARGENTINA**

PARAGUAY

Reprêsa Ilha Grande
Itaipu Res.
São

LOCATION

Lima is the capital and largest city of Peru and serves as the country's commercial and cultural center. Founded by Francisco Pizarro in 1535 on the ancient pre-Incan religious site of Pachacamac, the city soon became the capital of the Spanish empire in South America. Its close proximity to the vast resources of gold and silver in the Andes and its status as one of the finest ports on the western coast of South America made it an ideal location from which to administer the Spanish empire. Lima contains one third of Peru's population and workforce. Despite efforts to decentralize government agencies to other parts of the country, Lima remains the political, economic, and cultural center of Peru.

The city is located on the Rimac River 8 miles inland from the Pacific port of Callao, in Peru's arid coastal region. It represents the most densely populated and economically developed part of the country. Metropolitan Lima, which includes the provinces of Lima and Callao, covers a large area of 1,085 square miles (2,811 square kilometers) along the Pacific coast.

Despite its location in the tropics, Lima's climate is temperate, moderated by the cold Peruvian current that shuttles up the Pacific coast from Antarctica. The average temperature varies from 73.8 degrees Fahrenheit (23.2 degrees Celsius) in January to 63.3 degrees Fahrenheit (17.4 degrees Celsius) in July. From November to March, the city is warm during the day and cool in the evenings. During the cooler winter months from April to October, the coast is often obscured by dense fog. Rainfall is rare.

POPULATION AND DEMOGRAPHY

Lima's population increased from 4.1 million in 1981 to 6.8 million in 1996. The city's population is projected to grow by a cumulative 40.8 percent to 9.4 million in the year 2015. Since the 1940s, Lima's dramatic population growth has led to serious socioeconomic problems, including inadequate housing, water, and other services. During the 1960s, the population grew at a rate of 7 percent annually. This figure dropped to 5 percent in the 1970s and 4 percent in the 1980s. Annual growth was 2.7 percent in the early 1990s.

Lima's population density is 6,071 persons per square mile (2,343 per square kilometer). The age profile is quite young. About 43.4 percent of the population is under 20, 49.5 percent is between the ages of 20 and 60, and 7.1 percent is over 60. The birth rate is 27.1 per 1,000 births and the death rate is 6.1 per 1,000 deaths. The infant mortality rate is a high 57.5 deaths per 1,000 live births. The gender ratio is about even, at 49.5 males to 50.5 females. Ninety percent of the population is mestizo (of mixed European and Native American descent) There are also small minorities of whites, blacks, and Asians, mostly from Japan.

HISTORY

Lima was founded by conquistador Francisco Pizarro in 1535 and served as the colonial administrative center of Spanish-ruled South America for nearly three centuries, channeling its trade to Spain through Callao. The city expanded rapidly during the early colonial period as a commercial, cultural, and governmental center of the Viceroyalty of Peru. Toward the end of the colonial period, however, Lima's importance declined. When most of Latin America was struggling for independence, Lima became a hub for forces opposed to liberation from Spain. The city was eventually taken over by General José de San Martín, one of the leaders of the independence movement. In 1826, Lima became the capital of independent Peru. It was occupied for two years by Chilean forces in 1881, during the War of the Pacific.

The city maintained its dominant position as a major South American capital during the nineteenth century. Dramatic population growth and limited availability of housing and services during the twentieth century have led to squalor, misery, and ongoing instability for a large proportion of the population. In addition to the problems caused by uncontrolled growth, Lima suffers from pollution, crime, and social disorder. The city's colonial-era prominence has subsequently been eclipsed by Buenos Aires, São Paulo, and Rio de Janeiro, in Brazil.

The staggering poverty and economic inequality has contributed to the growth of military insurgencies and political terrorism in support of overthrowing the government. During the 1980s and 1990s, various insurrectionist groups including the Sendero Luminoso (Shining Path) and the Tupac Amaru, named after the last Inca emperor, have carried out numerous acts of sabotage including bombings, kidnappings, assassinations, and other attacks.

GOVERNMENT AND POLITICS

The politics of Lima and Peru have been quite tumultuous since independence. The country has seen numerous coups d'état since independence in the early nineteenth century. A recent return to civilian democratic rule has been marred by emergency measures taken by the current president, Alberto Fujimori. As far as metropolitan government is concerned, Lima is divided into forty-five municipal districts, including the adjoining port of Callao. The government of Lima unites municipal districts and coordinates some urban functions. Each municipal district elects a mayor and district council.

ECONOMY

Throughout its history, the city controlled great wealth due to the lucrative trade in gold and silver. In 1851, railroads connected Lima with other Peruvian cities, further helping the city prosper. Today, the vast majority of imports and exports pass through the port of Callao. An industrial belt almost 6 miles long links the port of Callao to downtown Lima.

Almost all of Peru's heavy industry is situated in and around Lima. These industries include textiles, clothing, processed foods, and some machinery and vehicles. Lima also serves as the center for finance as well as retail and wholesale trade. While the national government has traditionally served as one of the largest employers, during the 1990s there have been drastic cuts in the number of public sector jobs.

Lima accounts for more than two thirds of the nation's gross domestic product, tax revenue, bank deposits, and private investment. Of Lima's total civilian labor force of some 1,493,362 people, most are still employed in the public sector. Twenty-eight percent have jobs in trade, and another 4 percent are employed in finance, insurance, and real estate. Nevertheless, Lima suffers from severe unemployment (10 percent) and underemployment (50 percent).

TRANSPORTATION

Lima's streets are often clogged with traffic. Most of the city looks grimy because of automobile pollution and a lack of rain to wash away pollutants. There is no rapid-transit system and only one highway, which runs from the city center to the neighborhoods of Mira Flores and Barranco. Jorge Chavez International Airport is located on the northern edge of the city, and the Pan American Highway and the Central

Highway in the Andes connect Lima with the rest of the country. One railroad serves Lima, running from downtown Lima to the central Andes.

HEALTH CARE

There are 119 hospitals and 2.7 physicians per 1,000 residents. Lima's rapid population growth has generated severe problems in the metropolitan area: Access to basic services, including drinking water and sewage systems, is inadequate or absent in many neighborhoods, especially the *pueblos jovenes* (young cities). Nearby waters are severely polluted by sewage piped into the ocean, and this has contributed to recent outbreaks of cholera. Tuberculosis also is prevalent.

EDUCATION

Lima is home to the most prestigious universities in the country, including the oldest university in the Western Hemisphere, the National University of San Marcos (established in 1551). Also located in Lima are various private universities, including the National Engineering University and the La Molina National Agrarian University. While most of the city's children attend school at least part time, illiteracy rates remain high, even in comparison to other impoverished Latin American countries. About 52.4 percent of Lima's students are in primary school, 33 percent in secondary school, and 14.6 percent in higher education.

HOUSING

While some high-rise buildings dominate the skyline in affluent neighborhoods such as Mira Flores and San Isidro, as well as the downtown area, most of the city is characterized by low-density residential construction of one-, two-, and three-story buildings. Commercial districts are scattered throughout the downtown area and wealthy suburbs. The city is located in a seismically active zone and has experienced major earthquakes in 1687, 1746, and 1970. As a result, most structures do not predate the earthquake of 1746.

More than a third of the city's population lives in shanty towns known as *barriadas*. Since the early 1970s, the settlements are more euphemistically referred to as *pueblos jóvenes*, or "young towns." Housing is built using cardboard, reed mats, scrap lumber, and metal. Since the 1970s, vast areas of desert on the city's southern edges have been occupied. Decades after the settlements were established, some neighborhoods have been fortunate to be able to upgrade their homes with brick and mortar, steel, and concrete. Neighborhoods like Villa María del Triunfo and Villa El Salvador have gradually shed their humble structures and gained access to some services and infrastructure. Altogether, there are approximately 1,519,000 dwellings in the metropolitan area, with an average occupancy of 4.3 persons per unit.

CULTURE, THE ARTS, AND ENTERTAINMENT

With a rich historical past, Lima has been able to preserve much of its pre-Columbian and colonial cultural heritage in museums and archeological sites.

Lima's museums and galleries also feature art, music, and handicrafts from every region of the country.

Most of Lima's important historical and architectural landmarks are located in the city's colonial center, the Plaza de Armas, located just south of the Rimac River. Other landmarks include the cathedral, started after the earthquake in 1746; the archbishop's palace, decorated with typical elegant carved wood balconies; the governor's palace (1938), where the president lives; and the presidential palace, which was built on the site of Pizarro's house.

Cultural and recreational centers are scattered throughout the metropolitan area. They include the municipal theater, which hosts theater, symphony, opera, and ballet productions. There are numerous elaborate Catholic churches, including the massive San Francisco Church, famous for its catacombs and library.

CATEGORY	DATA	YEAR	AREA
LOCATION & ENVIRONMENT			
Area	1,085 square miles	1995	City
	2,811 square kilometers	1995	City
Elevation	394 feet/120 meters		City
January Temperature	73.8 degrees Fahrenheit		City
	23.2 degrees Celsius		City
July Temperature	63.3 degrees Fahrenheit		City
	17.4 degrees Celsius		City
POPULATION & DEMOGRAPHY			
Population	6,800,000	1996	City
Projected Population	9,400,000	2015	City
Growth Rate	2.7%	1990–1995	City
Growth Rate	40.8%	1995–2015	City
Density	6,071 per square mile	1992	City
	2,343 per square kilometer		
Gender			
Male	49.5%	1987	City
Female	50.5%	1987	City
Age			
Under 20	43.4%	1990	City
20–59	49.5%	1990	City
Over 60	7.1%	1990	City
VITAL STATISTICS			
Births per 1,000 Residents	27.1	1987	City
Deaths per 1,000 Residents	6.1	1987	City
Infant Mortality Rate	57.5 per 1,000 live births	1987	City

(continued)

CATEGORY	DATA	YEAR	AREA
ECONOMY			
Total Workforce	1,493,362	1987	City
Trade	28.5%	1987	City
Manufacturing	16.9%	1987	City
Services	2.7%	1987	City
Transport, Communications	4.8%	1987	City
Construction	0.7%	1987	City
Utilities	0.4%	1987	City
Mining	1.6%	1987	City
Government	42.0%	1987	City
TRANSPORTATION			
Passenger Journeys	1,429,000	1987	City
Rail	100%	1987	City
COMMUNICATIONS			
Telephones per 1,000 Residents	43.4	1987	City
HOUSING			
Total Housing Units	1,519,000	1992	City
Persons per Unit	4.3	1992	City
HEALTH CARE			
Hospitals	119	1990	City
Physicians per 1,000 Residents	2.7	1990	City
EDUCATION			
Total Students	1,640,956	1987	City
Primary	52.4%	1987	City
Secondary	33.0%	1987	City
Higher	14.6%	1987	City

Sources: Department of Economic and Social Affairs, Population Division. *Urban Agglomerations, 1996.* New York: United Nations, 1997. United Nations Center for Human Settlements. *Compendium of Human Settlements Statistics.* New York: United Nations, 1995.

Lisbon
PORTUGAL

LOCATION

Lisbon, the capital and largest city in Portugal, is built upon a series of terraces and low, rolling hills that rise from the banks of the Tagus River and the Mal da Palha (Sea of Straw), both of which are connected to the Atlantic Ocean some five miles to the west. While the port area of the city lies at sea level, most of the city is higher; thus, the average elevation is about 313 feet (113 meters) above sea level. The city is located approximately 320 miles west-southwest of Madrid, Spain, and some 275 miles northwest of Gibraltar. It covers approximately 32 square miles (86 square kilometers) of territory.

The city has a typical Mediterranean-type climate. Summers are hot and dry, with average July temperatures of about 71 degrees Fahrenheit (21.7 degrees Celsius). Winters are cool and rainy, with January temperatures averaging about 51 degrees Fahrenheit (10.6 degrees Celsius). The city receives approximately 27 inches (685.8 millimeters) of rain annually, most of it falling in the winter and spring.

POPULATION AND DEMOGRAPHY

The Lisbon metropolitan area has a population of approximately 1.9 million. It has experienced relatively rapid growth for a European city, about 2.3 percent annually in the 1990s. While this rate is expected to slow to 1 percent over the next twenty years, the population is still predicted to reach 2.3 million by the year 2015. The greater metropolitan area, which encompasses a great deal of rural land, has a density of 745 persons per square mile (276 per square kilometer), though the city center is extremely crowded. The city's age profile is situated somewhere between those of developing and developed world cities. Of the population, 33.2 percent are under the age of 20, while 13.5 percent are over the age of 60.

The vast majority of the city's population consists of Portuguese-speaking Roman Catholics. While religious attendance has been in decline in recent years, it continues at rates higher than in most of Europe. Other communities in the city include various peoples from Portugal's former empire, including Brazilians, Angolans, Mozambicans, and Timorese, as well as a small but ancient Jewish community.

HISTORY

Most historians and archeologists believe that Lisbon was established as a city by Phoenician traders around the year 1200 B.C. Legend has it that the city was founded by the Greek wanderer Odysseus. The city was under Roman rule from 205 B.C. to A.D. 409, but was then lost to the Visigoths, who, in turn, were conquered by Muslim Moorish invaders from North Africa in the early eighth century. Though Lisbon was occasionally occupied by invading Normans, Muslims maintained control of the city for some four hundred years, until it finally fell to the armies of the Portuguese Christian king Alfonso Henriques in 1147. The city, however, did not become the capital of Portugal until the court was moved there from Coimbra in 1256. The city was besieged and burned by invading Castilians in 1372, though the Portuguese kings never lost control of Lisbon.

With the beginning of the Portuguese age of exploration and conquest in the early 1400s, Lisbon grew in wealth and size. Under the reign of King Manuel I, from 1495 to 1521, the city saw the construction of numerous municipal buildings, palaces, and churches in the baroque style known as Manueline. The growing wealth and power of the kingdom was short-lived, however, brought down by profligate court spending and by the ouster of the Jews, many of whom ran the city's finances and businesses, in the early 1500s.

In order to keep Spain at bay, Portugal established a strategic alliance with Great Britain beginning in the seventeenth century, which led to more extensive trade between Lisbon and the ports of the United Kingdom. In 1755, the slow decline of the city was accelerated by a massive earthquake that killed 30,000 people and destroyed 9,000 buildings. While the city was rebuilt at a pace that surprised people of the age, the populace remained scarred by the event for generations.

Beginning with the peninsular wars of the early 1800s, following Napoleon's invasion of Spain, Lisbon and Portugal as a whole were rocked by revolution and civil conflict, though the city continued to expand in population. A major building program in the late 1800s gave much of the city its modern look of wide boulevards and blue mosaic sidewalks.

In 1908, the king and the crown prince of Portugal were assassinated in Lisbon; in 1910, the successor king gave up the throne and went into exile. These events inaugurated the country's first experiment with republican rule, an experiment that ended with the rise to power of the dictator Antonio Salazar in the 1920s. Together with his hand-picked successor, Marcelo Caetano, Salazar maintained a dictatorship, similar to Francisco Franco's in Spain, in Portugal until the bloodless Carnation Revolution of 1974. Under the liberal and socialist governments that followed,

Portugal began to shed its backward reputation. It quickly dissolved its overseas empire in Africa and Asia, and joined the European Union and NATO in the early 1980s.

GOVERNMENT AND POLITICS

Lisbon represents one of Portugal's twenty-one administrative districts. Each district is headed by a civil governor, appointed by the central government's Minister of the Interior. In turn, each district is divided into municipalities, which are further subdivided into wards and parishes. Representatives to the parish and ward councils are elected by popular vote. In addition, Lisbon has a municipal assembly whose representatives are chosen by parish committees and elected by universal suffrage. The assembly serves as the city's legislative branch of the local government and elects the Municipal Chamber, which serves as the city's executive branch and is headed by a president appointed by the district governor.

ECONOMY

Lisbon is the largest industrial center in Portugal. Its factories manufacture both heavy and light industrial products. Among the former are steel mills, munitions factories, a plastics plant, one of the world's largest cement plants, and a state-supported oil refinery. Light industries include glassmaking, electronics, food products, diamond cutting, soap, cooking oils, and the largest cork plant in the world. Some 16.5 percent of the workforce labors in industry. The city is also a major fishing center, with almost 10 percent of the population involved in sea-going ventures.

Since its incorporation into the European Union, Lisbon has grown as a financial and commercial city. Still, the largest portion of the nonindustrial workforce is employed in the city's service sector, much of which is devoted to the all-important tourist trade. In addition, as the city is the country's capital, a large proportion of Lisbon's labor force is employed in government offices and agencies.

TRANSPORTATION

Situated at the far end of the Iberian peninsula, Lisbon is the terminus for a number of highways and railways connecting the city to Spain and the rest of Europe. Much of this infrastructure is outdated, though the government has committed itself to major improvements over the past decade. By far, Lisbon's most important transportation sector is the port. With its 19 miles of docks and its special facilities for handling container ships, car ferries, and grain transport, Lisbon's harbor handles nearly 20 million metric tons of freight annually.

Metropolitan traffic is handled by a small system of expressways. The growing number of automobiles, the narrow streets, and the disjointed geography of the city make for bad traffic congestion. A bridge across the Tagus connects the city to suburbs and communities to the south. Several commuter rail lines, a system of buses, a small subway, and the city's quaint but dilapidated streetcars offer public transport.

HEALTH CARE

As the country's main urban area, Lisbon has a higher proportion of doctors and hospitals than the rest of Portugal. The ratio of 4 physicians per 1,000 residents, relatively high for Western Europe; the ratio of 0.8 hospital beds per 1,000 residents, also high. The city's hospitals include both government-operated and private facilities. The former, often strapped for funding, lack sufficient staff and equipment. Several small foreign clinics cater to the small communities of expatriates living in the city. Lisbon still suffers from minor outbreaks of typhus, cholera, and malaria, although these have declined dramatically in recent years.

EDUCATION

While education at the primary and secondary levels is officially free and compulsory for all children age 6 to 14, the city suffers from a lack of educational facilities. Many of the city's more elite citizens send their children to private academies. The city is home to several medieval- and modern-era institutions of higher learning. These include the University of Lisbon (the original university was founded in 1290, but it moved to Coimbra in the sixteenth century and was renamed the University of Coimbra; a second University of Lisbon was founded in 1911), the Technical University of Lisbon, and three other universities. While the city's population includes some 100,000 university students, demand continues to outpace the supply of places for students.

HOUSING

Lisbon's housing stock consists of some 1.4 million dwellings with an average occupancy of 2.3 persons per unit. In recent years, there has been a dramatic expansion of utility services throughout the city. As of 1992, some 92 percent of the dwellings had private baths. While much of the central city's population lives in nineteenth-century apartment buildings, new projects on the outskirts of the city shelter the majority of the region's people. These include new developments in the north and northwestern sectors of the city, built by the municipal government. Despite these developments, housing shortages remain, and a number of shantytowns have grown up around the periphery of the metropolitan area.

CULTURE, THE ARTS, AND ENTERTAINMENT

Lisbon enjoys a lively cafe culture and is home to most of the country's major institutions of higher culture. The city has over a dozen museums, featuring art and artifacts from the ancient, medieval, and modern eras of Portuguese history. Lisbon also boasts several musical and dramatic institutions, including the National Conservatory, the Municipal Orchestra, and the São Carlos and National Theaters.

Millions of tourists are drawn to Lisbon annually for its beautiful hilly setting and its many fine examples of baroque and classical architecture. While much of the former was destroyed in the 1755 earthquake, a fine extant example of baroque Manueline style is the São Roque Church. The city is also known for its exquisite tile work and mosaics, which grace many buildings and sidewalks.

CATEGORY	DATA	YEAR	AREA
LOCATION & ENVIRONMENT			
Area	32 square miles	1995	City
	86 square kilometers		City
Elevation	313 feet/113 meters		City
January Temperature	51 degrees Fahrenheit		City
	10.6 degrees Celsius		City
July Temperature	71 degrees Fahrenheit		City
	21.7 degrees Celsius		City
Annual Precipitation	27 inches/685.8 millimeters		City
POPULATION & DEMOGRAPHY			
Population	1,900,000	1996	Metro
Projected Population	2,300,000	2015	Metro
Growth Rate	2.3%	1990–1995	City
Growth Rate	21.9%	1995–2015	City
Density	745 per square mile	1992	Metro
	276 per square kilometer		
Gender			
Male	48.0%	1992	Metro
Female	52.0%	1992	Metro
Age			
Under 20	33.2%	1992	Metro
20–59	53.3%	1992	Metro
Over 60	13.5%	1992	Metro

(continued)

CATEGORY	DATA	YEAR	AREA
VITAL STATISTICS			
Births per 1,000 Residents	11	1992	Metro
Deaths per 1,000 Residents	10	1992	Metro
Infant Mortality Rate	10.9 per 1,000 live births	1992	Metro
Net Migration per 1,000 Residents	−0.5	1992	Metro
ECONOMY			
Workforce	1,358,000	1992	Metro
Agriculture	10.4%	1992	Metro
Manufacturing	16.5%	1992	Metro
Construction	9.6%	1992	Metro
Trade	40.3%	1992	Metro
Services	22.2%	1992	Metro
Utilities	1.0%	1992	Metro
HOUSING			
Housing Units	1,420,000	1992	Metro
New Housing Units	20,800	1992	Metro
Persons per Unit	2.3	1992	Metro
HEALTH CARE			
Physicians per 1,000 Residents	4	1992	Metro
Hospital Beds per 1,000 Residents	0.8	1992	Metro
EDUCATION			
Total Students	543,000	1992	Metro
Primary	49.7%	1992	Metro
Secondary	32.4%	1992	Metro
Higher	17.9%	1992	Metro

Sources: Department of Economic and Social Affairs, Population Division. *Urban Agglomerations, 1996.* New York: United Nations, 1997; United Nations Center for Human Settlements. *Compendium of Human Settlements Statistics.* New York: United Nations, 1995; and Eurostat *Regions Statistical Yearbook.* Brussels, Belgium: Statistical Office of European Communities, 1996.

Liverpool, Merseyside, England
UNITED KINGDOM

LOCATION

Liverpool is located in northwestern England, in the County of Merseyside. The city lies on the Cheshire Plain at an elevation of 198 feet along the northwestern shores of the Mersey Estuary, a wide channel that extends from the Irish Sea past the city's south and southeast, running about 20 miles before narrowing at the municipality of Runcorn. To Liverpool's immediate south is the Wirral Peninsula, which is connected to the city by three tunnels. Liverpool is the administrative center of Merseyside, a subregion that includes the municipalities of Knowsley, Sefton, St. Helens, and Wirral. The City of Liverpool covers a surface land area of 189 square miles (70 square kilometers). Liverpool is located 30 miles west of Manchester, 80 miles northwest of Birmingham, England's second most populous city, and approximately 175 miles northwest of London, the United Kingdom's capital and largest city. Dublin, Ireland, is located across the Irish Sea, 140 miles due west of Liverpool. The city's average temperature ranges from a low of 40 degrees Fahrenheit (4.4 degrees Celsius) in January to a high of 60.5 degrees Fahrenheit (15.8 degrees Celsius) in July. The city has an average annual precipitation of 28.9 inches (734.1 millimeters).

POPULATION AND DEMOGRAPHY

Between 1981 and 1995, the Merseyside regional population declined by 6.2 percent, to 1,427,000. This decline was reflected in all of the region's major cities: Knowsley, Liverpool, Sefton, St. Helens, and Wirral. Over the fifteen-year period, the central city population declined by 8.9 percent, to 471,000 in 1995. Liverpool has a density of 10,808 persons per square mile (4,173 persons per square kilometer), one of the highest densities in the United Kingdom outside of London. Liverpool's population is fairly evenly distributed across demographic groups: 20 percent of the city's population is under age 16, 64.4 percent is between 16 and 65 years of age, and 15.7 percent are over 65 years of age. Major factors in the population decline in Liverpool and the region as a whole are a declining birth rate and net out-migration. Between 1994 and 1995, the Merseyside region lost about 7,400 residents to other regions in the United Kingdom and abroad. In part the out-migration can be explained by continued economic decline, which limits employment opportunities in the region. Merseyside has a relatively small ethnic minority population of about

24,000, representing only 2 percent of the region's population.

HISTORY

In 1207 King John granted Liverpool free borough status. Growing trade with the Americas and the West Indies increased Liverpool's importance as a busy port city in the seventeenth and eighteenth centuries. The city's harbor facilities were used for trade in manufactured goods and slaves. Following the completion of the railway to Manchester in 1830, the city increased trade with the interior. In the nineteenth century Liverpool became a major European trading center. The city was bombed by German warplanes in the Second World War. After the war, Liverpool's manufacturing industries went into decline. In the 1960s, the Beatles rock group was formed in the city. The local infrastructure was eventually rebuilt through government development and slum clearance programs. However, the manufacturing sector continued to decline into the late twentieth century, contributing to double-digit unemployment.

GOVERNMENT AND POLITICS

The Liverpool City Council has ninety-eight members. The Labour and Liberal Democrat parties hold the vast majority of seats; there is just one Conservative member of the city council. The lord mayor is an ex-officio member of the city council committees.

ECONOMY

Though the city has experienced an economic decline in the post–World War II period, Liverpool is still a major English transportation and shipping center. Key manufacturing industries in the region are shipbuilding, petroleum refining, pharmaceuticals, electric equipment, motor vehicles, chemicals, refined sugar, flour, and rubber products. Since the contraction of the manufacturing industry that began following the end of the Second World War, Liverpool authorities and business have sought to develop new and more competitive industries. The city has sought to encourage the development of high-technology industries to replace the basic manufacturing industries that dominated the economy in previous centuries. The city's competitive industrial base includes pharmaceuticals, auto components, and civil engineering.

The wholesale and retail trade sector includes the development of new shopping and commercial venues and distribution, storage, and warehousing facilities. Other promising sectors include transport, shipping, and ports. Public authorities have sought to expand the regional arts and entertainment industry. The opening of a new convention center in 1996 has drawn visitors to the Merseyside region. Efforts have continued to upgrade the major sports and theater venues. The Merseyside Development Corporation is seeking to develop the Kings Waterfront with a large new complex slated to include theater, recreation, and restaurant facilities. Other projects are under way to improve the city center through hotel, office, and retail development.

In recent years, the Merseyside region has consistently had one of the highest unemployment rates in the United Kingdom. In the year ending May 1996, the regional unemployment rate was 13 percent, significantly higher than the national average of 8.5 percent. As a result, the Merseyside region and Liverpool in particular have had a smaller economically active population than most regions of the United Kingdom. The economically active population that is in the job market or seeking employment represented only 50.7 percent of the region's population in 1995 and 1996. Unemployment is concentrated among ethnic minorities. Due to the particularly high levels of unemployment, significantly higher proportions of the population are dependent on income support. As the Liverpool economy (and the rest of the United Kingdom's) is integrated into the European Union and the global market, the city has made an effort to promote local development, investment, and commerce. The efforts are aimed at stimulating business growth, encouraging arts and cultural industries, creating new opportunities for women, providing employment and training, and assisting the expansion of community-based economic development by offering financial assistance and advice.

The Merseyside region has historically had a high level of union membership. In 1996, 46 percent of Merseyside's workers were union members, a higher proportion than any other region in the United Kingdom. The decline in the manufacturing sector has reduced the number of workers in traditionally unionized industries; in 1996, 17.5 percent of Merseyside's labor force was employed in the manufacturing sector. The region has experienced higher levels of industrial strife during the 1980s and 1990s. In September 1995, over five hundred Liverpool dockworkers were locked out and replaced with replacement workers after they refused to cross picket lines. After

their firing, the dockworkers brought international attention to their fate with calls for worldwide port closures, work stoppages, and rallies. Over the next three years, several North American, European, and Australian ports were closed to demonstrate solidarity with the fired workers. In early 1998, after a long and drawn-out battle, the dispute was finally settled.

TRANSPORTATION

Residents in the region have a particularly high dependence on the public transportation system. Merseyside and London have the highest percentages of households without a car in the United Kingdom; in 1995 and 1996, 39 percent of Merseyside's households had no car. Manchester's airport is the major air transportation hub for Merseyside residents. The region is an important British road haulage and rail freight center. Liverpool has extensive port facilities that were redeveloped in the 1970s to increase capacity.

HEALTH CARE

Under British law, health care is guaranteed to all residents, regardless of ability to pay. Two health authorities operate in the Merseyside region: the North West Regional Health Authority and the South Sefton Health Authority. Fourteen community hospitals provide health care services to residents in the Liverpool region, including a children's hospital and a nursing home. Liverpool designates itself as a "healthy city." According to the World Health Organization (WHO), the goal of all governments for the year 2000 should be to bring all residents to a level of health that would permit them to lead a socially and economically productive life. Liverpool has joined twenty European "healthy cities" by signing on to the WHO goals. Liverpool's health authorities have committed themselves to the goal of providing health care for all, aiming to facilitate the development and implementation of health-oriented public policies through reducing inequalities in health care, promoting a holistic understanding of health, and encouraging collaborative local efforts. The regional emphasis on the provision of health care has produced positive results. The average infant mortality rate between 1993 and 1995 was 7.8 infant deaths per 1,000 live births, higher than the national infant mortality rate of 6.2 infant deaths per 1,000 live births, but significantly lower than the rate in most other urban regions. Over the period 1991 to 1995, Liverpool experienced a natural population decrease, as the death rate for the region declined marginally from 12.4 to 12.2 per 1,000 residents, while the birth rate decreased somewhat more, from 13.2 to 12.0 per 1,000 residents. Liverpool's drug clinic is considered by many health authorities to be a pioneer in innovative techniques for controlling the behavior of habitual drug users.

EDUCATION

The student/teacher ratio in regional Merseyside primary and secondary schools is slightly higher than the national average. About 75 percent of 16-year-olds in the Merseyside region continue to attend school after compulsory education ends at 15. Approximately 1,513,000 students attend primary and secondary schools in the region. The University of Liverpool is the leading postsecondary education institute in Merseyside. The region also has a number of technical colleges.

HOUSING

In 1995, housing associations and local authorities initiated about 36 percent of housing starts in Liverpool, with the private sector accounting for the remainder. In 1996, public authorities managed about 48,000 housing units in Liverpool. The average

household size in the central city of Liverpool was 2.42 persons, about the same as the national rate; one-person households accounted for 32.6 percent of all households. The regional household size was 2.5 persons in 1991. The average weekly rent for local authority tenants is comparatively higher than in other major cities, though lower than the average for the London region. Owner-occupied housing units represent 68 percent of the Merseyside regional housing stock. Between 1981 and 1995, the Merseyside housing stock increased by 4.1 percent, a lower level of increase than any other region in the United Kingdom.

CULTURE, THE ARTS, AND ENTERTAINMENT

The leading museums, arts institutions, and historical sites are the Walker Art Gallery, the Liverpool City Libraries, and the Merseyside County Museum. A major attraction is the Liverpool town hall, an ornate eighteenth-century building, and the Roman Catholic Cathedral of Christ the King. The city is home to the Liverpool Symphony Orchestra and several theater companies. The Liverpool region has two professional soccer teams, the Liverpool club and the Everton club. The city is a national and regional sports center, and leading sports include boxing, cricket, gymnastics, hockey, swimming, soccer, tennis, and volleyball.

CATEGORY	DATA	YEAR	AREA
LOCATION & ENVIRONMENT			
Area	42 square miles	1996	City
	113 square kilometers	1996	City
Elevation	198 feet/60.4 meters	1992	City
January Temperature	40 degrees Fahrenheit	1992	City
	4.4 degrees Celsius	1992	City
July Temperature	60.5 degrees Fahrenheit	1992	City
	15.8 degrees Celsius	1992	City
Annual Precipitation	28.9 inches/734.1 millimeters	1992	City
POPULATION & DEMOGRAPHY			
Regional Population	1,427,000	1995	Metro
Urban Population	471,000	1995	City
Rate of Decline	−8.9%	1981–1995	City
Density	10,808 per square mile	1995	Metro
	4,173 per square kilometer		
Gender			
Males	48.6%	1995	City
Females	51.4%	1995	City
Age			
Under 16	20.0%	1992	Metro
16–64	64.4%	1992	Metro
Over 65	15.7%	1992	Metro
VITAL STATISTICS			
Births per 1,000 Residents	12.0	1995	City
Death per 1,000 Residents	12.2	1995	City
Infant Mortality Rate	7.8 per 1,000 live births	1995	City
ECONOMY			
Total Workforce	614,000	1996	Metro
Manufacturing	17.5	1992	Metro
Construction	6.4%	1992	Metro
Utilities	1.8%	1992	Metro
Agriculture	1.1%	1992	Metro
TRANSPORTATION			
Passenger Vehicles	409,000	1995	City
HOUSING			
Total Housing Units	2,593,000	1991	Metro
Persons per Unit	2.5	1991	Metro
Owner-Occupied Units	68.0%	1991	Metro

(continued)

CATEGORY	DATA	YEAR	AREA
EDUCATION			
Total Students	1,513,000	1993	Metro
Primary	39.9%	1993	Metro
Secondary	50.1%	1993	Metro
Higher	10.1%	1993	Metro

Sources: Eurostat *Regions Statistical Yearbook.* Brussels, Belgium: Statistical Office of European Communities, 1996. Office for National Statistics. *Regional Trends 32.* London, England: The Stationery Office, 1997.

London, South East, England
UNITED KINGDOM

LOCATION

London, the capital and largest city of the United Kingdom, is located on the Thames River, at an elevation of 149 feet in southeast England's North Downs lowland region. Beyond the Thames River is the North Sea. The greater London metropolitan area is an urban region comprised of thirteen inner boroughs and nineteen outer boroughs. The city has a surface area of 609 square miles (1,578 square kilometers). The inner boroughs are Camden, Hackney, Hammersmith and Fulham, Haringey, Islington, Kensington and Chelsea, Lambeth, Lewisham, Newham, Southwark, Tower Hamlets, Wandsworth, and the City of Westminster. The outer boroughs are Barking and Dagenham, Barnet, Bexley, Brent, Bromley, Croydon, Ealing, Enfield, Greenwich, Harrow, Havering, Hillingdon, Hounslow, Kingston upon Thames, Merton, Redbridge, Richmond upon Thames, Sutton, and Waltham Forest. The English Channel is located 40 miles south of London. Liverpool and the Irish Sea are located 175 miles northwest of London, and Birmingham is located 130 miles northwest of London. Glasgow, the industrial center of Scotland, is located 350 miles to London's northwest. The "City of London" refers to a mile-square area, with a population of several thousand, that occupies the ancient walled city and currently is a global business and finance district, with the Museum of London, St. Paul's Cathedral, and the Tower of London. The principal shopping and theater areas are west of the city of London, in the City of Westminster, which is commonly referred to as the West End. "Greater London" refers to a thirty-two-borough area, including London and its suburbs, that until 1986 was administered by the Greater London Council. The average temperature ranges from a January low of 39.5 degrees Fahrenheit (4.2 degrees Celsius) to a July high of 64 degrees Fahrenheit (17.8 degrees Celsius). The average annual precipitation is 22.9 inches (581.7 millimeters).

POPULATION AND DEMOGRAPHY

Greater London is substantially larger than any other population center in the United Kingdom. London is more than three times as large as Birmingham, the country's second largest city. Between 1981 and 1995, greater London's population increased by 3 percent, to 7,007,000, reversing a moderate population decline from 1960 to 1980. The London metropolitan area has a population of 7,600,000. London is the only major British city with a population exceeding 400,000 that did not lose population between the period 1981 and 1995. Since 1960, a significant portion of greater London's population has shifted from the central city to the suburban and outlying areas of the region. The suburban growth trend is explained in part by government restrictions that have been placed on population growth within a greenbelt surrounding the city. In part, the area's stable population is explained by its expanded importance as an engine of the national economy. The central city area has a population density of 12,479 persons per square mile (4,816 persons per square kilometer). However, some London boroughs have considerably higher population densities. For example, the borough of Kensington and Chelsea has a density exceeding 3,700 persons per square mile (10,000 persons per square kilometer), as does Islington. In 1995, females comprised a slight majority, 51 percent, of greater London's population. The greater London area has a larger economically active population than any other U.K. city with a population in excess of 400,000. Fully 66 percent of greater London's population is between 16 and pension age (60 for women, 65 for men). Youth under age 16 comprise 18.8 percent of the region's residents, while seniors over 65 make up 15.2 percent of the population. London has the highest proportion of ethnic minorities in the United Kingdom. According to National Statistics, nearly one in four London residents is a member of an ethnic minority group. The leading ethnic minorities are blacks of African and West Indian descent, Indians, Pakistanis, and Bangladeshis. The national economic decline in the 1980s and 1990s has made minority populations a target of discrimination, intolerance, and police brutality.

HISTORY

London was founded in the first century A.D. by the Romans as a regional outpost and administrative center. The city became known as Fort Londinium. In the ninth century, King Alfred made the city the capital of England. London subsequently expanded into an important medieval town. The city's importance grew under a succession of national leaders. London's emergence as a major financial center emerged in the sixteenth century with the establishment of the Royal Exchange. The city expanded dramatically in the eighteenth and nineteenth centuries as a major global center. In the late eighteenth century, a vast construction boom greatly enlarged the downtown districts of the city. During the nineteenth century, London was the first major global city to develop suburbs in outlying areas. Initially the suburbs were intended for the poor and working class. However, in the nineteenth century the suburbs became popular with the affluent, who built country estates there. During the First and Second World Wars, many of London's buildings were destroyed by German bombings. Many buildings destroyed in the Second World War were rebuilt in the 1950s. The easing in construction codes for high-rise development contributed to the growth in high-rise building developments in the 1970s and 1980s, including the Canary Wharf project in the Docklands area on the outskirts of London. The Docklands is a major commercial development site, with offices and hotels, and is considered a symbol of a modern and revitalized London. The site is near the Millennium Dome, the world's largest indoor structure, which is scheduled to open at the turn of the century.

GOVERNMENT AND POLITICS

Since the early 1960s, the structure of greater London's government has shifted unstably between regional and local control. Today the fate of London's government continues to remain uncertain. In 1965, the London Government Act created a two-tiered government of thirty-two borough councils and the Greater London Council. Locally elected borough councils were accountable for local government, and the Greater London Council was accountable for regional government and service delivery. The Greater London Council had one hundred locally elected councilors and fifteen aldermen elected by councilors. In 1986, Margaret Thatcher abolished the Greater London Council and transferred regional political authority to thirty-three local authorities. The new authorities are responsible exclusively for developing policy in local areas, and their failure to adequately deliver regional services has galvanized public interest in reestablishing a regional London government. In addition, the local authorities have not successfully coordinated the promotion of London's image as a global city. In 1998, the newly elected Labour government of Prime Minister Tony Blair recommended the reestablishment of a regional London government to create a more sustainable city by improving the delivery and efficiency of regional service delivery. The Labour government has proposed to hold a referendum that will likely give London residents the right to directly elect a mayor of a greater London authority, like other major cities. Continued disagreement remains over the structure of the government; some favor a mayor without a local assembly, while others support a mayor checked by a local assembly.

ECONOMY

The enormous power of London's banking and finance sector confers on the city the status of a global city. The influence of the city's banking and finance sector extends well beyond the local, regional, and national borders to the international arena. As a result, London is clearly of national and international importance. However, due to the city's global reach, London and its residents are economically quite dependent on the international business environment. The greater London area is the largest and most dynamic regional economy in the United Kingdom and one of the three primary global centers, along with New York City and Tokyo, of international banking and finance. According to a government green paper, the London economy alone produces 15 percent of the United Kingdom's gross national product. The banking and finance industry produces a remarkable 43 percent of London's gross domestic product, followed by distribution, hotels, and catering (14 percent), manufacturing (13 percent), transport, storage, and communications (11 percent), and arts and culture (6 percent). Over 235,000 companies in greater London employ a workforce of about 3.4 million. As a major engine of the British economy, London's gross domestic product per person is about 25 percent higher than the national average. The leading components of the service sector are transportation, communications, insurance, banking, finance, business services, and public administration. As a leading global banking and financial center, London has a larger proportion of affluent residents than any other region in the United Kingdom.

Machinery, automobiles, clothing, printing and publishing, chemicals, petroleum and oil refining and processing, and textile products are the leading industries in greater London's manufacturing sector. The city is also a major producer of high-tech products, including aircraft, computers, electronic equipment, electrical engineering, and precision instruments. The growth of high technology is an important component of the revitalization of manufacturing in the region. However, it has not offset the steady decline in traditional manufacturing employment in basic industries.

Paradoxically, while London has the largest share of affluent residents in the United Kingdom, the regional economy also has serious unemployment and high poverty rates. According to International Labor

Office statistics, London's unemployment rate in the year ending May 1996 was 11.6 percent, considerably higher than the United Kingdom's national jobless rate of 8.5 percent. London has the second highest rate of unemployment in the United Kingdom. The growth of the service sector is not expected to compensate for the projected continued decline in basic manufacturing industries. Unemployment is therefore expected to continue to grow, particularly among low-income workers with fewer skills. Although unemployment has moderated in the 1990s, the problem of long-term joblessness is growing in severity. Greater London has a larger share of long-term unemployed than any region in the United Kingdom other than Northern Ireland. Still, a fairly large 64 percent of the population was economically active, a higher percentage than in other major British cities with populations exceeding 400,000 and higher than the national average. Household income in London is far greater than in other major urban centers and greater than the national average.

TRANSPORTATION

In 1890, the first electric underground railway in the world was built in London, connecting the central city with the outer boroughs. Although a larger percentage of London residents use public transportation than in any other British region, automobile use has increased rapidly in the last two decades of the twentieth century. The recent construction of a major motorway that encircles the greater London region is projected to further expand the use of motor vehicles. Still, Londoners have on average fewer automobiles per household, and nearly 40 percent of the region's households have no car at all. Greater London is a major auto, truck, and rail transportation hub, with motorways and rail lines extending from London to all regions of Britain. The Port of London Authority operates greater London's vast seaport and shipping facilities and two leading airports. Heathrow International Airport, west of London, has the largest number of domestic and international arrivals and departures in the nation. Gatwick International Airport, south of London, is the United Kingdom's second busiest international airport.

A growing dilemma for the region is the lack of an integrated transportation system. In addition, the growth of motor vehicle use on the regional roads and highways is causing higher levels of congestion and air pollution. The aging subway system, known as the Underground or "the tube," suffers from high levels of overcrowding. Some transportation analysts argue that London's underground rail transit system is in dire need of improvement and expansion.

HEALTH CARE

The greater London area continues to have a high natural population increase, with an excess of births over deaths. In 1981 there were 13.5 births and 11.4 deaths per 1,000 residents. By 1995, there were 14.9 births and 9.5 deaths per 1,000, representing a large natural population increase of 5.4 per 1,000. By comparison, the United Kingdom had a natural population increase of 1.6 per 1,000 residents. Greater London's average infant mortality rate between 1993 and 1995 was 9.5 infant deaths per 1,000 live births, higher than the national average of 8.9. In 1992, circulatory system deaths and cancers were London's leading causes of death. The region has the second highest rate of use of private medical insurance in the United Kingdom.

EDUCATION

According to national statistics, London has the most educated labor force in the nation, with more than one in five residents possessing a postsecondary or higher degree. London has a lower student/teacher ratio than the United Kingdom's national average. In the 1995–1996 school year, there were 21.6 students per teacher in primary schools and 15.8 students per teacher in secondary schools. Eighty-one percent of greater London's 16-year-olds continued to attend school following the completion of compulsory education at age 15, slightly higher than the national average of 80 percent. London's leading universities and specialized postsecondary educational institutions are the University of London, the London School of Economics, the Royal College of Art, the Royal Academy of Music, and the Royal Naval College.

HOUSING

According to National Statistics, 57 percent of dwellings in London are owner-occupied, a lower proportion of owner-occupied housing units than any other region in the United Kingdom. The amount of privately developed housing in greater London outnumbered housing developed by housing associations and local authorities by a ratio exceeding 2 to 1. The average of 2.5 persons per household in greater London exceeded the national average of 2.4 persons per household. However, the region had a larger proportion of one-person households than the nation as a whole. Differences in average household size vary greatly among London's boroughs. For example, the average household size in the City of London, the City of Westminster, and Kensington and Chelsea was below 2 persons, and about 50 percent of the three boroughs' households were occupied by only one person. Greater London faces two serious housing problems: a shortage of housing and the declining quality of the region's housing stock. London has the highest percentage of homelessness in the United Kingdom. In addition, 64 percent of the worst public housing stock in the United Kingdom is in London. London is home to sixteen of the twenty-two most deprived local authorities in the United Kingdom, and over 770,000 tenants receive housing subsidies. Public authorities have recently called on greater government investment in regenerating London's old and declining housing stock.

CULTURE, THE ARTS, AND ENTERTAINMENT

London is a leading international tourist destination, attracting 23 million visitors a year. Principal tourist sites include the Houses of Parliament, Westminster Abbey, Covent Garden, and Buckingham Palace. The arts and entertainment industries are major growth sectors of the regional economy. The city is a leading global center of culture, arts, and music. London's many museums include the British Museum, the Museum of the City of London, the Victoria and Albert Museum, the National Gallery, the National Portrait Gallery, the Tate Gallery, the Courtauld Institute Galleries, the Royal Academy of Arts, the Hayward Art Gallery, and Queens Gallery. The city's leading theaters include the National Theatre Company and the Royal Shakespeare Company. The London Symphony Orchestra, one of many orchestras in the city, is considered to be one of the finest in the world. London is also home to the London Opera and several ballet companies.

CATEGORY	DATA	YEAR	AREA
LOCATION & ENVIRONMENT			
Area	609 square miles	1996	City
	1,578 square kilometers		City
Elevation	149 feet/45 meters		City
January Temperature	39.5 degrees Fahrenheit		City
	4.2 degrees Celsius		City
July Temperature	64 degrees Fahrenheit		City
	17.8 degrees Celsius		City
Annual Precipitation	22.9 inches/581.7 millimeters		City
POPULATION & DEMOGRAPHY			
Population	7,600,000	1996	Metro
Projected Population	7,600,000	2015	Metro
Growth Rate	0.0%	1990–1995	Metro
Growth Rate	0.0%	1995–2015	Metro
Density	12,479 per square mile	1995	Metro
	4,816 per square kilometer		
Gender			
Males	48.9%	1992	Metro
Females	51.1%	1992	Metro
Age			
Under 16	18.8%	1992	Metro
16–64	66.0%	1992	Metro
Over 65	15.2%	1992	Metro

(continued)

CATEGORY	DATA	YEAR	AREA
VITAL STATISTICS			
Births per 1,000 Residents	14.9	1995	Metro
Deaths per 1,000 Residents	9.5	1995	Metro
Infant Mortality Rate	9.5 per 1,000 live births	1995	Metro
ECONOMY			
Total Workforce	3,503,000	1996	Metro
Manufacturing	17.2%	1992	Metro
Construction	5.9%	1992	Metro
Utilities	1.2%	1992	Metro
Agriculture	1.2%	1992	Metro
HOUSING			
Total Housing Units	7,287,000	1991	Metro
Persons per Unit	2.5	1991	Metro
Owner-Occupied Units	57.0%	1991	Metro
EDUCATION			
Total Students	3,734,000	1993	Metro
Primary	40.0%	1993	Metro
Secondary	48.7%	1993	Metro
Higher	11.2%	1993	Metro

Sources: Department of Economic and Social Affairs, Population Division. *Urban Agglomerations, 1996.* New York: United Nations, 1997; United Nations Center for Human Settlements. *Compendium of Human Settlements Statistics.* New York: United Nations, 1995; Eurostat *Regions Statistical Yearbook.* Brussels, Belgium: Statistical Office of European Communities, 1996; and Office for National Statistics. *Regional Trends 32.* London, England: The Stationery Office, 1997.

Los Angeles, California
USA

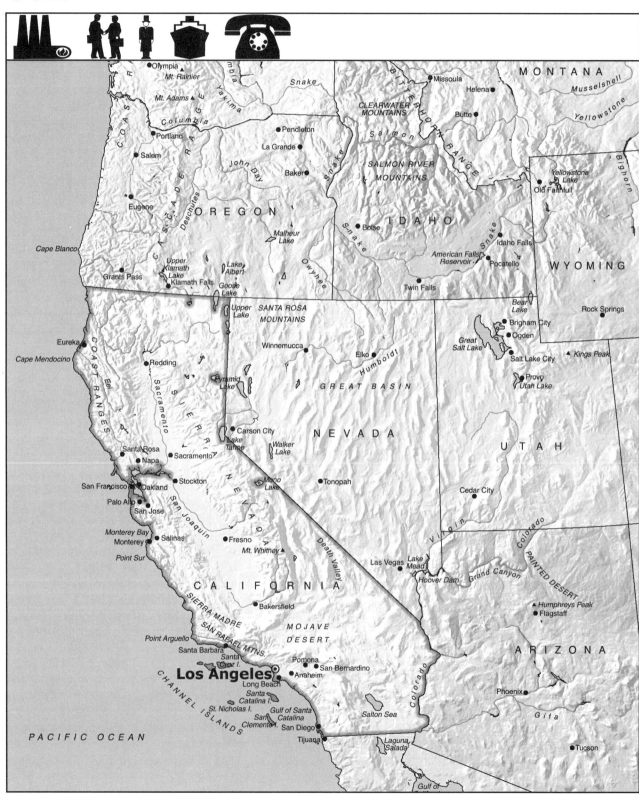

LOCATION

Los Angeles, California's largest city and the center of the second most populous region in the United States, is located amid a mountainous coastal plain on southern California's Pacific coast, south of the coast mountain range. The city's elevation is 97 feet above sea level. The 469.3-square-mile (1,215.5-square-kilometer) city lies at the center of a sprawling urban region that extends north to the San Fernando Valley, south to Orange County, west to the Santa Monica Mountains and Ventura County, and east to San Bernardino and Riverside Counties. Regional growth is so extensive that Los Angeles occupies the center of a megalopolis that extends 220 miles along the southern California coast from Santa Barbara, 90 miles to the northwest, to San Diego, 125 miles to the southeast. The city is 390 miles southeast of San Francisco and 380 miles southeast of Sacramento, California's state capital. A primary feature of Los Angeles is the innumerable freeways that connect the city to the suburbs and permit the growth of the formerly rural areas beyond the suburban perimeter. The unabated growth of Los Angeles's outlying areas has placed growing dependence on the automobile and produced serious transportation and pollution problems in the region. Los Angeles has a mild and comfortable climate, with temperatures ranging from a January average low of 58.3 degrees Fahrenheit (14.6 degrees Celsius) to a July average high of 74.3 degrees Fahrenheit (23.5 degrees Celsius). Precipitation is fairly moderate in Los Angeles, averaging under 14.8 inches (375 millimeters) of annual rainfall in the thirty years between 1961 and 1990.

POPULATION AND DEMOGRAPHY

The Los Angeles regional population has continued to grow at a rapid pace in the 1980s and 1990s, unlike that of many major U.S. cities in the Northeast and Midwest. The city's population expanded from 2,816,000 in 1970 to 3,489,779 in 1992, an increase of 19.3 percent. The rate of growth is expected to continue to increase into the next century. The regional population has grown even more dramatically. From 1970 to 1995, the Los Angeles regional population increased by over 43 percent, from 7,032,000 to over 12 million. Regional growth is projected to increase further over the next two decades, to over 14 million. The central city has a density of 7,436 persons per square mile (2,871 persons per square kilometer). By the year 2025, demographers project that the Los Angeles consolidated metropolitan statistical area—coupled with San Diego, to the city's south—will eclipse New York as the largest population center in the United States. A primary demographic feature of Los Angeles's continued growth is the expansion of the city's Hispanic population, which reached 40 percent of the central city's population in 1990 and is expected to overtake the white population by the beginning of the twenty-first century. A second factor in Los Angeles's continued population growth is the rapid expansion of the Asian population, which accounted for 10 percent of the city's residents in the early 1990s. The in-migration of Hispanic and Asian residents has been the primary factor in the city's continued growth during the last two decades of the twentieth century. Nearly 40 percent of Los Angeles's population is foreign-born, of which most are newcomers from Latin America (Mexico, Guatemala, El Salvador) and East Asia (Korea, China, Japan, and the Philippines). The city's white population has declined in recent years due to continued migration to the suburbs, the Pacific Northwest, and most recently outmigration to the Rocky Mountain states. The city's black population accounts for about 14 percent of the city's residents. Los Angeles has a larger proportion of males than females—a ratio of 100.8 males for every 100 females. Due to the large number of newcomers, who tend to be younger, the city's age distribution is more youthful than that of other major urban centers: 24.8 percent are under 18 years of age, 65 percent are between 18 and 64, and 10 percent are over 65 years of age.

HISTORY

Los Angeles was established as a Spanish outpost in 1781, and later came under Mexican and then American rule. Los Angeles was incorporated as a city in 1850 and grew in economic importance with the expansion of railroad links from San Francisco to the southern California region in the 1870s and 1880s. In the early twentieth century, Los Angeles became an important service, distribution, and financing center for the regional agricultural, oil, and gas industries. The temperate regional climate contributed to the city's population growth in the first half of the twentieth century. Los Angeles's population increased from 50,000 in 1890 to 1.5 million in 1940. The city's fortunes have also relied heavily on the growth of the film and television studio production industry in the early twentieth century. Since the 1960s, growing class inequality, racial conflict, and ethnic divisions have contributed to major violent street confrontations. The Watts riots of 1965, sparked by charges of police brutality, were one of the first urban social uprisings of the civil rights era. In 1992, the city exploded again in a major insurrection that followed the acquittal of police officers videotaped beating Rodney King, a black motorist. The uprising, which was not limited to blacks but included whites and Latinos, was concentrated in south-central Los Angeles but expanded widely into outlying poor and working-class neighborhoods. The latest series of uprisings, in the early 1990s, were suppressed with the help of the U.S. National Guard. Some commentators believe that local, state, and federal authorities have not adequately addressed the socioeconomic conditions of inequality contributing to the conflicts in Los Angeles. From the early 1990s through the end of the decade, Los Angeles public officials, often in concert with state and federal initiatives, have turned their attention to increasing public safety through expanding, diversifying, and modernizing the Los Angeles Police Department. In the wake of the January 17, 1994, earthquake, Los Angeles authorities have attempted to help the city's economy recover through public-private partnerships with local businesses.

GOVERNMENT AND POLITICS

Los Angeles has a mayoral–city council form of government. The mayor is responsible for executive and administrative functions. The mayor also recommends and submits the annual budget to the city council for adoption. The fifteen-member city council, elected on a district basis, is responsible for enacting ordinances subject to the approval or veto of the mayor. The mayor, city council, controller, and city attorney are elected to concurrent four-year terms. In the late 1990s, the city of Los Angeles formed the Commission on Charter Reform to evaluate government functions and suggest possible changes to improve government effectiveness. The city administers thirty-six departments, bureaus, and commissions and is responsible for the provision of public services.

ECONOMY

Los Angeles has a strong and diverse economic base across industrial sectors. Although the region was buffeted by a decline in aerospace and defense-related industries in the early 1990s, the regional base has diversified into new industries. The central city civilian labor market grew by 21.9 percent between 1980 and 1990, to 1,827,767. Although wholesale and retail trade was the largest employment sector in Los Angeles in 1990, with 20.2 percent of the city's labor force, the manufacturing sector has grown rapidly in recent years, reaching 18.4 percent of the labor force in 1990 and continuing to expand in the early 1990s. A large proportion of new growth is in basic manufacturing such as garment and furniture production, as employers have taken advantage of the access to low-cost Latin American workers who have migrated to the region in the last two decades. However, due to the growing integration of the North American market, manufacturers have greater access to workers in *maquiladoras*, factories clustered on the Mexican side of the U.S.-Mexico border, where employers are not subject to U.S. minimum wage laws. After the trade and manufacturing sectors, the leading employment sectors are finance, insurance, and real estate (8.1 percent), health services (7.1 percent), and public administration (2.2 percent). The end of the cold war in the early 1990s contributed to a dramatic decline in aerospace jobs, which had provided a solid core of employment for middle-class and upper-middle-class residents in the region. From 1990 to 1997, the city lost about 182,000 aerospace jobs. The loss in high-tech aerospace jobs has had a ripple effect throughout the regional economy. Los Angeles has a high unemployment rate relative to other regional cities, as well as a considerably higher poverty rate (18.9 percent), which tends to be even higher in areas with large concentrations of minorities.

Los Angeles County ranks first in the United States in manufacturing. The city's diverse industrial base includes aircraft, aircraft equipment, aluminum, dental equipment, games and toys, gas transmission and distribution equipment, guided missiles, space vehicles and propulsion units, and women's apparel. Other manufacturing industries include clothing, motion pictures, food processing, electric and electronic equipment, metal products, machinery, chemicals, printing and publishing, oil refining, and primary metals. The motion picture, television, and recording industries remain major cogs in the economy. To improve the local economy, city officials have attempted to form public-private partnerships to attract and retain businesses. On balance, although some service jobs have been gained as a result of free trade initiatives such as the North American Free Trade Agreement, the manufacturing sector has lost employment and remains under pressure from low-wage industries in Mexico.

TRANSPORTATION

From the early twentieth century, the automobile has been the trademark for commuters and travelers in the Los Angeles metropolitan region. The city of Los

Angeles has 6,400 miles of road and 160 freeway miles. The expansion of motor vehicle ownership in the region propelled growing urban sprawl and suburban settlement patterns. In 1990, only 10.5 percent of the city used public transportation as a means to travel to work, significantly less than the 53.4 percent of New York City residents who depend on public transportation to commute to their jobs. While the automobile will remain the dominant form of transportation in the region into the foreseeable future, the city has begun efforts to expand the availability of public transit. Before a rail transportation system opened in 1993, the city was one of the few major global cities not to have a passenger rail transit system. Still, the system is limited and incomplete. In the next century, the system is expected to expand to 23 miles of subway and 400 miles of commuter rail track. The city is a major distribution center. The Port of Los Angeles, at Long Beach, handles the largest volume of shipping tonnage in the United States. The city is a major rail and freight trucking transportation center. On the basis of air passengers, Los Angeles International Airport is one of the largest airports in the United States.

HEALTH CARE

The city of Los Angeles has twenty-eight community hospitals with 7,656 hospital beds, a rate of 220 hospital beds per 100,000 residents, and many more community and specialized hospitals serve residents in Los Angeles County. The city has a rate of 6.1 physicians per 1,000 residents. The reported infant mortality rate of 10.1 deaths per 1,000 live births compares favorably to that of other American cities with populations exceeding 200,000.

EDUCATION

The Los Angeles Unified School District is responsible for public education in the city and some outlying suburbs. The school district operates 539 primary and secondary schools throughout the region. Due to the city's youthful population, Los Angeles has a large school enrollment of 978,638, representing about 28 percent of the city's inhabitants. About 63 percent of all students are in primary and secondary schools, and 86.8 percent of them attend the city's public school system. The major postsecondary institutions in Los Angeles are the University of California at Los Angeles, Loyola Marymount University, the University of Southern California, Occidental College, and

California State University at Los Angeles and Northridge. Los Angeles has seven community colleges and numerous specialized postsecondary institutions in the fields of medicine, music, science, and theology. The city of Los Angeles has a lower rate of educational attainment than the more affluent outlying suburbs in the county. In 1990, 23 percent of the city's population age 25 and over held at least a bachelor's degree.

HOUSING

The Los Angeles metropolitan area has one of the highest residential housing costs in the United States. Among American cities with populations over 200,000, Los Angeles ranks fourth highest in median value of owner-occupied housing, and rental costs rank ninth highest in the nation. Between 1980 and 1990, Los Angeles's central city housing stock grew by 9.2 percent, to 1,299,963 units. Approximately 9 percent of Los Angeles's housing units are vacant. The city's owner-occupancy rate is 39.4 percent. The Los Angeles Housing Department is responsible for home ownership programs, neighborhood preservation and recovery, policy and planning, and rent stabilization programs. However, reductions in federal outlays for public housing programs have reduced the availability of affordable housing in the city and the region.

CULTURE, THE ARTS, AND ENTERTAINMENT

In addition to the large film, broadcasting, and recording industries, Los Angeles is a major and cultural center. Los Angeles's major museums are the Los Angeles County Museum of Art, Exposition Park, the Armand Hammer Museum of Art, and the J. Paul Getty Museum. The city is home to the Los Angeles Philharmonic and three major theater companies. The Los Angeles consolidated metropolitan statistical area has major league professional sports teams in three major sports, including the Los Angeles Dodgers and Anaheim Angels baseball teams, the Los Angeles Lakers and Los Angeles Clippers basketball teams, and the Los Angeles Kings and Anaheim Mighty Ducks hockey teams. City leaders are supporting efforts to attract a professional football team through building new arenas and modernizing existing sports facilities. Los Angeles was host to two summer Olympic Games in the last century, including the 1984 Summer Games.

CATEGORY	DATA	YEAR	AREA
LOCATION & ENVIRONMENT			
Area	469.3 square miles	1995	City
	1,215.5 square kilometers		City
Elevation	97 feet/29.6 meters		City
January Temperature	58.3 degrees Fahrenheit	1961–1990	City
	14.6 degrees Celsius	1961–1990	City
July Temperature	74.3 degrees Fahrenheit	1961–1990	City
	23.5 degrees Celsius	1961–1990	City
Annual Precipitation	14.8 inches/375 millimeters	1961–1990	City
POPULATION & DEMOGRAPHY			
Population	12,000,000	1996	Metro
Projected Population	14,200,000	2015	Metro
Growth Rate	1.6%	1990–1995	Metro
Growth Rate	14.6%	1995–2015	Metro
Density	7,436 per square mile	1992	City
	2,871 per square kilometer		
Gender			
Males	50.2%	1990	City
Females	49.8%	1990	City
Age			
Under 18	24.8%	1990	City
18–64	65.2%	1990	City
Over 65	10.0%	1990	City
VITAL STATISTICS			
Births per 1,000 Residents	22	1988	City
Deaths per 1,000 Residents	8	1988	City
Infant Mortality Rate	10.1 per 1,000 live births	1990	City
ECONOMY			
Total Workforce	1,827,767	1990	City
Trade	20.2%	1990	City
Manufacturing	18.4%	1990	City
Health Services	7.1%	1990	City
Finance, Insurance, Real Estate	8.1%	1990	City
Public Administration	2.2%	1990	City
TRANSPORTATION			
Passenger Journeys	497,158,000	1990	City
Buses	100.0%	1990	City
Passenger Vehicles	1,836,002	1990	City
COMMUNICATIONS			
Telephones per 1,000 Residents	1,119	1984	City
Televisions per 1,000 Residents	695	1984	City

(continued)

CATEGORY	DATA	YEAR	AREA
HOUSING			
Total Housing Units	1,299,963	1990	City
Persons per Unit	2.7	1990	City
Owner-Occupied Units	39.4%	1990	City
HEALTH CARE			
Hospitals	28	1991	City
Physicians per 1,000 Residents	6.1	1991	City
EDUCATION			
Total Students	978,638	1991	City
Primary and Secondary	63.0%	1991	City
Higher	32.4%	1991	City

Sources: Department of Economic and Social Affairs, Population Division. *Urban Agglomerations, 1996.* New York: United Nations, 1997; *Statistics of World Large Cities.* Tokyo, Japan: Tokyo Metropolitan Government, 1992 and 1994; U.S. Bureau of the Census. *County and City Data Book 1994.* Washington, DC: U.S. Government Printing Office, 1994; and United Nations Center for Human Settlements. *Compendium of Human Settlements Statistics.* New York: United Nations, 1995.